Signal Detection Theory

and Psychophysics

Signal Detection Theory and Psychophysics

DAVID M. GREEN

Professor of Psychology
University of California at San Diego
and Consultant
Bolt Beranek and Newman Inc
Cambridge, Massachusetts

JOHN A. SWETS

Director
Information Sciences Division
and Vice-President
Bolt Beranek and Newman Inc
Cambridge, Massachusetts

ROBERT E. KRIEGER PUBLISHING COMPANY
HUNTINGTON ● NEW YORK

Original Edition 1966
Reprint (with corrections) 1974

Printed and Published by
ROBERT E. KRIEGER PUBLISHING CO., INC.
BOX 542, HUNTINGTON, NEW YORK 11743

Library of Congress Catalog Card Number 66-21059
ISBN 0-88275-139-5

Printed in U.S.A. by
NOBLE OFFSET PRINTERS, INC.
New York, N.Y. 10003

Preface to Reprint

Seven years have passed from the first printing of this book to the present reprint. What have been the main trends in the application of detection theory in psychophysics—and in psychology—during those years? These trends can be discussed briefly in relation to the parts of the book.

Part I describes the early experiments, which were conducted primarily to illuminate the role of decision processes in detection and to determine how decision effects could be isolated in the study of sensory processes. In this regard, the fundamental results were evident by the time the book was first published; relatively little additional work has been done, and little has changed.

Part II is devoted to stimulus-oriented psychophysics, or to an understanding of sensory capability, highlighting the concept of the ideal observer. In this area we have seen a growing tendency to focus on the interaction of the stimulus and the sensory system. Detailed, specific assumptions have been made about neural correlates of the stimulus, such as pulse rate or interarrival times, and these correlates have been substituted for the likelihood ratio as the basic decision quantities. The development of substantive assumptions—to relate the formal theory to particular sensory modalities or particular perceptual tasks—was an inevitable outgrowth of the earlier, completely formal, decision-theoretic treatments. These detailed assumptions, of course, have resulted in more complex and more particular theories.

Part III presents applications of detection theory to long-standing problems in psychology, and it is in relation to such problems that the theory and techniques have been used most extensively in the last decade. The problem areas of vigilance, attention, reaction time, memory, and animal psychophysics—all discussed preliminarily in the concluding chapter—provide the chief examples.

One of the appendices discusses experimental techniques, and this has been another active area. Objective curve-fitting and estimation procedures have been developed; significance tests of observed differences in d' have been devised; and the sampling variability of some other measures of sensitivity has been examined.

In this reprint we have corrected several errors, mostly in equations, found in the first printing. We thank several people, especially James Egan, Lawrence Feth, and Gordon Wilcox, for pointing them out to us.

The addition to the book made in this reprint is a topical bibliography of some 400 articles published mainly between 1966 and 1973. The user should keep in mind that although many articles fit in several categories they are listed in just one.

D. M. G.
J. A. S.

Cambridge, Massachusetts
October, 1973

Preface

In the past twelve years many articles have been written on various aspects of signal detection theory in psychophysics. None of them deals with more than a small fraction of the material, and each assumes a background in certain branches of mathematics, electrical engineering, and psychology. This book gives a systematic presentation of the field. It contains introductions to probability theory, statistical decision theory, waveform analysis, and experimental techniques. It reviews the basic experiments that support the application of detection theory in psychophysics, and describes experimental applications of the theory to a variety of substantive problems in psychology. It considers the complexities and issues at the frontier of the field.

The timely appearance of this book was made possible by support from the National Aeronautics and Space Administration through a contract with Bolt Beranek and Newman Inc. We are grateful to Robert W. Taylor, of NASA's Office of Advanced Research and Technology, for initiating the project and for the encouragement and assistance that he gave us. Roger L. Winblade represented NASA in the closing stages of the project and was also very helpful. David M. Green held a faculty appointment in the Department of Psychology at the University of Pennsylvania, and benefited from a part-time leave as well as from the criticism and support of students and colleagues.

Several colleagues have kindly read and very ably criticized chapter drafts: Professors Wilson P. Tanner, Jr., Lloyd A. Jeffress, James P. Egan, Warren S. Torgerson, J. E. Keith Smith, David H. Raab, Irwin Pollack, Charles S. Watson, Arthur I. Schulman, Bert F. Green, Clyde H. Coombs,

Jacob Nachmias, and Drs. Saul Sternberg, Bruce Henning, and Joseph Markowitz. We are indebted to these friends for several positive contributions, and for saving us from many small, and some grievous, errors. Professor R. Duncan Luce read and commented thoughtfully on almost the entire first draft; his trail of red ink led us to many improvements in clarity and accuracy. Professors Alfred B. Kristofferson, William J. McGill, and Thomas Bizembender also gave us (and, we hope, the reader) the benefits of their advice on most of the manuscript. We wish to thank a majority of the persons named above and also Professors Richard C. Atkinson, Ronald A. Kinchla, Donald A. Norman, James D. Miller, J. A. Nevin together with Drs. Frank R. Clarke and Jane F. Mackworth for making some of their recent work available to us prior to its publication.

Various drafts of several chapters were typed by Audrey DiLeo, Cynthia Mullen, and Mary Lou Dampman at Bolt Beranek and Newman Inc. and by Barbara Kanalstein and Phyllis Ryan at the University of Pennsylvania, with coordination provided by Mrs. DiLeo. Florence Maurer of BBN implemented final revisions and prepared the index of names. We deeply appreciate their careful efforts. Joseph Markowitz labored hard and well to prepare an effective subject index. Edith L. Annin of Harvard's Psychology Department read the proofs with us and did much to make the book more readable.

It is a pleasure to recall contributions to this book made long before we thought of it. Both of us began working in psychophysics at the University of Michigan, as students in the Department of Psychology and as members of the Electronic Defense Group of the Department of Electrical Engineering, and we value many associates there among the faculty and our fellow students. We are pleased to acknowledge particularly our considerable debt to Wilson P. Tanner, Jr., the person most responsible for bringing signal detection theory into psychophysics. We worked closely with Spike Tanner for several years, and have often benefited more recently from his stimulation and criticism. Theodore G. Birdsall, a major contributor to the development of the theory in electrical engineering and another colleague at Michigan, was very helpful to us then and has been since that time.

We feel a special gratitude to our wives, Clara Green and Mickey Swets. Their cooperation and support also began in student days and did not waver during the many odd hours that went into writing this book. We dedicate this book to our children: Allan, Philip, Katherine, and George Green, and Stephen and Joel Swets.

Cambridge, Massachusetts
March 1966

D. M. G.
J. A. S.

Contents

Introduction   1

PART I   DECISION PROCESSES IN DETECTION   5

1.   Elements of Statistical Decision Theory   7

     1.1   Introduction   7
     1.2   A Simple Decision Problem   8
     1.3   Formal Discussion of the Decision Problem   11
     1.4   Notation   13
     1.5   Representation of Decision Outcomes   16
     1.6   Optimal Decision Making: Use of Likelihood Ratio   18
     1.7   Decision Goals   20
     1.8   Distribution of Likelihood Ratio   26
     1.9   Summary   26
     1.10   Appendix 1-A   27
          Problems   28

2.   Statistical Decision Theory and Psychophysical Procedures   30

     2.1   Introduction   30
     2.2   Yes-No Procedure   32
     2.3   Likelihood Ratio and the ROC Curve   36
     2.4   Rating Procedure   40
     2.5   Forced-Choice Procedure   43
     2.6   Relation between Forced-Choice Results and Yes-No or Rating ROC Curves   45
     2.7   Signal Strength and the ROC Curve   50

2.8 Summary 51
    Problems 52

3. Assumed Distribution of Signal and Noise   53

    3.1 Introduction 53
    3.2 The Gaussian Assumption 54
    3.3 Threshold Theory 69
    3.4 Exponential Model 78
    3.5 Luce's Choice Model 81
    3.6 Summary 84
        Problems 85

4. Basic Experiments: Separation of Sensory and Decision
    Processes   86

    4.1 Introduction 86
    4.2 The Yes-No Experiment 87
    4.3 The Rating Experiment 99
    4.4 The Forced-Choice Experiment 107
    4.5 Comparison of Indices of Sensitivity Obtained from the
         Three Experimental Procedures 110
    4.6 Summary 114
        Problems 115

5. The Sensory Threshold and Psychophysical Method   117

    5.1 Introduction 117
    5.2 Psychophysical Methods and Measures 121
    5.3 Threshold Existence and the Psychometric Function 126
    5.4 The High-Threshold Theory 127
    5.5 Quantal Theory 136
    5.6 Low-Threshold Theories 138
    5.7 Conclusions 146
        Problems 147

PART II SENSORY PROCESSES IN DETECTION   149

6. Theory of Ideal Observers   151

    6.1 Introduction 151
    6.2 Basic Paradigm of Ideal-Detector Analysis 152
    6.3 Representation of Noise 154
    6.4 Representation of Signal 162
    6.5 Ideal Detectors 162
    6.6 Criticism and Discussion of Ideal Detectors 175
    6.7 Summary 178
        Problems 178

7. Basic Experiments: Comparison of Ideal and Human
    Observers   180

    7.1 Introduction 180
    7.2 Two Experimental Conditions 181
    7.3 ROC Curves 185
    7.4 Psychometric Functions for Simple Detection Experiments 187
    7.5 Models for the Psychometric Function in Simple Detection
         Experiments 191
    7.6 Psychometric Functions for Increment-Detection Experiments 195
    7.7 The Product of Bandwidth and Signal Duration (WT) 206
    7.8 Weber's Law 206
    7.9 Summary 207
         Problems 208

8. Energy-Detection Model for Audition   209

    8.1   Introduction 209
    8.2   History of Concept and Previous Investigations 210
    8.3   The Energy-Detection Model 211
    8.4   Simple Detection Experiment 219
    8.5   The Increment-Detection Experiment 222
    8.6   Energy Detection and the Shape of the ROC Curve 224
    8.7   Increment Detection and Weber's Law 225
    8.8   Modifications of the Energy-Detection Model 226
    8.9   Reinterpretation of the Critical-Band Experiment 229
    8.10 Summary 231
          Problems 232

PART III   OTHER APPLICATIONS OF DETECTION THEORY 233

9. Multiple Observations   235

    9.1   Introduction 235
    9.2   Models for Combining Multiple Observations 237
    9.3   Multiple-Component Signals 243
    9.4   Multiple Observers 248
    9.5   Multiple Presentations: Fixed Number 253
    9.6   Multiple Presentations: Sequential Observation or Deferred
          Decision 259
    9.7   Extended Observation Intervals: Temporal Uncertainty 265
    9.8   Undefined Observation Intervals: Vigilance or Free Response 268
    9.9   Summary 270
    9.10 Appendix 9-A 271

10. Frequency Analysis   276

    10.1 Introduction 276
    10.2 History of the Frequency-Analysis Concept 277

10.3 The Critical Band   279
10.4 Interpretation and Extension of the Critical-Band-
      Concept—Experiments on Uncertain Signal Frequency   283
10.5 Detection of Multiple-Component Signals   289
10.6 Summary of Frequency-Analysis Experiments   293

11. Speech Communication   296

11.1 Introduction   296
11.2 Yes-No, Rating, and Second-Choice Procedures   299
11.3 Vocabulary Size and Uncertainty   306
11.4 Multiple Observations   309
11.5 Multivariate Analysis   311
11.6 Summary   313

12. Further Applications   315

12.1 Introduction   315
12.2 Animal Psychophysics   315
12.3 Sensory Physiology   319
12.4 Reaction Time   324
12.5 Time Discrimination   330
12.6 Vigilance   332
12.7 Stimulus Interaction and Attention   334
12.8 Subliminal Perception   335
12.9 Recognition Memory   337
12.10 Summary   345

APPENDICES

I. Elements of Probability Theory   349

I.1 Introduction   349
I.2 Basic Definitions and Theorems   350
I.3 Random Variables, Probability Functions, and Some
     Sampling Theory   358

II. Some Basic Concepts of Waveform Analysis   377

II.1 Introduction   377
II.2 Sinusoids   377
II.3 Addition of Two Sinusoids of the Same Frequency   379
II.4 Approximation of a Function   381
II.5 Noise   384
II.6 Stochastic Process   387
II.7 Representation of Noise   388
II.8 Summary   391

III. Experimental Techniques 392

    III.1 Introduction 392
    III.2 Data Collection 393
    III.3 Data Analysis 401
    III.4 Stimulus Measurement 411

References 417

Topical Bibliography (1967 — 1973) 437

Index 461

Introduction

This book describes the general theory of signal detectability and the application of the theory in psychophysical experiments. The theory provides a means of analyzing the essential structure of the observer's decisions in psychophysical tasks and specifies the optimal or ideal detection process in a variety of situations. Implicit in the theory are suggestions for appropriate procedures for data collection and analysis. These various aspects of the theory provide a quantitative framework for the study of a variety of substantive problems in sensory psychology.

The general theory of signal detectability was developed most fully in the early 1950's by mathematicians and engineers at the University of Michigan (Peterson, Birdsall, and Fox, 1954) and at Harvard and the Massachusetts Institute of Technology (Van Meter and Middleton, 1954). The basic papers, presented at the 1954 Symposium on Information Theory, drew upon work in mathematical statistics (notably by Neyman and Pearson, 1933; Wald, 1947, 1950; and Grenander, 1950), and from work on electronic communications (exemplified by Siegert's chapter in Lawson and Uhlenbeck, 1950; Shannon, 1948, 1949; Woodward and Davies, 1952; Reich and Swerling, 1953; Rice, 1944, 1945; North, 1943; and Middleton, 1953, 1954).

The part of the theory based in mathematical statistics is an almost direct translation of statistical decision theory, or of the theory of testing statistical hypotheses. Its application in psychology has much in common with the pioneering psychophysical work of Thurstone (1927a,b). This part of the theory provides a way of controlling and measuring the criterion the observer uses in making decisions about signal existence, and it

1

provides a measure of the observer's sensitivity that is independent of his decision criterion. This measure of sensitivity is practically invariant over several different psychophysical procedures, or detection tasks.

The part of the detection theory that grew from work on electronic communications specifies the mathematically ideal detector and hence the ideal sensitivity, as a function of measurable parameters of the signals and the interfering noise, for several kinds of signals. This theoretical structure defines relevant physical variables in quantitative terms. It also describes the effects of changes in these variables, and how uncertainty about the specific values of these variables will affect certain detectors. The normative standards of performance allow one to gauge how the efficiency of human sensory processes varies with changes in the stimulus and, thereby, to make inferences about the kind and extent of sensory information that is utilized by the observer, and about the nature of sensory processing.

Among the earliest applications of detection theory in psychology was an experiment in vision (Tanner and Swets, 1953, 1954a,b). About the same time, although conducted outside the context of the formal detection theory, two experiments demonstrated its applicability to audition (Smith and Wilson, 1953; Munson and Karlin, 1954). These three studies concentrated on the decision aspects of detection. Another early study, in audition, began to exploit in psychophysics the concept of ideally sensitive detectors (Marill, 1956). In the decade following, some 100 papers were published in this field. For ease of reference, about one third of these papers have been collected in a single volume (Swets, 1964). The present book is an attempt to give a relatively systematic and complete account of theory and experimental results and to assess the field as it appears in 1966.

Part I is devoted primarily to the role of decision processes in detection. There we present the elements of statistical decision theory that are basic to detection theory, and show how the procedures that they suggest yield independent measures of the observer's decision criterion and his sensitivity. We review the various experimental tests of detection theory, and compare and contrast the newer procedures and measures with those of classical psychophysics.

The direct contribution of the theory to an understanding of sensory processes in detection is emphasized in Part II. We first introduce concepts of ideal observers; that is, we define the most sensitive performance attainable, as a function of the signal-to-noise ratio, for a variety of different signals. We review experimental comparisons of ideal and human observers, and in the process examine some models for sensory aspects of auditory detection.

The remaining chapters, in Part III, present many applications of detection theory to long-standing problems in psychology—generally, to problems in which an examination of detection behavior is only a means to some more substantive end. One of these chapters is devoted to the integration of sensory information over time and space and to detection tasks that have more realism than those usually used in the laboratory. Another chapter reviews detection research on the problem of frequency analysis, and another takes up the application of detection theory to speech communication. The concluding chapter covers exploratory applications of the theory in such fields as animal psychophysics, sensory physiology, reaction time, attention, and recognition memory.

This volume, by virtue of the inclusion of three appendices, is largely self-contained. Appendix I lists the basic definitions and theorems of probability theory, and supplies at least the minimal prerequisite for an understanding of the material in Part I. It is included so that readers without training in probability will not have to begin elsewhere, and also to reassure readers with some knowledge of probability and statistics that their background is very probably adequate. Much of probability theory is not relevant, notably the counting techniques; and, indeed, calculus is not essential to Part I. Appendix II presents basic concepts of waveform analysis, and defines the minimally prerequisite knowledge for Part II. Understanding of this material will benefit from a greater facility in mathematics, but an attempt has been made throughout Part II to state verbally the problem, the nature of the attack on the problem, and the fundamental results. Appendix III draws together in one place and describes the more basic experimental techniques generally used in the experiments reported in this book, and does so with an attention to detail that is not usually given such matters in print. Appendix III is not strictly a prerequisite to Part III, but the significance of much of it depends upon the ideas developed in Parts I and II.

This volume should serve as a source book and also, it is hoped, as a textbook. To further the second aim, exercises for the reader follow the chapters in Parts I and II.

Part I

Decision Processes
in Detection

Chapter 1 presents the elements of statistical decision theory that are useful in analyzing detection processes. Chapter 2 shows how the statistical concept of the "operating characteristic" provides independent measures of the observer's sensitivity and of the criterion he uses in making decisions about signal existence. This chapter also shows how a distribution-free measure of sensitivity serves to unify the results obtained with three different psychophysical procedures. Some hypothetical distributions of sensory events are discussed in Chapter 3—particularly the normal distribution, which underlies the frequently used index of sensitivity termed d'. Chapter 4 reviews experimental results that support the psychophysical application of detection theory. Chapter 5 assays classical psychophysical procedures, and classical and modern views of the concept of a sensory threshold, in relation to the empirical evidence.

1

Elements of Statistical
Decision Theory

1.1   INTRODUCTION

A major part of detection theory is the application of the theory of decision making to situations in which certain waveforms called *signals* may or may not be added to a random background disturbance called *noise*. Thus we need to review briefly the theory of decision making, at least insofar as it is relevant to our purpose. We do not attempt a very extensive review of the topic. Such reviews may be found elsewhere (Luce and Raiffa, 1957; Raiffa and Schlaifer, 1961). We shall, instead, discuss a simple decision problem and introduce some of the terminology of *statistical decision theory*. The illustrative problem has obvious analogies to the problem an observer faces in trying to detect weak signals in noise. In tracing these similarities we concentrate on situations in which there is a single observation of fixed length, and in which a decision is required on the basis of that observation. Later (Chapter 9) we shall consider briefly another kind of decision procedure, in which the decision may be deferred until additional observations have been made.

The emphasis in this chapter is on the structural and formal features of decisions made in the face of ambiguous information. We follow closely the formulation of the statistical decision problem given by Wald (1950) rather than that of earlier statisticians. In the language of game theory, we shall study decisions made by individuals under conditions of risk and uncertainty. Our intention is twofold: (1) to introduce certain terminology so that this theoretical structure can be applied readily to psychophysical experiments in the following chapters and (2) to show that, despite vast

7

differences in the purposes or objectives of the decision maker, the quantity termed *likelihood ratio* is a variable of fundamental significance and usefulness in decision making.

1.2   A SIMPLE DECISION PROBLEM

A good way to begin the discussion is with an example. The example will illustrate without undue formalism those features of decision theory that are relevant to our application, and the example will also serve as a convenient referent for the terminology introduced later in the chapter.

Consider the following game of chance. Three dice are thrown. Two of the dice are ordinary dice with 1 to 6 spots appearing on their sides. The third die is unusual in that it has three spots on each of three of its sides and no spots on the remaining three sides. You as a player do not observe the throw of the dice. You are only informed of the total number of spots T showing on all three dice. From this single number T you must decide whether the odd die shows a "3" or a "0."

How do you play this game? At first you might merely guess more or less at random about the state of the odd die. As each number T was announced you might say "0" or "3" according to a momentary whim. But after a while you might become more reflective and try to formulate a definite policy or strategy that you would use in playing the game. To formulate such a policy you would clearly wish to compute the probabilities for the various values of T given the two possible states of the odd die.

Table 1-1 gives these computations in columns 2 and 3. You note that for $T = 2$, 3, or 4, there is no probability of the odd die being "3," because if the odd die were a "3" the other dice would have to total either -1, 0, or 1, and these totals are all impossible. Similarly, to achieve $T = 13$, 14, or 15 the odd die must be "3" and cannot possibly be "0." Given any number T between 4 and 12, however, it is impossible to be infallible in the choice between "0" and "3." For each of the numbers 4 to 12 there is some nonzero probability that the odd die is "0" and a nonzero probability that the odd die is "3." It is equally true that for some of these T it is more probable that the odd die is "0" than "3." If T is 9 or greater the probability is greater that the odd die is "3" rather than "0." The last column in Table 1-1 presents the ratios of the probabilities listed in columns 2 and 3, but we shall take up this column later.

How can you make judicious decisions about the number on the odd die, given only the total number T and the statistical information summarized in Table 1-1? What factors should influence the policy you adopt in this situation; that is, what are the relevant variables in a decision-making problem of this kind? Thus far you have no way of answering these questions because an essential part of the problem is unspecified. We have not, as yet, established the goal or objective that you as the decision maker are trying to achieve. What is the aim of your policy? Without specifying an objective there is no way to evaluate any decision procedure. Whether the rules that determine the decisions be capricious or systematic, an assessment of their worth implies a measure of excellence

TABLE 1-1. PROBABILITY OF VARIOUS TOTALS (T), GIVEN THAT ODD DIE COMES UP "0," "3" (MULTIPLY ENTRIES BY 1/36).

Total Spots on Three Dice T	Probability Given Odd Die Is:		Likelihood Ratio $l(T)$
	"3"	"0"	
2	0	1	0
3	0	2	0
4	0	3	0
5	1	4	1/4
6	2	5	2/5
7	3	6	3/6
8	4	5	4/5
9	5	4	5/4
10	6	3	6/3
11	5	2	5/2
12	4	1	4/1
13	3	0	∞
14	2	0	∞
15	1	0	∞
	36	36	

$$l(T) = \frac{f(T \mid \text{"3"})}{f(T \mid \text{"0"})}$$

whereby we can determine the relative merit of different decision procedures. Once the objective is stated—for example, making as many correct decisions as possible—then you can evaluate different policies and determine which one best fulfills the stated objective. Given the aim of trying to maximize the number of correct decisions, the best policy for our example turns out to be, as you might expect, saying "3" if T is 9 or greater and saying "0" if T is 8 or less.

The special property of the numbers 9 to 15 is that for any such number the probability of that number given "3" is greater than the probability of that number given "0." Similarly for the numbers less than 9 the probability is greater given "0" than the probability of that same number given "3." Consider the ratio of these two probabilities: (1) the probability of a particular number given that the odd die is "3" and (2) the probability of that same number given that the odd die is "0." This quantity is called *likelihood ratio*. It is denoted $l(T)$, and listed in the right-hand column of Table 1-1. The quantity is called likelihood ratio because the probabilities are sometimes called "likelihoods." It can be seen from the table that the policy that maximizes the percentage of correct decisions is to say "3" if the likelihood ratio exceeds 1 and to say "0" if it is less than 1.

Although this rule is correct for this simple situation, suppose that we alter the game in some way. Suppose, for example, that the odd die has only one side with 3 spots and five sides with no spots. Then, even before the dice are thrown, you know that the odds are 5 to 1 that the odd die is "0" rather than "3." Clearly, you would not wish to maintain the same decision rule that you used when the a priori probabilities of "0" and "3" were equal. Because the state "3" occurs so rarely, you would want to change your strategy in some way so that only very high likelihood ratios would lead you to say "3." Similarly, there might be different values and costs placed on the different decision outcomes. For example, the penalty associated with incorrectly responding "3" might be five times the penalty associated with incorrectly responding "0." If the values associated with the correct responses of "0" and "3" were the same, then this asymmetry in the cost of the errors would also induce you to adopt a policy that dictates responses of "3" only when the likelihood ratio is very high. Later in the chapter (Section 1.7) we consider a number of decision objectives, such as maximizing the percentage of correct choices and maximizing the expected payoff. For each objective it will be shown that there is an optimal policy or decision rule, one that best fulfills the objective. If the decision rule is stated in terms of likelihood ratio, it always has the same simple form: do one thing if the likelihood ratio is less than a certain number and do the other if the likelihood ratio is greater than that number. The only thing that is altered by the objective of the decision maker is this number, called the *criterion*, that divides the likelihood-ratio continuum in two.

When we speak of optimal decision rules we mean that no other rule can do better *on the average*. In any short period of time, random fluctuations may cause one decision rule to do better than another; for example, if a single decision is considered, the best rule is the one that is correct for that single decision. However, we are interested in decision performance in the long run, not in isolated decisions. We therefore consider the *expected value* of a decision rule. The expected value of a decision rule is a linear sum of the probabilities of all possible decision outcomes, each multiplied by the value (or cost) associated with that outcome. It is generally assumed that the probability of each event (in our example, each value of T), given either possible alternative (in our example, "0" or "3"), is constant throughout a sequence of decisions. This assumption is summarized by saying that the conditional probabilities are *stationary*. Many situations fall outside the range of application of decision theory simply because the assumption of stationarity is violated. Whether the assumption is justified in any particular situation is an empirical matter. A mathematical theory never guarantees any property of empirical process; what it says is that if certain assumptions are true, then certain results will follow.

1.3 FORMAL DISCUSSION OF THE DECISION PROBLEM

The example should help to make clear the essential structure of a typical decision problem as well as the variables one must consider in analyzing such a problem. We shall continue our discussion of these variables on a more general level and also make explicit the analogy between the simple decision game, as illustrated in our example, and a typical psychophysical procedure.

Like the single trial of a psychophysical experiment, a cycle in a decision problem begins with the presentation of some information or some stimulus and ends with the response of the decision maker. The minimal elements are: (1) two possible *states of the world*, (2) the *information*, and (3) the *decision*. In a typical psychophysical experiment the two states of the world are often the absence and the presence of a signal. An interval in time during which the observer attends some sensory display provides the information. We speak of the observer "making an observation" during this interval. Finally, the observer responds with a decision, possibly by stating "signal absent" or "signal present."

Presumably, the observer is fallible because some of his observations are the same whether a signal was sent or not. However, we may assume that different distributions of observations result when the state of the world is "signal" rather than "no signal." The character of the observation can be quite general; it might be a list of attributes having both qualitative and quantitative information. It need not be a single numeric variable such as T in our example. What is important and essential for our purposes is that there exist probability densities for each possible observation given both "signal" and "no signal" and, to make the situation nontrivial, that these densities differ. Thus an observation is like an event in probability theory (see Appendix I); it is an element of a set such that a probability can be defined for each event, and such that the probability of one of the events occurring on any trial is unity.

The response terminates a trial of the decision cycle. The responses available to the decision maker are determined by the nature of the decision task. Often they are in one-to-one correspondence with the possible states of the world. In this case it is easy to see that the response can be scored as correct or incorrect. The average numbers of correct and of incorrect responses are the major dependent variables in the analysis of psychophysical experiments.

We usually think of the response as being dictated by some policy or strategy on the part of the observer. Let us consider the general properties of such policies or, as we shall call them, *decision rules*.

Formally, a decision rule is simply a mathematical function that maps the space of observations onto the space of responses. In our example the response alternatives were "0" or "3" and T could equal 2, 3, . . . , 15. One decision rule was to say "0" if $T = 2, 3, 4, . . . , 8$, and to say "3" if $T = 9, 10, . . . , 15$. As the example illustrates, the range of the decision rule often has fewer elements than the domain. It is, therefore, convenient to consider the decision rule as a partition of the set of possible observations into a few subsets or equivalence classes. From this viewpoint, the decision rule of the example is the partition of the set of numbers T into two equivalence classes. All the decision rules considered in this book can be expressed as a function, or a simple partition, of the elements of the observation class. Technically, such decision rules are called *nonrandom* decision rules, that is, rules that prescribe a definite choice of one alternative for each observation.*

We have gone about as far as we can without introducing some notation and mathematical manipulation. In the next section, after establishing the notation, we consider in more detail the quantity *likelihood ratio* and its importance in decision making. First, we show that likelihood ratio is monotonically related to *a posteriori probability*, that is, to the apparent probability of a state of the world after the observation has been made.

---

* Rules are possible which cannot be simply represented by a function, for example, a rule of this type: if the kth member of the event set occurs, flip a coin and choose alternative A if the coin lands heads and alternative B if it lands tails. Actually, this rule can be viewed not as a random decision rule for the kth event, but as a mixture of two nonrandom rules. Consider two decision rules, D_1 and D_2, that agree on all decisions for all events except one, namely, the kth event. For event k, rule D_1 says, "Choose alternative A," whereas rule D_2 says, "Choose alternative B." Now if we flip a coin on each trial and use rule D_1 when the coin is heads and rule D_2 when the coin is tails, we generate the same decisions for all events save one, namely the kth event. When that event occurs, when the coin was heads we choose A, and when the coin was tails we choose B. Thus we have two fixed decision rules, chosen by a random process, and behaviorally equivalent to a single decision rule with one of the courses of action randomized. If we show that a fixed rule, say D_1, is better than all other fixed decision rules, then it is clearly better than D_2; hence the consistent use of D_1 is better than the random combination of D_1 and D_2.

Second, we show that decision rules based on likelihood ratio will (1) maximize a weighted combination, (2) maximize expected value, (3) maximize the percentage of correct responses, and (4) satisfy the Neyman-Pearson objective. At the end of the chapter we return to our example in discussing the probability density of likelihood ratio. These transformations often cause confusion and the simple example should help to clarify the situation.

1.4   NOTATION

A minimum of notation is needed for the mathematical development that follows, but three symbols must be introduced. Basically, all decision problems have the following structure: first there is some information or evidence, e_k, usually fallible, about a possible state of the world, h_i; from this information the decision maker selects an alternative, H_j, that may or may not be correct.

There must be at least two different states of the world, h_1 or h_2. The choice or response of the decision maker is to *accept one or another hypothesis* about the possible states of the world. We denote the response of the decision maker as a capital letter and use H_j to indicate the decision maker accepting the jth hypothesis. We use the small letter to indicate the states of the world; for example, h_j indicates that the world is in the jth state. When describing the decision maker's behavior we consider probabilities such as $P(H_i \mid h_j)$, which is the probability of the decision maker accepting the ith hypothesis about the state of the world, given that the world is in the jth state. If $i = j$ the response is correct.

The evidence or information that the decision maker uses in making his decision is denoted e_k if the information is discrete and e if it is continuous. It will become apparent in what follows that e_k plays the same role in decision theory as do the elements of a sample space in probability theory. The probability of the occurrence of any single piece of evidence e_k usually depends upon the state of the world. We shall often consider the probability of a certain event e_k occurring given that the world is in the jth state; that is, we consider the probability of e_k conditional on h_i, or $P(e_k \mid h_i)$. Generally, of course, $P(e_k \mid h_i) \neq P(e_k \mid h_j)$, and it is exactly this fact that leads us to describe e_k as evidence or information about the state of the world.

1.4.1   A priori probabilities

Various states of the world may occur with unequal frequency; for example, h_1 may occur more frequently than h_2. This probability of any particular state of the world *prior* to the observation is denoted $P(h_j)$ and is called the *a priori probability* of any particular hypothesis being true. It should be contrasted with the probability of the hypothesis after the observation, or the *a posteriori probability*, which we take up next.

1.4.2 A posteriori probabilities

In accepting or rejecting various hypotheses about the state of the world, we are interested in the probabilities of these hypotheses conditional upon the occurrence of the observation. These are the so-called *a posteriori probabilities:* the probabilities of the truth of each hypothesis after the event has occurred. The a posteriori probability of hypothesis h_i being true, given e_k, is denoted $P(h_i \mid e_k)$. How are the conditional probabilities and the a priori probabilities of the various hypotheses related to these a posteriori probabilities? First, note that, by definition,

$$P(h_i \cdot e_k) = P(e_k)P(h_i \mid e_k) \tag{1.1}$$

where $P(h_i \cdot e_k)$ denotes the probability of the joint occurrence of h_i and e_k. Second, by definition,

$$P(h_i \cdot e_k) = P(h_i)P(e_k \mid h_i) \tag{1.2}$$

And third, since event e_k can occur only if some hypothesis holds,

$$P(e_k) = \sum_i P(h_i)P(e_k \mid h_i) \tag{1.3}$$

Combining these equations,

$$P(h_i \mid e_k) = \frac{P(h_i)P(e_k \mid h_i)}{P(e_k)} = \frac{P(h_i)P(e_k \mid h_i)}{\sum_i P(h_i)P(e_k \mid h_i)} \tag{1.4}$$

This last equation is usually called Bayes' rule. The name honors the clergyman Thomas Bayes, who seems to have been the first to formalize this expression. Considerable dispute about this rule has occurred in the philosophy of science. The controversy centers on how the a priori probabilities can be determined and, indeed, since the world is in only one state, whether it is meaningful to think of the probability that different states of the world exist. We shall assume that the a priori probabilities are given as part of the specification of the decision problem and so avoid any argument.

The application of Bayes' rule can be illustrated with the material of our decision problem. The a priori probability of the odd die being a "3" is one half. After learning that T is equal to 10, the a posteriori probability of the odd die being a "3" is

$$P(h = \text{"3"} \mid T = 10) = \frac{\frac{1}{2} \times \frac{1}{6}}{\frac{1}{2} \times \frac{1}{6} + \frac{1}{2} \times \frac{1}{12}} = \frac{\frac{2}{24}}{\frac{3}{24}} = \frac{2}{3}$$

Similarly the a posteriori probability of the odd die being "0," given the same observation, is

$$P(h = \text{"0"} \mid T = 10) = \frac{\frac{1}{2} \times \frac{1}{12}}{\frac{1}{2} \times \frac{1}{6} + \frac{1}{2} \times \frac{1}{12}} = \frac{\frac{1}{24}}{\frac{3}{24}} = \frac{1}{3}$$

Whereas the initial or a priori probability that the odd die was "3" is one half, its probability after knowing the value of T is 0.67. The evidence provided by the event e_k changes the probabilities of the various hypotheses being true.

1.4.3   Likelihood ratio

The a posteriori probability is a function both of the a priori probability and of the information or event. Sometimes it is preferable to evaluate the evidence provided by an observation *independently* of the a priori probabilities of the hypotheses. That is, a quantity is desired that expresses the strength of evidence associated with each observation. Although no completely general measure seems to be known, if attention is restricted to two hypotheses, h_i and h_j, then the evidence provided by e_k relative to h_i and h_j is conveniently summarized by the likelihood ratio, which is defined as follows:

$$l_{ij}(e_k) = \frac{P(e_k \mid h_i)}{P(e_k \mid h_j)} = \frac{1}{l_{ji}(e_k)} \tag{1.5}$$

where $l_{ij}(e_k)$ is read "the likelihood ratio of event e_k for hypothesis i relative to hypothesis j." In the example just considered the likelihood ratio for number $T = 10$ is $6/3 = 2$.

If the a priori probability of each hypothesis is one half, then the likelihood ratio is the same as the "odds" of the given hypothesis. Likelihood ratio is a single number, the ratio of the probabilities of an event under two hypotheses.

Note that the dimensionality of the observation or event in no way influences the calculation of likelihood ratio. In our example, the observation was a single number, T. The observation might be very complicated, such as a certain configuration of pressure and temperature, the velocity of wind at certain altitudes, the time of year, and other factors. If only two hypotheses are considered—for instance, fair weather and foul—there are only two probabilities of the particular configurations of meteorological events occurring, one probability for each hypothesis. The likelihood ratio therefore remains a single real number no matter what the structure of the observation happens to be. If there are more than two alternatives, more likelihood ratios are needed to specify the decision problem completely. In general, the number of likelihood ratios required is one less than the number of hypotheses. For example, when there are four hypotheses, we can always find and compute only three likelihood ratios, so that any other likelihood ratio is determined by the first three. That is, if l_{12}, l_{13}, and l_{14} are known, then $l_{23} = l_{21}/l_{31}$ and $l_{34} = l_{14}/l_{13}$. In a two-hypothesis situation, such as drilling for oil at a particular location, one can sample as many sources of information as one likes—the events may represent an entire report filled with statistics about the situation. The decision should be based on the likelihood ratio, that is, the probability of these events given that there is oil divided by the probability of these events given that there is no oil. This likelihood ratio must be a single number.

1.5   REPRESENTATION OF DECISION OUTCOMES

In the decision situation that we are considering, any single decision is either right or wrong. Any sensible evaluation of the decision maker's performance, therefore, must be based on some function of the average number of correct and incorrect decisions that he makes. There are always at least two types of correct decisions that can be made and at least two .types of errors. Generally, when we decrease the probability of one type of error we increase the chance of an error of the other kind; or, what is equivalent: increasing the probability of both kinds of correct decisions cannot be carried out simultaneously.

Before turning to the problem of optimizing a decision rule, let us agree on a standard representation of these correct and incorrect decisions. Remember that we are assuming the probabilities involved in the decision process to be stationary and independent from trial to trial. Thus there is no information lost by ignoring the sequence of decisions. Decision outcomes in this case can always be represented by a matrix in which the rows are identified with the several potential states of the world and the columns are identified with the response alternatives available to the decision maker. Each instance of the decision process begins with an event drawn from the set of possible hypotheses (one hypothesis is true) and ends with the choice of a response alternative. Thus each decision cycle refers to only one cell of the matrix displayed in Fig. 1-1.

It is convenient to normalize the entries of the matrix so that they range between zero and one. The entries are the proportions of response alternatives chosen conditional upon a particular hypothesis. The notation uses the convention, adopted earlier, of representing the response of the decision maker by capital letter H_j and the state of the world by a small letter h_j. Thus, when alternative h_2 is presented 100 times and the decision maker chooses alternative H_3 twenty times, the entry is 0.20 in row 2, column 3 of the table. Given the conditional nature of the entries, the sum of all cell entries within a single row must equal one. This fact is indicated

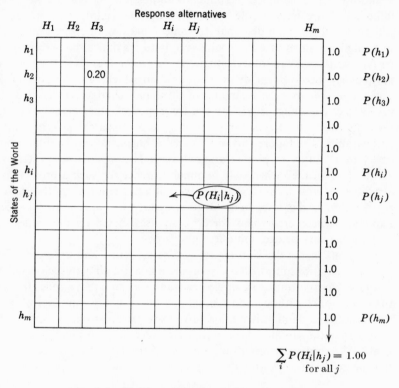

FIG. 1-1   Matrix representing decision outcomes.

by the number 1.0 which occurs at the end of each row. (*Note.* The sum of cell entries in any given column need not add up to any particular number.) Such a normalization causes us to lose all information about the a priori probabilities $P(h_k)$; we are therefore obliged to list these numbers separately at the end of the rows. The a priori probabilities can be estimated simply by counting the number of times each state of the world occurs and normalizing these numbers by the total number of decisions made. To determine the unconditional, or joint, probability of a given hypothesis-response pair, one multiplies the a priori probability $P(h_j)$ by the conditional probability of the desired pair. The product of $P(H_k \mid h_j)$ and $P(h_j)$ is the probability that response H_k was chosen *and* that the *j*th hypothesis was true.

The best we can hope for is a sequence of 1's down the main diagonal of the matrix. Since this forces all other entries to be 0, it means that all decisions are correct. It is rare always to be correct, and thus decision theory is devoted to providing judicious rules of decision for those more common situations where complete certainty is impossible. Given the necessary fallibility of any decision rule for situations of uncertainty, nonzero entries will occur off the main diagonal. In some situations all errors are equally unwanted, in which case the goal is simply to maximize the percentage of correct responses. In other situations, however, some errors may be particularly inconvenient or unacceptable, in which case the goal of the decision maker may be to minimize these particular errors even if this necessitates doubling or tripling the frequency of other errors and even lowering the total percent correct. A simple practical example is weather prediction, where failure to warn against a hurricane can be much more costly than failure to predict a sunny day. The weather forecaster may predict "hurricane" when only minimal evidence for such a prediction is available. Although this lowers his over-all average it insures that he will rarely fail to predict a storm in advance. Clearly, an appropriate balance is required between errors and correct responses, based on the values and costs of the various decision outcomes.

The goals of the decision maker can be as varied and different as the practical situations in which decisions are made. Faced with such diversity, is it possible to formulate a single decision procedure that applies to more than one goal? Although an unqualified "yes" is not possible, we shall show that the quantity likelihood ratio provides a convenient and simple means of stating optimal decision rules for several quite different decision goals. The particular criterion value is different for the different goals, but the general form of the decision rule is the same.

1.6   OPTIMAL DECISION MAKING: USE OF LIKELIHOOD RATIO

In the latter part of this chapter we list several goals and show how likelihood ratio can be used to achieve these goals. In what follows only two-hypothesis situations are considered. When the goal can be generalized to more than two alternatives, a generalization of the optimal decision rule exists that may be stated in terms of likelihood ratio. Before discussing how decisions can be optimized, let us introduce one more very important decision-theoretic concept—that of the equivalence of two decision rules.

Two decision rules are equivalent if for every event that can occur both rules dictate the choice of the same response alternative. For example, if $y = \log e_i$ and if the criterion value of e_i is k and the criterion value of y is $\log k$, then identical decisions will result. The two scales need only be monotonically related, for if the decision rule A is of the form "Choose H_1 if and only if $e > k$," and if another scale y exists so that $y(e_i)$ is a strictly monotonic function of e, then there exists another decision rule B of the form "Choose H_1 if and only if $y > t$," which is equivalent to decision rule A if $y = y(e_i)$ and $t = y(k)$.

Two variables that are monotonically related and are often used in decision making are likelihood ratio and a posteriori probability.

Rewriting Eq. 1.4 for the case of two alternatives, h_j and h_k, we have for e_i:

$$P(h_j \mid e_i) = \frac{P(h_j)P(e_i \mid h_j)}{P(h_j)P(e_i \mid h_j) + P(h_k)P(e_i \mid h_k)}$$

$$= \frac{1}{\dfrac{P(h_k)P(e_i \mid h_k)}{P(h_j)P(e_i \mid h_j)} + 1} \tag{1.6}$$

Using Eq. 1.5 we may write this in the form:

$$P(h_j \mid e_i) = \frac{1}{\dfrac{P(h_k)}{P(h_j)} l_{kj}(e_i) + 1} \tag{1.7}$$

The main point is that, if the a priori probabilities are nonzero, the a posteriori probability of the jth hypothesis, given the ith event, and the likelihood ratio of the ith event are monotonic functions of one another. Therefore, any decision procedure that operates by placing events in an acceptance class according to the magnitude of the a posteriori probability must be equivalent to some decision rule that places the events in classes according to the magnitude of the likelihood ratio. Another way to look at decision rules is in terms of partitions of the set of events e_i. As previously mentioned, it is often useful to think of decision rules as, in effect, labeling each element of the set whose elements are e_i. From this viewpoint, a decision rule partitions the event class into two mutually exclusive and exhaustive regions: those events that lead us to accept hypothesis j and those that do not. Two decision rules are equivalent if and only if they correspond to the same partition of the event set.

The exact form of this relation between likelihood ratio and a posteriori probability has several implications. We pursue these practical implications in more detail in Appendix 1-A, at the end of this chapter, where the formula for combining two or more independent likelihood ratios is developed. In addition, the equation relating a priori probability, a posteriori probability, and multiple likelihood ratio is developed in Appendix 1-A.

1.7 DECISION GOALS

The following sections give a precise statement of the decision maker's goal. The ensuing algebra either reveals that the decision rule attains the objective or proves that the stated rule is optimal. The observation e_i is considered discrete in all that follows, so that summations rather than integrals appear in all the equations. Thus probability theory and algebra are all that is required to follow the proofs. For those whose knowledge of probability theory is not recent, a brief review of that topic appears in Appendix I at the end of this book.

1.7.1 Maximize a weighted combination

Recall that in a two-alternative situation, where stationarity is assumed, the outcomes can be described by four probabilities. Only two of these four probabilities are independent because

$$P(H_0 \mid h_0) + P(H_1 \mid h_0) = 1$$

and

$$P(H_0 \mid h_1) + P(H_1 \mid h_1) = 1$$

One very desirable objective, were it possible, would be to maximize $P(H_1 \mid h_1)$ while minimizing $P(H_1 \mid h_0)$. Generally, however, we cannot achieve both objectives simultaneously. A somewhat weaker, but feasible, objective is to maximize the quantity

$$\{P(H_1 \mid h_1) - \beta P(H_1 \mid h_0)\}$$

where β is a constant, $\beta > 0$. Clearly, this is a reasonable goal, since it is achieved when $P(H_1 \mid h_1)$ is large and $P(H_1 \mid h_0)$ is small. The parameter β establishes the relative importance of these two objectives in the sense that when $P(H_1 \mid h_1)$ is increased by an amount Δ then $P(H_1 \mid h_0)$ should increase by no more than Δ/β for the change to be considered desirable.

Consider rules formulated in terms of the events that lead us to accept hypothesis h_1, that is, to choose response alternative H_1. If we designate as region A all those events which lead to the acceptance of h_1, then the probability that h_1 is accepted when h_1 is true is simply

$$\sum_{e_i \in A} P(e_i \mid h_1) = P(H_1 \mid h_1) \tag{1.8}$$

where the sum is over all those events e_i that lie within the acceptance region A. Thus A determines $P(H_1 \mid h_1)$.

Similarly, the probability of an incorrect acceptance of hypothesis h_1 is

$$P(H_1 \mid h_0) = \sum_{e_i \in A} P(e_i \mid h_0) \qquad (1.9)$$

To achieve the goal of maximizing $P(H_1 \mid h_1)$, we must select that region A so that

$$P(H_1 \mid h_1) - \beta P(H_1 \mid h_0) = \sum_{e_i \in A} P(e_i \mid h_1) - \beta \sum_{e_i \in A} P(e_i \mid h_0) \qquad (1.10)$$

is as large as possible.

How can we recognize whether an event e_i should be included with the acceptance region A? Consider a specific event e_k. It augments the total sum when

$$P(e_k \mid h_1) - \beta P(e_k \mid h_0) > 0 \qquad (1.11)$$

and it diminishes the sum when

$$P(e_k \mid h_1) - \beta P(e_k \mid h_0) < 0. \qquad (1.12)$$

Clearly we want to include in A only events of the first type, so e_k should be included in A if and only if*

$$\frac{P(e_k \mid h_1)}{P(e_k \mid h_0)} \geq \beta \qquad (1.13)$$

This is exactly equivalent to defining the acceptance region for the h_1 hypothesis as consisting of all events whose likelihood ratios equal or exceed β, where β is the criterion value.

Thus we have our first result: *A decision rule that maximizes $P(H_1 \mid h_1) - \beta P(H_1 \mid h_0)$ is to choose H_1 if and only if $l_{10}(e_i) \geq \beta$.*

1.7.2 Maximize expected value

Consider a binary decision situation for which certain values and costs are defined for each of the four possible outcomes. In the notation employed, the first subscript corresponds to the alternative presented and the second subscript to the alternative chosen.

---

* It does not matter how we allocate those events e_i for which $P(e_i \mid h_1) = \beta P(e_i \mid h_0)$ because they neither contribute to nor detract from the objective. We assume that they are in A.

V_{00} = value associated with a correct choice of H_0

V_{01} = value (cost) associated with an incorrect choice of H_1 (when, in fact, H_0 is the correct alternative); that is, the person loses V_{01} when this type of incorrect choice is made.

V_{11} = value associated with a correct choice of H_1

V_{10} = value (cost) associated with an incorrect choice of H_0 (when, in fact, H_1 is the correct alternative); that is, the person loses V_{10} when this type of incorrect choice is made.

The expected value of a decision strategy is the sum of four terms, each of which represents the value or cost associated with an outcome weighted by the probability of that outcome occurring under the strategy in question:

$$\text{Expected value} = V_{00}P(h_0)P(H_0 \mid h_0) + V_{11}P(h_1)P(H_1 \mid h_1)$$
$$- V_{10}P(h_1)P(H_0 \mid h_1) - V_{01}P(h_0)P(H_1 \mid h_0) \quad (1.14)$$

Suppose that the objective is to maximize the expected value; then the question is how to define the acceptance regions for h_0 and h_1 so as to achieve this goal. Although it probably is not yet apparent, we have in fact answered this question, because it turns out that to maximize the expected value, once the values, the costs, and the a priori probability are fixed, is equivalent to maximizing an expression of the form

$$P(H_1 \mid h_1) - \beta P(H_1 \mid h_0) \quad (1.15)$$

where β is a constant whose numerical value is determined by the a priori probability of the hypotheses and the values and costs associated with the various outcomes. According to the result of the previous section, maximizing Eq. 1.15 is achieved by placing in the acceptance class of h_1 all those events whose likelihood ratio of h_1 to h_0 is equal to or greater than β, and by placing all other events in the h_0 acceptance class.

We now prove this and at the same time determine the dependence of β on values, costs, and a priori probabilities. First we rewrite Eq. 1.14 solely in terms of $P(H_1 \mid h_1)$ and $P(H_1 \mid h_0)$, using the following identities:

$$P(H_0 \mid h_0) = 1 - P(H_1 \mid h_0) \quad (1.16)$$

and

$$P(H_0 \mid h_1) = 1 - P(H_1 \mid h_1) \quad (1.17)$$

This yields

$$\text{Expected value} = V_{00}P(h_0) - V_{00}P(h_0)P(H_1 \mid h_0) + V_{11}P(h_1)P(H_1 \mid h_1)$$
$$- V_{10}P(h_1) + V_{10}P(h_1)P(H_1 \mid h_1) - V_{01}P(h_0)P(H_1 \mid h_0) \quad (1.18)$$

Next note that $V_{00}P(h_0)$ and $V_{10}P(h_1)$ are constants, so that maximizing the expected value is equivalent to maximizing

$$[V_{11}P(h_1) + V_{10}P(h_1)]P(H_1 \mid h_1) - [V_{00}P(h_0) + V_{01}P(h_0)]P(H_1 \mid h_0) \quad (1.19)$$

By writing this in the form

$$P(H_1 \mid h_1) - \frac{(V_{00} + V_{01})P(h_0)}{(V_{11} + V_{10})P(h_1)} \cdot P(H_1 \mid h_0)$$

it is easily seen that maximizing the value of Eq. 1.19 is equivalent to maximizing an expression of the form given in Eq. 1.15 with

$$\beta = \frac{(V_{00} + V_{01})P(h_0)}{(V_{11} + V_{10})P(h_1)} \tag{1.20}$$

Therefore, the expected value is maximized by accepting as h_1 all those events whose likelihood ratio of h_1 to h_0 is equal to or greater than β as defined in Eq. 1.20.

Analysis of human behavior has often been interpreted as demonstrating that subjective probability, not actual probability, and subjective value or utility, not monetary value, determine the subject's decision. Let us assume, therefore, that nonlinear transformations of the values and costs, and of the a priori probabilities, ultimately determine behavior. Even if we assume four different transformations of the value scales and another transformation of the probability scale, the maximization of subjective value would still have the same form as that of Eq. 1.20. The only thing that changes is the numerical value of β. Although the particular criterion value for likelihood ratio may be altered, a likelihood-ratio criterion is still the optimal decision rule.

1.7.3   Maximize the percentage of correct responses

Often all the values associated with correct decisions are equally valued and all the errors are equally abhorred. If we set the value of being correct at unity and the cost of an error at zero, then we may realize that this is equivalent simply to maximizing the percentage of correct decisions. Inspection of Eq. 1.20 reveals that this condition is met if

$$\beta = \frac{P(h_0)}{P(h_1)} \tag{1.21}$$

If the a priori probabilities are equal, then $\beta = 1$; if they are unequal, then, as $P(h_1)$ increases, a smaller and smaller likelihood ratio is required for H_1 to be chosen.

1.7.4   Satisfy the Neyman-Pearson objective

The Neyman-Pearson objective is as follows: *for some constant k, $0 \le k \le 1$, set $P(H_1 \mid h_0) = k$ and then maximize $P(H_1 \mid h_1)$.* This goal is familiar to those who perform statistical tests. Usually k is set equal to 0.01 or 0.05 and then one endeavors to design a test to maximize the acceptance of h_1 when it is true, while holding the error rate at the level k. Neyman and Pearson suggested this objective in the classic paper of 1933 which, more than any other paper, established the fundamental significance of the decision procedure based on likelihood ratio.

To show that a likelihood-ratio criterion actually achieves the Neyman-Pearson objective is somewhat involved, but not really difficult. To begin, suppose that we rank all the events in terms of the likelihood ratio of hypothesis h_1 to h_0. Each likelihood ratio is composed of two probabilities: $P(e_k \mid h_1)$ in the numerator and $P(e_k \mid h_0)$ in the denominator. Given this ranking, we construct an acceptance class A for h_1 by adding the events one by one to the acceptance class, starting with the event having the largest likelihood ratio. Thus we will systematically increase the probability of incorrectly responding H_1 when H_0 is the correct alternative; in fact, the probability of this error is given by

$$P(H_1 \mid h_0) = \sum_{e_k \in A} P(e_k \mid h_0) \qquad (1.22)$$

When this sum equals the given constant k, we stop our construction of the acceptance class.† We denote β the smallest value (also the last value) of likelihood ratio included in our acceptance class. Our decision rule is, therefore: *Choose H_1 for all events whose likelihood ratio is equal to or exceeds β, where β is selected such that $P(H_1 \mid h_0) = k$.*

To show that this rule is optimal in the Neyman-Pearson sense, consider an alternative scheme that purports to do better. Denote its acceptance region A^*. The region A^* may include some of the events in A and may also include other events. Let

$$A - A^* = \text{the set of events in } A \text{ but not in } A^*$$
$$A \cap A^* = \text{the set of events both in } A \text{ and in } A^*$$
$$A^* - A = \text{the set of events in } A^* \text{ but not in } A$$

Recall that both decision rules A and A^* must have the common property that $P(H_1 \mid h_0) = k$; hence

$$\sum_{e_k \in A} P(e_k \mid h_0) = k = \sum_{e_k \in A^*} P(e_k \mid h_0) \qquad (1.23)$$

If we subtract from both sides of Eq. 1.23 the terms corresponding to the events common to both acceptance classes, that is, the $e_k \in A \cap A^*$, we

---

† We are implicitly assuming that e is continuous; thus the sum $P(H_1 \mid h_0)$ can be constructed to just equal k. The discrete proof is similar but more involved because the two kinds of inequalities as well as the equality must be considered.

have

$$\sum_{e_k \in A - A^*} P(e_k \mid h_0) = \sum_{e_k \in A^* - A} P(e_k \mid h_0) \qquad (1.24)$$

Now let us examine the difference between the probabilities of correct acceptance of h_1 under the two decision procedures. The probability of accepting h_1 when it is true is

$$\sum_{e_k \in A} P(e_k \mid h_1) \quad \text{for rule } A,$$

and is

$$\sum_{e_k \in A^*} P(e_k \mid h_1) \quad \text{for rule } A^*.$$

The difference is

$$\Delta = \sum_{e_k \in A^*} P(e_k \mid h_1) - \sum_{e_k \in A} P(e_k \mid h_1) \qquad (1.25)$$

Once again, if we subtract from both sums the common terms, that is, those terms corresponding to elements in the regions $A \cap A^*$, we do not alter the value of Δ:

$$\Delta = \sum_{e \in A^* - A} P(e_k \mid h_1) - \sum_{e_k \in A - A^*} P(e_k \mid h_1) \qquad (1.26)$$

By definition, region A consists of all those events such that

$$\frac{P(e_k \mid h_1)}{P(e_k \mid h_0)} \geq \beta \qquad (1.27)$$

The region $A - A^*$ consists only of events in A,

$$\sum_{e_k \in A - A^*} P(e_k \mid h_1) \geq \beta \sum_{e_k \in A - A^*} P(e_k \mid h_0) \qquad (1.28)$$

but from the fact that $A^* - A$ consists of events entirely outside A we have

$$\sum_{e_k \in A^* - A} P(e_k \mid h_1) \leq \beta \sum_{e_k \in A^* - A} P(e_k \mid h_0) \qquad (1.29)$$

Thus, by Eqs. 1.26, 1.28, and 1.29,

$$\Delta = \sum_{e_k \in A^* - A} P(e_k \mid h_1) - \sum_{e_k \in A - A^*} P(e_k \mid h_1)$$
$$\leq \beta \left[\sum_{e_k \in A^* - A} P(e_k \mid h_0) - \sum_{e_k \in A - A^*} P(e_k \mid h_0) \right] \qquad (1.30)$$

But by Eq. 1.24 the term within the square brackets is 0; thus $\Delta \leq 0$.

Therefore, at best, A^* does no better than A. Since A^* corresponds to an arbitrary decision rule, this result proves that A is the best region. We have therefore proved that the Neyman-Pearson criterion is equivalent to a decision rule based on the likelihood-ratio criterion.

1.8   DISTRIBUTION OF LIKELIHOOD RATIO

As the preceding derivations have demonstrated for several objectives, the best we can do is to adopt a policy or decision rule of the following kind: choose H_i if $l(e_k) \geq c$, where c is a constant, and choose H_j otherwise. The probability of a correct decision is then

$$\sum_{l(e_k) \geq c} P(l(e_k) \mid h_i) \tag{1.31}$$

which is a sum over the conditional probabilities of certain likelihood ratios given a particular hypothesis. In a two-alternative situation there are two such conditional probabilities, one for each hypothesis. We may also consider the likelihood ratio of the likelihood ratio. Let $P_1[l(e_k) \mid h_1]$ be the probability of likelihood ratio $l(e_k)$ given h_1, and let $P_2[l(e_k) \mid h_2]$ be the probability of likelihood ratio $l(e_k)$ given h_2. Then, to paraphrase Gertrude Stein, *the likelihood ratio of the likelihood ratio is the likelihood ratio.* That is,

$$l[l(e_k)] = \frac{P_1[l(e_k) \mid h_1]}{P_2[l(e_k) \mid h_2]} = l(e_k) \tag{1.32}$$

for all events e_k.

Since this relationship has puzzled some, it may be worth while to spend a little more time on it. In our example, given $T = 10$, we recall (see Table 1-1) that $P(T = 10 \mid \text{``3''}) = 6/36$, and $P(T = 10 \mid \text{``0''}) = 3/36$; thus $l(10) = 2$. Furthermore, $P(l = 2 \mid \text{``3''}) = 6/36$, since $l = 2$ only if $T = 10$, and $P(l = 2 \mid \text{``0''}) = 3/36$, for the same reason. Now we can consider the likelihood ratio of $l = 2$, and it must be

$$l(l = 2) = \frac{P(l = 2 \mid \text{``3''})}{P(l = 2 \mid \text{``0''})} = \frac{\frac{6}{36}}{\frac{3}{36}} = 2$$

When we consider the probability densities of the likelihood ratios given both hypotheses, we see that the ratio of the two conditional densities is simply the value of the argument. There is nothing mysterious or illogical about this relation; it is a natural consequence of our definitions. It is important that it be understood, as it will arise again when the topic of *receiver operating characteristics* is discussed in the next chapter.

1.9   SUMMARY

The latter part of this chapter has demonstrated that four distinct objectives all imply decision rules of the form

$$\text{Respond } H_1 \text{ if } l_{10}(e_i) \geq \beta$$

where the particular value of β is determined by the particular objective and where $l_{10}(e_i)$ is the likelihood ratio of hypothesis h_1 to h_0 for event e_i. The simplicity of decision rules of this form, coupled with the fact that such rules are appropriate in a variety of situations, is sufficient to establish the importance of likelihood ratio in decision-making problems of the type considered. Of course, the actual decision rule used by some device or person may not be phrased explicitly in terms of likelihood ratio. If the decision rule is equivalent to one based on likelihood ratio it will still achieve the decision objective best. The mere presence or absence of likelihood ratio in some decision rule is of no importance.

We use the terminology and definitions developed in this chapter to discuss the problem of human observers making decisions in the psychophysical task. The general structure developed here will, we hope, permit the reader to distinguish more clearly the empirical from the theoretical in the material that follows.

1.10   APPENDIX 1-A

Consider a decision maker who has two *independent* pieces of information, e_1 and e_2, both of which are relevant to a decision between two hypotheses, h_0 and h_1. How can these be combined to estimate the a posteriori probability, and how can the likelihood ratio be useful in this process?

Since, by assumption, e_1 and e_2 are independent, we know that

$$P(e_1, e_2 \mid h_0) = P(e_1 \mid h_0) \cdot P(e_2 \mid h_0) \tag{1A.1}$$

and

$$P(e_1, e_2 \mid h_1) = P(e_1 \mid h_1) \cdot P(e_1 \mid h_1) \tag{1A.2}$$

Note that we have assumed independence under both hypotheses. The a posteriori probability of h_0 is simply

$$P(h_0 \mid e_1, e_2) = \frac{P(h_0) \cdot P(e_1, e_2 \mid h_0)}{P(h_0)P(e_1, e_2 \mid h_0) + P(h_1)P(e_1, e_2 \mid h_1)} \tag{1A.3}$$

or, dividing both numerator and denominator by

$$P(h_0)P(e_1, e_2 \mid h_0)$$

we have

$$P(h_0 \mid e_1, e_2) = \frac{1}{1 + \dfrac{P(h_1)}{P(h_0)} l_{10}(e_1, e_2)} \tag{1A.4}$$

Since

$$l_{kj}(e_1, e_2) = \frac{P(e_1, e_2 \mid h_k)}{P(e_1, e_2 \mid h_j)} = \frac{P(e_1 \mid h_k)P(e_2 \mid h_k)}{P(e_1 \mid h_j)P(e_2 \mid h_j)} = l_{kj}(e_1)l_{kj}(e_2) \qquad (1A.5)$$

we have

$$P(h_0 \mid e_1, e_2) = \frac{1}{1 + \dfrac{P(h_1)}{P(h_0)} l_{10}(e_1)l_{10}(e_2)} \qquad (1A.6)$$

A simple induction shows that this result generalizes to any finite set of independent sources of information. Therefore, given n events, $e_1, e_2, \ldots, e_n$, each of which is independent under both hypotheses, the a posteriori probability of a hypothesis h_j is

$$P(h_j \mid e_1, e_2 \cdots e_i \cdots e_n) = \frac{1}{1 + \dfrac{P(h_k)}{P(h_j)} \displaystyle\prod_{i=1}^{n} l_{kj}(e_i)} \qquad (1A.7)$$

PROBLEMS*

1.1 Consider the following game of chance. Three dice are thrown. Two of the dice are ordinary dice with the numbers 1 through 6 appearing on their sides. The third die is unusual; either it has three spots on all six sides, or it has three sides with six spots and three sides with no spots. We may suppose that the die with three spots on each of its sides is black and that the other die having three "0's" and three "6's" is orange. The game is played as follows. Someone selects either the black or the orange die and, combining it with the two normal dice, rolls all three dice. You as a player do not observe the throw of the dice. You are only informed of the total number of spots (T) showing on all three dice. From this single number (T) you must guess whether the odd die is black or orange.

(a) List the probability of each value of T given each state of the world (i.e., orange or black), and derive the likelihood ratio for each value of T,

$$l(T) = P(T \mid h_b)/P(T \mid h_0).$$

(b) Two decision rules are equivalent if they always lead to the same decisions for all possible observations. Are the following decision rules equivalent?

> *Rule 1:* Say "black" if $T = 9$, 10 or 11; say "orange" otherwise.

> *Rule 2:* Say "black" if $l(T) \geq 1.50$; say "orange" otherwise.

1.2 The following table gives the probabilities (fictitious) of various heights conditional upon hair color.

* Problem solutions are on p. 429.

Hair Color

		Black	Blond	Red
Height	Greater than 5 ft	0.60	0.50	0.40
	Less than 5 ft	0.40	0.50	0.60
Relative frequency in population		0.40	0.40	0.20

(a) What is the likelihood ratio of a height greater than 5 ft to a height less than 5 ft given an observation of black hair; given red hair; given blond hair?

(b) What is the probability of a person being black-haired if his height is greater than 5 ft; a blond if less than 5 ft; a redhead if greater than 5 ft?

1.3 Suppose a gang of smugglers were trying illegally to export radioactive material. In an effort to try to stop this, you monitor with a Geiger counter every package leaving the country. For those packages without the radioactive material (NRA) the number of counts is given approximately by an exponential distribution. Letting x equal the number of counts:

$$f(x \mid \text{NRA}) \approx e^{-x}$$

For the package with radioactive material (RA):

$$f(x \mid \text{RA}) \approx \lambda e^{-\lambda x} \quad 0 < \lambda < 1.00$$

(a) What is the likelihood ratio of a package's containing radioactive material as opposed to its not containing radioactive material?

(b) If the a priori probability of a package's containing radioactive material is 1 in 10^6, and if

$100 is cost of opening a package and repacking
it if does not contain radioactive material
10^4 is value of catching a radioactive package
-10^6 is cost of letting a radioactive package
through
$0 is the value of letting a nonradioactive package
through

what value of likelihood ratio should lead one to ask that the package be opened?

(c) If $\lambda = \frac{1}{4}$, what value of x would one need to attain that value of likelihood ratio?

1.4 With reference to Problem 1.3, suppose your budget director gives you $100,000 per year, so that you can afford to open 1000 packages per year even if none is radioactive.

(a) What number of counts would you use on the assumption that 10^7 packages are processed each year?

(b) What is your probability of detecting a radioactive package if $\lambda = \frac{1}{3}$?

2

Statistical Decision Theory
and Psychophysical Procedures

2.1   INTRODUCTION

The preceding chapter presented material on statistical decision theory. In this chapter we consider one way of applying that material to the process of decision making as it occurs in psychophysical tasks.

The basic datum of classical psychophysics is the minimal signal energy that the observer can detect. According to detection theory, the observer's problem in detecting weak signals is to decide whether some sensory event was caused by a signal or by some random process, such as background noise. One example of the problem is the so-called *yes-no* task, in which the observer must say whether the single stimulus on each trial was a signal added to a background noise or simply noise alone. A variant of this task, also discussed in this chapter, is the *rating* task. In this case, too, the observer is presented a single stimulus on each trial, either signal plus noise or noise alone, but he can make one of many different responses. For example, the observer might be instructed to rate on a six-point scale the likelihood that the observation was caused by signal plus noise as opposed to noise alone. A third task included in this analysis is the *forced-choice* task, in which the signal is presented in one of two or more intervals (usually temporal, but sometimes spatial) and the observer is instructed to select the interval that he believes most likely to have contained the signal in addition to the noise. Usually, in all three procedures, the signal that is presented is specified for the observer in advance.

The statistical-decision analysis of these psychophysical procedures provides ways of predicting the results of one procedure from the results obtained in others. Comparing the results obtained from these different procedures is extremely important because such comparisons provide the major test of the validity of the decision-theory analysis. If the analysis is verified, it yields measures of the detectability of the signal that are independent of the procedure used to estimate these measures. Therefore, this analysis holds forth the possibility of psychophysical relations which are independent of procedure, a goal more often hoped for than achieved.

For those whose exclusive interest in psychophysics is to determine the particular signal level or increment in signal level that the observer can just reliably detect, this discussion can be interpreted as an analysis of the variables that influence the psychophysical judgment. The approach discussed here clearly isolates the inherent detectability of the signal from certain attitudinal or motivational variables that influence the observer's criteria for judgment. Furthermore, the analysis suggests ways of controlling, and hence eliminating, certain biases which will, unless measured and controlled, lead to spurious estimates of the signal's detectability. To the stimulus-oriented psychophysicist, this analysis is a methodological study, but one that is clearly pertinent since it claims to provide an unbiased estimate of what, for the stimulus-oriented psychophysicist, is the major dependent variable.

Before beginning the analysis, we must discuss a rather general assumption that underlies much of the following exposition. This assumption is that observers are able to distinguish among various sensory events, and that they can compare several such events with a scale that is monotonic with the likelihood ratio that a particular sensory event was caused by a signal rather than by noise. Presumably, the observers develop this ability by experience with the signals and the noise used in the particular experiment. The exact mechanisms responsible for this ability are not fully understood. We assume that, whatever the mechanisms, the observer develops such an ordinal scale of likelihood ratio. In particular, we assume that two sensory events can be compared and the sensory event associated with the larger likelihood ratio determined. This assumption needs to be made explicit, since the descriptions presented in this and later chapters are meant to apply to well-practiced observers. There is relatively little experimental evidence available on exactly how long a training procedure is necessary to obtain asymptotic performance in simple detection tasks (Appendix III). The available evidence from experiments on the detection of sinusoidal signals in noise suggests that two to four hours of training is sufficient.

This chapter begins with a fairly detailed description of three psychophysical procedures. Graphical treatment of the data obtained from the yes-no and rating procedures leads to a discussion of the *receiver operating characteristic* (ROC), which provides a natural distinction between the inherent detectability of the signal and the judgment, or decision, criterion of the subject. The third procedure, forced choice, is then discussed, and the expected relation between forced-choice results and the yes-no or rating ROC is described.

The unique feature of this presentation is that the results are completely independent of any assumption one might make about the statistical distributions of the sensory events produced by signal plus noise or by noise alone. The results are "distribution-free." In the next chapter specific assumptions, such as the normal or Gaussian assumption, are pursued. Here we consider only general relations.

2.2   YES-NO PROCEDURE

In a yes-no task, the observer is presented one of two mutually exclusive stimulus alternatives. He is asked to respond by selecting one of the two

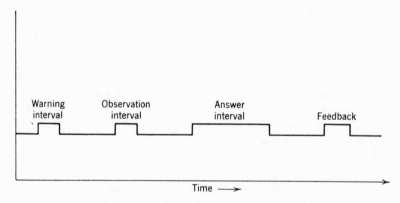

FIG. 2-1   Events in a trial of the yes-no procedure.

permissible response alternatives. Figure 2-1 shows a typical sequence of events within this binary detection task. Typically, the events are marked by lights in an auditory task and by sounds in a visual task.

An important element of the sequence is the *observation interval:* within this observation interval, which is clearly marked for the observer, one of the two possible stimulus alternatives occurs. This procedure is clearly not directly parallel to the usual, real-life, situation since one is seldom warned that a signal may or may not occur at some specific instant in time. We can suggest an analysis of the more natural situation, but it is rather complicated and is discussed elsewhere (Chapter 9). The clearly marked observation interval permits a much simpler analysis and is used in all the procedures discussed in this chapter.

The stimulus alternatives are denoted s and n. The stimulus alternative n might be the presentation of nothing, whereas s might be the presentation of a pulsed tone or a pulsed light. Actually, in many experiments a background noise is continuously present, and thus n represents a trial on which *no signal* is added to the noise, whereas s means *a signal* is added to the background noise during the observation interval.

The observer makes his response during the *answer interval*. This response is, in effect, the observer's decision that one or the other hypothesis is true. Thus the observer must accept either s or n. His responses are denoted with capital letters S and N. No other response is permitted in the simple detection task. In particular, the observer cannot fail to respond; that is, he cannot say "don't know."

In many psychophysical experiments, the observer is given *feedback*; that is, he is told whether or not his response is correct. The observer is also usually given a *warning* of some kind so that he will know when to expect the oncoming observation interval.

2.2.1 Stimulus-response matrix

Since on any one trial in the yes-no task there are two possible stimuli and two possible responses, each trial can be represented by the intersection of one of the stimulus alternatives and one of the response alternatives, as indicated in Fig. 2-2. On each trial of the task, either an s or an n stimulus is presented in the observation interval. Either the S or the N response must be selected, so that the conjunction of a stimulus and a response can be represented as one of the cells of the stimulus-response matrix. In the analysis made here, we ignore trial-by-trial effects and direct our attention to average behavior over a series of trials. The individual trials are averaged and estimates are made of the four probabilities represented in Fig. 2-2.

Note that the entries in the various cells of Fig. 2-2 are conditional probabilities. For example, we estimate $P(S \mid s)$, the probability that a given stimulus event s will evoke a response S. If the experimenter presents the observer with 100 instances of n and the observer chooses N 90 times, the observer must choose S 10 times; thus our estimate of $P(N \mid n)$ is 0.90 and our estimate of $P(S \mid n)$ is 0.10. Similarly, if the stimulus alternative s is presented 100 times and the observer chooses alternative S 45 times, he must choose the response alternative N 55 times, so that $P(S \mid s) = 0.45$ and $P(N \mid s) = 0.55$.

Only two numbers can be freely entered in the matrix. Once these two numbers are determined, the other two can be determined, since the rows must add to one. The matrix therefore has only two degrees of freedom, and not four as the number of cells might suggest.

The convention of using estimates of conditional probabilities rather than unconditional probabilities arises because we wish to focus our attention on the observer's behavior, and to suppress as much as possible any changes in the data caused by variation in the number of times either

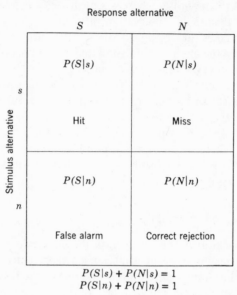

Response alternative

$$P(S|s) + P(N|s) = 1$$
$$P(S|n) + P(N|n) = 1$$

FIG. 2-2 The stimulus-response matrix of the yes-no procedure.

alternative is presented. The number of times the stimulus alternative s or n occurs is, of course, determined by the experimenter.

2.2.2 ROC curve

Because there are only two degrees of freedom in the stimulus-response matrix, we can represent all the information in the matrix as a point on a two-dimensional graph. Such a graph, with the coordinates labeled as in Fig. 2-3, has been called the "receiver-operating-characteristic" graph, or ROC graph. In the example discussed earlier, the estimate of the probability of the observer responding S when n was presented was 0.10, and the corresponding estimate of the probability of the observer responding S when s was presented was 0.45. This point on the ROC curve has the coordinate values 0.10 and 0.45 and is plotted as a circle in Fig. 2-3. Note

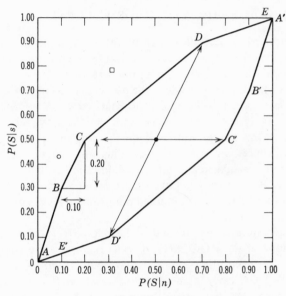

FIG. 2-3   The ROC graph.

that in this example the point is obtained on the basis of 200 observations, 100 observations of n and 100 observations of s.

Suppose that the observer is induced to change his decision behavior in some way. For example, he might increase the number of "yes" responses if he were indiscriminately rewarded for saying "yes." If he did thus, presumably both of the coordinate values of the circle plotted in Fig. 2-3 would increase. That is, the observer might increase the hit probability $P(S \mid s)$ from 0.45 to 0.80, but his false-alarm probability $P(S \mid n)$ would also increase, for instance, from 0.10 to 0.30. This new point is marked by a square in Fig. 2-3. This new point again would be estimated from several observations. By successively changing the instructions, which bias the observer's decision behavior, we can generate a point for each set of instructions. These points can be connected by a smooth curve which will represent the various modes of observing that the subject can adopt under particular, fixed stimulus conditions. For this reason it is called a receiver-operating-characteristic curve. The entire curve is generated without changing any physical parameter of the stimulus situation. The signal level and the noise level are the same for all the points—only the way the observer chooses to decide among the alternatives varies.

Let us now consider in more detail some of the properties of a realistic ROC curve and, in particular, how the various decision functions generate the different points obtained on the ROC curve.

2.3   LIKELIHOOD RATIO AND THE ROC CURVE

A very important aspect of the application of decision theory to psychophysical experiments is the relationship between certain properties of the points on the ROC curve and the structure of the underlying decision process. Each time we induce the observer to change his decision criterion, we generate a new point on the ROC curve. According to the decision-theory analysis, the decisions made by the observer represent decision rules, which are commitments on the part of the observer that he will make certain responses if certain stimulus inputs occur. As the rule is changed, different false-alarm and hit probabilities result; that is, different points on the ROC curve arise. Given these assumptions, let us explore the implied relation between the obtained points on an ROC curve and the underlying decision process.

The first implication to be stressed is the one concerning the relation between the slope of the ROC curve at some point and the value of the likelihood-ratio criterion that generates that point. It will be shown that *the slope of the ROC curve at any point is equal to the likelihood-ratio criterion that generates that point.* Consider the simple example shown in Table 2-1. Part (a) of the table lists four sensory events, labeled 1, 2, 3, and 4, along with their probabilities of occurrence conditional upon the truth of each hypothesis. As pointed out earlier, it is not necessary for the events to be unidimensional; rather, each of the four events could represent a point in a space having a large number of dimensions. In the fourth column the likelihood ratios of the various events are listed. Part (b) of the table lists five different decision rules, labeled *A, B, C, D,* and *E*. The decision rules are listed both in terms of their likelihood-ratio criterion and in equivalent statements phrased in terms of the sensory events for this particular example. Finally, part (c) of the table lists for each of the five decision rules the corresponding probabilities of a hit and a false alarm. As a specific example, consider decision rule *C*: "If the likelihood ratio of the event is greater than or equal to 2.00, respond *S*." From part (a) of the table we can determine the false-alarm probability given that the response is *S* when either event 1 or event 4 occurs. The second column of part (a) shows that $P(1 \mid n) = 0.10$ and that $P(4 \mid n) = 0.10$. Hence the total probability of a false alarm is the sum, or 0.20, $[P(S \mid n) = 0.20]$. Similarly, for the hit probability, $P(1 \mid s) = 0.20$ and $P(4 \mid s) = 0.30$. Hence the total probability of a hit is 0.50, $[P(S \mid s) = 0.50]$. Thus the coordinates of the point on the ROC curve corresponding to decision rule *C* are 0.20 and 0.50.

Figure 2-3 shows the ROC curve corresponding to the five decision rules (*A, B, C, D,* and *E*) given in Table 2-1. Note that the slope of the line

TABLE 2-1. A SIMPLE DECISION EXAMPLE

(a) Sensory events (e)	$P(e \mid n)$ = probability, given n, of e occurring	$P(e \mid s)$ = probability, given s, of e occurring	$l(e) = \dfrac{P(e \mid s)}{P(e \mid n)}$
$e = 1$	0.10	0.20	2.00
$e = 2$	0.30	0.10	0.33
$e = 3$	0.50	0.40	0.80
$e = 4$	0.10	0.30	3.00

(b) Decision rule Equivalent decision rule

	Decision rule	Equivalent decision rule
A	Say S if $l(e) > 3.00$	Never say S
B	Say S if $l(e) \geq 3.00$	Say S only if event 4 occurs
C	Say S if $l(e) \geq 2.00$	Say S only if event 1 or 4 occurs
D	Say S if $l(e) \geq 0.80$	Say S only if event 1, 3, or 4 occurs
E	Say S if $l(e) \geq 0.33$	Always say S

(c) Given decision rule	Probability, if n occurs, that response is S, a false alarm	Probability, if s occurs, that response is S, a hit
	$P(S \mid n)$	$P(S \mid s)$
A	0.00	0.00
B	0.10	0.30
C	0.20	0.50
D	0.70	0.90
E	1.00	1.00

connecting points B and C is 2.0, since the Δx increment from B to C is 0.10 and the Δy increment is 0.20. This slope is the same as the likelihood-ratio criterion that defines decision rule C. As can be verified from Table 2-1, this same relation between the likelihood-ratio criterion of the decision rule and the slope of the ROC curve holds for all of the decision rules of the example. When the events are continuous rather than discrete, the slope of the ROC curve at any point is exactly equal to the likelihood-ratio criterion that generates that point.

A proof of this correspondence for the continuous case is straightforward. Let $f(e \mid s)$ be the probability density given that the s hypothesis is true, and $f(e \mid n)$ the probability density given that the n hypothesis is true. Then, by definition,

$$l(e) = \frac{f(e \mid s)}{f(e \mid n)} \tag{2.1}$$

The coordinates of the ROC curve can be expressed as a function of the criterion k as follows:

$$P(S \mid s) = \int_k^{+\infty} f(e \mid s) \, de$$

$$P(S \mid n) = \int_k^{+\infty} f(e \mid n) \, de \tag{2.2}$$

The slope at the point determined by the criterion k is

$$\frac{dP(S \mid s)}{dP(S \mid n)}\bigg|_k = \frac{-f(k \mid s)}{-f(k \mid n)} = l(k) \tag{2.3}$$

In the discrete situation, the successive criteria on the likelihood-ratio axis determine the slopes between successive points on the ROC curve. Conversely, if there are several points on an ROC curve, and if the decision process is based on likelihood-ratio criteria, then the values of the likelihood-ratio criteria can be inferred from the slopes of the lines connecting successive points. The decision need not be based on likelihood ratio per se, but the decision rule must be equivalent to a likelihood-ratio criterion in order for this relation between likelihood ratio and the slope of the ROC curve to exist.

Consider the successive decision rules that generate the successive points along the ROC curve in our example. A conservative rule, such as B (see Table 2-1), has the second-highest likelihood-ratio criterion. There are few events in the acceptance class, so that both the probability of a hit and the probability of a false alarm are low. As the likelihood-ratio criterion decreases, more and more events are included in the set that leads to the acceptance of s. Thus both hit and false-alarm probabilities will increase. The slope of the line connecting successive points on the ROC curve will decrease, because it equals the likelihood-ratio criterion. Therefore, *an ROC curve based on likelihood-ratio criteria must have a hit probability that is a monotonically increasing function of the false-alarm probability, and a slope that is monotonically decreasing.*

It is important to realize that any point on a line connecting any two adjacent points on the ROC curve also represents a performance that can actually be obtained. The difference of criteria between two successive points on the ROC curve is that the higher point is generated by an acceptance class that includes all the events of the lower point *and* some additional events. If one uses a fixed decision rule and responds S each time an event occurs which is common to both acceptance classes, the hit and false-alarm probabilities must equal the coordinates of the lower point, since this is exactly the criterion that generated the lower point. If, in addition, one uses a random strategy and says S *sometimes* to the events appearing only in the larger acceptance class, then the false-alarm and hit probabilities will be located on a line connecting the lower to the higher point. For example, if the observer says S each time event 4 occurs and says S with probability p when event 1 occurs, then the false-alarm probability is $0.10 + (p)(0.10)$ and the hit probability is $0.30 + (p)(0.20)$. This point falls on the line connecting point B with C at a fractional distance p between the adjacent points B and C.

This same rule also holds for nonadjacent points, for example, decision rules A and D. Decision rule A contains *no* events that lead to acceptance of s, and decision rule D contains events 1, 3, and 4. If one says S with probability p only when event 1, 3, or 4 occurs, the point corresponding to this decision strategy will be given by the point with false-alarm probability $(p)(0.70)$ and with hit probability $(p)(0.90)$. In other words, the point lies on the line connecting point A and point D at the fractional distance p. Suppose that this probability is $1/7$; then the false-alarm probability is $(1/7)(0.70) = 0.10$ and the hit probability is $(1/7)(0.90) = 0.13$. The performance achieved with this strategy is far inferior to that expected from decision rule B, which achieves more than twice as many hits with exactly the same false-alarm probability. This deterioration of performance is to be expected, since the random mixture of decision rules A and D is not a likelihood-ratio criterion.

Decision procedures other than those based on likelihood-ratio criteria are difficult to discuss in general terms. Decision rules that are not equivalent to likelihood-ratio criteria always produce behavior that, on the average, is inferior to that obtained with likelihood-ratio criteria. The worst possible behavior is obtained by reversing the decisions that are dictated by a likelihood-ratio criterion. This reversal simply complements the x and y coordinates of the points and produces an ROC curve such that corresponding points lie at equal distances on a line through the midpoint $(0.50, 0.50)$ of the graph. Such an ROC curve is shown in Fig. 2-3 with the points corresponding to $A, \dots, E$ labeled $A', \dots, E'$. These decision rules are simply the complements of the decision rules discussed earlier. For example, B' amounts to saying S if $l(e) < 3.00$.

Even this very bad decision process has certain properties in common with the best decision procedures. For example, the hit probability for successive points on the ROC curve increases monotonically with the false-alarm probability. Although the monotonically increasing relation is not a necessary property of *all* decision rules, it is necessary for all those in which successive criteria are generated by adding new events to those already satisfying the previous criteria. In such cases the additional events can never decrease the false-alarm or hit probabilities; thus the hit probability must increase monotonically with the false-alarm probability.

For likelihood-ratio criteria, the slope of the ROC curve decreases monotonically with false-alarm probability. For nonlikelihood-ratio decision strategies, reversals in slope often occur. The worst possible ROC curve nicely illustrates this point. Instead of decreasing monotonically as the false-alarm probability increases, the slope of the ROC curve increases monotonically. Occasionally in psychophysical data we find low slopes for points obtained with low false-alarm probabilities and steeper slopes for higher false-alarm probabilities. Usually, however, these apparent inversions in slope disappear with further practice on the part of the observer. If the ROC curve does not show monotonically decreasing slopes, it is literally true that the observer can achieve better performance by reordering the events which lead to the acceptance of one of the hypotheses.

Thus far we have discussed only the results we might expect when the observer changes his criterion for the presence of a signal. The physical parameters of the situation have been constant; that is, the probabilities of the different sensory events under each hypothesis have been constant. Obviously, if the signal is made stronger, the decision problem becomes easier. That is, the hit probability relative to the false-alarm probability increases, and the ROC curve moves toward the upper left-hand corner of the graph. In applying decision theory to those psychophysical experiments in which we are interested in determining a signal level that the observer can reliably detect, we are especially interested in determining a single number from the ROC curve that will provide such a suitable measure of the detectability of the signal. The *area under the ROC curve* provides such a measure. It ranges from 0.50, when the hit probability equals the false-alarm probability, to 1.0, when the observer makes no errors whatsoever. There are other reasons to recommend this measure, but before discussing these reasons in more detail it is necessary to understand the detection-theory analysis of two other psychophysical procedures: rating and forced choice.

2.4 RATING PROCEDURE

In the yes-no detection task the observer chooses either S or N after each observation interval. From a large number of such decisions, we estimate the hit and false-alarm probabilities and thus determine the coordinates for a single point on the ROC curve. If the observer is induced to alter his criterion, new probabilities are estimated, and the coordinates for a second point on the ROC curve obtained from this second series of observations can be determined. Each experimental point may require two or three hundred observations, so that a single ROC curve estimated from only six or seven points may involve over two thousand observations.

Explicit in the general decision-theory approach is the assumption that likelihood ratio, or some monotonic function of it, is used by the observer in making his decision. Thus decision theory provides no reason to require only a binary response. Undoubtedly, both these reasons have led to the development of the rating procedure—a procedure in which the observer's response is essentially a report of likelihood ratio or of some discrete characterization of that quantity.

Note that, although the theoretical justification of the rating response is explicit in decision theory, it is a theoretical justification. There are cogent reasons why a multiple-response procedure might elicit from the observer quite different information from that obtained from the binary, yes-no, procedure. The actual equivalence of the binary and rating procedures demands empirical evidence. Though the evidence available at present does not contradict the assumption of equivalence, the assumption certainly has not been tested thoroughly in all situations. The evidence available is discussed in Chapter 4.

The use of a more-than-binary response in psychophysical experiments has a long history. Papers by Hennon (1911) and by Jersild (1929) present some of the earliest studies of the topic. Swets first used the procedure within the detection-theory framework, and Pollack and Egan have investigated the rating procedure more extensively, contributing considerable experimental data comparing this and other psychophysical procedures (Swets, Tanner, and Birdsall, 1955, 1961; Pollack and Decker, 1958; Decker and Pollack, 1958, 1959; Egan and Clarke, 1956; Egan, Clarke, and Carterette, 1956; Egan, Schulman, and Greenberg, 1959).

The rating procedure uses the same presentation format as the yes-no procedure; see Fig. 2-1. The sequence of physical events occurring in the two procedures is the same. What differs is the nature of the observer's response. In the yes-no experiment a binary decision is required, that is, the acceptance of one of the two hypotheses; in the rating procedure, theoretically at least, any number of responses may be available. Assume for a moment that six categories of response are employed by the observer. The first category represents almost certainty that s was presented, and the sixth almost certainty that s was *not* presented, that is, that n was. The categories between one and six represent smaller degrees of certainty about the occurrence or nonoccurrence of s. Figure 2-4a illustrates the stimulus-response matrix of the rating procedure.

The analysis of the rating task proceeds in the following way. In the yes-no task we assume that the observer reports a signal occurrence because the likelihood ratio, or some monotonic function of it, exceeds some criterion level. The same assumption is made with rating data. Thus the data are first analyzed on the assumption that the observer would say "yes" only on those trials where he reports that a signal was almost certainly present. That is, any trial on which the observer used the first category is treated as if the observer had said "yes," and all other trials on which the other five categories were used are treated as if the observer said "no." Analysis of the s and n trials in this manner allows one to estimate $P(S \mid s)$ and $P(S \mid n)$, respectively. The estimates define a single point on the ROC curve, that point corresponding to this very strict

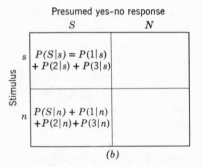

FIG. 2-4 (a) Illustrative stimulus-response matrix of the rating procedure. (b) Reduction of the matrix assuming that categories 1, 2, and 3 correspond to "yes" and that categories 4, 5, and 6 correspond to "no."

criterion. The criterion level can now be changed; for example, the experimenter can now assume that the observer would have said "yes" in a binary test whenever he responded with either the first or the second category in the rating test. This assumption generates a second pair of estimates for $P(S \mid s)$ and $P(S \mid n)$, and thus a second point on the ROC curve. Figure 2-4b illustrates the reduction of the original matrix assuming that the criterion is between the third and fourth categories.

Proceeding in this manner, the experimenter can calculate the corresponding probabilities for various criteria and obtain estimates for a number of points on an ROC graph. Notice that successive points are heavily interdependent. The number of times that the observer uses the first and second categories must include the number of times he uses the first category. Notice also that the number of points obtained is one less than the number of categories. If six categories are employed, five points on an ROC curve can be constructed from the observer's use of these six categories. The last point, the probability that one of the six categories was used under either hypothesis, is unity; thus the last point has coordinate values of 1.0, 1.0.

The outstanding virtue of the rating procedure is its obvious efficiency. To obtain five points on an ROC curve using a binary-decision procedure, five separate experimental conditions would have to be run, whereas with a rating procedure only one condition is necessary. Admittedly, some of the information on the nature of the observer's decision procedure is lost. The method of analysis, for example, *assumes* that all ratings larger than some arbitrary value would have led to an acceptance of the hypothesis *s* if a binary response had been employed rather than the rating response. It is possible that the observer might not display the consistency of decision strategy assumed by the model. There is, after all, a large experimental literature to suggest that observers do not always behave in an optimal manner in situations like this.* The issue, however, is not whether the observer is perfectly consistent, but whether he displays sufficient consistency to provide essentially the same information to the experimenter in the rating procedure as in the binary, or yes-no, procedure. The real issue is whether binary and rating procedures yield similar ROC curves. If the curves are similar, then the assumption of consistency, as made in the analysis of the rating procedure, apparently does not lead to an error large enough to imperil its usefulness.† Certainly the efficiency of the rating procedure for sensory experiments recommends its further investigation. The empirical work available on the comparison of the binary and the rating methods is discussed in Chapter 4.

2.5   FORCED-CHOICE PROCEDURE

Investigators whose primary interest is the sensory process and who wish to avoid the problem of determining the observer's criterion often

---

* Lee (1963) has recently investigated the consistency of the observer's binary decisions with stimuli (dot patterns) which permit direct calculation of the likelihood ratio.

† There is also a possibility that the two methods will agree because of a counter-balancing of errors. The rating procedure may suffer from inconsistency because of the number of categories. The yes-no procedure may suffer approximately the same degree of inconsistency because of the longer time period required to collect the data.

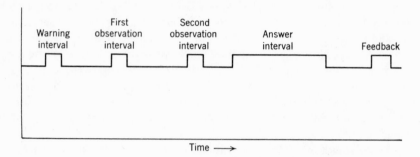

FIG. 2-5 Events in a trial of the forced-choice procedure.

use a forced-choice design as their psychophysical procedure. Forced-choice tasks differ from the yes-no and the rating tasks in that more than one observation interval precedes a response. Figure 2-5 shows a typical sequence of events within the two-alternative forced-choice (2AFC) procedure. Two observation intervals are provided. A signal always occurs in either the first or the second interval and the observer is forced to choose one of them. He is instructed to choose the interval most likely to have contained the signal. In the most general case, with m observation intervals, the signal occurs in exactly one interval, so that there are $m - 1$ instances of noise alone and a single interval in which the signal is added to the noise. Two and four intervals have been used most frequently in psychophysical experiments, but work also has been carried out with as many as eight observation intervals.

To analyze the forced-choice procedure in the utmost generality, one should redefine both the hypotheses and the sensory events. For the two-alternative forced-choice procedure, for example, one should define $\langle sn \rangle$ as the occurrence of the signal in the first observation interval and not in the second, and $\langle ns \rangle$ as the occurrence of the signal in the second observation interval and not in the first. The sensory effects of stimuli in the 2AFC task thus correspond to certain pairs of observations that occur during the two observation intervals. The acceptance of one or the other hypothesis could thus be considered, and a type of ROC curve could be generated. Thus, quantities analogous to a hit and a false alarm could be defined where, for example, incorrectly deciding that the signal occurred in the first temporal interval would be considered a false alarm, and a correct response that a signal occurred in the first interval would be considered a hit. In our presentation, however, we emphasize not this internal structure of forced-choice data, but the relation between the results obtained from the yes-no, rating, and forced-choice procedures.

Considerable simplicity in the exposition is achieved if we initially assume symmetry in the observer's decision—symmetry in the sense that there is no bias in the selection of one interval over any other. Thus, if the signal is equally likely to occur in each interval and if 80% of the signals are correctly detected when they occur in interval one, then 80% will also be correctly detected when they occur in interval two, in interval three, or in any other interval. The assumption of symmetry is dictated by our desire to present the relation between the forced-choice procedure and the yes-no and rating procedures in its simplest form. Once the relationship for this simple case is established, we can relax the assumption of symmetry and discuss the relationship without this assumption. This assumption is obviously restrictive, but it allows a very general development of the relation between the forced-choice and the other psychophysical tasks.*

Of course, the assumption of symmetry can be checked directly, since we can determine whether the subject has in fact detected more signals in one interval than in another. Therefore, one might choose to test first for symmetry, or to select data where the asymmetry is slight and use only such data to test further predictions of the theory.

2.6 RELATION BETWEEN FORCED-CHOICE RESULTS AND YES-NO OR RATING ROC CURVES

Let us begin our analysis of the forced-choice procedures by considering specifically a two-alternative forced-choice task. Once this analysis is completed, the generalization to more than two alternatives is obvious.

In a 2AFC task two sensory events e_1 and e_2, one corresponding to each observation interval, are of interest. The observer's task is to decide whether the first was a signal and the second a nonsignal, or the reverse. We assume that the observer's decision is determined by the likelihood ratios of the events where likelihood ratio is computed in the following way:

$$l(e_i) = \frac{f(e_i \mid s)}{f(e_i \mid n)} \qquad (i = 1, 2) \qquad (2.4)$$

---

* Luce (1959) has presented a very interesting algebraic model which easily incorporates asymmetries in m-alternative forced choice, although at the price of a parameter for each interval. His model is also very convenient for making comparisons between two-alternative forced choice and yes-no decision procedures. Unfortunately, from the experimental point of view, the predictions generated by detection theory are so close as to be almost indistinguishable. We may hope that a critical test of these two models will develop. As of this writing they appear to be two systems based on quite different assumptions which nonetheless generate remarkably similar predictions.

Note that the likelihood ratio of the event e_i has the same definition it had in the analysis of the single-observation procedure. This is because the states of the world are the same: s is the signal, n is noise alone. In two-alternative forced-choice tasks, however, there are two such likelihood ratios—one for each interval.

Assume that the observer chooses the first interval if and only if the likelihood ratio associated with the first interval is larger than the likelihood ratio associated with the second. This decision rule certainly has intuitive appeal—if the odds are 10 to 1 that the waveform in the first interval was a signal and only 1 to 1 that the waveform in the second interval was a signal, then one would probably respond that the first interval contained the signal. In fact, it can be shown that this decision rule maximizes the percentage of correct decisions.

We now want to compute the percentage of correct decisions in the forced-choice task and to determine how that percentage is related to quantities we have already considered in our analysis of the yes-no and rating tasks. If the observer's decision rule is to select the interval producing the larger likelihood ratio, he will be correct if the likelihood ratio associated with the signal-plus-noise distribution is greater than the likelihood ratio associated with the nonsignal, or noise-alone, distribution. That is, the two intervals of the forced-choice task can be likened to two random samples from two statistical distributions: one a signal distribution, the other a nonsignal distribution. Only if the sample from the signal distribution has a higher likelihood ratio than the sample from the noise distribution will the observer be correct. Realizing this fact, we can compute the probability of a correct decision. Suppose that the value of likelihood ratio sampled from the signal distribution is k; then the observer will be correct if the value sampled from the nonsignal distribution is less than k. Let the sample of likelihood ratio from the signal distribution be called l_s and, similarly, let the sample from the nonsignal or noise distribution be called l_n. The observer will be correct if $l_s = k$ and $l_n < k$.

Now if the two samples are independent, the probability of this joint occurrence will be the product of the two probabilities. That is, denoting the probability of a correct response in the two-alternative forced-choice task as $P_2(C)$:

$$P_2(C) = P(l_s = k) \cdot P(l_n < k) \tag{2.5}$$

Since the numerical value of l_s is clearly immaterial, the total probability of being correct is simply this expression summed over all possible values for k, namely:

$$P_2(C) = \int_{-\infty}^{+\infty} [P(l_s = k) \cdot P(l_n < k)] \, dk \tag{2.6}$$

Since l_s and l_n are distributed as $f(e \mid s)$ and $f(e \mid n)$ respectively, we can write Eq. 2.6 as

$$P_2(C) = \int_{-\infty}^{+\infty} f(k \mid s) \left[\int_{-\infty}^{k} f(e \mid n) \, de \right] dk \tag{2.7}$$

Now the correspondence between the forced-choice percentage correct and the binary and rating ROC curves begins to emerge because, as we shall show, the right-hand side of Eq. 2.7 involves quantities given by the ROC curve. If the criterion of the observer is k, the probability of a false alarm is simply $P(l_n > k)$, that is,

$$P(l_n > k) = \int_{k}^{\infty} f(e \mid n) \, de = P_k(S \mid n) \tag{2.8}$$

or

$$P(l_n < k) = \int_{-\infty}^{k} f(e \mid n) \, de = 1 - P_k(S \mid n) \tag{2.9}$$

and

$$\left. \frac{dP(S \mid s)}{dk} \right|_k = \frac{d}{dk} \int_{k}^{\infty} f(e \mid s) \, de = -f(k \mid s) \tag{2.10}$$

We now can use these equations and substitute into Eq. 2.7. Note that Eq. 2.10 gives us the relations between k and $P(S \mid s)$, so that the limits of integration can be determined. When k is positive and very large, $P(S \mid s)$ is zero and, similarly, for large negative values of k, $P(S \mid s)$ approaches unity. Thus

$$P_2(C) = -\int_{1}^{0} [1 - P_k(S \mid n)] \, dP_k(S \mid s) \tag{2.11a}$$

or, more conveniently,

$$P_2(C) = \int_{0}^{1} [1 - P_k(S \mid n)] \, dP_k(S \mid s) \tag{2.11b}$$

Thus, as Fig. 2-6 illustrates, *the percentage correct in a two-alternative forced-choice task is simply the area under the yes-no or rating ROC curve.*

The argument is easily extended to give the percentage correct in m-alternative forced-choice experiments; in this case we consider the probability that $l_s = k$ and $l_n < k$ where there are $m - 1$ likelihood ratios of the latter kind. Once more we assume that the events are independent, and hence

$$P_m(C) = P(l_s = k)P(l_n < k)^{m-1} \tag{2.12}$$

Likewise, making substitutions as before,

$$P_m(C) = \int_{0}^{1} [1 - P_k(S \mid n)]^{m-1} \, dP_k(S \mid s) \tag{2.13}$$

Thus detection theory provides a means of predicting the percentage of correct detections in forced choice from the yes-no or rating ROC curve.

Two important assumptions have been made in the above derivation. First, the decision in the m-alternative forced-choice task is unbiased—the interval with the largest likelihood ratio is chosen as the most likely signal interval. Second, all observation intervals in the forced-choice task are treated as statistically independent.

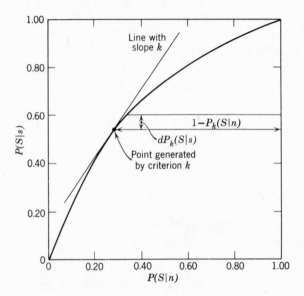

FIG. 2-6   To illustrate the relationship between the percentage of correct responses in a two-alternative forced-choice task and the area under the yes-no or rating ROC curve.

The assumption of symmetry can be relaxed, as we shall now demonstrate. Consider a decision rule of this type: accept the hypothesis that the signal is in the first interval if and only if the likelihood ratio of the first observation is c times the likelihood ratio of the second observation, where c is some constant bias parameter. If the signal occurs in the first interval, then a choice of the first interval—denoted $R1$—will occur only if $l_s = k$ and $l_n < ck$. Proceeding as before, we have

$$P(R1 \mid \langle sn \rangle) = \int_0^1 1 - P_{k/c}(S \mid n) \, dP_k(S \mid s)$$

$$= 1 - \int_0^1 P_{k/c}(S \mid n) \, dP_k(S \mid s)$$

$$(2.14)$$

Similarly, if the signal occurs in the second interval, then an $R1$ response will occur only if $l_s = k$ and $l_n > ck$. Thus

$$P(R1 \mid \langle ns \rangle) = \int_0^1 P_{ck}(S \mid n) \, dP_k(S \mid n) \tag{2.15}$$

These two probabilities, $P(R1 \mid \langle sn \rangle)$ and $P(R1 \mid \langle ns \rangle)$, completely describe the observer's average behavior in a two-alternative forced-choice task, since

$$P(R1 \mid \langle sn \rangle) + P(R2 \mid \langle sn \rangle) = 1$$

$$P(R1 \mid \langle ns \rangle) + P(R2 \mid \langle ns \rangle) = 1$$

These same two probabilities can, therefore, be used as the coordinates of an ROC curve for the 2AFC task. The equations above indicate that the values of the coordinates of the two-interval forced-choice ROC curve may be determined by integration from the single-interval ROC curve. Specifically, to determine $P(R1 \mid \langle sn \rangle)$, multiply the small increment in $P(S \mid s)$ occurring at the line of slope k by the value of $[1 - P(S \mid n)]$ occurring at the slope k/c, and sum all such products. A corresponding summation determines $P(R1 \mid \langle ns \rangle)$.

Some study of the quantities defining the coordinates of the forced-choice ROC curve reveals that the curve is symmetric about the negative diagonal. Algebraically, such symmetry amounts to a complementary relation between the coordinates of the corresponding points. That is, if one point has coordinates (x, y), then the corresponding symmetric point (x', y') has coordinates $x' = 1 - y$ and $y' = 1 - x$. Thus if we denote the corresponding probabilities by primes, we require

$$P'(R1 \mid \langle sn \rangle) = 1 - P(R1 \mid \langle ns \rangle) \tag{2.16}$$

$$P'(R1 \mid \langle ns \rangle) = 1 - P(R1 \mid \langle sn \rangle) \tag{2.17}$$

But the definition of these quantities reveals that $P'(R1 \mid \langle sn \rangle)$ and $P'(R1 \mid \langle ns \rangle)$ are generated by decision rules where the criterion c' is the reciprocal of the constant c used to determine the quantities $P(R1 \mid \langle sn \rangle)$ and $P(R1 \mid \langle ns \rangle)$. Hence we have proved that *the two-alternative forced-choice ROC curve is symmetric about the negative diagonal.*

Note that in all cases the derivation is independent of the distribution associated with either hypothesis. In particular, the distributions have not been assumed to be normal (or Gaussian). The assumption of normality is so frequently made in the literature that it is important for us to discuss the specific results that can be derived when this assumption is made; however, we postpone this discussion to the next chapter.

2.7   SIGNAL STRENGTH AND THE ROC CURVE

The entire analysis of the yes-no, rating, and forced-choice tasks has assumed a fixed and constant experimental situation. The noise distribution was assumed fixed, as was the signal distribution—what changed was the observer's criterion for the acceptance of certain hypotheses. In much psychophysical research the level of the signal is systematically changed in the course of the experiment. Changing the signal level would change the signal distribution, since a stronger signal should, on the average, lead to larger values of likelihood ratio than a weaker signal. What is desired is some simple measure that is easily understood and that summarizes this statistical aspect of the signal and noise distributions.

In the forced-choice task, a stronger signal leads to a greater percentage correct than a weaker signal, so that there is no difficulty in providing a simple summary measure of the detectability of a signal. The percentage correct obtained in, for example, a two-alternative forced-choice task provides a scale of signal detectability. Such a scale of detectability ranges from 50% to 100%. The lower number represents chance performance, or zero detectability, and the upper number represents complete or perfect ability to discriminate signal from noise.

We see now that this same measure, *percentage correct*, is also applicable to the single-observation task where the data are summarized by an ROC curve. The area under the ROC curve should be equal to the percentage correct in the two-alternative forced-choice task. If the area is nearly 100%, the ROC curve follows the extreme left and top coordinates of the graph; that is, at a false-alarm probability of zero, the hit probability is one, or nearly one. If the area is nearly 50%, the ROC curve falls near the major diagonal; the hit and false-alarm probabilities are nearly equal.

As indicated by Eq. 2.13, there exists a relation between the area under the ROC curve and the percentage correct for any number of alternatives in the forced-choice task. Given an ROC curve, for each coordinate value of $[1 - P(S \mid n)]$ we can plot a new value at $P'(S \mid n) = [1 - P(S \mid n)]^{m-1}$. The area under the new curve is the expected percentage correct in an m-alternative forced-choice task. Figure 2-7 shows this transformation used to predict four-alternative forced-choice values.

Therefore, the area under the yes-no or rating ROC curve provides a convenient and simple index of the detectability of the signal. It is distribution-free, since no assumption about the form or character of the underlying distributions is made by calculating the area. Finally, the area under a yes-no or rating ROC curve is a directly observable quantity, and thus differences in this quantity can be easily interpreted. The *empirical*

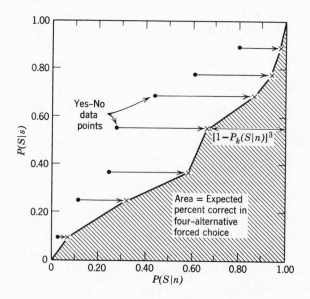

FIG. 2-7 To illustrate the relationship between the percentage of correct responses in a four-alternative forced-choice task and the area under the yes-no or rating ROC curve.

relation between signal strength and percentage correct is discussed in Chapter 7.

2.8   SUMMARY

Three psychophysical procedures have been discussed: the yes-no, rating, and forced-choice procedures. The first two use a single observation interval. Either a signal is presented during the observation interval or it is not. The yes-no procedure uses two possible responses to these stimulus alternatives; the rating procedure uses many responses. Data from either procedure can be used to construct ROC curves. An ROC curve, if based on likelihood ratio or any quantity montonic with likelihood ratio, displays a hit probability that is a monotonically increasing function of the false-alarm probability, and a slope that is a monotonically decreasing function of these two probabilities. Forced-choice tasks employ two or more observation intervals. The signal is presented in one and only one interval. The usual dependent variable is the percentage of trials on which the observer correctly identifies the signal interval.

The detection-theory analysis shows how all three tasks can be united by a single number. This number, which does not depend on any assumptions about the form of the statistical distributions of signal and noise, represents the inherent detectability of the signal. Such a summary measure holds promise for psychophysical results that are independent of the method used to obtain them. We investigate this promise in Chapter 4.

In the next chapter we explore assumptions about the form of the statistical distributions of signal and noise. This exploration provides the more complete theoretical background that is needed before we review certain results that have been obtained with the various procedures.

PROBLEMS

2.1   Using the data provided in the first problem of the previous chapter (Problem 1.1), construct a yes-no ROC curve [coordinates $P(B \mid b)$ and $P(B \mid o)$].

2.2   For the preceding example, verify that the slope between two successive points on the ROC curve is the likelihood ratio associated with the higher point.

2.3   Given the following three points on an ROC curve, what is the predicted percentage of correct responses in a two-alternative forced-choice task?

(a) $P(S \mid n) = 0, P(S \mid s) = 0$

(b) $P(S \mid n) = 0.20, P(S \mid s) = 0.70$

(c) $P(S \mid n) = 1.00, P(S \mid s) = 1.00$

2.4   Sketch two Gaussian distributions with unequal variance. (Be sure that the area under each distribution is unity.) Now plot likelihood ratio as a function of x for the graphs you have drawn. Is likelihood ratio a monotonic function of x?

3

Assumed Distribution
of Signal and Noise

3.1 INTRODUCTION

Thus far we have used decision theory to identify the relevant variables of different experimental procedures, and to predict relations between parameters of the observer's sensory system as estimated from data collected by different procedures. The relations stressed in the last chapter were distribution-free; that is, no particular form for the probability distribution of sensory events was assumed. One need assume only that the observer partitions sensory events into equivalence classes. For each equivalence class there is an associated response. A stimulus causes an event that falls into either one or the other of these classes, and the response associated with that class is then produced.

Although the distribution-free approach has a certain elegance as well as the safety of implying no commitment to any particular distribution, there are many problems or research questions that necessitate very specific assumptions. Such questions arise when the aim of the psychophysical investigation is more substantive than methodological. We may desire to know, for example, how the signal duration or some other parameter of the signal affects the detectability of the signal. With such concerns we might assume some particular form for the probability distribution of sensory events and then assume that a parameter of this distribution has some specific relation to the experimental variable. These assumptions lead to predictions about how changes in this physical variable will influence the observer's ability to detect the signal. Indeed, as we shall see in a later chapter, the ultimate aim of detection theory is to discover the exact form of the distributions using (1) the physical parameters of the signal and noise and (2) the character of the sensory detector. Once the distribution of sensory effects is specified, it is a simple calculation to determine the probabilities of the various responses in a psychophysical task and thus to predict any given experimental data. The major obstacle to this endeavor is, of course, our ignorance about the nature of the sensory detector.

One way to overcome this obstacle is to make guesses about the underlying distribution of sensory events. The accuracy of these conjectures is determined by comparing the deductions made from them with empirical data. Such inferences are no different, in kind, from any other hypotheses about the sensory system and, indeed, they share all the usual weaknesses inherent in any such inferential approach.

This chapter covers some of the more commonly advanced hypotheses about the distribution of sensory events in psychophysical experiments. Our discussion is centered largely on how the expected shape of the ROC curve and the expected results obtained in forced-choice experiments depend on these hypotheses. Specifically, the Gaussian or normal assumption is discussed, and particular emphasis is directed to how the variances of the distributions of signal and noise affect the shape of the ROC curve. Next, the classical threshold theory and its more modern counterparts are reviewed. Finally, the single-parameter exponential model and Luce's choice model are briefly discussed. We begin with a very old assumption, namely, that the distribution of sensory effects is Gaussian. This assumption and its implications were most precisely stated by Thurstone in his classical work. The assumption is frequently made by investigators in detection theory. Because the assumption is so general, we briefly discuss its background.

3.2   THE GAUSSIAN ASSUMPTION

3.2.1   History of the Gaussian assumption—Thurstone

Thurstone (1927a,b) developed an analysis of two very general judgmental methods. In the first—comparative judgment—the subject makes a binary choice between two stimuli. In these tasks he is asked to state whether one tone is louder than a second, one painting more beautiful than another, one sentence more representative of the subject's opinion than another, and the like. A specific example of a comparative-judgment situation is a two-alternative forced-choice task in which two sinusoidal signals of the same frequency, but of different intensities, are presented in the two intervals. The subject is asked to say whether the stimulus in the first interval is louder or softer than the one in the second interval.

The second method—categorical judgment—requires a categorical response from the subject to the presentation of one of a number of stimuli. The subject is asked to place a particular stimulus in the appropriate category. A specific example of a categorical judgment is a yes-no task in which, on any single trial, one of the two sinusoidal signals mentioned earlier is used. The subject is asked to say whether the stimulus presented on a given trial is the more or the less intense sinusoid.

Thurstone analyzed both of these methods in terms of a concept he called "discriminal dispersion." The essence of this concept is that the effects of stimulation can be represented as a random variable. The stimulus has a mean value on the relevant psychological scale but, for various reasons, its exact value fluctuates from moment to moment. Thus it is assumed that stimulation produces a distribution of effects. Thurstone assumed the distribution to be Gaussian, and thus the distribution caused by any stimulus is completely characterized by two parameters, a mean and a variance.

Thurstone developed equations for both methods. In the general comparative-judgment situation, the equations relate the probability of choices between two stimuli to the parameters of the stimulus distributions. In the categorical-judgment method, the equations relate the probability of choosing a category to parameters of the stimulus distributions and the category boundaries. These equations, which are known respectively as the "law of comparative judgment" and the "law of categorical judgment," use the number of times stimulus A is confused with stimulus B to determine, for example, the mean subjective distance between A and B. Thus, by analyzing the subject's confusion using Thurstone's equations, one could relate a physical measure of the stimulus intensity to a psychological scale value of inferred loudness. The unit of measurement is an arbitrary scalar and is directly related to the confusability of the stimulus. Ultimately, then, Thurstone's procedure rests on the two assumptions: (1) that similar stimuli tend to be confused and (2) that distance can be used to represent similarity.

Although Thurstone's model was originally formulated as a psychophysical theory, it has not been widely used as such. Rather, it has been used mainly to scale stimuli that are not easily represented in physical terms. For instance, the technique has been used to scale attitudes, opinions, handwriting, and other psychological attributes that are difficult to quantify. The number of parameters in the model is one reason that it has not been widely used to analyze psychophysical data. Even when very strong assumptions are introduced about the relation among the parameters of the distributions, the number of free parameters is very large. Only when both a large number of stimuli are used and strong assumptions are made does the ratio of free parameters to free data points become small enough to invite empirical investigation.

Another reason that Thurstone's model failed to generate much enthusiasm among psychophysicists was a general reaction against the so-called "indirect" psychophysical techniques. These indirect techniques use the confusion among stimuli to determine their scale values. There are two general criticisms of this procedure; both arise because the technique tries to use data obtained from local regions of the scale to infer something about the entire scale. The first criticism is simply that it is poor measurement technique to use local measures to infer global ones. To measure a house with a six-inch rule is possible, but it requires a great deal of caution. The second criticism is more fundamental. Sensation, it is claimed, is not so constituted that small sensations placed end to end can represent bigger sensations. William James (1890) has most effectively expressed this point of view.

Impatient with indirect methods of measurement, psychophysicists created other techniques to provide more direct estimates of psychological magnitudes without measuring, by pairs, a large number of intervening stimuli. The most direct method is the recent technique of Stevens (1956), known as magnitude estimation, where one simply tells the subject that A is 10 units and asks, "How many units is B?"

By suitable averaging of these estimates of magnitude, Stevens and others have obtained remarkably stable relations between physical scale values and these estimates over a wide variety of sensory continua. Some psychologists, however, feel as much trepidation about the direct procedures as do their champions about the indirect techniques. Basically, the issue is far deeper than the question of sensory scaling. The differences can be traced to two general attitudes that psychophysicists hold about sensation and sensory processes. Torgerson (1958, Chapter 5) has discussed these attitudes in some detail. The crux of the difference is illustrated in the attitudes towards the "stimulus error." According to the indirect school, the observer should be asked to make as careful and sensitive discriminations as possible. If the observer knows that the smaller stimulus occurs in the first interval with probability 0.8, this knowledge should influence his décision. For the classical, or direct, psychophysicist such a view is anathema. The subject, indeed, may take such information into account in making his response, but that has nothing to do with the sensory process. The subject is committing the stimulus error when he lets his sensory judgments be biased by nonsensory information such as the a priori probability that a certain stimulus will occur. He is not judging what he sees or hears, but what he guesses or knows about the stimulus. There is little doubt that subjects can make such judgments, but they are not sensory judgments.

The relative strength of these two positions has varied over the years. Thurstone's technique is not enjoying a great deal of popularity among psychophysicists at this time. Rather, adherents of the direct techniques are having more and more influence in sensory scaling.

Detection theory has never really used the scaling aspect of the general Thurstone model. Although Gaussian distributions of sensory effects have frequently been assumed, the emphasis, at least in the yes-no experiment, has been on how the location of the category boundaries affects the false-alarm and hit probabilities (ROC curve). Indeed, the physical conditions of the experiment often are held fixed and thus, presumably, the two distributions are constant; in particular, the distance between their means is supposedly constant. Similarly, the aim in conducting forced-choice experiments is frequently to determine how some physical parameter such as signal duration might affect the variance of the assumed distribution, rather than to measure the distance per se. Seldom has the inferred distance been extrapolated to generate the entire psychophysical scale. Such an extension of the local measurements appears to be of little interest to detection theorists.

Philosophically, however, detection theory joins Thurstone and others in seeing the need for an indirect approach to the analysis of sensory experience. Detection theory, in fact, goes beyond Thurstone in one respect, in that it admits a criterion, that is, a definition of category boundaries, even in paired-comparison tasks. For example, in a two-alternative forced-choice task, the observer may establish as his criterion for choosing the first interval that the likelihood ratio of a signal in that interval be five times greater than the likelihood ratio in the second interval. This emphasis on judgmental determinants as well as on sensory determinants definitely places detection theory among the indirect psychophysical analyses.

It is hoped that this brief historical digression will have clarified to some extent the relation of detection theory to Thurstone's scaling theory. The difference, it should be apparent, is one of emphasis rather than content. But despite this difference in emphasis there is, basically, considerable agreement about the underlying philosophical questions concerning the nature of an adequate theory of the measurement of sensory phenomena.

3.2.2 Justification of the Gaussian assumption

There are two reasons to assume that the underlying distributions of sensory events are Gaussian; one is theoretical and the other is practical. The theoretical reason is the so-called "central limit theorem." The central limit theorem is a description for a collection of theorems giving the asymptotic behavior of a sum of random variables. One of the earliest results was that of deMoive, who showed that the number of successes in m independent Bernoulli trials tends toward a Gaussian distribution as m increases. Since then a large number of theorems have been proved. One general result is that if the random variables of the sum are independent and all have the same distribution, then, whatever this distribution, the sum of such variables approaches a Gaussian distribution as the number of variables increases indefinitely. There are, in addition, a variety of special conditions on the random variables, which, if satisfied, guarantee that the sum will tend towards a Gaussian distribution. Since we often think that sensory events are composed of a multitude of similar, smaller events, which are by and large independent, the central limit theorem might be invoked to justify the assumption of a Gaussian distribution of net effects. While it may be true that some circumstances warrant the Gaussian assumption, we should not believe that all sums of random variables tend to be Gaussian, since they do not (Cramér, 1946; Gnedenko and Kolmogorov, 1954). Similarly, while some experimental procedures may establish conditions such that the distribution of sensory events is Gaussian, there may also be some circumstances where these conditions do not occur.

The practical reason for assuming that the underlying distribution is Gaussian is that this assumption allows one to derive results that would be difficult or impossible to derive under other assumptions. The facts that Gaussian variables are easy to manipulate and that the parameters are additive under linear operations are often advantages not easily ignored. But this rationale, like the preceding one, is not absolute; there are other distributions, and some have equally attractive mathematical properties.

Ultimately, the justification of any scientific assumption is pragmatic, and we shall attempt no further a priori rationalizations of this assumption. Rather, we turn to some of its implications.

3.2.3   The Gaussian assumption and the single-observation task

When considering two alternative hypotheses, as we do for the most part, we may assume that the various sensory events can be mapped on a single line that we call x. The numerical value of an observed sensory event affects the observer's confidence about which hypothesis is true. Indeed, we assume that he has a criterion k such that he will choose h_0, or n, whenever $x < k$ and will choose h_1, or s, whenever $x > k$. The variable x may or may not be likelihood ratio; whether or not it is depends on a further assumption that will be discussed shortly. We may now state the Gaussian assumption in precise form: the distribution of the random variable x is Gaussian under each hypothesis. Specifically, under hypothesis n, x has a Gaussian distribution with mean m_n and standard deviation σ_n and, under hypothesis s, x has a Gaussian distribution with mean m_s and standard deviation σ_s. Repeated in equation form, the assumption is that

$$f(x \mid n) = (2\pi\sigma_n{}^2)^{-\frac{1}{2}} \exp\left[-\frac{(x - m_n)^2}{2\sigma_n{}^2} \right]$$

$$f(x \mid s) = (2\pi\sigma_s{}^2)^{-\frac{1}{2}} \exp\left[-\frac{(x - m_s)^2}{2\sigma_s{}^2} \right]$$

(3.1)

where $\exp x$ is e^x.

The coordinates of the ROC curve are uniquely determined from our assumptions since, for any given criterion k, we know that

$$P(S \mid s) = \int_k^\infty f(x \mid s)\, dx = \Phi\left(\frac{k - m_s}{\sigma_s} \right)$$

and

(3.2)

$$P(S \mid n) = \int_k^\infty f(x \mid n)\, dx = \Phi\left(\frac{k - m_n}{\sigma_n} \right)$$

where Φ is the integral of the standard normal deviate (see Appendix I). Although the basic equations for the two probabilities appear to contain four parameters related to the two Gaussian distributions, in fact only two parameters are relevant. Since the underlying distribution is not directly observed, we can always scale the underlying variable x so that m_n is at zero and σ_n is one unit on our new scale. That is, let y be the following linear transformation of x:

$$y = \frac{1}{\sigma_n}(x - m_n)$$

The mean of the second distribution is then $(m_s - m_n)/\sigma_n$ and its standard deviation is then σ_s/σ_n. The criterion k can also be transformed by this same equation to make the two probabilities, $P(S \mid s)$ and $P(S \mid n)$, remain the same. This equivalent transformation reveals that the distance between the two means $(m_s - m_n)$, and the ratio of standard deviations (σ_s/σ_n) are the parameters of interest.

3.2.3.1 EQUAL-VARIANCE CASE: $(\sigma_n = \sigma_s)$. We begin with the assumption that $\sigma_s = \sigma_n$ and, after deriving the likelihood ratio and the ROC curve for this simple case, we explore how a change in this assumption complicates the resulting relations. Since σ_n and σ_s, as well as $m_s - m_n$, are measured in the units of x, it will simplify our work to choose that unit to equal $1/\sigma_n$; then $\sigma_n = \sigma_s = 1$. We now compute the likelihood

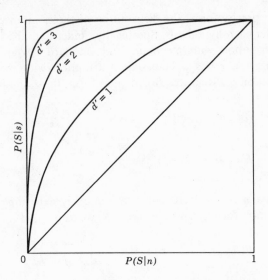

FIG. 3-1 Receiver-operating-characteristic (ROC) curves assuming that the two underlying distributions are Gaussian with equal variance. The hit and false-alarm probabilities are plotted on linear scales. The parameter d' is the distance between the means of the two distributions divided by the common standard deviation.

ratio, $l(x)$:

$$l(x) = \exp\left[(m_s - m_n)x - \tfrac{1}{2}(m_s^2 - m_n^2)\right] \tag{3.3a}$$

Since the only parameter is $(m_s - m_n)$, it is convenient to let $m_s = d'/2$ and $m_n = -d'/2$; then

$$l(x) = e^{d'x} \qquad \text{or} \qquad \ln l(x) = d'x \tag{3.3b}$$

Equation 3.3b has two important implications. First, note that likelihood ratio and the quantity x are monotonically related; thus decision criteria such as "say S if $x > k$" are optimal criteria if k is properly chosen. Second, it is easy to show that likelihood ratio is not monotonic with x unless $\sigma_n = \sigma_s$; thus we can also say that the assumption that x is monotonic with likelihood ratio implies $\sigma_n = \sigma_s$.

The form of the ROC curve generated by these assumptions is easy to determine. We use the relation that the slope of the ROC curve is equal to likelihood ratio to know that unit slope occurs when $x = 0$. Furthermore, since $e^{d'x} = 1/e^{-d'x}$, the slope of the ROC curve is reciprocally related for plus and minus values of x. The ROC curve is, therefore, symmetric about the negative diagonal. Figure 3-1 shows in some detail the ROC curves plotted on linear paper. The parameter d' is the difference between the means of the two distributions, $m_s - m_n$, divided by the standard

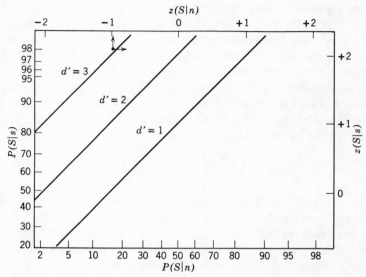

FIG. 3-2 Receiver-operating-characteristic (ROC) curves for the equal-variance Gaussian case plotted on double-probability paper. These are the same curves plotted in Fig. 3-1 except that the Gaussian transform has been used to scale the ordinate and abscissa. For an explanation of these transformations see the text.

deviation. As is apparent from the graph, the more the means of the two statistical hypotheses are separated, the larger the area beneath the ROC curve.

Another, and for some purposes more convenient, way of plotting data is to use double-probability paper. A probability scale is constructed by calculating a value z for each value of P according to the following equation:

$$P(z) = \frac{100}{(2\pi)^{1/2}} \int_{-\infty}^{z} e^{-x^2/2} \, dx \qquad (3.4)$$

but denoting each distance on z with its P value. Double-probability paper uses probability scales along each axis. Figure 3-2 shows ROC curves corresponding to a d' of 1, 2, and 3 plotted on such scales. The advantage of such graph paper when the underlying decision functions are Gaussian is obvious; the ROC curve is a straight line, and the mean separation between the two distributions can be read off such graph paper by simply subtracting the ordinate scale value $z(S\,|\,s)$ from the abscissa scale value $z(S\,|\,n)$.

The point $P(S\,|\,s) = 0.98$ and $P(S\,|\,n) = 0.16$, for example, lies near the $d' = 3$ line (see Fig. 3-2). The z value associated with $P(S\,|\,n)$ is -1;

see the top scale of the graph. The z value associated with $P(S \mid s)$ is $+2$; see the right scale of the graph. Thus $+2 - (-1) = +3$, as it should.*

3.2.3.2   UNEQUAL-VARIANCE CASE: $(\sigma_n \neq \sigma_s)$. First, we know that if $\sigma_n \neq \sigma_s$, then likelihood ratio is not monotonic with x. Thus ROC curves generated from criteria of the type "say S if $x > k$" will not have slopes that are monotonically decreasing. To see exactly how the ratio of the standard deviation affects the ROC curve, it is easiest to proceed geometrically. The slope of the ROC curve at any criterion k is still the ratio of the densities at that value of k; that is,

$$\frac{dP(S \mid s)}{dP(S \mid n)}\bigg|_k = \frac{f(k \mid s)}{f(k \mid n)}$$

This result is demonstrated by using Eq. 3.2 and repeating the argument of the previous section. Figure 3.3 shows the three possible relations between the magnitudes of σ_n and σ_s. First the densities of x are drawn under both hypotheses. The ratio of the densities determines the slope of the ROC curve that accompanies each assumption.

At the top of the figure, σ_s is greater than σ_n; thus the ROC curve accelerates rapidly until point b is reached, at which point the likelihood ratio, and hence the slope, is unity. Between b and a the likelihood ratio is less than one, and hence the ROC curve in this region has a shallow slope. The curve will actually cross the major diagonal between b and a. From point a to the extreme right-hand corner the curve again accelerates. In the bottom curve, σ_n is greater than σ_s, and the results are similar to the top curve except that the x scale has been turned around and the ROC curve has been reflected about the minor diagonal. In the middle of the figure, $\sigma_s = \sigma_n$; the ROC curve is symmetric about the minor diagonal and achieves a slope of one at the point marked c, which is located on the minor diagonal. Only when $\sigma_s = \sigma_n$ is the slope of the ROC curve monotonically decreasing.

Unfortunately for the experimentalist, the ratio σ_s/σ_n must be considerably different from unity before a departure from monotonicity in the slope can be detected in experimental ROC curves. If, for example, the total area under the ROC curve is 0.75 and σ_s is twice σ_n, then the rapid acceleration of the ROC curve near the right-hand corner (point a) occurs for values of $P(S \mid s)$ between 0.96 and 1. To detect experimentally such an increase in slope requires at least third-place accuracy. On the

---

* The actual definitions of the ordinate and abscissa of the Codex No. 41453 paper are somewhat inappropriate for our purpose, since the direction of integration is opposite to our definition of the hit and false-alarm probabilities. Nevertheless, since both scales are affected if the z value associated with $P(S \mid n)$ is subtracted from the z value associated with $P(S \mid s)$, the correct value for d' is determined.

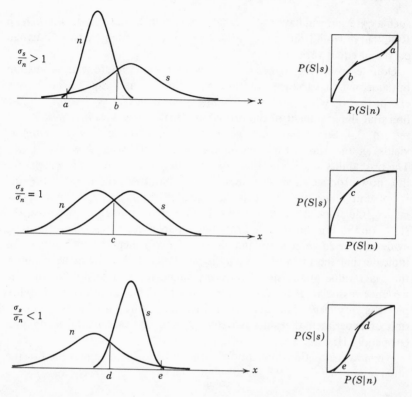

FIG. 3-3   The expected ROC curve for the unequal-variance Gaussian case. At the top of the figure the distribution under s has a variance larger than the variance under the n hypothesis. At the points marked a and b on the variable x the probability density given either hypothesis is the same; hence the likelihood ratio is 1. These two points are labeled in the ROC curve to the right of the distribution and, as indicated, the slope of the ROC curve is unity at the points marked a and b. In the middle of the figure is shown the equal-variance Gaussian case. Only at the point c is the likelihood ratio equal to 1. At higher values of x the likelihood ratio is greater than 1, and at lower values the likelihood ratio is less than 1. On the ROC curve the only point at which the slope is 1 is marked on the graph. The slopes below and above that point are less than 1 and greater than 1, respectively. At the bottom of the figure we consider the case in which the variance under s is smaller than the variance under n. At the points marked e and d the likelihood ratio is 1; thus the slope of the ROC curve is 1 at these points, as indicated in the accompanying ROC curve.

other hand, if the ratio of the sigmas is very extreme, for instance 4 to 10, then it seems plausible, although no experimental evidence is available, that the subject will modify his decision rule and respond N only if x is in or near the region between a and b. That is, he will adopt a decision axis nearly monotonic with likelihood ratio. The ROC curve produced from such a criterion will have a slope that monotonically decreases, and such an ROC curve would differ very little from one generated by two Gaussian curves of equal variance.

Double-probability paper is useful when the distributions are Gaussian but unequal in variance. Suppose that Eq. 3.1 and Eq. 3.2 hold true, except that $\sigma_s \neq \sigma_n$. Making a change of variables, $z_y = (k - m_s)/\sigma_s$, we find that the argument of the probability scale z becomes $k = \sigma_s z_y + m_s$; see Eq. 3.4. Similarly, a change in the other variable $z_x = (k - m_n)/\sigma_n$ yields as the transformation of the probability scale $k = \sigma_n z_x + m_n$. The probability scales are still linearly related, but because a given change in k now produces a smaller change in z_y than in z_x, the slope of the line is not unity. The slope is easily calculated: since $\Delta k = \sigma_s \Delta z_y$ and $\Delta k = \sigma_n \Delta z_x$, the slope $\Delta z_y/\Delta z_x = \sigma_n/\sigma_s$. Thus as the ratio σ_s/σ_n increases, the slope of the line on double-probability paper decreases. There is some evidence, based largely on the slopes of experimental ROC curves, to indicate that the ratio of σ_s to σ_n is not unity. It is difficult to establish the exact value of the slope from any single set of data points, and the variance associated with extreme probabilities on double-probability paper is very large. This question is discussed more fully in the presentation of experimental results (Chapter 4) and of experimental techniques (Appendix III).

We now trace the implications of the Gaussian assumption for the observer's behavior in the forced-choice tasks.

3.2.4 Gaussian assumption and forced-choice tasks

In a forced-choice task two or more observation intervals are defined for the subject. All observation intervals except one are samples from the same hypothesis, which is denoted n; the other interval contains a sample from a different hypothesis, which is denoted s. In a three-alternative forced-choice task, for example, the three possible composite hypotheses are $\langle snn \rangle$, $\langle nsn \rangle$, or $\langle nns \rangle$, which represent, respectively, the occurrence of s in the first, second, or third interval.

Assume that each observation produces a sensory effect and that these effects can be mapped to a single dimension, as previously assumed in the yes-no task. Denote by x_i the sensory effect corresponding to the ith observation interval. Thus, in a three-alternative forced-choice task the trio of numbers $\langle x_1, x_2, x_3 \rangle$ represent the total observation made on a single trial.

The most general analysis of a forced-choice task with m alternatives involves, therefore, a choice from among m hypotheses based on an observation that is an m-dimensional vector of real numbers. The hypotheses are $h_1 = \langle s_1 n_2 n_3 \cdots n_m \rangle$, $h_2 = \langle n_1 s_2 n_3 \cdots n_m \rangle$, and $h_m = \langle n_1 n_2 \cdots s_m \rangle$; the observation is $\langle x_1, x_2, \ldots, x_m \rangle$. This multitude of hypotheses complicates the analysis, since we must specify $m - 1$ mutually exclusive criterion regions in the m-dimensional real vector space. If the observation falls within one of the $m - 1$ regions, we accept the hypothesis corresponding to that region; if it falls outside, then we accept the sole remaining hypothesis. For certain well-defined objectives, such as maximizing expected value, the optimum acceptance regions can be specified (Anderson, 1958). Once these regions are given, the probabilities can be determined by integration over the appropriate regions for each hypothesis. Finding the answer may be difficult, since the integration is in a space of m dimensions and the area under a Gaussian function of one dimension must either be looked up in a table or be approximated by some numerical method. Certainly, determining the probabilities will be lengthy because there are so many independent probabilities. However, the multiplicity of hypotheses is a difficulty of complication only. There are more fundamental problems with the general m-alternative forced-choice analysis; the number of parameters is enormous.

A one-dimensional Gaussian variable has only two parameters: a mean and a standard deviation. An m-component Gaussian variable has m means, m standard deviations, and $m(m - 1)/2$ correlations. Each cross product of the type $x_i x_j$, $i > j$, produces a correlation term. Thus, to represent the distribution of an m-component Gaussian variable requires $2m + m(m - 1)/2$ parameters. Furthermore, these correlations, means, and variances may, in the most general cases, depend on the hypothesis. Even the correlation between the third and the fourth variable, $r_{x_3 x_4}$, might be different if $\langle snnn \rangle$ rather than $\langle nsnn \rangle$ were true. In total, then, $m\{2m + m(m - 1)/2\} = \frac{1}{2}(m^3 + 3m^2)$ parameters must be specified in the most general case.

The data of a general m-alternative forced-choice task consist of $m^2 - m$ probabilities; the term m^2 arises because there are m responses that the observer can choose, given any one of the m stimulus sequences; the term $-m$ arises because he must always choose one of the responses. Since there are many more parameters than observations, the Gaussian model will be useful only if some assumptions are made to reduce drastically the number of parameters.

Several assumptions are possible, and each one has its own particular strengths and weaknesses. Many of them are discussed by Torgerson (1958) in his treatment of the analogous problem faced by the Thurstonian models. The first assumption that we make can be called the homogeneity-of-noise assumption. We assume that in the forced-choice task each of the noise intervals has the same distribution of effects, independently of its location in the sequence of intervals. A precise statement of this assumption for the most general case would be, first, that the expected cross product $E(n_i n_j)$ is some constant k_1 for $i = j$, and some other constant k_2 for $i \neq j$. One realization of this assumption is when the noise components of the vector are independent and have equal variance for all hypotheses. Actually, the noise components could be correlated if the variances were all equal, since a linear transformation could render them uncorrelated and still preserve the equality of variance. Second, we assume that the correlation of a noise component with any signal component is the same for all noise components. In short, one noise interval is like any other. Thus there are basically only two hypotheses, s and n. Since, by assumption, only two hypotheses are different, the analysis of a two-interval forced-choice task illustrates the most general case.

We use the following notation. The occurrence of the signal in the first interval is denoted $\langle sn \rangle$, and in the second interval $\langle ns \rangle$. Choosing the first interval is denoted $R1$, and the second $R2$. The probability of choosing interval 1 when $\langle sn \rangle$ is presented, $P(R1 \mid \langle sn \rangle)$, and the probability of choosing the same interval when $\langle ns \rangle$ is presented, $P(R1 \mid \langle ns \rangle)$, are, respectively, the ordinate and abscissa of the forced-choice ROC curve. Remember that the two remaining probabilities are determined directly from these because $P(R2 \mid \langle sn \rangle) = 1 - P(R1 \mid \langle sn \rangle)$ and $P(R2 \mid \langle ns \rangle) = 1 - P(R1 \mid \langle ns \rangle)$.

There are basically two distributions, $f(x_1, x_2 \mid \langle sn \rangle)$ and $f(x_1, x_2 \mid \langle ns \rangle)$. The likelihood ratio is defined as the former density divided by the latter; thus the likelihood ratio of a signal in the first interval rather than the second is

$$l(x_1, x_2) = \frac{f(x_1, x_2 \mid \langle sn \rangle)}{f(x_1, x_2 \mid \langle ns \rangle)} \tag{3.5}$$

or

$$l(x_1, x_2) = \frac{\dfrac{1}{2\pi\sigma_s\sigma_n(1 - r^2)^{1/2}} \exp\left\{-\dfrac{1}{2(1 - r^2)}\left[\left(\dfrac{x_1 - m_s}{\sigma_s}\right)^2 - 2r\left(\dfrac{x_1 - m_s}{\sigma_s}\right)\left(\dfrac{x_2 - m_n}{\sigma_n}\right) + \left(\dfrac{x_2 - m_n}{\sigma_n}\right)^2\right]\right\}}{\dfrac{1}{2\pi\sigma_s\sigma_n(1 - r^2)^{1/2}} \exp\left\{-\dfrac{1}{2(1 - r^2)}\left[\left(\dfrac{x_1 - m_n}{\sigma_n}\right)^2 - 2r\left(\dfrac{x_1 - m_n}{\sigma_n}\right)\left(\dfrac{x_2 - m_s}{\sigma_s}\right) + \left(\dfrac{x_2 - m_s}{\sigma_s}\right)^2\right]\right\}} \tag{3.6}$$

where m_s and σ_s represent the Gaussian parameters if s is true, and m_n and σ_n represent the Gaussian parameters if n is true. The correlation term r is defined as the expected value of the cross product of the normalized variables.

We are implicitly assuming that temporal factors play no role. The parameter values of the distributions depend upon s and n alone, not on the order of presentation. Constant values of likelihood ratio are quadratic functions of the random variables x_1 and x_2. The logarithm of likelihood ratio makes this relation clear:

$$2 (1 - r^2) \ln l(x_1, x_2) = (x_1{}^2 - x_2{}^2)\left(\frac{\sigma_s{}^2 - \sigma_n{}^2}{\sigma_n{}^2 \sigma_s{}^2}\right)$$

$$+ (x_1 - x_2)\left[2\left(\frac{m_s \sigma_n{}^2 - m_n \sigma_s{}^2}{\sigma_n{}^2 \sigma_s{}^2}\right) + 2r\left(\frac{m_s - m_n}{\sigma_n{}^2 \sigma_s{}^2}\right)\right] \quad (3.7)$$

When σ_s does not equal σ_n, extreme values of the random variable are given disproportionate weight.

As in the yes-no analysis, we assume $\sigma_s = \sigma_n$. Since the exact value of the common standard deviation is only a scale value, it is convenient to set $\sigma_s = \sigma_n = 1$. The likelihood ratio then becomes

$$\ln l(x_1, x_2) = (x_1 - x_2)(m_s - m_n)/(1 - r) \quad (3.8)$$

Equation 3.8 indicates that, given the same values of x_1 and x_2, the likelihood ratio can range from plus to minus infinity, depending on the value of r. A detailed analysis of the effects of correlation would lead us too far afield. Suffice it to say that these effects may be quite profound. If $m_s - m_n$ is a constant less than zero, and if the correlation of x_1 and x_2 under both hypotheses is positive, then detection may be better than if x_1 and x_2 are independent. If, as is generally the case, $m_s - m_n > 0$ and the correlation is negative, then detection is poorer than would be the case if x_1 and x_2 were independent. We assume here that the correlation is zero, $r = 0$. Then the quantity $x_1 - x_2$ is strictly monotonic with likelihood ratio.

Since both x_1 and x_2 are Gaussian, their difference is Gaussian (see Appendix I).

If $\langle sn \rangle$ is true, then

$$E(x_1 - x_2) = E(x_1) - E(x_2) = m_s - m_n$$

$$\text{variance } (x_1 - x_2) = \sigma_s{}^2 + \sigma_n{}^2 = 2$$

If $\langle ns \rangle$ is true, then

$$E(x_1 - x_2) = E(x_1) - E(x_2) = +m_n - m_s = -(m_s - m_n)$$

$$\text{var } (x_1 - x_2) = \sigma_s{}^2 + \sigma_n{}^2 = 2$$

The separation of means, $2(m_s - m_n)$, divided by the common standard deviation is $\sqrt{2}$ larger than the corresponding variable (d') of the yes-no task.

As an alternative to the analysis just given, one might forgo any concern with likelihood ratio and simply assume that the observer uses a decision variable x such that yes-no decisions are based on the magnitude of x and forced-choice decisions are based on the difference in magnitude $(x_1 - x_2)$. The same statistics for the difference distribution arise if the correlation is assumed to be zero, except that now σ_s need not equal σ_n. Whatever the actual values of the standard deviations, the standard deviation of the difference $\sigma_{x_1-x_2}$ is equal to the square root of the sum of squares of σ_n and σ_s, and thus is the same under both hypotheses $\langle sn \rangle$ and $\langle ns \rangle$. Therefore, even if the yes-no ROC curve is not symmetric, the two-alternative forced-choice curve will be symmetric.

Given either set of assumptions,

$$P(R1 \mid \langle sn \rangle) = \int_c^{+\infty} f(x_1 - x_2 \mid \langle sn \rangle) = \int_c^{+\infty} \phi \left\{ \frac{x - (m_s - m_n)}{\sigma_{x_1-x_2}} \right\} dx$$

and

$$P(R1 \mid \langle ns \rangle) = \int_c^{+\infty} f(x_1 - x_2 \mid \langle ns \rangle) = \int_c^{+\infty} \phi \left\{ \frac{x + (m_s - m_n)}{\sigma_{x_1-x_2}} \right\} dx \quad (3.9)$$

The forced-choice ROC curve is symmetric and, as remarked earlier, if $\sigma_s = \sigma_n$ the curve will appear to follow a yes-no ROC curve with the d' parameter $\sqrt{2}$ larger than the corresponding yes-no value. This result is reasonable, since we assume that the combination of the observations from each interval is linear, that the observations are independent ($r = 0$), and that each observation is given equal weight. Almost no studies have reported forced-choice ROC curves.* This lack is unfortunate since, as our later analysis of the threshold model will indicate, the most divergent predictions between detection and threshold theories arise over the shape of the two-alternative forced-choice ROC curves.

Forced-choice experiments have enjoyed a general popularity among sensory psychologists. They do not usually obtain the complete ROC curve, but merely instruct their subjects to try to maintain equal percentages of correct responses in each interval. They then use the total percent correct, averaged over the two intervals, as the main dependent

* The notable exception is the data collected by Elizabeth F. Shipley on the detection of a pulsed 1000-cps tone in noise. The data appear in Figures 12, 13, and 14 in an article by Norman (1964b).

variable. A general treatment of the m-alternative forced-choice case involves a great many parameters, as we have discussed earlier. Even if the statistical parameters were all known, the process of predicting each of the entries in the mth order matrix representing the various stimuli and responses possible in m-alternative forced-choice tasks would be quite formidable.

If we make some very strong simplifying assumptions above and beyond the Gaussian one, we can determine the expected probability of a correct response in an m-alternative forced-choice task. First, we assume that the observation vector $X = (x_1, x_2, x_3, \ldots, x_m)$ has m components, x_i, that are Gaussian random variables, uncorrelated with each other, and all having equal variance. If the components of the vector represent the n hypothesis, we assume a zero mean. The presence of the signal in the jth interval causes the mean of the jth component to increase to a value mean d', which we assume is independent of the particular interval. The final assumption is that the decision rule in the m-alternative forced-choice experiment is simply to select the hypothesis corresponding to the interval that has the largest component.

The probability of being correct in an m-alternative forced-choice task is equal to the probability that the sample associated with the signal, x_s, is greater than the maximum of the $m - 1$ samples from the noise, x_n. This probability in integral form is

$$P_m(C) = \int_{-\infty}^{+\infty} \phi(x_n - d')[1 - \Phi(x_n)]^{m-1} \, dx \qquad (3.10)$$

Various approximations to this relation have been computed (Green and Birdsall, 1958). Tables relating d' to $P_m(C)$, calculated by Elliott, are given by Swets (1964).

The preceding derivations have traced the assumption of an underlying Gaussian distribution in both yes-no and forced-choice tasks. How various assumptions about the values of, or relationships among, the parameters of the distribution affect the expected results have been derived. We turn next to a quite different set of assumptions concerning the underlying distribution, to the so-called threshold model.

3.3   THRESHOLD THEORY

3.3.1   Introduction and background

Threshold theory is the name for a set of assumptions that appear implicitly in a variety of psychophysical theories. In Chapter 5 we review this theory in greater detail and contrast its predictions with available data. It is not an exaggeration to say that there is little evidence to support the old, classical theory of the threshold and, hence, some psychophysical procedures that depend upon it. There are, however, recent modifications of threshold theory which are still viable. Luce (1963a,b) has recently restated the essentials of threshold theory in the most complete and precise presentation it has ever received. Because we discuss classical threshold theory in Chapter 5, we shall not review it here. Rather, the development in this section will emphasize that threshold theory, both the classical and the recent versions, can be represented by a certain kind of assumption concerning the assumed distribution of signal and noise. Secondly, we show that Luce's theory assumes an adjustable threshold and that, far from defending the classical psychophysical procedures, it suggests that a stable estimate of the threshold value can only be obtained if more trials are devoted to estimating the false-alarm proportion than the hit proportion. Thus Luce's theory joins with detection theory in recommending that the false-alarm proportion be an essential ingredient in specifying the sensory detection process.

Threshold theory assumes a very sparse range of sensory experience in the detection task. Either the stimulus produces a sensory event of sufficient magnitude for the observer to think a stimulus was there (a detect state), or the sensory event is so weak as to produce the opposite state (a nondetect state). Classical threshold theory seemed to imply an almost continuous gradation of sensory information above the threshold. Luce's theory, in a desire to preserve some simplicity and parsimony, assumes only one state above the absolute threshold, a detect state. Luce would, of course, be forced to abandon this simple two-state theory if the threshold itself were fixed. The easiest way to see the difficulty is to consider a situation in which a false-alarm proportion of 0.10 is found in a yes-no experiment. If the threshold were fixed, we might expect that same false-alarm proportion even when the signal was made extremely easy to detect. Empirically, we know that subjects achieve hit proportions of 1.0 and false-alarm proportions of 0 when given very easy signals. This can only happen in a two-state model if the threshold itself is adjustable. Actually, the threshold parameter in Luce's theory is not continuously adjustable but may be selected from among a set of fixed values. The threshold parameter is determined by the sensory criterion, which is the number of neural-quantum units that the subject demands to define the detect state. Once this criterion is fixed, only detect and nondetect states are used as sensory information. The theory can then be characterized by the assumption that the observer's sensory processing produces only two values of likelihood ratio. In the detect state, the likelihood ratio is high; in the nondetect state, the likelihood ratio is low. The sensory processing results in one of these two values. To understand the remainder of the theory, we must turn to a specific experimental procedure such as the yes-no procedure.

3.3.2   Two-state threshold theory and the yes-no ROC curve

In the yes-no experiment the subject is asked to vary the false-alarm and hit proportions. How can such instructions be carried out by an observer who, according to modern threshold theory, recognizes only two possible likelihood ratios? Obviously, his reports cannot perfectly mirror his sensory experience, because then the ROC curve would consist of only one point, which is contrary to empirical fact. Specifically, the hit proportion $P(S \mid s)$ would be the probability of a detect state given the presentation of a signal, that is, $P(D \mid s)$; and the false-alarm proportion $P(S \mid n)$ would be the probability of a detect state given noise alone, that is, $P(D \mid n)$. The subject must therefore be guessing, or changing some of his reports to contradict his sensory experience and to comply with the experimental instructions. The important point is that, because no gradation of sensory experience is allowed within these two categories of the model, *the guessing mechanism cannot operate on any sensory basis*. Therefore, we may assume that the guessing mechanism is *independent* of the sensory mechanism. Two guessing parameters need to be specified: the probability of saying "yes" in the nondetect state, and the probability of saying "no" in the detect state. The sum of the product of these probabilities, multiplied by the conditional probability of that state given signal or noise, provides the relevant probability of the yes-no experiment. The product of the probabilities is used because, according to the model, the guessing process must be independent of the sensory process.

We could at this point, using only algebra, write out all the required probabilities. Instead, we introduce some assumptions about hypothetical, underlying distributions. Given these assumptions, we can generate all the predictions of Luce's threshold model, but we shall use geometric rather than algebraic arguments. The equations generated by these distributions are identical to those derived by Luce; the comparison will be facilitated by the fact that we have used Luce's notation for parameters of the geometric model. The motivation for this particular method of presentation is to preserve continuity with the material presented earlier. It will also seem familiar to those who know neural-quantum theory. The assumed distributions will be used to generate the coordinates of the ROC curve, just as the Gaussian model was used to generate its predictions. However, the reader should be warned at the outset that the distributions cannot be based on sensory effects. The distributions must have reference to some

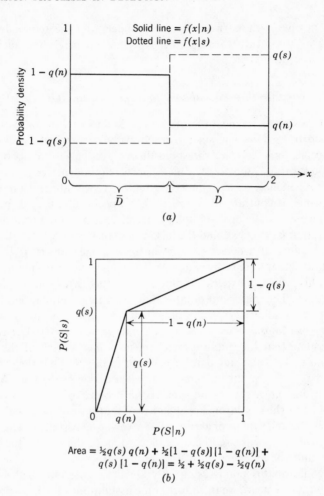

FIG. 3-4 A possible interpretation of the underlying density functions for Luce's two-state threshold theory. In part (a) the detect state is assumed to exist if x is between 1 and 2, and the non-detect state is assumed to exist if x is between 0 and 1. The probability densities for the signal hypothesis are represented by the dashed lines; the probability density associated with the noise-alone hypothesis is represented by solid lines. In part (b) of the figure the ROC curve generated by moving the criterion along different values of x is indicated. If the criterion is set at the point $x = 1$, the probability of a hit is $q(s)$ and the probability of a false alarm is $q(n)$. The area under the yes-no ROC curve is calculated on the basis of the rectangle and two triangles, as indicated in the drawing. This area is equal to the expected percentage correct in two-alternative forced choice, given a symmetric decision criterion.

inferred response or guessing mechanism. The distributions look, super-ficially, as if they might refer to sensory effects, but we shall later point to the essential features of the model that belie this impression.

Consider the two probability densities displayed in Fig. 3-4a. Both are uniform over the interval 0 to 1 and also uniform over the interval 1 to 2. Specifically, if hypothesis n is true:

$$f(x) = 1 - q(n) \quad \text{if} \quad 0 \leq x \leq 1 \tag{3.11}$$

$$f(x) = q(n) \quad \text{if} \quad 1 < x \leq 2$$

and if hypothesis s is true:

$$f(x) = 1 - q(s) \quad \text{if} \quad 0 \leq x \leq 1 \tag{3.12}$$

$$f(x) = q(s) \quad \text{if} \quad 1 < x \leq 2$$

There is nothing significant about the selection of unit intervals; any two other unit intervals would be as good. It is convenient that they are unit intervals, since then the parameters can refer to probability as well as probability density; for example, the probability, given hypothesis s, that $x > 1$ is $q(s)$.

Given any stimulus, one of two likelihood ratios results: either $q(s)/q(n)$ or $\{1 - q(s)\}/\{1 - q(n)\}$. We associate the former likelihood ratio, which is greater than one, with the detect state D and the smaller likelihood ratio with the nondetect state $\bar{D}$. The variable x can take on any value in the interval 0 to 2, but only two likelihood ratios can result. As will become evident, the uniform distributions over the unit intervals 0 to 1 and 1 to 2 represent the independent guessing mechanism. The subject can be assumed to set a criterion t such that if $x > t$ he says "yes." Thus the description of the observer's behavior is the same as with the Gaussian model; only the density function differs.

It is easy to derive the two coordinates of the ROC curve given these assumptions. The decision rule is to say "yes" when $x > t$. Then

$$P(S \mid s) = \int_t^2 q(s)\, dx = q(s)(2 - t)$$

and
$$1 \leq t \leq 2$$

$$P(S \mid n) = \int_t^2 q(n)\, dx = q(n)(2 - t)$$

or

$$P(S \mid s) = q(s) + \int_{t'}^1 1 - q(s)\, dx = q(s) + (1 - t')[1 - q(s)]$$

and
$$0 \leq t' \leq 1$$

$$P(S \mid n) = q(n) + \int_{t'}^1 1 - q(n)\, dx = q(n) + (1 - t')[1 - q(n)] \tag{3.13}$$

The quantity $(2 - t)$, $0 \leq (2 - t) \leq 1$, and the quantity $(1 - t')$, $0 \leq (1 - t') \leq 1$, represent the tendencies to respond "yes" in the detect and nondetect states, respectively. The ROC curve resulting from these assumptions is displayed in Fig. 3-4b. It consists of two straight lines connected at the point $q(s)$, $q(n)$. With a high criterion, $2 > t > 1$, the observer is not always responding "yes" even when the detect state occurs. Some point of this lower limb of the ROC curve is generated which depends on the exact value of the criterion. Similarly, with a low criterion, $0 < t' < 1$, the subject is sometimes saying "yes" even when the nondetect state occurs. Some point on the upper limb of the ROC curve is generated which corresponds to the value of the criterion. Only if the criterion is set exactly at the value $x = 1$ will the response faithfully mirror the sensory events; then a detect state produces a "yes" response, and a nondetect state produces a "no" response. Any other criterion value obscures the sensory events by imposing a response bias between the sensory event and the observer's report. Note that, since there are only two values of likelihood ratio, this model preserves the paucity of sensory information which is central to any threshold theory. It is also easy to see that x cannot represent a sensory event since, for either state, the sensory probabilities, $q(s)$, $q(n)$, etc., are independent of x. The variable x, therefore, must refer to some guessing or response mechanism.

3.3.3   Two-state threshold theory and the forced-choice procedure

Next we consider an application of this model to a two-alternative forced-choice task. A pair of observations, x_1 and x_2, occur in the two intervals of the forced-choice trial. The likelihood ratio is defined as before, and the value of likelihood ratio is given for the four possible observations that can arise. The likelihood ratio is

$$l(x_1, x_2) = \frac{f(x_1, x_2 \mid \langle sn \rangle)}{f(x_1, x_2 \mid \langle ns \rangle)}$$

Assuming $q(s) > q(n)$,

$$l(x_1, x_2) = \begin{cases} l_1 = \dfrac{q(s)[1 - q(n)]}{[1 - q(s)]q(n)} & > 1 \quad x_1 > 1 \quad x_2 < 1 \\[2mm] l_2 = \dfrac{q(s)q(n)}{q(n)q(s)} & = 1 \quad x_1 > 1 \quad x_2 > 1 \\[2mm] l_2 = \dfrac{[1 - q(s)][1 - q(n)]}{[1 - q(n)][1 - q(s)]} & = 1 \quad x_1 < 1 \quad x_2 < 1 \\[2mm] l_3 = \dfrac{[1 - q(s)]q(n)}{[1 - q(n)]q(s)} & < 1 \quad x_1 < 1 \quad x_2 > 1 \end{cases} \qquad (3.14)$$

As the equations indicate, three values of likelihood ratio can result: a likelihood ratio equal to one, less than one, or greater than one. The two values of likelihood ratio equal to one come about because the detect or nondetect state arises in both intervals. Given that the subject cannot make distinctions within either state, there is no sensory information upon which the subject can base his decision. The likelihood ratio greater than one occurs when the first observation lies in the detect state and the second does not. The likelihood ratio less than one occurs when the second observation lies in the detect state and the first does not. Thus two of the three likelihood ratios yield some positive sensory information about the probabilities of signals in the first or second intervals. The two middle cases yield no sensory information and thus, we would expect, would be most subject to response or guessing biases.

As the two coordinates of the forced-choice ROC curve, we use the probability of saying "interval one" when the stimulus sequence was $\langle sn \rangle$, $P(R1 \mid \langle sn \rangle)$, and the probability of saying "interval one" when it was $\langle ns \rangle$, $P(R1 \mid \langle ns \rangle)$. These probabilities can be easily computed from the original density functions for successive criterion values on likelihood ratio. The most stringent criterion demands so large a likelihood ratio that no likelihood ratio can occur that exceeds or equals the criterion. The subject never makes response $R1$. If the observer's criterion is to make response $R1$ whenever the likelihood ratio is equal to l_1, then the probability of an $R1$ response given the stimulus pair $\langle sn \rangle$ is $q(s)[1 - q(n)]$. Likewise, the probability of $R1$ when the reverse stimulus sequence occurs, namely, $\langle ns \rangle$, is $q(n)[1 - q(s)]$. The next criterion would be to make response $R1$ when the likelihood ratio exceeds one and to make response $R1$ on some proportion of the trials, for instance, v, when the likelihood ratio is equal to one. As the bias parameter v increases, the observer chooses the first interval with greater frequency until finally he is responding $R1$ on all occasions. Then his decision rule is to respond $R1$ whenever the likelihood ratio is equal to one or more. Finally, the most inclusive category is one in which subject responds $R1$ no matter what the value of likelihood ratio, in short, on all trials. The probabilities for the two-alternative forced-choice task are given in equations that follow.

If the decision rule is to choose $R1$ with probability α when $l(x_1, x_2) > 1$, then

$$P(R1 \mid \langle sn \rangle) = \alpha q(s)[1 - q(n)]$$

and   (3.15a)

$$P(R1 \mid \langle ns \rangle) = \alpha q(n)[1 - q(s)]$$

If the decision rule is to choose $R1$ when $l(x_1, x_2) > 1$, never to choose $R1$ when $l(x_1, x_2) < 1$, and to choose $R1$ with probability v when $l(x_1, x_2) = 1$, then

$$P(R1 \mid \langle sn \rangle) = q(s)[1 - q(n)] + vq(s)q(n) + v[1 - q(s)][1 - q(n)]$$

and   (3.15b)

$$P(R1 \mid \langle ns \rangle) = q(n)[1 - q(s)] + vq(n)q(s) + v[1 - q(n)][1 - q(s)]$$

If the decision rule is to choose $R1$ when $l(x_1, x_2) > 1$, and to choose $R1$ with probability β when $l(x_1, x_2) < 1$, then

$$\begin{aligned} P(R1 \mid \langle sn \rangle) = {} & q(s)[1 - q(n)] + q(s)q(n) \\ & + [1 - q(s)][1 - q(n)] + \beta[1 - q(s)]q(n) \end{aligned}$$

and   (3.15c)

$$\begin{aligned} P(R1 \mid \langle ns \rangle) = {} & q(n)[1 - q(s)] + q(n)q(s) \\ & + [1 - q(n)][1 - q(s)] + \beta[1 - q(n)]q(s) \end{aligned}$$

The plethora of terms should not intimidate the reader. The expressions for the probabilities have been left unsimplified to reveal the simple structure of the relations. The probability associated with each decision rule is the weighted sum of the probability of the likelihood ratio given the hypothesis, weighted by the probability of the choice given that likelihood ratio. These conditional probabilities of the choice, given the likelihoods β, α, and v, are response biases, since they change the probabilities of certain responses and are independent of the sensory events. Each succeeding equation from Eqs. 3.15a to Eq. 3.15c is simply the preceding equation with the response bias set equal to one, plus a term arising from the extension of the decision criterion to include another value of likelihood ratio.

Figure 3-5 shows the ROC curve for the two-alternative forced-choice case. The slope of the ROC curve is the value of likelihood ratio used in the decision rule. For the major part of the curve the likelihood ratio is one. This portion of the curve is undoubtedly the one most likely to be encountered in experimental work. Luce, in his analysis, ignores the possibility of the segments with slope greater or less than unity. There is no reason to exclude these possibilities; Luce probably omitted them to keep the development somewhat simpler. Moreover, he does not use a likelihood ratio approach, and thus distinguishes between trials which yield two detect (x_1 and $x_2 > 1$) states and trials which yield two nondetect (x_1 and $x_2 < 1$) states. He thus invokes two bias parameters, w and v, instead of the one, v, as used in this development. This difference between the two presentations arises because we emphasize the likelihood-ratio approach, and thus map both the double detect and double nondetect trials to a

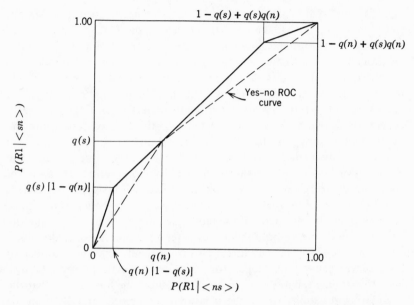

FIG. 3-5 The ROC curve for two-alternative forced choice assuming Luce's two-state threshold model. The ordinate is the probability of a correct response given that the signal occurred in the first interval. The abscissa is the probability of that same response ($R1$) given that the signal occurred in the second interval (an error). The dashed curve shows the yes-no ROC curve if the hit and false-alarm proportions of the yes-no experiment are used as the ordinate and abscissa respectively. At the point $q(s), q(n)$ the yes-no curve just touches the two-alternative forced-choice curve.

single observation with likelihood ratio equal to one. The parameter v then refers to the tendency to guess, given a sensory event which is equally likely to be signal or noise.

The relation between yes-no and forced-choice procedures for the two-state threshold model deserves some discussion. When

$$v = q(s)q(n)/\{q(n)q(s) + [1 - q(n)][1 - q(s)]\}$$

then $P(R1 \mid \langle sn \rangle) = q(s)$ and $P(R1 \mid \langle ns \rangle) = q(n)$. For the classical, or "high-threshold," theory, $q(n) = 0$ and the forced-choice ROC curve should rise with slope one until $P(R1 \mid \langle sn \rangle) = 1$. For any value of $q(n)$, the forced-choice ROC curve lies above the yes-no ROC curve everywhere but at this one single point. A symmetric decision rule results when $v = \frac{1}{2}$ in Eq. 3.15b. Then

$$P(R1 \mid \langle sn \rangle) = \tfrac{1}{2} + \tfrac{1}{2}q(s) - \tfrac{1}{2}q(n)$$

and

$$P(R1 \mid \langle ns \rangle) = \tfrac{1}{2} - \tfrac{1}{2}q(s) + \tfrac{1}{2}q(n)$$

Since for the symmetric point the total percentage correct is simply $P(R1 \mid \langle sn \rangle)$, we see that the area under the yes-no ROC curve gives the percentage correct for the symmetric forced-choice criterion, as it should.

Although the continuous-detection and the discrete-threshold models are formally quite different, it should be apparent that, experimentally, their predictions are remarkably similar. Given the inevitable scatter of empirical data, it is difficult to design experiments that will distinguish clearly between these two possibilities. We take up the task of comparing the models with existing data later, in Chapters 4 and 5.

Luce's threshold theory and signal detection theory agree on the basic dependent variables; they are the hit probability $P(S \mid s)$ and the false-alarm probability $P(S \mid n)$. They disagree on how these two variables are related. Since low values of false-alarm probability lead to very poor estimates of the corresponding parameter of the model, it is impossible, even within the context of modern threshold theory, to defend the practice of maintaining near-zero false-alarm probabilities. This is especially true since almost all ROC curves show high slopes for very low false-alarm probabilities. Thus, to estimate reliably a given hit probability, one must argue that the false-alarm probability should be measured even more carefully than the hit probability.

Before leaving the two-state threshold model, we should mention that Luce has attempted to extend it by assuming a (linear) learning mechanism which, in turn, determines the response-bias parameters. Such a model is much easier to attach to a threshold model, with only two possible sensory states, than to a detection model, with a continuum of possible sensory events.* It is too early to judge the success of this model, but such developments must be carefully watched. If the learning part of this threshold model produces interesting experimental results, then it may prove, for some purposes, to be a more useful first approximation—even if ultimately it is rejected as a sensory model. Certainly, there are interesting problems for which the discrete features of the threshold model make the mathematical analysis vastly more tractable.

3.4   EXPONENTIAL MODEL

Very early in the history of detection theory, some empirical ROC curves were obtained that did not appear to fit the Gaussian model with equal variances. The most common departure is that the data, although apparently straight lines on double-probability paper, have a slope less than

---

* However, one should not believe that it is impossible to generate a learning model in which the sensory events are assumed to be continuous; for example, see Schoeffler (1965).

one. To fit the data, the Gaussian model with unequal variances has often been used. The ratio of the noise standard deviation to the signal standard deviation is then equal to the obtained slope on double-probability coordinates.

Not only does this ad hoc assumption introduce another free parameter, but it creates a set of rather knotty theoretical problems. If the ratios of the standard deviations of the noise and signal distributions are unequal, then, as discussed above, the decision axis x is no longer monotonic with likelihood ratio. It seems peculiar that an observer with sufficient training cannot learn to re-order his decision axis so that when very low values of x occur he responds "yes" instead of "no." The theory assumes that the observer's behavior is influenced by these low values of x since, presumably, the criterion can be placed at this as well as any other value of the scale. Why, then, does the observer persist in responding "no," when the probability of a signal given such a low value is three or four times the conditional probability of noise given that same value? We can hardly argue that he is insensitive to such ratios since, presumably, ratios of the same magnitude lead him to respond in the other manner for higher values of x.

The justification for the Gaussian model with unequal variance is, we believe, not to be made on theoretical but rather on practical grounds. It is a simple, convenient way to summarize the empirical data with the addition of a single parameter. Many practical questions about statistical processes can be answered from information about their first and second moments. The assumption of a Gaussian distribution with unequal variance seems to be motivated by the same pragmatic goals.

As another way of summarizing yes-no data, we introduce an exponential distribution that has, we feel, many advantages over the Gaussian assumption with unequal variance. First, the decision axis is monotonic with likelihood ratio. Second, this distribution arises in a natural way in many counting processes and may, therefore, generate interesting hypotheses about the sensory mechanisms. Third, and equally important, it is a one-parameter distribution, and thus the ROC curve can be summarized by one parameter rather than by two. The parsimony gained, however, entails the risk that the new distribution may fit fewer data than two-parameter models.

Specifically, we assume that x has an exponential distribution

$$f(x \mid n) = e^{-x}$$
$$f(x \mid s) = ke^{-kx} \qquad k < 1$$

The likelihood ratio then is

$$l(x) = ke^{-(k-1)x}$$

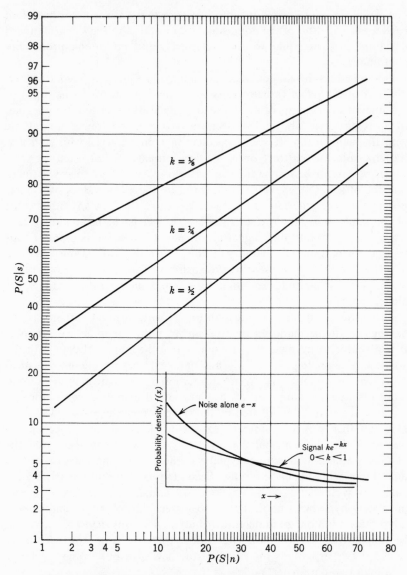

FIG. 3-6 The ROC curve associated with the exponential model, plotted on double-probability paper. The insert shows the assumed distributions of noise and signal plus noise. The ROC curve displays the expected hit and false-alarm probabilities as a function of the criterion for a fixed parameter k. The parameter k is a measure of the signal's detectability.

so that $l(x) = 1$ when $x = \ln k/(k - 1)$. Figure 3-6 shows the ROC curve for the yes-no task for three values of k. These values of k correspond to values of d' of about 1.8, 1.1, and 0.6. The graph shows that the slope decreases with decreasing k; some data have shown the same trend.

In addition, consider the relation of $P(S \mid s)$ to $P(S \mid n)$. Since

$$P(S \mid n) = \int_t^\infty e^{-x}\, dx = e^{-t}$$

and

$$P(S \mid s) = \int_t^\infty ke^{-kx}\, dx = e^{-kt} = (e^{-t})^k$$

therefore

$$P(S \mid n) = P(S \mid s)^{1/k} \qquad 1/k > 1$$

That is, the ROC curve is a power function of the two coordinates. This relation is assumed by Egan, Greenberg, and Schulman (1961b) and is discussed in Chapter 9, Section 9.8.

3.5 LUCE'S CHOICE MODEL

Before concluding our discussion of forms of the assumed underlying distribution, we discuss one other assumption about the form of the underlying distribution. This assumption is of interest because it generates predictions similar to those obtained from the choice theory developed by Luce (1959). The basic density function for the assumed distributions is

$$f(x) = \frac{\lambda}{(\lambda + x)^2} \qquad \lambda \geq 1 \tag{3.16}$$

where λ is a constant. For the noise distribution we set $\lambda = 1$; the signal distribution has $\lambda \geq 1$, its exact size depending on the magnitude of the signal. Figure 3-7 shows the distribution of x for several values of the parameter λ.

Likelihood ratio is given by

$$l(x) = \frac{f(x \mid s)}{f(x \mid n)} = \frac{\lambda(1 + 2x + x^2)}{\lambda^2 + 2x\lambda + x^2} \tag{3.17}$$

from which one can easily show that likelihood ratio is strictly monotonic with x and that likelihood ratio equals one when $x = \sqrt{\lambda}$.

Suppose that the observer adopts a certain value b of x as a criterion, and responds "yes" whenever $x \geq b$. The two coordinates of the yes-no ROC curve can be determined by simply integrating the appropriate

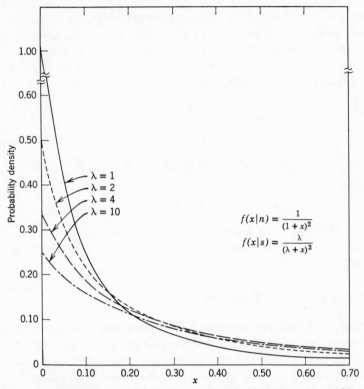

FIG. 3-7   Possible probability densities associated with the yes-no part of Luce's choice model. The formulas and graphs for the two densities corresponding to noise alone and signal plus noise are indicated.

density function from b to ∞,

$$\int_b^\infty \frac{\lambda}{(\lambda + x)^2}\, dx = \frac{-\lambda}{x + \lambda}\Bigg]_b^\infty = \frac{\lambda}{b + \lambda}$$

Thus

$$P(S \mid n) = \frac{1}{b + 1}$$

and

$$P(S \mid s) = \frac{\lambda}{b + \lambda} \tag{3.18}$$

These two expressions for $P(S \mid n)$ and $P(S \mid s)$ are identical to the equations given by Luce.* To make the correspondence, one identifies λ_n with η

* For an application of a learning model to this theory, see Bush, Luce, and Rose (1964).

for the noise hypothesis and, when signal plus noise is presented, one sets $\lambda_s = 1/\eta$. Thus our assumed density function (Eq. 3.16) and a detection-theory analysis yield equations that, in the yes-no task, are identical to those obtained in Luce's choice theory. We next pursue this similarity between the assumed distributions and choice theory to the forced-choice procedure. Application to forced choice reveals an essential difference.

Using the assumed density function, we can generate predictions for the two probabilities of the forced-choice task, namely, $P(R1 \mid \langle sn \rangle)$ and $P(R1 \mid \langle ns \rangle)$. If we do so, we find that the probabilities given by using our assumed density and those derived by Luce are different. This result clearly indicates that the density given in Eq. 3.16 is not isomorphic with choice theory; but perhaps we started with the wrong assumption about the underlying density function. The density function given in Eq. 3.16 is not the only function that, when integrated, yields yes-no predictions equivalent to those suggested by the choice model. The form we used is only one of a class of distributions. In general we need two distributions, $g(x \mid n)$ and $g(x \mid s)$, such that

$$\int_b^\infty g(x \mid s)\, dx = \frac{1}{1 + \eta g(b)}$$

and

$$\int_b^\infty g(x \mid n)\, dx = \frac{1}{1 + g(b)}$$

(3.19)

Given these requirements we know that

$$g(b \mid s) = \frac{\eta g'(b)}{[1 + \eta g(b)]^2} = \frac{1/\eta g'(b)}{[1/\eta + g(b)]^2}$$

and

$$g(b \mid n) = \frac{\eta g'(b)}{[\eta + g(b)]^2}$$

(3.20)

Thus, any distribution of the form

$$g(x \mid s) = \frac{k g'(x)}{[k + g(x)]^2}$$

(3.21)

generates the required yes-no equations, by setting $k = \eta$ for the noise hypothesis and $k = 1/\eta$ for the signal hypothesis. The question at issue is whether there is any function $g(x)$ that will also satisfy the forced-choice equations given by the choice theory. That is, is there any assumption about an underlying density function that will yield predictions which are the same as those generated by choice theory? We now show that no such function exists.

This impossibility is proved by recalling that, for any assumption about the underlying distribution, one can show that the area under the yes-no ROC curve is the percentage correct in the symmetric two-alternative forced-choice task. If any distribution $g(x)$ exists, we must be able to predict the symmetric forced-choice results for the choice theory on the basis of the given yes-no probabilities.

Table 3-1 compares the two sets of predictions—one from the area analysis and the other from Luce's choice theory—for a variety of values

TABLE 3-1. COMPARISON OF PREDICTIONS FROM THE AREA AND CHOICE MODELS.

η	Area Analysis $P_2(C)$	Choice Theory $P_2'(C)$	Difference $P_2'(C) - P_2(C)$
0.9	0.526	0.537	0.011
0.8	0.573	0.578	0.005
0.7	0.614	0.623	0.009
0.6	0.665	0.673	0.008
0.5	0.718	0.727	0.009
0.4	0.775	0.786	0.011
0.3	0.837	0.845	0.008
0.2	0.902	0.906	0.004
0.1	0.963	0.963	0.000

of η. The largest difference is about eleven thousandths. Thus no function $g(x)$ exists that will generate all of the predictions of choice theory. Choice theory is, therefore, a very different theoretical approach to the explanation of detection behavior from either detection theory or threshold theory. It would be desirable to know exactly what aspect of choice theory prevents it from being related to the assumption of some underlying density function. We have not as yet been able to characterize this difference in any succinct form.

3.6 SUMMARY

In this chapter we discussed four general models in terms of assumptions about underlying distributions of signal and noise. With the exception of Luce's choice model, we were able to show a correspondence between assumptions about the underlying distribution and the predictions of these models in the yes-no and forced-choice tasks. The Gaussian and exponential models assume a continuous representation of sensory experience, whereas the threshold model assumes a discrete representation. Despite this difference, all agree that a careful measurement of the false-alarm proportion is essential in accurately specifying the parameters of the sensory system. Thus, on methodological grounds, there is complete agreement.

The difference between these first three theories and choice theory is not easily summarized. The theories are fundamentally different, yet their predictions are remarkably close.

PROBLEMS

3.1   Assume that the density function for signal plus noise, $f(x \mid s)$, is given as follows:

$$f(x \mid s) = 2x \qquad \text{where} \quad 0 < x < 1$$

Assume that the density function for noise alone is

$$f(x \mid n) = 1 \qquad \text{where} \quad 0 < x < 1$$

(a) What is the likelihood ratio?

(b) Plot the yes-no ROC curve on linear scales and on probability scales, assuming that the decision rule is to say "yes" if and only if $x > k$.

3.2   Let $P(R1 \mid \langle sn \rangle)$ and $P(R1 \mid \langle ns \rangle)$ be the coordinates of a two-alternative forced-choice ROC curve. If the observer adopts a symmetric criterion, then the number correct in each interval is the same. Where does such a point lie on the forced-choice ROC curve?

3.3   Show that symmetric behavior in a two-alternative forced-choice task is equivalent to choosing $R1$ if and only if $x_1 - x_2 > 0$, when the distributions of signal plus noise and of noise alone are Gaussian.

3.4   Assume that the underlying distributions of both s and n are Gaussian with equal variance. Show how, for the symmetric criterion, assuming some small Gaussian error in the criterion is equivalent to assuming added variability in the distributions of s and n.

3.5   Derive the answer to Problem 2.3 (p. 52) from an application of two-state threshold theory.

3.6   Derive the yes-no ROC curve for a three-state threshold model and draw the underlying distributions that represent such a model.

4

Basic Experiments:

Separation of Sensory

and Decision Processes

4.1   INTRODUCTION

Presented here are the results of typical experiments which employed the three psychophysical procedures introduced previously: yes-no, rating, and forced choice. Data obtained from yes-no experiments, in which the observer was induced to vary his decision criterion under constant signal conditions, are displayed in the form of ROC graphs. Also shown are the ROC graphs that result when the observer is asked to maintain several decision criteria simultaneously in a rating task. The discussion of results obtained using the forced-choice procedure emphasizes a particular variant of the procedure, a variant in which a trial contains more than two alternatives and in which the observer is asked to make a second as well as a first choice. This experiment, like the yes-no and rating experiments, tests the assumption that the observer can rank his observations according to signal likelihood. The chapter concludes with a comparison of estimates of sensitivity obtained from the three procedures.

We note before proceeding that, in order to preserve continuity of the major ideas, the data are presented here with only a cursory discussion of the experimental conditions under which they were collected. Appendix III contains a detailed discussion of the laboratory procedures generally followed in the experiments reported in this book. We also note that, although a distribution-free measure of sensitivity (area under the ROC curve) is available (see Chapter 2), extensive use is made here and in subsequent chapters of the measure d', which is based on the assumption of normal probability distributions (see Chapter 3). The measure d' is used, in part, because the *area* measure was developed only recently, in the process of writing this book, and almost all the results in the prior literature are reported in terms of d'. More important, in many instances the assumptions of this measure seem to be met reasonably well. When they are, there are good reasons, as discussed in Chapter 3, for taking advantage of them. Finally, we note that the theoretical curves fitted to ROC data in the following pages are fitted solely on the basis of visual inspection; Appendix III, on experimental techniques, presents the reasons for this seemingly casual procedure.

4.2   THE YES-NO EXPERIMENT

4.2.1   Changing the decision criterion

The simplest and most direct test of the decision-theory analysis of the yes-no task is to trace out an empirical ROC curve for a signal (and noise background) of a given strength. To obtain this curve, the observer must change his decision criterion from one set of trials to another, thus producing several different points in the unit square having the proportion of hits, $P(S \mid s)$, as the ordinate and the proportion of false alarms, $P(S \mid n)$, as the abscissa. The form of the empirical ROC curve can be compared with the form that is predicted by decision theory, and with the forms that are predicted by alternative theories of the detection process. In this chapter we consider only the predictions of decision theory; in the chapter immediately following, the data are related to the predictions of several alternative theories.

The observer can be induced to change his decision criterion in any of several ways. He can simply be asked to adopt a "strict" or a "medium" or a "lax" criterion (Egan, Schulman, and Greenberg, 1959). These instructions may be amplified by further verbal instructions to the effect that "strict" means "press the *yes* key only when you are very certain that a signal was presented," and that "lax" means "press the *yes* key each time there was the slightest indication that a signal was presented." Within the framework of such instructions, "medium strict" and "medium lax" can also be given a fairly clear meaning. The observer can, instead, be asked to maximize the proportion of hits while approximating a specified proportion of false alarms. In this case the observer is asked, in effect, to adopt the decision goal that was defined by Neyman and Pearson, as discussed in Chapter 1. This numerical approach, which prescribes the desired false-alarm rate, can be used in conjunction with the verbal instructions—"strict," "medium," and "lax"—to lend them greater precision.

Other decision goals discussed in Chapter 1 suggest other practical ways of manipulating the decision criterion. The experimenter may vary the a priori probability of signal occurrence, and instruct the observer to maximize the percentage of correct responses. Or variable values and costs may be assigned to the four possible decision outcomes, and the observer may be instructed to maximize the expected value. A common practice is to state these values and costs in terms of cents payable at the end of the experimental session, and then to invite the observer to maximize his take-home pay.

4.2.2 Empirical ROC curves

The data shown in Fig. 4-1 were generated by varying the a priori probability of signal occurrence. The leftmost point was obtained from a group of trials having a low probability of signal occurrence, 0.10. Moving to the right, the successive points were based on successively higher

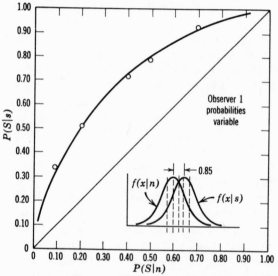

FIG. 4-1 An empirical ROC graph and a theoretical curve based on normal distributions of equal variance. The data points were obtained by varying the a priori probability of signal occurrence. Each point is based on 600 trials. The vertical dashed lines in the insert at lower right represent the decision criteria corresponding to the data points. The data were obtained in an auditory experiment. (Data from Tanner, Swets, and Green, 1956.)

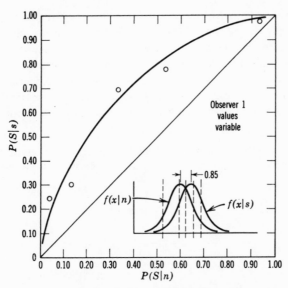

FIG. 4-2 ROC data obtained, from the same observer as in Fig. 4-1, by varying the values of the decision outcomes. Each point is based on 600 trials. The theoretical curve is the same as shown in Fig. 4-1. The vertical dashed lines in the insert represent the decision criteria. (Previously unpublished data collected by the authors.)

a priori probabilities: 0.30, 0.50, 0.70, and 0.90, respectively. The curve shown in the figure is the theoretical curve, assuming normal probability functions of equal variance, that appears to fit the data points best. The insert at lower right shows the probability distributions underlying the curve. The distance between the means of the two distributions is shown as 0.85; this distance is equal to d' under the convention that the standard deviation of the noise distribution is unity. These data were obtained in an auditory experiment in which the observer attempted to detect a tone burst in a background of white noise.

In a second part of this experiment, with the same physical conditions, the a priori probability of signal occurrence was held at 0.50, and the values of the decision outcomes were varied from one group of trials to another. The same observer as in Fig. 4-1 produced the data shown in Fig. 4-2. The leftmost point was obtained when there was a high premium on being correct when noise alone was presented. Moving to the right, the successive points were obtained as the premium on being correct when a signal was presented was successively increased relative to the premium on being

correct when noise alone was presented. As in Fig. 4-1, the curve is the
theoretical curve based on normal probability distributions of equal
variance that corresponds to a d' of 0.85.

The vertical dashed lines shown on the probability distributions in the
inserts at the lower right in Figs. 4-1 and 4-2 represent the decision criteria
corresponding to the various data points (assuming normal probability
distributions); we shall discuss shortly the decision criteria adopted by the

TABLE 4-1. THE DATA SHOWN IN FIGS. 4-1 AND 4-2 AND THE DECISION
PARAMETERS OF THE VARIOUS CONDITIONS WHICH PRODUCED THEM.

| | | Values | | | Optimal | Obtained | | |
$P(s)$	$n \cdot N$	$n \cdot S$	$s \cdot S$	$s \cdot N$	β	β	$P(S \mid n)$	$P(S \mid s)$
0.10	1	−1	1	−1	9.00	2.20	0.090	0.335
0.30	1	−1	1	−1	2.33	1.40	0.205	0.510
0.50	1	−1	1	−1	1.00	0.88	0.400	0.715
0.70	1	−1	1	−1	0.43	0.74	0.490	0.785
0.90	1	−1	1	−1	0.11	0.46	0.690	0.925
0.50	9	−9	1	−1	9.00	2.80	0.040	0.245
0.50	2	−2	1	−1	2.00	2.15	0.130	0.300
0.50	1	−1	1	−1	1.00	0.98	0.335	0.695
0.50	1	−1	2	−2	0.50	0.69	0.535	0.780
0.50	1	−1	9	−9	0.11	0.19	0.935	0.975

observer and their relationship to the optimal criteria. For now, let us
simply observe that the data plotted on a ROC graph follow the smoothly
increasing course (a curve with monotonically decreasing slope) that is
expected, under decision theory, to result from the adoption of likelihood-
ratio criteria. In particular, the data are fitted reasonably well by an ROC
curve derived from normal probability distributions.

The data of Figs. 4-1 and 4-2 are reproduced, along with the decision
parameters, in Table 4-1. The top part of the table shows the hit and
false-alarm proportions obtained when the a priori probability of signal
occurrence varied while the values placed on the decision outcomes were
held constant. The bottom part of the table shows the hit and false-alarm
proportions obtained when the values were varied and the a priori probability was fixed. Each decision condition, corresponding to a row in
the table and to a point in one of the two preceding figures, was in effect

for 600 trials. The decision conditions in each part of the experiment, probabilities varying and values varying, were presented in a random order, rather than in the order in which they are listed in the table.

4.2.3   Approach to optimal behavior

Consider now the columns in Table 4-1 labeled *optimal* β and *obtained* β. It will be recalled from the discussion of decision goals in Chapter 1 that β is equal to the critical value of likelihood ratio $[f(x \mid s)/f(x \mid n)]$ which corresponds to the decision criterion, and that the value of β is equal to the slope of that ROC curve at the point which results from a decision criterion set at that value of β on the likelihood-ratio axis. The optimal value of β when the a priori probabilities vary and when the values are fixed and symmetrical is the ratio $P(n)/P(s)$, as given in Eq. 1.21. The expression for the optimal value of β which applies when the values are not symmetrical is

$$\frac{(V_{n \cdot N} + V_{n \cdot S})P(n)}{(V_{s \cdot S} + V_{s \cdot N})P(s)}$$

as given in Eq. 1.20. As can be seen in Table 4-1, the a priori probabilities and values of decision outcomes were selected to yield similar values of the optimal β in the two parts of the experiment.

The criteria actually used by the observer, whether or not they are optimal, can be indexed by the quantity β. One simply estimates the slope of the empirical ROC curve at a given data point; this value represents the critical value of likelihood ratio, β, that was used by the observer in producing that data point. The dashed vertical lines in Figs. 4-1 and 4-2 indicate the various decision criteria used by the observer in the present experiment. The values listed in the table under the heading *obtained* β correspond to the ratios $f(x \mid s)/f(x \mid n)$ at which the vertical dashed lines are placed.

The relationship between the optimal and the obtained decision criteria that appears in these data is typical. It is more easily examined in graphical form, as in Fig. 4-3. The decision conditions which employ moderate probabilities and moderate decision values lead to actual criteria quite similar to the optimal ones. The observer tends to avoid extreme criteria: when the optimal β is relatively large, his actual criterion is not so high as the optimal criterion, and when the optimal β is relatively small, his criterion is not so low as the optimal criterion. Although this pattern is consistent with studies of decision making under uncertainty which do not involve ambiguous sensory information, the significance of its appearance here is not totally clear. It may be suspected that the subject's natural disinclination to make the same response on all trials is strengthened by his awareness that the experimenter's principal interest is in a sensory process. He probably finds it difficult to believe that he would be performing responsibly if the sensory distinctions he makes are exactly those that he could make by removing the earphones in an auditory experiment or by turning his back on a visual signal.

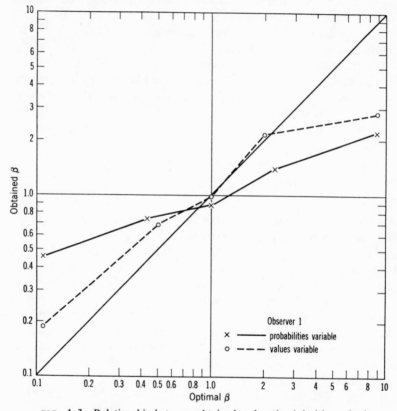

FIG. 4-3   Relationship between obtained and optimal decision criteria.

Another factor which supports the conservative behavior of the observer is the shape of the expected-value function. This function is quite flat for an appreciable range about its maximum. Therefore, the observer can adopt criteria considerably less extreme than those which approach a pure strategy (all "yes" or all "no"), and lose only a small percentage of the maximum payoff (see Green, 1960b).

The fact that the expected-value function is flat also for moderate probabilities and decision values makes it difficult to investigate in any more than a correlational sense the correspondence between obtained and optimal criteria. For example, for $P(s) = 0.50$, symmetrical values and costs, and $d' = 0.85$, any false-alarm proportion within a range from 0.15 to 0.50 will achieve at least 90% of the maximum payoff. Nonetheless, as illustrated in Table 4-1, experimental observers typically adopt criteria that are perfectly ranked with respect to the optimal criteria for as many as five different decision conditions. Other data show that, even for ten different decision conditions, the rank-order correlation between optimal and obtained values of β is near unity.

In considering the relation between optimal and obtained decision criteria in a detection task, it is important to place that relation in the perspective of sensory theory. From the standpoint of sensory theory, the decision goals defined within statistical decision theory simply suggest convenient ways of generating an empirical ROC curve. For sensory theory, it is important to obtain various decision criteria, each of them relatively stable, which span a range that is sufficient to define clearly an ROC curve; how these decision criteria are obtained is of little or no concern. We have said that verbal instructions such as "strict," "medium," and "lax" are entirely adequate for the purpose. Thus, the well-known fact that human decision makers commonly introduce a subjective transformation of real probabilities and of real decision values is not necessarily salient in the detection setting. Although more sophisticated theories of human decision making, which take into account the subjective transformations, might be fruitfully applied in real detection situations, students of sensory functions working within the framework of decision theory have not viewed them as essential to the idealized detection problems constructed for experimental purposes.

Exact optimal calculations notwithstanding, the fact that the rank-order correlation between optimal and obtained values of β is nearly unity means that the observer can adjust his decision criterion in a detection experiment with a high degree of precision. He can evidently partition his observations, including those which result from noise alone, rather finely—more finely than would be expected on the basis of alternative theories, as we shall see in the next chapter.

Additional evidence on this point is supplied by a visual experiment in which four observers were instructed to adopt the Neyman-Pearson decision goal, that is, to maximize the hit proportion while holding the false-alarm proportion within narrow bounds. Specifically, for four different decision conditions, the observers were instructed that the acceptable range for the false-alarm proportion was 0.0–0.07, 0.21–0.28, 0.43–0.50, or 0.64–0.71. In Fig. 4-4 the false-alarm proportions obtained are plotted against the restricted ranges of false-alarm proportion. The

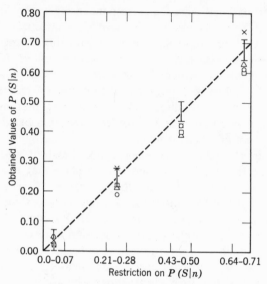

FIG. 4-4 Data from four observers attempting to reproduce specified false-alarm proportions. (From Swets, Tanner, and Birdsall, 1961.)

four observers are represented by different symbols; the vertical bars designate the acceptable range. It can be seen that the largest deviation from the range stipulated is 0.04.

4.2.4 Asymmetrical ROC curves

Let us turn our attention again to the form of the empirical ROC curve, and consider a commonly observed variant of the form shown in Fig. 4-1. The theoretical curve sketched in Fig. 4-1 is symmetrical about the negative diagonal of the ROC graph. The results obtained from a second observer in the same experiment, displayed in Fig. 4-5, are better fitted by a curve that is not symmetrical about the negative diagonal.

As discussed in Chapters 3 and 6, an asymmetrical curve having a form approximating the curve of Fig. 4-5 can be generated theoretically in at least two ways. One way is to assume that the probability distributions underlying the ROC curve, rather than being normal distributions, are exponential distributions (Chapter 3) or Rayleigh distributions (Chapter 6). An alternative is to retain the assumption of normal distributions and to allow the noise-alone and signal-plus-noise distributions to have different variances.

As stated earlier, and as illustrated in the insert at lower right of Fig. 4-1, the symmetrical ROC curve shown there is based on the assumption of normal distributions of equal variance. An empirical ROC curve which diverges from the symmetrical curve in the manner of the curve shown in Fig. 4-5 may be accounted for by assuming that the variance of the signal-plus-noise distribution is greater than the variance of the noise-alone distribution. This assumption is illustrated in the insert at lower right of

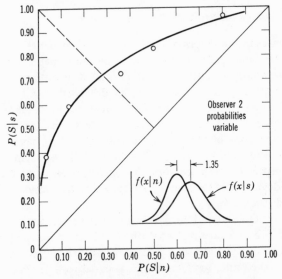

FIG. 4-5 ROC data obtained from a second observer in the auditory experiment under discussion, and a theoretical curve assuming normal probability distributions of unequal variance. Specifically, the curve is based on the assumption that $\Delta m/\Delta \sigma = 4$. Each point is based on 600 trials. (Data from Tanner, Swets, and Green, 1956.)

Fig. 4-5. Specifically, the theoretical ROC curve of Fig. 4-5 is predicated on the assumption that the variance of the signal-plus-noise distribution increases with increases in its mean—that the ratio of the increment in the mean to the increment in the standard deviaton is equal to some constant. More specifically, the ROC curve in Fig. 4-5 is based on the assumption that this ratio, $\Delta m/\Delta \sigma$, is equal to four.

We shall see shortly that the assumption that $\Delta m/\Delta \sigma = 4$ fits quite well the data obtained in a variety of experiments. Later, in the discussion in Part II of the theory of ideal observers (ideal with respect to sensitivity), we consider a rationale for the assumption of unequal variance. It is shown there that the theory of ideal observers leads to the prediction of distributions of equal variance and, therefore, to a symmetrical ROC curve when the observer has full knowledge of a signal all of whose characteristics are specified exactly. The same theory leads to the prediction of unequal variance and, therefore, to an asymmetrical ROC curve when one or more of the dimensions of the signal are specified only statistically rather than exactly, or when the observer is unable to make use of exact information about one or more of the signal's dimensions.

4.2.5   ROC curves on probability scales

The differences in the shapes of the ROC curves are better seen in a plot on double-probability graph paper, that is, on graph paper which spaces linearly the standard deviations of the normal distribution (the normal deviates, or z-scores). On these scales, as discussed in Chapter 3, the normal ROC curves are straight lines. ROC curves based on the assumption of equal variance have a slope of unity on these scales; the ROC curves based on assumptions of unequal variances ($\sigma_s{}^2 > \sigma_n{}^2$) have slopes less than unity. As shown in Chapter 3 (Section 3.2.3.2), the reciprocal of the slope, with respect to the normal-deviate scales, is equal to the ratio of the standard deviation of the signal distribution to the standard deviation of the noise distribution, σ_s/σ_n.

The data for Observers 1 and 2 in the experiment under discussion (Fig. 4-1 and Fig. 4-5) are replotted on double-probability graph paper in Fig. 4-6. The slope of the solid line, for Observer 1, is equal to 1. The slope of the dashed line, for Observer 2, is equal to 0.75. The reciprocal of this slope, which is σ_s/σ_n, is approximately 1.33. If we set $\sigma_n = 1$, then $\sigma_s = 1.33$. To see that this value of σ_s obtained from the slope is consistent with the assumption of $\Delta m/\Delta \sigma = 4$, or $\Delta \sigma = 1/4\, \Delta m$, note that Δm is given in Fig. 4-5 as 1.35; $\Delta \sigma$ therefore equals 0.33, and $\sigma_s = 1.33$.

The symbol Δm is used here to denote the difference between the means of (normal) distributions of unequal variance, so that the symbol d' may be reserved for equal-variance (normal) distributions. It seems advisable also to make explicit the second parameter of asymmetrical ROC curves, or ROC curves having slopes less than unity. Therefore, we introduce the notation $D(\Delta m, s)$ to summarize such curves: Δm, like d', is the difference between the means of the signal and noise distributions; s is the slope of the ROC curve. The value of s can be taken simply as an empirical description; alternatively, it can be converted to the ratio of standard deviations, σ_s/σ_n, or to the "mean-to-sigma" ratio, $\Delta m/\Delta \sigma$.

Note that some arbitrary convention must be adopted to determine Δm from a plot of data on double-probability scales. The value of d' is equal to the absolute value of the difference between $z(S \mid s)$ and $z(S \mid n)$, but this quantity is not constant along a curve with slope other than

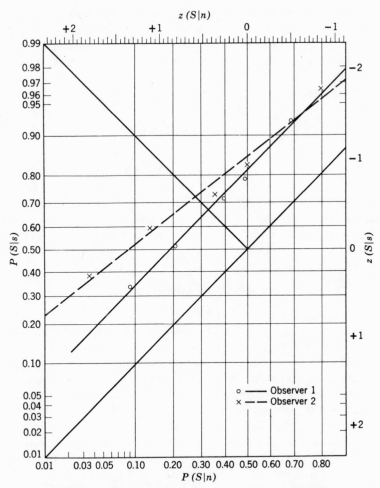

FIG. 4-6   The ROC data from the two observers in the auditory experiment under discussion plotted on linear normal-deviate scales. The straight lines are consistent with normal probability distributions; the slopes of these lines may be taken as representing the relative variance of the two probability distributions. (Data from Tanner, Swets, and Green, 1956.)

unity. The convention followed here, in the measure $D(\Delta m, s)$, is to read Δm at the point where $P(S \mid s) = 0.50$ or, equivalently, where $z(S \mid s) = 0$. This procedure scales Δm in the unit of the noise distribution, $\sigma_n = 1.0$. To exercise immediately this new notation and procedure for calculation, note in Fig. 4-6 that, whereas Observer 1 yields a $d' = 0.85$, Observer 2 yields a $D(\Delta m, s) = 1.35, 0.75$.

An alternative convention frequently used in the literature of detection theory (suggested by J. P. Egan) is to read the sensitivity index (corresponding to Δm) from the point where the curve crosses the negative diagonal. This measure, which has been denoted d_e', and sometimes $(d_e)^{1/2}$ or d_s, gives equal weight to the units of the noise and signal-plus-noise distributions. The conversion formulas are

$$\Delta m = \frac{d_e'}{2}\left(\frac{1}{s}\right) + \frac{d_e'}{2}$$

and

$$d_e' = 2 \, \Delta m \left(\frac{s}{1+s}\right)$$

In the present example $D(\Delta m, s) = 1.35, 0.75$ corresponds to $d_e' = 1.23$. It can be seen in Fig. 4-6 that the absolute value of the difference between $z(S \mid n)$ and $z(S \mid s)$ at the negative diagonal for Observer 2 is approximately 1.23.

4.2.6   Individual and modality differences

We have said that some empirical ROC curves are symmetrical and consistent with the assumption of equal-variance (normal) density functions, whereas others are asymmetrical and consistent with the assumption that $\Delta m/\Delta \sigma = 4$. Note first that the constant 4 is strictly empirical; any theoretical significance it may have has not been established. Note also that the constant 4 is an approximation; available data are insufficient to establish that 4 uniformly provides a better fit than 3 or 5. Indeed, we might expect that the value of $\Delta m/\Delta \sigma$ will vary with stimulus parameters—given the fact in statistical theory that variance depends upon sample size, we might expect that the ratio $\Delta m/\Delta \sigma$ will vary with the duration of the signal, and with its area or bandwidth.

It is not totally clear what factors determine the occurrence of symmetrical and asymmetrical ROC curves. To the extent that there is a pattern in existent data, it is as follows. Visual signals, perhaps without exception, yield asymmetrical curves. Examples are shown in the remainder of this chapter. Auditory signals frequently yield asymmetrical curves, but some observers, as seen above, produce symmetrical curves.

Two ROC curves have been obtained in another sensory modality, namely, taste. Figure 4-7 shows that, as in audition, there are individual differences. The curve fitted to the data of Observer 1 is based on the assumption that $\Delta m/\Delta \sigma = 4$; the curve fitted to the data of Observer 2 assumes density functions of equal variance. The data were obtained by setting the a priori probability of signal occurrence at 0.1, 0.3, 0.5, 0.7,

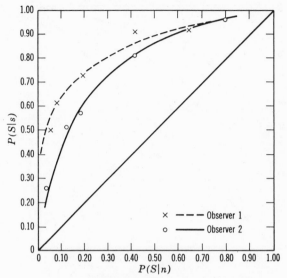

FIG. 4-7   ROC curves from two observers in a yes-no experiment on taste. The data were obtained by varying the a priori probability of signal occurrence. The theoretical curve for Observer 1 is based on the assumption that $\Delta m/\Delta \sigma = 4$; the curve for Observer 2 assumes normal distributions of equal variance. The number of trials varied from one point to another, with a minimum of 280. (After Linker, Moore, and Galanter, 1964.)

and 0.9, with values and costs held constant. For Observer 1, $D(\Delta m, s) =$ 1.70, 0.70; for Observer 2, $d' = 1.20$.

In brief, the shape of the ROC curve seems to depend to some extent on the sensory modality and to some extent on the observer. Further work is necessary to specify the nature of these dependencies.

4.3   THE RATING EXPERIMENT

4.3.1   The observer's task

The rating task requires that the observer maintain several decision criteria simultaneously. He must place each observation in the one of several categories that best represents his degree of certainty that the observation resulted from the presentation of a signal in addition to the noise.

In the form of this task described within the general theory of signal detectability, the observer reports the *a posteriori probability* that the

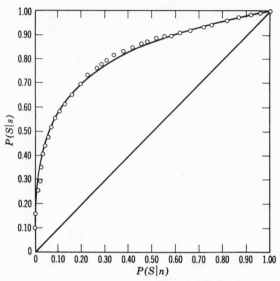

FIG. 4-8   An empirical ROC graph obtained by
the rating method using a scale and sliding pointer.
The theoretical curve is based on the assumption
of normal probability distributions of unequal
variance, specifically on the assumption that
$\Delta m/\Delta \sigma = 4$. One thousand observations were
made. (Data from Watson, Rilling, and Bourbon,
1964.)

observation resulted from the occurrence of a signal. As discussed in
Chapter 1, the a posteriori probability of signal occurrence is a monotonic
function of the likelihood ratio, and statistical theory specifies a particular
relationship between these two variables. Thus, as we did in the case of
decision goals which require that a single criterion be in effect at any
given time, we can examine the relationship that holds between the
decision behavior that is stipulated by theory and the behavior that is
observed in an experiment. It is again the case, however, that the extent
to which the human observer approaches the statistically defined decision
behavior is of secondary importance to studies of sensory processes. And,
again, experimenters have employed not only the quantitative instructions
suggested by the theory, but simple verbal instructions as well. Thus, for
example, the observer may be given a scale and a sliding pointer which
permit him to indicate a posteriori probability with a high degree of
precision. Or he may be instructed to place each observation in one of
five categories of a posteriori probability, say: 0.0–0.20, 0.21–0.40,

0.41–0.60, 0.61–0.80, 0.81–1.00. Alternatively, six categories of certainty may be defined by the terms "strict," "medium strict," "medium," "medium lax," and "lax." Such verbal instructions are entirely appropriate in instances in which the exact relationship between the observer's behavior and the likelihood ratio is of no concern—in which the aim is simply to generate an ROC curve. In this case, it is sufficient to assume that the observer's sensory scale, although monotonically related to signal likelihood, is only an ordinal scale.

The procedure in which the observer positions a slider along a scale is of interest because it yields a relatively detailed definition of the ROC curve. In an auditory experiment the slider positions set by the observer were assigned by the experimenter to 36 categories. The ROC curve obtained from one observer in this experiment is shown in Fig. 4-8. The curve shown in the figure is the theoretical curve for $D(\Delta m, s) = 1.50, 0.73$, based on the same assumption of increasing variance ($\Delta m / \Delta \sigma = 4$) that we used before. This curve deviates systematically from the data (and the best-fitting theoretical curves of this kind for three observers at each of two signal levels show deviations of the same sort) but, on the whole, this curve fits quite well. We shall consider later the possibility of obtaining a better fit to these data (Chapter 7).

4.3.2 Calculation of the ROC curve

Consider next a visual experiment in which the observer placed his observations in one of six categories defined by ranges of a posteriori probability. Four observers participated in this experiment, and the results obtained from each of them will be shown. We concentrate, however, on the data obtained from only one of the observers (Observer 1) to illustrate concretely the calculations made in the construction of an empirical ROC graph from rating data.

These calculations for Observer 1 are shown as part of Table 4-2. The columns of the table are headed by the ranges of a posteriori probability that defined the six rating categories. The first section, consisting of the first row of the table, lists the frequency with which each rating category R_i was employed. The second section shows four quantities based on trials containing the signal; and the third shows the corresponding quantities based on trials containing noise alone.

Before discussing the construction of the ROC graph, let us consider a calculation which displays more directly the observer's ability to use the rating scale given him. The first row in section (2), labeled $f(s \cdot R_i)$, shows the frequency of the compound occurrence of a signal presentation and the use of category R_i. The row beneath it lists estimates of the conditional

TABLE 4-2. CALCULATIONS BASED ON DATA OBTAINED BY THE RATING METHOD FROM OBSERVER 1. SECTION (2) OF THE TABLE IS BASED ON 597 SIGNAL TRIALS, AND SECTION (3), ON 591 NOISE TRIALS. (DATA FROM SWETS, TANNER, AND BIRDSALL, 1961.)

A Posteriori Probability	0.0–0.04	0.05–0.19	0.20–0.39	0.40–0.59	0.60–0.79	0.80–1.0
(1) $f(R_i)$	220	229	170	193	195	181
(2) $f(s \cdot R_i)$	46	57	66	101	154	173
$P(s \mid R_i)$	0.21	0.25	0.39	0.52	0.78	0.96
$P(R_i \mid s)$	0.07	0.09	0.11	0.18	0.26	0.29
$P(S \mid s)$	1.00	0.93	0.84	0.73	0.55	0.29
(3) $f(n \cdot R_i)$	174	172	104	92	41	8
$P(n \mid R_i)$	0.79	0.75	0.61	0.48	0.22	0.04
$P(R_i \mid n)$	0.29	0.29	0.18	0.16	0.07	0.01
$P(S \mid n)$	1.00	0.71	0.42	0.24	0.08	0.01

probability $P(s \mid R_i)$; specifically, it shows the proportion of the observations placed in each category that resulted from the occurrence of a signal. For example, the figure 0.96 in the rightmost column is obtained by dividing the compound frequency (173) by the total number of observations placed in that category (181). It may be observed that the quantity $P(s \mid R_i)$ increases monotonically with increases in the a posteriori probabilities that define the categories. This result indicates that the observer is using the rating categories as intended, at least roughly. It indicates an ability to rank observations according to signal likelihood, at least to the extent of partitioning them into approximately six categories. It indicates, further, that the observer can maintain five criteria simultaneously. Figure 4-9 shows $P(s \mid R_i)$ plotted against the announced categories of a posteriori probability for each of the four observers. Two of the curves increase monotonically; each of the other two shows a single reversal.

The last two rows in Sections (2) and (3) of Table 4-2 illustrate the calculation of the proportions of hits and false alarms. The third row in each section, $P(R_i \mid s)$ and $P(R_i \mid n)$, is the reverse of the conditional probability just considered. Thus, for example, the figure 0.29 in the rightmost column of Section 2 is obtained by dividing the number of signal observations placed in that category (173) by the total number of signals presented (597). The fourth row in each section, the hit and false-alarm proportions corresponding to each of the five decision criteria, is a cumulation of the quantities in the third row, moving from right to left in the

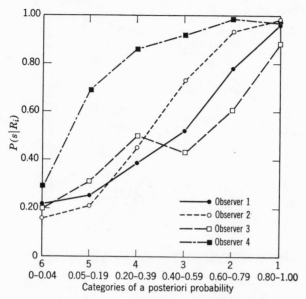

FIG. 4-9 The proportion of the observations placed in each rating category that resulted from presentation of a signal. Data from four observers. (From Swets, Tanner, and Birdsall, 1961.)

table. It represents the procedure of compressing rating data into yes-no data by considering successively each of the five category boundaries as defining a yes-no criterion.

4.3.3 Empirical ROC curves

The hit and false-alarm proportions calculated for Observer 1 in Table 4-2 are shown in the form of an ROC curve in Fig. 4-10a. The other three parts of the figure show the results of the other three observers in the experiment. In each case the data are fitted by a theoretical curve based on normal probability distributions, and on the assumption of unequal variance ($\Delta m/\Delta \sigma = 4$) that we have used before.

It is apparent from Fig. 4-10 that the variability of the data points about the best-fitting theoretical curve is very small. Such a small degree of variability—noticeably less than that typically obtained in yes-no experiments—is consistently obtained in rating experiments. It is important to note that the reduced variability is largely due to the way in which ROC curves are calculated from rating data; the cumulative process that is used smooths the data and, indeed, permits only a monotonically increasing

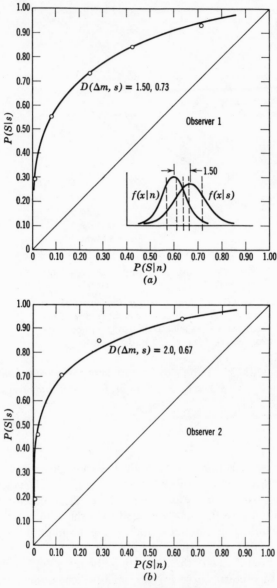

FIG. 4-10 ROC data obtained by the rating procedure from four observers; 1188 observations were made. The theoretical curves assume normal probability distributions of unequal variance, with $\Delta m/\Delta\sigma = 4$. (Data from Swets, Tanner, and Birdsall, 1961.)

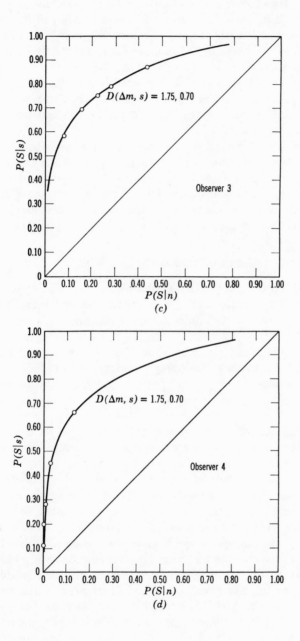

(c)

(d)

curve to result. However, the substantial difference in variability is obtained even when the rating data are based on as few as one-fourth the number of observations made in a yes-no experiment. Whether or not one can, in practice, take advantage of the economy provided by the rating procedure in defining ROC curves that are to be interpreted as yes-no ROC curves is a pragmatic question. It depends on whether or not rating and yes-no experiments yield essentially the same ROC curves for the case at hand. We shall discuss shortly the evidence on this question for the cases that have been examined.

Rating ROC curves have been obtained with visual signals, from dark-adapted observers, by Nachmias and Steinman (1963). Their article shows eight curves (three signal levels for two observers and two signal levels for a third) on double-probability plots. The three points making up each curve lie *on* a straight line. The slopes of the curves decrease with increasing signal strength, and are consistent with the assumption that $\Delta m/\Delta \sigma = 4$.

4.3.4   Objective and subjective probabilities

It was mentioned earlier that the multiple criteria used by observers under the rating procedure could be compared with the criteria specified by statistical theory. The data obtained in the experiment discussed above can be used for this purpose. In this experiment, since the a priori probabilities of signal and noise were equal [$P(s) = P(n) = 0.50$], the theoretical relationship between a posteriori probability and likelihood ratio may be simply expressed as

$$P(s \mid x) = \frac{l(x)}{l(x) + 1}$$

Given that the value of $l(x)$ is equal to the slope of the ROC curve at a point representing a criterion, the value of $P(s \mid x)$ corresponding to each criterion used by an observer can be calculated. The calculated values can be compared with the values of $P(s \mid x)$ that were announced as marking off the categories. The results are shown in Fig. 4-11, where the announced category boundaries are given on the ordinate and the obtained category boundaries are given on the abscissa. The data obtained from Observers 1, 2, and 3 are consistent with a decision function similar to likelihood ratio and with approximately the theoretically specified relationship between a posteriori probability and likelihood ratio. Observers 1 and 3 exhibit the pattern we have discussed before as typical of experiments requiring estimates of probability. The data from Observer 4, as may also be seen in Figs. 4-9 and 4-10d, deviate from the data obtained from the other three observers; his tendency is consistently to underestimate the a posteriori probability, that is, to set very strict criteria.

The demonstrated ability of the human observer to report a quantity that is monotonically related to the likelihood ratio may have important implications for practical detection problems. Because it permits separation of the observation and decision-making functions, the observations can be made by one person and the decisions may be reserved for another— perhaps for a person who has more information about the pertinent probabilities and values, or more responsibility. It will become apparent

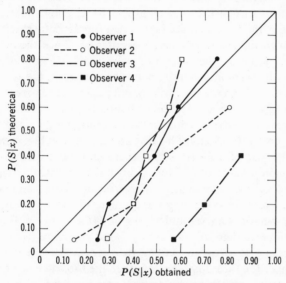

FIG. 4-11 Comparison of theoretical and obtained decision criteria in a rating task. (Data from Swets, Tanner, and Birdsall, 1961.)

that the use of multiple observers, who transmit the results of their observations to a single decision maker, is also facilitated by the ability to report likelihood ratios—multiple likelihood ratios can be combined into a single decision quantity with greater precision than can multiple binary judgments. We discuss this point in more detail later, in Chapter 9.

4.4   THE FORCED-CHOICE EXPERIMENT

4.4.1   Economy of forced-choice procedure

In the forced-choice task, two or more stimulus alternatives are presented; one of the alternatives is signal plus noise and the others are noise alone. The alternatives may be defined by regions of space but, in the more common form of the task, they are defined by intervals of time. The signal on any given trial may be selected from a specified set of signals but, as in the case of the yes-no and rating tasks, a single signal is ordinarily used throughout a series of trials.

The two-alternative forced-choice task is like the yes-no task in certain formal respects. It is possible to vary the a priori probability of occurrence of the signal in the first interval relative to the second interval, and to vary the value of a correct response in the first interval relative to the second interval, and thus to construct an empirical ROC graph. However, the principal value of the forced-choice task is that it practically eliminates the need to deal with the observer's decision criterion. Since the errors in a forced-choice task, unlike the errors in a yes-no task, do not differ intrinsically in cost, observers find it more natural to maintain the symmetrical criterion. Occasionally an observer will show a preference for one or another interval; such a preference is usually eliminated with further practice, particularly because no harm is done if the experimenter gives the observer a running account of the extent of his bias and encourages him to reduce it.

The consistent use of a nearly symmetrical decision criterion makes it possible to obtain a value of d' from a single data point, that is, from a single estimate of the probability of correct response. Appendix III outlines a procedure for correcting the estimate of $P(C)$ for any interval bias that may persist. Graphs and tables of $P(C)$ versus d' for various numbers of stimulus alternatives may be found elsewhere (Swets, 1964).

It will be clear that, if we are willing to forgo a determination of the ROC curve under the forced-choice task, then the forced-choice task has a distinct advantage over the yes-no task in economy and in simplicity of data analysis. It is favored by experimenters in studies wholly concerned with sensory processes, in which it is desirable to minimize motivational and response processes. As remarked earlier, if it can be established that forced-choice procedures produce estimates of sensitivity comparable to those obtained from yes-no and rating procedures, then forced-choice results can be used to predict performances in situations in which motivational and response processes play a significant role. We shall examine the evidence on this question later in this chapter.

4.4.2   Second choices

Consider a four-alternative forced-choice task in which the observer is asked not simply to choose the interval most likely to contain the signal, but to rank the four intervals with respect to signal likelihood. Analyses of the resulting data will disclose how fully the observer can distinguish and rank sensory events. It is usually assumed in applications of detection

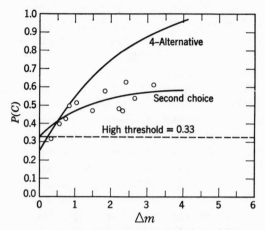

FIG. 4-12 Data on second choices with two predictions based on differing abilities to rank observations according to signal likelihood. (Data from Swets, Tanner, and Birdsall, 1961.)

theory that sensory events can be ranked throughout the range of likelihood ratios, but different assumptions lead to different predictions for this task. If, for example, the observer cannot distinguish sensory events that fall below the mean of the noise distribution, then his performance in this task will differ noticeably from the performance that would result from complete ranking. Any test of the assumption that is made about the observer's ability to rank his observations is of interest, because this assumption distinguishes the detection theory based on statistical decision theory from some other theories of the detection process that have been proposed. As will be discussed in more detail in the next chapter, some alternative theories place strict limitations on the observer's capability in this regard.

The particular experiment to be considered here is a visual experiment. The signal was a spot of light of fixed intensity presented on a uniformly illuminated background. Each trial consisted of four temporal intervals. The observer was asked to choose the interval most likely to contain the signal, and then to choose the interval he believed second most likely to have contained the signal. He was not asked in this experiment to distinguish his third and fourth choices. A control condition, in which the observer indicated only his first choice, established that the act of making a second choice did not depress the proportion of correct first choices.

Figure 4-12 shows the results of the experiment. The top curve shows the relationship between the proportion of correct first choices and Δm that is predicted by the theory of signal detectability under the assumption of increasing variance ($\Delta m/\Delta \sigma = 4$) previously discussed. The second curve from the top shows the relationship between the proportion of correct second choices and Δm that is predicted by the theory, under the same assumption of increasing variance, if the observer is able to rank his observations completely. The points on the graph represent the proportions of correct second choices obtained by experiment. They are plotted at the value of Δm corresponding to the observed proportion of correct first choices. The variation in Δm that is evident in the figure came about, despite the constant signal strength, because four observers were used and the distance of the observers from the screen was varied.

The horizontal dashed line at $P(C) = 0.33$ provides a standard of comparison. The data points would fall along this line if the observer were unable to rank observations below a cutoff point three standard deviations above the mean of the noise distribution. Such a cutoff point would be exceeded by observations of noise alone on a negligible proportion of the trials, so that only very rarely would the observer have other than a random basis for making a second choice. Under these conditions, if his first choice were incorrect, his second choice would be correct with a probability of 0.33, the chance probability.

The data points are fitted well by the curve predicted by the theory of signal detectability. The rather large variability of the points is attributable to the fact that each of the second-choice proportions obtained in this experiment is based on fewer than 100 trials. It is clear that the points deviate significantly from the horizontal dashed line; combining all the data yields a second-choice proportion of 0.46.

The result of this second-choice experiment indicates an ability to rank observations likely to result from noise alone. This result has been confirmed in a more extensive visual experiment (Kincaid and Hamilton, 1959) and in experiments on touch and temperature (Eijkman and Vendrik, 1963). An auditory experiment in which the observer made only a fourth choice, in which he tried to be wrong, led to the same conclusion (Tanner, Swets, and Green, 1956).

4.5   COMPARISON OF INDICES OF SENSITIVITY OBTAINED FROM THE THREE EXPERIMENTAL PROCEDURES

According to detection theory, the index of sensitivity should remain invariant with changes in the decision criterion. Of course, some variability has to be tolerated in practice, but there should be no systematic error. Several experiments have shown Δm, or $D(\Delta m, s)$, to remain relatively constant while the decision criterion varies.

The detection theory passes a still more severe test if its index of sensitivity, for a given signal-to-noise ratio and for a given observer, is independent of the particular psychophysical procedure used to collect the data. Again, happily, a considerable body of evidence indicates that this is the case. Some of this evidence is reviewed in the following paragraphs.

Table 4-3 shows the results of an auditory experiment in which a tone burst was presented in a background of white noise. Values of Δm and σ_s/σ_n (or $1/s$) are given, for yes-no and rating tasks, for three observers. It can be seen that the values obtained from the two procedures are very

TABLE 4-3.   VALUES OF Δm AND σ_s/σ_n OBTAINED BY THE YES-NO AND RATING PROCEDURES. EACH ENTRY IS BASED ON 240 OBSERVATIONS. (DATA FROM EGAN, SCHULMAN, AND GREENBERG, 1959.)

Observer	Δm		σ_s/σ_n	
	Yes-No	Rating	Yes-No	Rating
1	1.30	1.42	1.03	1.11
2	1.52	1.36	1.06	1.13
3	1.85	1.82	1.36	1.06
Mean	1.56	1.53	1.15	1.10

nearly the same. The *largest* discrepancy between the two estimates of Δm is 0.16. Since, as will be discussed in more detail in Chapter 7, Δm (as well as d') is approximately proportional to signal power, the difference of 0.16 is equivalent to a difference of 0.5 decibel in signal power. Such accuracy is more than adequate for most psychophysical experiments, and such differences are considerably smaller than we had come to expect of psychophysical data collected by two different procedures.

Table 4-4 shows the results of an auditory experiment in which values of d' were obtained from yes-no, two-alternative forced-choice, and four-alternative forced-choice procedures. Again, the results are very similar. In only one case (Observer 2 at signal level 1) is the discrepancy equivalent to more than one decibel in signal power. In six of the 11 rows in the table, the largest difference is equivalent to less than 0.5 decibel.

Another auditory experiment compared the results obtained from forced-choice procedures with two, three, four, six, and eight temporal alternatives. The results for the three observers are shown in Fig. 4-13. The two smooth curves shown are theoretical curves of constant d'. The two curves, which bound the large majority of the data points, represent values of d' of 1.50 and 1.70; these values differ by the equivalent of 0.5 decibel.

The last experiment to be mentioned under this topic is a visual form-discrimination experiment in which the observers were required to discriminate a square and a nearly-square rectangle. In brief, the values of Δm and the values of σ_s/σ_n obtained from the yes-no procedure and from

TABLE 4-4. VALUES OF d' OBTAINED BY THREE DIFFERENT PROCEDURES. EACH ENTRY IS BASED ON 500 OBSERVATIONS. (DATA FROM SWETS, 1959.)

Signal Level	Observer	d'		
		Yes-No	2AFC	4AFC
1	1	1.57	1.30	1.23
	2	1.24	1.03	0.91
	3	1.48	1.45	1.41
	Mean	1.43	1.26	1.18
2	1	—	—	—
	2	1.40	1.15	1.24
	3	1.64	1.57	1.63
	Mean	1.52	1.36	1.44
3	1	2.05	2.17	1.95
	2	1.51	1.52	1.68
	3	1.90	1.98	2.10
	Mean	1.82	1.89	1.91
4	1	2.47	2.28	2.31
	2	1.83	1.82	1.86
	3	1.98	2.42	2.38
	Mean	2.09	2.17	2.18

three- and four-category rating procedures are nearly identical. The constancy of Δm was further tested by inserting, in certain conditions of the experiment, extraneous stimuli in the form of rectangles that were either more or less discriminable from the square than was the standard rectangle used throughout the experiment. When the observer was uninformed, and unaware, of the extraneous stimuli, these stimuli had no effect on the value of Δm or on the value of σ_s/σ_n obtained from trials containing the standard rectangle, and they had no effect on the observer's use of the rating categories. When the observers were informed of the extraneous stimuli,

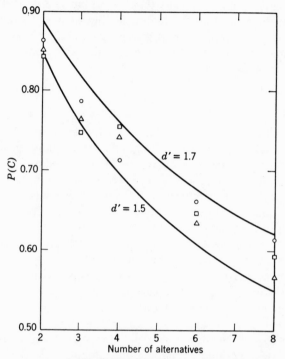

FIG. 4-13 Proportion of correct detections obtained from three observers in forced-choice tasks
with different numbers of alternatives. Number of
observations varied with number of alternatives:
2AFC—300, 3AFC—500, 4AFC—600, 6AFC—
900, and 8AFC—1200. The two theoretical curves
are curves of constant d'. (Data from Swets, 1959.)

their use of the rating categories (their decision criteria) changed considerably, but the two measures of sensitivity were unaffected (Weintraub and
Hake, 1962).

The demonstrated constancy of the sensitivity indices d' and $D(\Delta m, s)$,
obtained by any of the several procedures we have discussed, represents a
substantial advance in psychophysical technique. Prior to this development,
it had become a commonplace that the prominent psychophysical procedures yield different values for the sensory threshold, and there was a
tendency to regard the results of a psychophysical experiment as meaning-
less except in relation to the specific procedure used. It is now the case that
half a dozen laboratories, which have been using the procedures and the
measures associated with the theory of signal detectability in auditory

experiments, regularly obtain results that are within one decibel of one another. It may be noted that the favorable comparison of values of d' and $D(\Delta m, s)$ obtained from different procedures and in different laboratories means that the distribution-free index, the area under the ROC curve, would also show a favorable comparison.

4.6 SUMMARY

This chapter has presented the results of illustrative psychophysical experiments employing the yes-no, rating, and forced-choice procedures.

The yes-no procedure yields ROC curves of monotonically decreasing slope, that is, curves of the general form predicted by the theory of signal detectability. The data are fitted well by theoretical curves based on normal probability distributions. In some instances the data are consistent with the assumption of noise and signal distributions of equal variance; then the measure d' is applicable. In other instances the data are consistent with a greater variance of the signal distribution than of the noise distribution; then the two-parameter measure $D(\Delta m, s)$ is appropriate. It is clear that the human observer can adopt, and can readopt at a later time, any of several decision criteria; these criteria are ranked in accordance with instructions given him. The ability to measure and control the observer's decision criterion, and the ability to obtain a measure of sensitivity that is independent of the criterion, are major contributions of the theory.

The same remarks apply to results obtained by means of the rating procedure. The results of this procedure show, in addition, that the observer can maintain several criteria simultaneously. The rating procedure has the advantage, in the laboratory, of economy; it produces ROC data as reliable as those produced by the yes-no procedure, with fewer observations. In practical detection situations, the advantage of the rating procedure is that it permits separation of the responsibilities for observation and for decision.

Because its decision outcomes are intrinsically symmetrical, the forced-choice procedure minimizes the concern for the observer's decision criterion. Consequently, it is not necessary to trace out an ROC curve—a reliable measure of sensitivity can be based on the number of observations that are required to determine a single point on an ROC curve. The forced-choice procedure is therefore the best available for studies concerned with sensory, rather than with motivational or response, processes. Although the results of the yes-no and rating procedures demonstrate extensive capability to rank observations according to signal likelihood, a variant of the forced-choice procedure, in which the observer ranks the alternatives on this basis, demonstrates the capability in a more direct way.

For a signal and noise of given strengths, and for a given observer, the three procedures yield essentially the same index of sensitivity. Such consistency of results obtained by different techniques is not easy to attain in the measurement of complex physical phenomena, and it has been very rare, perhaps nonexistent, in the measurement of human behavior. This result gives promise of a rigorous, quantitative science of psychophysics.

PROBLEMS

The first few problems below are based on the results of an experiment conducted after this book had gone to press (Markowitz and Swets, unpublished). The experiment provides ROC curves at six intensities of a tone burst in white noise, for each of four different psychophysical procedures. Three of the procedures were yes-no, rating, and two-alternative forced-choice, with formats as discussed in foregoing chapters. The fourth procedure had the stimulus-presentation structure of the (temporal) two-alternative forced-choice task, but the observer made a rating response.

The ROC curves for the procedure with two observation intervals and a binary response were plotted by considering as a "hit" a correct decision that the signal occurred in the first interval, and by considering as a "false alarm" an incorrect decision that the signal occurred in the first interval. In the notation of Chapter 2 (Section 2.6), $P(R1 \mid \langle sn \rangle)$ was plotted against $P(R1 \mid \langle ns \rangle)$. For the ROC curves of the two-interval-rating procedure, the conditioning events were likewise $\langle sn \rangle$ on the ordinate and $\langle ns \rangle$ on the abscissa, but in accordance with the usual rating analysis the response $R1$ was successively redefined to include more rating categories.

The two procedures with rating responses were conducted with $P(s) = 0.50$; four rating categories provided three points on the ROC curve at each signal intensity. The two procedures with binary responses also provided three points on each ROC curve, attained by values of $P(s) = 0.20$, 0.50, and 0.80. In the rating-response procedures there were 1200 trials at each signal level; in the binary-response procedures there were 800 trials at each value of $P(s)$ and thus 2400 trials at each signal level.

The values of $D(\Delta m, s)$ obtained from one of the three observers are given in Table 4-5.

4.1   Consider first the one-interval-rating procedure, and note that the slopes tend to decrease as Δm increases. Does the assumption of $\Delta m / \Delta \sigma = 4$ provide a good fit to the data? How about $\Delta m / \Delta \sigma = 2$? Or $\Delta m / \Delta \sigma = 6$? Calculate a predicted slope at each obtained value of Δm for each of the three constant ratios mentioned, and determine the closeness of fit by inspection.

4.2   Consider next the two-interval-rating procedure, and note that again the slopes tend to decrease as Δm increases. Does the assumption of $\Delta m / \Delta \sigma = 2$ provide a close fit to the data?

TABLE 4-5

Signal Level	Procedure							
	One Observation Interval				Two Observation Intervals			
	Rating Response		Binary Response		Rating Response		Binary Response	
	Δm	s	Δm	s	Δm	s	Δm	s
1	0.08	1.03	0.03	0.92	0.33	0.93	0.17	0.91
2	0.49	0.82	0.52	0.86	0.46	0.97	0.40	0.87
3	0.72	0.78	0.55	0.91	0.62	0.74	0.67	0.85
4	1.13	0.84	1.08	0.88	0.83	0.64	1.09	0.72
5	1.64	0.77	1.10	0.90	1.81	0.52	1.11	1.24
6	2.23	0.71	1.49	1.01	2.17	0.46	1.50	1.09

4.3   Look now at the slopes obtained from the two binary-response procedures. (a) Do they tend to decrease as Δm increases? (b) Are the results of the two-interval-binary procedure consistent with the prediction of Chapter 2 (Eqs. 2.16 and 2.17 and surrounding text), that the two-alternative forced-choice ROC curve is symmetric about the negative diagonal?

4.4   (a) Are the values of Δm obtained from the two binary-response procedures similar? (b) Ignoring the lowest signal level, which signal level led to the largest difference in Δm, in terms of decibels of signal power?

4.5   There remains the puzzle as to why the rating response led to higher values of Δm than the binary response in both the one-interval and the two-interval tasks. Can you think of any way to account for this result?

4.6   In another experiment, on the temperature sense, observers were asked to make a second as well as a first choice in a four-alternative forced-choice procedure (Eijkman and Vendrik, 1963). Two observers were presented two different signal intensities, and two observers were presented three different signal intensities, to yield ten pairs of proportions. These ten pairs, with the proportion of correct first choices listed first, and the proportion of correct second choices (given an incorrect first choice) listed second, are: (0.36, 0.40), (0.38, 0.42), (0.38, 0.35), (0.42, 0.50), (0.42, 0.41), (0.50, 0.48), (0.62, 0.40), (0.65, 0.57), (0.71, 0.55), and (0.84, 0.75). Plot these points on the coordinates of Fig. 4-12, and estimate the mean deviation from: (a) the high-threshold prediction and (b) the detection-theory prediction assuming $\Delta m/\Delta \sigma = 4$.

5

The Sensory Threshold

and Psychophysical Method

5.1 INTRODUCTION

Psychophysics was conceived by Gustav Theodor Fechner in 1850. His *Elemente der Psychophysik*, published 10 years later, marks the beginning of experimental psychology. Strangely, the *Elemente* is not merely a classic. The concepts and methods that it specified have been dominant in the study of sensory and perceptual functions ever since. In fact, they were without serious rivals until the early 1950's.

For Fechner, a central concept was the *sensory threshold*. This concept, of course, was not invented by Fechner; it appeared in Greek philosophy and again in the writings of Leibnitz and Herbart. Nor did the methods described by Fechner originate with him. The method of adjustment (average error, reproduction), the method of serial exploration (limits, minimal changes), and the method of constant stimuli (right and wrong cases) had been introduced for various purposes from 5 to 150 years before Fechner began his work. But Fechner refined the threshold concept, worked out details of the methods, and showed how all three methods could be used to obtain a measure of the sensory threshold. In general, the sensory threshold was measured by determining the intensity required for a signal to be just detectable, or by determining the difference between two signals necessary for the two to be just noticeably different.

Although Fechner considered the possibility of "negative," or sub-threshold, sensations, the threshold was generally regarded, in the root sense of the word, as a barrier that has to be overcome. Signals too weak to exceed the threshold were supposed to have no effect on the organism.

By analogy with the all-or-none action of neurons, a signal presented to a sense organ is either detected or not detected, with no shades in between.

The first experiments showed that a given signal did not produce a consistent "yes" ("I detect it") or a consistent "no" ("I do not detect it") response. It was therefore immediately clear that the sensory threshold was unstable, that it varied randomly over time. Plots of the psychometric function—the proportion of "yes" responses as a function of signal magnitude—were in the form of an ogive, which suggested an underlying bell-shaped distribution of the level of the sensory threshold. Such a distribution is in accordance with the fact of continuous physiological change in large numbers of similar receptive and nervous elements. Thus, psychophysical methods had to be carefully designed to provide a good estimate of the mean and the variance of the threshold distribution.

An even greater problem than physiological variability that had to be faced in the design of psychophysical methods was the problem of psychological variability. It was obvious from the start that the calculated value of the sensory threshold is heavily influenced by "nonsensory" factors. The history of psychophysics is in large part a history of analytical and experimental critique of methods centered about this problem. The basic methods have been refined again and again to minimize such extraneous contributions to the calculated value of the threshold as the subject's "timidity, warming up, and anxiety" (Titchener, 1905, p. 150), and his conscious and unconscious criteria for making a positive response (Guilford, 1936, p. 204). A discouragingly large number of factors that affect the subject's set, attitude, or motivation had to be controlled. Should the subject, working under the methods of limits or constants, be allowed to make a response of "doubtful" or "equal"? Should the trials on which such a response is made be presented again, and should the subject be told that the experimenter plans to present those trials again? What is to be done if the subject reports that he detected a signal when no signal was present? These questions illustrate some of the many problems that arose. The reader is referred to Guilford (1936, 1954) and Woodworth (1938) for a fuller discussion of these problems.

It will be apparent from the foregoing chapters that a principal advantage of modern detection theory is that it shows how to compress a host of factors which affect the observer's attitude into a single variable, called the decision or response *criterion*, and how to use false-alarm responses to estimate the level of the criterion. By extracting two parameters from the data—one related to attitude and one to sensitivity—instead of just a single sensitivity (threshold) parameter, the procedures of detection theory isolate nonsensory factors, so that a relatively pure measure of sensitivity remains. These procedures, in other words, provide an analytical technique for separating two distinct processes, and thus allow us to measure each process independently of the other. Although not a logical necessity, in defining a response criterion, or "response threshold," detection theory gives up the concept of a sensory threshold—substituting for it the concept of continuously variable, nondichotomized sensitivity.

The existence of a sensory threshold, or the desirability of basing a psychophysics on the concept of the sensory threshold, was brought into question long before the development of modern detection theory. For example, Jastrow in 1888 criticized the concept as a misconception which stemmed from the method of serial exploration. He believed that no point on the sensory continuum had peculiar characteristics, that there was no threshold in any true sense, and that applying discrete notions to the stimulus and sensory continua could only lead to confusion. Urban in 1930 regarded the sensory threshold as a superfluous hypothesis and predicted the development of a psychophysics without this notion as its cornerstone. (See Corso, 1963, for an historical review of the threshold concept.) Moreover, measures of sensitivity that are relatively free from nonsensory influences have been available since the late 1800's, and the possibility of extracting two parameters from the data, in order to secure independent indices of sensory and nonsensory aspects of behavior, was considered in the literature of the 1930's.

Unfortunately, the early arguments against the threshold concept were given little attention in written histories of psychology and in secondary sourcebooks on sensation and perception, and the first relatively pure measures of sensitivity were not widely used. By and large, the men who developed these measures had only a glancing contact with psychophysics; they worked at first in the mental-test tradition and, after refining psychophysical methods to their satisfaction, went off to work on psychometrics, on the scaling of stimuli not amenable to physical measurement.

The next section of this chapter presents a brief review of the classical psychophysical methods. It also reviews threshold measures and the measures proposed within the mental-test, or psychometric, framework, and compares and contrasts these with the measures of detection theory. The remainder of the chapter is devoted to a discussion of theories of the sensory threshold that are more explicit than the classical theory. Five such theories have been developed within the past 30 years, and three of these within the past 10 years.

The first considered is the so-called *high-threshold* theory. This theory represents the view that is implied by the more common forms of the classical methods and measures—the view that a sensory threshold exists which is rarely if ever exceeded when no signal is present. The next theory discussed is also closely related to the classical view: the theory of the *neural quantum*. Quantal theory, as the name indicates, proposes that sensory representation of stimulus magnitude is discrete throughout its range, and that many thresholds exist. The other theories discussed have been termed *low-threshold* theories. Although each of them can be regarded as an adaptation of high-threshold theory or of quantal theory, or of both, in an important sense they all have a closer kinship with detection theory. They agree in asserting that false-alarm responses, in substantial proportions, may have a sensory basis.

Throughout the chapter we are concerned with the questions raised by Jastrow and Urban. Do sensory thresholds exist? If they do exist, can they be measured precisely enough to serve as a cornerstone for psychophysical science? It will be clear that the care given here to the concept of the sensory threshold is necessary for several reasons. One reason is the great durability of the concept. As indicated, it was among the first quantitative concepts established in experimental psychology and, despite considerable criticism almost from its inception, it is widely used today. The notion of some limit on sensitivity is, of course, highly likely on a priori grounds, but whether or not there exists a limit in the sense of the threshold is a very intricate question. That a crucial experiment has not been devised is indicated by the fact that when the classical view appeared again recently to be in jeopardy, several modified versions, consistent with the new data, were soon developed. Clearly, a blanket denial of sensory thresholds of any sort is not to be accepted in advance of a protracted period of study. However, if the classical view of the threshold is incorrect, then it is important to spell out the ramifications of this result, since they are many and not all are obvious. Perhaps the most important implications are for measurement. Suffice it to say now that the classical threshold is not merely a statistical construct; the conceptual neurophysiology on which it is based is directly reflected in some popular forms of psychophysical methods and measures; if the concept is not valid, then these methods and measures are inappropriate. The classical threshold concept has also had an extensive influence on theory in several areas. Estes (1962) has recently reviewed its place in learning theory. To take an example from sensory theory, one pursued further in Chapter 9, the concept has supported for years a prediction which has been applied to multiple observations, multiple observers, and multicomponent signals, although a large share of the data relevant to the prediction are contradictory to it. It may also be noted that the classical view of the threshold has fostered the large literature on subliminal, or subthreshold, perception.

5.2   PSYCHOPHYSICAL METHODS AND MEASURES

5.2.1   *The classical methods and measures*

When applied to the measurement of the sensory threshold, the common aim of the three classical methods is to determine the physical value of the stimulus or stimulus difference that is noticed, that elicits a positive response, some fixed percentage (usually 50%) of the time. In measuring the "absolute threshold," only a variable stimulus is presented; in measuring the "difference threshold," a fixed, or standard, stimulus is also presented, and the signal consists of a variation from this standard.

Under the method of adjustment, the subject manipulates a continuously variable stimulus. He may be asked to adjust the stimulus so that it is just noticeable, or just noticeably different from a standard, or he may be asked to set the variable stimulus so that it is equal to a standard. Under the method of serial exploration, the variable stimulus is presented by the experimenter in steps, from values below the point of 50% response to values above that point. Alternatively, the experimenter may present values of the stimulus in a descending order, or the two types of series may be interleaved. Under the method of constant stimuli, the experimenter presents several values of the stimulus in a random or semirandom order. In both of the last two methods, the subject responds, in effect, "yes" or "no"—he may or may not be permitted to say "doubtful" when the absolute threshold is measured, or "equal" when the difference threshold is measured.

The sensory threshold can be measured in various ways, depending upon what the subject is asked or allowed to do. Thus, if the subject is attempting to set a variable stimulus equal to a standard stimulus under the method of adjustment, the threshold may be taken as the *probable error* of the distribution of settings. (The probable error equals about two-thirds of the standard deviation; if the distribution is normal, 50% of the settings fall between plus and minus one probable error.) The computation of the threshold value under the other two methods depends upon whether or not the subject is allowed to make a judgment of "doubtful" or "equal." In any case, the data obtained from all three methods can be plotted as psychometric functions, and the value of the signal corresponding to 50% response can be determined. If the subject is allowed the third (uncertain) category of response, "upper" and "lower" thresholds are obtained, which can be combined by taking the mean of the two. If the subject must say whether the second, or variable, stimulus is greater than or less than the first stimulus presented, the psychometric functions for "greater than" and "less than" responses cross at the 50% point; in this case the sensory threshold is redefined as the signal value corresponding to the point of 75% response.

The procedure of taking the threshold as the point of 75% response, when 50% response represents chance performance, is equivalent to using the probable error, an index of variability in general use prior to 1930, as a measure of sensitivity; we shall have more to say about this and similar measures shortly. When the procedure is generalized, as it usually is if a threshold measure is sought, so that the proportion of responses taken as defining the threshold lies halfway between chance and perfect performance irrespective of the number of response categories, then the procedure is equivalent to making a "correction for chance success." As we shall see, the use of this correction implies a view of the threshold that is made explicit in the high-threshold theory.

As indicated above, the relative advantages and disadvantages of the three methods have been subjected to careful scrutiny. The method of adjustment is economical, but contaminated by "uncertainty of the hand." The method of serial exploration applies generally to qualitative and quantitative variables, but the extensive knowledge that the subject possesses about the progression of signal values may induce errors such as "habituation" and "expectation." The method of constant stimuli leaves the subject properly uncertain about the size of the signal to be presented next, but a large number of trials is required. And so on.

5.2.2   Relation of classical and detection-theory methods

From the point of view of the theory of signal detectability, both the serial-exploration and the constant-stimulus methods are adequate—if "blank trials," trials containing no signal, are presented in sufficient numbers to allow us to determine reliably the proportion of false-positive responses, so that a quantitative estimate of the observer's response criterion can be obtained. If the yes-no forms of the method of limits and the method of constant stimuli are used with no, or very few, blank trials, then the single (threshold) parameter that is extracted from the data is heavily dependent on an indeterminate response criterion. Although it might be assumed that a practiced observer will maintain an invariant response criterion from one session to another and from one experimental condition to another, different observers in different laboratories certainly cannot be expected to maintain the same response criterion. Similarly, the three-category method of constant stimuli without blank trials yields a single measure—the average of the upper and lower thresholds, or half of the interval of uncertainty—that is influenced heavily by an unmeasured response criterion. (The threshold goes to zero if the observer gives no "doubtful" judgments.)

The use of a large number of blank trials does not, by itself, insure adequate separation of sensory and nonsensory factors. The proportion of false-positive responses is often taken as a measure of pure response bias rather than as a measure of an adjustable criterion applied to sensory inputs. That is, the proportion of false-positive responses is taken as an estimate of the proportion of correct positive responses that are correct by chance, and this chance factor is used to adjust the latter proportion in order to remove a supposedly spurious contribution. As discussed in the next section, this procedure assumes the existence of a "high" threshold that is independent of the proportion of false-positive responses. In short, detection theory is inconsistent with several classical and current psychophysical practices, for these practices imply, and depend upon, the existence of a sensory threshold that is rarely exceeded on trials not containing a signal.

5.2.3   Objective versus classical psychophysics

Implicit in the foregoing discussion contrasting the classical and detection-theory methods is the fact that in one case the observer is trusted and in the other case he is not. Forms of Fechner's methods in general use, without a substantial number of blank trials, do not permit an objective check on the observer's report. Their use assumes that, although the observer will sometimes be confounded by psychological factors, he is generally able to say whether or not he is aware of the signal that he knows is present. And their use with blank trials, but without a treatment of the data that permits an index of the response criterion, assumes that the observer will rarely if ever have valid sensory reasons for deciding that a signal is present when none is; that is to say, it is assumed that if noise alone can exceed the threshold, it will do so on a negligible proportion of trials. Of course, the fact that detection-theory methods do not trust the observer to differentiate signal and noise reliably is not a comment on his character; they assume that sensory events caused by noise can exactly duplicate any sensory event caused by the signal and that the observer, therefore, is constitutionally incapable of determining whether any given sensory event was caused by noise or by the signal.

It is important to note that the objectivity of detection-theory methods does not require that the experimenter be able to score the subject as right or wrong; he need only know which value of the signal he presented on each trial. The experimenter cannot score the subject as right or wrong when he is measuring a transition from hot to cold, from not painful to painful, from beats to roughness, or from achromaticity to chromaticity. He can, however, determine the reliability with which an observer can discriminate between any two signals on one of these continua, by determining an ROC curve—by plotting the conditional probability that signal A is called signal A against the conditional probability that signal B is called signal A, as the criterion is varied from one set of trials to another.

If the experimenter is not interested in the discriminability of two signals, but is interested rather in finding out what an observer will call a given signal, for instance "hot" or "cold," then he is faced with a problem of nominal scaling. In this case, although the experimenter may want to avoid idiosyncratic criteria, in the final analysis his goal is an estimation of the observer's criterion, and sensitivity is involved only indirectly. The availability of the detection-theory methods means that problems in which sensitivity is the primary concern do not have to be handled as if they were problems of nominal scaling; if sensitivity is the concern, the observer's responses can be scored objectively, and a measure of sensitivity can be obtained that is independent of his criterion.

The distinction between subjective and objective approaches did not first become apparent with the contrast between classical threshold theory and modern detection theory—as indicated in Chapter 3, it has been a matter of considerable controversy almost since psychophysics began. At issue was whether the observer should judge sensations or stimuli (the stimulus error), and whether the experimenter should measure the threshold or should use another measure, a measure of resolving power. We shall not review this history here; the particulars of disagreement over method are treated fully by Guilford (1936, 1954) and Woodworth (1938), and Torgerson (1958) has recently given an excellent summary of the two points of view.

5.2.4   Early objective methods

It is essential, however, to point out here that the members of the objective school (which included Jastrow, Cattell, Thorndike, and Thurstone) arrived at a method and a measure that were relatively insensitive to variations in the observer's attitude. Their preferred method was the two-category method of constant stimuli, or the method of paired comparisons; and their preferred measure was a measure of response (or momentary threshold) variability, such as the probable error or the standard deviation. The probable error and standard deviation are, like the threshold, inverse measures of sensitivity; the less the momentary threshold varies, the keener is the discrimination. A similar measure, but one directly related to sensitivity, is the maximum slope of the psychometric function. A measure sometimes used in the late 1800's and early 1900's was the measure h—also a measure of precision rather than scatter, $h = 1/\sqrt{2}\sigma$—the measure advocated by Fechner. That the measure d' of detection theory is closely related to these measures, particularly h and σ, comes as no surprise when it is recalled that Thurstone linked the early and recent versions of the objective approach.

It will also be apparent that the two-category method of constant stimuli, when applied to the differential threshold, is similar to what has been called here the forced-choice method. Both minimize attitudinal factors or response biases; that is, they facilitate shaping behavior to approximate a symmetrical response criterion. The use of a measure of variability makes a further contribution to reducing attitudinal effects. Kellogg (1930) showed that the measure σ obtained from the same observers differed very little in two- and three-category experiments. Fernberger (1931) studied directly the effects of variation in the response criterion; he applied three sets of instructions to obtain three different frequencies of "doubtful" judgments, and found the measure σ relatively unaffected. It was Fernberger's study that led to the suggestion that the threshold calculated in the three-category method, though not a valid measure of sensitivity because it varies directly with the frequency of "doubtful" judgments, might have value as a measure of attitude (Woodworth, 1938, p. 425). The suggestion seems not to have been pursued.

There is some reason to question the idea that measuring only variability provides an entirely adequate index of sensitivity. Consider the direct index provided by the maximum slope of the psychometric function. Hecht, Shlaer, and Pirenne (1942) calculated psychometric functions for the ideal observer in a vision experiment who responds consistently to one quantum absorption, or to two, or three, and so forth. As the observer requires fewer quanta for a positive response, the psychometric function moves to the left—the mean or threshold value decreases—but, at the same time, the slope *decreases*. It might be expected that a factor which increases sensitivity will have more effect on the lower, left portion of the function than on the upper, right portion, and will serve, therefore, to increase the range of the function. In the engineering literature, the relation of increasing slope to decreasing sensitivity is referred to as "weak-signal suppression." We shall see in Chapter 7 that human observers yield psychometric functions of less and less slope as conditions are changed to permit them to approach more nearly the calculated ideal sensitivity.

However that may be, the point of discussion now is that a psychophysical method and a sensitivity measure relatively uninfluenced by criterion variations, at least under some conditions, have been available since the turn of the century. Such methods and measures were not invented by detection theorists. The contribution of detection theory in this context is that it rescues the yes-no method and provides a detectability measure which unifies the yes-no, forced-choice, and rating methods. Note, again, that neither did detection theory first bring into question the existence of a sensory threshold. We should remember in the following discussion that some early objective psychophysicists did not advocate high-threshold theory or low-threshold theory or any other kind of threshold theory—they simply measured the sensitivity, or discrimination capacity, of the organism.

5.3   THRESHOLD EXISTENCE AND THE PSYCHOMETRIC FUNCTION

The remainder of the chapter considers several threshold theories, partly in an attempt to answer the question of whether a sensory threshold, or a practicably measurable sensory threshold, exists. Consideration of several theories is a complicated way of attempting to answer the question; therefore, let us first establish that what appears to be a simple way is not satisfactory.

A seemingly direct way to determine threshold existence is to examine some empirical psychometric functions. Does the psychometric function intersect the origin of the plot, or does it intersect the abscissa to the right of the origin? We have seen that the answer to this question helps us little if the ordinate of the plot is the proportion of positive responses. A function which intersects the abscissa to the right of the origin does not imply that some low signal magnitudes are too weak ever to elicit a positive response. Such a finding suggests, instead, a very strict criterion, and too few trials. Under ordinary circumstances blank trials often elicit positive responses; in fact, it is difficult to eliminate all false-alarm responses while retaining some correct positive responses.

Therefore, to overcome criterion effects, it is necessary to use as the ordinate of the function a measure like d' in a yes-no test, or a measure like percentage correct in a forced-choice test. Then, in principle, it is possible to determine whether or not an infinitesimally small signal is detected with greater-than-chance probability. Unfortunately, to establish the statistical significance of a difference of 0.01, between the hit proportion $P(S \mid s)$ and the false-alarm proportion $P(S \mid n)$, requires thousands of trials. The same is true of an attempt to establish that $P(C) = 0.51$ is significantly different from $P(C) = 0.50$ in a two-alternative forced-choice test. This is the case even if one assumes binomial variance and, clearly, 1,000 trials

is many more than one could obtain with any assurance of stable physiological, psychological, or physical conditions.

Thus we are constrained to extrapolate to the intersection a function
determined by points in a measurable range. As we shall see later (Chapter
7), there is some evidence that empirical plots of d' versus signal power
are fitted reasonably well by theoretical curves which intersect the origin.
Of course, the use of an arbitrary theoretical function, combined with the
large range over which the extrapolation must be made, makes this result
less than compelling evidence against the existence of a sensory threshold.
The evidence is no more compelling when the choice of a different theoretical function produces an intersection to the right of the origin.

To deal with the question of the threshold, we must compare theories
which incorporate a threshold with one that does not, and determine the
relative success with which these theories predict the results of several
experiments. In the following sections, detection theory, which assumes that
the observer can completely order sensory events, is compared with
threshold theories, which place a limit on the ability to order sensory
events—in relation to results of yes-no, forced-choice, and rating experiments. One of the questions asked is: What is the upper lower bound
on the observer's criterion? That is: How high (relative to the hypothetical
distribution of noise-determined sensory events) can a cutoff exist, below
which the observer is incapable of ordering sensory events?

We consider first the high-threshold theory proposed by Blackwell
(1953, 1963), then the quantal theory proposed by von Békésy (1930) and
advocated by Stevens (1961) and others, and finally three low-threshold
theories proposed, respectively, by Swets, Tanner, and Birdsall (1955,
1961), Luce (1963a,b), and Atkinson (1963).

5.4   THE HIGH-THRESHOLD THEORY

5.4.1   An interpretation of the threshold

The classical threshold is a statistical construct—the signal value
corresponding to some arbitrary percentage of (correct) positive responses.
Underlying this construct, however, is some conceptual neurophysiology,
according to which the sensory threshold is a cutoff level of sensory
excitation which is either exceeded or not exceeded by the sensory effect
of a signal. If that cutoff level is exceeded, the observer notices, or detects,
the signal; if that cutoff level is not exceeded, the signal has no effect
whatsoever on the observer.

A common interpretation of the threshold is that a signal which is
nominally the same signal from one presentation to another, and which has

presumably the same sensory effect from one presentation to another, may sometimes exceed the cutoff level and sometimes not, because that threshold level varies randomly over time. An alternative conception, which is equivalent for some purposes, is to assume that the sensory effect of a given signal varies randomly over time (exhibits a variable "discriminal process," in Thurstone's terms), and that the threshold remains fixed. (It might be assumed that both the sensory effect of a given signal and the threshold vary in time, but this interpretation is not necessarily different from the one just stated, since the variance of the threshold may be viewed as variance added to the variance of the sensory effect.) The second way of stating the threshold concept permits a direct comparison with the theory of signal detectability. This view of the threshold may be represented by a "continuum" of sensory events and two probability distributions of these events, one corresponding to noise alone and the other to signal plus noise. The threshold view differs from detection theory in that, instead of a variable criterion, there exists a fixed cutoff below which sensory events are indiscriminable from one another.

5.4.2   True detection responses and the correction for chance

The high-threshold theory represents the classical view that the fixed cutoff is rarely or never exceeded on presentations of noise alone. (When normal probability distributions are assumed, the cutoff may be located in this representation at approximately three standard deviations above the mean of the noise distribution.) There is thus a "true" value of the false-alarm proportion—call it $P^*(S \mid n)$—that for practical purposes is equal to zero. Corresponding to $P^*(S \mid n)$, there is some true proportion of hits, $P^*(S \mid s)$, the value of which depends on the difference between the means of the two probability distributions, that is, on the strength of the signal.

If, in an experiment with blank trials, the observer exhibits a false-alarm proportion greater than zero, then according to this view he is responding "yes" to sensory events which fail to exceed the threshold. Since he is unable to discriminate among these events, his "yes" responses to them are merely guesses, and they will be correct only by chance. If the observer guesses, the observed proportion of hits will be an overestimate of the true proportion of hits. Specifically, the observed proportion of hits is equal to the true proportion of hits plus a guessing factor which operates in the absence of a true hit. The rational equation of the high-threshold theory is

$$P(S \mid s) = P^*(S \mid s) + P(S \mid n)[1 - P^*(S \mid s)] \qquad (5.1)$$

A rearrangement of Eq. 5.1 yields the familiar correction for chance success:

$$P^*(S \mid s) = \frac{P(S \mid s) - P(S \mid n)}{1 - P(S \mid n)} \qquad (5.2)$$

It may be seen that the correction adjusts the observed proportion of hits according to the observed proportion of false alarms to obtain the true proportion of hits.

In the forced-choice task, where there are no false alarms, the chance factor is taken as $1/m$ where m is the number of alternatives. The rational equation for forced choice is

$$P(C) = P^*(C) + \frac{1}{m}[1 - P^*(C)] \qquad (5.3)$$

and the correction for chance is

$$P^*(C) = \frac{P(C) - 1/m}{1 - 1/m} \qquad (5.4)$$

By inserting various values in this last equation, the reader may determine that defining the threshold proportion to be halfway between chance and perfect performance is tantamount to applying the chance correction. That is, if $P(C) = \frac{1}{2}(1/m + 1)$ then $P^*(C) = \frac{1}{2}$.

5.4.3 Assumption of independence of false alarms and true hits

The basic assumption of the high-threshold theory is that false alarms and true hits are independent—the guessing mechanism, which produces false alarms, operates only when there is no sensory basis for a response, and is therefore independent of the sensory mechanism. Because all the experimental tests which compare high-threshold theory and detection theory are essentially tests of this assumption, let us pursue the matter a little further, in order to see how the assumption is reflected in the formal statement of the high-threshold theory.

Note simply that the rational equation and the chance correction, Eqs. 5.1 and 5.2, can be written in the form

$$1 - P(S \mid s) = [1 - P(S \mid n)][1 - P^*(S \mid s)] \qquad (5.5)$$

This equation demonstrates that the events involved in $[1 - P(S \mid n)]$ and the events involved in $[1 - P^*(S \mid s)]$ are assumed to be independent, since their compound probability is equal to the product of their probabilities taken singly. As indicated in Appendix I, if these events are independent, then the complementary events—that is, the proportion of false alarms and the true or corrected proportion of hits—are also independent. We shall examine the implications of this assumption for data in various forms.

5.4.4 Predictions and data—yes-no experiments

Equation 5.1, the rational equation, expresses $P(S \mid s)$ as a linear function of $P(S \mid n)$. Thus the ROC curves based on high-threshold theory, for yes-no data, are straight lines on linear coordinates. These straight lines

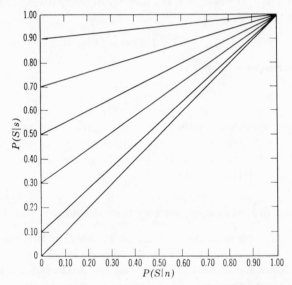

FIG. 5-1a   ROC curves based on the high-threshold theory.

run from various values on the left-hand vertical axis, the particular value depending on the signal strength, to the upper right-hand corner of the plot. A family of these ROC curves is shown in Fig. 5-1a. It can be observed that if the chance correction is applied to these linear ROC curves—that is, if $P^*(S \mid s)$ is substituted for $P(S \mid s)$ on the ordinate—then the curves become horizontal lines at the level of their left-hand intercepts. The horizontal lines further illustrate the assumed independence of $P^*(S \mid s)$ and $P(S \mid n)$.

Data presented in Chapter 4 are inconsistent with this assumption of independence. The ROC data shown there, in Figs. 4-1, 4-2, 4-5, and 4-7, are fitted reasonably well by the curvilinear ROC curves of detection theory, and very poorly by the straight lines of Fig. 5-1a. Figure 5-1b shows the

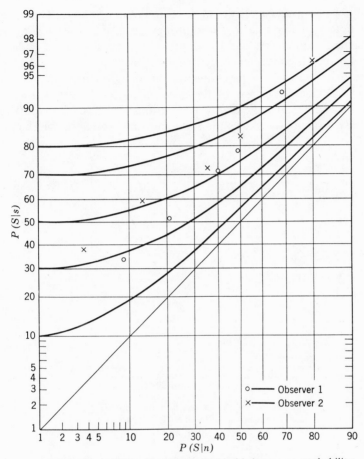

FIG. 5-1*b*   ROC curves of high-threshold theory, on probability
scales. Data from two observers in an auditory experiment, taken
from Figs. 4-1 and 4-5.

high-threshold ROC curves on probability scales. Also shown in this
figure are the data from two observers in an auditory experiment, the same
data as shown in Figs. 4-1 and 4-5. It may be seen that, rather than being
fitted by one of the theoretical curves, the data cut across several of them.

Another way of examining the validity of the assumption of independence, as Smith and Wilson (1953) have pointed out, is to apply the chance
correction to psychometric functions based on different proportions of
false alarms, that is, to psychometric functions having different intercepts
on the left vertical axis. The correction normalizes the various functions
so that they all intersect the origin. If the assumption of independence were

valid, all the corrected curves would lie on top of one another. The signal strength corresponding to a corrected proportion of hits of 0.50 will then be the same for all curves, and the threshold can be determined without concern for the observer's tendency to guess.

Figure 5-2a shows three psychometric functions obtained in a visual experiment. Values and costs of the decision outcomes were varied to obtain three different false-alarm proportions: 0.35, 0.25, and 0.04, respectively. Figure 5-2b shows the same functions corrected for chance,

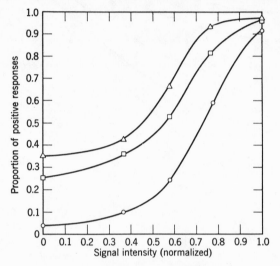

FIG. 5-2a Psychometric functions showing false-alarm proportions of 0.35, 0.25, and 0.04. (Data from Swets, Tanner, and Birdsall, 1961.)

and demonstrates the failure of the prediction of high-threshold theory. The corrected curves do not lie practically on top of one another; they diverge in the direction predicted by detection theory. According to the data, if the threshold is taken at the point of 50% response, then the higher the false-alarm proportion, the lower the calculated threshold. Apparently, if the observer is induced to say "yes" more frequently, he does not have to do so on a chance basis; he can, in effect, adopt a lower criterion.

The tests, just examined, of the assumed independence of the false alarm and true hits are conceptually appropriate. Perhaps the strongest test, however, is achieved by calculating the coefficient of correlation between the corrected proportion of hits and the false-alarm proportion. Several experiments have yielded correlation coefficients on the order of 0.90, with about 10 degrees of freedom. These coefficients are statistically very significant; if the true correlation were 0, coefficients of this size would

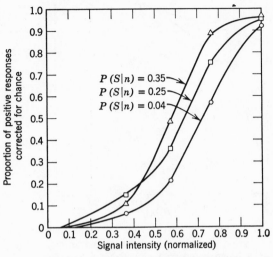

FIG. 5-2b The psychometric functions of Fig. 5-2a corrected for chance success, by Eq. 5.2.

arise with a probability of considerably less than 0.001. It is quite clear that the corrected proportion of hits and the false-alarm proportion are not independent.

5.4.5   Extent of dependence of calculated threshold on false-alarm proportion

If we assume, for the purpose of this discussion, the validity of the detection-theory analysis, then we can state quantitatively the extent of the dependence on the false-alarm proportion of the corrected proportion of hits or of the calculated threshold. Figure 5-3a shows three of the linear ROC curves based upon the high-threshold theory, and the curvilinear ROC curve of detection theory (assuming normal density functions of equal variance) that corresponds to $d' = 1.0$. The points of intersection of the three straight lines with the curved line represent, in terms of detection theory, three different locations of the criterion for a given signal intensity. If detection theory is correct, then the three values of $P^*(S \mid s)$ that would be obtained from a signal of a given intensity, for the three different locations of the criterion, correspond to the intercepts of the three straight lines and the ordinate. The correlation between this proportion and the criterion is obvious; $P^*(S \mid s)$ varies from 0 to 1.0 as the criterion varies from very strict to very lenient.

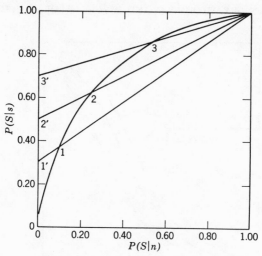

FIG. 5-3*a* The curved ROC is based on detection theory, $d' = 1.0$. The three linear ROC's are based on high-threshold theory. The values of $P(S \mid s)$ at the points 1, 2, and 3, upon correction for chance successes, become the values of $P^*(S \mid s)$ at points 1′, 2′, and 3′, respectively. The figure illustrates the dependence of $P^*(S \mid s)$ on the observer's criterion. (From Egan and Clarke, 1966.)

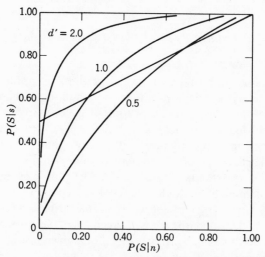

FIG. 5-3*b* The curvilinear ROC curves are based on detection theory. The linear ROC curve is based on high-threshold theory; $P^*(S \mid s) = 0.50$.

The graph shown in Fig. 5-3b is similar, except that it contains a family of the curvilinear ROC curves based on detection theory, and only a single linear ROC curve based on the high-threshold theory, namely, the one which intersects the ordinate at 0.50. This single linear ROC curve is the one which corresponds to $P^*(S \mid s) = 0.50$, the usual threshold proportion. If we note which curvilinear ROC curves the single linear curve intersects, we see how the value of d' which corresponds to the threshold varies with

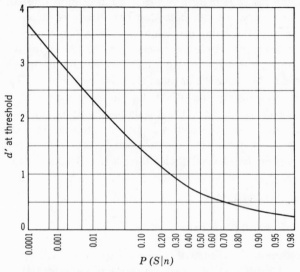

FIG. 5-3c The relationship between d', at the threshold calculated under high-threshold theory, and the false-alarm proportion.

the false-alarm proportion. This variation is shown in Fig. 5-3c; d' at threshold is a monotonic function which ranges from infinity to zero as the false-alarm proportion ranges from 0 to 1.0. According to detection theory, an infinitely strong signal is required to exceed the "high" threshold if no false-alarm responses are to be made, and an infinitely weak signal will exceed this threshold if the criterion adopted yields a false-alarm proportion of 1.0. Given that d' is approximately proportional to signal power (see Chapter 7), a change in the false-alarm proportion from, say, 0.25 to 0.001 will result in a change in the calculated threshold of a factor of 3, or a change of 5 db. Variation in the false-alarm proportion in a range below 0.01, which could not be measured in an experimentally feasible number of trials even if a large number of blank trials were used, could easily lead to much greater variation in the calculated threshold. In clinical audiometry, or in measuring the course of dark adaptation, a variability of 5 db is not crucial; on the other hand, as we shall see in later chapters, it is often the case that grossly different hypotheses about sensory processes can be distinguished only if a reliability of about 1 db can be achieved.

5.4.6 Predictions and data—rating and forced-choice experiments

In concluding the examination of the relation of data to predictions of high-threshold theory, we can note that the theory is inconsistent with data obtained from the rating procedure, and with data on second-choice responses in a four-alternative forced-choice task. The rating data shown in Fig. 4-10 indicate ordering of values of sensory excitation well below a threshold fixed at 3σ above the mean of the noise distribution. The second-choice results deviate significantly from the high-threshold prediction shown in Fig. 4-12. A related fact that is damaging to the theory is that the forced-choice and yes-no procedures do not lead to the same value of the calculated threshold; yes-no thresholds based on low false-alarm rates are consistently higher than forced-choice thresholds (Blackwell, 1953).

5.5 QUANTAL THEORY

5.5.1 Neural-quantum theory

Our discussion of the theory of the neural quantum will be brief, for it has been fully presented elsewhere. Proposed by von Békésy (1930), the theory has been revised and tested by Stevens, Morgan, and Volkmann (1941), by Miller and Garner (1944), by Norman (1963), and by Larkin and Norman (1964), among others. Reviews of the successes and failures of the theory have recently been made by Corso (1956) and Stevens (1961).

Quantal theory postulates that sensory representation of stimulus magnitude is discrete throughout its range, in other words, that multiple thresholds exist. It will evidently be very difficult to distinguish between a multi-threshold theory, with a small quantum size, and the assumption of continuity made in detection theory. In fact, all the data reported in Chapter 4 as supporting detection theory could have been obtained if there exist N thresholds and $N + 1$ discriminable categories of sensory excitation—with N as small as 5 or 6—and none of the uses that have been made of detection theory is incompatible with such a discrete process.

A central feature of quantal theory, in the present context, is that it is in the classical, or subjective, tradition. Though it acknowledges explicitly the possibility of variation in the observer's response criterion, it provides a single measure of performance that depends on the criterion as well as on sensitivity. The measure is the quantum, defined operationally as the difference between the smallest signal which always produces a "yes" response and the largest signal which never produces a "yes" response.

The prescription for experimental procedure that has accompanied quantal theory precludes the possibility of obtaining an independent, objective measure of the response criterion because it specifies a yes-no procedure and prohibits the use of blank trials. It has been recommended that, in testing the theory, signals of the same magnitude be presented on all trials of a series, and that this fact be made known to the observer. This procedure is followed in order to avoid undue distraction of the observer, since it is believed that obtaining results consistent with the theory demands extremely careful attention on the part of the observer (Stevens, 1961). However, it may fairly be argued that blank trials will not affect the observer's detections if he cannot distinguish between a failure to detect and the absence of a signal; and recently some experiments have been conducted to test quantal theory with a procedure including blank trials. The results of these experiments are mixed: Larkin and Norman (1964) obtained evidence in support of the quantal hypothesis, but an extended experiment and analysis conducted by Norman (1963) did not disclose multiple discontinuities.

Quantal theory differs from detection theory, and from the low-threshold theories to be described, in that it is a theory of an almost noiseless observer, whereas the other theories assume that a substantial amount of noise is always present, inside as well as outside the observer. Because experiments conducted to test detection theory and the various low-threshold theories, in which a background of noise is deliberately added, cannot be expected to reveal the fine-grained action of the nervous system, or the existence of a neural quantum, it has been possible to suppose that detection theory is applicable when the problem is one of detecting signals in noise, and that quantal theory applies when attempts to eliminate external noise, and such internal noise as may be due to lapses of attention, are successful (Stevens, 1961). However, there is reason to doubt that external noise can be sufficiently reduced to reveal quantal nervous action in a psychological experiment, and it may be that, even on the level of the single neuron, the problem of detection is inherently one of extracting signals from noise (see, for example, FitzHugh, 1957, and Chapter 12). The possibility that the two theories may have complementary scopes is also lessened by the results of a study in which detection theory was tested without deliberately added background noise. This study of absolute visual detection (Nachmias and Steinman, 1963) provides support for detection theory.

Several studies have supported the quantal hypothesis, and about the same number have failed to provide support (Corso, 1956). It has been suspected that the negative instances resulted from a failure to meet the exacting conditions which are necessary to demonstrate this threshold (Stevens, 1961). In any case, the quantal threshold is clearly very difficult to measure. Although the theory of the neural quantum cannot be discounted, it will not serve as a basis for the study of substantive problems of sensory functions until the conditions of measurement are brought under adequate control.

5.5.2   Physical-quantum theory

Barlow (1956) has discussed the relationship between detection theory and the physical-quantum theory that has developed in the study of vision. Within the framework of this theory, Hecht, Shlaer, and Pirenne (1942) have proposed that coincident absorption of five to eight quanta are required to exceed the threshold, whereas Bouman and van der Velden (1947) believed that the absorption of two quanta is sufficient to exceed the threshold. Barlow argues that visual detection is a problem of discriminating signals from noise, and supports the argument with data, obtained by means of a three-category rating scale, which show the value of the calculated threshold to depend upon the observer's criterion. His further analyses of the data of Hecht, Shlaer, and Pirenne, indicating five or more quanta, and of the data of Bouman and van der Velden, indicating only two quanta, lead to the conclusion that the difference results from the difference in the response criteria used by the observers in the two experiments.

5.6   LOW-THRESHOLD THEORIES

Within the past few years, three threshold theories have been proposed as alternatives to the classical view and to the high-threshold and quantal theories. They differ in several respects. One of them postulates a single threshold; the other two postulate more than one threshold. Two of them are "dynamic" theories which postulate a particular learning process; the third is "static," and intended to describe only asymptotic behavior. The three theories differ in the precision and detail with which they have been formulated, and they differ in the range of data that they are supposed to encompass. They are alike in one respect—they specify a threshold which is exceeded a substantial portion of the time when only noise is present—and thus they may be considered together as "low-threshold" theories.

5.6.1   Single-threshold multi-state theory

One of the low-threshold theories is like the high-threshold theory in that it assumes a single threshold with a continuous gradation of sensory events above this threshold, and no gradation below. It is also like the high-threshold theory in assuming that a guessing, or chance, mechanism underlies "yes" responses made to sensory events which do not exceed the threshold. This theory differs, as indicated, in placing the threshold at a lower point relative to the probability distribution of sensory events caused by noise. Furthermore, it assumes that the processes described by detection theory are operative when sensory events exceed the low threshold. In other words, this theory assumes that there is a lower limit on the response criterion that an observer can adopt; he cannot lower his criterion below a certain point because all sensory events below that point, below the sensory threshold, are indistinguishable.*

Data indicate that the threshold of this theory should be assumed to lie somewhere between the mean of the noise distribution and a point one standard deviation above the mean. The ROC curves of this theory for yes-no data would have a curvilinear portion, similar to the detection-theory ROC curves, extending from a false-alarm proportion of zero to a false-alarm proportion somewhere between 0.16 (corresponding to 1σ) and 0.50 (corresponding to the mean). The other portion of this ROC curve, extending over higher false-alarm proportions, would be a straight line, like the high-threshold ROC curve. The curvilinear portion of the curve represents an ability to rank values of sensory excitation higher than some point, and the linear portion reflects the necessity to rely on guesses if "yes" responses are to be made to values of sensory excitation below that point.

It may be seen that the empirical ROC curves illustrated in Chapter 4 are fitted well by such a theoretical curve. In particular, the theoretical curves of detection theory based on a mean-to-sigma ratio have nearly the shape just described. It appears to be the case for some of the empirical curves shown in Chapter 4, and is quite clear for other curves that have been obtained, that they are fitted well by a straight line above a false-alarm proportion of 0.16—a result consistent with the existence of a sensory threshold located one standard deviation above the mean of the noise distribution.

To the best of our knowledge, this theory is consistent with all available data, including data obtained in rating experiments and on second choices

* This theory grew out of a discussion in which several persons participated; among them, it may be noted, was Professor Robert Thrall. The theory was described in publications by Swets, Tanner, and Birdsall (1955, 1961).

in forced-choice experiments (see Chapter 4). Rating data do not clearly indicate an ordering of sensory events below the mean of the noise distribution, and further analyses of the second-choice data show that they might be obtained with a sensory threshold at approximately this point. We shall not reproduce the analyses here, but it can be noted that the second-choice data reported in Chapter 4 are consistent with the hypothesis of complete ordering of sensory events only if a mean-to-sigma ratio is assumed. The proportions of correct second choices fall below the theoretical curve predicated on distributions of equal variance. In general, proportions of correct second choices fall midway between the theoretical curve of high-threshold theory and the theoretical curve of detection theory based on distributions of equal variance (see, for example, Eijkman and Vendrik, 1963).

Although this low-threshold theory is consistent with data at hand, the threshold it postulates will be difficult to measure. How do we go about obtaining from a yes-no experiment the physical value of the signal that corresponds to this threshold? The theory assumes a guessing mechanism, but not one which permits use of the standard chance correction because only some of the false alarms are supposed to be guesses. How does one estimate this threshold in a forced-choice experiment? It was shown in Chapter 4 that the observer conveys less information about his ordering of sensory events than he is capable of conveying, if only a first choice is required; several experiments have shown the second choice to contain information, and one has shown that the observer can order four choices. It is not obvious how to determine when enough information has been extracted from forced choices to yield a good estimate of a low threshold. Moreover, even if an adequate measure could be obtained, it would be insufficient—yes-no data resulting from a suprathreshold criterion would depend upon the criterion, but would be completely independent of the threshold value.

5.6.2   Multi-threshold two-state theory

As discussed in Chapter 3, Luce (1963a,b) has also proposed a threshold theory which places a threshold somewhere between the middle and the upper end of the noise distribution; it differs in assuming that values of sensory excitation above, as well as below, the threshold are indistinguishable. Thus, in this theory, the guessing mechanism works both ways. The observer achieves a proportion of false alarms that is higher than the true proportion by saying "yes" on a random basis to some of the sensory events below the threshold, and he achieves a proportion of false alarms lower than the true proportion by saying "no" on a random basis to some of the sensory events that exceed the threshold.

This theory, in part an adaptation of high-threshold theory, is also in part an adaptation of neural-quantum theory. Like quantal theory, it is a "multi-threshold" theory; it postulates a discrete representation of sensory events and, in particular, a discrete analogue of the continuous distributions of noise and signal plus noise found in detection theory. However, it may be viewed also as a "two-state" theory because, for reasons of simplicity, only two of the many possible states of sensory excitation are considered.

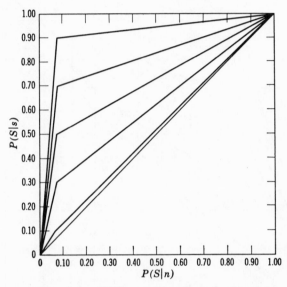

FIG. 5-4a   ROC curves based on the two-state theory. The curves assume a threshold which is exceeded on 7% of the presentations of noise alone.

The ROC curves of this theory, for yes-no data, are composed of two linear segments, which run from points at a given false-alarm proportion to the upper right-hand corner of the ROC graph, and to the lower left-hand corner, respectively. A family of such curves is shown in Fig. 5-4a. The same ROC curves, when plotted on probability scales, are nearly straight lines at low and high values of the false-alarm proportion, but show a scallop at the false-alarm proportion corresponding to the location of the threshold. The scallop is almost unnoticeable at low signal intensities, but is quite pronounced at high signal intensities, as can be seen in Fig. 5-4b.

In drawing Figs. 5-4a and 5-4b to represent the two-state theory, the threshold was taken as corresponding to $P(S \mid n) = 0.07$. The theory does not specify this value or any other value; the true "stimulus-determined" threshold probabilities, $P^*(S \mid s)$ and $P^*(S \mid n)$, must be estimated from data. The value of 0.07, however, is a reasonable one for illustrative purposes. Luce (1963a, p. 67) has fitted the two-linear-segment ROC

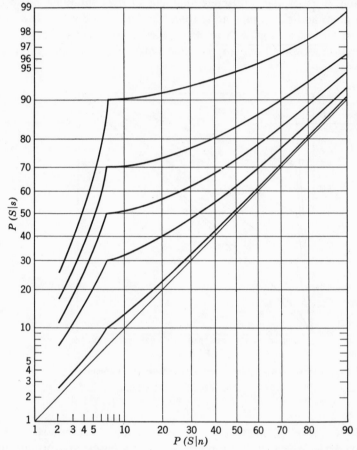

FIG. 5-4b ROC curves from two-state theory—on probability scales—assuming a threshold which is exceeded on 7% of the presentations of noise alone.

curve to visual and auditory data: for the visual data the break in the curve occurs at values of $P(S \mid n)$ of approximately 0.05; for the auditory data the breaks occur between 0.10 and 0.25.

An examination of the data from yes-no experiments presented in Chapter 4 (Figs. 4-1, 4-2, 4-5) shows that the two-limb ROC curves fit those data reasonably well—perhaps as well as the curvilinear curves of detection theory or the hybrid curves of the threshold theory described in the preceding section. Certainly, data will have to be obtained with much greater detail before the theories can be confidently distinguished on the basis of yes-no ROC curves. Moreover, given the low threshold, this theory is also consistent with a proportion of second choices greater than chance in a four-alternative forced-choice experiment.

The restriction to only two states makes this theory evidently inconsistent with data obtained in rating experiments, since these data indicate more than two discriminable classes of sensory events (see Chapter 4). Although Luce had no intention of encompassing the results of rating experiments with the two-state theory, this fact was clearer to some of his readers after the second presentation of the theory (1963b) than after the first (1960, 1963a). In the interim, Broadbent and Gregory (1963a), Nachmias and Steinman (1963), Swets (1961) and Watson, Rilling, and Bourbon (1964) regarded rating experiments as legitimate tests of Luce's theory and found the theory to be at odds with rating data.* It is, in a sense, unfortunate that rating data are irrelevant to the two-state theory, since rating ROC curves could provide the detail needed to distinguish between the two-limb curve and the curvilinear curve of detection theory (see Figs. 4-8 and 12-14).

Despite the fact that rating experiments lie outside the intended scope of the two-state theory, one of the results obtained by Nachmias and Steinman can legitimately be related to the theory. These investigators found that the probability that the threshold is exceeded on noise trials is not independent of the strength of the signal presented on signal trials. This agrees with the observation made by Swets (1961) that, since yes-no ROC data are fitted quite well by the curvilinear curves of detection theory, the intersection of the two straight lines which best fit the data varies with signal intensity. In particular, two-state ROC curves fitted to the data that have been obtained show a decreasing false-alarm proportion with increasing signal strength. The theory has to suppose that the level of the threshold is affected by the strength of the signal being presented.

The deliberate limitation of two-state theory, which excludes some sensory data, raises a question about the basis for evaluating sensory theories that we have not considered in discussing the other theories. The question is one that we shall also need to consider in connection with the threshold theory to be discussed next. There is a strong possibility that the particular limitation may be more than offset by permitting an increase in scope in another direction. As pointed out in Chapter 3, Luce has combined the two-state sensory theory with a theory of learning. We shall not discuss the learning theory here, but it will be clear that simplifying the statistics of the sensory theory (by considering just two rather than a

* See also Norman and Wickelgren (1965), or Chapter 12, Section 12.9.2.

continuum of sensory states), and thereby simplifying the calculations, greatly heightens the chances of relating learning processes to sensory processes. We repeat the opinion, expressed in Chapter 3, that it will be important to watch carefully any further developments along these lines. An oversimplification of sensory theory can be tolerated if the values outweigh the costs.

Moreover, although it may be evident that the observer is capable of distinguishing more than two classes of sensory events, he may in fact not do so in certain sensory tasks. The observer may find it convenient to assign sensory events in a yes-no task, with a weak signal, to either a "detect" or a "nondetect" class. Of course, we should like to be able to define the conditions under which he tends to use two states and the conditions under which he tends to use more than two states. The two-state theory cannot apply, for example, to the whole range of signal strengths typically used in a forced-choice task. If the threshold dividing the two states is low, that is, if it is exceeded by noise on a significant portion of the trials, then the observer cannot reach a proportion correct of nearly 1.0. If the threshold is exceeded on, for example, 7% of the noise trials, then, for a strong signal, on 7% of the trials two sensory events will fall in the detect state, and the observer will be in doubt. Then, no matter how strong the signal, the observer using two states cannot exceed a percentage correct of 0.965. If the observer can set the boundary separating the detect and nondetect states at any place he chooses, then this boundary is a response threshold rather than a physiologically determined sensory threshold, and a major difference between the two-state theory and detection theory evaporates.

Aside from the measurement problem presented by the dependence of the threshold on the magnitude of the signal, the prospects for obtaining a valid estimate of this low threshold are obscure. While expanding on the response aspects of detection to include learning, the theory slights stimulus aspects of detection. The theory of signal detectability is stimulus-oriented as well as response-oriented. As the next chapter shows, it stipulates the characteristics of the signal and noise to be measured, and specifies the psychometric function in relation to particular values of the signal-to-noise ratio, for each of several different kinds of signal. In contrast, this low-threshold theory, like the other low-threshold theories discussed, makes no reference to physical parameters of the signal other than to the fact that the signal can vary in magnitude. We have discussed the difficulties inherent in using the psychometric function to estimate a threshold value and, in this case, some accommodation would have to be made of the fact that the theory produces estimates of two different sensitivity parameters. Luce (1963a,b) has discussed some other sources of ambiguity in estimating the true hit and false-alarm probabilities which define this threshold.

In concluding this discussion of two-state theory, let us consider a possible objection to the present treatment of the theory and a related objection to the treatment of neural-quantum theory in Section 5.5.1. We have criticized two-state theory for failing to deal in quantitative terms with the stimulus, and have not particularly commended it for suggesting a means of dealing with false-alarm responses or with response biases. Neural-quantum theory, it might be said, got it the other way around—that theory was presented as dealing inadequately with response biases, and was not complimented for deriving a psychometric function. One can hold the view, as Luce (1963b) does, that the two theories can be combined in such a way as to overcome the a priori objections to both. Our opinion is that the combination leaves something to be desired. We have indicated in the foregoing our reservations about the way in which two-state theory handles response biases. We point out now that the neural-quantum theory does not specify in advance how the physical stimulus is to be measured; it does not specify in advance what transformation of the physical scale will yield the predicted rectilinear form of the psychometric function.

5.6.3   Two-threshold three-state (variable-sensitivity) theory

Atkinson (1963) has also combined a new theory of detection and a theory of learning. The stochastic theory of Bush and Mosteller (1955) served as a model for Luce's (1963a,b) learning theory; Estes' stimulus-sampling theory (1950) served as a model for Atkinson's learning theory.

In this theory, the stimulus leads to a detect state and a "yes" response, or to a nondetect state and a "no" response, or to an uncertain state in which a conditioning process determines either a "yes" or "no" response in accordance with the recent history of stimuli and responses. This theory may thus be characterized as a "two-threshold three-state" theory. Atkinson applies the term "variable sensitivity" to his theory because the observer is regarded as adjusting his level of sensitivity according to whether he has recently been emitting correct or incorrect responses.

We shall not show here how ROC curves are derived from this theory. The ROC curves for yes-no data look very much like the ROC curves of detection theory based on the assumption of unequal variance, in particular the curves based on a mean-to-sigma ratio of 4.0. The forced-choice ROC curves of this theory have the appearance of the equal-variance, symmetrical ROC curves of detection theory.

The theory is consistent with second-choice data but, as currently formulated, it does not encompass rating data. Again, certain simplifications in representing the sensory process are made in order to treat the learning process. A major aim of the theory is to predict sequences of responses in yes-no and forced-choice tasks. Sequential effects, or trial-by-trial phenomena, constitute a source of information about the detection process of a kind that cannot be obtained from the grosser statistics of hit and false-alarm proportions.

Concerning the practicalities of threshold measurement, this theory is subject to limitations that we have mentioned in connection with the other low-threshold theories. In its present form, it has little to say about the stimulus or about the shape of the psychometric function, and it contains two different sensitivity parameters. A measurement problem peculiar to this theory arises from its assumption that the family of ROC curves, which in other theories correspond to different signal magnitudes, can be generated with a fixed signal by manipulating the general level of the observer's motivation. Data presented in Appendix III show that the ROC curve obtained with a constant signal is quite insensitive to attempts to manipulate motivation.

A recent, unpublished revision of the theory does not incorporate the concept of variable sensitivity. In its modified form, the theory is basically similar to that of Luce. The predictions of the theory for sequential effects will be developed further; present plans do not call for further development of stimulus aspects of the theory (Atkinson, personal communication, 1964).

5.7 CONCLUSIONS

There may be a sensory threshold. One of the low-threshold theories is consistent with all the data collected to date. The other two low-threshold theories are consistent with most of the data, and could be made consistent with all available data by removing a restriction placed on them to facilitate the study of learning processes in detection. There may be several (quantal) thresholds; experimental evidence does not clearly distinguish between a continuous representation of signal magnitude and a discrete representation with several states.

On the other hand, the existence of a sensory threshold has not been demonstrated. Furthermore—and this is the moral of the story—the threshold that is tenable is not compatible with several commonly used forms of the classical psychophysical methods. A threshold likely to be exceeded in the absence of a signal is not measured by the yes-no forms of the methods of limits or constants without a large number of blank trials, nor by means of the correction for chance success.

The classical view of the threshold, the explicit high-threshold theory, and early forms of neural-quantum theory can be contrasted with the low-threshold theories and detection theory. The evidence favors the latter position. The low-threshold theories (including recent adaptations of quantal theory) and detection theory agree in prescribing presentation of a large number of blank trials, in order to obtain a good estimate of the probability of a false-alarm response, and they agree on the fundamental importance of using this estimate to isolate effectively judgmental factors from the index of sensitivity. The yes-no experiments conducted in the framework of detection theory have typically included as many blank trials as signal trials, and Luce (personal communication, 1964) has observed that the rapid rise of the initial segment of the ROC curve suggests measuring false alarms even more accurately than hits. If it were shown that many thresholds exist, the measurement procedures stipulated by detection theory would be unaffected.

Although tenable, a low threshold has not been shown to be a good building block for a quantitative science. None of the low-threshold theories supplies, for more than one psychophysical procedure, a means of accurately estimating the signal strength that corresponds to the threshold. Two of them give promise of illuminating learning processes in the detection setting, but in their present forms the low-threshold theories do not provide an adequate basis for experimentation on substantive problems in sensory psychology.

PROBLEMS

5.1 Apply the correction for chance to the data points shown in Fig. 5-2a. Do the resulting data points agree with those shown in Fig. 5-2b?

5.2 Two experiments have been conducted recently to determine the adequacy of detection theory for visual signals presented on a low-intensity or zero-intensity background. Nachmias and Steinman (1963) found their empirical ROC plots to be fitted very well by straight lines on probability scales. Hohle (1965) plotted his ROC data on linear scales and found them to be in better agreement with the straight-line prediction of high-threshold theory than with the curved-line prediction of detection theory. Refer to the original articles and attempt to resolve the conflict.

5.3 One can derive from physical-quantum theory the prediction that the variance of the signal distribution will increase as the mean of this distribution increases; that is, that σ_s/σ_n will increase with Δm. The hypothesized density functions of the theory are Poisson distributions, for which the variance is equal to the mean. The predicted rate of growth of σ_s/σ_n with Δm varies depending upon the mean assumed for the noise distribution, or the assumed average number of quanta absorbed from noise alone, and this number, in turn, depends upon the conditions of stimulation: whether the signal is presented to the fovea or the periphery of the retina, and whether the signal is presented against a dark background ("absolute") or as an increment to a standard stimulus ("increment").

Nachmias (unpublished) has collected data in the three conditions: "foveal absolute," "foveal increment," and "peripheral absolute." Listing Δm first, and σ_s/σ_n second, the values he obtained are as follows: Foveal absolute: (0.35, 1.00), (0.45, 1.15), (0.58, 1.26), (0.70, 1.18), (0.75, 1.23), (0.78, 1.17), (1.00, 1.48), (1.15, 1.42), (1.15, 1.40), (1.17, 1.23), (1.40, 1.48), (1.55, 1.45), (1.87, 1.45), (1.95, 1.60), (2.10, 1.58), (2.30, 1.30), (2.45, 1.60), and (2.70, 1.45). Foveal increment: (0.40, 1.18), (0.45, 1.38), (0.55, 1.15), (0.85, 1.13), (0.85, 1.27), and (1.85, 1.47). Peripheral absolute: (0.97, 1.13), (1.15, 1.45), (1.90, 1.48), (2.17, 1.75), and (3.45, 1.90).

Plot these data, keying differently the points for the three different conditions of stimulation. (a) Does the relationship between σ_s/σ_n and Δm depend in a systematic way on the condition of stimulation? (b) Which integer value of k in the equation $\Delta m/\Delta \sigma_s = k$ provides the best fit to all of the data?

5.4   It was stated in the discussion of two-state theory (in Section 7.6.2) that if two-limb ROC curves are fitted to empirical ROC data, one finds that the intersection of the two lines moves to the left as signal strength increases; that is, the false-alarm proportion at the intersection declines as signal strength increases. How might one account for this result in terms of the two-state theory?

Part II

Sensory Processes
in Detection

Chapter 6 defines detectors that are ideal with respect to sensitivity for a variety of detection situations; the situations differ in the amount of information that the detector is assumed to have about signal parameters. The explicit, quantitative models specified in this way are compared with human performance in Chapter 7. Specifically, the shapes of psychometric functions that are obtained in simple detection experiments and in increment-detection experiments are compared with predictions from two models, one involving a cross-correlation process and the other an envelope-detection process. A third model, based on an energy-detection process, is discussed in more detail in a separate chapter; Chapter 8 presents the statistics of this model and the results of its application to a variety of psychoacoustic data.

6

Theory of Ideal Observers

6.1 INTRODUCTION

A concept of central importance in detection theory is that of an ideal or optimal detector. Such a concept serves as an absolute standard of reference by which human performance can be evaluated and, since different devices are optimal for different situations, the analysis provides a means of comparing human performance with a variety of different nonoptimal detection devices. The chapter begins with a review of the basic principles of ideal-detector analysis.

Basic to any model of any detection system is how the noise waveform is represented. Once this representation of the noise is given, the optimal or ideal detectors are derived for a variety of specific detection situations. These derivations should dispel any impression that there is only one ideal detector. There are many; the adjective "ideal" refers to the best possible performance in detecting signals under specified conditions. For example, we can study the detection of signals of an exactly specified (exactly known) waveform, detection of sinusoids of random phase, detection of signals that are samples of noise, and so forth. Each detection situation, which is characterized by the detector's knowledge or uncertainty about certain signal parameters, requires a different detector to achieve optimal performance. Since the optimal detection device is determined from a knowledge of the signal parameters, we can anticipate that signal uncertainty leads to a decrement, even in this optimal performance. Finally, criticisms of this general approach are considered. Because these criticisms have been of a fundamental nature, they receive careful discussion. Most

151

of the criticisms center on the stochastic process used to represent the noise. We therefore take particular pains to clarify the exact assumptions made in our representation of the noise waveforms.

A question that commonly arises when optimal detection systems are discussed is why we should be interested in ideal observers. Why should we study ideal observers when we are really interested in describing a real observer? The reply to that question is that ideal detectors serve as baselines, as standards of comparison, for human detection performance. If a change in the stimulus situation makes the signal harder to detect for the ideal observer, then we shall not be surprised if the same change makes the signal harder to detect for the human observer. The principle is parsimony—it is unnecessary to invent psychological mechanisms to explain a change that may be traced to the stimulus situation itself. Naturally, if the ideal detectors were particularly esoteric or unusual, then their applicability to real observers would probably be minimal. But when the ideal observers for the three situations discussed in this chapter turn out to be (1) a cross-correlation receiver, (2) an envelope detector, and (3) an energy detector, it is clear that they are both germane and interesting.

The emphasis in this chapter is on auditory detection. Among the early papers on this topic are those by Marill (1956), Tanner and Birdsall (1958), and Tanner, Clarke, and Birdsall (1960). An article by Tanner and Jones (1959) provides an introduction to the several studies in which the concept of ideal observers is applied to visual detection. Voelcker (1961) has applied the concept to sound lateralization, and Green, Wolf, and White (1959) have used it in studying the recognition of patterns in a matrix of dots.

6.2 BASIC PARADIGM OF IDEAL-DETECTOR ANALYSIS

To clarify the exact procedures involved in calculating what kind of signal processing is optimal or ideal for each particular situation, consider the following basic paradigm. The detection problem begins with an observed waveform, $x(t)$, defined over some finite interval of time, 0 to T. The detector must decide between two possible states of the world on the basis of this waveform; either the waveform arose from (1) n, noise alone, or (2) s, signal plus noise. The signal may be a single waveform or one of a number of possible waveforms. For the present, consider it to be a single definite waveform.

Our problem is to determine how the detector should process the waveform $x(t)$ so that the decision it makes will be optimum. We assume that our criterion for optimality is included among the broad set of objectives considered in Part I. If this is true, we know that the best detector will base its decisions on likelihood ratio or on some monotonic function of likelihood ratio.

We use the following notation: $f[x(t) \mid n]$ denotes the conditional density of $x(t)$ occurring when noise alone is present, and $f[x(t) \mid s]$ denotes the conditional density when signal plus noise is present. The likelihood ratio is, therefore

$$l[x(t)] = \frac{f[x(t) \mid s]}{f[x(t) \mid n]} \tag{6.1}$$

The ideal detector either computes $l[x(t)]$ or processes the waveform in such a way as to obtain a quantity that is monotonic with $l[x(t)]$. The likelihood ratio is a positive real number, even though it is a function of the waveform $x(t)$. Once the likelihood ratio is computed, it is compared with a decision criterion, and response S is made only if $l[x(t)]$ exceeds the criterion k. The hit and false-alarm probabilities are determined by the following integrals:

$$P(S \mid s) = \int_{k}^{+\infty} g\{l[x(t)] \mid s\} \, dl[x(t)]$$
$$P(S \mid n) = \int_{k}^{+\infty} g\{l[x(t)] \mid n\} \, dl[x(t)] \tag{6.2}$$

where $g\{l[x(t)] \mid s\}$ and $g\{l[x(t)] \mid n\}$ are the conditional density functions for the likelihood ratio of the waveform $x(t)$, given s or n.

In principle, then, the basic paradigm used to evaluate an ideal detector is as follows.

(1) Determine the densities under each hypothesis, $f[x(t) \mid n]$ and $f[x(t) \mid s]$.

(2) Determine likelihood ratio $l[x(t)] = f[x(t) \mid s]/f[x(t) \mid n]$, or a function $z[x(t)]$ which is monotonic with $l[x(t)]$.

(3) Determine $P(S \mid s)$ and $P(S \mid n)$, which are obtained by integrating either $g[l(x) \mid s]$ and $g[l(x) \mid n]$ or the conditional densities of z, $f(z \mid s)$ and $f(z \mid n)$.

Steps 1 and 2 are sufficient to determine how the waveform should be processed. Step 3 is essential in evaluating the performance of the ideal detectors, that is, in relating the probabilities of the various decisions to the physical parameters of signal and noise. The basic paradigm will be followed for each of the specific situations considered in Section 6.5. Before we proceed to this analysis, however, we must explain in some detail our representation of signal and noise waveforms.

6.3   REPRESENTATION OF NOISE

We now present a model of the noise used in psychoacoustic experiments. We denote the actual waveform used in any experiment as $x(t)$. Our representation, a stochastic process, is a model of this waveform, and we denote it $\hat{x}(t)$ to indicate that it is an approximation of the real waveform. For a brief discussion of stochastic waveforms, see Appendix II.

It should not be surprising that the noise waveform, like other waveforms, can be expressed either in time or in frequency, that is, as $\hat{x}(t)$ or as $\hat{y}(f)$. We shall go to some length to spell out very clearly the exact form of the representation in both the time and frequency domains, since any answers we compute will only be as good as is our approximation $\hat{x}(t)$ to the real waveform $x(t)$. For some problems the quality of the approximation is best judged by considering the temporal representation of the waveform; for other problems the frequency representation is most convenient.

The basic idea behind our representation is as follows. Imagine a noise waveform, filtered by a band-limited device such as an amplifier or the earphones in a psychoacoustic experiment. Figure 6-1 displays a typical waveform. Because the waveform is filtered, we do not expect any very high-frequency components to be present. The illustrated filtered waveform, for example, might well arise by passing noise through a 500-cps low-pass filter. The 1000-cycle-per-second waveform sketched in Fig. 6-1 shows a much faster variation as a function of time than any part of the sampled noise waveform. A direct implication of the predominantly low-frequency content of the waveform is that two values of the waveform taken at sufficiently small separations in time will be very nearly the same. Thus if $t_1 - t_0$ is sufficiently small, the value $x(t_1)$ will be almost perfectly predictable from a knowledge of $x(t_0)$. This fact suggests that we might try to approximate the entire waveform by specifying only a finite number of points along the waveform. It is plausible that the density of points (number of points per unit time) will be directly proportional to the highest-frequency component present in the waveform.

Those familiar with the early work in information theory will recognize the similarity of the previous argument to the idea implicit in the so-called sampling theorems (Nyquist, 1924; Hartley, 1928; Gabor, 1946; Shannon, 1949; Shannon and Weaver, 1949). These theorems prove that if $x(t)$ contains no frequencies higher than W, then $x(t)$ can be exactly reconstructed from the value of the waveform at discrete, equally spaced intervals in time. This theorem cannot be invoked for the case that we are considering here, since we are dealing with waveforms defined over a finite interval $(0, T)$ rather than over the infinite interval $(-\infty, +\infty)$. Since we do not know the sample values over the infinite interval, we cannot exactly reconstruct the waveform during the finite interval in question. Nevertheless, for the purposes of psychoacoustics, a finite representation of the waveform may be sufficiently detailed to allow us to calculate interesting answers. For the following discussion we assume that only frequencies up to W cps are present in the noise waveform, and we use a finite Fourier

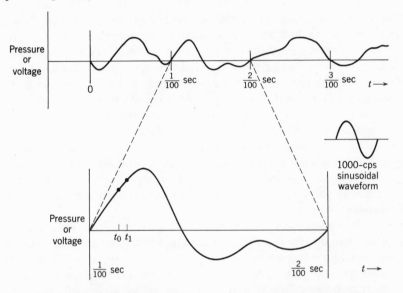

FIG. 6-1 An intuitive justification of the sampling theorem. The waveform at the top of the figure contains no frequency higher than 1000 cycles per second. In the second part of the figure we draw an expanded version of this same waveform. The value of the waveform is essentially the same at two successive time intervals if the interval chosen is small enough, for instance t_0 and t_1. The ability to predict the value of the waveform at t_1 from the knowledge of its value at t_0 suggests that a finite number of points might be sufficient to contain all the information in the waveform.

series to represent the noise. From the finite-frequency representation, we develop an equivalent representation based on the value of the waveform at equally spaced intervals in time.

6.3.1 Frequency representation

We use the following model of Gaussian noise:

$$\hat{x}(t) = \sum_{k=1}^{WT} a_k \cos \frac{2\pi}{T} kt + b_k \sin \frac{2\pi}{T} kt \qquad 0 \le t \le T \qquad (6.3)$$

where

$$a_k = \frac{2}{T} \int_0^T x(t) \cos \frac{2\pi}{T} kt \, dt$$

and

$$b_k = \frac{2}{T} \int_0^T x(t) \sin \frac{2\pi}{T} kt \, dt$$

Thus, given any actual waveform $x(t)$ defined on the interval $(0, T)$, we can use Eq. 6.3 to develop $2WT$ constants a_k, b_k such that $\hat{x}(t)$ is approximately equal to $x(t)$. Furthermore, we assume that a_k, b_k are all independent Gaussian variables having mean zero and variance σ_k^2. In other words, we assume that $x(t)$ can be closely approximated by a finite Fourier series containing no term with frequency higher than W; the lowest frequency is $1/T$ and the frequency between successive components is equal to $1/T$. Note that we mean "approximate" in two different senses. First, we mean that we can determine $2WT$ constants, $a_1, a_2, \ldots, a_{WT}, b_1, b_2, \ldots, b_{WT}$, such that the difference between $\hat{x}(t)$ and $x(t)$ is small. Secondly, we mean that if we do so repeatedly, the constants a_k, b_k will be Gaussianly distributed with the correct mean and variance, and each constant will be independent of all others.

Since the variances of the constants, σ_k^2, are unspecified, let us choose them so that the finite series will have a second moment that closely approximates the second moment of $x(t)$. Most noise in psychoacoustic experiments generates approximately equal power in equal frequency intervals throughout the spectrum, at least up to some high frequency W (see Appendix II). Thus $x(t)$ measured across a 1-ohm resistor will have a total noise power of approximately $N_0 W$, where N_0 is the noise power in a 1-cps band. Since $\hat{x}(t)$ should mimic $x(t)$, we want

$$E\left\{\frac{1}{T} \int_0^T [\hat{x}(t)]^2 \, dt\right\} = WN_0 \tag{6.4}$$

or, writing $\hat{x}(t)$ as in Eq. 6.3 and expanding, we have*

$$[\hat{x}(t)]^2 = \sum_{k=1}^{WT} \frac{a_k^2}{2} + \sum_{k=1}^{WT} \left(\frac{a_k^2}{2}\right) \cos\left(\frac{2\pi}{T} 2kt\right)$$

$$+ \sum_{k=1}^{WT} \frac{b_k^2}{2} - \sum_{k=1}^{WT} \left(\frac{b_k^2}{2}\right) \cos\left(\frac{2\pi}{T} 2kt\right)$$

$$+ \sum_{j=1}^{WT} \sum_{k=1}^{WT} 2a_k b_j \left(\cos \frac{2\pi}{T} kt\right) \sin\left(\frac{2\pi}{T} jt\right) \qquad j \neq k \tag{6.5}$$

* We are using the following trigonometric identities: $\sin^2 \alpha = 1/2 - 1/2 \cos 2\alpha$, and $\cos^2 \alpha = 1/2 + 1/2 \cos 2\alpha$.

Since all but the first and third terms integrate to zero, the integral of $\hat{x}^2(t)$ is therefore

$$\int_0^T \hat{x}(t)^2 \, dt = \sum_{k=1}^{WT} \left(\frac{a_k^2}{2} + \frac{b_k^2}{2} \right) T \tag{6.6}$$

Now, using Eq. 6.4, we have

$$E\left[\frac{1}{T} \int_0^T \hat{x}^2(t) \, dt \right] = \frac{1}{T} WT \left[E\left(\frac{a_k^2}{2} \right) + E\left(\frac{b_k^2}{2} \right) \right] T = WN_0$$

Thus $E(a_k^2/2) + E(b_k^2/2) = N_0/T$. Since, by assumption, $E(a_k^2) = E(b_k^2)$,

$$E(a_k^2) = \frac{N_0}{T} = E(b_k^2) \tag{6.7}$$

Thus, because $E(a_k) = E(b_k) = 0$, we must set $\sigma_k^2 = N_0/T$ in order for the second moments of the random variables a_k, b_k to have the desired values.

The average power at the sine part of the kth component is $E(a_k^2/2) = N_0/2T$ and the average power at the cosine part of the kth component is $E(b_k^2/2) = N_0/2T$; thus the total power at that component, sine plus cosine part, is N_0/T. There are WT components in all, and therefore, N_0W is the total average power of the noise.

6.3.2 Temporal representation

We next develop a more intuitive representation of the process $\hat{x}(t)$. This representation, a temporal one, will be useful in our later discussion of ideal detectors. From the Fourier-series representation we may derive a set of functions $\Psi_m(t)$, $m = 1, 2, \ldots, 2WT$, as follows:

$$\Psi_m(t) = \sum_{n=1}^{WT} a(m)_n \cos \frac{2\pi}{T} nt + b(m)_n \sin \frac{2\pi}{T} nt \qquad 0 < t < T$$

where

$$a(m)_n = \frac{2}{T} \int_0^T \Psi_m(t) \cos \frac{2\pi}{T} nt \, dt$$

$$b(m)_n = \frac{2}{T} \int_0^T \Psi_m(t) \sin \frac{2\pi}{T} nt \, dt \tag{6.8}$$

The functions $\Psi_m(t)$ are called *interpolation functions* for reasons that will become apparent. For our purposes, we need know only two properties of the interpolation functions. The first property concerns the value of the interpolation function at equally spaced intervals in time. These equally spaced intervals occur at each $1/2W$ seconds, and there are $m = 2WT$ intervals in all. The mth interpolation function is, it so happens, unity at the mth time period. Further, it is zero at all the other periods; that is,

$$\Psi_m\left(\frac{m}{2W}\right) = 1.0 \qquad m = 1, 2, \ldots, 2WT$$

$$\Psi_m\left(\frac{n}{2W}\right) = 0 \qquad m \neq n \quad m = 1, 2, \ldots, 2WT$$

$$n = 1, 2, \ldots, 2WT$$

Now since both $\Psi_m(t)$ and $\hat{x}(t)$ can be written in terms of the same set of sinusoidal components, we can write $\hat{x}(t)$ in terms of $\Psi_m(t)$, for instance,

$$\hat{x}(t) = \sum_{m=1}^{2WT} h_m \Psi_m(t) \tag{6.9}$$

where h_m can be determined from Eqs. 6.3 and 6.8. To see how this is done, consider the function $\hat{x}(t)$ at equally spaced points in time ($t = 1/2W$, $2/2W, \ldots, i/2W, \ldots, 2WT/2W$). Using these sample points successively, we may determine each of the constants h_m of Eq. 6.9. For example,

$$\hat{x}(1/2W) = h_1 1 + h_2 \cdot 0 + \cdots + h_i 0 + \cdots + h_m \cdot 0 = h_1$$

$$\hat{x}(2/2W) = h_1 0 + h_2 \cdot 1 + \cdots + h_i 0 + \cdots + h_m \cdot 0 = h_2 \tag{6.10}$$

$$\hat{x}(i/2W) = h_1 0 + h_2 \cdot 0 + \cdots + h_i 1 + \cdots + h_m \cdot 0 = h_i$$

because of the peculiar property of the functions $\Psi_m(t)$. We see now why $\Psi_m(t)$ is called an interpolation function. We can write $\hat{x}(t)$ in the following way:

$$\hat{x}(t) = \sum_{m=1}^{2WT} \hat{x}\left(\frac{m}{2W}\right)\Psi_m(t) \tag{6.11}$$

This representation is analogous to the Fourier-series representation except that the constant terms of the series, $\hat{x}(m/2W)$, are simply the values of the waveform $\hat{x}(t)$ at $m = 2WT$ different points in time. The functions, $\Psi_m(t)$, interpolate between these equally spaced values.

A second property of the interpolation functions is that they are orthogonal; that is

$$\int_0^T \Psi_m(t)\Psi_n(t)\, dt = 0 \qquad \text{for} \quad m \neq n$$

$$\int_0^T \Psi_m^2(t)\, dt = \frac{1}{2W} \qquad \text{for} \quad \text{all } m \tag{6.12}$$

This property, along with Eqs. 6.3 and 6.9, allows one to determine the probability density of the temporal sample values $x(i/2W)$. Consider the two representations of $\hat{x}(t)$, Eqs. 6.3 and 6.11:

$$\sum_{m=1}^{2WT} \hat{x}\left(\frac{m}{2W}\right)\Psi_m(t) = \sum_{k=1}^{WT} a_k \cos\frac{2\pi}{T}kt + b_k \sin\frac{2\pi}{T}kt \qquad 0 < t < T \quad (6.13)$$

Now, if we multiply each side of Eq. 6.13 by $\Psi_m(t)$, and then integrate from 0 to T, by the orthogonality property of $\Psi_m(t)$,

$$\hat{x}(m/2W)\frac{1}{2W} = \sum_{k=1}^{WT} a_k \int_0^T \Psi_m(t)\cos\frac{2\pi}{T}kt\,dt + b_k\int_0^T \Psi_m(t)\cos\frac{2\pi}{T}kt\,dt$$

$$(6.14a)$$

But according to Eq. 6.8 the integrals are equal to the constants $a(m)_k T/2$ and $b(m)_k T/2$; thus we may write

$$\hat{x}(m/2W)\frac{1}{2W} = \sum_{k=1}^{WT}\left[a_k a(m)_k \frac{T}{2} + b_k b(m)_k \frac{T}{2}\right] \qquad (6.14b)$$

The temporal sample $\hat{x}(m/2W)$ is therefore a linear function of the Gaussian variables a_k and b_k; hence $\hat{x}(m/2W)$ is Gaussian.

Let us determine the parameters of this Gaussian variable. The expected value of $\hat{x}(m/2W)$ is easily calculated from Eq. 6.14b:

$$E[x(m/2W)] = WT\sum_{k=1}^{WT} a(m)_k E(a_k) + b(m)_k E(b_k) = 0 \qquad (6.15)$$

The variance of $\hat{x}(m/2W)$ is, therefore, $E\{[\hat{x}(m/2W)]^2\}$, and it too can be calculated from Eq. 6.14b:

$$E\left\{\left[\hat{x}\left(\frac{m}{2W}\right)\right]^2\right\} = W^2T^2 E\left\{\sum_{k=1}^{WT}[a_k a(m)_k + b_k b(m)_k]^2\right\}$$

$$= W^2T^2 E\left[\sum_{k=1}^{WT} a_k^2 a^2(m)_k + \sum_{k=1}^{WT} b_k^2 b^2(m)_k\right.$$

$$\left. + 2\sum_{k\neq j}^{WT}\sum^{WT} a_k a(m)_k b_j b(m)_k\right] \qquad (6.16)$$

$$= W^2T^2 \sum_{k=1}^{WT}[a^2(m)_k E(a_k^2) + b^2(m)_k E(b_k^2)]$$

$$= W^2T^2 \frac{N_0}{T}\sum_{k=1}^{WT} a^2(m)_k + b^2(m)_k$$

But from Eq. 6.6 we know that a sum of squares of the coefficients of a Fourier series is proportional to the integral of the square of the function,

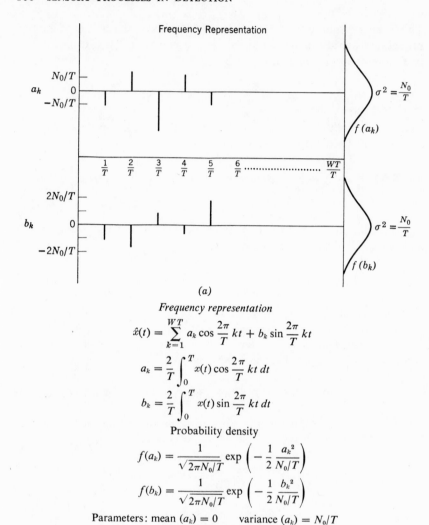

$$\hat{x}(t) = \sum_{k=1}^{WT} a_k \cos \frac{2\pi}{T} kt + b_k \sin \frac{2\pi}{T} kt$$

$$a_k = \frac{2}{T} \int_0^T x(t) \cos \frac{2\pi}{T} kt \, dt$$

$$b_k = \frac{2}{T} \int_0^T x(t) \sin \frac{2\pi}{T} kt \, dt$$

Probability density

$$f(a_k) = \frac{1}{\sqrt{2\pi N_0/T}} \exp \left(-\frac{1}{2} \frac{a_k^2}{N_0/T} \right)$$

$$f(b_k) = \frac{1}{\sqrt{2\pi N_0/T}} \exp \left(-\frac{1}{2} \frac{b_k^2}{N_0/T} \right)$$

Parameters: mean $(a_k) = 0$ variance $(a_k) = N_0/T$
mean $(b_k) = 0$ variance $(b_k) = N_0/T$
a_k and b_k all independent

FIG. 6-2   Two equivalent representations of the waveform. Part (a) of the figure shows the finite frequency representation of the waveform. The waveform is represented by a Fourier series having a fundamental frequency of $1/T$ and containing the indicated value at all harmonics of this fundamental. The value of a_k is the contribution of the cosine component; the value of b_k is the contribution of the sine component. Given noise alone, the distribution of the values in frequency is assumed to be Gaussian with mean 0 and standard deviation $\sqrt{N_0/T}$. Part (b) of the figure shows a finite temporal representation of the waveform; that is simply the value of the waveform at successive, equally spaced intervals in time. The distribution of these samples is assumed to be Gaussian with mean 0 and variance WN_0.

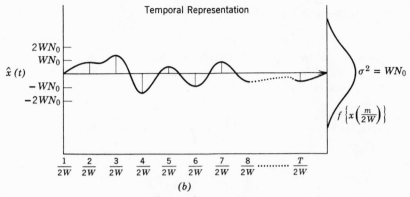

(b)
Temporal representation

$$\hat{x}(t) = \sum_{m=1}^{2WT} \hat{x}\left(\frac{m}{2W}\right) \Psi_m(t)$$

$$f\left\{x\left(\frac{m}{2W}\right)\right\} = \frac{1}{\sqrt{2\pi N_0 W}} \exp\left\{-\frac{1}{2}\frac{\left[x\left(\frac{m}{2W}\right)\right]^2}{N_0 W}\right\}$$

Parameters: mean $\left\{x\left(\frac{m}{2W}\right)\right\} = 0$ variance $\left\{x\left(\frac{m}{2W}\right)\right\} = N_0 W$

all $\left\{x\left(\frac{m}{2W}\right)\right\}$ are independent of one another

FIG. 6-2   (*concluded*).

and from Eq. 6.12 we know that this integral is equal to $1/2W$; that is,

$$\sum_{k=1}^{WT} a^2(m)_k + b^2(m)_k = \frac{2}{T}\int_0^T \Psi_m{}^2(t)\,dt = \frac{1}{WT} \qquad (6.17)$$

Using this result in Eq. 6.16 we obtain, finally,

$$E\left\{\left[\hat{x}\left(\frac{m}{2W}\right)\right]^2\right\} = W^2 T^2 \frac{N_0}{T}\cdot\frac{1}{WT} = WN_0 \qquad (6.18)$$

Furthermore, one can demonstrate that different sample points $\hat{x}(m/2W)$ and $\hat{x}(n/2W)$ are independent, since they are Gaussian and the expected value of the cross product is zero.

We have therefore established two equivalent but different ways to describe the sample space used to generate the stochastic process $\hat{x}(t)$. Figure 6-2a, b gives a summary of these two representations along with the probability densities, and parameters, of the representation.

6.4   REPRESENTATION OF SIGNAL

We assume that the signals we wish to investigate can be represented in the same way as the noise. If the signal is some fixed and definite waveform, such as a sinusoid of fixed amplitude, frequency, and phase, we assume that it can be represented as

$$s(t) = \sum_{n=1}^{WT} \left[a_n \cos \left(\frac{2\pi}{T} n t \right) + b_n \sin \left(\frac{2\pi}{T} n t \right) \right]$$

or

$$s(t) = \sum_{i=1}^{WT} s \left(\frac{i}{2W} \right) \Psi_i(t) \tag{6.19}$$

where s_i is the value of the signal at the ith temporal sample interval, $s_i = s(i/2W)$. If the signal is from some stochastic process, we assume that the sample space of the stochastic process can be specified in terms of the random variables a_n, b_n or in terms of $s(i/2W)$. Since we are assuming a 1-ohm impedance, the energy of the signal, E_s, is given by

$$E_s = \int_0^T s^2(t) \, dt = \sum_{i=1}^{WT} s_i^2 \, \Delta t = \frac{1}{2W} \sum_{i=1}^{WT} s_i^2 \tag{6.20}$$

6.5   IDEAL DETECTORS

In this section we derive the optimal detector for several specific detection tasks. That is, the basic paradigm is applied to several specific situations, situations that differ in the amount and kind of information the detector has about the signal. We shall emphasize those aspects of the derivation that are of general interest and, in particular, we emphasize how the detector's uncertainty about the signal parameters affects its performance.

6.5.1   Signal specified exactly

For the case of the signal specified exactly, the observed waveform, $x(t)$, is noise alone, or signal plus noise. The signal, $s(t)$, $0 < t < T$, is specified exactly and is known to the detector in the following sense. Using the temporal representation of the signal, the detector knows that if the signal is sent it will have a certain value $s_i = s(i/2W)$, $i = 1, 2, \ldots,$ $2WT$, at each of the sample points.

The density function for each hypothesis can now be expressed using the temporal representation of the waveform and equal-interval samples.

Consider a single sample point $x_m = x(m/2W)$. Given noise alone,

$$f\{x_m \mid n\} = \frac{1}{\sqrt{2\pi N_0 W}} \exp\left(-\frac{1}{2}\frac{x_m^2}{N_0 W}\right) \tag{6.21}$$

Given signal plus noise,

$$f\{x_m \mid s\} = \frac{1}{\sqrt{2\pi N_0 W}} \exp\left[-\frac{1}{2}\frac{(x_m - s_m)^2}{N_0 W}\right] \tag{6.22}$$

The total waveform $x(t)$ may be represented by the collection of sample values x_m, $m = 1, 2, 3, \ldots, 2WT$. The entire collection or vector has a probability density, given noise alone, of

$$f\{\hat{x}(t) \mid n\} = \prod_{m=1}^{2WT} f\{x_m \mid n\} \tag{6.23}$$

or, given signal plus noise, of

$$f\{\hat{x}(t) \mid s\} = \prod_{m=1}^{2WT} f\{x_m \mid s\} \tag{6.24}$$

We multiply the sample densities together because our representation makes each sample point independent of all others. The likelihood ratio is then

$$l[\hat{x}(t)] = \frac{f[\hat{x}(t) \mid s]}{f[\hat{x}(t) \mid n]} = \prod_{m=1}^{2WT} \exp\left(\frac{1}{2}\frac{x_m^2}{N_0 W}\right) \exp\left[-\frac{1}{2}\frac{(x_m - s_m)^2}{N_0 W}\right] \tag{6.25}$$

Taking the natural logarithm of likelihood ratio, and simplifying,

$$\ln l[x(t)] = \frac{1}{N_0 W}\left(\sum_{m=1}^{2WT} x_m s_m - \frac{1}{2}\sum_{m=1}^{2WT} s_m^2\right) \tag{6.26}$$

Because the term $\Sigma\, s_m^2$ is a constant, the cross correlation between the expected sample s_m and the received signal x_m is monotonic with likelihood ratio.* The optimal detection scheme for the signal specified exactly is therefore cross correlation between the expected signal and the received waveform. If the receiver computes the cross correlation and accepts the hypothesis that the signal was present only when the cross correlation is above some criterion value, it will be the optimal detector.

This result does not imply that some other receiver may not also be optimal. In fact, if we had used the Fourier-series representation of $x(t)$, we would have received a different configuration for the optimal detector.

---

* The cross correlation of two waveforms, $h(t)$, $0 < t < T$, and $g(t)$, $0 < t < T$, is the integral of the product of the two waveforms,

$$\int_0^T h(t)g(t)\, dt$$

(See Appendix II.)

Here the sample values a_k and b_k are Gaussianly distributed; a single sample, for example a_k, has the following distribution under each hypothesis. Given noise alone,

$$f[a_k \mid n] = \frac{1}{\sqrt{2\pi N_0/T}} \exp\left(-\frac{1}{2}\frac{a_k^2}{N_0/T}\right) \tag{6.27}$$

and given signal plus noise,

$$f(a_k \mid s) = \frac{1}{\sqrt{2\pi N_0/T}} \exp\left(-\frac{1}{2}\frac{(a_k - a_k^s)^2}{N_0/T}\right) \tag{6.28}$$

where a_k^s is the kth Fourier-series term in the representation of the signal. The densities for b_k are similar, except that b_k would replace a_k and b_k^s would replace a_k^s.

As in the previous derivation, the samples are independent, and thus the logarithm of likelihood ratio is

$$\ln l[x(t)] = \frac{T}{N_0}\left\{\sum_{k=1}^{WT} a_k a_k^s - \frac{1}{2}\sum_{k=1}^{WT}[a_k^s]^2 + \sum_{k=1}^{WT} b_k b_k^s - \frac{1}{2}\sum_{k=1}^{WT}[b_k^s]^2\right\} \tag{6.29}$$

Once more the optimal detector cross-correlates the received signal, represented by a_i, b_i, $i = 1, 2, 3, \ldots, WT$, with the expected signal, represented by a_i^s and b_i^s, but the elements of the cross product come from the frequency domain rather than the time domain.

Often the expected signal $s(t)$ is of such a form that a filter can be constructed so that the response of the filter $h(t)$ to an impulse is equal to the expected signal played backward in time; that is,

$$h(t) = s(T - t) \tag{6.30}$$

When this is the case, we can proceed as follows: the response $y(t)$ of the filter to an input voltage $x(t)$ is known to be*

$$y(T) = \int_{-\infty}^{T} x(\alpha)h(T - \alpha)\, d\alpha \tag{6.31}$$

If we gate into this filter the observed waveform, we produce as an input to the filter:

$$x(t) = x(t) \qquad 0 \leq t \leq T$$
$$x(t) = 0 \qquad \text{otherwise} \tag{6.32}$$

The output is determined by letting $x(t)$ replace $x(\alpha)$ in Eq. 6.31, and also substituting $s(\alpha) = h(T - \alpha)$, as Eq. 6.30 indicates; then

$$y(T) = \int_{-\infty}^{T} x(\alpha)s(\alpha)\, d\alpha \tag{6.33}$$

---

* For those who are not familiar with filters and filter theory, Chapter 13 of Lee (1960) is highly recommended.

is the desired cross product. This is called "matched filtering," and it illustrates a filtering technique to detect a signal specified exactly.

All three of these techniques—cross correlation in time, cross correlation in frequency, and matched filtering—compute a quantity that is monotonic with likelihood ratio; thus they are all optimal detectors.

Now let us evaluate the performance of these detectors. Likelihood ratio is monotonic with the following quantity:

$$z = \sum_{m=1}^{2WT} x_m s_m \tag{6.34}$$

Therefore, we need to determine the distribution of z under both hypotheses. This is not difficult since z is a sum of Gaussian variables x_i; thus we know that z is Gaussian.

Given noise alone,

$$E(x_i) = 0, \qquad E(x_i^2) = N_0 W$$

Therefore

$$E(z_n) = 0 \quad \text{and} \quad \text{var } z_n = E(z_n - 0)^2 = N_0 W \sum_{i=1}^{2WT} s_i^2$$

Now, since

$$\sum_{i=1}^{2WT} s_i^2 = 2WE_s$$

it follows that

$$\text{var } (z_n) = 2W^2 N_0 E_s \tag{6.35}$$

Given signal plus noise,

$$E(x_i) = s_i \quad \text{and} \quad E(x_i - s_i)^2 = N_0 W$$

Then

$$E(z_s) = \sum_{m=1}^{2WT} E(x_m) s_m = \sum_{m=1}^{2WT} s_m^2 = 2WE_s$$

$$\text{var } (z_s) = E \left(\sum_{m=1}^{2WT} x_m s_m - \sum_{m=1}^{2WT} s_m^2 \right)^2 = \sum_{m=1}^{2WT} s_m^2 E(x_m - s_m)^2 = 2W^2 N_0 E_s \tag{6.36}$$

The difference in the means divided by the common standard deviation, d', is a convenient quantity:

$$d' = \Delta m / \sigma = \frac{2WE_s}{\sqrt{2N_0 W^2 E_s}} = \sqrt{\frac{2E_s}{N_0}} \tag{6.37}$$

We have now related the signal energy, E_s, and the noise power density, N_0, to the distributions of signal and noise on a decision axis that is monotonic with likelihood ratio. For this signal-specified-exactly case, the distributions are Gaussian and have equal variance. We therefore can predict the shape of the ROC curve and the percentage correct in 2AFC from a knowledge of the physical parameters of the signal (Eq. 6.37). This relation, Eq. 6.37, is for the ideal detector of the signal specified exactly. To see how these predictions depend upon details of the detection system, we must investigate other detectors, each ideal but possessing less information about the exact character of the signal.

6.5.2 Signal specified statistically

Often the signal is not a single, known waveform, but only one from a particular class of waveforms. We assume that members of this class are selected at random and that each member is used with equal probability as the signal. In this section we discuss the ideal detection of such statistically specified signals. Actually, the detector's uncertainty about the signal presents no new problem to analysis other than complication.

Suppose that the signal is known up to some parameter, α, which is distributed according to some density function, $g(\alpha)$. That is, $g(\alpha_0)\,d\alpha_0$ is the probability that the signal parameter is α_0, and hence that the signal waveform is $s(t, \alpha_0)$.

Given the waveform $x(t)$, the probability density of the waveform given noise alone is, by definition,

$$f[x(t)\,|\,n] \tag{6.38}$$

Suppose that the observed waveform $x(t)$ has a signal added to it and suppose that the signal parameter is α; then the probability density of the waveform conditional on the parameter α is

$$f[x(t)\,|\,s(t,\alpha)] = f[x(t) - s(t,\alpha)\,|\,n] \tag{6.39}$$

This equation for the conditional density may need some explanation. The waveform $x(t)$ is either noise alone or signal plus noise. If $x(t)$ is signal plus noise and we subtract the signal from $x(t)$, we are left with noise, so that the conditional density is the same as if noise alone had been presented. Since α occurs with probability $g(\alpha)\,d\alpha$, we may also write

$$f[x(t)\,|\,s] = \int_{\alpha} f[x(t) - s(t,\alpha)\,|\,n]g(\alpha)\,d\alpha \tag{6.40}$$

where the integration is over all the possible signals. If α is discrete, a summation would be used.

Once the density of the waveform given the signal parameter is obtained, the likelihood ratio is determined, and the performance of the detector is evaluated as we discussed in the basic paradigm.

6.5.2.1 SIGNAL SPECIFIED EXACTLY EXCEPT FOR PHASE. Suppose that the signal is a sinusoid of known and fixed frequency but of unknown phase; that is, let

$$s(t) = A \cos (2\pi l t - \theta) \qquad (6.41)$$

where A is the amplitude of the signal, l is the frequency, and θ the phase.* The probability density of the unknown parameter θ is

$$g(\theta) = \frac{1}{2\pi} \qquad 0 < \theta < 2\pi \qquad (6.42)$$

The frequency representation, rather than temporal representation, of the noise will be used; thus, let us express the signal in these terms:

$$s(t) = a_l(\theta) \cos 2\pi l t + b_l(\theta) \sin 2\pi l t \qquad (6.43)$$

where

$$a_l(\theta) = A \cos \theta \qquad \text{and} \quad b_l(\theta) = A \sin \theta$$

and

$$\frac{a_l^2(\theta) + b_l^2(\theta)}{2} = \frac{A^2}{2} = \frac{E_s}{T}$$

Using the Fourier-series form for noise (Eq. 6.3), the density function given noise alone is

$$f[\hat{x}(t) \mid n] = \prod_{k=1}^{WT} f(a_k) f(b_k) \qquad (6.44)$$

where $f(a_k)$ and $f(b_k)$ are the densities of the random variables a_k and b_k. They are Gaussian, independent, and have mean zero and variance N_0/T (see Eq. 6.27).

The density function given signal plus noise can be obtained by applying Eq. 6.40 to this specific case:

$$f[\hat{x}(t) \mid s] = \int_0^{2\pi} \prod_{k \neq l}^{WT} f(a_k) f[a_l - a_l(\theta)] f(b_k) f[b_l - b_l(\theta)] \frac{1}{2\pi} d\theta \qquad (6.45)$$

The likelihood ratio (using Eqs. 6.27 and 6.28) is

$$l[x(t)] = \frac{1}{2\pi} \int_0^{2\pi} \exp \left\{ + \frac{2[a_l a_l(\theta) + b_l b_l(\theta)]T}{2N_0} \right\}$$

$$\times \exp \left\{ - \frac{[a_l^2(\theta) + b_l^2(\theta)]T}{2N_0} \right\} d\theta$$

* We shall use the symbol l to denote frequency, as well as likelihood ratio, throughout this section.

and, using Eq. 6.43,

$$l[x(t)] = \frac{1}{2\pi} \int_0^{2\pi} \exp\left\{ + \frac{2[a_l a_l(\theta) + b_l b_l(\theta)]T}{2N_0} \right\} \exp\left(-\frac{E_s}{N_0}\right) d\theta \quad (6.46)$$

The components of the observation, a_l, b_l, at the signal frequency can be used to express the observed component in terms of an amplitude and phase, as follows:

$$a_l \cos 2\pi l t + b_l \sin 2\pi l t = x_l \cos (2\pi l t - \gamma)$$

where
$$a_l = x_l \cos \gamma \quad \text{and} \quad b_l = x_l \sin \gamma \quad (6.47)$$

Combining this with the signal, Eq. 6.43, we see that

$$a_l a_l(\theta) + b_l b_l(\theta) = x_l A \cos (\theta - \gamma)$$

Using this in Eq. 6.46, we have

$$l[x(t)] = \frac{1}{2\pi} \int_0^{2\pi} \exp\left[\frac{2x_l AT}{2N_0} \cos (\theta - \gamma)\right] \exp\left(-\frac{E_s}{N_0}\right) d\theta$$

Now, by definition,

$$I_0(x) = \frac{1}{2\pi} \int_0^{2\pi} e^{x \cos \theta} d\theta$$

where $I_0(x)$ is the modified Bessel function of zero order. $I_0(x)$ is a monotonically increasing function of x; some values are: $I_0(0) = 1.0$; $I_0(1) = 1.26$; $I_0(2) = 2.27$; $I_0(5) = 27.2$; $I_0(10) = 281.6$. (See Abramowitz and Stegun, 1965, p. 374, Fig. 9-7.)

Thus, using this definition, we may write

$$l[\hat{x}(t)] = I_0\left(\frac{x_l AT}{N_0}\right) \exp\left(-\frac{E_s}{N_0}\right) \quad (6.48)$$

Now, since I_0 is strictly monotonically increasing, we see that the likelihood ratio is a monotonic function of x_l, the magnitude of the sinusoid at the frequency of the signal. The quantity x_l is the envelope of the waveform at the signal frequency (see Appendix II). This result should surprise no one; if signal phase is unknown but signal frequency is known, then an optimal procedure is to measure the magnitude of the sinusoid at the signal frequency. The magnitude is independent of phase and is monotonic with likelihood ratio.

Next we shall derive the density of this envelope, x_l, under each hypothesis. The derivation is somewhat tedious, but because this approach is unfamiliar to many, we proceed very slowly.

6.5.2.1.1 *Given noise alone.* The distribution of x_l, the amplitude of the sinusoid at the kth frequency, can be determined from the densities of

a_l and b_l. Using Eq. 6.47 we see that

$$x_l^2 = a_l^2 + b_l^2 \tag{6.49}$$

The square of a normalized Gaussian variable is chi square with one degree of freedom (Appendix I) and the sum is a chi-square distribution with two degrees of freedom; that is,

$$f\{(x_l/\sigma)^2 \mid n\} = \tfrac{1}{2}e^{-\frac{1}{2}[x_l/\sigma]^2} \tag{6.50}$$

Now we want the density of the envelope x_l, not $t = (x_l/\sigma)^2$. Given that the density of t is $f(t)$ and that $t = g(x)$, then the density of x is $f_R(x_l) = f(t)\left|\dfrac{dt}{dx}\right|$. Thus

$$f_R(x_l) = f(t)\left|\frac{dt}{dx}\right| = \frac{1}{2}\exp\left\{\left[-\frac{1}{2}\left(\frac{x_l}{\sigma}\right)^2\right]\frac{2x_l}{\sigma^2}\right\} = \frac{x_l}{\sigma^2}\exp\left[-\frac{1}{2}\left(\frac{x_l}{\sigma}\right)^2\right] \tag{6.51}$$

This distribution is known as the Rayleigh distribution in honor of Lord Rayleigh* (see Appendix II).

6.5.2.1.2 *Given signal plus noise.* When a signal is added to the noise, the amplitude of the observed envelope, x_l, depends on the phase angle between the signal and noise. Since the phase angle of the noise is im-material, we might set it equal to zero. Then, to find the density of this resultant, using Eq. 6.40, we wish to evaluate

$$f(x_l \mid s) = \int_0^{2\pi} f_R(x_l - A\cos\theta)\frac{1}{2\pi}\,d\theta \tag{6.52}$$

Direct integration is difficult, and thus we use the following approach to lighten our labors. Recall that

$$l[x(t)] = \frac{f[x(t) \mid s]}{f[x(t) \mid n]}$$

and, as long as $f[x(t) \mid n]$ is never zero,

$$f[x(t) \mid s] = l[x(t)]f[x(t) \mid n]$$

For the case at hand, $l[x(t)]$ is the same as $l(x_l)$; that is, only the magnitude of the envelope at the frequency l affects likelihood ratio. Thus $f[x_l \mid s] = l[x_l]f[x_l \mid n]$ and, specifically,

$$f[x_l \mid s] = I_0\left(\frac{x_l A T}{N_0}\right)\exp\left[-\frac{E_s}{N_0}\right]\frac{x_l}{\sigma^2}\exp\left[-\frac{1}{2}\left(\frac{x_l}{\sigma}\right)^2\right] \tag{6.53}$$

* See Rayleigh (1894, p. 40), Davenport and Root (1958, p. 161), and Jeffress (1964, p. 766).

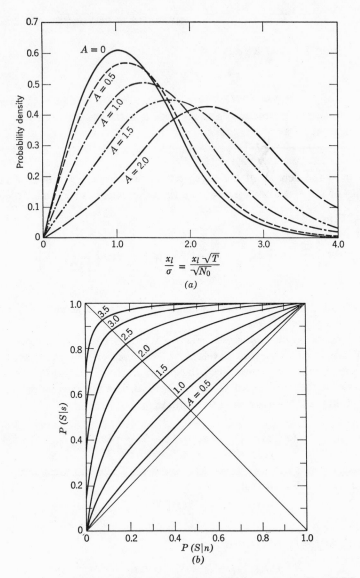

FIG. 6-3 The distribution function and the corresponding ROC curve for the envelope detector. Part (a) of the figure shows the probability density of the amplitude of the envelope of a narrow-band Gaussian process. The parameter, A, is the amplitude of the sinusoidal signal relative to the rms value of the noise. The curve A = 0 is the distribution for the case of noise alone. The curve labeled A = 2 is the density when a sinusoid with amplitude twice the rms noise voltage is added to the noise. The ROC curves corresponding to selected values of signal amplitude are shown in part (b) of the figure. (After Jeffress, 1964.)

Using the fact that $E_s = A^2 T/2$, and that $\sigma^2 = N_0/T$, we have

$$f[x_l \mid s] = \frac{x_l T}{N_0} I_0\left(\frac{x_l A T}{N_0}\right) \exp\left[\left(-\frac{A^2 + x_l^2}{2}\right)\frac{T}{N_0}\right] \tag{6.54}$$

The density functions and ROC curve associated with these density functions are shown in Fig. 6-3.

As A, the signal amplitude, increases, the density of x_l becomes essentially normal. This is because $I_0(x) \approx e^x/(2\pi x)^{1/2}$ for $x > 1$; thus since $AT/N_0 \gg 1$, we have

$$f[x_l \mid s] = \frac{x_l T}{N_0}\left(\frac{N_0}{2\pi x_l A T}\right)^{1/2} \exp\left[\left(-\frac{A^2 + x_l^2}{2}\right)\frac{T}{N_0} + \frac{x_l A T}{N_0}\right]$$

$$= \left(\frac{x_l}{A}\right)^{1/2}\left(\frac{1}{2\pi\sigma^2}\right)^{1/2} \exp\left[-\frac{1}{2}\left(\frac{x_l - A}{\sigma}\right)^2\right]$$

Thus for x_l near A and $A \gg \sigma^2 = N_0/T$, the envelope is approximately Gaussian with mean A and variance $\sigma^2 = N_0/T$.

6.5.2.1.3 *The envelope density and a narrow-band filter.* The equations just developed for the signal-specified-except-for-phase detector are approximations to the densities of the envelope of the output of a narrow filter excited by Gaussian noise. Rice (1944) derived the argument originally; the following presentation is similar to that of Davenport and Root (1958), to whom the reader is referred for more detail.

Consider a narrow-band filter centered at f_c and excited by white Gaussian noise. The output of the filter can be written

$$y(t) = \sum_{n=1}^{\infty}(a_n \cos nf_0 t + b_n \sin nf_0 t) \tag{6.55}$$

where f_0 is some low frequency and where a_n and b_n are defined in the usual way. Using the following identity:

$$nf_0 = (nf_0 - f_c) + f_c \tag{6.56}$$

we may rewrite Eq. 6.55 as follows:

$$y(t) = A \cos f_c t + B \sin f_c t$$

where

$$A = \sum_{n=1}^{\infty}[a_n \cos (nf_0 - f_c)t + b_n \sin (nf_0 - f_c)t]$$

$$B = \sum_{n=1}^{\infty}[a_n \sin (nf_0 - f_c)t + b_n \cos (nf_0 - f_c)t]$$

Alternatively

$$y(t) = V(t) \cos [2\pi f_c t + \theta(t)]$$

where

$$V(t) = \sqrt{A^2 + B^2} \quad \text{and} \quad \theta(t) = \tan^{-1} \frac{B}{A} \qquad (6.57)$$

By hypothesis, A and B contain only low-frequency terms, since the only components passed by the filter are in a narrow interval about f_c. Thus $V(t)$ and $\theta(t)$ are slowly changing, compared with f_c. A and B are both Gaussian since they are the sum of Gaussian variables a_n and b_n. Using the argument expressed in Eqs. 6.49, 6.50, and 6.51, we conclude that the probability density for the envelope $V(t)$ is a Rayleigh distribution as given in Eq. 6.51. If a signal of frequency f_c is added to the input of the filter, the envelope distribution is given by Eq. 6.54.

Jeffress (1964) has recently compared the envelope detector with the human observer listening for sinusoidal signals in noise. This model was also suggested by Marill (1956). These applications are considered in more detail in the next chapter.

6.5.3   Signal one of M orthogonal signals

The next two sections cover how detection changes as the receiver becomes more and more uncertain about the exact form of the signal. This uncertainty is characterized by a single number M that represents the number of waveforms in the class of potential signals. The answers obtained for this and the following case, which were first derived by Peterson and Birdsall (1953), are approximations. We shall not derive them, but merely state the assumptions of the derivation and the results.

We first assume that the noise can be closely represented by a finite Fourier series, as discussed earlier. The signal will be one and only one of M possible signals; we denote the ith signal $s_i(t)$, $i = 1, 2, 3, \ldots, M$. Two rather strong assumptions are made about members of this signal class. First, they are orthogonal, that is,

$$\int_0^T s_i(t)s_j(t)\, dt = 0 \qquad i \neq j \qquad (6.58)$$

and second, they all have equal energy:

$$\int_0^T s_i^2(t)\, dt = E \qquad i = 1, 2, \ldots, M \qquad (6.59)$$

Finally, we assume that the logarithm of likelihood ratio is approximately normal. This last condition is a technical assumption that is made to enable us to use certain approximations to the moments of the noise and signal-plus-noise distributions. One circumstance in which this assumption is true is if the distributions of signal plus noise and of noise alone can be transformed so that they are both Gaussian with equal variance. In short, if both distributions were normal and differed only in their means, then the logarithm of likelihood ratio is also Gaussian (see Chapter 3). Given these assumptions, the variable d', which is the separation between the means of the two distributions divided by the standard deviation, is related to the signal energy E and the noise power density N_0, by the following equation:

$$\frac{2E}{N_0} = \ln \{1 + M[e^{(d')^2} - 1]\} \tag{6.60}$$

where M is the number of potential signals. Thus if detectability is held constant, that is, if d' is held constant, we may investigate how the signal level E varies with M, the uncertainty parameter. For values of M much greater than two, the quantity within the brackets of Eq. 6.60 is essentially $M \cdot k$ where k is a constant. Thus the signal energy is roughly proportional to the logarithm of M; that is, the signal intensity in decibels changes as the log log M. Hence, once signal uncertainty exceeds some small value, large changes in the amount of signal uncertainty can be counterbalanced by a very small change in signal level, and the detectability of the signals will remain unchanged.

6.5.4 Signal one of M orthogonal signals of unknown phase

This case is similar to the immediately preceding one except that the signal *phase* is unknown. The assumptions are the same as those made in the preceding section. One realization of this case is a receiver that is insensitive to phase, that is, a receiver which merely monitors the envelopes of several potential signal frequencies.

Once more, because it is assumed that the signal-plus-noise distribution and the noise-alone distribution differ only in their means, the parameter d' summarizes completely the detectability of the signal. The result for this case is that

$$(d')^2 = \ln \left[1 - \frac{1}{M} + \frac{1}{M} I_0\left(\frac{2E}{N_0}\right) \right] \tag{6.61}$$

If the detectability is held constant, say at unity, then

$$M\left(2.71 - 1 + \frac{1}{M}\right) = I_0\left(\frac{2E}{N_0}\right) \tag{6.62}$$

and

$$\ln M \approx \ln I_0\left(\frac{2E}{N_0}\right) - 0.5$$

Once more, because $I_0(x)$ is nearly linear for small values of x, we find that the signal energy is nearly proportional to log M. The signal intensity in decibels therefore covaries as the log log M. The detectability of the signal may be held constant, despite large changes in the amount of signal uncertainty, by very small changes in signal level. We discuss this relation in a more detailed form when we take up a comparison of these models and human detection performance in the next chapter.

6.5.5 Signal a sample of noise

We come now to that signal which is simply a sample of noise. When such a signal is added to the noise, the total power increases; thus, intuitively, we know that the ideal detector will base its judgment on power or on some variable monotonic with waveform power. The two hypotheses are

$$f(x_m \mid n) = \frac{1}{\sqrt{2\pi W N_0}} \exp\left(-\frac{1}{2}\frac{x_m{}^2}{W N_0}\right)$$

$$f(x_m \mid s) = \frac{1}{\sqrt{2\pi W(N_0 + S_0)}} \exp\left[-\frac{1}{2}\frac{x_m{}^2}{W(N_0 + S_0)}\right]$$

(6.63)

where N_0 is the noise-power density of the background and S_0 is the noise-power density of the noise signal. Likelihood ratio is then

$$l[x(t)] = \frac{\displaystyle\prod_{m=1}^{2WT} f(x_m \mid s)}{\displaystyle\prod_{m=1}^{2WT} f(x_m \mid n)} = \left(\frac{N_0}{N_0 + S_0}\right)^{WT} \exp\left[\frac{1}{2}\frac{S_0 \displaystyle\sum_{m=1}^{2WT} x_m{}^2}{W(N_0 + S_0)N_0}\right] \quad (6.64)$$

Since N_0, S_0, and WT are all constants, it is easy to see that likelihood ratio is monotonic with

$$\sum_{m=1}^{2WT} x_m{}^2$$

which is proportional to the energy of the waveform. Thus the ideal detector for a signal which is a sample of noise simply measures the energy of the waveform and responds "signal" when that quantity exceeds some criterion value.

The distribution of a quantity such as

$$\sum_{m=1}^{2WT} x_m{}^2$$

is easily determined since the x_m's are independent and Gaussian under both hypotheses. If we normalize each x_m so that it has unit variance, then, since each is Gaussian with zero mean, $x_m{}^2$ is distributed as chi square with one degree of freedom (Appendix I).

There are $2WT$ such terms in the sum and they are all independent of each other; hence the sum is also distributed as chi square with $2WT$ degrees of freedom. Recalling that the mean of a chi-square distribution equals the number of degrees of freedom, and that the variance is twice the mean, we can readily determine the first two moments of the distribution. Also, since a chi-square distribution with more than 10 degrees of freedom is essentially normal, we can obtain the entire ROC curve for this case.

Applying these observations to the noise-alone hypothesis,

$$\sum_{m=1}^{2WT}\left(\frac{x_m}{\sqrt{WN_0}}\right)^2 \quad \text{is chi square with } 2WT\,d.f.,$$

$$E(\sum x_m{}^2) = WN_0 2WT$$

and

$$\text{var}(\sum x_m{}^2) = W^2 N_0{}^2 4WT \tag{6.65}$$

Given signal plus noise,

$$\sum_{m=1}^{2WT}\left(\frac{x_m}{\sqrt{WN_0 + S_0}}\right)^2 \quad \text{is chi square with } 2WT\,d.f.,$$

$$E(\sum x_m{}^2) = W(N_0 + S_0)2WT$$

and

$$\text{var}(\sum x_m{}^2) = W^2(N_0 + S_0)^2 4WT \tag{6.66}$$

For $S_0 \ll N_0$, the two variances are nearly the same and thus

$$d' = \frac{\Delta m}{\sigma} = \frac{WS_0 2WT}{WN_0 2\sqrt{WT}} = \frac{S_0}{N_0}\sqrt{WT} \tag{6.67}$$

Several aspects of this model have been compared with data on human observers (Green, 1960a). Unlike the ideal observer for the signal-specified-exactly case, in which d' is proportional to the square root of signal energy, the d' for this noise signal should vary directly with the average signal power. The noise signal gives a kind of lower limit on the continuum of possible signal uncertainty. The receiver knows neither frequency, phase, nor any other detail of the waveform. Only the energy of the waveform is used to decide among the hypotheses.

6.6   CRITICISM AND DISCUSSION OF IDEAL DETECTORS

Before closing our discussion of ideal detection systems, we must discuss some of the criticisms that have been made of this concept. In the course of the discussion we shall review our assumption concerning the finite representation of the signal and noise waveforms.

The ideal detector is defined by the type and amount of information that the detection device possesses about the signal waveform. If we limit the information enough, then ultimately there will be some circumstances under which the received information is equivocal—either hypothesis is possible—and mistakes will arise. The device that does best under these circumstances, that makes the fewest possible errors, is by definition the ideal observer. But what limits the information? Why must the information be equivocal? Basically, the answer to these questions lies in the model of noise we use, the finite-series representation of noise. The model of noise we use can be represented by a finite-dimensional vector; the components of the vector are determined from samples of the waveform either in time or in frequency. The signal can be represented in the same coordinate system. The reason that the observation is always equivocal is that any point in the space has finite probability under either hypothesis. Thus the likelihood ratio of any point is always finite. As the signal energy goes to zero, the likelihood ratio for all points approaches one; no matter where the observation lies in the space, it is equally likely to be noise or signal.

Some detection problems, in which the noise cannot be represented by a finite vector, lead to rather surprising results. Suppose, for example, that the problem is to detect a gated sinusoidal signal in a noise whose spectrum is shaped by a low-pass, RC filter. One would suppose that some errors might result in this situation, at least for small signal-to-noise ratios, even for the "ideal detector." Martel and Mathews (1961), however, have shown that if the detector can differentiate the observed waveforms an infinite number of times, then the detector need make *no* errors even if the signal-to-noise ratio is infinitely small.

This fact does not mean that all detection problems lead to singular results. Middleton (1961) has suggested some general constraints that allow one to determine in advance whether this singular case—perfect detection at all signal levels—will result in any particular detection task. This is an area of some subtlety, and we shall not be able to cover more than a small portion of it. Indeed, the fundamentals are still subject to debate and new results are still being proved.

In our treatment we have used a representation of the signal and of noise that *never* leads to singular results. We have then analyzed the ideal detectors, given this representation, for a variety of specific signal uncertainties. Thus, our ideal detectors will make mistakes at certain signal-to-noise ratios. The variation of these errors with the signal-to-noise ratio, or with M, the amount of uncertainty, is the essential subject matter of this chapter.

But how good is this finite representation of the noise? One should not expect an unqualified answer to such a question, any more than one expects an unqualified answer to the question of how good is a given theory. The representation of the noise makes certain assumptions, as does any theory. If we invalidate these assumptions, the theory no longer applies. The uncomfortable feature of ideal detection schemes is that even very small changes in certain minor assumptions lead to violently different results, for example, perfect detection at all signal-to-noise ratios. The theoretical development is new, and an exploration of the sensitivity of certain assumptions will undoubtedly arise. As yet, no such systematic treatment is available. There are some rather obvious points that can be made about the finite-series representation, and these will have to serve as the only caveats available at this time.

The greatest weakness with a finite-series model of noise is that we cannot guarantee that the representation $\hat{x}(t)$ will converge to $x(t)$ even if $x(t)$ is a very smooth, well-behaved function. This is because we have a finite-, not infinite-, series approximation. An *infinite* Fourier-series, or Fourier-integral, representation will converge to any waveform of practical interest. For exact restrictions, see Carslaw (1930) or Goldman (1948). The finite representation that we use may not exactly equal extremely well-behaved functions; for example, suppose $x(t)$ is $\sin 2\pi(1000.5)t$. If T is 1 second and W is 20,000 cps, then $\hat{x}(t)$ will not exactly equal $x(t)$. The waveform $x(t)$ is simply not a linear combination of $\sin 2\pi nt$ or cosine $2\pi nt$ where n is an integer between 1 and 20,000. Thus, $\hat{x}(t)$ will not, in general, be a perfect replica of $x(t)$. Of course, $x(t)$ may be closely approximated by $\hat{x}(t)$, and we can appreciate the degree of approximation by thinking of $x(t)$ as represented by discrete temporal samples. There are 40,000 equally spaced samples in the temporal representation of $x(t)$, or about 40 samples to each cycle of our 1000.5-cps waveform. Even though $\hat{x}(t)$ will not exactly equal $x(t)$, it will closely approximate it. Obviously, extreme examples can be devised which can only be poorly approximated by the representation waveform $\hat{x}(t)$.

If $\hat{x}(t)$ and $x(t)$ were exactly equal, the statistics of each stochastic process would be the same. Since $\hat{x}(t)$ may not exactly equal $x(t)$, a second, more crucial problem arises. This problem, unfortunately a little more removed from intuitive grasp, is whether or not the representation $\hat{x}(t)$—and the attendant assumptions about the sample space of the random variables a_k and b_k—is a very useful representation of the statistical character of the actual waveform $x(t)$. The reader should be very clear about this problem. Any detector searching for a signal in the waveform $x(t)$ will try to compute various statistics of the waveform. On the basis of these computations it will try to determine whether $x(t)$ is a sample of noise alone or signal plus noise. The waveform $\hat{x}(t)$ will be a useful representation of $x(t)$ only if the computed statistics are the same using either $x(t)$ or $\hat{x}(t)$. We know, for example, that the first and second moments of $x(t)$ and $\hat{x}(t)$ are the same, since we set the mean and variance of $\hat{x}(t)$ to equal measured parameters of the actual process. We cannot make any sweeping generalization about the other parameters of the process. Whether or not the finite-series representation is a reasonable compromise is still in dispute. Although a resolution to the dispute would be desirable, it does not seem likely in the next few years; the most prudent course, in the meantime, is to understand and appreciate the basic issues and assumptions.

Our personal feelings about this issue are as follows. First, we feel that if the finite Fourier-series model of noise is used with care, it is likely to lead to answers that are very near those obtained with more sophisticated but more complicated analyses. Secondly, the very simplicity of the finite-series model recommends it as a pedagogical device to introduce the study of ideal detectors.

6.7 SUMMARY

Detection of signals in noise has been reviewed for a variety of detectors. All of the detectors are ideal, or optimal, for the detection case considered; that is, each detector uses likelihood ratio or some monotonic function of likelihood ratio as its basis for deciding between the two hypotheses. The finite representation of the noise and signal waveforms has been emphasized, both because it provides an easy intuitive approach to stochastic processes and because this aspect of the ideal-detector analysis has come under attack. Several different cases have been considered; they varied in the amount of knowledge or information that the receiver has about the character or form of the signal. The results of these evaluations will be useful in our attempts to analyze human detection performance, a topic that we take up in the next chapter.

PROBLEMS

6.1 According to the finite representation of noise discussed in this chapter, if the noise bandwidth is 4000 cps wide and the signal duration is 1/10 second, how many sample values are used to represent the noise waveform in time, in frequency? What is the distance between the Fourier components? What is the interval in time between successive sample values?

6.2 Suppose that the noise can be represented by a vector $\vec{N}$, having a multivariate density $f(\vec{N})$, and that the signal $\vec{S}$ can be described in the same vector space.

(a) If the observed vector is $\vec{X}$, what is the density of $\vec{X}$, given that the signal has occurred?

(b) Suppose that the signal might be $\vec{S}_1$ or $\vec{S}_2$ with equal probability; what is the density of $\vec{X}$ given that one or the other signal has occurred?

6.3   Is there any difference between the envelope detector (the optimal detector for a sinusoidal signal specified except for phase) and a receiver that measures energy at the signal frequency?

6.4   What is the mean-to-sigma ratio of the energy of successive samples of white Gaussian noise if the bandwidth of the sampled noise is 4000 cps and the signal duration is 1/10 sec? Could an increase of 10% be reliably detected?

7

Basic Experiments:

Comparison of Ideal

and Human Observers

7.1 INTRODUCTION

In this chapter we apply the analysis of optimal or ideal detection systems, covered in the last chapter, to the data obtained from human observers in psychoacoustic experiments. This application will parallel the application of decision theory to the analysis of various psychophysical methods as presented in Part I. From the standpoint of a sensory psychologist, those chapters deal primarily with methodology. Certainly, decision theory is largely concerned with how values, costs, and a priori probabilities influence the response criterion, given that the stimulus is held constant. While the same experiments may also be relevant to certain basic assumptions about the nature of the human sensory system—for example, whether sensory information is better treated as a discrete quantity, as it is in threshold models, or as a continuous quantity, as the Gaussian assumption would imply—the main purpose of the application of decision theory is to separate the detectability of the signal, a sensory process, from the decision criterion of the subject, a response or motivational process. In this chapter we consider the application of ideal-detector analysis to the study of sensory processes. That is, assuming that the response criterion is constant, how does a change in the physical stimulus alter detection performance?

It will soon become apparent that fewer data are available on this topic than in other areas of detection theory. Several reasons can be suggested for the paucity of data comparing human performance to optimal detection systems. One is that much of the theoretical material arose from an analysis of radar and other information systems and is foreign to many sensory psychologists. Thus, comparisons of human data with quantitative detection systems are often not made because the investigator fails to recognize the pertinence of these quantitative models to his problem. Certainly, the analysis of optimal detection systems often involves mathematics less familiar to the sensory psychologist than that used in the application of decision theory. Nevertheless, the comparison of variation in human sensory performance with explicit, quantitative models of optimal detection systems is an important and useful tool of analysis.

In this chapter we review some of the work that is most relevant in this comparison of human and ideal detection. To avoid confusion we must first distinguish carefully between two different detection tasks.

7.2   TWO EXPERIMENTAL CONDITIONS

Nearly all of the empirical data discussed in this chapter were collected in one of two experimental conditions. One we call the "simple detection experiment"; the other we call the "increment-detection, or pedestal, experiment." It is necessary to distinguish between these two conditions because the results obtained in the two are somewhat different. In describing the two experimental conditions, we shall also define the physical parameters relevant in each. In the following descriptions it is convenient to assume that a two-alternative forced-choice procedure is used as the psychophysical procedure in both experimental conditions. This assumption is consistent with our general purpose, which is to analyze stimulus rather than response determinants of performance. Thus we assume that through either instructions or training, the observer maintains a symmetric response criterion. If the likelihood of the signal's being in the first interval is greater than the likelihood of its being in the second interval, the observer will choose the first interval. If the opposite is true he will choose the second interval. It is, of course, important to monitor the actual behavior of a subject in any experiment to insure that this symmetry actually exists, but for the purposes of this exposition we assume that it does.

7.2.1   Simple detection experiment

In the simple detection experiment, one of the hypotheses is simply that noise alone occurred in a particular one of the two forced-choice intervals. The noise usually has a fairly flat frequency spectrum; that is, the average power in a one-cycle band is approximately the same at all audible frequencies. Generally, the noise is continuous throughout a given experimental session, although in some experiments it might be

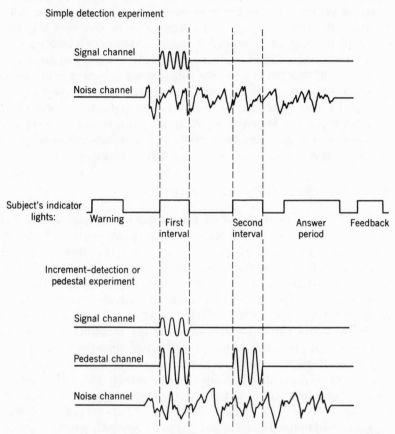

FIG. 7-1 Diagram of stimulus events in a simple detection experiment and in an increment-detection experiment. The middle portion shows the temporal events within a single trial cycle; they are: (1) a warning light, (2) a first observation interval, (3) a second observation interval, (4) an answer period, and (5) a feedback period. For the simple detection experiment, displayed in the upper section of the figure, the noise is continuous and the signal is added to the noise either in the first observation interval (as shown) or in the second observation interval. The increment-detection experiment, displayed in the lower section of the figure, also has continuous noise, but a pedestal is added to noise in both observation intervals. The signal is added to the noise and pedestal either in the first observation interval (as shown) or in the second interval. The figure indicates a *gated* pedestal experiment. Alternatively, the pedestal could be *continuous*, as is the noise.

pulsed for the duration of the first observation interval, removed, and then pulsed again for the duration of the second interval. The important point is that in what we call a "simple detection" experiment nothing other than noise occurs during one of the observation intervals.

The second hypothesis is that a signal is added to the noise during a particular one of the intervals. The observer's task is to select the interval containing the signal. Often the signal is a sinusoid and, in that case, the experiment consists of adding, in one of two temporal intervals, a gated sinusoid to continuous noise. The subject is asked to select the interval in which he considers it more likely that the gated sinusoid is added. In all cases the two intervals are marked for the observers by lights, so that the starting time and duration of the possible signal are indicated. Figure 7-1, top, shows schematically the sequence of events within a typical trial cycle.

If a sinusoid or another definite waveform is used as signal, the usual measure of the intensive aspect of the signal is the time integral of its power, that is, the energy of the signal, which we denote E_s. Assuming a one-ohm impedance, if $s(t)$ is the voltage or pressure waveform of the signal, then

$$E_s = \int_0^T s^2(t)\, dt \qquad (7.1)$$

where T is the duration of the signal.

7.2.2   Increment-detection or pedestal experiment

In the increment-detection experiment, as in the simple detection experiment, there are a signal interval and a nonsignal interval, both of which contain noise. In addition to the noise some constant waveform, often a sinusoid, appears in *both* observation intervals. This constant waveform is referred to as the "pedestal" because the signal consists of an increment to this waveform, the increment occurring in either the first or second of the two observation intervals. Thus the nonsignal interval contains both the noise and the constant waveform or pedestal. The signal interval contains the noise, the pedestal and, in addition, the increment to the pedestal, or signal. Figure 7-1, bottom, displays the events within a typical trial cycle.

In one example of such an experiment, the nonsignal interval contains a noise plus a 1000-cps sinewave of fixed amplitude. The signal, also a 1000-cps sinewave, is added in phase to the sinusoid of fixed amplitude; thus the signal simply adds an increment to the amplitude of the pedestal. The observer is instructed to detect the increment or, what is equivalent, to select the interval with the more intense 1000-cps component. Sometimes the fixed waveform is continuous; sometimes, as in Fig. 7-1, it is presented only for the duration of the observation interval. These two conditions have been called the "continuous" and "gated" pedestal experiments, respectively.

7.2.3 Measurement of quantities in the increment-detection experiment

No standard terminology has evolved for referring to the various quantities involved in the increment-detection experiment. We therefore take some care in defining the relevant physical parameters. If we denote the pedestal as $c(t)$, then two hypotheses can occur: the observation, $x(t)$, can be either

$$H_n: n(t) + c(t) \qquad 0 < t < T$$

or

$$H_s: n(t) + c(t) + s(t) \qquad 0 < t < T$$

Since we have already defined the signal energy as the time integral of $s^2(t)$ (see Eq. 7.1), we keep that notation; similarly, we define

$$E_c = \int_0^T c^2(t)\, dt \tag{7.2}$$

as the energy of the pedestal. Sometimes, for example, if $c(t)$ and $s(t)$ are in-phase sinewaves, the integral of the cross product is not zero and then the energy of the increment is, by definition,

$$\Delta E = \int_0^T [c(t) + s(t)]^2\, dt - \int_0^T c^2(t)\, dt \tag{7.3}$$

$$\Delta E = 2\int_0^T c(t)s(t)\, dt + E_s \tag{7.4}$$

The increment in energy, ΔE, will clearly depend on the correlation between the signal and the pedestal and thus may be different from the signal energy E_s.

These definitions are purely formal. Experiments may show that the increment in energy, ΔE, may be a more meaningful definition of the effective signal energy than E_s (Raab, Osman, and Rich, 1963). The best definition of "effective" signal level is an empirical one and, hopefully, it can be determined once the formal definitions are clear.

If the signal is a slight increment in the constant signal, say $s(t) = kc(t)$ where k is some constant, then

$$\Delta E = 2kE_c + E_s$$

or

$$\Delta E = 2kE_c + k^2E_c \qquad \text{if} \quad E_c > 0 \qquad (7.5)$$

Usually the pedestal is fixed and the signal level is varied by changing k. If k is much less than one, then ΔE is proportional to kE_c and, since k is proportional to signal voltage or pressure, ΔE is also proportional to signal voltage. In the simple detection condition the increment in energy is simply E_s, because E_c is zero, and thus ΔE is proportional to signal energy or power.

In the remainder of the chapter we discuss data obtained in one or the other of these two experimental conditions, simple detection or increment detection, and contrast the results with various models of the detection process.

7.3   ROC CURVES

One means of gaining information about the character of a detector is to compare the shape of the empirical ROC curve with that predicted by a variety of detection devices. Such comparisons are already familiar, since they were used earlier to contrast continuous and discrete models of the human sensory system (Chapters 3 and 5). There our attention centered largely on the issue of whether the slope of the ROC curve was continuously varying or whether the curve was composed of a few linear segments. These differences in the predicted shape of the ROC curve were traced to different assumptions concerning the underlying distributions of sensory events.

The immediately preceding chapter demonstrated that these distributions depend upon both the character of the detector and the statistical characteristics of the input waveforms, namely, the signal and the noise. If enough were known about the detection system, the shape of the ROC curve could be predicted from physical measurements of the signal and the noise. Thus the ROC curve may change if the physical conditions of the experiment are varied. A sufficiently detailed model of the detection system may, therefore, permit us not only to deduce the typical shape of the ROC curve but also to predict certain systematic changes in that shape as conditions of the experiment change.

One such model is the model for a signal specified except for phase, that is, the envelope detector. For the simple detection experiment, the distribution of noise alone is a Rayleigh distribution (see Rayleigh, 1894). The signal-plus-noise distribution is skewed to the right (see Chapter 6, Fig. 6-3). In the increment-detection condition, however, the distribution becomes Gaussian, so that if a sufficiently large pedestal is used the two distributions will be Gaussian with equal variance. Thus the envelope-detection model predicts that the shape of the ROC curve for the simple detection experiment will differ from that for the increment-detection experiment.

In a recent paper, Jeffress (1964) has argued that the envelope detector is a reasonably good model of the human auditory detection system. A

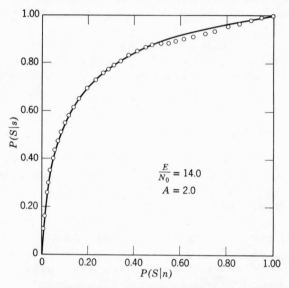

FIG. 7-2 Rating data fitted by the envelope-detection model. The data were obtained from an observer listening for a weak sinusoidal signal in noise. The ratio of signal energy to noise-power density, E/N_0, is 14.0. The theoretical ROC curve is for an envelope detector of a sinewave whose amplitude is twice the rms value of the narrow-band noise process ($A = 2.0$). Data from Watson, Rilling, and Bourbon (1964). (After Jeffress, 1964.)

compelling part of his argument is the rather favorable comparison between the envelope-detector model and data from the rating experiment of Watson, Rilling, and Bourbon (1964). Illustrative results from one observer are shown in Fig. 7-2. The ROC curve, as can be seen, is asymmetric about the negative diagonal. The ROC curve is not very different from the curve that we would expect if the underlying distributions were Gaussian, but with the variance of the signal distribution greater than that of the noise distribution. In fact, the same data are fitted quite well by the Gaussian model assuming unequal variance (see Chapter 4,

Fig. 4-8). The important difference between the Gaussian, unequal-variance model and the envelope-detector model of Jeffress is that the latter model makes explicit predictions about how the distribution of likelihood ratio depends on signal and pedestal amplitude. The envelope model predicts that if the amplitude is large, the ROC curve will be approximately symmetric, since the Gaussian distributions associated with the two hypotheses will have approximately equal standard deviations. The unequal-variance Gaussian model makes no predictions for the pedestal experiment. Whether or not such a systematic change in the empirical ROC curve exists is not yet known. The experiment is an important one because not only does the envelope-detector model predict such a change, but several other models predict similar systematic changes in the shape of the ROC curve with signal level (see Chapter 8).

There is, as yet, no systematic study comparing the shape of the ROC curves obtained in the simple detection and the pedestal conditions. Most ROC curves have been obtained for sinusoidal signals in noise, that is, in simple detection experiments. For the simple detection experiment, asymmetric ROC curves seem to be the general rule. Whether the ROC curve changes in shape for different conditions, or is characteristic of the individual observer, is not known.

7.4   PSYCHOMETRIC FUNCTIONS FOR SIMPLE DETECTION EXPERIMENTS

Although systematic studies of the shape of the ROC curve have not been carried out, there is ample evidence that a classical relation of sensory psychology, the psychometric function, does depend on the experimental condition. In particular, the slope of the psychometric function in a simple detection experiment is different from the slope in an increment-detection experiment.

Recall that the psychometric function relates the percentage of positive reports to the level of signal intensity. Usage is not standard, and "psychophysical function," as well as "frequency-of-seeing curve" (in vision), is sometimes used to designate this same graph. It is a remarkable invariance of psychoacoustic data that for a wide variety of signal frequencies, signal durations, and noise levels the resulting psychometric functions look remarkably similar—if the logarithm of the ratio of signal energy to noise-power density is plotted as the abscissa and the percentage correct in a two-alternative forced-choice task is plotted as the ordinate. Figure 7-3 shows this typical function for a signal that is a pulsed sinusoid of 100-ms duration and 1000-cps frequency. The noise had a spectrum level of 40 db SPL (sound pressure level). That is, the noise in a 1-cps band

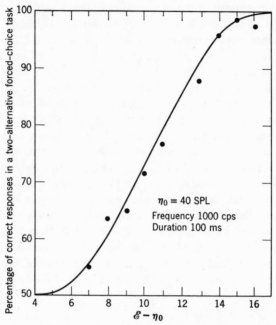

FIG. 7-3 Typical psychometric function for the simple detection experiment. The percentage of correct responses in the two-alternative forced-choice task is plotted against $\varepsilon - \eta_0 = 10 \log E/N_0$. E/N_0 is the ratio of signal energy to noise-power density. As the signal increases about 10 db, the percentage of correct responses rises from near chance to 100% correct. The signal parameters are indicated on the graph. About 400 observations were used to estimate each point. The spectrum level of the noise was 40 db SPL; that is, the noise power in a 1-cps band had an average power equal to a sinusoid of 40 db re 0.0002 dyne/cm². (After Green, 1960b.)

generated the same average power as a continuous sinusoid of 40 db re 0.0002 dy/cm². The abscissa $\varepsilon - \eta_0$ is $10 \log E_s/N_0$, where E_s is the signal energy and N_0 is the noise-power density. The data were collected using a two-alternative forced-choice procedure. Notice that the ordinate ranges from 50% or chance performance to 100% or perfect detection, and thus it is not strictly comparable to the older, classical psychometric function, which is usually based on the percentage of affirmative responses in a yes-no procedure. The curve may be described, at least roughly, as a monotonically increasing function, rising from 50% to 100%. To cover this range of percentage correct responses, a change in $\varepsilon - \eta_0$ of about 10 db appears to be required.

Another way to examine the same relation is to use a different measure of sensitivity, for example d' or d_e' rather than percentage correct, as the ordinate of the graph, and to determine how this inferred parameter changes with the ratio of signal energy to noise-power density. (Chapter 4, Section 4.2.5, defines d_e'.) Figure 7-4 shows different data plotted in this manner. This study concerned the effects of uncertainty about the time of occurrence of the signals. The equations of the fitted straight lines are given on the graphs; they provide a fair first approximation to the form of the psychometric function. The range of E/N_0 covered in this study is only about 6 db, so that whether this simple linear approximation is correct over the entire 10-db variation of signal energy cannot be decided from these data. To establish the true relation between d_e' and signal intensity for the entire range of the function is a difficult experimental question. The variability in the estimates of d_e' at high signal levels is heavily skewed towards large values of d_e', and the variability of the estimates at low signal levels tends to be very great, either for statistical reasons or because these conditions are very tedious for the subjects, or both. It is entirely plausible that the function relating d_e' and E/N_0 is a polynomial with a strong square or cubic term.

Figure 7-5 shows considerable data collected from three subjects at several signal durations and several frequencies. A constant has been added to or subtracted from the abscissa in order to make the point corresponding to $d' = 1.00$, which is 76% correct in two-alternative forced choice, occur near the middle of the scale (0 db). Although the data were collected at signal frequencies that differ by a factor of 20, and durations that vary by a factor of 100, all the psychometric functions appear to be roughly similar in shape. The solid line is the linear relation $d' = kE/N_0$. The fit of the line to the data is best in the region between $d' = 1$ and $d' = 2$, which was the range of the data shown in Fig. 7-4. At extremely high or low values of d', the linear approximation does not provide a very accurate representation of the data. One should appreciate that the regions of probable error change as a function of the percentage correct; this is shown at these levels by the vertical lines extending between the $\pm 1\sigma$ marks, which assume only binomial variation. While the scatter of these data points is considerable, probably larger than binomial variation, there does not appear to be any consistent trend in the slope of the psychometric function as a function of either signal frequency or duration.

Other pertinent data are shown in Figs. 2 and 3 of Chapter 8. These data show that neither frequency nor frequency uncertainty appears to affect the shape of the psychometric function. In summary, for the simple detection task, the shape of the psychometric function appears to be remarkably invariant over changes in the noise level, the signal frequency,

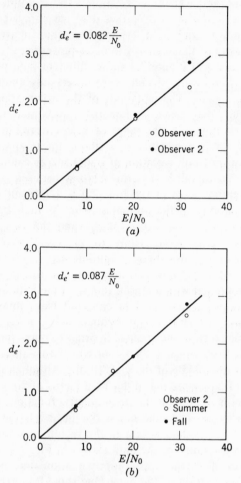

FIG 7-4 Psychometric functions, showing d_e' versus E/N_0, obtained by the yes-no procedure. The ordinate d_e' is an inferred measure of the detectability of the signal. The abscissa is the ratio of signal energy E to noise-power density N_0. The parameter d_e' is approximately linear with E/N_0 for a change in signal energy of about 4 to 1. When d_e' is 3.00, the area under the ROC curve is 0.985; when $d_e' = 0.80$, the area is about 0.71. (After Egan, Greenberg, and Schulman, 1961a.)

the signal duration, and the observer's uncertainty about either signal duration or signal frequency. The psychometric function, in all cases, appears to cover a range of about 10 db and, to a first approximation, d' and related measures appear to be nearly linearly related to E/N_0, at least in the middle range of the function.

7.5   MODELS FOR THE PSYCHOMETRIC FUNCTION IN SIMPLE DETECTION EXPERIMENTS

Psychometric functions for a variety of detection models are presented in Fig. 7-6. Two classes of models are presented in the figure. The first is a type of cross-correlation receiver. This receiver compares the observed waveform $x(t)$ with the M possible signals $s_i(t)$, $i = 1, 2, 3, \ldots, M$, by multiplying $x(t)$ by $s_i(t)$ and integrating the product over the duration of the interval.

If only one signal is expected by the receiver, only one cross-product is computed, and the curve labelled $M = 1$, for the signal known exactly, should result. If the signal is one of M possible signals, then the curve labelled with the proper value of M should result. For details of the assumptions of this model, see Chapter 6, Section 6.5.3.

The decision about the existence of the signal is based on a comparison of the expected and the received waveforms. Such a comparison, which is sensitive to the detailed waveshape of the received signal, may not be an appropriate model for the human auditory system because the ear may be phase-deaf, as Helmholtz (1885) suggested. Nevertheless, for the present we shall entertain this model and determine whether, using detection data, any strong evidence can be developed against this hypothesis.

The second class of models is like the first except that the detection device is assumed to be insensitive to phase; only envelope information is relevant. If, for example, the expected signal is one particular frequency, then the dotted curve labelled $M = 1$ is the same as the curve from the signal-specified-except-for-phase model.* If signal frequency is unknown, that is, if the signal might be any one of M different frequencies, all with unknown phase, then the dotted curve with M corresponding to the number of possible signals should result. All of the M signals must be orthogonal, that is, the integral of their cross-products must be zero.

---

* Two curves are displayed in Fig. 7-6 for the case of unknown phase, $M = 1$. One is an approximation; the other is an exact calculation. It is known that the approximation becomes better as M increases; thus the largest difference between the exact and approximate curves for $M = 1$ is an upper bound on the error of the approximation at all M. This upper bound is at most about 1 db, as can be seen from the figure. For $M = 256$ the error is probably less than $1/10$ db at all values of $\varepsilon - \eta_0$.

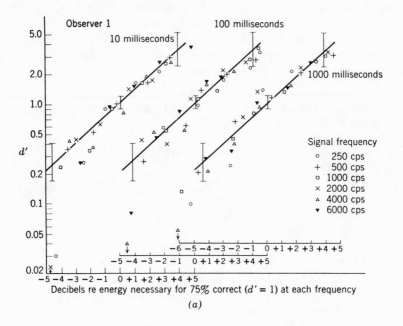

Decibels re energy necessary for 75% correct ($d' = 1$) at each frequency

(a)

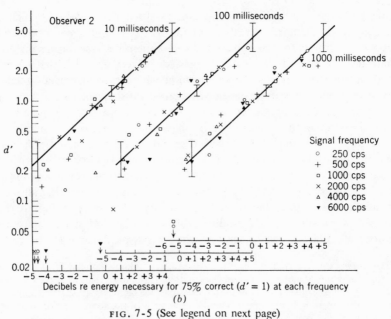

Decibels re energy necessary for 75% correct ($d' = 1$) at each frequency

(b)

FIG. 7-5 (See legend on next page)

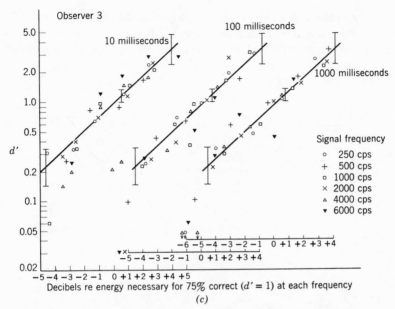

(c)

FIG. 7-5 Psychometric functions, for three observers, for the simple detection experiment. These functions were obtained at three durations and with six different signal frequencies, as indicated. The masker was continuous noise. The percentage of correct responses obtained in two-alternative forced choice was converted to the inferred measure of detectability, d', plotted on the abscissa. The signal intensity in decibels is plotted along the ordinate. The ordinate is scaled so that zero db corresponds to $d' = 1$; that is, a constant has been added to the scale of $\varepsilon - \eta_0 = 10 \log E/N_0$ so that all the psychometric functions meet in the center. As can be seen, all the functions appear to have essentially the same shape and do not appear to change with either signal frequency or signal duration. The solid line is the equation $d' = cE/N_0$ where c, a constant, depends on signal frequency and duration. This equation seems to fit best for moderate values of d' (as in Fig. 7-4); a more complicated expression seems necessary to fit the entire function. The short vertical bars attached to the solid lines represent the expected variability assuming a binomial process for the percentage of correct responses. (Green, previously unpublished data.)

Thus, all of the set of possible signals might have the same frequency but occur in nonoverlapping segments of time. A simple example of the latter would be the set of one-second signals that are exactly zero in three quarters of the intervals and have a fixed-frequency sinusoid in the remaining quarter. The first signal would occur in the first quarter of the interval, the second in the second quarter, and so on.

A third model, the energy detector, which is the optimal detector for a noise signal, could be considered here, but because of the importance of that model we devote the whole of Chapter 8 to a careful consideration of it.

A comparison of the theoretical psychometric functions with the empirical psychometric function (Fig. 7-3) for a simple detection task

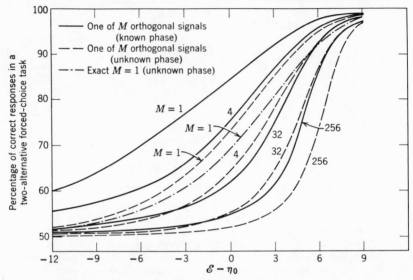

FIG. 7-6   Theoretical functions for various models for the case of one-of-M-orthogonal signals. The detector expects one of M equal-energy, orthogonal signals. The phase of the signal is either known or unknown. The curves give the expected percentage of correct responses in two-alternative forced choice as a function of $\varepsilon - \eta_0 = 10 \log E/N_0$, where E is the energy of the signal and N_0 is the noise-power density. The parameter M is the number of potential signals. For $M = 1$, phase unknown, two calculations are shown. One is exact; the other is an approximation used to generate the curves for higher values of M. The approximation is known to improve as M increases. The difference between these two curves for $M = 1$ is an upper bound on the error involved in the approximation.

leads to the following general conclusion. A valid model for the human observer will probably have to postulate some uncertainty about the signal parameters. It seems unlikely that either of the above models, cross-correlation or envelope detection, can account for human detection performance without assuming M to be at least 4. Once M exceeds 8 or so, the functions have very similar shapes and hence the psychometric function should be nearly the same, independent of the amount of uncertainty about signal parameters that is introduced experimentally. Moreover, such uncertainty will change the absolute level of the detection very little. When the number of uncertain signals increases from $M = 32$ to $M = 256$ then, for a cross-correlation detector, a change of 2 db in signal level is sufficient to maintain the level of correct detections at 75% (see Fig. 7-6). This rather meager effect of signal uncertainty is consistent with experimental data (Egan, Greenberg, and Schulman, 1961a; Green, 1961).

The energy-detector model does not explicitly assume uncertainty about the signal parameters; however, the bandwidth and time constant of the postdetection integrator can be chosen in such a way as to mimic changes in the psychometric function that are produced by variations of M in the cross-correlation or envelope-detector models. The psychometric functions predicted by the cross-correlation and envelope-detector models are sufficiently similar, for appropriate choices of the parameter values, that it would be impossible to distinguish between them on the basis of their shape. Fortunately, some other results obtained in the pedestal experiment clearly indicate the inadequacy of the cross-correlation model.

7.6   PSYCHOMETRIC FUNCTIONS FOR INCREMENT-DETECTION EXPERIMENTS

The use of the increment-detection experiment to decide among the several hypotheses was suggested by Julian Bigelow (personal communication) shortly after some of the results with gated sinusoidal signals in noise were reported. The psychometric functions using the pedestal procedure are quite different from those obtained in simple detection experiments. Figure 7-7 shows some typical results.

The difference between the two procedures can be appreciated by comparing Fig. 7-7 and Fig. 7-3. The coordinates of both graphs are the same, although the scale of the abscissa, $\varepsilon-\eta_0$, has been changed to encompass the larger range of the psychometric function obtained with the increment-detection condition. In the simple detection condition, Fig. 7-3, the psychometric function covers a range of about 10 db in $\varepsilon-\eta_0$. In the pedestal condition, Fig. 7-7, the psychometric function covers a range of about 25 db. Note that the other physical parameters (noise level, signal duration, and signal frequency) are the same.

The reader should not infer from a comparison of Figs. 7-7 and 7-3 that the human observer's performance is always more nearly optimal in the pedestal experiment than in the simple detection experiment. The size of the pedestal heavily determines how near the observer's performance is to that of the optimal or ideal observer. As the pedestal amplitude increases from the value shown in Fig. 7-7, the signal level needed to achieve any given percentage correct also increases (Tanner, 1961a; Pfafflin and Mathews, 1962). The psychometric function will retain the

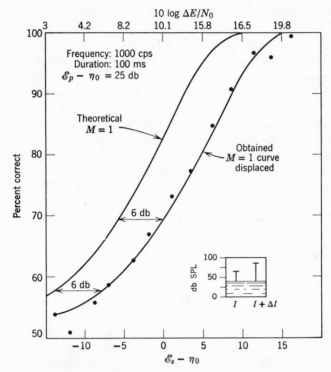

FIG. 7-7 Typical psychometric functions for the increment-detection, or pedestal, experiment. The percentage of
correct responses in a two-alternative forced-choice task as a
function of $\varepsilon_s-\eta_0$ (lower abscissa), $10 \log E_s/N_0$, where N_0 is
the noise-power density and where E_s is the signal energy,
that is, the energy of the signal added in-phase to the pedestal.
The theoretical curve for the signal-specified-exactly receiver
is shown as the solid line labeled "theoretical $M = 1$." The
curve fitted to the data is the solid curve displaced 6 db. The
amount of displacement depends on $\varepsilon_p-\eta_0$, $10 \log E_p/N_0$, where
E_p is the energy of the pedestal and N_0 is the noise-power density. The upper abscissa gives the value of $10 \log \Delta E/N_0$. The
quantity ΔE is the increment in energy caused by adding the
signal to the pedestal. Because the signal and the pedestal are
correlated, $\Delta E > E_s$. The signal parameters (duration and
frequency) are the same as those used in Fig. 7-3, as is the
observer. Thus one can compare the shape of the psychometric functions in these two tasks. (After Green, 1960b.)

same shape but will progressively shift to the right as the pedestal amplitude increases. This empirical constancy between the ratio of signal and pedestal amplitude for constant detectability is described by Weber's Law. We discuss this topic in more detail in Section 7.8.

The difference between the *range* of the psychometric function for the simple detection and the pedestal experiments is not dependent on the particular measurement of signal-energy-to-noise-power density. Other methods of calculating the effective signal-to-noise ratio support the same conclusion. A strong alternative candidate for the measurement of the signal is the increment in energy caused by the signal, ΔE. In the simple detection experiment the signal is added to the noise and, because the signal and noise are orthogonal, increment energy and the energy of the signal are the same quantity. The abscissa of Fig. 7-3 would, therefore, remain unchanged if this new measure of the signal were used. In the pedestal experiment the signal and the pedestal are not orthogonal, and the increment in energy caused by adding the signal to the pedestal is not the same as the signal energy alone. The abscissa of Fig. 7-7 would, therefore, be altered if the increment in energy were used as the measure of the signal. At the top of Fig. 7-7 we have indicated the values of this new scale. As can be seen, even if this new scale were employed, the range of the psychometric function would be larger in the pedestal experiment (17 db) than in the simple detection experiment (10 db).

Because the pedestal technique is unfamiliar to many, we shall review rather carefully the measured quantities displayed in Fig. 7-7. The noise-power density was 40 db SPL (sound pressure level); that is, the noise generates the same average power in a 1-cps band as a continuous sinusoid of 40 db re 0.0002 dynes per square centimeter. For convenience, let us define a power scale such that 40 db re 0.0002 dynes corresponds to unity on this scale. As the small insert in Fig. 7-7 indicates, the pedestal is 25 db above the noise, so that the pedestal is 317 units on this same scale (10 log 317 = 25 db). The signal, for instance at $\varepsilon - \eta_0 = 3$ db, is twice the noise density, or 2 units of energy (10 log 2 = 3 db).* Since the signal is only $\frac{1}{10}$ second, the average signal power (while the signal is on) is 20 units. To calculate the increment in power that is produced when the signal is added to the pedestal, we must convert the signal and pedestal powers to voltages, add the two quantities, and then transform the result back to power. Our scale of power will be useful now, since we may transform both powers to the same scale of voltage by simply taking the square root

---

* Again we remind the reader that N_0 measures noise power per cycle per second, and thus has the dimensions of energy. We multiply the noise density by 1 sec to determine its average power. See Appendices II and III for further discussion of the measurement of signal and noise.

of the power units. Thus the pedestal is $\sqrt{317} = 17.8$ units and the signal voltage $\sqrt{20} = 4.5$ units. The total power of signal and pedestal is then $(22.3)^2$ or 497 power units. The pedestal power is 317, and thus the increment in power caused by the addition of the signal is 180 units. Since the increment lasts $\frac{1}{10}$ sec, the energy of the increment is 18 units. The increment in energy is 12.6 db above the noise density ($10 \log \Delta E/N_0 = 10 \log 18 = 12.6$ db). The upper scale of Fig. 7-7 shows this scale, in decibels, of the increment energy with respect to the noise-power density.

Whatever scale is used, either $10 \log E/N_0$ or $10 \log \Delta E/N_0$, the psychometric functions for the pedestal and for the simple detection experiment are different. What conclusion can we draw from this difference in the shape of the psychometric functions? Unfortunately the result, in itself, would be more informative if it came out some other way, because almost all the models predict that the increment-detection experiment should come out the way it did. Consider first the cross-correlation detector. Clearly, the results are consistent with this model, since the solid curve running parallel to the psychometric function, in Fig. 7-7, is the cross-correlation model with $M = 1$. We could expect the increment-detection experiment to reduce uncertainty about starting time and duration, because the occurrences of the two pedestals precisely mark off the observation intervals. Information about signal frequency is also conveyed by the pedestal.

The same arguments apply to the model for "one-of-M-orthogonal signals," assuming unknown phase. In fact, the coherence between the pedestal and the signal makes this model, which is normally phase-insensitive, essentially a phase-sensitive detection system. Briefly, this occurs because the detector measures the amplitude of the envelope at the signal frequency. Normally, the signal when added to noise can increase or decrease the envelope magnitude. In the pedestal experiment, however, the pedestal is large compared with the noise, so that variation of the noise is minimized, and the fact that the signal is added in phase to the pedestal means that the signal must increase, *and only increase*, the envelope magnitude. Thus the statistics of the detection process are altered, and the detector will perform as well as one that is phase-sensitive.

A more concrete understanding of these processes can be gained by considering the following geometrical interpretation of the detection process. Consider first the cross-correlation receiver. It bases its decision on the quantity

$$\int_0^T s(t)x(t)\,dt \tag{7.6}$$

where $s(t)$ is the signal waveform, $x(t)$ is the observed waveform, and the interval 0 to T is the observation interval. Suppose that the signal has a frequency k cps and phase θ, with an amplitude V; then

$$s(t) = V \cos(2\pi kt + \theta)$$
$$= V(\cos \theta \cos 2\pi kt + \sin \theta \sin 2\pi kt)$$
$$= V(a_k^s \cos 2\pi kt + b_k^s \sin 2\pi kt) \tag{7.7}$$

where $a_k^s = \cos \theta$ and $b_k^s = \sin \theta$.

The observed waveform $x(t)$ can, by assumption, also be represented as a finite Fourier series; let

$$x(t) = \sum_{k=1}^{WT} a_k \cos 2\pi kt + b_k \sin 2\pi kt \tag{7.8}$$

The cross-product of $x(t)$ and $s(t)$ contains terms of several different types. All of the terms will integrate to zero except the following:

$$\int_0^T s(t)x(t)\,dt = \int_0^T V a_k^s a_k \cos^2 2\pi kt\,dt + \int_0^T V b_k^s b_k \sin^2 2\pi kt\,dt$$
$$= \frac{V}{2}(a_k^s a_k + b_k^s b_k) \tag{7.9}$$

Because $V/2$ is simply a scalar, consider the expression within the brackets. This can be recognized as the scalar product of two vectors (a_k^s, b_k^s) and (a_k, b_k): the former vector is the signal vector, the latter is that part of the total observation $x(t)$ that is correlated with the signal and hence relevant to the decision. We may call (a_k, b_k) the observation vector, although actually it is only a small part of the total observation $x(t) = (a_1, b_1, a_2, b_2, \ldots, a_k, b_k, \ldots, a_{WT}, b_{WT})$, because (a_k, b_k) is the only part correlated with the signal.

The scalar product of two vectors equals the product of the magnitude of each vector times the cosine of the angle between them. In our case the magnitude of the signal vector (a_k^s, b_k^s) is unity ($\cos^2 \theta + \sin^2 \theta = 1$; see Eq. 7.7); hence the scalar product of (a_k, b_k) and (a_k^s, b_k^s) is simply the magnitude of (a_k, b_k) times the cosine of the angle between the two vectors. Figure 7-8 shows this result pictorially. The cross-correlation receiver bases its decision on a quantity that is proportional to the magnitude of the projection of the observation vector on the signal axis.

In the simple detection experiment the part of the observation vector correlated with the signal (a_k, b_k) will be either noise alone or signal plus noise. If it is noise alone, then the two components (a_k, b_k) will be Gaussian with equal variance and the distribution of such observations will be bivariate normal (see Appendix I). Figure 7-9 shows how that would appear. This bird's-eye view of a three-dimensional surface uses circles to represent contours of equal probability density. When the signal plus noise occurs, the observation (a_s, b_s) contains a signal added to the noise.

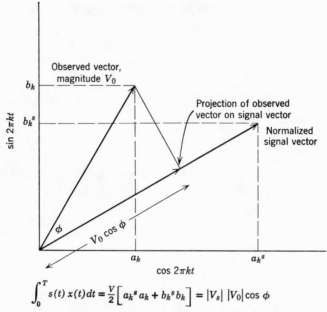

$$\int_0^T s(t)\, x(t)\, dt = \frac{V}{2}\left[a_k{}^s a_k + b_k{}^s b_k \right] = |V_s|\,|V_0|\cos\phi$$

FIG. 7-8   A representation of the observation for a signal specified exactly. A Fourier-series representation for the observed waveform shows that only components at the signal frequency are relevant in making the decision. Thus a_k, the cosine component, and b_k, the sine component, are used as coordinates of the graph. The normalized signal vector has coordinates $a_k{}^s$ and $b_k{}^s$. The observed vector a_k, b_k has magnitude $|V_0|$. The quantity monotonic with likelihood ratio is the cross-correlation between the observed and the expected waveforms. As the equation in the figure shows, this quantity is proportional to the product of the magnitude of the two vectors times the cosine of the angle between them, ϕ. Since the projection of V_0 on V_s is $|V_0|\cos\phi$ and since $|V_s|$, the signal magnitude, is a constant, we see that the projection of the observed vector on the signal vector is monotonic with likelihood ratio. Thus optimal decisions can be made simply on the basis of the magnitude of the projection of V_0 on the normalized signal vector.

The average value of a_k will be $Va_k{}^s$, the signal magnitude along the cosine component, and the average value of $b_k = Vb_k{}^s$, the signal magnitude along the sine component. The average magnitude of the vector is therefore $[V^2/2(a_k{}^2 + b_k{}^2)]^{1/2} = V/\sqrt{2}$, which is the root-mean-squared (rms) signal voltage ($V^2T/2$ is the signal energy). Once again the distribution of observations about this point is normal and the bivariate normal contours are drawn in Fig. 7-9.

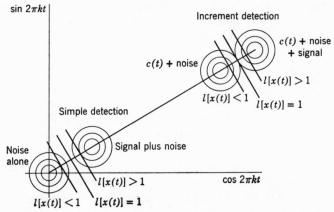

FIG. 7-9   Representation of the density functions for the signal specified exactly in the simple detection experiment and in the increment-
detection experiment. As was shown in the preceding figure, the
information in the observed waveform for the signal-specified-exactly
case may be plotted as a point in a two space using the frequency representation of the waveform. The magnitude along the cosine and sine
components at the signal frequency contains all the information
relevant to making a decision. Given noise alone, the distribution is
centered at the origin in this space, and lines of equal probability
density are circles centered at the origin. (Simple bivariate normal with
zero correlation and equal variance.) The signal vector displaces this
density to a point centered about the tip of the signal vector, but again
with circles representing lines of equal probability. Because likelihood
ratio is monotonic with the magnitude of the projection of any observed
waveform on the signal vector, lines of constant likelihood ratio are
perpendicular to the signal vector. For the increment-detection experiment, the pedestal displaces the noise-alone distribution along the
signal vector to a point labeled $c(t)$ plus noise. Again, circles represent
lines of constant probability density. The signal when added to the
pedestal displaces the vector still further, and again circles represent
lines of equal probability density. Likelihood ratio is still perpendicular
to the signal vector.

Since likelihood ratio is monotonically related to the cross correlation
of the signal with the observation, and since we have shown how this
cross correlation is proportional to the magnitude of the projection on the
signal vector, we have also established that lines of equal likelihood ratio
are perpendicular to the signal axis. Figure 7-9 shows a few of these lines.
Lines of equal likelihood ratio for the cross-correlation receiver are
perpendicular to the vector representing the signal.

For the increment-detection experiment nothing is changed except the
mean location of the two hypotheses. The pedestal waveform $c(t)$ causes a

considerable displacement of the observation vector along the direction of the signal. (The pedestal and signal waveforms are in phase.) Figure 7-9 also shows the new location of this density function, which is labelled $c(t)$ + noise. When the signal is added to the noise and pedestal, the mean of the distribution is displaced, but the decision axis and the lines of the constant likelihood ratio remain perpendicular to the signal axis.

Consider next the envelope detector or ideal detector for a signal specified except for phase. We may assume that the signal is a sinusoid, as given in Eq. 7.7, except that θ is a random variable with a uniform density function.

In Chapter 6 we proved that, in the case of a sinusoidal signal specified except for phase, the magnitude of the envelope at the signal frequency was monotonic with likelihood ratio. The magnitude of the envelope is proportional to the quantity $(a_k{}^2 + b_k{}^2)^{1/2}$, where a_k is the magnitude of the cosine component at the signal frequency k, and b_k is the magnitude of the sine component at that same frequency. Thus lines of equal likelihood ratio are circles centered about the origin in the space determined by the two coordinates of the observation, as shown in Fig. 7-10.

Once more our bird's-eye view shows the contours of the noise-alone distribution as circles centered about the origin. A signal-plus-noise distribution is also depicted for some particular value of phase angle. For the case of the sinusoidal signal, specified except for phase, the phase angle is a random variable, and on the next trial the signal might appear at a different phase angle. It is this uncertainty about the phase angle that causes the lines of constant likelihood ratio to be circles rather than straight lines, as they are for the correlation receiver; compare Fig. 7-9 and Fig. 7-10.

Note that the probability densities for noise and for signal plus noise are exactly the same, because the cross-correlation receiver is attempting to detect a signal of known phase (Fig. 7-9) and the densities drawn for the envelope detector are *conditional* on some particular phase angle. The probabilities of interest are the areas of the densities falling above some criterion value for likelihood ratio. For the cross-correlation receiver this area is the region to the right and above the straight line chosen as the criterion value on likelihood ratio. For the envelope detector it is the entire plane, with the exception of a circle about the origin. Thus the performance of the two detectors will differ, because their areas of integrations are quite different.

Consider, however, the increment-detection experiment. Figure 7-10 also shows the density for the pedestal-plus-noise and for the pedestal-plus-signal-plus-noise. Again the picture is drawn assuming one particular phase for the pedestal. The signal, if it occurs, must add to the vector

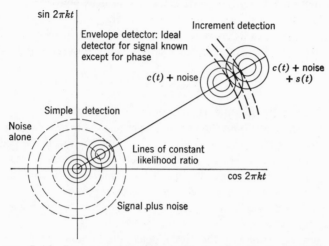

For either simple detection or increment detection
lines of equal likelihood ratio lie on circles; the larger
the ratio of the circles the larger the likelihood

FIG. 7-10   Representation of the density functions for the envelope
detector in the simple detection experiment and in the increment-
detection experiment. The coordinates and densities are the same as
shown in Fig. 7-9. We have to consider these densities for a single
trial. Thus ϕ, the signal phase, is fixed, and since the pedestal is in
phase with the signal, the same densities as shown in Fig. 7-9 would
result. Given another trial, the phase of the signal might change; the
picture would have the same general appearance, except that the
circles of constant probability density would have centers falling on
another line. Since all phase angles are equally likely, only the magnitude of the observed vector is relevant and lines of constant likelihood
are circles centered at the origin. For the simple detection experiment
the probability densities falling inside or outside a given likelihood-
ratio criterion are quite different. If, however, the pedestal amplitude
is large enough, the parts of the circles indicating lines of constant
likelihood for the pedestal experiment are essentially straight lines.
Thus the pedestal has converted the envelope detector to a signal-
known-exactly detector.

representing the pedestal, since the signal is added in phase to the pedestal.
The addition of the pedestal, if large enough, will make the performance of
the envelope detector essentially the same as the cross-correlation detector.
That is because the circles will have such a large radius compared to the
probability densities that the regions of integration for the envelope and
cross-correlation receivers will be the same. In fact, for practically all
observations, the individual decisions generated by the envelope and the

cross-correlation receivers will be identical. They will therefore have nearly identical psychometric functions.

An entirely similar argument can be invoked to show that the psychometric function for the energy detector will also be similar to that of the envelope or the cross-correlation detector in the pedestal experiment. The energy detector bases its decision on the sum of squares of many observation components, for example, the r components between l and $l + r$,

$$\sum_{k=l}^{l+r} a_k{}^2 + b_k{}^2$$

A constant likelihood ratio is, therefore, a hypersphere in a space of r dimensions centered about the origin. The criterion of the cross-correlation detector is a hyperplane in this same space. Once again, if the pedestal is large enough, then in the small region where the probability densities lie, the surface of the energy detector's hypersphere will very nearly be the same as some cross-correlation detector's hyperplane. Thus the pedestal will also make the energy detector behave as if it were phase-sensitive.

In summary, although the three detection systems predict different psychometric functions for the simple detection experiment, they all predict the same psychometric function for the increment-detection situation.

In an attempt to choose among these theoretical alternatives, Pfafflin and Mathews (1962) investigated an experimental situation like the increment-detection experiment except that the signal was always 90° out of phase with the pedestal. The cross-correlation detector should not be affected by this change in phase between the signal and the pedestal—the receiver should still cross-correlate the expected signal with the received waveform. Since the pedestal is 90° out of phase with the signal, it would have no projection on the signal axis and, therefore, would never contribute to the decision. Detection of the signal should, therefore, be the same whether the pedestal is in phase with the signal or 90° out of phase.

For the envelope and energy-detection systems the phase between signal and pedestal is crucial. Consider first the envelope-detection model. Figure 7-11 shows the signal $s(t)$ added 90° out of phase with the pedestal $c(t)$. The envelope detector measures only the magnitude of the observation; thus the change in average magnitude caused by adding a signal to the pedestal is essentially a change in the mean of the two signal distributions, and the amount of this change is indicated by Δ on the graph. The size of Δ can be calculated from geometry. The magnitude of $c(t)$ and the magnitude of $s(t)$ form two sides of a right triangle. The length of the hypotenuse minus the magnitude of $c(t)$ is the size of Δ. Let A be the magnitude of $c(t)$ and V be the magnitude of $s(t)$; then, as the geometry associated with Fig. 7-9 shows, and assuming θ is small, $\Delta = V^2/2A$. Clearly, when the signal is added 90° out of phase to the pedestal, it is considerably less detectable than when it is added in phase. (The comparable quantity for the in-phase condition is $\Delta = (V + A)^2$.) Furthermore, if the pedestal is held constant and the magnitude of the signal varied,

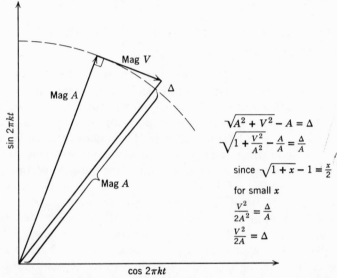

FIG. 7-11 Derivation showing how the increment in the pedestal experiment (when pedestal and signal are 90° out of phase) depends upon size of signal, V, and size of pedestal amplitude, A.

then the distance between the means divided by the common standard deviation, d', varies proportionally with signal power when the pedestal is 90° out of phase with the signal.

A similar conclusion can be reached for the energy-detection model. (The derivation is presented in Chapter 8.) When the signal and pedestal are in phase, d' varies proportionally with signal voltage; when they are 90° out of phase, d' varies as signal voltage squared, or signal power.

Pfafflin and Mathews (1962) held the signal level constant and gradually increased the pedestal amplitude. For the 90°-out-of-phase condition, the detectability of the signal appeared to remain at about the same level (55% in a two-alternative forced-choice task) and did not change as a function of pedestal amplitude. When, in another condition, they added the signal in phase with the pedestal, they found that the detectability increased markedly with pedestal amplitude, rising from 55% to nearly 95%. They did not obtain complete psychometric functions for the in-phase and 90°-out-of-phase conditions, but presumably the two functions would be different.

These results seem to rule out any cross-correlation detector as a realistic model of human detection performance. Either an envelope detector or an energy detector would appear to be a more reasonable analogue of human detection performance.

7.7 THE PRODUCT OF BANDWIDTH AND SIGNAL DURATION (WT)

The next logical step is to devise experiments to distinguish between the envelope detector and the energy detector as models of the human observer's performance. This appears to be a difficult task, because formally both models are very similar: each assumes an initial filter, a nonlinear device, and some postdetection filtering. The difference arises in specific assumptions about the size of parameters of the process. One parameter of particular importance is the bandwidth of the initial filter, or a related quantity, the product of bandwidth times the signal duration (WT). This quantity (WT) is of particular interest because it is the number of degrees of freedom in the stochastic process that the energy detector uses as a basis for making its decisions. For the analysis of the energy detector to be valid, this number must be large (see Chapter 8). For the analysis of the envelope detector to be valid, the number must be small (see Chapter 6). We can, of course, take some empirical data and try to estimate the size of this parameter from the data. But what model should we use in making the estimates? As might be expected, if we use the energy model to make our estimates, we infer that this product is much larger than if the envelope model is used.

Jeffress (1964), using the envelope model, estimates a bandwidth of 50 cps for a $\frac{1}{10}$-second, 1000-cps signal. Using data similar to those used by Jeffress, the energy model leads to the conclusion that the bandwidth is nearly 500 cps for a $\frac{1}{10}$-second signal at a signal frequency of 1000 cps. The duration-bandwidth product is therefore 50. As yet there are no data available to give a clear choice between these models.

7.8 WEBER'S LAW

Up to this point we have considered only the shape of the psychometric function; we have ignored the absolute levels of performance. This neglect has been largely dictated by the simple fact that any inferences based on absolute levels depend heavily on estimates of other detection parameters, such as the predetection bandwidth and the level of internal noise. There is still considerable disagreement about the correct values of these sensory parameters.

Furthermore, there is one very salient characteristic of practically all sensory devices that is not included in any of the simple detection devices we have mentioned thus far. Consider the increment-detection experiment. To maintain a constant level of detectability, we know that the signal level must be increased as the pedestal level is increased, and in such a way that the ratio of increment energy to background energy remains nearly constant. This constancy of the ratio of increment energy to background energy is known as Weber's law, and although the law is not exactly true, it is certainly a good first approximation. Clearly, it is a more descriptive rule than the one that characterizes ideal detection systems, namely, that detection is determined by the amount of change, independent of the value of the initial point.

This unrealistic rule arises simply because the devices are ideal, and thus they are assumed to measure with infinite accuracy and with no computation errors. It is not difficult to modify any of the models to make them more realistic. A very appealing assumption is that there is "internal noise" or variability in the observation interval that is proportional to the quantity being measured. If this assumption is made, it follows that the amount of increment needed to reach a certain level of detectability is proportional to the starting point. Thus Weber's law can be explained by assuming an amount of internal noise that is proportional to the average level of the external noise plus pedestal. Examples of this assumption can be seen in papers by Tanner (1961a) and by Pfafflin and Mathews (1962). There is also some independent evidence from quite different areas that the internal and external noise levels are related (see Chapter 9). Once again, however, the exact values assumed for the constant of proportionality are affected considerably by the exact assumptions we make about the other parameters of the sensory system, such as predetection bandwidth and postdetection integration. Although a specific theory complete with explicit values of all the parameters seems tantalizingly close, no one has yet proposed it.

7.9   SUMMARY

A variety of detector systems were compared with data obtained from human observers in two general experimental conditions: the simple detection of a gated sinusoid in noise, and the increment-detection task, in which the signal is added to another constant signal, or pedestal.

The psychometric functions, relating the percentage of correct detections to the ratio of signal energy to noise-power density, for these two situations, were described. For the simple detection task, the curve rises abruptly from near chance to almost perfect performance in a range of about 10 db. For the increment-detection task the psychometric function ascends much more gradually and spans a range of about 25 db.

Two general models, the envelope detector and the cross-correlation detector, were compared with the data. Based on results of some increment-detection experiments, the envelope detector appears to be the more likely model. The psychometric functions for simple detection experiments indicate that the detector tests for a variety of possible signals even if only one is used as the signal in the experiment; that is, the detector appears uncertain about the exact character of the signal. The energy detector is also a likely candidate, but we postpone further discussion of that model until Chapter 8.

The amount of progress in this area has not been very great; yet, given the rather small number of studies, the amount of progress appears quite encouraging. It seems likely that the next few years will indicate that this is an area of considerable research potential.

PROBLEMS

7.1   Explain the difference between signal energy, E_s, and increment energy, ΔE. State the conditions under which the two quantities are equal.

7.2   According to the model for 1-of-M orthogonal signals (known phase), how much will one need to increase the signal level to compensate for a fourfold increase in the number of uncertain signals?

7.3   Of the several detector systems discussed in Chapter 7, which one gives results consistent with Weber's law and for what kind of signal?

8

Energy-Detection Model
for Audition

8.1   INTRODUCTION

This chapter is devoted to a detailed analysis of a simple energy-detection system. This system, it is argued, provides a rather good analogue of the human auditory detection process. The energy-detection system is composed of three separate parts: a first stage of filtering (a predetection filter), a square-law device (or detector in the radio-communication sense), and a final integrator (or postdetection filter). The predetection filter is suggested by the critical-band concept. Part of the chapter will be devoted to an estimate of the bandwidth of this filter. The square-law device acts as a nonlinear element to provide a quantity whose average value is monotonically related to the intensity of the signal. The particular nonlinear characteristic assumed, a square law, is dictated mostly by mathematical convenience. If we were to assume that the nonlinear element was a half-wave rectifier, the assumption might be more realistic from the physiological standpoint, but mathematical analysis would be more difficult. The last of the three elements, the integrator, simply averages or smooths the value of the test statistics provided by the first two processes. This integrated value provides the basis for the final decision.

The derivations that follow must, of necessity, be specific. The derivation will, however, be of general use, because the three parts of this model are present in all detection devices. Furthermore, the particular relations suggested here are in no way atypical of detection devices in general. It is not our intention to suggest that this particular model is a very detailed or complete analogue of the human detection process. It is felt, however, that this model does contain the minimal elements for a more realistic and a more detailed model. The important point is to understand quantitatively how parameter values of the elements of this system influence detection performance. Similar variations will be true of a variety of the other models. In accordance with this aim, we shall attempt to simplify the resulting equations as much as possible. Good first-order approximations will be preferred to more accurate, but more complicated, expressions.

The model and equations will be illustrated by discussing the implications of such a model for the following set of phenomena:

(1) The detection of a pulsed sine wave in noise.

(2) The detection of an increment in a large pulsed sinusoid present in a background noise.

(3) The detection of a sinusoid in noise of various bandwidths—that is, Fletcher's (1940) critical-band experiment.

8.2 HISTORY OF CONCEPT AND PREVIOUS INVESTIGATIONS

There is a long history to the use of a filter, followed by an energy detector, as an analogue to the auditory detection mechanism. The hypothesis was credible shortly after the first careful consideration of the auditory process. First-stage filtering was implicit in the ideas of Helmholtz and, in particular, his resonance theory of hearing (Helmholtz, 1885). Detection by some sort of nonlinear device is hardly novel. In more recent times, this general analogue has been explicitly suggested by many authors. Among the earliest, probably, were Schafer, Gales, Shewmaker, and Thompson (1950). Jeffress, Blodgett, Sandel, and Wood (1956) have suggested a detailed model of this sort for both monaural and binaural hearing. Sherwin, Kodman, Kovaly, Prothe, and Melrose (1956) have attempted to analyze the individual responses of subjects with such a model. Green (1960a) has attempted to explain the detection of noise signals in noise with such a model. Urick and Stocklin (1962) use this general model in analyzing some psychoacoustic data and, finally, the recent paper of Pfafflin and Mathews (1962) has provided considerable quantitative detail for the behavior of such a detection process in at least two general experimental situations. Raab, Osman, and Rich (1963) have also endorsed an energy detector, although some details of their arguments are faulty (Green, in press).

We follow the spirit of these previous investigators. The use of the discrete representation of the noise and signal waveforms, along with the assumption of a rectangular filter, allows us to derive the results in particularly simple form. These results are very nearly the same as those derived by Pfafflin and Mathews. In their limiting form, the results of Pfafflin and Mathews differ from ours by a factor of $\sqrt{2}$; this difference arises because of small differences in our assumptions about the shape of the critical band (Pfafflin and Mathews, 1966).

The first part of the chapter is devoted to deriving the statistics of the energy-detection process. Secondly, the results of this analysis are applied to a variety of psychoacoustic data. The resulting application leads to an unusually large estimate of the size of the critical band. Finally, the discrepancy between this new estimate and the older estimates leads us to re-evaluate Fletcher's (1940) critical-band experiment. The argument advanced in this re-evaluation is essentially the same as the one expressed by DeBoer (1962).

8.3   THE ENERGY-DETECTION MODEL

The flow diagram of Fig. 8-1 indicates components of the model. The input signal passes through an internal filter with unity gain and bandwidth W_I. The output of this internal filter is denoted $x(t)$. We make here the same assumptions about $x(t)$ as we did in Chapter 6. Specifically, we assume that $x(t)$ is Fourier-series band-limited, with bandwidth W. The bandwidth W, in most cases, refers to the internal bandwidth W_I, but in some cases, such as the critical-band experiment, the signals are filtered by an external filter of bandwidth W_E. We assume that the external

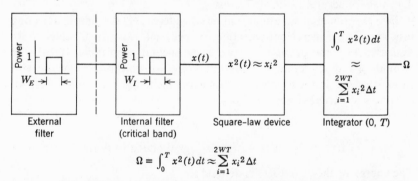

$$\Omega = \int_0^T x^2(t)\,dt \approx \sum_{i=1}^{2WT} x_i^2 \Delta t$$

FIG. 8-1   Flow diagram of the energy-detection model. The assumed components are to the right of the dotted line. The first stage is an internal filter. It is, as a first approximation, assumed to have a square bandwidth of width W_I cps and unity gain. The output of the internal filter is squared and passes to an integrator. The integrator begins integration at the start of the signal 0, and ends at the termination of the signal T. The output Ω is the quantity used in deciding whether or not a signal is present. In some experiments an external filter is employed. We can, for simplicity, assume the external filter to be square with bandwidth W_E cps and unity gain. The internal and external filters will have the same center frequency for all the experiments that we discuss.

filter is rectangular with unity gain, and thus the effective bandwidth W is either W_I or W_E, whichever is smaller. As in Chapter 6, we assume that $x(t)$ can be approximated by measuring $x(t)$ at discrete samples in time spaced $1/2W$ seconds apart. The variance of the sample, given that only noise is present, is denoted σ_n^2. This quantity is also the average power of $x(t)$. If $W_I < W_E$, the average power in $x(t)$ is $W_I N_0$; if $W_E < W_I$, the average power in $x(t)$ is $W_E N_0$. We shall use the unscripted letter W to indicate the smaller of these two bandwidths in most of the discussion that follows. For a variety of experiments W_E may be considered the bandwidth of the power amplifier used by the experimenter; thus W_E may be at least two orders of magnitude larger than W_I. In the critical-band experiment itself, however, W_E is systematically varied, and its explicit recognition at this point will simplify our later discussion of that experiment. The waveform $x(t)$, after emerging from the internal filter, is squared and then integrated for the signal duration T. We thus assume that the observer knows the signal interval almost exactly, since his decision is based on information only during the signal interval $(0 - T)$.

The output of the integrator is represented by a real number, the quantity Ω.* The problem is to decide from the magnitude of the statistic Ω which of the two possible hypotheses is true. This decision is determined by the conditional probability density of Ω under the two hypotheses. In the next section we derive an approximation to these probability densities for several cases of interest.

Two experimental situations will be considered: (1) the simple detection task and (2) the increment-detection, or pedestal, task. In Chapter 7 we discussed in some detail these two experimental conditions. As a brief reminder, and to define some terminology, we quickly review the two situations here. In the simple detection experiment one of the following two hypotheses is true; either

$$x(t) \quad \text{is} \quad n(t) \qquad \text{noise alone}$$

or

$$x(t) \quad \text{is} \quad n(t) + s(t) \qquad \text{signal added to noise.}$$

The energy of the signal $s(t)$ is defined as

$$E_s = \int_0^T s^2(t)\, dt \approx \sum_{i=1}^{2WT} s_i^2 \,\Delta t \tag{8.1}$$

* We designate the statistic Ω, the energy of $x(t)$, to avoid confusion with measured quantities such as E_s, the energy of the signal, and E_c, the energy of the pedestal. The energy quantities are subscripted to avoid confusion with the symbol for the expected value of a random variable such as $E(\Omega)$, the expectation of the energy of the stochastic process, $x(t)$.

In the increment-detection or pedestal experiment, one of the following two hypotheses is true; either

$$x(t) \quad \text{is} \quad n(t) + c(t) \qquad \text{noise plus pedestal}$$

or

$$x(t) \quad \text{is} \quad n(t) + c(t) + s(t) \qquad \text{noise plus pedestal plus signal.}$$

The energy of the pedestal $c(t)$ is defined as $E_c = \int_0^T c^2(t)\, dt$. When both signal and pedestal are presented together, the energy of the combination is

$$E_{c+s} = \int_0^T [c(t) + s(t)]^2\, dt = E_c + E_s + 2\int_0^T s(t)c(t)\, dt \qquad (8.2)$$

We define

$$2\int_0^T s(t)c(t)\, dt = 2r_{sc} \qquad (8.3)$$

Thus

$$E_{c+s} = E_c + E_s + 2r_{sc} \qquad (8.4)$$

Sometimes the signal is an attenuated copy of the pedestal, $s(t) = kc(t)$, where k is a constant, $k < 1$; then

$$2r_{sc} = 2kE_c \qquad \text{and} \quad E_s = k^2 E_c \qquad (8.5)$$

Thus

$$E_{c+s} = E_c + k^2 E_c + 2kE_c = (1 + 2k + k^2)E_c \qquad (8.6)$$

The increment in energy caused by adding $s(t)$ to $c(t)$ is

$$\Delta E = E_{c+s} - E_c = (2k + k^2)E_c \qquad (8.7)$$

or, in general,

$$E_{c+s} - E_c = E_s + 2r_{sc} \qquad (8.8)$$

Only if there is no correlation between pedestal and signal is the increment in energy, ΔE, equal to the signal energy E_s.

The definitions listed above are used as we derive the conditional probability of the quantity Ω for the simple detection and the pedestal experiments. There are four conditional density functions of the statistic Ω: two hypotheses for each of the two experimental situations.

8.3.1 Conditional probabilities for Ω

8.3.1.1 GIVEN NOISE ALONE, $n(t)$. If $x(t)$ is noise alone, $n(t)$, we want to determine the density of Ω:

$$\Omega_n = \int_0^T n^2(t)\, dt \qquad (8.9a)$$

First we approximate Ω_n by a finite sum:

$$\Omega_n = \sum_{i=1}^{2WT} n_i^2 \Delta t \tag{8.9b}$$

Observe that n_i is Gaussian and independent of all other terms in the sum. By definition, the square of a normalized Gaussian variable is distributed as chi square. Furthermore, if two variables are independent and both are distributed as chi square, then their sum is also distributed as chi square with degrees of freedom equal to the sum of degrees of freedom of the independent variables. Thus, since $\sigma_n^2 = N_0 W$,

$$\frac{\Omega_n}{\Delta t N_0 W} = \sum_{i=1}^{2WT} \left(\frac{n_i}{\sigma_n}\right)^2 \tag{8.10}$$

is χ^2 with $2WT$ degrees of freedom. Using the equality $\Delta t = 1/2W$ we have $2\Omega_n/N_0$, which is χ^2 with $2WT$ degrees of freedom. The expected value of a chi-square distribution is the number of the degrees of freedom. The variance is twice the number of the degrees of freedom. Thus,

$$E\left(\frac{2\Omega_n}{N_0}\right) = 2WT$$

$$\text{var}\left(\frac{2\Omega_n}{N_0}\right) = 4WT$$

The expected value of $\Omega_n [E(\Omega_n) = TWN_0]$ checks with our earlier definitions (see Chapter 6, Eq. 6.4). We set the noise power per component at $N_0/2T$. The average energy per component is therefore $N_0/2$. The total noise energy is the number of components, $2WT$, multiplied by the average energy per component, or $2WT \cdot N_0/2 = TWN_0$.

The mean-to-sigma ratio of Ω is proportional to the square root of the quantity WT. An energy measurement of noise 1000 cps wide, and $\frac{1}{10}$ second in duration, will have a mean-to-sigma ratio of approximately 10 to 1. Thus, if the true average were 10 watt-seconds, one would often measure values between 9 and 11 watt-seconds, but one third of the measurements would exceed these bounds.

8.3.1.2   GIVEN SIGNAL PLUS NOISE, $s(t) + n(t)$. We next derive the probability density when the waveform is $n(t) + s(t)$. For this case our approximation to the energy Ω_{s+n} is

$$\Omega_{s+n} = \sum_{i=1}^{2WT} (n_i + s_i)^2 \Delta t \tag{8.11a}$$

Once again the expected value of n_i is zero, and the variance is WN_0. We again normalize the terms in the sum:

$$\frac{\Omega_{s+n}}{\Delta t N_0 W} = \sum_{i=1}^{2WT} \left(\frac{n_i + s_i}{\sigma_n}\right)^2 \tag{8.11b}$$

This quantity is a sum of squares of independent normal deviates; each deviate has mean s_i/σ_n and variance unity. The probability density of this sum is a noncentral chi square with $2WT$ degrees of freedom and noncentral parameter

$$\frac{1}{\sigma_n^2} \sum_{i=1}^{2WT} s_i^2 = \lambda$$

The noncentral chi-square distribution may be approximated by a Gaussian distribution if the number of the degrees of freedom is large.* The mean is the number of degrees of freedom plus the noncentral parameter, which is denoted by λ. The variance is twice the number of degrees of freedom plus four times the noncentral parameter (see Abramowitz and Stegun, 1965, p. 942). The noncentral parameter λ is

$$\lambda = \frac{1}{\sigma_n^2} \sum_{i=1}^{2WT} s_i^2 = \frac{1}{N_0 W} \frac{1}{\Delta t} E_s$$

$$\lambda = \frac{2E_s}{N_0}$$

Therefore

$$E\left(\frac{2\Omega_{n+s}}{N_0}\right) = 2WT + \frac{2E_s}{N_0}$$

$$\text{var}\ \left(\frac{2\Omega_{n+s}}{N_0}\right) = 4WT + \frac{8E_s}{N_0} \tag{8.12}$$

which is not surprising, since the mean is the normalized energy of the noise, as in the previous case, plus the standardized energy of the signal. The variance is almost the same, except for the addition of some variability caused by adding the sinusoidal signal to the noise.

8.3.1.3 GIVEN PEDESTAL PLUS NOISE, $c(t) + n(t)$. In the pedestal experiment, if the first hypothesis is true then $x(t) = n(t) + c(t)$. There is no need for further labor to derive the conditional density of the statistic Ω_{n+c}. The quantity $c(t)$ may be identified with $s(t)$ as in the previous

---

* For further information both about the noncentral chi square and about approximations to it, Kendall (1947), Patnaik (1949), and Sankaran (1963) are recommended. We are indebted to Dr. Saul Sternberg for pointing out these approximations.

TABLE 8-1.   CONDITIONAL DENSITY OF ENERGY, Ω, GIVEN VARIOUS HYPOTHESES.

Random Variable	Hypothesis True	Mean	Variance	Distribution for $2WT > 10$
Simple detection experiment				
$\dfrac{2\Omega_n}{N_0}$	$x(t) = n(t)$	$2WT$	$4WT$	Approximately Gaussian
$\dfrac{2\Omega_{n+s}}{N_0}$	$x(t) = n(t) + s(t)$	$2WT + \dfrac{2E_s}{N_0}$	$4WT + \dfrac{8E_s}{N_0}$	Approximately Gaussian
Pedestal experiment				
$\dfrac{2\Omega_{n+c}}{N_0}$	$x(t) = n(t) + c(t)$	$2WT + \dfrac{2E_c}{N_0}$	$4WT + \dfrac{8E_c}{N_0}$	Approximately Gaussian
$\dfrac{2\Omega_{n+c+s}}{N_0}$	$x(t) = n(t) + c(t) + s(t)$	$2WT + \dfrac{2E_{s+c}}{N_0}$	$4WT + \dfrac{8E_{c+s}}{N_0}$	Approximately Gaussian

derivation. We therefore have

$$E\left(\frac{2\Omega_{n+c}}{N_0}\right) = 2WT + \frac{2E_c}{N_0}$$

$$\text{var}\left(\frac{2\Omega_{n+c}}{N_0}\right) = 4WT + \frac{8E_c}{N_0}$$

8.3.1.4 GIVEN SIGNAL PLUS PEDESTAL PLUS NOISE, $s(t) + c(t) + n(t)$. If the second hypothesis of the pedestal experiment is true, then $x(t) = s(t) + c(t) + n(t)$. Again we use our previous derivation of the density given $n(t) + s(t)$, but identify $c(t) + s(t)$ as the signal waveform. Then,

$$E\left(\frac{2\Omega_{n+s+c}}{N_0}\right) = 2WT + \frac{2E_{s+c}}{N_0}$$

$$\text{var}\left(\frac{2\Omega_{n+s+c}}{N_0}\right) = 4WT + \frac{8E_{s+c}}{N_0}$$

Table 8-1 summarizes these derivations for the conditional probabilities of the statistic Ω for all hypotheses and experiments.

8.3.2 Percent correct in two-alternative forced-choice procedure

The derivations just concluded give us the densities of a quantity proportional to energy for two experimental situations. Our next task is to relate these densities to some measurable aspect of the detector's behavior in the psychophysical task. There are several ways we might proceed. We could, for example, simply plot ROC curves for a variety of physical parameters in both experimental situations. Such plots would be rather cumbersome and would hardly facilitate a comparison of the results with the physical parameters of signal and noise. For this reason we use the *area under the ROC curve* as our summary parameter. Thus the area is used as the measure of the detector's performance and this parameter, or a quantity monotonically related to it, is used in the discussion that follows. The area under the yes-no ROC curve is the expected percentage correct in a two-alternative forced-choice task, if a symmetric decision rule is used. We now derive this percentage correct.

For either the simple detection experiment or the pedestal experiment, the two observation intervals of the forced-choice task yield two samples for the energy Ω. One of the samples contains a signal; the other does not. If the observer selects the interval associated with the larger sample, then he will be correct if and only if the larger sample comes from the signal-plus-background distribution. The probability that $y > x$ is most easily determined by computing the probability that $y - x > 0$. When y and x

TABLE 8-2. DIFFERENCE DISTRIBUTIONS FOR SIMPLE DETECTION AND PEDESTAL EXPERIMENTS.

	Random Variable	Mean of h_i	Variance of h_i
Simple detection experiment	$h_1 = \dfrac{2}{N_0}(\Omega_{n+s} - \Omega_n)$	$2E_s/N_0$	$8WT + \dfrac{8E_s}{N_0}$ $4\left(2WT + \dfrac{2E_s}{N_0}\right)$
Pedestal experiment	$h_2 = \dfrac{2}{N_0}(\Omega_{n+c+s} - \Omega_{n+c})$	$\dfrac{2E_{s+c} - 2E_c}{N_0}$ $\dfrac{2(E_s + 2r_{sc})}{N_0}$	$8WT + \dfrac{8E_c}{N_0} + \dfrac{8E_{c+s}}{N_0}$ $4\left(2WT + \dfrac{2E_c}{N_0} + \dfrac{2E_{c+s}}{N_0}\right)$

If $s(t) = kc(t)$, then $2r_{sc} = 2kE_c$ and $E_s = k^2E_c$

$$\frac{2(k^2 + 2k)E_c}{N_0} \qquad 4\left\{2WT + \frac{2E_c}{N_0}(2 + k^2 + 2k)\right\}$$

are normal and independent this probability is easily determined, since the difference distribution is also normal and has a mean equal to the difference in the means and a variance equal to the sum of the variances. If the number of degrees of freedom is large, that is, if $2WT > 10$, then the chi square and the noncentral chi square are approximately normal. Table 8-2 gives the parameters of these difference distributions for the two experimental situations. The probability of being correct is the probability that h is greater than zero, where h is Gaussian. Thus for the simple detection experiment

$$P_2(C) = \Phi(h_1)$$

where

$$h_1 = \frac{E_s/N_0}{(2WT + 2E_s/N_0)^{1/2}} \tag{8.13}$$

and for the pedestal experiment

$$P_2(C) = \Phi(h_2)$$

where

$$h_2 = \frac{(E_{c+s} - E_c)/N_0}{(2WT + 2E_c/N_0 + 2E_{c+s}/N_0)^{1/2}} \tag{8.14}$$

A brief table of $P_2(C)$ and h follows:

h	$P_2(C)$
0.25	60
0.68	75
0.70	76
1.28	90

Because h is a parameter of the difference distribution, it is exactly equal to $\sqrt{2}$ times the normalized difference between the means of the original distribution, if both distributions have equal variance. Thus $\sqrt{2}h \approx d'$. Since h is monotonically related to the expected percentage correct, and is directly equal to the physical parameters of the experimental situation, it is frequently employed in the discussion that follows.

In summary, Eqs. 8.13 and 8.14 are the two basic equations of this chapter. In the remainder of the chapter we compare these two equations with a variety of experimental results.

8.4   SIMPLE DETECTION EXPERIMENT

Briefly, the experimental situation is as follows. The observer is listening to a continuous, white Gaussian noise. At certain intervals in time, marked by brief light flashes, a pulsed sinusoidal signal may be presented. The observer's task is to detect this signal.

The two questions we wish to investigate are (1) how does the detectability of the signal change with changes in signal intensity, or what is the psychometric function? and (2) what is the signal energy to noise-power density at a particular level of detectability, say 76% correct? The relation between E_s/N_0 and $2WT$ is given by Eq. 8.13; if $2WT > 2E_s/N_0$, then it can be approximated very accurately by neglecting the term $(2E_s/N_0)$ in the denominator, so that

$$E_s/N_0 \approx h_1(2WT)^{1/2} \tag{8.15}$$

or, in decibels,

$$\varepsilon - \eta_0 = 10 \log E_s/N_0 \approx 10 \log h_1 + 10 \log (2WT)^{1/2} \tag{8.16}$$

For 76% correct, $h_1 = 1/\sqrt{2}$; thus

$$\varepsilon - \eta_0 \approx 10 \log (WT)^{1/2}$$

or

$$E_s/N_0 \approx (WT)^{1/2} \tag{8.17}$$

As previously observed, $P_2(C)$ is a Gaussian function of h and, since h is a linear function of E_s/N_0 (Eq. 8.9), the percentage correct in a two-alternative forced-choice task is a cumulative Gaussian function when

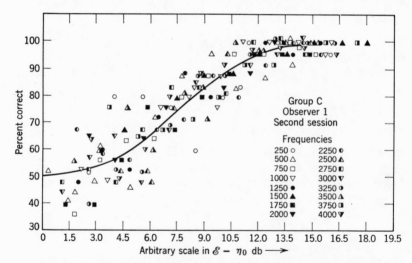

FIG. 8-2 Psychometric functions for a single observer at a variety of signal frequencies. The signal, a pulsed sinusoid of 1/10-sec duration, was partially masked by noise. The percentage of correct responses as a function of the signal energy in decibels is displayed. At each frequency the scale of $\varepsilon - \eta_0 = 10 \log E/N_0$ has been displaced by an attenuation constant. Each point is defined by the percentage correct in 25 trials. The solid line is the theoretical psychometric function for the energy detector. (After Green, McKey, and Licklider, 1959.)

plotted against signal energy. Alternatively, we may say that *the psychometric function is a Gaussian function when plotted on a scale of E_s/N_0.* Note, however, that only one half of the Gaussian function is integrated; this psychometric function starts at 50% correct.

There are considerable experimental data to indicate that this relation is approximately correct for the detection of a pulsed sinusoid in noise.

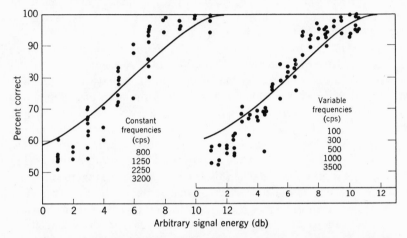

FIG. 8-3   Psychometric functions for a typical observer for "constant" and "variable" frequencies. In the case of constant frequency, the signal frequency was fixed at one of the values indicated (800, 1250, 2250, 3200 cps), and was the same from trial to trial. In the case of variable frequency, the signal frequency was changed from trial to trial, and was chosen from a range of frequencies as indicated (100, 300, 500, 1000, 3500 cps); the center frequency of each range was 2250 cps. The ordinate is the percentage correct in two-alternative forced-choice trials. Each point is based on 300 observations. The abscissa is the ratio of signal energy to noise-power density in decibels. The abscissa has been shifted to the left or right so that the curves are grouped together. The solid lines are the theoretical curves from the energy-detection model. (After Green, 1961.)

Figure 8-2 shows actual data from a single subject at 16 different frequencies, in a two-alternative forced-choice task. The signal duration is $\frac{1}{10}$ sec. The data show considerable scatter because only 25 observations are used to estimate each point. Figure 8-3 shows data based on 300 observations per point. Other data support this same relationship.

Having considered how the detectability changes with signal intensity, consider now the specific values of the parameters at a single level of detectability. In particular, what do values of E, N_0, and h_1 imply about the remaining terms in Eq. 8.15, namely T and W? Solving Eq. 8.15 for

TW is reminiscent of what Zwicker, Flottorp, and Stevens (1957) called the critical-ratio method of determining the width of the critical band.

Fletcher (1940) originally argued that the masked threshold for the tone occurred when the signal power was equal to the total noise power in a critical band. Thus, for a wide-band noise of power density N_0, the threshold signal power P_s was equal to the critical bandwidth W_c multiplied by the noise power density ($P_s/N_0 = W_c$). In Fletcher's experiment the signal duration was unlimited; the subjects adjusted the signal level P_s so that the tone was just detectable in the noise.

In Eq. 8.17 the integration time of the hypothetical integrator (see Fig. 8-1) is assumed to equal the duration of the signal T. Given this assumption, we can determine the bandwidth of the hypothetical filter. At a signal frequency of 1000 cps and a signal duration of $\frac{1}{10}$ sec, about 76% correct is obtained with an $E_s/N_0 = 10$. Solving Eq. 8.17, we have $WT \approx 100$ or, since $T = \frac{1}{10}$, $W = 1000$ cps. This estimate of the critical bandwidth is about 16 times larger than Fletcher's estimate of 60 cps, and about 5 times larger than the estimate of Zwicker and others (1957). Our estimate is probably inflated. It is generous to assume that the observer integrates for a period of time exactly equal to the signal duration. More probably he integrates for a somewhat longer period of time, so that overlap with the signal interval is assured. It is easy to show that, if the integrator samples a period of time $T' > T$, the equations are exactly the same, except that T' replaces T.* Thus, if the effective period of integration is $\frac{2}{10}$ sec, rather than the actual signal duration of $\frac{1}{10}$ sec, the estimated bandwidth would be 500 cps rather than 1000 cps. Although 500 cps is still considerably larger than most other estimates, we have other ways of estimating bandwidth, and these other methods also support this figure. Furthermore, in a later section, where the critical-band experiment is reanalyzed, we try to reconcile these diverse estimates. Before we do so, however, we consider a slightly different psychoacoustic detection situation, the detection of the more intense of two tone bursts.

8.5   THE INCREMENT-DETECTION EXPERIMENT

The procedure of the increment-detection, or pedestal, experiment is like that of the simple detection experiment except that a constant waveform $c(t)$ occurs in both temporal intervals. The observer's task is still to indicate the interval containing the signal. Often the signal and the pedestal are the same frequency and the signal is added, in phase, to one

---

* The energy of the signal is $E_s = P_s T$, so that if the results are expressed in terms of signal power P_s, we must note that the multiplier is T, the actual duration of the signal, rather than T', the interval of integration.

of the two pedestals. The signal then adds a small increment to one of these pedestals. When this is the case, the signal $s(t)$ can be described in terms of the pedestal $s(t) = kc(t)$. Then Eq. 8.14 applies and, rewriting E_{c+s} in terms of k and E_c by Eqs. 8.4 and 8.6, we have

$$h_2 = \frac{(k^2 + 2k)E_c/N_0}{[2WT + 2E_c/N_0(2 + k^2 + 2k)]^{1/2}} \tag{8.18}$$

(See also Table 8-2.) Typically, k is small ($k \approx \frac{1}{20}$); thus when the pedestal is large compared with $2WT$,

$$h_2 \approx \frac{2k(E_c/N_0)}{(4E_c/N_0)^{1/2}} \qquad 2WT \ll \frac{2E_c}{N_0} \quad \text{and} \quad k \ll 1 \tag{8.19}$$

and, since $E_s^{1/2} = k \cdot E_c^{1/2}$,

$$h_2 \approx \sqrt{\frac{E_s}{N_0}} \tag{8.20}$$

This last expression indicates that the energy detector shows the same variation with signal energy E_s as that displayed by the cross-correlation detector, or the ideal observer for signal specified exactly (see Chapter 6). The large pedestal has converted the energy detector to a signal-specified-exactly receiver. Figure 7-7 shows some typical data for the pedestal experiment in which the signal is an attenuated version of the pedestal $[s(t) = kc(t)]$.*

For cases in which the signal is completely or partially uncorrelated with the pedestal, the variation of percentage correct in a 2AFC task is as follows:

$$P_2(C) = \Phi(h_2) = \Phi\left[\frac{(E_s + r_{sc})/N_0}{(2WT + 2E_c/N_0 + 2E_{c+s}/N_0)^{1/2}}\right] \tag{8.21}$$

Unless r_{sc} is exactly zero, it may vary with the magnitude of both the signal and the pedestal. When r_{sc} is zero, the term within brackets will vary linearly with E_s, rather than $(E_s)^{1/2}$. Thus the energy-detection model clearly predicts a difference in the shape of the psychometric function depending on the correlation of the pedestal and the signal. Pfafflin and Mathews' (1962) data show that the change of detectability with pedestal amplitude is different for the correlated and uncorrelated conditions. There are no data directly testing the prediction that the shape of the psychometric function for the uncorrelated condition varies as Eq. 8.21 would indicate.

* Note the difference between the shape of the psychometric function for the simple detection and for the increment-detection task. In the former, the psychometric function covers a range of signal variation of about 10 db; in the increment-detection task this range is nearly 25 db.

8.6   ENERGY DETECTION AND THE SHAPE OF THE ROC CURVE

The energy-detection model might also predict that the shape of the ROC curve changes as a function of the amplitude of the pedestal. The tentative nature of this statement is necessary because we are not sure of the exact value of the critical band, or more precisely the parameter WT, the product of bandwidth and integration time. The shape of the distribution of the parameter Ω is approximately Gaussian for all the experimental conditions. What changes is the ratio of signal variance to nonsignal variance in the various tasks. For the simple detection task this ratio of signal to nonsignal variance (see Table 8-1) is

$$\frac{\sigma_{n+s}}{\sigma_n} = \left(\frac{4WT + 8E_s/N_0}{4WT}\right)^{\frac{1}{2}} \tag{8.22}$$

The following table relates typical values of E_s/N_0 and $P_2(C)$, and determines σ_{n+s}/σ_n for a sinusoidal signal of 1000 cps and $\frac{1}{10}$ sec duration. We assume that $W = 500$ for this calculation.

$P_2(C)$	E_s/N_0	(σ_{n+s}/σ_n)
64	5	1.1
76	10	1.2
93	20	1.3
99	40	1.6

If, on the other hand, we assume with Fletcher that $W = 60$ cps, then $WT = 6$, and even if E_s/N_0 is only 10, the ratio of signal to nonsignal variance is $\frac{104}{24} \approx 4$, or the ratio of sigmas is as much as 2.

For the pedestal experiment the ratio of variances is

$$\frac{\sigma_{n+c+s}}{\sigma_{n+c}} = \left[\frac{4WT + 8E_c/N_0}{4WT + 8E_{c+s}/N_0}\right]^{\frac{1}{2}} = \left[\frac{4WT + 8E_c/N_0}{4WT + 8E_c/N_0(1 + 2k + k^2)}\right]^{\frac{1}{2}} \tag{8.23}$$

where $k = s(t)/c(t)$. Since $k \approx \frac{1}{20}$ and $E_c/N_0 \gg 4WT$, the ratio becomes nearly 1. The sure prediction for the energy-detection system is that, as the pedestal gets very large, the ratio of the variances becomes nearly unity. Thus the ROC curve becomes symmetric about the minor diagonal. This result is also predicted by the cross-correlation and envelope-detection models.

We turn now to some experimental data that simply cannot be handled by the simple energy-detection model. There is no room for doubt about the lack of correspondence between data and theory in this area. The model must be modified.

8.7 INCREMENT DETECTION AND WEBER'S LAW

Weber's law is an empirical generalization that is approximately true for a variety of sense modalities. The law says that the intensity of a stimulus change needed to be just detectably different from the background intensity is a *constant fraction* of this background intensity. For example, with light intensity, if I is the standard or original intensity and ΔI is the amount added to I to evoke a just noticeable change, then we find $\Delta I/I$ to be approximately the same for various values of I. In acoustics the fraction is sometimes stated in power or energy terms and sometimes as a pressure ratio. This leads to a rather serious ambiguity, because the former, the energy ratio, is twice the latter or pressure ratio.* We shall use the notation $\Delta E/E_c$ throughout this discussion, and this is an energy ratio.

Consider the model's prediction as we let the pedestal get larger and larger with respect to the noise. We know that ultimately Weber's law will hold. Consideration of Eq. 8.14 shows that the simple energy-detection model will *not* predict Weber's law. In fact, let us write Weber's fraction explicitly and derive the model's prediction for the size of the Weber fraction as a function of E_c. By definition,

$$\text{Weber's fraction} = \frac{E_{c+s} - E_c}{E_c} = c$$

and substituting this in Eq. 8.14, we find

$$h_2 = \frac{cE_c/N_0}{[2WT + 2E_c/N_0 + 2E_c/N_0(1 + 2k + k^2)]^{1/2}} \qquad (8.24)$$

$$h_2 \approx \frac{c(E_c/N_0)^{1/2}}{2} \qquad \text{for large } E_c/N_o \qquad (8.25)$$

Suppose that the Weber fraction is measured at several values of pedestal magnitude with the percentage correct held constant; i.e., h_2 is constant.

* Consider a constant background pressure P_c to which we add (in phase) a small pressure P_s. The increment in pressure ΔP is simply P_s, and the ratio is simply $\Delta P/P_c = P_s/P_c$. Now consider the quantities on an energy scale. First, $E_c = P_c{}^2$ and $E_s = P_s{}^2$, but $E_{c+s} = (P_c + P_s)^2 = P_c{}^2 + 2P_cP_s + P_s{}^2$. Therefore, $\Delta E = E_c - E_s = 2P_cP_s + P_s{}^2$ and $\Delta E/E_c = (2P_cP_s + P_s{}^2)/P_c{}^2 = 2P_s/P_c + P_s{}^2/P_c{}^2$. Furthermore, since $P_s{}^2 \ll P_c{}^2$, we have, approximately, $\Delta E/E_c \approx 2P_s/P_c = 2\Delta P/P_c$. Thus, on a scale of voltage or pressure, $\Delta P/P$ is about one-half the same ratio measured on an energy or power scale.

Then c is inversely related to $(E_c/N_0)^{1/2}$. The Weber fraction should decrease as the square root of energy of the pedestal. Such a variation is clearly inconsistent with the data.

8.8 MODIFICATIONS OF THE ENERGY-DETECTION MODEL

There are, however, two very plausible ways to modify the basic model to make its predictions consistent with the data. The first method of amendment is to maintain that the device is incapable of measuring infinitely small differences in the test quantity Ω.

The argument is briefly as follows. As the equation of Table 8-1 indicates, for low values of E_c/N_0 the variability of the energy tends to be great compared with the mean; hence, even if there are finite bounds to the resolution of Ω, it is unlikely that two independent samples of Ω will be very near one another. As the signal energies increase, however, the variability of the distribution, relative to the mean, decreases. The sigma-to-mean ratio is proportional to $1/(E_c/N_0)^{1/2}$ as E_c gets very large. The two hypotheses become point distributions; the variation is essentially zero with respect to the means. Their mean separation is essentially $4kE_c/N_0$, that is,

$$\frac{2E_{s+c} - 2E_c}{N_0} = \frac{2[1 + 2k + k^2]E_c - 2E_c}{N_0} \approx \frac{4kE_c}{N_0},$$

and the two hypotheses can be reliably distinguished from one another only if $4kE_c/N_0$ is greater than the resolution of the measuring device. Equation 8.25 can be used to indicate when these resolution limits are reached. For signal durations of about $\frac{1}{10}$ sec, we know that $c \approx \frac{1}{10}$ and $h_2 = 1\sqrt{2}$ for $P_2(C) = 76\%$; thus $E_c/N_0 \approx 200$. Therefore, when E_c is 23 db above N_0 ($10 \log 200 \approx 23$), we might expect factors of resolution to play a more important part in detection of the increment than does variability of the stimulus.

Unfortunately, this appeal to factors of resolution, although it provides a reasonable excuse for the failure of the energy model, does not of itself predict that the Weber fraction will be constant as the signal intensity E_c is raised. To account for Weber's law, we might assume that the resolution is proportional to the mean. This assumption, also, is very reasonable, but it represents a second, ad hoc assumption. Let us postpone further discussion of this modification until an alternative modification has been presented.

The assumption that the resolution is proportional to the mean suggests another way in which we might amend the energy-detection model to account for Weber's law. The second approach makes no assumption about resolution limit; rather it postulates a particular form of internal variability.* Specifically, we assume the existence of some internal variability whose magnitude is dependent on the size of the stimulus. Given some variability, it is not uncommon for the standard deviation of the variability to be related to the mean value of the process.† We assume that the standard deviation of the internal noise is equal to a constant multiplied by the mean value of the process, Ω. This internal noise, we assume, is independent of the external noise, so that the total variance of Ω is the sum of internal and external variance. The standard deviation of Ω is, therefore, the square root of this total variance.

The equations that follow express the mean and variance under each hypothesis; σ_E is variability caused by the external stimulus, and σ_I is variability caused by the internal stimulus:

(a) $\dfrac{2\Omega_n}{N_0}$ mean $2WT$

$$\sigma_E{}^2 = 4WT$$
$$\sigma_I{}^2 = c_1{}^2(2WT)^2$$

combined variance

$$\sigma^2 = \sigma_E{}^2 + \sigma_I{}^2$$
$$\sigma^2 = 4WT + c_1{}^2(WT)^2 = 4WT(1 + c_1{}^2WT)$$

(b) $\dfrac{2\Omega_{n+s}}{N_0}$ mean $2WT + \dfrac{2E_s}{N_0}$

$$\sigma_E{}^2 = 4WT + \frac{8E_s}{N_0}$$

$$\sigma_I{}^2 = c_1{}^2\left(2WT + \frac{2E_s}{N_0}\right)^2$$

$$= c_1{}^2\left[4(WT)^2 + 8WT\frac{E_s}{N_0} + 4\left(\frac{E_s}{N_0}\right)^2\right]$$

$$\sigma^2 = 4WT(1 + c_1{}^2WT) + \frac{4E_s}{N_0}\left[2 + 2c_1{}^2WT + c_1{}^2\left(\frac{E_s}{N_0}\right)\right]$$

(c) $\dfrac{2\Omega_{n+c}}{N_0}$ is same as Ω_{n+s} except that c replaces s.

(d) $\dfrac{2\Omega_{n+c+s}}{N_0}$ is same as Ω_{n+s} except that $c + s$ replaces s. (8.26)

* There are still other ways to account for Weber's law. Treisman (1964b) has suggested a plausible neurological model for visual data.
† Expressing the tolerance of a measurement as a percentage implicitly recognizes this fact. A 1% measurement means that the mean-to-sigma ratio is about 100 to 1.

These equations become somewhat less forbidding if we immediately derive the difference distribution $2/N_0(\Omega_{n+c+s} - \Omega_{n+c}) = h_2'$. This derivation also relates the constant c_1 to a well-known experimental value. As E_c/N_0 becomes larger, we need consider only terms such as $(E_c/N_0)^2$ and $(E_{c+s}/N_0)^2$:

$$h_2' = \frac{2(E_{s+c} - E_c)/N_0}{[4c_1{}^2(E_{s+c}/N_0)^2 + 4c_1{}^2(E_c/N_0)^2]^{\frac{1}{2}}} \approx \frac{2\Delta E/N_0}{2c_1(E_c/N_0)(2)^{\frac{1}{2}}} \quad (8.27)$$

Thus

$$h_2' \approx \frac{1}{c_1}\frac{\Delta E}{E_c}\frac{1}{\sqrt{2}} \quad (8.28)$$

but, for 76% correct, $h_2' = 1/\sqrt{2}$; thus $c_1 = \Delta E/E_c = c$. The proportionality constant c_1 is simply Weber's fraction c.

Note that Eq. 8.28 indicates that the detection of the increment in the sine wave is independent of the size of the critical band. This is clearly reasonable since, as we keep increasing E_c, practically all the energy, and indeed practically all the variation in energy, is associated with this single frequency.

Returning to our consideration of Eq. 8.26, suppose that the signal frequency is 1000 cps and that the duration is $\frac{1}{10}$ sec. Then $c \approx \frac{1}{10}$, and WT is probably between 50 and 100. The term c^2WT is probably negligible in all situations. For values of $E_s/N_0 < 20$ the squared terms can be ignored and for extremely large values of E_s/N_0, Eq. 8.28 has already been derived.

For moderate values of E_s/N_0, say in the range from 100 to 1000, the cross-product term $WT(E_c/N_0)$ is as important as $c_1{}^2E_s/N_0$. This fact indicates that the Weber fraction becomes essentially constant only when $E_s/N_0 > 1000$, or when $\varepsilon - \eta_0 \geq 30$ db. This suggestion is consonant with empirical data.

Returning to the simple detection experiment and neglecting the term $c_1{}^2(WT)$, we have

$$h_1' = \frac{2E_s/N_0}{[8WT + 8E_s/N_0 + 4c_1{}^2(E_s/N_0)^2]^{\frac{1}{2}}} \quad (8.29)$$

The term $E_s/N_0 \approx 10$, and $c_1{}^2 \approx \frac{1}{100}$; thus if $WT \approx 50$, that term will dominate and the effects of internal noise can be ignored. Then Eq. 8.15 should be approximately correct.

In summary, either the assumption of finite resolution or the assumption of internal noise could be used to modify the energy-detection model to make it consistent with Weber's law. At present there is little objective evidence that might be used to choose between these two modifications of the energy-detection model. Both modifications are a priori reasonable; it seems likely that there is some internal noise, just as it seems likely that there is some lower limit to a difference in sensation that one can distinguish. The question is not one of existence but one of quantity. How much internal noise? How small is the quantum size?

This topic has recently been the subject of several experimental and theoretical papers and, if activity is indicative of progress, we may soon achieve a more complete and comprehensive answer to some of our questions. In the meantime, let us concentrate our attention on the size of the parameter W. To do so, we reanalyze the original critical-band experiment of Fletcher in terms of the energy-detection model.

8.9   REINTERPRETATION OF THE CRITICAL-BAND EXPERIMENT

Fletcher's (1940) critical-band experiment was a classical work in psychoacoustics. Fletcher demonstrated that only a narrow band of noise, centered about the frequency of the sinusoidal signal, was effective as a masker. He did so by systematically varying the bandwidth of the noise and determining the detectability of the sinusoidal signal for various values of the noise bandwidth. The original experiment and replications of it are discussed in more detail in Chapter 10, on Frequency Analysis. Here, we contrast Fletcher's results with the energy-detection model and, in particular, use the energy model to estimate the size of the critical band. Most of the following argument was first developed by deBoer (1962).

Since the experiment is basically the detection of the presence of signal in noise, Eq. 8.13 is applicable, at least for low values of E_s/N_0. If we assume an internal noise whose standard deviation is proportional to the mean, then Eq. 8.29 should be used. Generally, however, for the conditions we shall discuss, $E_s/N_0 \approx 10$, so that the terms $c_1{}^2(E_s/N_0)^2$ and $2c_1{}^2WTE_s/N_0$ can both be neglected. Equation 8.13 will therefore be used, but we may consider it as an approximation to Eq. 8.29.

In applying these equations to this experiment, in which the external bandwidth is systematically varied, we must remember that the parameter W refers either to the external or to the internal bandwidth, depending on which is smaller. Figure 8-1 depicts the flow diagram and reminds us that this analysis can be considered only a first approximation, since the transient behavior of the filters has been ignored and an idealized square filter is assumed.

Given these approximations, the energy-detection model predicts the following relation between bandwidth W_E and E_s/N_0 for a constant level of detectability:

$$\frac{E_s}{N_0} = h_1 \left(2W_E T + \frac{2E_s}{N_0} \right)^{\!1/2} \qquad W_E < W_I$$

$$\frac{E_s}{N_0} = h_1 \left(2W_I T + \frac{2E_s}{N_0} \right)^{\!1/2} \qquad W_I < W_E \qquad (8.30)$$

where h_1 defines the level of detectability used to obtain the relations (for example, 75% correct).

Fletcher also assumed a square filter and suggested two formulas to fit the data of his experiment. Exact comparison with his equation is impossible, since signal duration was ignored in his analysis. The observer in Fletcher's experiment simply adjusted the power level of the signal until he could just hear it in the noise. Nevertheless, we state Fletcher's

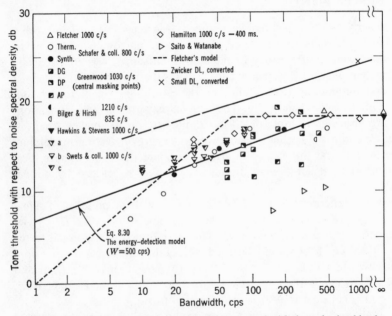

FIG. 8-4   The energy-detection model compared with data obtained in the original critical-band experiment and in several repetitions of it. The ordinate is the intensity in decibels of a sinusoidal signal (near 1000 cps) that is just detectable in a band of noise whose width is indicated by the abscissa. The noise density is constant through any one series of experiments. The data indicate that as the noise band becomes narrower, the signal becomes easier to hear. The heavy solid line is the prediction of the energy-detection model, assuming that the internal filter is 500 cps wide. The dotted line is Fletcher's approximation to his data. From Fletcher's curve one would assume that the internal filter is 60 cps wide. (After deBoer, 1962.)

equation in energy terms to facilitate comparison with Eq. 8.24. Fletcher's equations are:

$$E_s/N_0 = h_1 t' W_E \qquad W_E < W_I$$

$$E_s/N_0 = h_1 t' W_I \qquad W_I < W_E \qquad (8.31)$$

where t' is some constant related to signal duration. Obviously the two sets of predictions, Eq. 8.30 and Eq. 8.31, are quite different. Surprisingly, data from the critical-band experiment do not strongly suggest that one prediction is much better than the other. Figure 8-4 shows the two sets of predictions for two different assumptions about the size of the critical band (W_I), and some representative data. Fletcher, using his approximation, suggests the critical band is 60 cps wide. The energy-model prediction is based on the assumption of a 500-cps bandwidth. Although the models disagree as to the size of the critical band by about an order of magnitude, we see that the data do not clearly support one hypothesis over the other.

In summary, the energy model conceives of two processes as occurring when we change the external bandwidth. First, if $W_E < W_I$ and W_E is increased, the average power ($W_E N_0$) delivered to the detector increases. According to the energy model this increase in power is not relevant. Whatever the value of this average power, the signal will still add to this average power an increment equal to the signal power. What is important about increasing the external bandwidth is increasing the number of sample points, $2W_E T$. This increase, in turn, allows us to estimate the average power better and, hence, to detect smaller increments when they are added to this background level. In short, increasing the bandwidth increases the mean-to-sigma ratio of Ω and, thereby, allows us to make more precise measurements of Ω.

8.10   SUMMARY

The energy-detection model has been analyzed, and its predictions for both the simple detection task and the pedestal task have been derived. The approximate shape of the psychometric function is predicted for both tasks. Predictions were also derived from the model for the shape of the ROC curve.

Although the shapes of the psychometric functions seem to be correct, the actual level of detection that is predicted leads to two problems. For the simple detection experiment, the energy-detection model leads to a rather large estimate of the size of the critical band: about 500 cps wide at a center frequency of 1000 cps. This apparent anomaly led us to reinterpret Fletcher's experiment on the size of the critical band. The energy-detection model gives a plausible account of how critical-band data might be reinterpreted in terms of much larger critical bands.

A similar consideration of the actual level of detection in the pedestal, or increment-detection, experiment shows the largest discrepancy between the model and the data. Clearly, some modification of the general model is required, because it does not predict Weber's law. Two modifications were considered, and the predictions based on one of those modifications were derived. With these ad hoc assumptions, the theoretical predictions will mirror the empirical results but, obviously, this area remains the least satisfactory part of the general energy-detection model.

PROBLEMS

8.1   (a) Given that $W = 4000$ cps and $T = 1/10$ sec, calculate h_1 for $E_s/N_0 = 20$ according to Eqs. 8.13 and 8.15.

(b) Perform the same calculation where $T = 1/100$ instead of $1/10$ sec.

8.2   Suppose that the critical band were 60 cps wide at 1000 cps, as Fletcher's original experiment suggested, and assume that the signal duration is $1/10$ or $1/100$ sec. Discuss how these parameter values would affect the validity of the approximation used in deriving the density functions for noise and for signal plus noise.

Part III

Other Applications
of Detection Theory

Chapter 9 relates two models for combining observations to performance data on multiple-component signals, multiple-observer teams, and repeated stimulus presentations. Also considered are detection tasks with varying degrees of temporal structure. In Chapter 10, data on multiple-component signals and on signals of uncertain frequency are used to define further the concept of the "critical band" in auditory frequency analysis. Chapter 11 shows how many of the ideas and procedures of detection theory can be applied to speech recognition. Chapter 12 reviews preliminary applications of the theory to a variety of substantive problems that border on psychophysics, including sensory physiology, animal discrimination learning, reaction time, attention, and recognition memory.

9

Multiple Observations

9.1 INTRODUCTION

Detection theory is a formal structure, and as such provides an abstract means of analyzing detection problems. One of the terms of analysis, taken from statistical decision theory, is the concept of an observation. The theory does not specify the nature of the observation, but rather treats it in a general way as providing evidence or information which the decision maker uses in choosing among the available alternatives. The specific information used as the observation will depend upon the nature of the detection task. The formal theory does not treat the substantive aspects of the detection situation.

Despite this lack of specificity, the theory is often useful in interpreting particular experimental results, because we can often interpret a change in an experimental situation as a change in the amount of information provided by an observation, or as a change in the number of observations that contribute to a decision. If, for example, the observer makes two successive observations rather than a single observation of a given stimulus, then, assuming that these observations are independent, the theory can be used to make quite specific predictions about how the detectability of the signal will change. Extensions of the signal in time, area, or frequency range are other examples of experiments that can be interpreted in this manner. Detection theory provides a means of analyzing these situations because it prescribes how multiple observations should be combined to arrive at a single decision.

Actually, there are two distinct notions about the combination of observations that can be recognized in the literature of psychophysics. One of them is akin to the process envisioned in detection theory. It suggests that observations are accumulated and that the total weight of the evidence is used as the basis for a decision. The other notion arises from threshold theory. According to this conception, each of the several observations leads to a decision, and it is the decisions rather than the observations themselves that are combined. In the simplest form of this approach, the rule is to respond affirmatively if any one of the observations indicates the presence of a signal.

Often these two conceptions have not been explicitly recognized. Certainly, the differences in both the basic formulation and the predictions generated by these notions have not received the attention they deserve. The questions raised by these two approaches are basic in a wide variety of experimental situations. They are pertinent when the area of a target in a visual display is extended, when the number of components of a complex signal is increased, when several observers are used as a detection team, or when the observation is simply repeated a number of different times. All of these situations are potentially amenable to analysis in terms of how the multiple observations are combined and what effect the combination has on the resulting decision.

Bordering on these questions are broader issues concerning the structure of the detection task itself. In the simplest task a single observation interval, or a single stimulus, is presented in each trial, and on the basis of an observation taken during the interval the observer is expected to make a decision. In a seemingly trivial extension of this task, the stimulus may be repeated a number of times, allowing the observer to make repeated observations and to base his decision on several of them. Even this small variation of the task raises a basic question as to how many observations should be taken before a decision is reached. Now that time has been added to the experimental picture, we have, at least potentially, a question of how to balance speed and accuracy. A question of real and fundamental importance is how the observation sequence should be structured to make best use of the knowledge available. One general answer is provided by the theory of sequential analysis as developed in mathematical statistics. Here, after any given observation, three decisions can be reached. The decision maker can make a terminal decision, by accepting one or the other of the two hypotheses, or he may decide to continue the observation sequence and take one more observation before making a terminal decision. As Wald (1947) has shown, the sequential observation procedure is better than any procedure having a fixed number of observations, in the sense that the sequential procedure leads to a given level of accuracy, on the average, in fewer trials.

Finally, the exploration of sequential decision procedures brings us to the problem of procedures with very little structure, in which the observation interval is almost completely undefined. These unstructured situations, in which the occurrence of a signal is random in time, can also be thought of as involving multiple observations. In this case, instead of combining observations that are known to arise from the same source, the observer must select among multiple observations the small proportion that are relevant to a detection decision. Increasing the observation time, or the number of observations, decreases rather than increases detectability. The analysis of such unstructured tasks is a problem that is largely unsolved. Nevertheless, a general discussion of this area is required because of its importance; it is currently an area of active research interest.

Thus, in this chapter we go beyond the highly idealized detection paradigms that were emphasized in preceding chapters to some variations of experimental procedure that reflect more nearly real detection problems and everyday perception. Where before we focused on relatively simple signals presented in well-defined observation intervals, and on simple detection responses made at specified times, we consider now complex signals that consist of several components, ill-defined observation intervals, responses that depend upon several observations, and responses made at times determined by the observer.

We begin with a discussion of models for combining observations, and then apply this analysis to several experimental situations. Taken up in turn are multiple-component signals, multiple-observer teams, and repeated stimulus presentations. The last of these topics leads to a consideration of various sequential decision procedures. The chapter then concludes with a brief discussion of the available analyses of the temporally unstructured detection task.

9.2   MODELS FOR COMBINING MULTIPLE OBSERVATIONS

Given the opportunity to take multiple observations, how does the observer combine them to arrive at a single, overall decision? The first general answer is that the overall decision is solely a function of the individual decisions that are based on individual observations. This model, which originated with the classical threshold theory, stipulates that the only aspect of an observation used in making the combined decision is the decision, usually a binary decision, to which the observation led. The second general answer, more compatible with detection theory, is that the information in multiple observations is pooled and the sum of the information determines the overall decision. According to this model, instead of considering only binary representations of individual observations, finer-grained representations are combined in a way that preserves more information. For example, if the individual observations are independent, then the overall decision is based on the product of their likelihood ratios.

Whether threshold theory is correct in assuming that sensory events are discrete is not relevant to this discussion. Here we are concerned with decision thresholds which may or may not depend upon sensory thresholds. The model for combination which specifies that the overall decision is determined by individual decisions could be associated with a sensory model that assumes a continuous representation of sensory events. One might assume, specifically, that the storage or memory of the individual sensory events, or observations, is binary. The issue is whether or not decisions are made on the basis of individual observations and only the decisions retained for further processing.

In presenting the two models of combination, we intend to trace the rationale for the two forms of analysis, and to contrast the predictions of the two models. As we shall see, under certain conditions the predictions are virtually indistinguishable, and data on multiple observations do not make possible a clear choice between the detection-theory and threshold models of combination. Let us begin with the detection-theory model, which is termed "the integration model."

9.2.1 The integration model

The name of this model reflects its assumption that information from individual observations is added together to form the accumulation of evidence that is used to make an overall decision. In order to derive specific predictions from this model it is necessary to make some further assumptions. A general assumption which we shall not relax in this discussion is that observations are combined with no loss of information. In the case of successive observations, for example, the observer is assumed to have perfect memory; the first observation is added to the sum of the evidence with the same fidelity as the last. Unfortunately, this is a rather strong asumption and one that cannot always be tested in isolation. A second assumption, one that we shall modify in a later discussion, is that the individual observations are independent, so that the various components of the sum are statistically independent of one another. The third and last assumption is that each observation is normally distributed with the same variance under noise alone and signal plus noise. This assumption allows us to associate with each observation a detectability index d', a measure of the separation between the means of the noise and signal distributions divided by the common standard deviation.

Given these three assumptions, a specific prediction is easily derived. When n observations are combined, the combined value of d', denoted d_n', is equal to the square root of the sum of the squares of the individual values of d':

$$d_n' = \left[\sum_{i=1}^{n}(d_i')^2\right]^{1/2} \qquad (9.1)$$

In deriving this formula, it is assumed that the individual observations are combined via likelihood ratio or, equivalently, that an optimal linear combination of the individual observations is made. Appendix 9-A gives the derivation using both assumptions.

It can be seen that when all the values of d' are equal, then d_n' increases as the square root of n. This result is basically similar to the result in statistical theory (Appendix I, Eq. I.36) stating that the mean of a population is estimated with a precision that increases as the square root of the number of observations in the sample.

9.2.2   The decision-threshold model

According to the decision-threshold model, an increase in detectability results from multiple observations, not because they are integrated to form a single basis for decision, but rather because each additional observation presents another independent detection opportunity. Thus, in its basic form, this model also assumes statistically independent observations. When sensory thresholds are assumed, it is supposed that they fluctuate over time, and that the levels of the individual thresholds are independent from one observation to another.

The rule used most frequently to combine decisions is to make a positive response if any one of the several decisions is positive, if any one of the sensory measures exceeds a threshold. Under this rule the probability of detection based on n observations is equal to one minus the product of the probabilities that detection will not occur on any of the n observations:

$$p_n = 1 - \prod_{i=1}^{n}(1 - p_i) \qquad (9.2)$$

If the individual probabilities are all equal, this formula becomes

$$p_n = 1 - (1 - p)^n \qquad (9.3)$$

To treat the forced-choice task with this model, it may be noted that the probability of a correct response on a single trial is, by Eq. 5.3 of Chapter 5,

$$P(C) = p + \left(\frac{1}{m}\right)(1 - p) \qquad (5.3)$$

where m is the number of intervals in a trial. Hence, the expression for $P_n(C)$ can be written by substituting p_n of Eq. 9.2 for p in the foregoing equation, with the result that

$$P_n(C) = 1 - \prod_{i=1}^{n} (1 - p_i) + \frac{1}{m} \prod_{i=1}^{n} (1 - p_i) \qquad (9.4)$$

We can consider, at the other extreme of rules for combination, the rule which states that a positive response is made after multiple observations only if all the individual decisions are positive. The resulting formula, again assuming independence, is

$$p_n = \prod_{i=1}^{n} p_i \qquad (9.5)$$

9.2.3   Comparison of predictions

The prediction of the decision-threshold model, usually in the form of Eq. 9.3, has been used as a rule of thumb in a variety of situations (see, for example, Koopman, 1956). It is typically used in the context of high-threshold theory (Chapter 5) with the assumption that false-alarm responses are negligible (either because they are discouraged or because the correction for chance is applied). It is clear that if Eq. 9.3 is applied only to correct positive responses, or to hits, then the supposed gain from additional observations is very large. Indeed, according to this formula, if a signal is detected 50% of the time on a single observation, only 4 observations are required to reach 93.75% detection, and 10 observations will yield 99% detection. This rate of gain is noticeably greater than the increase expected under the optimal integration model.

It can be shown that if the equations of this model are used in conjunction with a low-threshold theory (Chapters 3, 5), then the predicted gain is less optimistic. Similarly, if these equations are applied to false alarms as well as to hits, and the result is plotted in the form of an ROC graph, the expected gain is less than that of the integration model. Figure 9-1 shows a comparison of the predictions, for two observations, at various levels of detectability. Each of the solid lines, at $d' = 1$, 2, and 3, has associated another solid line at a value of d' that is $\sqrt{2}$ greater, namely, the prediction of the integration model. The dashed lines at each level of detectability are two predictions from the decision-threshold model. The lightly dashed line represents Eq. 9.3; a positive decision is based on the union of two decisions, that is, the overall decision is positive if *either* individual decision is positive. The heavy dashed line represents Eq. 9.5; a positive decision is based on the intersection of two decisions, that is, the overall decision is positive only if *both* individual decisions are positive.

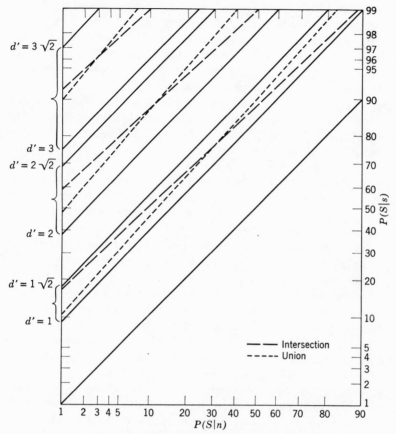

FIG. 9-1   A comparison of predictions from the integration and decision-threshold models of combination, for the combination of two observations. The lower solid lines in each of the three bands represent levels of detectability indexed as $d' = 1, 2$, and 3. The upper solid lines in each band are the predictions of the integration model, Eq. 9.1. The dashed lines are the predictions under two decision rules from the decision-threshold model. The line keyed as the union is based on Eq. 9.3; the line keyed as the intersection is based on Eq. 9.5 (After Birdsall, unpublished work, 1955; see also Pollack and Madans, 1964.)

These two predictions assume that the two individual decisions result from thresholds, or decision criteria, at the same level. Given that d' is approximately proportional to signal power for human observers (see Chapter 7), the predicted gain under the integration model is about 1.5 db. The gain expected under the decision-threshold model varies with the false-alarm rate but, on the average, is about half the figure of 1.5 db.

Let us also briefly compare the two models of combination as they apply to the forced-choice task. In this case we find that, even when a high threshold is assumed throughout, the decision-threshold model predicts a greater gain than does the integration model under some circumstances, and less gain under other circumstances. In the most frequent case, with a high chance probability of detection, or a small number of alternatives, the decision-threshold model predicts uniformly greater rates of improvement for all initial detection probabilities. For example, setting $P(C) = 0.60$ and $m = 2$ in Eq. 5.3 of Chapter 5 (which is reproduced in the preceding section, Section 9.2.2) yields $p = 0.20$. Setting $p = 0.20$ in Eq. 9.4 and taking $n = 1, \ldots, 5$, we find $P_n(C) = 0.60$, 0.68, 0.74, 0.80, and 0.84. Under the integration model $P(C) = 0.60$ in two-alternative forced choice corresponds to $d' = 0.36$. If we calculate values of d' for $n = 1, \ldots, 5$ by Eq. 9.1 and then convert these back to probabilities, we have $P_n(C) = 0.60$, 0.64, 0.67, 0.69, and 0.71. For five observations, the prediction of the decision-threshold model exceeds the integration-model prediction by 0.13. However, the two models predict roughly the same gain for an ensemble of eight alternatives, and the decision-threshold model predicts less gain for a signal ensemble of 200 alternatives, as might be used in a word-recognition test (see Chapter 11), for all but very low initial detection probabilities.

Briefly, in yes-no procedures, the prediction of the decision-threshold model exceeds the prediction of the integration model if false alarms are ignored, and falls below the latter prediction when false alarms are taken into account. In forced-choice procedures, even considering only the high-threshold sensory model, which of the two models predicts the greater gain depends upon the chance probability and the initial probability of detection. (Note that the decision-threshold model, in connection with a high-threshold sensory model, can lead to a predicted gain that is greater than the gain predicted by the optimal integration model, because the correction for chance, in effect, ignores false-alarm responses. Specifically, use of the correction for chance assumes that noise alone will almost never produce a suprathreshold sensory event; see Chapter 5.) In many instances, the predictions are too close to distinguish experimentally, and most of the available, relevant data have come from experiments in which attempts were not made to maximize the difference in predictions. It is clear, however, that although the prediction of the decision-threshold model appears to be met under some conditions, its accuracy cannot be taken for granted in all situations.

To this point we have considered, for both models, only the case of complete statistical independence of individual observations. The assumption of independence is sometimes met, but often it is not. We shall not attempt here to treat predictions based on varying degrees of dependence. We shall simply make some observations about what can be expected if individual observations are completely correlated. It is obvious that if the observers in a multiple-observer team are completely correlated, then one is as good as several. We should expect no increase in detectability to result from additional observers if all receive precisely the same information. Similarly, no gain will result from repeating the stimulus several times if the several observations of it are completely correlated. Any degree of correlation in these experimental situations will serve to reduce the gain in detectability to a level below the gain predicted, by either model, under the assumption of independence. The case of multiple-component signals is somewhat different. Consider a two-component signal with components of equal energy. Here we might expect independence of the observations of the two components if the two components are sufficiently separated in space to be outside the range of areal summation, or sufficiently separated in frequency to lie in nonoverlapping critical bands. The correlation of the observations would increase as one of the components is moved closer to the other until, finally, the observations were completely correlated. Then, however, the effect would be the same as doubling the energy of a single component. The effect of doubling energy is outside the scope of the two models for combination, and may be expected to vary from one sense modality to another. Simply as one standard of comparison, we shall consider, in the section to which we turn now, a simple addition of values of d'.

9.3   MULTIPLE-COMPONENT SIGNALS

9.3.1   Visual signals

We consider first the detection of two-point signals, with varying distances between the points, and then a comparison of single-point signals presented monocularly and binocularly.*

The experiments on two-point signals were reported by Kristofferson and Dember (1958). The points were one minute in diameter and, in different experimental conditions, were presented to the fovea with 3.5, 8, 12, 16, 32, 44, and 64 minutes of vertical separation. Two experiments are discussed here. They are identical in all essential respects. The differences between them were in the particular observers used, the number of observers, the number of trials in a given experimental condition, and the spatial separations. These differences are ignored, and the results of the

---

* These data were brought to our attention by Professor A. B. Kristofferson, who has kindly reanalyzed them in terms of the integration model.

two experiments are pooled, in the subsequent analyses. It should be noted, however, that in most instances the estimates of probability were based on relatively few (50) trials.

Figure 9-2 shows obtained values of d' plotted against predicted values of d'—for the smaller separations, 3.5' and 8'—with predictions made on two bases. The circles in the figure represent the integration model's

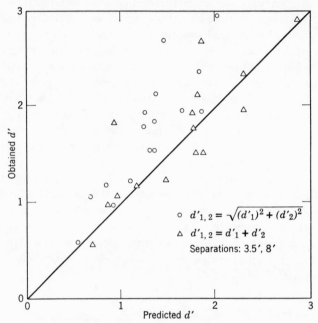

FIG. 9-2 Obtained versus predicted values of d', for two-point visual signals with small separation, based on two predictions from the integration model. (Data from Kristofferson and Dember, 1958.)

prediction of square-root improvement as given in Eq. 9.1. The triangles represent a simple d' summation. It can be seen that the second prediction is more successful for the small separations in question. Whereas there are 10 triangles above the line and 6 below, all 16 circles are above the line. The data suggest that the assumption of independence of observations is not met at separations less than about 8 minutes of arc.

The results obtained from larger separations—12' to 64'—are shown in the same form in Fig. 9-3. The results related to the two predictions are on different graphs in this figure because of the large number of points involved. Figure 9-3a indicates that the prediction of square-root improvement in d', and therefore the assumption of independence, is reasonably

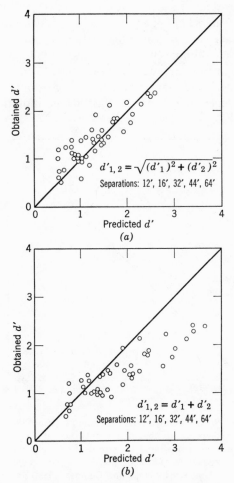

FIG. 9-3 Obtained versus predicted
values of d', for two-point visual signals
with large separation, based on two
predictions from the integration model.
(Data from Kristofferson and Dember,
1958.)

accurate for larger separations. Of 45 points, 27 are above the line and 18
are below. In Fig. 9-3b, based on a simple summation of d', the points
split with 8 above and 37 below the line.

On the whole, the data for larger separations match quite well the
prediction of square-root improvement in d', and fall well short of simple
d' summation. Do they reach the level of performance predicted by the

decision-threshold model? Figure 9-4, which shows detection probabilities corrected for chance success, leaves the answer in some doubt, but tends to indicate that they do not. Of the 45 circles, 29 fall below the line and show less improvement than predicted by Eq. 9.4; 13 circles are above the line. For the smaller separations, where we have reason to believe that the assumption of independence is not satisfied, the decision-threshold model

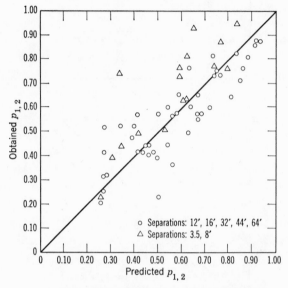

FIG. 9-4 Obtained versus predicted values of the true detection probability, for two-point visual signals with small and large separation, based on the prediction of the decision-threshold model. (Data from Kristofferson and Dember, 1958.)

clearly fails: 13 of 16 triangles are above the line, and the other 3 are only slightly below it.

The experiment on binocular summation considered here used a zero-illumination background, four dark-adapted observers, the peripheral retina, four signal diameters, five signal luminances, and the four-alternative forced-choice procedure. Each probability estimate was based on 50 trials. Again, all the data are pooled for the present analyses.

Figure 9-5 shows obtained versus predicted values of the binocular d'. (Fewer than $4 \times 4 \times 5 = 80$ points appear, because some proportions were at the chance level and some fall off the scale at the upper end.) Figure 9-5a shows clearly that the prediction of square-root improvement

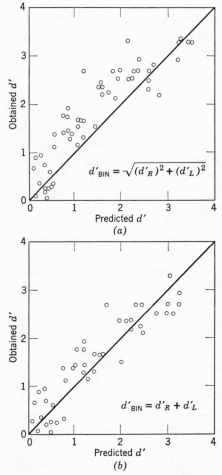

FIG. 9-5 Obtained versus predicted values of d', for visual signals presented binocularly, based on two predictions from the integration model. (Data from Kristofferson, 1958.)

in d' underestimates the amount of summation obtained: 41 points are above the line and 13 are below. Figure 9-5b shows a better fit for the prediction of simple d' summation: 27 points are above the line and 18 are below, a 60–40 split. The decision-threshold model also underestimates the amount of summation that is obtained; the predicted-versus-obtained graph for this model (not given here) shows 49 points above the line and 24 below, a 67–33 split. Essentially the same results were obtained in a replication of the experiment with foveal signals and a moderately high background luminance (10 foot-lamberts). The relation of the data to the prediction of the decision-threshold model in both experiments is in detailed agreement with the earlier results of Collier (1954).

9.3.2 Auditory signals

A few experiments have been conducted to determine the detectability of auditory signals consisting of various numbers of sinusoids with varying frequency separation. Their results are discussed in the context of frequency analysis (Chapter 10), and thus they are treated very briefly here. In general, the experimental results on signals with two to eight widely-separated components are in quite good agreement with both models of combination (Schafer and Gales, 1949; Green, 1958). One experiment showed a simple summation of values of d' for two components close together in frequency (Marill, 1956). A study of 16-component signals gave results which agreed with the predictions of the integration model to within 0.5 db (Green, McKey, and Licklider, 1959). These authors also showed that the decision-threshold model leads to the prediction that the psychometric function for a compound signal will be considerably steeper than the function for a single-component signal. This prediction was not supported; the psychometric functions in the two cases were not noticeably different in slope.

9.4 MULTIPLE OBSERVERS

The classical view of the threshold makes it tempting to use teams of observers in practical detection problems. If one observer fails to detect a signal because his threshold is momentarily at a high level, it is unlikely that all the others will. If two independent observers each have a probability of detection of 0.50, then the probability that both will fail to detect this signal is 0.25, so that the probability that one or the other or both will detect the signal is 0.75. Whether so large a gain in detectability will be realized is worth careful study, particularly in those detection situations in which observers appear to be independent.

9.4.1 History of research

The first systematic research on the problem was conducted by Schafer (1949). In an auditory experiment with sinusoidal signals, he found that multiple-observer teams showed less than the expected improvement. There were a number of reasons for suspecting that the observers were not independent of one another in this case. Schafer pointed out that all the observers were listening to the same noise background, that they had similar biases in generating a series of responses, and that they were similarly affected by practice and fatigue. A more extensive study of auditory signals was carried out by Smith and Wilson (1953). These investigators provided a theoretical and empirical treatment of correlation among observers, and they raised the problem of the relationship between sensitivity and the proportion of false-alarm responses.

This study of multiple observers was the context in which Smith and Wilson, as pointed out in the introductory chapter, proposed a view of the detection process very similar to that developed in the general theory of signal detectability. They were led to this view by the finding that the correction for chance failed to superimpose psychometric functions based on different proportions of false-alarm responses. They presented data like those shown in Figs. 5-2a and 5-2b, which indicated that greater sensitivity resulted from higher false-alarm proportions, that is, that a false-alarm response is more than a guess based on no sensory information. In order, therefore, to determine the effectiveness of multiple-observer teams relative to single observers, another way had to be found to equate the false-alarm proportions of the psychometric functions under comparison. Smith and Wilson dealt with the problem by instructing one group of five observers to maintain a strict criterion, and another group of five observers to maintain a liberal criterion. The average false-alarm proportions that resulted were approximately 0.03 for the first group and 0.25 for the second group. Each of these average curves was compared with the multiple-observer curve which showed approximately the same false-alarm proportion. Thus, for example, the multiple-observer curve for four or more observers reporting "yes" under the liberal criterion, and the multiple-observer curve for two or more observers reporting "yes" under the strict criterion, showed false-alarm proportions approximating 0.03, the average figure for the individual observers working under the strict criterion.

The gain of the team over the average of the individuals was found to be approximately 1 db at a positive-report proportion of 0.50, and approximately 2 db at a positive-report proportion of 0.95. This amount of improvement was regarded as disappointingly small. Indeed, a gain of 1 or 2 db is not of obvious practical importance—perhaps not worth the room and board of four additional observers.

To what extent was the gain depressed by a correlation among observers? The average (tetrachoric) intercorrelation among the observers was 0.55. However, Smith and Wilson calculated from their data that if the correlation could be reduced to zero, and if individual variability were four times greater than it was, then the gain from four extra observers would be no more than 2 or 3 db. Neither are these figures very large. They may be compared, for example, with the range of the psychometric function, which is about 10 to 12 db (see Chapter 7).

Figure 9-6 shows previously unpublished data obtained with visual signals that are similar to the data on tones obtained by Smith and Wilson.

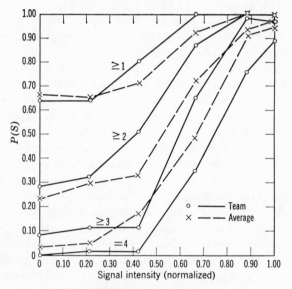

FIG. 9-6 Psychometric functions for a 4-observer team, when the average proportion of false alarms for individuals was 0.23, and for the average of 4 individuals with various proportions of false alarms. Each signal level was presented 60 times; there were 250 presentations of noise alone. (Swets, previously unpublished data.)

The solid lines, reading from top to bottom, are curves based respectively on one or more, two or more, three or more, and four observers reporting "yes," in a four-observer team, where the average of the individual false-alarm proportions was 0.23. The figure also shows average results for the same four observers (considered individually, not as a team) working under various criteria which yielded, respectively, false-alarm proportions of 0.66, 0.23, and 0.03. Again, it can be seen that the team is very little better than the average individual when false-alarm proportions are equated. The team, of course, shows an even smaller advantage over the best of the individual observers.

9.4.2 ROC data

In the framework of detection theory the problem of varying false-alarm proportions is handled by plotting ROC curves. Illustrative predictions of the integration model were shown in Fig. 9-1. Recall that the lower bound of each region in the figure is the ROC curve describing the individual performances of two observers with equal sensitivity, or d'. The upper bound of each region is the ROC curve that would be obtained from two independent observers—if they report likelihood ratios to a decision maker who optimally combines the two reports. The upper bound has a value of d' associated with it that is $\sqrt{2}$ times the value of d' of the individual observers.

The only data available to us for comparison with the predictions of the integration model are yes-no data on visual signals. They are more variable than we should like, but they are adequate to show approximately the extent of improvement in d' that results from an additional observer. They can, in particular, be compared with the maximum improvement expected, that is, with $\sqrt{n}$ improvement in d'.

Figure 9-7 shows ROC data for each of two observers, and for the two-observer team, at two signal levels. At each signal level there are four points for each observer, four points representing the union (when either observer says "yes"), and four points representing the intersection (when both observers say "yes"). A pair of ROC curves is shown for each signal level: the lower curve of each pair is the average of the two observers considered individually. The upper curve is the maximum predicted for the team, namely, $\sqrt{2}$ times the average of the individual curves. It can be seen that the team does not surpass $\sqrt{2}$ improvement. The results are consistent with the decision-threshold model, provided that the equations of the model are applied to false alarms as well as hits (compare Fig. 9-1). The results are also consistent with those of Smith and Wilson in showing a small improvement to result from an additional observer.

Note that at the higher signal level the ROC curve fitted to the individual data and the curve for the predicted maximum have a slope less than one. These curves are consistent with a greater variance of the signal than of the noise distribution; they represent some liberty that we have taken with the integration model, since this model assumes equal variance of signal and noise distributions. It can also be noted that the assumption of equally sensitive observers was not met very well at the higher signal level. The average $d' = 1.85$; d' for Observer 1 is 1.60 and for Observer 2 it is 2.0. However, if we take the differing values of d' into account in deriving the predicted maximum, the prediction ($d' = 2.60$) changes only in the second decimal place.

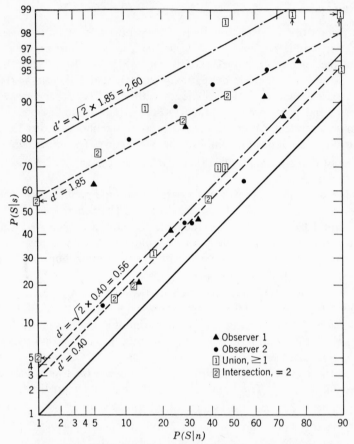

FIG. 9-7 ROC data for each of 2 observers, and for the 2-observer team, at 2 signal levels. At each signal level, there are 4 points for each observer, 4 points representing the union, and 4 points representing the intersection. Each point is based on 200 presentations of the signal and 200 presentations of noise alone. A pair of ROC curves is shown for each signal level: the lower curve of each pair is the average ROC curve of the two observers considered individually; the upper curve of each pair represents the maximum performance for the 2-observer team as predicted by the integration model. The upper curve is based on the assumption that the observers are independent and that they report likelihood ratios. (Swets, previously unpublished data.)

A correlational analysis of these visual data does not reject the hypothesis of independent observers. Fourfold point correlation coefficients, ϕ, vary between 0.01 and 0.13. None of them reaches significance at the 0.05 level of confidence, nor does their combination. The levels of significance show an approximately rectangular distribution over the range from 0.90 to 0.10.

Considering the difference between white (auditory) noise and white light, we should expect the results that were obtained: a significant correlation among observers in audition and an insignificant correlation among observers in vision. The auditory stimulus is the same in all earphones, whereas the photon absorption differs for different eyes. The essential result is that the improvement from multiple observers was found to be no more than $\sqrt{n}$ in d' even when the assumption of independence appeared to be met. This amount of improvement is considerably smaller than the familiar prediction of the decision-threshold model (Eq. 9.3) when the equation is applied only to hits, as it often has been, and is not large for practical purposes.

9.5   MULTIPLE PRESENTATIONS: FIXED NUMBER

In this section we consider the effect of a fixed number of successive presentations of a given signal: first, a simple auditory signal in white noise, and then words displayed visually.

9.5.1   Sinusoids in white noise

9.5.1.1   INDEPENDENT NOISE.   In the experiment to be discussed, a trial consisted of five observations; each observation consisted of four temporal intervals, one of which contained the signal. The observer made a forced choice among the four intervals after each observation. The observer knew that the signal would occur in the same interval in all five observations of a given trial; he was asked to base his decision after each observation on all observations he had made previously within the trial. The observer was asked to make a decision after each observation, instead of only after the last observation, so that the single experiment in which a trial contained five observations could be analyzed to indicate the results that would be obtained in experiments having trials containing fewer observations.

The signal was a 1000-cps pulse of 0.1-second duration. It was presented in a background of white noise. The term "independent noise" in the heading of this section signifies that the samples of noise in the different intervals were statistically independent of one another. Since the signal was of constant strength, we can assume that the values of d' for the several observations are equal. The integration model of detection theory thus predicts that d' will increase as $\sqrt{n}$.

Figure 9-8 displays the results obtained from three observers. The solid lines in the figure represent the prediction of $\sqrt{n}$ improvement. (Given logarithmic scales, this prediction is represented by lines with a slope of 1/2. However, the scale on the ordinate is twice that of the abscissa; thus the square-root improvement is represented by a line with a slope of one.) Note that the lines have been made to intercept the vertical axis at the value of d' corresponding to $n = 1$ and are, therefore, not necessarily the best-fitting lines, with the predicted slope, to the obtained data points. Clearly, the data obtained from the second observer would be fitted better by the predicted line if this restriction had not been made.

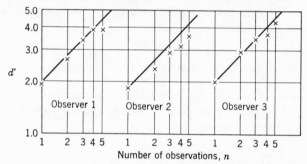

FIG. 9-8 The increase in detectability over 5 successive observations of a signal presented in independent noise. The line represents the $\sqrt{n}$ prediction for the increase in d'; this line has been forced through the obtained value of d' at $n = 1$. It should be noted that the scale of the ordinate is twice the scale of the abscissa, so that a slope of $\frac{1}{2}$ appears as a slope of 1. (From Swets, Shipley, McKey, and Green, 1959.)

Figure 9-8 shows data in reasonably close agreement with the prediction of $\sqrt{n}$ improvement. It agrees in this respect with the results of an earlier experiment of the same type (Schafer and Shewmaker, 1953). However, the data do not distinguish between the predictions of the integration and decision-threshold models. The value of $P(C)$ for the first observation (0.80) is too high for a sensitive test of this difference with a four-alternative procedure. In terms of $P(C)$, the decision-threshold model overestimates the results by about one percentage point more than does the integration model.

9.5.1.2 CONSTANT NOISE. A similar experiment was conducted, with the difference that the samples of background noise were not independent; in fact, they were identical. That is, the four intervals making up a single observation were recorded on tape, and a trial consisted of the same four intervals repeated five times. The samples of noise in a given interval were therefore identical, within the limits of the equipment.

This experiment, like the one just described, does not distinguish between the two models. Both models would assume a high correlation among observations and little gain. The experiment is considered because it provides one means of estimating the degree of correlation among observations. In particular, it can be analyzed to indicate the portion of total noise in the observation that originates within the observer. The result, of course, is specific to the kind of stimulus used, but for a given kind of stimulus it gives an upper bound on the correlation among successive observations or multiple observers. Incidentally, the result also indicates the limitations of what has been termed "molecular psychophysics" (Green, 1964), that is, the attempt to predict an individual's trial-by-trial detection behavior on the basis of some trial-by-trial measure of the stimulus.

When the same background noise is presented on each observation, the integration model again assumes that the observer makes his choice on the basis of a linear combination of the sensory measures obtained from the different intervals. In this case, however, the variability of the sensory measures from one observation to another for a given interval is determined only by variability within the observer, or by "internal noise." Any improvement in detectability over multiple observations under "constant" external noise must, under the integration model, result from integrating over internal noise only. Thus, if the integration model is assumed, the amount of improvement in detectability can be used to indicate the amount of internal noise.

The data from this experiment, using the same three observers, show $P(C)$ and d' to increase over additional observations, but considerably less than under independent noise. The values of $P_1(C)$ are comparable for the different noises, but $P_5(C)$ is approximately 0.86 under constant noise, as opposed to 0.99 under independent noise. Similarly, the ratio d_5'/d_1' under constant noise is approximately 1.20, as compared with 2.0 under independent noise.

Consider how these data can yield an estimate of the amount of internal noise. In the following, external noise is denoted by E, internal noise by I, and the mean of the signal distribution by $\bar{x}$. Assuming that internal noise adds to external noise, the value of d' on the first observation is

$$d_1' = \frac{\bar{x}}{(\sigma_E^2 + \sigma_I^2)^{1/2}} \tag{9.6}$$

and the value of d' on the nth observation is

$$d_n' = \frac{n \cdot \bar{x}}{(n^2 \sigma_E^2 + n \sigma_I^2)^{1/2}} \tag{9.7}$$

Combining the two equations, we have

$$\frac{d_n'}{d_1'} = \frac{n \cdot \bar{x}/(n^2\sigma_E^2 + n\sigma_I^2)^{1/2}}{\bar{x}/(\sigma_E^2 + \sigma_I^2)^{1/2}} = \frac{[1 + (\sigma_I^2/\sigma_E^2)]^{1/2}}{[1 + (\sigma_I^2/\sigma_E^2)(1/n)]^{1/2}} \quad (9.8)$$

Let $k = \sigma_I^2/\sigma_E^2$; then

$$\frac{d_n'}{d_1'} = \frac{(1 + k)^{1/2}}{(1 + k/n)^{1/2}} \quad (9.9)$$

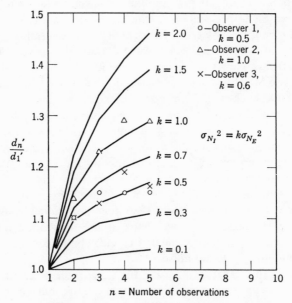

FIG. 9-9 The determination of k, the ratio of internal to external noise, using 5 successive observations of a signal in constant noise. (From Swets, Shipley, McKey, and Green, 1959.)

Thus, by plotting empirical values of d_n'/d_1' against n for various assumed values of k, the value of k which gives the best estimate of the ratio of internal to external noise can be determined. The data of this experiment are plotted in this fashion in Fig. 9-9. The estimates of k range from 0.5 to 1.0. Roughly speaking, the internal noise must be approximately equal to the external noise at the level of external noise used in the experiment.

If the amount of internal noise remains constant over various conditions, then, with smaller values of external noise, the internal noise will constitute a larger proportion of the total noise; that is, k will be larger. Another experiment was conducted similar to the one just described in all respects except that the external noise was attenuated by approximately 20 db. This is a substantial reduction in the variance of the external noise, so that should we expect a noticeable increase in k if the variance of internal noise is constant. It may be seen in Fig. 9-10 that the values of k obtained

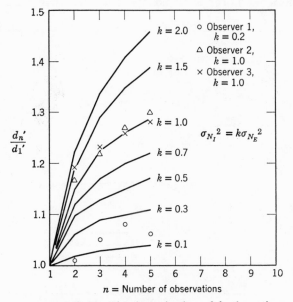

FIG. 9-10   The determination of k, the ratio of internal to external noise, at a lower level of external noise. (From Swets, Shipley, McKey, and Green, 1959.)

in this experiment are in approximately the same range as those obtained in the previous experiment. Apparently, given the model, internal noise is not constant, but is proportional to the amount of external noise.

9.5.2   Word recognition

The effect of successive presentations of words displayed visually was examined by Haber (1964). Most experiments on word recognition have used the ascending method of limits, a method in which the intensity or duration of a given word is increased on each successive presentation until the word is correctly reported. As Haber pointed out, if repetition alone leads to increased perceptibility, without changes in intensity or duration, then an important variable in these studies has been ignored. If repetition alone leads to increased perceptibility, then the method of limits confuses the effects of repetition with the effects of changes in intensity or duration.

The experiment used 288 seven-letter words. Half of the words were English words with a relatively high frequency of occurrence as determined from the Thorndike-Lorge word counts. The other half were Turkish

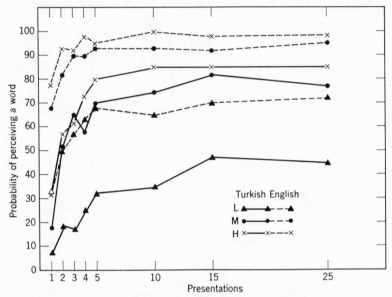

FIG. 9-11 Proportion of words correctly identified as a function of the number of repetitions. (From Haber, 1964.)

words. The subject reported after each presentation the letters that he saw; his response was scored as correct when he reported correctly all seven letters. The intensity of the stimulus was held fixed throughout the experiment; three durations, designated L, M, and H, were used.

The results are shown in Fig. 9-11. Repetition alone increased perceptibility, whether or not the subject knew the meaning of the words, and at a similar rate for the two languages and the three durations.

In all cases the probability of a correct response after five presentations is nearly that attained after 25 presentations, even when the final probability does not approach unity. Clearly, then, neither of the models we are considering provides an adequate description of the data over the full range of 25 presentations. For five or fewer presentations, the integration model gives a better fit in some instances, and the decision-threshold model gives a better fit in others. In this range, the two predictions do not differ by much, and neither is particularly good or bad; deviations between predicted and obtained proportions are on the order of 0.03 to 0.05.

9.6 MULTIPLE PRESENTATIONS: SEQUENTIAL OBSERVATION OR DEFERRED DECISION

9.6.1 The sequential task

In a sequential detection task, a trial consists of a sequence of independent observation intervals. The intervals in a given sequence are alike in that all of them contain noise alone, or all of them contain a signal in addition to the noise. The observer bases his decision on all the preceding intervals in the immediate sequence. He may make one of two *terminal* decisions: "yes" (a signal is present in this sequence of intervals) or "no" (a signal is not present in this sequence of intervals). Alternatively, he may respond "continue," which means that he wishes to defer a terminal decision until he has had the opportunity to observe at least one more interval. There may or may not be an upper limit on the number of intervals he can observe before making a terminal decision.

The feature of this task that makes it of special interest in psychology is that it provides a structure for study of the trading relationship between the two principal measures of behavior, namely, *time* and *error*. Many behavioral studies employ only one of these measures. In mental testing, for example, "speed" tests are contrasted with "power" tests. Similarly, in sensory testing, the response time is fixed and the error rate is observed; or the task is made simple so that errors will be negligible, and then the reaction time is recorded. In the studies in which both of these measures are employed, conditions are usually arranged so that they will vary directly: they vary directly in sensory studies when the signal strength or the number of response alternatives is manipulated, and they vary directly in studies of learning as practice proceeds. Nonetheless, in most of the tasks that we perform, perceptual as well as motor or intellectual tasks, we must choose either to proceed with care, and thereby reduce the likelihood of a mistake, or to buy time at the cost of error. Thus, a theoretical and experimental framework for examining the balance between time and accuracy is of general value in experimental psychology.

9.6.2 Sequential-observation theory

The early developments in statistical theory were those made by Dodge and Romig (1929) and Bertky (1943). The major work was Wald's book *Sequential Analysis* (1947). Recently, Goode (1961) and Birdsall and Roberts (1965), using results obtained by Bellman (1957) and Blackwell and Girshick (1954), have advanced the theory of sequential analysis and have spelled out its application to signal detection.

Birdsall and Roberts distinguish three observation procedures. (1) In the *fixed-observation* procedure, the usual procedure considered in connection with signal detection, the only concern is for the accuracy of the decision. The observer is instructed to maximize the number of correct decisions, or the expected value of the decisions. The optimal procedure is to observe for as long as possible before making a decision. (2) The *predetermined-observation* procedure recognizes the competing goal of time. The observer under this procedure is instructed to balance the loss due to a terminal decision error and the cost of observing, by selecting the optimal observation length before the observation begins. The optimal observation length depends upon the signal-to-noise ratio and the cost of observing, as well as upon the values of the terminal decision outcomes and the a priori probability of signal occurrence. This is the general nonsequential observation procedure, for the observation length selected may be the maximum allowed, or any length short of the maximum. (3) In the *sequential-observation* procedure there is a continuous balancing of the potential terminal error losses and the cost of observing, depending upon what has already been observed. The observation length is a random variable; it depends upon the same factors that determine observation length in the predetermined-observation procedure and, in addition, upon the observation itself.

The three procedures may be compared on the basis of two types of decisions: one which determines the observation length and one which is a terminal, yes-no decision. In the first procedure, only the yes-no decision is made. In the second procedure the observer makes both types of decision, but he makes the decision as to observation length only once for each terminal decision. In the third procedure the decision as to observation length is made many times for each terminal, yes-no decision. The first two procedures are thus special cases of the third.

Two kinds of sequential-observation procedure can be distinguished. In the first kind, which is Wald's procedure, the observation length, or the available time to make a terminal decision, is unbounded. In the second kind, considered by Birdsall and Roberts, the terminal decision cannot be postponed indefinitely. It is assumed in all of this work, in order to make the mathematics and the computations feasible, that observations may be treated as if they are discrete, or at least that the decision whether or not to terminate is made in discrete steps. Thus, in Wald's procedure the number of observations or decisions that can be made in a given sequence is unlimited, whereas in the deferred-decision procedure of Birdsall and Roberts the maximum number of observations or decisions that can be made is fixed in advance and known to the observer.

In Wald's theory, formulas for determining the decision criteria are developed on the assumption that the error probabilities are given. Wald chose a pair of error probabilities—in effect, a point on the ROC curve—and then obtained the decision criteria, irrespective of error costs, observation costs, and a priori probabilities, by minimizing the average number of observations. Birdsall and Roberts take the Bayesian standpoint. They assume knowledge of the error costs, the observation costs, and the a priori probabilities, and from these determine the ROC curve, the average number of observations, and the decision criteria which maximize the total expected value. The Bayesian view permits an extensive generalization of Wald's sequential theory. Instead of holding constant the density functions of the observed variable, the losses due to errors, the value of d' associated with a single observation, and the cost of a single observation, all these parameters are allowed to vary in an arbitrary manner with the number of observations. The ability to treat a relatively large number of parameters, which may vary during a given sequence of observations, is made possible by establishing an upper limit on the number of observations. An important result, especially for detection problems, is that reliable calculations of optimal performance can be made even when the number of observations is very small. This is an advance, because the calculations made in Wald's theory are based on approximations that are unreliable for such small numbers of observations as are typical, or realistic, in a detection problem.

9.6.3   A sequential-observation experiment

The only sequential-observation experiment in a detection setting with human observers was conducted before Goode and Birdsall and Roberts had developed the theory of deferred decision for signal detection (Swets and Green, 1961). (For other psychological experiments on sequential observation, not in a detection setting, see Irwin and Smith, 1957, and Becker, 1958; for a sequential-observation experiment in speech recognition, see Pollack, 1959b, and Chapter 11, Section 11.4.) The experiment was intended to provide qualitative results in relation to two predictions derived from Wald's theory. The first of these is that, for a given signal strength, the error proportions and the average number of observations preceding a terminal decision will vary inversely. The second is that to yield the same error proportions, sequential tests will require fewer observations on the average than tests of fixed length. The basis for the second prediction is that sequential tests can take advantage of sequences in which the evidence happens to be very persuasive at an early stage of observation. The experiment went a step beyond Wald's theory, in that values were assigned the four possible outcomes of a terminal decision, and a cost was levied for each additional observation that was made. Qualitative results are thus available in relation to a third prediction, namely, that the average number of observations per sequence will increase and the error proportions will decrease as the values of the decision outcomes are increased relative to the cost of an additional observation.

The data of this experiment were also analyzed to determine whether the observer integrated the information obtained from the successive observations in a sequence, or made a terminal decision whenever the evidence from a single observation was sufficiently persuasive, independent of the preceding evidence. It is possible for the data to agree with the predictions of sequential theory just listed, yet not to support the assumption of sequential theory that successive observations are integrated. The data may agree qualitatively with predictions about error proportions and average numbers of observations and, at the same time, support the assumption of no integration that is made in the decision-threshold model.

Table 9-1 displays some illustrative results of this experiment. Sections (1) and (3) of the table show the results of fixed-observation tests (two-alternative forced-choice tests) that were conducted before and after the sequential tests; they indicate a good stability of equipment and observers. The signal was a pulsed tone of 1000 cps, with a duration of 0.1 second, and was presented in a continuous background of white noise.

The second section of Table 9-1 gives the results of sequential tests. Throughout these tests the a priori probability of signal occurrence was fixed at 0.50, and the cost of each additional observation was fixed at 1.0. The payoff matrices were symmetrical; that is, the four possible decision outcomes always had equal values, although the values were positive for correct decisions and negative for incorrect decisions. These values are shown in the left column of the middle section of the table. Although the five values are listed in increasing order, the conditions they represent were presented in random order.

Each condition yielded four quantities for each of two observers. These are the false-alarm and miss proportions, and the average numbers of observations preceding a terminal decision in noise and in signal sequences, denoted $\bar{x}_n$ and $\bar{x}_s$. It can be seen that, as the decision values increase, the error proportions tend to decrease and the mean number of observations tends to increase, in accordance with sequential theory.

Another phase of the experiment, with different observers, yielded data on the relative efficiency of sequential tests and tests of fixed length.

TABLE 9-1. THE RESULTS OF A SEQUENTIAL-OBSERVATION EXPERIMENT. SECTION (2) SHOWS ERROR PROPORTIONS, AND AVERAGE NUMBERS OF OBSERVATIONS PRECEDING A TERMINAL DECISION IN BOTH NOISE AND SIGNAL SEQUENCES, FOR FIVE CONDITIONS IN WHICH DIFFERENT VALUES WERE PLACED ON THE OUTCOMES OF A DECISION. THE RESULTS OF FIXED-LENGTH TESTS CONDUCTED BEFORE AND AFTER THE SEQUENTIAL TESTS ARE SHOWN IN SECTIONS (1) AND (3), RESPECTIVELY. (DATA FROM SWETS AND GREEN, 1961.)

		Observer 1				Observer 2			
	Forced choice								
(1)	$P(C)$	0.83				0.81			
	d'	1.33				1.23			
						(800 observations)			
	Sequential decision								
	V	$P(S\mid n)$	$P(N\mid s)$	$\bar{x}_n$	$\bar{x}_s$	$P(S\mid n)$	$P(N\mid s)$	$\bar{x}_n$	$\bar{x}_s$
	5	0.22	0.22	1.2	1.1	0.30	0.29	1.0	1.0
	10	0.16	0.17	1.7	1.4	0.22	0.20	1.9	1.6
(2)	15	0.18	0.19	1.8	1.5	0.26	0.17	2.1	1.7
	25	0.17	0.13	2.2	1.6	0.22	0.27	2.0	1.5
	60	0.11	0.11	4.3	3.0	0.11	0.13	3.8	2.4
						(400 sequences of observations in each of the four conditions)			
	Forced choice								
(3)	$P(C)$	0.83				0.82			
	d'	1.33				1.31			
						(600 observations)			

The results are shown in Fig. 9-12, which shows the error rates corresponding to different numbers of observations. It is apparent that the error rates in the sequential tests are generally lower than those in the tests of fixed length. It is also apparent that no simple generalization describes the amount of savings effected by the sequential tests in this experiment.

Let us consider now the experimental results with regard to the question of integration. The data from three phases of the experiment similar to the one just described were analyzed to determine the number of terminal decisions made at each observation stage. In every case, plots of the frequency of termination versus the observation stage showed an exponential function. This is the function that would result if the observer failed to integrate the successive observations, that is, if he set constant criteria and made a terminal decision when and only when a criterion was exceeded by a single observation. This is equivalent to ignoring, if an observation falls in the "continue" or "defer" region, just where in that region it

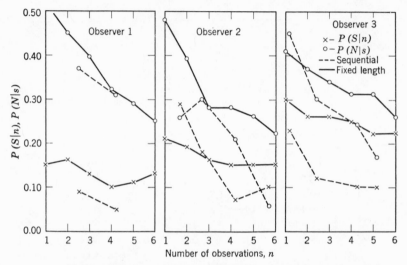

FIG. 9-12. The observed error rates as a function of the number of observations, in sequential tests and tests of fixed length, for three observers. (After Swets and Green, 1961.)

falls. Thus, the data are consistent with the decision-threshold model of multiple observations. In order to determine whether or not the exponential function is also consistent with an integration of the successive observations, as assumed by the statistical and detection theories, further analysis is required.

This analysis is accomplished by determining whether or not the number of terminations at each stage can be predicted from the observed error proportions at each stage, under the assumption that d' remains constant over successive observations. We shall not develop here the rationale for this procedure (see Swets and Green, 1961). Suffice it to say that if the number of terminations at each stage is adequately predicted by this procedure, then the decision-threshold model is supported at the expense of the integration model. The results of applying this predictive procedure to the first two phases of the sequential-observation experiment show the predictions to be quite accurate. Coefficients of correlation between predicted and obtained values are on the order of 0.90. Thus, for these two phases of the experiment, the assumption of no integration over successive observations is a good assumption.

The third phase of the experiment was conducted with this result in hand, and the observers were given explicit instructions to attempt to integrate over successive observations. In the third phase, then, we were not asking if human observers in a sequential-observation task would integrate if left to their own devices, but if they could integrate when encouraged to do so. The outcome was that the termination data from the third phase could not be predicted by the procedure which assumed that d' remained constant over successive observations. There were many more terminations at each observation stage than would result from no integration. Apparently the payoff structure, or the variability of sensory measures, in this kind of experiment is such that the benefits to be obtained from integration, if there are benefits, are not clear to the observers. Nonetheless, in the third phase the observers gave evidence that they were capable of integrating the information in successive observations.

It is clear that the existing experimental results on sequential observation leave several loose ends. For reasons that have been discussed, however, the sequential-observation task is of special interest. With an adequate theory now available, we are certain to see more experimental activity in this problem area in the near future.

9.7   EXTENDED OBSERVATION INTERVALS: TEMPORAL UNCERTAINTY

In preceding pages we examined a variety of ways in which the simplest detection tasks may be extended. We considered, as parameters of the detection task, the number of successive presentations of a given stimulus, the number of observers, and the number of signal components. The various parameters were linked by the question of whether or not the several observations entering a single decision are integrated, that is, whether or not they are combined into a single measure, a single basis for a decision.

The basic detection tasks can also be modified better to reflect everyday perceptual problems by introducing uncertainty about the time of signal occurrence. Three experiments have been conducted to study the effects of progressive deterioration in the observer's knowledge of the time of signal occurrence. In the first, the signal could occur anywhere in a defined interval that was considerably longer than the signal (Egan, Greenberg, and Schulman, 1961a). In the second, the observer was informed of the observation interval a fixed time before or after its occurrence (Egan, Schulman, and Greenberg, 1961). In the third experiment of this series the observation interval was not fixed, nor was it defined for the observer; the signal was presented several times at random, unspecified moments in a relatively long (two-minute) observation interval (Egan, Greenberg, and Schulman, 1961b). The essential results of the first two experiments are briefly reviewed in this section. The results of the third experiment, in which a version of the familiar "vigilance" problem was studied, are

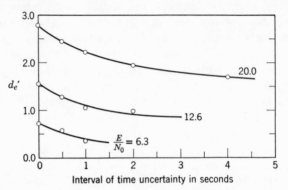

FIG. 9-13 The detectability index d_e' as a function of the interval of time uncertainty. Each point is based on 8 observers; 500 stimuli were presented to each observer at each point. (After Egan, Greenberg, and Schulman, 1961a.)

discussed in the next section; the emphasis in that discussion is on method, that is, on one possible method for determining the quantity d', or $D(\Delta m, s)$ or d_e', when the observation and response intervals are undefined.

The first study determined how d_e' varies as a function of the length of the interval in which the signal can occur. The length of the observation interval was held constant in a given series of trials, and was known to the observer. Considering the interval during which the signal may have its onset, the interval lengths examined were 0.0, 0.5, 1.0, 2.0, and 4.0 seconds; the signal was a tone with a duration of 0.25 second.

The average of the results obtained from eight subjects, at three signal-to-noise ratios, is shown in Fig. 9-13. Apparently, even a small amount of deliberately introduced uncertainty about the time of signal onset results in a decrement in performance. Further analyses indicate that the decrement for the longer observation intervals does not result from increased fatigue or flagging attention. It seems reasonable to suppose that, as the interval increases, the number of stimulus alternatives increases; that is, more samples of noise are available to be confused with the signal.

This conclusion is consistent with the detection model for "one-of-M-orthogonal signals" and with the results of the "pedestal" experiments discussed in Chapter 7.

In the second experiment the observation intervals occurred at random times. In some conditions the observer was warned that the observation interval would occur after a fixed time. In other conditions the observer was alerted that the observation interval had already occurred some

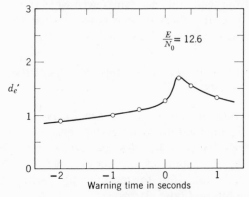

FIG. 9-14   The index d_e' as a function of the time at which the observer is informed that an observation interval will occur, or has occurred. Negative values indicate marking of the observation interval after the signal has occurred. Each point is based on 8 observers, and on approximately 400 presentations of the stimulus to each observer. (After Egan, Schulman, and Greenberg, 1961.)

fixed time before the alert. In three different conditions, each in force throughout a series of trials, the warning light was presented 1.0, 0.5, or 0.25 seconds before the observation interval. In three other conditions the alerting light was presented 0.5, 1.0, or 2.0 seconds after the observation interval. In a seventh condition the indicator light occurred exactly at the onset of the observation interval. The interval was 0.25 second in duration, the same as the duration of the sinusoidal signal.

Figure 9-14 shows the results obtained from the same eight observers as in the previous figure. From left to right, the first three data points were obtained when the observers were alerted after the occurrence of the observation interval; the fourth point was obtained when indicator light and observation interval had the same onset; the last three points resulted when the observers were warned prior to the observation interval. As Egan, Schulman, and Greenberg have pointed out, there are probably two kinds of uncertainty at work here: the observer has neither a perfect memory for the stimulus waveform, nor an unerring sense of the time of onset of the observation interval.

The two experiments discussed in this section show that a change in performance of a factor of 2, in d_e' or in signal power—that is, a change of 3 db—can result from the introduction of a relatively small amount of temporal uncertainty. The argument is advanced in Chapter 7 that the observer suffers from temporal uncertainty even when none is deliberately introduced, and that the effect of this possibly irreducible amount of initial uncertainty is larger than 3 db.

9.8   UNDEFINED OBSERVATION INTERVALS: VIGILANCE OR FREE RESPONSE

If the observer does not know when a signal may occur or how many signals may be presented during the observing session, and if he responds whenever he believes that according to some decision criterion a signal has occurred, then the evaluation of his performance depends upon the ability to devise some procedure for meaningfully partitioning the "yes" responses between hits and false alarms.

Egan, Greenberg, and Schulman (1961b) have proposed and examined one such procedure. Under this procedure, one counts the numbers of responses in an interval immediately after the occurrence of each signal, and in another interval long after the occurrence of each signal but before the occurrence of the next signal. The rates of responding in these two intervals are cumulated to provide estimates of the probabilities $P(S \mid s)$ and $P(S \mid n)$, respectively, and thus a point on the ROC curve. The model on which this procedure is based contains some assumptions which are difficult to test, and the procedure has some evident limitations. However, the model is spelled out in some detail, and it has received support from experimental results.

Denote the interval immediately after the occurrence of a signal as i_1, and the interval taken later as i_2. Examination of the number of responses in each of the two intervals, for a number of signal presentations, shows that the number of responses in each is increased if the observer adopts a more lenient decision criterion, and that the number of responses in each is decreased if the observer adopts a more stringent criterion. Although the model does not permit a direct evaluation of the criterion, it states an assumed relation between the number of responses in i_1 and the number of responses in i_2 as the criterion is varied. The assumption is that the relationship between these two quantities can be described by a power function. This assumption is based on the fact that empirical ROC curves in fixed-interval experiments are reasonably well described by a power function (see Chapters 3 and 4). A complete family of ROC curves can be generated by varying the exponent of the power function between one and zero, so that the relationship between d_e', or $D(\Delta m, s)$, and the exponent of the power function can be determined. The rates of responding in i_1 and i_2 yield an estimate of the exponent of the power function, and thus an estimate of the quantity d_e'.

Figure 9-15 shows some illustrative results relating the rate of responding

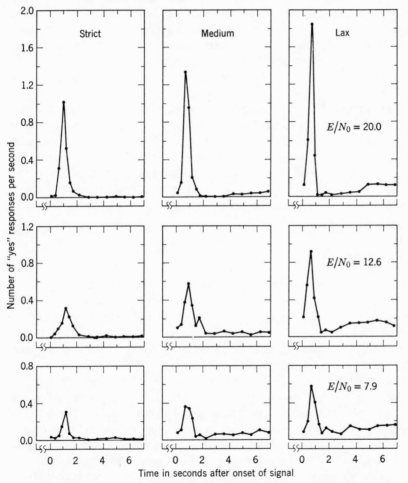

FIG. 9-15 Illustrative results of an experiment on vigilance. Rate of response is shown as a function of the time after the onset of a signal. Three signal intensities and three criteria are shown. (After Egan, Greenberg, and Schulman, 1961b.)

to the time after the onset of the signal. Three criteria, defined as "strict," "medium," and "lax," and three levels of signal intensity are represented. It is clear that the instructions to adopt different criteria, and the use of different signal intensities, affect the rate of responding in a predictable way. For each criterion at each signal level, a quantity comparable to the hit proportion is obtained by taking the area under the peak of the curve, and a quantity comparable to the false-alarm proportion is obtained by taking the average value of the rate from a level portion of the curve at some predetermined interval well to the right of its peak. The three ROC points obtained from each signal intensity establish the exponent of the power function relating the points; this exponent is then converted to d_e'. The model underlying this procedure is supported by the fact that estimates of d_e' obtained in this way are linearly related to E/N_0, as is the case in experiments with fixed and specified observation intervals (see Chapter 7).

Luce (1966) has proposed an alternative model which differs fundamentally in that the temporally continuous task is not reduced to a discrete one. This model uses data on the stimulus and response time series to estimate certain interresponse and stimulus-response distributions, and derives some theoretical relations among these distributions. The overall process is viewed as a renewal counting process in the technical sense. Chapter 12 may be consulted for other applications of counter theory in psychophysics.

9.9   SUMMARY

The simple detection tasks emphasized in preceding chapters can be modified in several ways. As one example, a single decision about the presence or location of the signal can be preceded by more than one observation. In this case the experimenter may arbitrarily fix in advance the number of observations to be made on all trials; or the observer may determine after each observation of a sequence whether or not to make another, basing his judgment on what he has already observed in the immediate sequence as well as on such variables as the values and costs, the a priori probabilities, and the expected signal strength. The simplest detection tasks can also be modified by increasing the number of observers attending to the same stimulus; the members of the observing team report to a decision maker who makes the final decision by taking into account, according to some rule, the several reports that he receives. Similarly, one can extend the signal in time, in space, or in frequency content. For each of the three general kinds of modification listed, a major problem is to determine how multiple observations are combined. The objective is to arrive at some general principles which state how the detectability of the signal is affected by increasing the number of observations.

The so-called integration model associated with detection theory assumes in each instance that the multiple observations are linearly combined to form a single basis for decision. A contrasting model, the decision-threshold model, is associated with classical psychophysical theory. The basis for improvement in this model is the assumption that making additional observations simply increases the probability that at least one of the observations will exceed a sensory or decision threshold. In most typical situations, the second model predicts a greater gain in detectability than the first, when false-alarm responses are ignored. If false-alarms are taken into account (either by means of a low-threshold sensory theory or by means of an ROC plot), the second model predicts less gain than the first, but the differences in prediction are small in most situations.

The simplest detection tasks may also be modified in the direction of realism by introducing various degrees of uncertainty about the time of the observation interval. This chapter presented results of experiments in which the signal could occur anywhere in an interval of greater duration than the signal, and the results of experiments in which the observation interval was marked at various times before or after the signal's occurrence. This chapter also presented the results of an experiment in which several signals (and responses) could occur in a relatively long interval without any indicators to mark their occurrence. This is the well-known problem of "vigilance." We described a method recently developed for constructing an ROC curve from data obtained in a vigilance task. The objective of such a method is to derive a measure of sensitivity that is unaffected by the observer's criterion for making a response, even though a direct evaluation of the criterion is not possible. Another method designed to reach the same objective was briefly characterized; this method differs basically from the first in that it does not attempt to reduce the temporally continuous case to the discrete one. Further applications of detection theory to vigilance problems are considered in Chapter 12.

9.10   APPENDIX 9-A

We derive here the prediction of the integration model for the increase in detectability that results from the combination of independent observations. The prediction is derived in two ways; the first is an approach through likelihood ratio; the second is based on linear combination of observations.

Consider the combination of two observations, x_1 and x_2. If they are independent, then $l(x_1, x_2) = l(x_1)l(x_2)$, as shown in the appendix to Chapter 1. Then

$$P[l(x_1, x_2) > t] = P[l(x_1)l(x_2) > t]$$
$$= P[\ln l(x_1) + \ln l(x_2) > c] \qquad (9A.1)$$

where $c = \ln t$.

Let us determine the density of $\ln l(x_1)$:

$$\ln l(x_1) = \ln \frac{f(x \mid s)}{f(x \mid n)} = \ln \frac{e^{-\frac{1}{2}[(x-\mu_s)/\sigma_s]^2}}{e^{-\frac{1}{2}[(x-\mu_n)/\sigma_n]^2}} \qquad (9A.2)$$

Letting $\sigma_s = \sigma_n = \sigma_1$,

$$\begin{aligned}
\ln l(x_1) &= -\frac{1}{2}\frac{x^2}{\sigma_1^2} + \frac{x\mu_s}{\sigma_1^2} - \frac{1}{2}\frac{\mu_s^2}{\sigma_1^2} + \frac{1}{2}\frac{x^2}{\sigma_1^2} - \frac{\mu_n x}{\sigma_1^2} + \frac{1}{2}\frac{\mu_n^2}{\sigma_1^2} \\
&= x\left(\frac{\mu_s}{\sigma_1^2} - \frac{\mu_n}{\sigma_1^2}\right) - \frac{1}{2}\frac{\mu_s^2}{\sigma_1^2} + \frac{1}{2}\frac{\mu_n^2}{\sigma_1^2} \\
&= \frac{x}{\sigma_1}\frac{\mu_s - \mu_n}{\sigma_1} - \frac{1}{2}\left[\left(\frac{\mu_s - \mu_n}{\sigma_1}\right)\left(\frac{\mu_s + \mu_n}{\sigma_1}\right)\right] \\
&= \frac{\mu_s - \mu_n}{\sigma_1}\left[\frac{x}{\sigma_1} - \frac{\mu_s + \mu_n}{2\sigma_1}\right]
\end{aligned} \qquad (9A.3)$$

Since $\dfrac{\mu_n - \mu_s}{\sigma_1} = d_1'$,

$$\ln l(x_1) = d_1'\left[\frac{x}{\sigma_1} - \frac{\mu_s + \mu_n}{2\sigma_1}\right] \qquad (9A.4)$$

If the noise-alone hypothesis, or H_0, is true, then

$$E[\ln l(x_1)] = d_1'\left(\frac{\mu_n}{\sigma_1} - \frac{\mu_n - \mu_s}{2\sigma_1}\right) = d'\left(\frac{\mu_n - \mu_s}{2\sigma_1}\right) = -\frac{(d_1')^2}{2} \qquad (9A.5)$$

Since, if x has variance σ_1^2, $ax + b$ has variance $a^2\sigma_1^2$,

$$\operatorname{var} \ln l(x_1) = \frac{(d_1')^2}{\sigma_1^2}\sigma_1^2 = (d_1')^2$$

If H_1 is true, then

$$E[\ln l(x_1)] = d_1'\left(\frac{\mu_s}{\sigma_1} - \frac{\mu_s + \mu_n}{2\sigma_1}\right) = d_1'\left(\frac{\mu_s - \mu_n}{2\sigma_1}\right) = +\frac{(d_1')^2}{2}$$

and

$$\operatorname{var} \ln l(x_1) = \frac{(d_1')^2}{\sigma_1^2}\sigma_1^2 = (d_1')^2 \qquad (9A.6)$$

By similar development for x_2, if H_0 is true,

$$E[\ln l(x_2)] = d_2' \left(\frac{\mu_n - \mu_s}{2\sigma_2} \right) = - \frac{(d_2')^2}{2} \qquad (9A.7)$$

and

$$\text{var } \ln l(x_2) = (d_2')^2$$

and, if H_1 is true,

$$E[\ln l(x_2)] = d_2' \left(\frac{\mu_s - \mu_n}{2\sigma_2} \right) = \frac{(d_2')^2}{2} \qquad (9A.8)$$

and

$$\text{var } \ln l(x_2) = (d_2')^2$$

Since both $\ln l(x_1)$ and $\ln l(x_2)$ are Gaussian under both hypotheses, their sum, $\ln l(x_1) + \ln l(x_2)$, is Gaussian. If H_0 is true, the combined variable has a mean:

$$- \frac{(d_1')^2}{2} - \frac{(d_2')^2}{2}$$

and variance

$$(d_1')^2 + (d_2')^2$$

If H_1 is true, the combined variable has a mean

$$\frac{(d_1')^2}{2} + \frac{(d_2')^2}{2}$$

and variance

$$(d_1')^2 + (d_2')^2$$

Therefore

$$d'_{x_1, x_2} = \frac{\Delta m}{\sigma} = \frac{(d_1')^2 + (d_2')^2}{\sqrt{(d_1')^2 + (d_2')^2}} = \sqrt{(d_1')^2 + (d_2')^2} \qquad (9A.9)$$

that is, the combined d' is the square root of the sum of the squares.

As an alternative derivation, consider a linear combination of the two independent Gaussian variables x_1 and x_2, for example,

$$y = ax_1 + bx_2 \qquad (9A.10)$$

We wish to choose a and b to maximize the percentage of correct detections or, equivalently, to maximize d_y'. Since x_1 and x_2 are Gaussian, their sum is Gaussian. Hence

$$d_y' = \frac{a \, \Delta x_1 + b \, \Delta x_2}{\sqrt{a^2 \sigma_1^2 + b^2 \sigma_2^2}} \qquad (9A.11)$$

where $\Delta x_1 = \mu_1{}^s - \mu_1{}^n$ and $\Delta x_2 = \mu_2{}^s - \mu_2{}^n$, and where

$$\text{var } x_1 = \sigma_1{}^2 \quad \text{and} \quad \text{var } x_2 = \sigma_2{}^2$$

Now

$$\frac{\partial d_y{}'}{\partial a} = \frac{\Delta x_1 \sqrt{a^2\sigma_1{}^2 + b^2\sigma_2{}^2} - (1/2)2a\sigma_1{}^2(a^2\sigma_1{}^2 + b^2\sigma_2{}^2)^{-\frac12}(a\,\Delta x_1 + b\,\Delta x_2)}{a_1{}^2\sigma_1{}^2 + b^2\sigma_2{}^2} \tag{9A.12}$$

and

$$\frac{\partial d_y{}'}{\partial b} = \frac{\Delta x_2 \sqrt{a^2\sigma_1{}^2 + b^2\sigma_2{}^2} - (1/2)2b\sigma_2{}^2(a^2\sigma_1{}^2 + b^2\sigma_2{}^2)^{-\frac12}(a\,\Delta x_1 + b\,\Delta x_2)}{a_1{}^2\sigma_1{}^2 + b^2\sigma_2{}^2}$$

The maximum occurs when the two numerators are simultaneously zero, that is, when

$$\Delta x_1(a^2\sigma_1{}^2 + b^2\sigma_2{}^2)^{\frac12} = a\sigma_1{}^2(a\,\Delta x_1 + b\,\Delta x_2)(a^2\sigma_1{}^2 + b^2\sigma_2{}^2)^{-\frac12} \tag{9A.13}$$

and

$$\Delta x_2(a^2\sigma_1{}^2 + b^2\sigma_2{}^2)^{\frac12} = b\sigma_2{}^2(a\,\Delta x_1 + b\,\Delta x_2)(a^2\sigma_1{}^2 + b^2\sigma_2{}^2)^{-\frac12} \tag{9A.14}$$

Thus

$$\Delta x_1(a^2\sigma_1{}^2 + b^2\sigma_2{}^2) = a\sigma_1{}^2(a\,\Delta x_1 + b\,\Delta x_2) \tag{9A.15}$$

and

$$\Delta x_2(a^2\sigma_1{}^2 + b^2\sigma_2{}^2) = b\sigma_2{}^2(a\,\Delta x_1 + b\,\Delta x_2) \tag{9A.16}$$

Now, if

$$a = \frac{\Delta x_1}{\sigma_1{}^2} \quad \text{and} \quad b = \frac{\Delta x_2}{\sigma_2{}^2}$$

by substitution in Eqs. 9A.15 and 9A.16,

$$\Delta x_1\left[\left(\frac{\Delta x_1}{\sigma_1}\right)^2 + \left(\frac{\Delta x_2}{\sigma_2}\right)^2\right] = \Delta x_1\left[\left(\frac{\Delta x_1}{\sigma_1}\right)^2 + \left(\frac{\Delta x_2}{\sigma_2}\right)^2\right]$$

and

$$\Delta x_2\left[\left(\frac{\Delta x_1}{\sigma_1}\right)^2 + \left(\frac{\Delta x_2}{\sigma_2}\right)^2\right] = \Delta x_2\left[\left(\frac{\Delta x_1}{\sigma_1}\right)^2 + \left(\frac{\Delta x_2}{\sigma_2}\right)^2\right]$$

Thus, because $\Delta x_1/\sigma_1 = d_1{}'$ and $\Delta x_2/\sigma_2 = d_2{}'$, we may substitute in Eq. 9A.11 to obtain

$$d_y{}' = \frac{(d_1{}')^2 + (d_2{}')^2}{\sqrt{(d_1{}')^2 + (d_2{}')^2}} = \sqrt{(d_1{}')^2 + (d_2{}')^2} \tag{9A.17}$$

Equation 9A.17 is identical to Eq. 9A.9; the optimal linear combination is a likelihood-ratio solution.

The extension to n variables is immediate. If $n = 3$,

$$d'_{x_1, x_2, x_3} = \sqrt{(d'_{x_1, x_2})^2 + (d'_{x_3})^2}$$
$$= \sqrt{(d_1')^2 + (d_2')^2 + (d_3')^2}$$

and so on. Hence, when n observations $(x_1, x_2, \ldots, x_i, \ldots, x_n)$ are combined,

$$d_n' = \left[\sum_{i=1}^{n} (d_i)^2 \right]^{1/2} \tag{9A.18}$$

10

Frequency Analysis

10.1   INTRODUCTION

In the earlier chapters (Part I) the decision and detection theories were used as a means of analyzing a variety of psychophysical methods. The emphasis placed on methodology in these early chapters should not obscure the fact that the decision and detection theories may also be useful in the analysis of substantive problems. The applications of ideal-observer theory to the shape of the psychometric function and to other similar problems have already been illustrated in Chapter 7. In this chapter we consider the topic of auditory frequency analysis.

Auditory frequency analysis is certainly one of the oldest topics, and probably the most important, in audition. As von Békésy's observations have indicated, there is a spatial pattern of excitation along the basilar membrane in response to a steady sinusoidal stimulus, and the location of that pattern is determined by the frequency of the sound. What is still unknown is how these patterns are processed by the nervous system, and whether multiple modes of processing are possible. On the psychological side, frequency analysis is evident in the ability to distinguish among different parts of a complex sound stimulus, and in the ability to ignore unwanted, interfering sounds and hence to listen to only certain aspects of the total stimulus configuration. What are still unknown are the specifics of this process—what is the extent of this ability to ignore unwanted sounds, and how good is this ability in a variety of stimulus situations? To begin the discussion let us consider, at least briefly, some of the history of the topic of auditory frequency analysis.

10.2   HISTORY OF THE FREQUENCY-ANALYSIS CONCEPT

The central phenomenon of hearing is frequency analysis—the ability of the observer to separate a complex sound into components and to identify each of these separate components. The visual sense integrates a complex spectrum, and thus we do not analyze a color sensation; rather we see a single, unitary color or hue, whether the spectrum is complex or simple. The laws of color mixture are, in one sense, simply a quantitative analysis of this failure of the visual sense to separate a complex spectrum into components of radiant energy at the various frequencies or wavelengths. But sounds are quite different. One can, with practice, virtually ignore the various components of a complex sound and listen to one or more components of the complex spectra at will. This striking ability was, in fact, the substance of the first law of psychoacoustics. In the middle of the nineteenth century Ohm described frequency analysis in his acoustic law, which stated, in effect, that the ear could act as a kind of Fourier-analysis device. Thus Ohm's law asserted that auditory perception of a continuous periodic sound wave could be completely described by the amount of power at the fundamental frequency and the power at all the harmonics of the fundamental. The great Helmholtz announced the first theory of hearing, and this theory was simply a plausible physiological mechanism to accomplish this frequency analysis.

Helmholtz, at least in the earlier versions of his theories, assumed that the basilar membrane could be likened to a harp, with the various strings of the harp tuned to the different frequencies. When a complex sound is presented to such a structure, the various frequency components of the sound vibrate the corresponding, sympathetic fibers of the harp. Every periodic vibration is therefore represented on the basilar membrane by a particular configuration of excitation along the extent of the membrane. The peaks and valleys of this excitation correspond to the frequencies present and absent in the sound. This is the so-called "place theory" of hearing; each frequency of vibration is represented by a corresponding place along the membrane. For over 50 years the classical theory of hearing was synonymous with a physiological and mechanical explanation of how the ear performs this frequency analysis.

Despite the central importance of this topic, there was from 1863, when Helmholtz's theory was first published, until the early 1920's very little *quantitative* data on the exact limits or extent of this frequency-analysis ability. One of the most direct and straightforward ways of determining something about the quantitative limits of frequency analysis is to present two sounds simultaneously and ask the subject if he hears one in the presence of the other. That is, one sound is singled out as a signal, and the subject is asked whether he hears that sound in the presence of the other sound. This other sound tends to disrupt or "mask" the signal.

Such a simple masking experiment, as it is now called, is not at all difficult with modern electronic equipment, but it was very difficult in the days of Ohm. A masking experiment presupposed the ability to control and measure at least two independent sources and to manipulate one or the other so that the subject could judge whether or not he could hear the signal. It was several years after Helmholtz that Mayer (1876) first announced what is the most obvious fact about pure-tone masking, namely, that low-frequency sounds are more successful in masking high-frequency sounds than the reverse. That is, at least for loud maskers, there is an asymmetry in the frequency-analysis ability. It was not until much later that Wegel and Lane (1924), using sound generated by an electronic oscillator, systematically investigated the ability of one sinusoidal sound to mask or obscure another. Many introductory texts show their results. They confirmed Mayer's findings that high-frequency sounds are less effective in masking low-frequency sounds than the reverse, once the intensity of the masker is 60 or 70 decibels above the intensity at which it can just be heard.

Wegel and Lane also showed that at moderate and lower sound levels the sinusoidal masker would completely obscure or mask only a signal sinusoid located in a range of frequencies near the frequency of the masker. Thus, whereas a 1200-cps tone at a very low level would have no effect on the detection of a very weak sound at 2400 cps, nor on a sound at 600 cps, those frequencies in a narrower range around 1200 cps, for instance from 800 cps to 2000 cps, would be affected by the 1200-cps sinusoid used as the masker.

There are, however, certain disadvantages to using sinusoids as both the signal and the masking sounds. In particular, when they are very close together, they interact with each other to produce a waxing and waning of intensity called *beats*. These beats somewhat complicate the interpretation of the masking data. Fletcher (1940) used wide-band noise as a masker of a sinusoidal signal. He manipulated the frequency spectrum of the noise and investigated, for example, how the detection of a sinusoid located in the middle of the noise band depended on the bandwidth of the noise. The results led Fletcher to infer that the ear possessed a critical range of frequency, or a *critical band*. Using the results of several experiments, he tried to estimate the width of this critical band at several different frequencies. Because Fletcher's experiment and its interpretation are so central to the later work reviewed in this chapter, we shall consider Fletcher's experiment in some detail.

10.3 THE CRITICAL BAND

Fletcher began by taking a sine wave as the signal and masking it with a wide-band noise. He had the subject adjust a continuous sinusoid until it was just detectable in the presence of the masking noise. If we do thus with a 1000-cps signal and a wide-band masking noise, the subject will set the signal-to-noise ratio at about 18 db (the ratio of the signal power to the noise power in a one-cycle band will be 18 db). Fletcher continued the experiment by filtering the noise so that, instead of a wide-band masking noise, he had a masking noise approximately 1000 cps wide. The spectrum level of the noise was held constant throughout the experiment. Thus the noise extended from about 500 cps up to 1500 cps, the signal still being the 1000-cps tone. Once again the subject adjusted the intensity of the signal until it could just be heard in this masking noise, and once again the result was that the signal-to-noise ratio, where the noise was measured in one-cycle bands, was still the same, about 18 db. The experiment continued by further filtering the noise, using, for example, a 200-cps filter, so that the noise extended only from 900 cps to 1100 cps, with the signal still set at 1000 cps. Once again we find that the signal-to-noise ratio in a one-cycle band is approximately 18 db. Finally, when the signal is filtered to an even narrower width, for example, to a band only 30 cps wide, we notice an improvement in the ability of the subject to hear the signal in the noise; that is, the subject will adjust the signal intensity to a lower value and still be able to hear it in this masking noise. If we consider the ratio of the signal power to the noise-power density, the ratio is reduced to approximately 15 db.

Thus, as we diminish the bandwidth of the noise while maintaining a constant spectral level, we find that the threshold for the tone is not affected until a certain critical bandwidth is reached. At this bandwidth the signal level needed to hear the tone in the noise diminishes approximately linearly with further decreases in the bandwidth of the noise. This bandwidth at which the signal becomes easier to hear is the width Fletcher called the *critical band*. Figure 8-4 of Chapter 8 shows the original data. The dotted line of that figure shows Fletcher's approximation to the result.

One way of interpreting this experiment, suggested by Fletcher, is to assume that the ear acts as a narrow filter with a width equal to the critical bandwidth. Only noise within the critical band is effective in masking the signal. The signal level needed to just hear the signal is assumed to be some constant proportion of the effective noise. The signal level needed to just hear the signal will therefore be independent of bandwidth if the noise masker is wider than the critical band, and will vary inversely with the external bandwidth once the masking noise is less than the critical band. Fletcher estimated the width of the critical band as 60 cps at a center frequency of 1000 cps.

He varied the noise bandwidth at a variety of center frequencies and found that the width of the critical band appeared to depend upon the frequency of the signal. It was approximately 200 cps wide at 4000 cps; that is, at 4000 cps the signal intensity needed to hear the signal and the noise was independent of the width of the band, for bandwidths greater than about 200 cps. The second column of Table 10-1 lists the width of

TABLE 10-1. VARIOUS ESTIMATES OF THE CRITICAL BAND

Center Frequency	Fletcher	Hawkins and Stevens (Critical-Ratio Method)	Zwicker, Flottorp, and Stevens
250	51	39	95
500	51	50	110
1000	63	79	160
2000	98	126	295
3000	141	200	450
4000	204	314	680

the critical band as estimated at several center frequencies from Fletcher's original experiment.

There is also another way of determining the width of the critical band from the data obtained in Fletcher's experiment. Consider the results obtained at 1000 cps. With a wide-band noise, the ratio of signal power to noise power in a one-cycle band that was needed to just hear the signal was 63, or about 18 db. Now, if we assume that the subject can just hear the signal when the signal power is equal to the total noise coming through the critical band, then, by reversing the arithmetic, we can determine the critical bandwidth from the ratio of signal power to noise power in the one-cycle band. That is, if the critical band is 63 cps wide, then the total noise power will just equal the signal power when the signal is 63 times more intense than the noise power in a one-cycle band. At 4000 cps we find the subject needs about 200 times as much signal power as noise-power density, and so we conclude from this ratio that the critical band is about 200 cps wide. In fact, Fletcher's estimates of the critical bandwidth have been heavily influenced by this ratio, and some later writers appear to believe that the experiment in which the bandwidth of the noise was varied had little effect on his estimates of the critical band (Zwicker, Flottorp, and Stevens, 1957; Scharf, 1961; Greenwood, 1961a,b).

Obviously, the idea that the signal is just detectable when the signal power equals the total effective noise is an assumption. Its support lies in the data collected in the experiment in which the noise was filtered to reveal a critical region. The data obtained in this experiment are somewhat scanty, but they do exist. In any case, determining the critical bandwidth

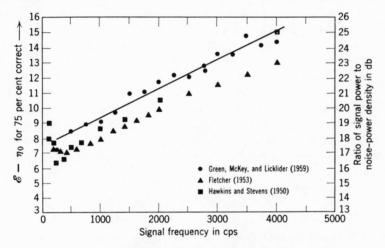

FIG. 10-1   A comparison of data from three experiments. The solid line is the best-fitting linear function to the average data (filled dots) obtained by Green, McKey, and Licklider (1959). The key explains the source of the various data points.

from the signal-to-noise ratio deserves a special name; the "critical-ratio method" has been suggested (Zwicker, Flottorp, and Stevens, 1957).

One of the most complete studies of this critical ratio is the work of Hawkins and Stevens (1950) in which they determined the signal-to-noise ratios needed to hear sine waves in noise at a variety of noise levels and signal frequencies. Once the noise level is 30 or 40 db above the absolute threshold, the signal-to-noise ratio needed to just hear the signal is largely independent of level of the noise. In general, the results are consistent with Fletcher's, as shown in Table 10-1 and Fig. 10-1, where the results of Hawkins and Stevens are presented along with the results of Fletcher's original experiment. The graph also shows the results of an experiment by Green, McKey, and Licklider (1959). In their study, only one noise level was used, and the signal was a gated sinusoid of $\frac{1}{10}$ second duration. As we can see from the graph, the fact that the signal is of fixed duration does not appreciably alter the way in which the detectability of the signal changes with frequency.

Since the early papers of Fletcher and his collaborators at the Bell Telephone Laboratories, the critical band has received considerable attention. The concept has been utilized with particular vigor and elegance by Zwicker, Gässler, and others of the Technical Institute at Stuttgart. They have used a variety of experimental techniques including masking, loudness balancing, and perception of phase changes to determine the critical frequency difference, or "Frequenzegruppe," as they call it. Their experiments suggest that the critical band is about two to three times wider than first suggested by Fletcher. Table 10-1 also presents these later estimates of critical bandwidth, or Frequenzegruppe. These estimates are taken from the paper by Zwicker, Flottorp, and Stevens (1957).

Why there is this discrepancy between the critical band and the Frequenzegruppe is not at all clear. Some have suggested that the critical band may have no fixed width but may be changed by the observer to suit best the task in which it is used (Swets, Green, and Tanner, 1962; Swets, 1963a). Generally, the critical band is measured in an experimental situation in which it is desirable to have as small a band as possible, for example, in detecting a continuous sine wave in noise. But suppose that the same observer is listening for a sinusoid that may appear anywhere in a range of frequencies, or is listening to a complex sound composed of several different sinusoids spread over a wide frequency range. How will the observer operate in these situations? The narrow-band filter of the fixed-sinusoid experiment is clearly inappropriate.

If possible, the observer should either widen his band somehow to encompass the range of potential signal frequencies, or base his response on the output of more than one narrow critical band. The next section reviews a series of experiments aimed at determining how the observer operates in these situations in which the signal occupies a wide range of frequencies. Clearly, a study of these situations is necessary if we are ever to make any practical use of the critical-band concept, that is, if we are to extend the concept beyond the experiments in which it was originally discovered.

For the reader interested in more detailed information about the critical-band concept, there are several excellent reviews available on the topic. Zwicker, Flottorp, and Stevens (1957) review much of the German work. Scharf's (1961) review is also very complete. For arguments that the bands may be adjustable, the papers by Green (1960a), Swets (1963a), Jeffress (1964), and van den Brink (1964) may be consulted. For another discussion of the size of the critical band and a reinterpretation of Fletcher's original experiment, see Chapter 8.

10.4   INTERPRETATION AND EXTENSION OF THE CRITICAL-BAND CONCEPT—EXPERIMENTS ON UNCERTAIN SIGNAL FREQUENCY

The critical-band experiment suggests that the auditory mechanism can be likened to a narrow-band-pass filter, at least for the condition in which the signal is a sinusoid and the noise has a wide band. Such an analogy implies that the ear is insensitive to sounds outside the frequency region of the critical band. This interpretation is strengthened when we consider the results of the experiment by Webster, Miller, Thompson, and Davenport (1952), who investigated the converse situation, a masking situation in which the noise has a deep notch in the power spectrum of the noise at the signal frequency. The observer was asked in this experiment to set the level of the signal that he needed for the signal to be heard in this noise. The results were, in the main, consistent with the simple filter interpretation. Thus only a narrow range of frequencies, centered about the tone to be detected, seem to play a role in the masking of the signal.

We can hardly quarrel with this interpretation in this experimental context. But as with any argument from analogy, the crucial test is how far one can extend this analogy. What is of interest is the generality of the results. If the signal occupies a wide range of frequencies, will the ear still act as a narrow-band-pass receiver?

A consideration of this question led to the so-called one-of-two-frequencies experiments. In these experiments there are two signal frequencies, but only one of these frequencies occurs on any single trial of the forced-choice procedure. Let us assume, for example, that the frequencies are 1000 and 2000 cps. The signal frequency is selected at random on each trial. On any one trial, then, the observer knows that one of the two frequencies will be presented, but he does not know which. His task is to select the temporal interval in the forced-choice procedure in which he thinks the signal occurs. He is not asked to recognize the signal; that is, he is *not* asked to state which frequency occurred, 1000 or 2000 cps, but only to detect its presence by indicating its location in time—first or second interval. Will such a procedure lead to a lower percentage of correct responses than the subject would achieve if the signal frequency were fixed, and if so, by how much?

In one of the early experiments on signal uncertainty, the signal was 0.1 second in duration, and the two possible signal frequencies were 1000 and 500 cps. The signal levels were set so that the observers could obtain about 95% correct in a two-alternative forced-choice procedure when the signal frequency was fixed at 500 and about the same percent correct when the signal was fixed at 1000 cps. When the signal frequency was uncertain, the percent correct dropped to about 73 %. This is approximately the percent correct that the observer would achieve if he were listening to only one frequency region on any given trial in the forced-choice test. On about one half of the trials he is listening at the right frequency and will be correct about 95 %, whereas on the remaining trials, he is at the wrong frequency and thus will be correct only by chance, or 50 %. The net percent correct will be one-half the combined probabilities (48 + 25), or about 73 %.

We call this hypothetical account of the data the *single-band* model, since it assumes that the observer acts as a narrow-band-pass receiver. This is clearly not a model of optimal behavior, since the frequency of the signal is not constrained to lie within a narrow frequency region. The model assumes that the center of this band-pass filter can be adjusted so that if, for example, the observer were informed before each trial of the frequency of the signal, he could adjust the center frequency of this filter to the correct frequency and thus improve the percentage of correct detections. Given these assumptions, the prediction of the amount of decrement encountered in the one-of-two-frequencies experiments is straightforward and, as we have just discussed, a decrement of about 22 %, from 95 % to 73 % correct, can be expected in a two-alternative forced-choice procedure.

This, however, is not the only hypothesis we can entertain to explain the decrement caused by the variation in the frequency location of the signal. Another very simple model is the so-called *multiple-band* model. This model assumes, along with the single-band model, that the ear can act as a narrow-band-pass receiver when listening to a narrow signal in wide-band noise. It differs from the single-band model in assuming that, should the signal frequency occupy a larger frequency region, more than one of the narrow filters can be utilized at one time. Physiologically, we can think of the different tuned filters as representing different locations along the cochlea. The single-band model assumes that the observer, in effect, monitors only one region at any one time; the multiple-band model assumes that the observer can monitor several different frequency regions simultaneously. Specifically, it is assumed that the outputs of any number of regions can be linearly combined, with appropriate weight constants for each channel.

Now, if the signal occupies only a single frequency region, then only one filter is used to listen to the signal. We then listen to a signal in some effective noise which is determined by the width of the critical band. This effective noise is, therefore, less than the total power in the wide-band masking noise. When the signal can be at either of two frequencies, two filters must be employed; and thus, at any given instant in time, roughly twice as much masking noise is effective in masking the signal. The signal level stays the same, since on any one trial only one signal is presented. Thus, when the signal frequency is uncertain, the observer is listening to twice as much effective noise as in the single-frequency case. We can work out from this model the numerical predictions of the decrement that we should expect in the uncertain frequency case; and, to consider our example, if the detectability of both frequencies is 95%, the predicted percent correct on the basis of the multiple-band model is 85%.

The single-band and multiband hypotheses do not exhaust the set of alternative models. Shipley (1960) has recently proposed an extension of Luce's (1959) choice model that will also account for the decrement encountered with the one-of-two possible signal frequencies. Her model completely ignores the stimulus situation, except to observe that both a detection and a recognition experiment are potentially involved in the forced-choice procedure in which one of two possible signal frequencies is sent. She assumes that an implicit recognition response is made even though it is not required in the experiment, writes out in full form the response matrix* based on Luce's choice model and then, making plausible assumptions, reduces the full matrix to the responses allowed in the detection task, namely, the choice of the first or second interval. A reduction in the percentage of correct detections can be expected from this collapsing of the original matrix. The strong point of her model is the fact that the explanation of the decrement does not involve assumptions about processes outside the scope of the model. The decrement is explained by a straightforward extension of the basic choice axiom. We shall not review the details of the derivation here; it is presented very clearly by Shipley (1960).

Actually two predictions can be made from Shipley's choice model. These two predictions are determined by whichever of two assumptions is made within the model. One of the predictions made on the basis of the choice model is almost indistinguishable from that made by the multiple-band model. The other solution of the choice model generates exactly the same prediction as the single-band model. The difference between the multiple-band model and the choice theory is so small, about 3% at most, that no existing data could distinguish between them. There is, however, a somewhat larger difference between the predictions of the two forms of the choice model, and between the predictions of the single-band and multiple-band models. As in the example just above where the initial probability is

---

* A four-by-four matrix whose rows and columns are the stimulus and response alternatives corresponding to the stimulus presented, either high or low frequency, and either the first or the second interval.

95%, the single-band model predicts 73% correct in the one-of-two experiments, whereas the multiple-band model predicts 85%, a difference in prediction of 12%. Let us now review some of the existing empirical data in order to evaluate these two theories.

The first experimental evidence was presented along with the introduction of the single-band model by Tanner, Swets, and Green (1956) and indicated that the decrement due to signal uncertainty was dependent upon the frequency separation between the two possible signal frequencies and perhaps also dependent upon the duration of the signal. The evidence is best described as scanty; it clearly establishes that there is a decrement associated with the uncertain frequency condition, but the exact magnitude of this decrement was not carefully estimated.

Veniar (1958a,b) reported several experiments, some of them repetitions of the conditions used by Tanner et al., and others in which the number of possible signal frequencies was extended to four and eight. A simple summary of the experimental data is impossible. There is considerable scatter, and there are some differences among observers; for example, two observers show that the decrement associated with signal uncertainty is greater as the separation in frequency between the two signals increases, whereas one observer does not.

Creelman (1960) has reported an extensive investigation aimed particularly at establishing whether the decrement caused by signal uncertainty is a function of the separation in frequency between the signals. Once again, there is considerably variability in the data, and he was unable to establish any single variable in the experiment that would explain the various results. Whether or not the decrement is dependent upon the separation of the frequencies of the signals is fairly important since, potentially at least, it provides a way of choosing between the choice model and the signal-detection models.

Creelman, in the report of his experiment, advances a fifth hypothesis concerning the decrement encountered in the uncertain-frequency condition. He suggests, as does the multiple-band model, that the observer can monitor several frequency channels simultaneously. However, in Creelman's model it is supposed that the maximum output of each band is noted for both the first and the second interval of the forced-choice trial. With two possible signal frequencies and two possible time intervals, a total of four observations are taken. The largest output is then determined, and the temporal interval associated with this largest output is chosen by the observer. This model predicts less decrement than the multiple-band model, and thus considerably less decrement than the single-band model. In general, Creelman's results are more consistent with the multiple-band model or his own model than with the single-band model. The multiple-band model and Creelman's model are similar in that both are based on a combination of the outputs of several critical bands. Other multiple-band models could be generated by suggesting other rules of combination. The important point is that all maintain that several critical bands can be monitored simultaneously.

As pointed out earlier, the single-band and multiple-band models generate predictions that are very similar to two versions of choice theory. While the differences between the two pairs of models are small, the theories are quite different in conception, since both the multiple-band and the single-band models are essentially *stimulus* theories. Choice theory, on the other hand, is based upon an analysis of *response* determinants. One possibility of testing the models is to determine how *cues* would affect the decrement that is due to uncertainty. In particular, telling the observer the frequency that was presented after the observation interval (but before the response) should have no effect according to the stimulus model, whereas under choice theory such information could be used to determine how the observer reduces the full choice matrix, and thus such information should influence the percentage of correct decisions. Swets and Sewall (1961) have attempted to investigate this aspect of the problem by presenting frequency cues at different times within the trial cycle. Specifically, they cued the subject (by lights or by the frequencies themselves) as to the frequency presented, both before and after the stimulus presentation. The results are equivocal; some of the results favor each theory. However, one empirical result that emerged from this study is of considerable importance. This result was that a decrement in performance occurred in the situation when the signal was randomly varied in frequency from trial to trial, even though the subject knew in advance which frequency to expect on any given trial. That is, the observer had lower percentages correct when the signal frequency was varied from trial to trial—even when the signal frequency was presented as a cue before each trial—than when the signal frequency was fixed for the entire series of trials. This result is not predicted by any of the theories and may be the reason for the ambiguity encountered in the interpretation of the earlier experiments. It may mean that all the performance baselines for generating the predictions in all models are too high, and thus all decrements caused by frequency uncertainty are in fact less than they have appeared to be.

Another effort to test two theories that predict similarly in the one-of-two-frequencies experiment is to analyze the trial-by-trial responses of the subject. Any version of the multiple-band model, since all channels are being monitored at all times, must predict that the probability of a correct response is independent of the signal frequency presented on the previous trial, whether the subject was right or wrong on that previous trial. The single-band model, on the other hand, would suggest that frequency cues are important, since the single filter is constantly searching out the signal frequency. Thus, if the subject were correct on the previous trial, and if the same signal frequency were presented on the present trial, we might expect a higher percent correct than if the same frequency were presented but the previous response were incorrect. These two probabilities are in fact different for all three observers, the average difference being about 8% near 70%. Equally conclusive is the opposite pattern of results, when the frequency changes between the previous and present trials. Here the percentage of correct responses is higher on the present trials if the response on the previous trials was incorrect. The average difference, consistent for all three observers, is about 12% at about 70%. This more detailed analysis clearly supports a single-band, as opposed to a multiple-band, model (Swets, Shipley, McKey, and Green, 1959).

In still another effort to throw some light on the experimental problem, Green (1961) abandoned the usual paradigm of determining the decrement by comparing the detection of a single fixed frequency with that obtained when one of two possible signals is presented. He used a two-alternative forced-choice technique and, on any trial, presented a signal frequency selected from a *range* of permissible frequencies. Thus, in one condition of this experiment, the signal frequency might be any frequency in a range between 500 cps and 4000 cps. This range of 3500 cps corresponds to something on the order of 20 to 30 critical bands, depending upon what assumption is made about the exact width of a critical band (see Table 10-1).

Assuming that 20 critical bands are involved in the frequency range 500 to 4000 cps, the single-band model predicts that, even if the subject is getting nearly 100% correct with the single frequencies in that band, the uncertainty will reduce his chances of being correct to 1/20 of 100% plus 19/20 of 50%, or essentially 53% correct. This result occurs because the probability of the observer's being at the right frequency is 1/20, and at the wrong frequency, 19/20. The multiple-band model predicts a decrement almost as large: if 20 critical bands are involved, the predicted decrement is about 10 db. Creelman's model would predict decrements of about the same size. Predictions based on the choice model are not as clear, since it is not at all evident how many implicit recognitions would result from a signal in the frequency range 500 to 4000 cps. The difficulty, of course, is that the choice model is not stimulus-oriented and thus is somewhat ambiguous when changes are made in the stimulus situation.

The empirical results indicate that the subjects needed about 3 db more signal energy in order to maintain the same percent correct when the signal appeared anywhere in the band from 500 to 4000 cps as when it was fixed in frequency. As part of the experiment, the width of the frequency band was varied; that is, signal frequency widths of 100, 300, 500, and 1000 cps centered about 2250 cps, the linear center of the band, were investigated. These ranges of signal uncertainty produced even less decrement. For example, at 500 cps the decrement was about 1 to 1.5 db. Signal duration was also varied in the investigation; there was no tendency for the amount of decrement to be dependent upon the duration of the signal.

This surprisingly small decrement, compared with the predictions of at least 10 db by the various models, is also consistent with the previous findings by Veniar that there is only a slight increase in the decrement caused by adding uncertainty of 4 or 8 frequencies. It is advisable to postpone further analysis of these results until we review another kind of experiment: the detection of multiple-component signals in noise.

10.5   DETECTION OF MULTIPLE-COMPONENT SIGNALS

Studies of the detection of signals of uncertain frequency represent one way to gain insight into the frequency-analysis mechanism of the ear. A second approach uses the data on the detection of wide-band signals in masking noise. Suppose that the signal has a broad spectrum with frequency components in several critical bands. Will the ear maintain the narrowly tuned configuration appropriate to a single sinusoid, or will it change to match the spectral composition of the signal? Surprisingly enough, there has been comparatively little work on this problem, and almost all of it has occurred since 1949. There are, as far as we know, five studies on this issue; a brief review of their results follows.

Schafer and Gales (1949) studied the detectability of two-, four-, and eight-component tones in noise. The complex signal was generated simply by adding the components together. The question at issue is whether the complex sound is any more detectable than the most detectable member of the complex. The detectability of this most detectable component represents the lower limits of detectability, since no one doubts that, as a minimum, the observer can simply listen to this most detectable component of the complex. The question is whether the observer can do any better than this lower limit. If the observer's performance is no better than this minimum, then he is effectively ignoring all the components of the signal other than this most detectable one. Schafer and Gales found that a two-component signal, with each component as detectable as the other, was on the average 1.5 db more easily detected than either component of the pair. There was considerable variability in their data, and in their conclusion they state that the improvement was in the range between 0 and 2 db. If the lower number (0 db) is accepted, in effect there is no improvement—the observer listens to only one of the signals.

With four to eight components in the complex sounds, the increase in detectability was between 0 and 3 db, with something nearer 2 to 2.5 db improvement on the average. Schafer and Gales suggest that this improvement in the detectability of the multiple-component signal is the result of a statistical process, assuming an independence among the thresholds for the signal in several critical bands. This argument is reviewed in some detail in Chapter 9. Assume that the probability of missing the signal in one critical band is q; then, since the signal in the other band has the same detectability, the probability of missing the signal in the other band is also q. If the two critical bands are independent, the probability of missing the signal in *both* bands is q^2; and hence the probability of *not* missing the signal in either band, that is, the probability of detecting the signal, is $1 - q^2$. With a single-component signal, the probability of detection is $1 - q$, and thus the increment in detectability caused by adding the second component to the signal is the difference between $1 - q$ and $1 - q^2$.

Schafer and Gales did not specifically study the question of the detectability of complex signals in which both components of the signal are within the critical band. The implication from the model of the critical band is that signal energy is the only determinant of detectability within the critical band. Thus, if two sinusoids fall within a single critical band, their detectability in noise would be the same as a single component whose energy is equal to the energy of the complex signal.

The next study was reported by Gassler (1954), who determined the detectability of a complex signal composed of many added sinusoids. He determined how the detectability of this complex signal varied with the number of sinusoidal components. An ordered series of signals was used. Each successive signal was generated by adding another sinusoidal component 20 cps higher than the last component in the sequence. For example, the first signal might be 1000 cps; the next signal, a complex signal generated by adding 1000 and 1020 cps; and the third signal, the combination of 1000, 1020, and 1040 cps. As more signals are added, the complex signal becomes more and more detectable and, in fact, up to a point, the increase in detectability supports the energy-summation hypothesis; that is, the complex signal seems to increase 3 db in detectability with each doubling of energy.

As this process continues, the complex signal extends over a wider and wider frequency range. Finally, the complex signal does not increase in detectability as additional components are added to the signal. Gassler's results suggest that the detectability of the complex is independent of the frequency range of the signal once this frequency limit is exceeded. Thus, according to Gassler, there is energy summation within a certain frequency region; outside this region the ear ignores energy. This region defines for Gassler the critical band. The results obviously suggest that the observer uses only one critical band even when the signal energy exists outside that critical bandwidth.

Marill (1956) made a direct experimental determination of this hypothesis. He used three complex signals, each composed of two frequencies. For the complex signals that were very close together in frequency (500 cps and 540 cps, or 1100 cps and 1060 cps) there was complete energy summation. However, the pair of signals separated by more than several critical bands (500 cps and 1100 cps) was no more detectable than the more detectable member of the pair.

Green (1958) investigated this same question, also with pairs of sinusoidal signals sampled from various points on the spectrum. He found that even signal pairs widely separated in frequency were more detectable than the more detectable member of the pair. Thus his results for signals widely separated in frequency are contrary to those obtained by Marill and Gassler. Green applied the multiple-band model to this result. According to this model, signal energy is the prime determinant of detectability within a critical band. If components fall into different critical bands, the detection process common to each band would occur, and the outputs of each critical band would be linearly combined. Thus, because of a kind of postdetection integration, some increase in the detectability of the signal would result. The crucial assumptions of the model are that the combination of the two filter outputs is linear and that an optimal weighting of the channels is used; that is, the channel with the more detectable signal is given more weight in the decision. These assumptions generate the following equation for the detectability of complex signals (Chapter 9 reviews the rationale and may be consulted for the derivation of this formula):

$$d_c' = (\sum d_i^2)^{1/2}$$

where d_c' is the detectability of the complex signal and d_i' is the detectability of the ith component of the complex signal. If two component signals are equally detectable, then $d_c' = \sqrt{2}\, d_i'$ and, since d' is roughly proportional to signal energy, the complex will be about 1.5 db more detectable than either component separately.

Finally, Green, McKey, and Licklider (1959) determined the detectability of a complex signal generated by adding the sixteen harmonics of a 250-cps sine wave, that is, 250, 500, 750, 1000, . . . , 3750, and 4000 cps. The components were adjusted so that each component had about the same detectability as every other in the noise. The detectability of the total complex was about 6 db better than any single component of the complex.

A twelve-component complex, generated by turning off every other component of the high-frequency part of the signal (so that the high-frequency part of the complex now consisted of 2000, 2500, 3000, 3500, and 4000 cps) was about 4.5 db more detectable than any single component in the complex. In this experiment independent phase control of each component was possible. The detectability of the complex signal was determined for a variety of phase patterns. There was no significant change in detectability for the various phase patterns explored. The result of the experimentation with the harmonic signals was compared with the summation (multiple-band) model suggested by Green; the average difference between predicted and obtained results was about one fourth of a decibel.

In summary, all studies agree that there is perfect power summation within the critical band. If all the components of a complex signal fall within a single critical band, then the detectability of that complex is equivalent to a single sinusoidal signal of the same total energy as the complex signal. Disagreement arises on the question of what happens when the energy of the complex sound is spread over more than one critical band, for example, when two equally detectable sinusoids fall in two different critical bands. Two of the studies, by Gassler and by Marill, suggest that the detectability of the complex is no better than the more detectable member of the pair. The other three studies suggest that, although the detectability of the complex is not the same as would result from complete power summation, the ear does not completely ignore the other components.

There is no certain explanation of the differences found between the studies. Gassler used a steady signal and had the subject adjust the signal level to obtain the just-detectable signal in the noise. Green and Marill, like Schafer and Gales, used a constant-stimulus method; in fact, Green and Marill, who disagree on results, used the same procedure, a two-alternative forced-choice test.

We might possibly criticize the results that showed summation with the 16-component signal, all harmonics of 250 cps, on the grounds that some of the higher components would have fallen within a single critical band. There is some disagreement over the exact size of the critical band (see Table 10-1), but the Frequenzegruppe, the larger critical band, suggests a 600 cps band at 3500 cps. Thus only three components could be within the critical band, and one would expect only 4.5 db summation. The net summation was, as we have said, about 6 db. Furthermore, when odd harmonics at the high frequencies were removed, the complex was 4.5 db rather than 3 db more detectable.

Gassler's results may depend heavily upon his technique, although there is no particular reason to believe so. One possibility is that he did not extend the frequency range of his complex far enough to notice the small statistical summation from several critical bands. According to the statistical model, the trading relation is 3 db for each double in the number of components within the critical band and only 1.5 db per double once the critical band is exceeded. If the energy of the signal were plotted as a function of frequency, both models would predict a break point at the same frequency. Gassler may not have extended the range far enough to note the smaller drop in signal level once the critical band is exceeded. There is, however, no evidence of any such improvement in detectability in a close inspection of the data published in his article.

10.6 SUMMARY OF FREQUENCY-ANALYSIS EXPERIMENTS

Psychoacoustic work on the problem of the frequency-analysis mechanism suggests the following picture. First, the ear may be likened to a narrow-band-pass filter followed by some sort of nonlinear process and an integrator. This general model will account for the detectability of a narrow-band signal in wide-band noise. The observer listens to only a narrow frequency range in order to maximize the signal-to-noise ratio in the listening band, and bases his decision only on the energy present in that band. On these general notions there is complete agreement.

Disagreement arises as to the details of the process. There is, as we reviewed briefly, some disagreement as to the exact width of the critical band. In general, it seems that techniques such as adjustment or tracking, as in the von Békésy audiometer, produce larger critical bands than the constant-stimulus methods, such as forced choice. The wider critical bands, however, do have the support of the data on loudness and of data on differences in quality of AM-FM modulation; and thus for many problems a wider critical band, the Frequenzegruppe of the Stuttgart group, is often used.

The other area of disagreement concerns how the ear operates when the signal does not occupy a narrow frequency region. Two separate approaches to this problem have been reviewed. One is the uncertainty technique, where the signal can occur at any one of a number of different frequencies. The other is the detectability of multiple-component signals in noise. Determination of how the ear operates in either of these situations is extremely critical if we are ever to make any practical use of the data on the widths of critical bands. Almost any question of interest eventually involves the question of how the ear treats signals distributed in various frequency regions. Unfortunately, in neither area can we give a completely certain answer. The most striking characteristic of the data in both areas is the way the results of one experiment will flatly contradict the results obtained from another experiment. Such contradictions lead us to suspect that some important, unknown variable is operating in these situations.

In the one-of-two-frequencies experiment, Shipley's response model generates two predictions, depending upon which of the two prior assumptions is made. Her first prediction is identical to the single-band model; the second prediction is very close to the prediction of the multiple-band model. In the stimulus models, we can maintain that the observer on some occasions listens with only one critical band, and that on other occasions he can try to combine the outputs of several critical bands if the conditions of the experiment warrant it. He may, therefore, be operating at a given time in one of two possible modes. But what variables are important in determining which mode is used? There also appear to be strong individual differences which are consistent over different experiments (Swets, 1963a). Whether these differences are sensory in nature or reflect different decision strategies is not clear. These remain questions that we cannot answer at all fully at this time.

Perhaps the present ambiguity rests upon a failure to understand in detail the exact mechanism of the critical band. For example, up to this point our summary of the critical-band concept has been a first-stage filter followed by some sort of detection process and then an integrator. One possibility is that, by clarifying the exact details of the detection mechanism, the questions of the combination of several bands and the possibilities for such combinations will explain some of the apparent contradictions. One such clarification has been carried out in Chapter 8, where the energy detector was explored in some detail. Using this model, the estimate of the critical band at 1000 cps was 500 cps, almost 3 times larger than the large estimate of the Stuttgart group.

Many of the experiments designed to test questions about the mechanism of frequency analysis were executed with the implicit assumption that the critical band is no bigger than the Frequenzegruppe, which is roughly three times the size of Fletcher's critical bandwidth. For example, one typically assumed that the critical bandwidth is no wider than about 180 cps at 1000 cps. Thus, in the study by Green, McKey, and Licklider (1959), a multicomponent signal with all 16 harmonics of 250 cps was used to determine the detectability of a signal whose energy was supposed to fall in different critical bands. The amplitude of each component was adjusted to produce roughly the same detectability for any single signal. The results indicated that the complex signal was about 6 db easier to detect than any single component of the compound. Given the implicit assumption about the size of the critical band, these results are extremely damaging to the single-band scanning model. However, if the critical band is 500 cps at 1000 cps, it is probably large enough at 4000 cps so that four components could fall within the same critical band. Thus we might expect the detectability to increase about 6 db, as it did.*

In the uncertain-frequency study, in which the pulsed signal might occur anywhere between 500 cps and 4000 cps, detectability was decreased by only about 3 db. This result is impossible if 20 or 30 critical bands must be combined, as in the multiple-band model. With the very wide critical band estimated on the basis of the energy-detection model, we can make a very plausible case that between four and six critical bands can be arranged to cover the frequency region from 500 cps to 4000 cps. Such an arrangement would lead us to expect a decrement of from 3 db to 5 db because of frequency uncertainty, and this prediction is consistent with the data.

Unfortunately, the assumption of a much wider critical band does not clarify the exact nature of the frequency-analysis mechanism. If anything, it produces somewhat the opposite result, since it reprieves two models that had been somewhat damaged by experimental evidence. The salutory influence of this model is that it indicates a connection between several previously diverse areas of auditory psychophysics and demonstrates how assumptions about the details of the detection mechanism heavily influence the estimates of parameter values. These diverse estimates of the parameter values, in turn, imply vastly different models of the auditory system.

As more experimental data become available we should be able to obtain more precise estimates of the parameter values. What is equally clear is the need for more theoretical work to help us understand the implication of slightly different assumptions about the form or detail of the detection system. As such models develop, the experimenter will be given models that generate quite different predictions over wide ranges of the physical stimulus. Up to this point most of the models of the detection process were remarkably vague about the physical stimulus. Detailed analysis of a variety of detection systems will rectify this deficit, and should therefore promote more incisive experimentation.

---

* In another condition of the experiment the components 2250, 2750, 3250, and 3750 cps were removed because at the highest frequencies it was possible that more than one component was falling in the same band. The increment was 4.5 db, which is also consistent with the hypothesis that three components are within one critical band.

11

Speech Communication

11.1 INTRODUCTION

Our discussion of speech communication in this chapter is parallel to the treatment of simpler signals in the foregoing chapters. Recent studies of the recognition of spoken messages have employed the yes-no, rating, and second-choice procedures and the ROC analysis, which are the concern of the chapters in Part I. Although, in general, the speech signal cannot be specified precisely enough to allow calculation of the performance of an ideal observer, one of the ideal detection models discussed in Part II—namely, the model for "one-of-M-orthogonal signals"—has proved useful in analyzing a general result of experiments on speech recognition. Studies of speech have also used the procedures and models of multiple observations and deferred decision that were introduced in Chapter 9. The theory of multivariate statistical analysis, which extends decision theory from two to several stimulus alternatives, is currently being applied to automatic speech recognition.

Before considering these procedures and models in any detail, let us discuss the topic in more general terms, in order to determine how the new procedures are related to the standard procedure for studying speech recognition, and to consider their relation to realistic communication situations. This discussion will serve to lead into the more detailed analyses suggested by the various models.

In the standard procedure for studying speech recognition, a speaker reads a list of carefully chosen words to a listener who records what he hears. The speech signals are intercepted by the experimenter and modified in various ways, or they are presented in a background of noise. In any event, identification of the spoken word is relatively difficult, and the usual dependent variable of the procedure is the percentage of words on the speaker's list that appear in the appropriate place on the listener's list. This procedure is often called an "articulation test," a term which reflects the origin of the procedure in the engineering concern for testing telephonic communication systems (Fletcher, 1953). Another term commonly used is "speech-intelligibility test." These terms are sometimes more apt than the listener-oriented designations—"speech-recognition test" or "speech-perception test"—because they are suggestive of practical communication settings, and they serve as a reminder that the test score applies not only to the listener, but also to the speaker and to the electrical apparatus that intervenes between speaker and listener.

The articulation test is not a completely faithful representation of the realistic communication situation, since usually the receiver of a communication can decide whether or not he has correctly identified a given item and, ordinarily, he can take an action based on the decision. One action the receiver can take, for example, is to ask the source of the communication to repeat the item to him so that he may confirm his identification. Alternatively, the receiver may repeat to the source what he believes he heard, and ask for the source's confirmation. In the latter event, the source must also make a yes-no decision about the correctness of the reception. Thus, at least in many realistic settings, both participants in the communication process face the problem of setting a decision criterion. The detection-theory procedures for control and analysis of the decision criterion make it possible to extend the standard articulation test to include this variable (Egan, Clarke, and Carterette, 1956; Egan and Clarke, 1956). It must be noted that application of detection theory to the kind of decision criterion under discussion depends upon the identification of correct and incorrect confirmations with hits and false alarms, respectively. As we shall see, the analogy is appropriate for the source, but it is not exact for the receiver of a communication, and the analogy must be approached with some caution.

The analysis of the confirmation criterion in speech recognition is carried out by means of the operating characteristic. Most of the operating-characteristic curves that have been obtained experimentally have been obtained with the rating procedure (Pollack and Decker, 1958; Clarke, 1960; Carterette and Cole, 1962). Ratings are used in preference to yes-no decisions because of the economy they afford. If the listener in an articulation test is required to give a confidence rating for each identification response, additional information is gained at little cost.

When the receiver's first response—his identification response—is in error, this identification response may itself contain some residual information. Speech signals are obviously not completely orthogonal and, indeed, distinct clusters of errors are often apparent in the stimulus-response matrices obtained by experiment. In a vocabulary composed of digits, for example, "five" and "nine" are confused more often with each other than with the other digits. If the test vocabulary is known to the receiver, as it usually is, then the articulation test has the structure of a forced-choice task, and the receiver can reasonably be asked to give a second-choice as well as a first-choice identification response. Since the receiver has some knowledge of which items tend to be confused with each other, his second choice may be determined entirely by his first choice. On the other hand, the receiver may have some information about the signal that is not contained in his first choice, and may convey this information in a second choice. The second-choice identification response has been studied as an alternative to a second response in the form of a confidence rating (Clarke, 1960).

It is well known that the intelligibility score is dependent upon the size of the test vocabulary; the proportion of correct identifications decreases quite sharply as the number of possible items increases (Miller, Heise, and Lichten, 1951). This is the basis for an analysis of results in terms of the detection model for "one-of-M-orthogonal signals." Although the assumption of orthogonality is known to be too strong, it provides a reasonable starting point. Here the issue is whether or not there exists a single detectability parameter, such as d', that will remain invariant over vocabulary size (Tanner, unpublished note, 1954; Green and Birdsall, 1958). A related question concerns the familiar finding that high-probability items yield higher intelligibility scores than low-probability items. Are high-probability items more readily perceived, in fact, or have they only been made to appear so because of a response bias that is inherent in conventional intelligibility measures (Pollack, 1964)? Another related question is whether the number of possible stimuli or the number of responses available to the receiver is the critical determinant of message reception (Pollack, 1959a).

In the laboratory and in practical communication problems, the gain in recognition probability that results from repeated presentations is of interest. The early telephone studies showed that the number of repetitions required to reach a given level of correctness is a good measure of communications performance (Martin, 1931; McKnown and Emling, 1933). More recently, repetition has been investigated as one possible procedure for overcoming unfavorable conditions of communication (Pollack, 1958). Of relevance to our present purposes is a study which determined the rate of improvement over a number of repetitions that was fixed by the experimenter, and compared the results to the predictions of detection theory (Pollack, 1959b). Other relevant studies have examined the results of repetitions made at the discretion of the source—if he does not confirm the receiver's identification (Egan, Clarke, and Carterette, 1956)—and the results of repetitions made at the discretion of the receiver—if he lacks confidence in his identification (Carterette, 1958; Pollack, 1959b). The latter studies show that the rate of improvement with repetition can be either large or small and that there may even be a decrement with repetition, depending on the decision criterion that the receiver adopts for terminating a trial.

The detection model for "one-of-M-orthogonal signals" gives one means of analyzing the problem of identifying one of many stimuli. Another model with attractive possibilities as a general model for perception is provided by the theory of multivariate statistical analysis (Anderson, 1958; Marill and Green, 1960; Rodwan and Hake, 1964). We shall discuss briefly the applications of this model to date in studies of speech recognition (Smith, 1962; Smith and Klem, 1961).

11.2   YES-NO, RATING, AND SECOND-CHOICE PROCEDURES

11.2.1   Yes-no decisions and ROC analysis

Consider an expanded articulation test, with both vocabulary size and speech-to-noise ratio fixed, in which (1) a source sends a message item to a receiver; (2) the receiver makes a forced choice from a known message set, and records the item he believes he heard, that is, his identification response; (3) the receiver records a yes-no decision about the correctness of his identification response; (4) the receiver repeats his identification response to the source; and (5) the source records a yes-no decision about the correctness of the receiver's identification response. Let us ignore the index of performance that can be obtained from the operation described in (2)—namely, the articulation score $P(C)$—and examine the indices of performance that can be obtained from the receiver's and source's yes-no decisions as described in (3) and (5).

In order to isolate the effects of the communicator's decision criteria, both communicators are asked to vary their criteria from one set of trials to another, and the results are analyzed by means of the operating characteristic. Figures 11-1a and 11-1b show the results of one such test. In the figure the proportions of correct confirmations ("hits") are plotted against the proportions of incorrect confirmations ("false alarms"). Figure 11-1a shows data from six receivers; the curve drawn through the data is labelled "ROC," where "R," as usual, denotes "receiver." Figure

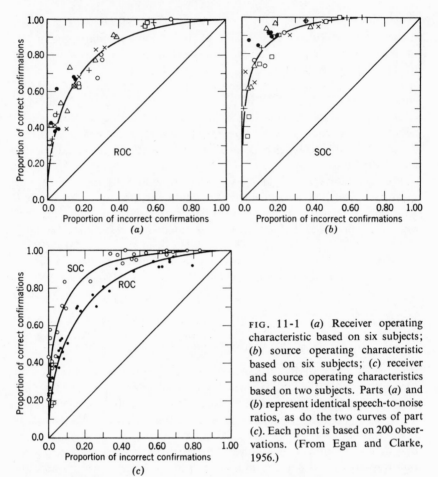

FIG. 11-1 (a) Receiver operating characteristic based on six subjects; (b) source operating characteristic based on six subjects; (c) receiver and source operating characteristics based on two subjects. Parts (a) and (b) represent identical speech-to-noise ratios, as do the two curves of part (c). Each point is based on 200 observations. (From Egan and Clarke, 1956.)

11-1b shows data from six sources; the curve is labelled "SOC," where "S" signifies "source." The two curves represent the same speech-to-noise ratio. Figure 11-1c shows ROC and SOC data obtained in another test from two highly-trained speakers and listeners; the data of the two are similar and are not distinguished in the figure. Again, the two curves are based on identical speech-to-noise ratios.

Two features of the data are readily apparent. First, the data are fitted to a first approximation by operating-characteristic curves based on normal distributions of equal variance. Second, the receivers perform less well than the sources. If we calculate values of d' in the usual manner, the value for the six receivers is 1.4, and the value for the six sources is 2.1. In Fig. 11-1c the receivers' d' is 1.3 and the sources' d' is 1.9. That the sources perform better than the receivers seems reasonable when it is recalled that the source has only to decide if the message he hears corresponds to the one he sent; the receiver must select one from several (in this case, 50) alternatives and then decide whether he has made a correct choice.

Of the several thoughts expressed in the preceding paragraph, only one does not require qualification, namely, the fact that the sources perform better than the receivers—in the sense that their data points lie farther away from the diagonal representing chance performance. The remarks about the shape of the distributions underlying the operating-characteristic curve, about the index d', and about the difference between the tasks of the source and receiver—all these require further discussion. We shall see that they are intimately related.

The first point to note is that a receiver's task is very different from that of a source, or from that of an observer in a typical yes-no detection problem (Clarke, Birdsall, and Tanner, 1959; Pollack, 1959c). A source, like an observer in a typical detection problem, attempts to discriminate between stimuli—whereas a receiver of the sort just described attempts to discriminate between his correct and incorrect responses. The operating characteristic for such a receiver is based upon response-response contingencies rather than upon the familiar stimulus-response contingencies. The difference, from the point of view of analysis, is greater than it seems at first glance and, indeed, was not at first apparent to workers in this field.

The receiver, as we have said, first selects the response most likely to be correct and then evaluates it with respect to all other possible responses. An exact mathematical analysis of this two-stage decision process is very difficult to present unless severe simplifying assumptions are made. One set of assumptions leads to probability density functions which are not normal and of equal variance, but exponential (Clarke, Birdsall, and Tanner, 1959). In this case, as discussed also in Chapter 3, the theoretical operating-characteristic curve is nearly linear on normal coordinates, with a slope that decreases systematically as the curve diverges farther from the chance diagonal. If the specified relationship between slope and distance from diagonal holds in practice, then the empirical curve can be described by a single parameter k. If the relationship observed is not the one specified in the exponential model, then a two-parameter index can be used. In any event, it is clear that the measure d', which has a distinct meaning when derived from stimulus-response contingencies, should not be applied to operating-characteristic data based on response-response contingencies. As indicated, this fact was not appreciated at first, and the reader should bear that in mind when examining the primary literature.*

The problems associated with distinguishing different types of operating characteristics and indices of performance, while knotty, by no means preclude application of the detection-theory analysis in studies of speech. Before proceeding to other examples, we mention another common speech task which requires yes-no decisions. This is the so-called monitoring task, in which the observer must receive and identify messages in a given set while ignoring all other, irrelevant messages. Varying the decision criterion for acceptance of a word as a member of the set to be monitored results in data that are fitted very closely by normal operating-characteristic curves (Egan, 1957).

11.2.2   Ratings and ROC analysis

The addition of ratings of response correctness to an articulation test, like the addition of yes-no decisions about response correctness, does not appear to depress the articulation score (Egan and Clarke, 1956; Pollack

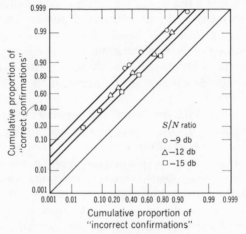

FIG. 11-2   ROC results, for one observer, of a rating scale applied to speech recognition. The parameter is speech-to-noise ratio. Each curve is based on 1350 observations. (From Pollack and Decker, 1958.)

---

* The literature contains several suggestions for notation related to this issue. Clarke, Birdsall, and Tanner (1959) have called the ROC curve based on response-response contingencies a "Type II ROC curve." The index taken from the intersection of this kind of curve with the negative diagonal has been called d_r (Pollack, 1959c) and $(d_e)^{1/2}$ or d_e' (Clarke et al., 1959).

and Decker, 1958). The ROC curves obtained with confidence ratings are very similar to those obtained from binary decisions, as illustrated in Fig. 11-2. The results shown are from one observer; two other observers in the experiment yielded very similar results. The curves fitted to the data have a slope of one; at the lowest and highest speech-to-noise ratios, better fits would be obtained with curves of slope less than one. In another experiment, as shown in Fig. 11-3, five observers yielded ROC curves with slopes less than one. A similar result is obtained from words presented in brief visual exposures, as shown in Fig. 11-4.

Figure 11-5 shows, for three observers and three speech-to-noise ratios, the proportion of correct responses in each rating category. It can be seen that the confidence rating is directly related to recognition accuracy, and practically independent of speech-to-noise ratio. A similar result was obtained in the study of visual word recognition, as shown in Fig. 11-6.

In concluding the discussion of rating scales applied to speech recognition, we should mention that similar results are obtained when speech is degraded by filtering instead of by background noise (Decker and Pollack, 1958), and that confidence ratings can be used to improve substantially the probability of correct message reception in the absence of agreement among multiple observers (Decker and Pollack, 1959).

11.2.3 Second choice in intelligibility tests

Data presented in Chapter 4 on the detection of simple signals showed that when the first choice in a four-alternative forced-choice test is incorrect, the second choice is correct with greater than chance probability. Another study mentioned in Chapter 4 showed that when the observer tried to be wrong, that is, when he made only a fourth choice, he was wrong more often than he could have been if he were limited by a "high" threshold. These studies indicate that the observer can rank sensory events below a high threshold and that he can discriminate among sensory events likely to result from noise alone. As Clarke (1960) has pointed out, this interpretation depends on the assumption that the first and second choices are independent. Stated otherwise, the assumption made is that when the second choice is correct with greater than chance probability, it contains information that is independent of the information contained in the first choice.

The assumption of independence of choices seems reasonable enough in the context of temporal-alternative forced-choice detection of simple signals; it is consistent with the assumption that the sensory events arising from different temporal alternatives are independent, an assumption that is basic to the standard analysis of forced choices. However, as Clarke

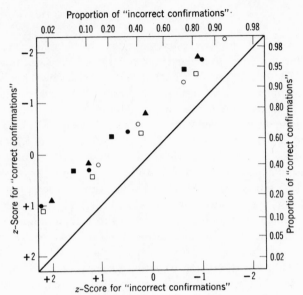

FIG. 11-3 ROC results, from 5 observers and 1650 observations, of a rating scale applied to word recognition. (From Clarke, 1960.)

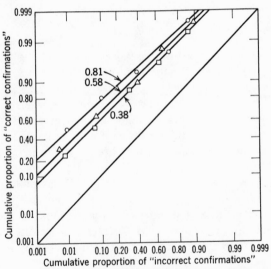

FIG. 11-4 ROC results, the average of three observers, of a rating scale applied to visual word recognition. The parameter is $P(C)$, the proportion of correct identification responses. Each curve is based on 1440 observations. (From Carterette and Cole, 1962.)

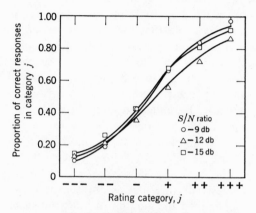

FIG. 11-5 Proportion of correct responses in each rating category. The figure shows the average of three observers at each of three speech-to-noise ratios. (From Pollack and Decker, 1958.)

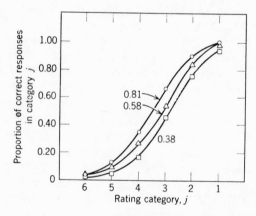

FIG. 11-6 Proportion of correct responses in each rating category—visual word recognition. The figure shows the average of three observers at each of three durations of exposure. The labels on the curves are $P(C)$, the proportions of correct identification responses. (From Carterette and Cole, 1962.)

noticed, it is unlikely that the assumption holds in word-recognition tests. Given different patterns of word confusability, and the observer's knowledge of these, it is quite possible that most of his second choices are ·determined, not by the stimulation, but rather by his first-choice response. If, in identifying spoken digits, the observer gives a second choice of "nine" after a first choice of "five," then his second choice will likely be correct with greater than chance probability while conveying very little, if any, information not already contained in the first choice. Indeed, a second observer who hears the first observer's first choice, but not the stimulus, will make the second choice correctly more often than chance would have it—and, clearly, would add nothing at all to the information in the first choice.

Clarke used the analysis of information transmission presented by Shannon (1948). He determined the amount of independent information (in terms of bits per item) in the second choice by subtracting the information in the first choice from the information in the first and second responses considered jointly. A speech-to-noise ratio was chosen to maximize the independent information in the second choice. When the first choice was incorrect, the second was correct with probability 0.39, where 0.25 represents chance performance. It was found that the second choice conveyed, on the average, 0.025 bit of independent information. This amount of information is highly significant statistically, but it is very small. Further analysis showed that only about 7% of the information in a second choice was independent of the first-choice information, and that, of the information carried jointly by the first and second choices, over 97% was carried by the first choice alone. This result may be compared with the result of rating responses, in another part of the same experiment, which carried, on the average, 0.127 bit of information beyond that contained in the first choice. Thus a second response in the form of a rating response carried six times as much independent information as a second identification response. Although the generality of the quantitative result is limited by the size of the message set and the speech-to-noise ratio that were used, it seems clear that little is to be gained by requiring a second identification response in an articulation test.

11.3   VOCABULARY SIZE AND UNCERTAINTY

11.3.1   One-of-M-orthogonal signals

The probability of correctly identifying an item in an intelligibility test depends not so much on what was presented as on what might have been presented (Miller, 1951). The intelligibility of a given item, with fixed signal and noise characteristics, depends critically upon the size of the vocabulary used in the test or, at another level of discourse, upon the observer's uncertainty. The magnitude of the effect is illustrated by the finding of Miller, Heise and Lichten (1951) that, in order to get 90% of monosyllabic words correct, the words in a set of 256 had to be approximately 20 db more intense than the words in a set of 4. Taking a cut in the other direction, at one speech-to-noise ratio, the set of 4 words gave a $P(C)$ of approximately 0.75 and the set of 256 words gave a $P(C)$ of approximately 0.15.

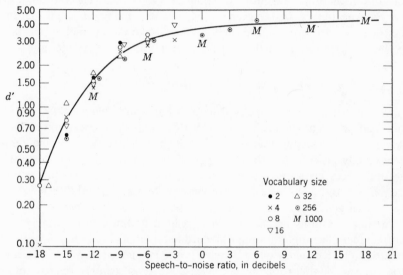

FIG. 11-7 d' versus speech-to-noise ratio for various vocabulary sizes. (Data from Miller, Heise, and Lichten, 1951; analysis from Green and Birdsall, 1958.)

The detection model for "one-of-M-orthogonal signals" provides one possible way to analyze the effects of this uncertainty. We know that the assumption of orthogonality is not met here, but the interrelations of alternative words are so complex that it seems judicious to test the simple model before trying to cope with the complexities—the assumption might not be critical in this instance. To test the model, we can take the values of $P(C)$, for each of several vocabulary sizes and speech-to-noise ratios, that were obtained by Miller, Heise, and Lichten, and use them as entries in the tables showing $P(C)$ versus d' for different numbers of orthogonal alternatives (Swets, 1964). The question is whether or not a given speech-to-noise ratio produces essentially the same d' for a wide range of vocabulary sizes.

The values of d' obtained in this way are plotted against speech-to-noise ratio in Fig. 11-7. The line drawn through the data points fits them reasonably well. The departure of the points denoted M is attributable to the fact that the 1000-word message set was not defined for the observer; that is, the observer was not given a list of these words in advance. These points would lie close to the curve if the effective vocabulary size in this condition were assumed to be between 2000 and 4000 words. (Some data points at a vocabulary of size 2 are not shown in Fig. 11-7 because the values of d' were too small to appear on the plot.)

The index d' is not alone in transforming the articulation scores from different vocabulary sizes to a single function. For example, the number of bits of information transmitted (Shannon, 1948) is relatively constant over varying vocabulary size (Garner, 1962). However, the point here is that the detection model does achieve such an invariance; its range of application is thereby extended to include a general result in speech recognition.

11.3.2   The effect of a priori probability

Why is a given item, under fixed acoustic conditions, recognized correctly much more often when it is a member of a small set of possibilities than when it is embedded in a larger set? It may be the case that expected items are actually easier to hear than unexpected items, that is, that the observer's set influences his sensory apparatus. On the other hand, it may simply be that when the observer does not hear an item at all, and thus is forced to make a guess, the odds of guessing correctly favor the smaller set.

Similar questions pertain to other, related findings. For example, the correct identification of an English word in an intelligibility test is strongly related to its frequency of occurrence in the language (Howes, 1957), and the correct identification of a nonsense word is strongly related to its familiarity as influenced by pretraining (Solomon and Postman, 1952). In neither case is it clear that a sensory rather than a response process is affected, since a word's frequency in the language is strongly related to the frequency with which it appears as an incorrect response in an intelligibility test (Pollack, Rubenstein, and Decker, 1960), and the results of the nonsense-word experiment can be duplicated without presenting any differential stimuli (Goldiamond and Hawkins, 1958).

In short, the standard intelligibility measure $P(C)$ is subject to the bias of differential response probability. Will high-probability items yield higher intelligibility scores than low-probability items when measures are used that are relatively free of response bias? Pollack (1964) has shown that they will. He applied four different measures—including d' as determined from ROC curves, and the uncertainty measure derived from information theory (Shannon, 1948)—to tests in which words occurred with different frequencies. All four measures showed intelligibility to be positively related to word probability. This result supports the initial interpretation according to which the a priori probability of a stimulus, in word-recognition tests, genuinely modifies the sensory discriminability of the stimulus.

11.3.3 Stimulus versus response uncertainty

When defined vocabularies are tested under fixed acoustic conditions, it has often been assumed that the number of different stimuli determines the probability of recognition. A logical alternative is that the number of different responses available to the observer is the principal factor. Pollack (1959a) has recently produced evidence that the number of available responses is largely responsible for the recognition score, and that the number of stimuli is not critical.

In an experiment which used a relatively large set of stimulus words known to the observer, he was informed after an item was received that the correct response was to be selected from a smaller set of response words. The observed $P(C)$ was nearly independent of the size of the stimulus ensemble (up to 64 words) when the number of possible responses was fixed. Transformation of $P(C)$ into d' according to the model for "one-of-M-orthogonal signals" yielded a nearly constant d' for all the response sets examined (2–64 words). A later study showed that the selection of words from a limited and defined set was not essential to the result—the same result was obtained when the words were selected at random from the entire language (Pollack, 1960).

11.4 MULTIPLE OBSERVATIONS

Another study made by Pollack (1959b) provides a wealth of information about multiple observations of speech signals. He examined successive presentations of a given message in independent and in repeated ("constant") samples of noise, the effects of multiple presentations on recognition probability and on the observer's ability to discriminate among his correct and incorrect responses, and the differential effects of fixed and observer-determined numbers of observations.

Figure 11-8 shows how d', as determined from $P(C)$ according to the model for "one-of-M-orthogonal signals," increases with successive presentations when the number of presentations is fixed (at 6). Three conditions represented in the figure are constant (i.e., taped) signal and independent noise (S, n), independent signal and independent noise (s, n), and constant signal and constant noise (S, N). The dotted line, labelled "Theory," represents improvement proportional to the square root of the number of presentations—the rate of improvement predicted from statistical theory for independent samples of noise. As with sinusoidal signals (Chapter 9), the rate of improvement is less under constant than under independent noise. Unlike sinusoidal signals, speech signals fail to show the full square-root improvement. The recognition of speech

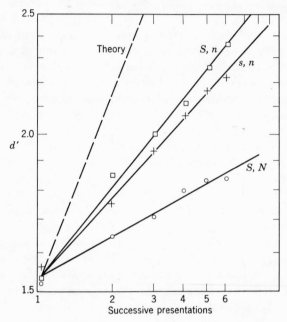

FIG. 11-8 d' on successive presentations for various conditions of constant and independent signal and noise (see text). (From Pollack, 1959b.)

signals, also, does not improve as rapidly as predicted under the decision-threshold model (see Chapter 9). The predicted gain under the decision-threshold model, in this instance (with an ensemble of 32 words), is nearly the same as that predicted by the statistical (square-root) model.

The observers in this experiment gave confidence ratings on the correctness of their identification responses. Operating characteristics constructed from the ratings show that response discriminability increased regularly with successive presentations under independent noise, but did not increase under constant noise. Again, the observers used the ratings in a consistent manner: the average intelligibility of the messages assigned a given rating was practically invariant over the six successive presentations, and over the three conditions of constant and independent signal and noise.

The device of requiring confidence ratings in addition to the identification response permits us to treat the results of a test with a fixed number of repetitions as a test in which the observer determines the number of repetitions on each trial. In studying sequential observation, or deferred decision, the six rating categories that were used are viewed as giving terminations of a trial according to each of five criteria. It is assumed that the observer would have terminated a trial if he assigned a given rating, or a higher rating, during the trial. The results are that $P(C)$ increased substantially with additional presentations, more so under independent than under constant noise, when a strict criterion of response acceptance was employed. Less and less gain is evidenced with successively more lenient criteria, and no gain resulted from the most lenient criteria. Indeed, under constant noise, $P(C)$ *decreased* over successive presentations for moderate and lenient criteria.

11.5   MULTIVARIATE ANALYSIS

Detection theory can be extended from detection, or from two-alternative recognition, to perception, or the identification of one of many alternatives, by generalizing statistical decision theory from two hypotheses to several. This generalization has been achieved with contributions from several persons; Anderson (1958) has provided a very lucid summary.

In multivariate analysis, each observation consists of a vector of numbers. These numbers might represent measurements of various aspects of the stimulus. The elements of the observation vector determine a point in a space which has as many dimensions as the vector. Critical regions in this observation space are defined in terms of likelihood ratio, and are determined by the a priori probabilities of the alternative hypotheses and the values and costs of the decision outcomes.

To date, the application of multivariate analysis to speech identification has been confined to automatic identification. The literature includes reports by Sebestyen (1962), Welch and Wimpress (1961), and Pruzansky and Mathews (1964). We briefly discuss here two applications: to the identification of vowel sounds (Smith and Klem, 1961) and to the identification of speakers (Smith, 1962). In both cases the outputs of 35 band-pass filters were used to estimate a multivariate distribution function—for each vowel sound, in the one case, and for each speaker, in the other. After an initial sequence of utterances is analyzed to estimate the proper statistical parameters and, hence, the proper critical regions, a new sample of speech is presented. The likelihood that the new sample arose from each of the previously identified alternatives is computed, and a decision is made according to some pre-established rule.

In the study of vowel-sound identification, the decision rule was simply to choose the alternative that yielded the largest likelihood. The system was tested with 10 vowels produced by 21 speakers, both male and female. The performance of the system was evaluated under two different assumptions. The first was that the multivariate distributions can be approximated by multivariate normal distributions, with different parameters for each hypothesis. It can be shown that in this case the decision rests upon, at most, a quadratic function of the filter outputs, that is, upon a quadratic discriminant function. The second assumption was that the distributions under all hypotheses have the *same* variance-covariance matrices. That is, the pattern of correlations among the measures is *independent* of the hypothesis. In this case it can be shown that a linear discriminant function is sufficient. Analysis by means of the linear discriminant function, with a pooled estimate of the variance-covariance matrix, yielded 87% correct responses. Application of the quadratic discriminant function, with individual estimates of the variance-covariance matrices for each vowel, yielded 94% correct responses.

These levels of performance, and also the kinds of confusions, are similar to those of systems that do not make use of decision theory. This result can be seen in the work of Forgie and Forgie (1959), in which exactly the same utterances were used. Typically, however, the development of automatic speech recognizers has depended upon the abstraction from speech spectra of distinctive features, or information-bearing elements, by expert phoneticians, and upon the ability to devise measures of speech spectra that are sensitive to these features. A possible advantage of the approach through decision theory is that it does not require such human analysis and invention; the abstraction of significant features and the design of measures are accomplished by the application of statistical procedures.

In the study of speaker identification, the likelihoods of the various alternatives were not only compared with each other, but with the likelihood that the sample arose from *none* of the previously identified alternatives. Values and costs were applied to decision outcomes, and a maximum-expected-value decision was made. The operator of the system confirmed or corrected each decision and thereby supplied new data which were combined with data received earlier. In this way the performance of the system could be continually improved.

The leads given by studies like these for the design of studies and models for human speech perception have not yet been pursued. Although this pursuit is not a simple matter, we should be able to expect some progress in the not-too-distant future.

11.6 SUMMARY

Several of the procedures developed to study the detection of simple signals have been applied to the recognition of speech, including yes-no decisions, ratings, second choices, multiple observations, and deferred decisions. Analytical techniques developed in the context of decision theory and applied to speech include the operating characteristic and models for the effects of uncertainty, for improvement with repeated observations, and for multivariate problems.

Yes-no decisions are made by the receiver of a communication when he must take one or another action based on his degree of confidence in the correctness of his identification response. Similarly, when the receiver sends back his identification to the source, the source may be required to confirm or reject it. The analogy between correct confirmations and hits, and between incorrect confirmations and false alarms, has led to analyses in terms of the operating characteristic. Although the analogy is not exact in the case of the receiver, based as it is on a discrimination between responses rather than between stimuli, the operating-characteristic analysis serves its major purpose.

In most experiments the operating characteristics have been obtained from rating responses. The empirical curves are approximately linear on a double-probability graph, with slopes usually less than unity. This is the case for words presented visually as well as for spoken words. In both modalities the confidence rating is directly related to the accuracy of identification, independent of the signal-to-noise ratio.

Adding the requirement of a rating response to the standard articulation test appears not to depress identification performance, and produces a substantial amount of additional information. A second choice, or second identification response, on the other hand, has been found to carry very little information independent of that carried by the first identification response. Apparently, the patterning among confusions of speech alternatives is strong enough for the second response to be determined largely by the first response.

Despite the fact that the assumption of orthogonal signal alternatives is not met in speech identification, the detection model for "one-of-M-orthogonal signals" has been applied successfully. The index d', as calculated under the model, transforms to a single function the widely varying articulation scores that are obtained from vocabularies of different sizes. It has been found that the articulation score depends on the number of responses available to the observer rather than on the number of possible stimuli; the model for "one-of-M-orthogonal signals" yields a practically constant value of d' for response sets of different sizes. The measure d', along with some other measures relatively free of response bias, has been employed to buttress the hypothesis that high-probability words are more intelligible than low-probability words.

Speech signals repeated a fixed number of times in independent samples of noise show more improvement than those repeated in the same sample of noise, a result consistent with studies of sinusoidal signals. The rate of improvement, however, is less than that predicted under the models discussed in Chapter 9. When the observer determines the number of repetitions, the rate of improvement depends on his decision criteria for termination of the sequence: less gain is shown with more lenient criteria, and a decrement results from the most lenient criteria.

To date, multivariate statistical analysis and discriminant-function analysis have been applied to automatic speech recognition but not to human speech recognition. We look forward to the development of a multivariate statistical theory for human speech perception.

12

Further Applications

12.1 INTRODUCTION

We consider in this concluding chapter the application of detection theory to animal psychophysics, sensory physiology, reaction time, time discrimination, vigilance, attention, subliminal perception, and recognition memory. The thread relating these diverse topics is the need in each to separate discriminal processes from motivational, judgmental, or response processes. Three of them—sensory physiology, reaction time, and time discrimination—are also linked in suggesting another specific model for an ideal observer, a model based on the theory of counting mechanisms. This suggestion, discussed only briefly here, is pursued further by Creelman (1962) and, in considerable detail, by McGill (1966).

These topics are somewhat peripheral to the main stream of detection-theory applications, and for most of them only fragmentary data are now available. Indeed, it must be understood that there is no intention, on the part of either the original investigators or the present authors, of representing these data as strong evidence for the applicability of the concepts of detection theory. The point of the discussion is rather that the theory appears to have some potential value for the problem areas mentioned, and that attempts are being made to assess this potential. The results of the preliminary attempts are, at least, encouraging.

12.2 ANIMAL PSYCHOPHYSICS

Behavioral studies of the sensitivity of animals necessarily involve both probabilistic signal presentation and payoffs. They can, therefore, be

315

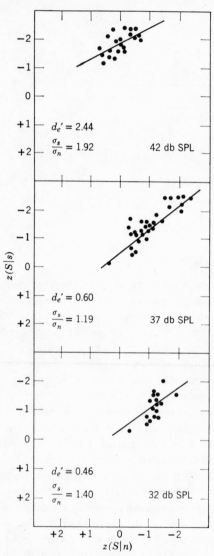

FIG. 12-1 ROC curves for Rat 1 at three signal intensities. The signal intensities are expressed in terms of the sound pressure level: in decibels re 0.0002 dyne/cm². (After Hack, 1963.)

interpreted as presenting the subject with a decision problem. The animal can respond as if to a signal when no signal is present, and receive nothing in return for its effort. If the animal responds to the presence of a signal, it must be, at least intermittently, rewarded. Detection theory suggests a way of determining sensitivity that is independent of the pattern of reinforcement and independent of changes in behavior (for example, in studies of the effects of drugs) that might properly be attributed to changes in the animal's criterion for making a response.

The two relevant animal studies reported to date examined the discrimination behavior of rats in Skinner boxes. In one, the signal-presentation probability was varied while the probability of reinforcement was held

TABLE 12-1. VALUES OF d_e' AND σ_s/σ_n AS A FUNCTION OF SOUND PRESSURE LEVEL (IN DECIBELS RE 0.0002 DYNE PER CM^2) FOR THREE RATS. (FROM HACK, 1963.)

	Subject		
SPL	1	2	3
42	2.44, 1.92	2.50, 3.23	1.96, 1.75
37	0.60, 1.19		
32	0.46, 1.40	1.50, 2.22	0.95, 1.72
27		0.46, 0.96	0.73, 1.69

constant (Hack, 1963). In the other, the probability of reinforcement was varied, with the signal-presentation probability fixed (Nevin, 1964).

In Hack's experiment the first press of the right-hand lever after a seven-second interval turned on a small lamp for one second. After the lamp went off, the signal—a two-second tone of 2000 cps—appeared or did not appear according to an a priori probability established by the experimenter. This a priori probability was varied from session to session over a range of 0.14 to 0.75. If the signal was presented, and if the rat then pressed the left lever, its thirst was reduced by one drop of water. Pressing the left lever in the absence of a signal went unrewarded.

The ROC curves obtained from one of the four subjects in the experiment, at each of three signal intensities, are shown on probability scales in Fig. 12-1. The figure indicates a tendency for hits and false alarms to vary together. At each signal level, a straight line was fitted to the data points and used to determine the sensitivity index denoted d_e'. (Chapter 4, Section 4.2.5, gives the definition of d_e'.) It can be seen that d_e' decreases as the signal intensity decreases.

Table 12-1 shows d_e' and the reciprocal of the slope, $1/s$—interpreted as the ratio of the standard deviations of density functions for noise and signal—for three subjects. (The fourth subject responded 100% of the time at all a priori probabilities.) In addition to showing the covariation of d_e' and signal intensity for three subjects, the table shows the tendency usually observed in human subjects for d_e' (or Δm) and σ_s/σ_n to vary directly with one another.

In Nevin's experiment, in each 20-second interval, the rat's pressing one lever produced a signal—a fixed increment in the illumination of the box for two seconds—with probability 0.50. Presses of a second lever during the

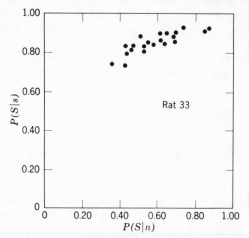

FIG. 12-2   ROC curve obtained from a rat by varying the reinforcement probability. (After Nevin, 1964.)

increased illumination were reinforced with probability 1.00 (11 sessions), 0.50 (11 sessions), or 0.20 (8 sessions). Figure 12-2 shows a graph of the hit and false-alarm probabilities for the single rat studied, for the last 7 sessions under each reinforcement schedule. Again there is a tendency for hits and false alarms to vary together. Nevin states that there was a positive correlation between each of these response proportions and the reinforcement probability.

The data of Figs. 12-1 and 12-2 illustrate our introductory remark that the evidence is more encouraging than conclusive. Further study is clearly indicated. Again, the basic need is to separate explicitly sensory processes from the processes influenced by reward, and detection theory provides one means of satisfying the need.*

* In another study, published since this writing, the ROC analysis was applied to the discrimination by pigeons of two fixed-ratio reinforcement schedules, with varying difference between the two ratios (Rilling and McDiarmid, 1965).

12.3   SENSORY PHYSIOLOGY

Several studies have shown the existence of maintained nervous activity in sense organs of vertebrates and invertebrates, apparently in the absence of any external stimulation. Much of the evidence is reviewed in Granit's (1955) book. A more recent study of note is that of Kuffler, FitzHugh, and Barlow (1957).

According to the physical-quantum theory proposed by Hecht, Shlaer, and Pirenne (1942; see Chapter 5), variability in the visual threshold is attributable to variation in the physical stimulus rather than to sources of variation within the organism. However, there is growing evidence that variation in the sensory nervous system is large enough to play a substantial part in limiting sensitivity—one line of evidence is the large variability observed in the maintained discharge from single ganglion cells in the cat's retina (Granit, 1947; Kuffler, 1952, 1953)—and later writings of Hecht and his associates (Hecht, 1945; Pirenne and Marriott, 1959) have considered this possibility.

Another implication of the relatively recent results from single-cell recording is that we can no longer look to physiology for collateral support of the threshold concept. It seems clear that sensory information is not conveyed merely by the all-or-none firing of an impulse in neurons limited by thresholds, but rather by a modulation of the maintained, or "spontaneous," rate of discharge. The distribution of the rates of firing in the absence of a signal overlaps the distributions observed in the presence of weak signals, and thus the problem for the "analyzer" is one of extracting signals from noise, that is, a problem of statistical decision.

We review here a study of nervous discharge undertaken in the context of detection theory by FitzHugh (1957). Impulses were recorded from single ganglion cells in the retinas of cats, both in the dark and in the presence of some background illumination. The data reproduced here were obtained from a cell in total darkness.

Light flashes of 5 milliseconds in duration were delivered repetitively at the rate of one per second for 10 successive flashes. Five different signal intensities were used: they were 1.74, 3.09, 5.50, and 8.51 times a base intensity, and the base intensity itself, which was taken as 1.00. The base intensity was the intensity at which the experimenter, and other observers, detected a response (in the form of a change in frequency or in the distribution of intervals between impulses) to roughly half of the flashes, upon watching them on an oscilloscope and simultaneously listening to them over a loudspeaker. The responses to these five signal intensities were compared to the responses at zero intensity.

The photograph in Fig. 12-3 illustrates the responses observed. Shown there are responses to five successive flashes at signal intensity 1.74. From records like these, the number of impulses occurring in each 10-millisecond period, from 100 milliseconds before the flash to 400 milliseconds after it,

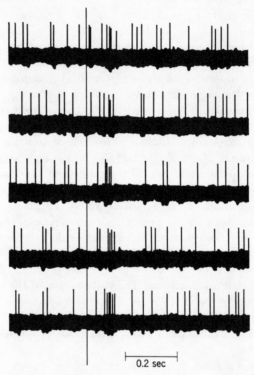

0.2 sec

FIG. 12-3 Photographs of the impulses recorded from an on-center ganglion cell in response to five successive flashes given at a rate of one per second. Flash duration 5 msec; flashes occur at long vertical line. Stimulus intensity 1.74 times base. The abscissa is time. Retouched photographs. (From FitzHugh, 1957.)

was determined The number of impulses occurring in each period, averaged over 10 successive flashes, is shown in Fig. 12-4. These data suggested defining an index of the response, x, as the number of impulses occurring in the period from 70 to 100 milliseconds after the beginning of the flash. This index, of course, does not reflect the detailed course of rise and fall of average frequency; it also neglects the latency of the burst and the length of the pause after the burst, both of which are correlated with

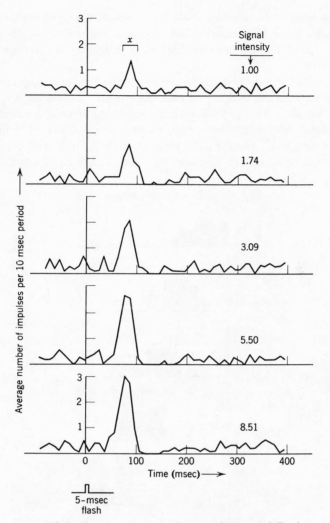

FIG. 12-4 Transient changes of average frequency following 5-msec flashes, plotted from data such as those of Fig. 12-3. On the vertical axis is plotted the mean number of impulses in each 10-msec period obtained by averaging over 10 successive flashes. The relative signal intensity for each curve is as shown, with base taken as 1.00. The number of impulses (x) occurring in each discharge during the critical period marked at the top of the figure was used as an index of the response. (After FitzHugh, 1957.)

signal intensity. Nonetheless, this index was shown to provide a satis-factory basis for data analysis. We may note that it is a possible physical interpretation of the decision axis in a detection theory for human observers.

Figure 12-5 shows the distributions of x in the form of histograms for ten successive flashes at each signal intensity. At zero intensity x was defined by ten 30-millisecond periods spaced one second apart in a record of the maintained discharge. This figure shows the possibility of defining an index similar to d', which FitzHugh called d, as the difference between the mean of a signal distribution and the mean of the noise distribution. It

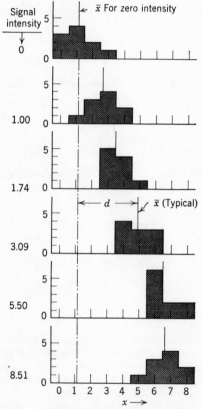

FIG. 12-5 Experimental dis-tributions of the index x (see Fig. 12-4), obtained from rec-ords like those of Fig. 12-3 for six signal intensities. (After FitzHugh, 1957.)

can be seen in the figure that d increases monotonically with intensity: the slope of the function relating d to intensity, on logarithmic scales, varies from 0.5 to 1.5 for four cells studied. The analysis in terms of d was found to be relatively insensitive to changes in the conditions which are taken as defining the index x.

FitzHugh analyzed his results in terms of the information measure presented by Shannon (1948). He found that the information transmission increased from 0 bits at zero intensity to the maximum of one bit at intensity 3.09. For intensity 1.00, the number of bits transmitted was determined as a function of the number of successive flash presentations; the number of bits increased regularly with additional presentations. Specifically, the information in one flash was approximately 0.4 bit, and the information in a block of six flashes was estimated to be about 0.95 bit, or near certainty.

This last result suggests that the information analysis based on x will provide the physiologist with a measure useful in experiments on neural recording. The informational analysis is at least as sensitive as the subjective method used by the experimenters, since they observed intensity 1.00 for five to ten flashes before deciding whether or not the neural response reached their criterion of acceptance.

In further work, FitzHugh (1958) has proposed a mathematical model of the central neural mechanism which must analyze sensory nerve messages of the kind just described. The model is an electrical filter which converts the time scale of the impulsive input into the running average frequency of the impulses, that is, into a single variable related to signal likelihood. This filter is assumed to be adjustable so that it is ideal for (or can be matched to) any expected signal. A different approach to the nerve-message analyzer has been taken by Creelman (1962) and McGill (1966), who define an ideal analyzer based on the theory of counting mechanisms. Creelman has applied this model in experiments on time discrimination, and McGill has applied it to a wide range of experimental results in physiology and sensory psychology.

FitzHugh, in developing his model, was principally concerned with the calculation of signal likelihoods. He treats three cases: detection of a signal of known intensity and time of occurrence, detection of the time of occurrence of a signal of known intensity, and estimation of the intensity of a signal occurring at a known time. He, and also Creelman, devotes little attention to the problem of determining a criterion for response; they both consider as possibilities the various definitions of the optimal (likelihood-ratio) criterion given in decision theory. McGill considers the pros and cons of some of the definitions of the optimal criterion that are given in decision theory, and also of a rather automatic mechanism for determination of the criterion that is derived from statistical learning theory. (See Chapter 5 for a partial discussion of the relationship of detection and learning models.) His study leads him to prefer the learning-model approach for those situations in which there are complete feedback, or knowledge of results, and fixed values associated with the decision outcomes. McGill's concern for the determination of the criterion is evidenced in his separation of a signal-acceptance criterion, which he views as a sensory mechanism, from a mechanism of response bias, and in his discussion relating the operation of the two mechanisms to the shape of the psychometric function.

The idea of a counting mechanism for signal detection grew, in part, out of studies of reaction time, a topic to which we now turn.

12.4   REACTION TIME

12.4.1   The criterion problem

In experiments on both simple and choice reaction time, the subject is typically instructed to avoid premature responses. In studies of choice reaction the subject is often further instructed to make no incorrect choices. It seems likely that variation in observed reaction times, within and between subjects, is due in part to variation in the criterion adopted by the subject for making a response. Mean reaction times could vary along with the criterion without producing a direct reflection of the different criteria in the data, that is, in the absence of any premature or incorrect responses. And it seems clear that the policy of ignoring premature or incorrect responses, or discarding data in which they are too frequent, will bias the results to an undetermined extent, to an extent which might vary from one experimental condition to another.

There is some reason to believe that differences in response criteria will not cause great differences in the summary statistics of reaction times. As in sensory studies, differences in criteria very probably do not influence to any substantial extent the interpretation of "main effects" that are large. Examples of large main effects come from studies in which the signal intensity is varied over a range of, for instance, 80 decibels, and in which the number of stimulus and response alternatives varies from one to many.

On the other hand, differences in response criteria might produce differences in reaction times that are considerable in an absolute sense and, almost surely, they produce differences that are significant relative to small, but nonetheless important, main effects. The familiar attempts to apportion parts of an observed reaction time to "sense time, nerve time, brain time, and muscle time" are examples of studies where the main effects are small.

Donders, who devised the choice reaction-time experiment, and later Wundt, attempted to delve into the "brain time" to measure such mental operations as attention, perception, association, and choice. The importance of "preparatory set" in experiments on reaction time—and the result that a "motor," as opposed to a "sensory," attitude leads to a decrease in reaction time and an increase in the number of premature responses—is quite a clear indication that a concern for the response criterion in reaction time is worth while.

Although detection theory suggests some ways of dealing with the response criterion in studies of reaction time, the implications for experimental method are not clear in detail. It may not be as easy, for example, to vary the proportion of premature reactions in a reaction-time experiment as it is to vary the proportion of false alarms in a fixed-interval detection experiment. Whether or not one could extract a useful measure of reaction time, one that is independent of the response criterion, from a curve analogous to an ROC curve is an open question. It does seem that the experimenter ought to control the criterion so that it is in a measurable range even if he does not attempt to vary it systematically. One way to do so, perhaps, is to give a monetary bonus which reflects both time and accuracy, and establishes the desired balance point with respect to the trading relationship between the two. Or the subject could be instructed to respond as quickly as is consistent with a given proportion (less than 1.0) of correct responses. An attempt of this sort was made in an experiment that is described in Section 12.4.5.

12.4.2 The sequential-decision model

According to the sequential-analysis or deferred-decision model (see Chapter 9), the length of the observation preceding a yes-no decision, as well as the error probabilities, is a function of the a priori probabilities of signal presentation, the cost of observing, the values of the various decision outcomes, and the strength of the signal. The application of this model to reaction time has been spelled out by Stone (1960). Stone also developed the application of the fixed-sample detection model for "one-of-M-orthogonal signals" (see Chapters 6 and 7) to reaction-time experiments with more than two choices, deriving the relation between decision time, error probabilities, and the number of alternatives. Other models of reaction time that emphasize the decision process have been presented by Christie and Luce (1956) and by Audley (1960). To date, few data have been collected specifically to test these decision models. The only experiment of which we are aware that was conducted in the context of the sequential-decision model is that of Fitts, Peterson, and Wolpe (1963). This experiment explored the relation between reaction time and the amount of redundancy in the sequence of stimuli; the results are in qualitative agreement with the sequential model.

12.4.3   The counting model for the mechanism of sequential decision in reaction time

McGill (1963, 1966) has added some restrictive assumptions to Stone's (1960) model, and principally a model of the neural mechanism for the decision process in reaction time. This is the neural "counter" to which we referred earlier in the discussion of sensory physiology.

McGill conceives of two counters which accumulate impulse counts over time: one registers only noise, the other registers signal plus noise. The detection of a signal is based on the observation of a systematic divergence of the two readings. It is assumed that a decision to respond is made when the difference reaches an arbitrary criterion, the criterion being determined by instructions and rewards.

This model is in agreement with several results of reaction-time experiments. It says that weak stimuli yield larger reaction times, because the counter readings diverge, and reach the criterion, less rapidly. It predicts the comparatively large variability of reaction times to weak signals. It says that varying the noise level while holding constant the detectability of the signal—that is, the signal-to-noise ratio—leads to constant reaction-time distributions. Further, it says that reaction time will increase with the number of alternatives, since there must emerge the criterion difference between the reading of the signal counter and the largest reading of the noise counters; the latter will increase with the number of alternatives.

We return to a consideration of the counting model when we take up the topic of time discrimination in Section 12.5.

12.4.4   An index of performance in detection experiments

"One of the most available response variables for experimental psychology is speed. The reason is obvious: every act takes time, and time can be measured. . . . Speed is a useful measure in two ways; as an index of achievement . . . and also as an index of the complexity of the inner process by which a result is accomplished, for the more complicated the process, the longer time it will take" (Woodworth and Schlosberg, 1954, p. 8).

The promise that additional information may be obtained by measuring reaction time, as well as various response probabilities, has not often been pursued in studies of detection. There are two apparently good reasons for keeping the possibility in mind. They are related, respectively, to the "achievement" and the "complexity of the inner process" of which Woodworth and Schlosberg speak.

One reason for measuring reaction times in detection experiments is that reaction times have a greater range than the proportion of correct responses, or d'. Reaction times vary about as sharply as detection probabilities when detection is a problem and, as signal intensity is increased further, reaction times continue to decrease after $P(C)$ reaches 1.0. They may continue to decrease long after $P(C)$ reaches 1.0, as in audition experiments (Chocholle, 1945; McGill, 1961), or not so long, as in judgments of the comparative lengths of lines (Johnson, 1939). An interesting result obtained in Johnson's experiment is that reaction times had a range twice as large as $P(C)$, and a range identical to that of the observer's ratings of confidence in his judgments. As others have suggested, reaction times may thus provide a link between studies of weak and strong signals.

A second reason for measuring reaction times in detection experiments is that there are sometimes alternative models for a given detection experiment, which differ substantially in the nature of the process that is envisioned, but which predict very nearly the same relationship between an independent variable and the proportion of correct responses. An example comes from the detection of one of two specified frequencies (see Chapter 10). In this case the predictions for $P(C)$ of the single-band, scanning model and the multiband model (both developed in the context of detection theory) differ by very little, and the response-oriented model developed by Shipley (1960) in the context of choice theory (Luce, 1959) leads to two predictions, one exactly like that of the scanning model and the other practically coincident with that of the multiband model. It seems at least plausible that models such as these could be extended to show some implications for the complexity of the process, and therefore of the time required, as a function of various manipulations of independent variables.

12.4.5 Detection of one of two frequencies

Actually, an attempt was made to distinguish experimentally between the single-band and multiband models on the basis of differential predictions for the complexity of the processes involved, and therefore for certain characteristics of the reaction-time distributions (Swets, Schouten, and Lopes-Cardozo, unpublished work, 1958). The results relative to these predictions were ambiguous, so that the rather intricate derivations of the predictions are not discussed here. However, certain aspects of the method and data bear discussion for other reasons.

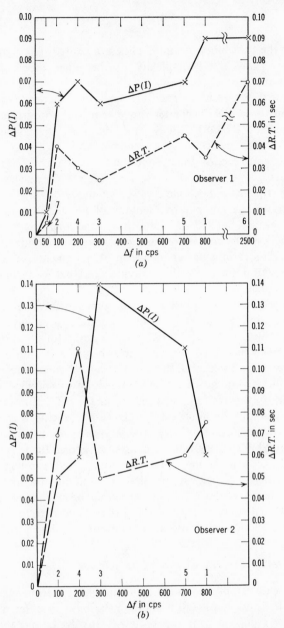

FIG. 12-6 (*a,b*) The increment in the proportion of incorrect responses and in the mean reaction time, when the signal is either of two frequencies instead of a fixed frequency, as a function of the separation of the two frequencies: (*a*) Observer 1, (*b*) Observer 2. Each datum point is based on 200 trials with f_1, 200 trials with f_2, and 400 trials with f_1 or f_2. The order of presentation of the different values of Δf is shown on the abscissa. (Swets, Schouten, and Lopes-Cardozo, unpublished work, 1958.)

The problem of the response criterion was treated more or less successfully by including blank, or no-signal, trials and by giving quantitative instructions about the relationship between time and accuracy. The experiment had the structure of a yes-no experiment, with 50% blank trials, and the observer pressed either the "yes" or the "no" button on every trial. The observer was instructed to maximize a score, which was defined as a specific descending function of both reaction time and proportion of errors.

In a given experimental condition, sessions containing a single frequency as the signal—f_1 in some sessions and f_2 in others—were intermixed with sessions in which the signal was either f_1 or f_2. In the latter case, f_1 occurred on 25% of the trials, f_2 occurred on 25% of the trials, and no signal occurred on 50% of the trials—the observer pressed the "yes" or "no" button to indicate his decision about signal existence, *without regard to the frequency of the signal*. The frequencies f_1 and f_2 were varied from one condition to another to give various separations, Δf, centered approximately (except for the largest Δf) about 1000 cps.

The observers maintained a nearly symmetrical response criterion, with respect to errors, throughout the experiment. That is, the proportion of misses and the proportion of false alarms were nearly equal. The signal-to-noise ratios chosen yielded a proportion of incorrect responses of both types, $P(I)$, of approximately 0.15 in the single-frequency sessions. The mean reaction time in these sessions was about 0.40 seconds. As an aside, we mention that the observers took, on the average, 0.05 seconds longer to respond "no" to noise than "yes" to signal.

The results as indexed by reaction times provide corroboration of the earlier finding in terms of incorrect responses, namely, that performance suffers when the signal is either of two frequencies, relative to sessions in which only one frequency is used. For one of the two observers, the reaction times are also in agreement with some previous results in indicating that the decrement in performance increases with the separation of the two frequencies. These results are consistent with both the single-band and multiband models: the former says that greater separations will require increased scanning time; the latter says that greater separations, up to a point, will introduce more noise and thus bring about a lower effective signal-to-noise ratio.

The results for the two observers are shown in Fig. 12-6 (*a,b*). The figures show the increment in the proportion of incorrect responses and the increment in reaction time that are caused by frequency uncertainty. The figures show the mean reaction times for correct "yes" responses (hits) only. For Observer 1, $\Delta P(I)$ and $\Delta R.T.$ are positively correlated and indicate a fairly stable response criterion with respect to time versus accuracy. Both measures tend to increase with Δf. Observer 2 shows a decrement in performance resulting from frequency uncertainty, but the decrement does not appear to be correlated with Δf in the range (between 100 and 800 cps) for which data on him are available. The existence of such a correlation for Observer 2 is obscure because he shows a distinctly unstable response criterion with respect to the trading relationship between time and accuracy.

12.5   TIME DISCRIMINATION

Creelman (1962) performed a series of experiments to determine the human observer's ability to discriminate between durations of auditory signals presented in a noise background. Separate experiments showed the effect on discrimination of the base duration T, of the increment duration

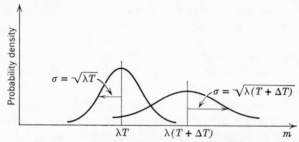

FIG. 12-7   Probability density distributions of the number of counts from a random source depending on whether it is active for T or for $T + \Delta T$. (From Creelman, 1962.)

ΔT, and of signal strength. The results were related to a detection model in which the theory of counting mechanisms is used to specify the statistical properties of the density functions of T and ΔT.

The model pictures the observer as measuring short durations by means of a mechanism that counts incoming pulses throughout the duration to be judged. Assuming that the source of pulses contains a large number of independent elements with randomly distributed firing times, and that each element has a fixed probability λ of firing at any given moment, then the probability of m counts occurring in an interval T is (Feller, 1957):

$$P(m) = \left[\frac{\lambda T^m}{m!}\right][\exp(-\lambda T)]$$

This is the Poisson distribution, having both mean and variance equal to λT. The distribution is approximately normal for large λT.

Figure 12-7 represents the decision problem. The distribution on the left is the distribution of the number of counts when duration T is presented;

on the right is shown the distribution of counts when duration $T + \Delta T$ is presented. The figure illustrates the dependence of the variance on the mean.

Under the two-alternative forced-choice procedure, the observer is supposed to make two observations and to indicate as longer the observation that yields the larger count. He will be correct when the observation of $T + \Delta T$ produces a larger number than the observation of T or, equivalently, when the difference between the two numbers is greater than

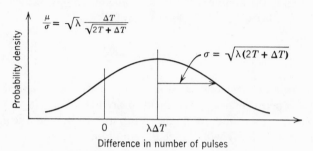

FIG. 12-8 Probability density distribution for differences in the number of counts from the distributions of Fig. 12-7. (From Creelman, 1962.)

zero (see Chapter 3). The density function of the difference is shown in Fig. 12-8. The probability of a correct response is equal to the area under the curve to the right of zero.

Creelman defined an index $d'_{1,2}$ as $\sqrt{2}$ times the distance from zero to the mean of the difference distribution divided by the standard deviation.* That is,

$$\text{(expected) } d'_{1,2} = (2\lambda)^{\frac{1}{2}} \frac{\Delta T}{(2T + \Delta T)^{\frac{1}{2}}} \qquad (12.1)$$

The formula shows the value of $d'_{1,2}$ that is expected under the counting model from an ideal observer. The human observer will do less well if he has some difficulty preserving the number of counts obtained from the first interval while listening to the second interval, and if he does not have

* This definition follows from the theory of recognition developed by Tanner (1956). The values of this index are larger by $\sqrt{2}$ than the values relating d' to $P(C)$ given in published forced-choice tables (Swets, 1964). Essentially, this index is the one obtained when forced-choice data are used to estimate hit and false-alarm probabilities, which are then used to enter yes-no tables of d'. The use of yes-no tables of d' with forced-choice data provides one way of correcting for a response bias in forced-choice experiments, as discussed in Appendix III, Section III.3.4.

exact knowledge of the starting and ending times of the signal. Under the assumption that longer base times place a greater strain on memory, Eq. 12.1 is modified to include a constant K associated with memory. The modified formula, squared to eliminate radicals, is

$$(d'_{1,2})^2 = \frac{1}{1 + KT} \frac{2\lambda\,\Delta T^2}{2T + \Delta T} \tag{12.2}$$

Ambiguity in the starting and ending times of the signals may be expected to add variance to the number of counts, in an amount inversely related to signal strength. This suggests the final formula

$$(d'_{1,2})^2 = \frac{1}{1 + KT} \frac{2\lambda\,\Delta T^2}{2T + \Delta T + \sigma^2} \tag{12.3}$$

Creelman estimated the constants λ, K, and σ for individual observers in one set of experiments and used them to predict the results of another set. The model was found to predict both the form and the level of performance over a fairly wide range of conditions.

12.6 VIGILANCE

The detection problem referred to as "vigilance" is characterized by extended periods of continuous observation. Signals can occur at any time during the long period, without warning and without marking of the interval of the signal. Relative to standard kinds of psychophysical testing, signals occur infrequently, and the term "low-probability watch" is also used to describe this problem. The practical significance of this detection problem is obvious. In the real setting the a priori probability of signal occurrence is low but not definitely low, and the values and costs associated with the decision outcomes may be enormous.

A fairly large literature testifies to the fact that there is a decrement in performance—as measured by the proportion of correct detections, or hits—as the watch proceeds. The analytical techniques of detection theory make it possible to determine experimentally whether the observed decrement in performance is due entirely to a decrement in sensitivity, the usual interpretation, or in part to a change in the response criterion. If a substantial part of the decrement over time reflects a gradually tightening criterion, the possibility exists of taking a corrective action to reduce the decrement.

In Chapter 9 we discussed two methods of analysis which yield a measure of vigilance sensitivity that is influenced minimally, if at all, by the response criterion. The concern here is with data: with experimental determinations of both hit and false-alarm probabilities as a function of time. The data collected to date are sparse, but they clearly support the notion that the decrease over time in the proportion of hits is not the whole story. In each of the experiments that included an attempt to estimate the false-alarm probability, this probability was found to decrease along with the hit probability.

Mackworth and Taylor (1963) defined a false alarm by marking successive five-second intervals for the observers and by informing them that no more than one signal would occur in each interval. In one of their experiments the rate and regularity of signal presentation were varied over six conditions, and the hit and false-alarm probabilities were estimated for the first and second halves of a one-hour session. The average decrement in the proportion of hits was 0.11 (from 0.45 to 0.34). This was accompanied by an average decrement in the proportion of false alarms of 0.013 (from 0.054 to 0.041). These figures correspond to a decrement in d' of 0.14 (from 1.47 to 1.33)—which is clearly not very large.

In a further analysis the same quantities were estimated for the first 5 minutes, the second 5 minutes, and for each of the five 10-minute periods in the remainder of the hour (Mackworth, 1962). These estimates are considerably less accurate, but are worth examination. We report the decrements from the first 5-minute period to the last 10-minute period, averaged over those four of the six conditions that yielded an adequate amount of data. The proportion of hits dropped 0.22 (0.66 to 0.44); the proportion of false alarms dropped 0.021 (0.050 to 0.029); d' dropped 0.30 (2.05 to 1.75). As in two other experiments reported by Mackworth and Taylor (1963), most of the decrease in d' occurred in the first 10 minutes of the hour.

It is evident in these data that much of the decrement over time in the hit proportion is due to an increasing strictness in the response criterion, rather than to decreasing sensitivity. The result is a general one: it is confirmed in studies reported by Broadbent and Gregory (1963a, 1965), Colquhoun and Baddeley (1964), and Loeb and Binford (1964).

A somewhat different application of decision theory to the vigilance problem is represented in the work of Jerison and Pickett (1963). Their interest focuses less on the observer's detection decision than on his decision whether or not to *attend* to the signal display. They develop the model for attention in this setting, or for what has been called an "observing response," and review the vigilance literature from this point of view. Later articles report experimental results which lend support to their approach (Jerison and Pickett, 1964; Jerison, Pickett, and Stenson, 1965). Other applications of decision theory to the process of attention are reviewed in the following section.

12.7   STIMULUS INTERACTION AND ATTENTION

Studies recently conducted in England have initiated the application of detection theory to problems in stimulus interaction and attention. We discuss briefly three of them.

M. Treisman (1964a) has re-examined, from the vantage point of detection theory, the results of some earlier studies of the effect of one stimulus on the threshold for another. The earlier experiments showed that the stimulus threshold (measured by the method of limits) is reduced if this "critical" stimulus is regularly preceded at a fixed interval by an "accessory" stimulus. The threshold was found to decrease gradually at first and then more rapidly as the interval between the two stimuli was shortened from nine seconds to one second. The effect was independent of the modality of the two stimuli (Howarth and Treisman, 1958).

Treisman concludes upon reanalysis that the decrease in threshold is attributable to changes in the observer's response criterion rather than to changes in sensitivity. There are, however, some problems with this interpretation remaining to be solved. If, as the authors suggest, the results can be thought of in terms of the effect of the warning interval, or the precision with which the signal interval is defined for the observer, then these results should be considered along with the similar results of Egan, Greenberg, and Schulman (see Chapter 9, Section 9.7). Egan and his colleagues, also working in the framework of detection theory, attributed their results to a change in sensitivity.

In another paper, Treisman (1963) incorporates detection theory in a model he has devised to account for some interaural effects. Specifically, the model predicts that the masking of a tone in one ear by a tone in the other ear will be reduced by adding white noise at the masking ear and, further, that the extent of the "unmasking" will decrease with practice.

Several studies of attention have used the technique of presenting different information simultaneously to the two ears. Broadbent (1957, 1958) has reviewed many of the results and has proposed a filter model to account for them. According to this model, information is filtered peripherally, at the level of the sense organ, so that rejected information does not proceed farther into the nervous system to elicit a response, and thus has no effect on the observer. Broadbent and Gregory (1963b) recently reported an experiment which, along with other evidence, has led them to a revision of this interpretation. In brief, Broadbent now views information at the unattended ear as attenuated rather than completely blocked. He states that under his earlier model a diversion of attention would be expected to bring about a marked increase in the response criterion—in his present thinking, a diversion of attention affects sensitivity rather than the response criterion.

It may be recalled from the preceding section that recent experiments on vigilance have shown a substantial effect on the response criterion. In fact, Broadbent and Gregory (1963a) observed a change in the criterion and no change in d'. In view of the diverging results of vigilance and attention experiments, Broadbent has now questioned the suggestion in his book (1958) that the deterioration in performance during vigilance can be attributed to a diversion of attention. We shall probably see further work on these problems in the near future.

12.8 SUBLIMINAL PERCEPTION

The reader no doubt has some acquaintance with the extensive literature on subliminal (or subthreshold) perception, and is aware of the recent public interest in the concept. Several good reviews of the literature are available, so that we shall not attempt a summary here. Of particular relevance to our present concern, because they consider the literature in terms of recent developments in psychophysics, are the critical reviews by Goldiamond (1958, 1963), Eriksen (1960), Hake (1962), and Pierce (1963). However, a brief characterization of the methods used in the major studies is possible, and is in order.

Many of the studies that have been put forward as evidence for subliminal perception depend on the finding that a subject who first reports no stimulus can then identify the stimulus with greater than chance accuracy when forced to make a choice from a limited set. This interpretation is particularly clear in the case of the earlier studies (see Miller, 1942). Other studies which have been viewed as supporting the concept have shown that when the subject's verbal report (a single identification response) is incorrect, some other kind of response (e.g., the galvanic skin response) indicates an awareness of the stimulus presented, or of the class to which the stimulus belongs. This result suggests the term "discrimination without awareness"; the term "subception" is also applied (e.g., Lazarus and McCleary, 1951).

Certain results in psychophysics suggest a different interpretation of these studies (Swets, Tanner, and Birdsall, 1955, 1961). First, it is often observed, with signals such as lights and tones in the standard forced-choice procedure, that subjects respond with greater than chance accuracy when they profess not to see or not to hear the signal. This result has not been pursued systematically in experiments with simple signals, so that it has only the status of an anecdote in that context. The point, however, is that this result is not taken as evidence for subthreshold perception.

There is little basis to contend that the signal is subthreshold if it is above the forced-choice threshold, or if it is reliably identified with more than chance accuracy in the forced-choice procedure. A related result, with a sounder footing in data, is that stimulus thresholds determined by the yes-no procedure are higher than those determined by the forced-choice procedure (Blackwell, 1953). In the terms of detection theory, this result is to be expected on the grounds that observers who are left to set their (yes-no) criterion wherever they choose will tend to adopt a fairly strict criterion, and that the threshold, calculated with the correction for chance, varies directly with the criterion (see Fig. 5-3c). There are two reasons for the observer to adopt a strict criterion in the yes-no procedure: traditionally, observers have been explicitly instructed to avoid false alarms, and it seems likely that in the absence of such instructions they will regard a miss as less opprobrious than a false alarm. At worst, a miss indicates a minor sensory deficit; a false alarm, for the naive observer, is a falsehood.

Another result of psychophysical studies with simple signals that may be adduced specifically in this context is that when the first (forced) choice is incorrect, the second choice is correct with greater than chance accuracy (Chapter 4). An incorrect first-identification response does not imply a below-threshold stimulus. The observer may gain some information about the stimulus which he can make evident at the level of verbal report, or "awareness," if given an opportunity (by a second-choice identification response), as well as at a level presumably below the level of awareness (by a galvanic skin response). Bricker and Chapanis (1953) have criticized the subception experiments on exactly this count and have shown the second-choice effect with the kind of stimuli (words presented visually) usually used in these experiments. Howes (1954) has developed a probability model for this procedure in its application to word perception.

Of course, any doubts about the existence of a sensory threshold bring into question the existence of subthreshold perception. The ability to perceive stimuli below the threshold loses its mystery if the threshold is merely a construct of the data analysis. As reviewed in Chapter 5, it is reasonable to suppose in the light of present evidence that sensory information is continuous, and that there is no inherent dichotomy between seeing and not seeing, or hearing and not hearing. A signal which produces relatively fragmentary or ambiguous sensory information will surpass a response criterion relatively infrequently. There is no clear need to postulate a physiologically determined threshold, or a separate psychological or physiological process such as subliminal perception.

Concurrent with and related to the recent interest in subliminal perception was the so-called "new look" in perception, a school of thought which stressed processes of perceptual sensitization and defense and, in general, emphasized such internal states as needs, values, and emotions as determinants of perception. Studies in this area have relied on demonstrations of threshold differences between stimuli of different affect. These studies have been criticized on several grounds and, in the more recent and more prevalent view, internal states are regarded as affecting response systems rather than perception per se. This view is consonant with the "old look" in perception as well as with modern psychophysics. The review articles by Goldiamond (1958) and Pierce (1963) include a discussion of this topic.

12.9   RECOGNITION MEMORY

In order to obtain a more sensitive measure of retention than is provided by a direct measure of unaided recall, a variant of the recognition procedure is often used. In one form of the recognition procedure, the subject's ability to remember stimuli to which he has been exposed is tested by presenting those stimuli intermixed with other stimuli to which he has not been exposed, and by requiring him to state for each stimulus whether it is "old" or "new" (Woodworth and Schlosberg, 1954). The subject, in effect, responds "yes" or "no" depending on whether or not he thinks the stimulus is an old one. This memory task is much like the yes-no task of detection in psychophysics and, understandably, models of the memory process have developed in parallel with models of the detection process. Specifically, recognition memory has long been viewed as a threshold process, and the data have commonly been subjected to a correction for chance success. Decision theory plays the same role as it does in psychophysics: it provides an estimate of the subject's discrimination that is relatively unaffected by his response criterion. It separates the degree of recognizability of the old stimuli, which depends upon the amount of learning and the similarity of old and new stimuli, from the response criterion, which depends upon the a priori probabilities of the two types of stimuli and upon the values and costs of the various stimulus-response combinations.

The application of decision theory to recognition memory was proposed and developed by Egan. His work appeared in a technical report of limited circulation (Egan, 1958), and thus we reproduce the essentials here. The following section is mainly a summary of Egan's report.

12.9.1   Threshold and decision-theoretic models for recognition memory; an application to verbal materials

Under the threshold model, the correction for chance success, or for guessing, is applied as follows to obtain the "true" recognition score

(Woodworth and Schlosberg, 1954, p. 700):

True Score = (percent of old stimuli recognized)

— (percent of new stimuli falsely recognized)   (12.4)

This model assumes that the observed proportion $P(O \mid o)$ is made up of true recognitions $P^*(O \mid o)$ and guesses P_G:

$$P(O \mid o) = P^*(O \mid o) + P_G[1 - P^*(O \mid o)]   \qquad (12.5)$$

Expressing the threshold of new stimuli as $P^*(N \mid n)$ we have

$$P(O \mid n) = P_G[1 - P^*(N \mid n)]   \qquad (12.6)$$

In Eqs. 12.5 and 12.6 the probability of a guess is modified by the opportunity for guessing to occur, namely, when neither of the thresholds—for old and new stimuli—is exceeded.

If it is assumed, for the moment, that the subject cannot recognize new stimuli as such, then $P^*(N \mid n) = 0$. Solving Eq. 12.6 for P_G and substituting it in Eq. 12.5, we obtain:

$$P(O \mid o) = P^*(O \mid o) + P(O \mid n)[1 - P^*(O \mid o)]   \qquad (12.7)$$

This equation is identical to Eq. 5.1, and leads to the family of ROC curves shown in Fig. 5-1a. The y-intercepts represent various true thresholds for the old stimuli, $P^*(O \mid o)$; the slopes of the lines are equal to $1 - P^*(O \mid o)$.

A more reasonable assumption is that new stimuli have a threshold which may be exceeded, that $P^*(N \mid n) > 0$. Assuming that $P^*(N \mid n) = P^*(O \mid o)$, Eq. 12.5 becomes:

$$P(O \mid o) = P^*(O \mid o) + P(O \mid n)   \qquad (12.8)$$

This equation is identical to Eq. 12.4, the formula for computing the *true score*. The ROC curves implied by this model have the form shown in Fig. 12-9.

If the thresholds for old and new stimuli are allowed to differ, we can write:

$$P^*(N \mid n) = kP^*(O \mid o)   \qquad (12.9)$$

Assuming that the new stimuli have a higher threshold than the old, $0 < k < 1$. When $k = 0$, Eq. 12.7 and the ROC curves of Fig. 5-1a are obtained. When $k = 1$, Eq. 12.8 and the ROC curves of Fig. 12-9 are obtained. When k lies between zero and one, with a fixed value of $P^*(O \mid o)$, the ROC curves intersect the ordinate at $P^*(O \mid o)$ and have a slope which changes with k according to:

$$\text{Slope} = \frac{[1 - P^*(O \mid o)]}{[1 - kP^*(O \mid o)]}   \qquad (12.10)$$

According to the decision-theory model, on the other hand, the information available to the subject is not limited to the three categories "truly old," "truly new," and "uncertain." The subject can adopt a response criterion other than that corresponding to a fixed (and "high") threshold. If he relaxes his criterion, he can utilize varying degrees of certainty to

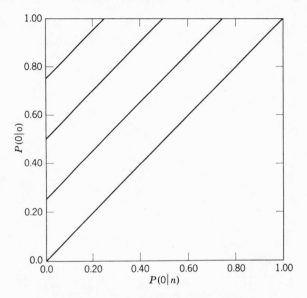

FIG. 12-9 ROC curves predicated on the classical formula for the correction for guessing in recognition memory. The curves, which assume thresholds for both old and new stimuli, are described by Eq. 12.8. (After Egan, 1958.)

perform better than guessing will allow. The ROC curve will have a large slope at low values of $P(O \mid o)$ and will decrease continually as $P(O \mid n)$ increases.

Egan reported data which were obtained using monosyllabic words presented visually: 100 words in the old set, and 100 in the new. One group of 16 subjects was given one presentation, and a second group of 16 subjects was given two presentations of the 100 words to be remembered, before the 200-word recognition test. ROC curves were generated from responses given on a 7-point rating scale.

The ROC curves from 4 of the 16 subjects given one presentation before the test are shown in Fig. 12-10. These subjects were those with performance scores in the first quartile, where performance was measured by the ability to discriminate old and new stimuli. It is clear that the data points follow a curve of decreasing slope rather than a straight line. The form of the curve is familiar; it is consistent with hypothetical distributions of stimuli having greater variance for old than for new stimuli.

The average result for each of the quartiles of subjects is shown—on probability scales—in Fig. 12-11. The points obtained from each of the

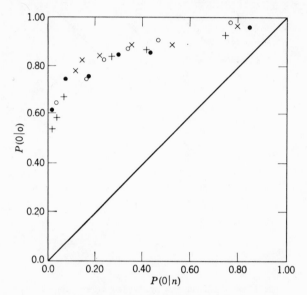

FIG. 12-10   ROC curves obtained from the four subjects in the first quartile, given one presentation of 100 words before the 200-word recognition test. (After Egan, 1958.)

top three quartiles clearly define a straight line; it will be recalled that a straight line, on these scales, is consistent with a decision model that assumes normal density functions. The points obtained from the bottom quartile show a slight tendency for the upward curvature that is predicted by the threshold models (see Fig. 5-1b). The data show, as detection data frequently do, a decreasing slope with increasing discriminability.

The effect of the amount of learning is shown in Fig. 12-12, which compares the result for subjects given one presentation with the result for subjects given two presentations before the recognition test. These ROC curves are the average for the middle 50% of the subjects in each case. The discrimination index $D(\Delta m, s)$ is 1.45, 0.71 for one presentation, and 2.75, 0.67 for two presentations.

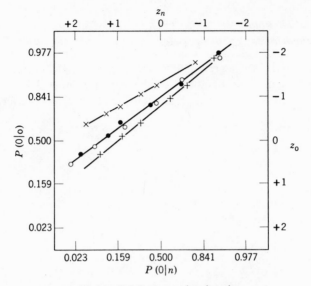

FIG. 12-11   ROC curves showing the average result in each quartile of subjects, given one presentation. (After Egan, 1958.)

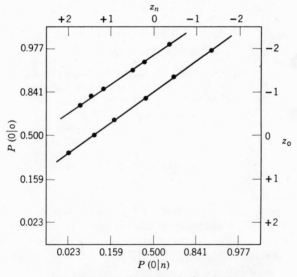

FIG. 12-12   Lower curve is the average result for middle 50% of subjects given one presentation; upper curve is the average result for middle 50% of subjects given two presentations. (After Egan, 1958.)

12.9.2 Other applications of threshold and decision theories to verbal materials

Norman and Wickelgren (1965) applied the ROC analysis to the recognition of a single item and to the recognition of a pair of items. They presented a sequence of 5 spoken digits, then an interfering task,

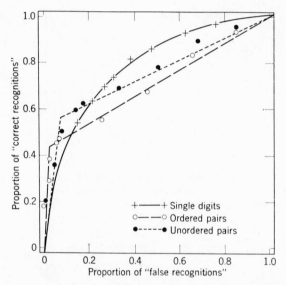

FIG. 12-13 Average ROC curves obtained by a 10-point rating scale for single digits, ordered pairs, and unordered pairs. The curve fitted to the points representing single digits is based on the decision model assuming normal, equal-variance density functions. The curves fitted to points representing pairs of digits are based on two-state threshold theory. (After Norman and Wickelgren, 1965.)

and then a test of recognition memory for one or two digits. The subjects responded "yes" or "no," and in either case gave their decision a rating of confidence on a 5-point scale; in effect, they used a 10-point rating scale. When two digits were presented on the test, the subjects were required to state whether or not the two were in the same order as in the original presentation.

Figure 12-13 shows the average results from 29 subjects. The curve fitted to the plus signs representing single digits is a theoretical curve from decision theory based on normal probability density functions of equal variance. The curves fitted to the open and filled circles for pairs of digits are curves based on Luce's two-state threshold model (see Chapter 5, Section 5.6.2).

The curves shown appear to provide reasonably good fits. It is clear, at least, that single items and pairs of items lead to ROC curves of different forms. However, one cannot assess very accurately on these plots the fit of

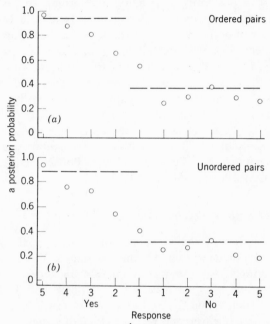

FIG. 12-14   A posteriori probability of correct recognition as a function of the rating category for ordered and unordered pairs of digits. The dotted lines are predictions from two-state threshold theory. (After Norman and Wickelgren, 1965.)

the lower limb—the points above threshold—of the two-linear-segment curves. We determine more easily the accuracy of this fit by considering for each rating category the a posteriori probability of correct recognition or the proportion of items assigned each category that were old items. Results in this form are shown in Fig. 12-14. As Nachmias and Steinman (1963) have pointed out, the two-state threshold model predicts an a posteriori probability function of two horizontal lines representing the two states (or two values of likelihood ratio, a variable that is monotonic with a posteriori probability; see Chapter 3). Decision theory, on the other hand, predicts a monotonically decreasing function representing a continuum of information or many states. It can be seen that the points in the region of a "yes" decision decrease monotonically; this indicates that the points on the lower limb in Fig. 12-13 are not fitted well by a straight line. The points in the region of a "no" decision (generally corresponding to the upper limb of Fig. 12-13) are approximated by a straight line, and thus indicate a lack of discrimination below a threshold.

The analysis of a posteriori probability, as Norman and Wickelgren state, shows the data for pairs to be inconsistent both with Luce's two-state theory and with decision theory. It must be recalled, however, that Luce did not intend an application of his theory to rating experiments (Chapter 5, Section 5.6.2). The data for pairs are consistent with the multi-state threshold theories proposed by Norman (1963) and by Swets, Tanner, and Birdsall (1955, 1961; see Chapter 5, Section 5.6.1). Norman and Wickelgren (1965) have presented what they call an "all-or-none incremental model" of memory which is also consistent with their results.

Other applications of the ROC analysis to recognition memory are presented by Nachmias and Sternberg (1963), Pollack, Galanter, and Norman (1964a), Murdock (1965), and Parks (1966).

12.9.3   Application to nonverbal sounds

Experimental studies of the identification of nonverbal sounds are usually limited, if not hampered, by the assignment to the sounds of arbitrary designations, for example, numerals, in order to give the observer some means of identification (e.g. Pollack and Ficks, 1954; Swets, Millman, Fletcher, and Green, 1962). Pollack (1959d) has suggested that this limitation can be overcome by the method of recognition memory. He tested his suggestion with tones differing in loudness, and for exposure sets of various sizes. The ROC curves obtained by means of a rating scale were suitably linear on probability scales. The recognition-memory procedure was also used successfully in a test of retention of complex sounds after one month; in this case it was reasonable to suppose that the subjects might remember the sounds while forgetting their arbitrary, and nonsensical, designations (Swets, Millman, Fletcher, and Green, 1962).

12.9.4   Nonparametric measures of recognition

A nonparametric analysis of ROC data, as described in Chapter 2, is of course applicable to ROC data from any source, including experiments on signal detection and recognition memory and, in fact, on information retrieval (see Swets, 1963b). However, such an analysis is perhaps especially appropriate in areas other than detection. In the case of detection, there exist well-defined models (of various ideal and threshold detectors) that specify probability distributions, and hence ROC curves, of various particular forms. In the other areas there is little, if any, basis for expecting a particular kind of ROC curve. We therefore recall at this point the nonparametric (area) analysis of Chapter 2 and the related measures proposed by Norman (1964a) and by Pollack and Norman (1964).

12.10   SUMMARY

Animal psychophysics, sensory physiology, reaction time, time discrimination, vigilance, attention, subliminal perception, recognition memory—we have left out only cabbages and kings. None of the topics discussed here fits naturally into any one of the preceding eleven chapters, but it seems that all of them would benefit from an analysis that separates sensory from nonsensory processes. Detection theory, therefore, may find an application in each case, and preliminary studies have been undertaken to explore the nature of the application.

Results to date in *animal psychophysics* are barely suggestive of possibilities. Rewards, which are essential to studies of animal behavior, are viewed as affecting the response system. The ROC analysis provides a means, as it were, of looking through the response system into the sensory system. *Physiologically*, sensory information consists, apparently, of changes in the maintained (background) rate of nervous discharge. The central "analyzer" may thus be profitably viewed as extracting signals from noise, as making statistical decisions. The study of *reaction time* requires a consideration of the trading relationship between time and accuracy, and is currently being conducted in the framework of statistical models for sequential analysis or deferred decision. *Judgment of time intervals*, another problem with a long history, is important to theories of detection because detection depends heavily upon the observer's ability to estimate accurately the length of the interval during which the signal can occur or, more generally, the duration of the signal. Relative durations provide cues to stress and inflection in the perception of English speech and, in some languages, they signal differences in linguistic meaning. *Vigilance* is the practical detection problem. It appears that not all of the decrement over time in vigilance performance is due to decreasing sensitivity; the decrease in the hit proportion is accompanied by a decrease in the false-alarm proportion. It may be, therefore, that the observer gradually tightens his response criterion as the watch proceeds. Alternatively, a diversion of *attention* may depress both hits and false alarms. Some evidence on attention, on the other hand, suggests that its diversion results in attenuation rather than complete blocking of the signal, and that it may not be chiefly responsible for the decrement in vigilance. The presumed existence of *subliminal perception*, and of affective determinants of perception, is currently being questioned on the basis of results obtained in more standard psychophysical studies. Subliminal and "new-look" perception clearly require more careful consideration than they received at first. Studies of *recognition memory* have extended the ROC analysis to processes more cognitive than perceptual, and are currently exciting much interest. These studies have promoted the development of non-parametric measures of discrimination. Three of the topics considered— sensory physiology, reaction time, and time discrimination—have led to the development of an ideal observer based on a counting mechanism.

Appendices

Appendix I briefly reviews the concepts of probability theory that are basic to the psychophysical application of detection theory. Appendix II is a primer on waveform analysis; it presents ideas about the representation of signals and noise that are fundamental to the definition of ideally-sensitive detectors. Appendix III describes in some detail experimental techniques that are relevant to data collection, data analysis, and stimulus measurement in psychophysics.

APPENDIX I

Elements of Probability Theory

I.1 INTRODUCTION

As indicated in the Introduction, the general theory of signal detectability is composed of two distinct mathematical theories. For our purposes in psychophysics, it thus provides two distinct mathematical models. One of the mathematical models is, specifically, a probability model; it is a direct translation of the theory of statistical decision, or of the theory of statistical inference. The second model, of ideal observers, is based to a large extent on the first. Therefore, probability theory is used as a basic tool throughout this book. So that the book may be self-contained, this appendix presents the essentials of probability theory.

We shall need to have at our command a substantial portion of the theory of probability. Every chapter makes use of its basic definitions and many of its theorems. They depend upon a knowledge of random variables, and of properties of their distributions. They utilize continuous, as well as discrete, random variables, and also some sampling theory. Since space is limited relative to these requirements, a rigorous presentation of probability theory is not attempted here. Neither are many examples included. This treatment of probability consists of a compact listing and discussion of the basic concepts.*

* Several excellent textbooks are available for supplementary reading on the theory of probability. Goldberg (1960), Hodges and Lehman (1964), and Mosteller, Rourke, and Thomas (1961) provide introductions that do not depend upon a knowledge of calculus. The more advanced text by Feller (1957) is a classic, as is the considerably more advanced book by Cramér (1946).

Historically, the theory of probability has its basis in some heuristic observations made in the study of games of chance. Although the early theory enjoyed considerable success in scientific applications, its lack of a strictly rational, mathematical basis led ultimately to various paradoxes and inconsistencies. Fortunately, probability theory has since been developed as an axiomatic, mathematical theory so that a sound basis now exists for applications of the theory.

In formulating the mathematical theory of probability, it is possible to begin with set theory and to develop the basic theorems in that context. Probability theory may then be articulated with set theory through measure theory, that is, by considering the magnitude of a set or, strictly, by introducing a measure function which associates a real number (meeting certain conditions) with each subset. Field theory may also play a part in the formulation, and if it does the probability measure is defined on a collection of subsets which meet the requirements for a Borel field.

An alternative way of presenting the mathematical theory of probability, which is quite adequate and better suits the present purposes, is to begin directly in the probability context—to begin with *sample spaces* rather than with sets. The sample spaces contain *sample points* which represent the possible *outcomes* of an idealized, random *experiment*. *Events* consist of certain classes of outcomes, or contain certain sample points. In short, the following presentation strikes a balance between the primitive and mathematical theories of probability—it uses a vocabulary with intuitive appeal in the probability setting, but one which corresponds to the undefined terms (elements and sets or points and point sets) that are basic to all of mathematics. The conventions and theorems of set theory that are basic to probability theory are presented here in the language of probability.

In this discussion of fundamentals, attention is restricted to finite and discrete experiments, that is, to sample spaces consisting of a finite number of isolated points. For our purposes, this is not a severe restriction. It permits us to concentrate on the essential ideas of probability theory without concern for some purely technical considerations. Only a change in the technical tools is required when these ideas are applied to continuous sample spaces.

I.2   BASIC DEFINITIONS AND THEOREMS

I.2.1   Sample space

The term *experiment* describes an act or an observation that can be repeated under the same conditions. The exact result of the act, or the outcome, cannot be predicted with certainty. An experiment and a sample space are related by the following definition:

A sample space of an experiment is a collection S of points such that any outcome of the experiment corresponds to exactly one point in the collection.

We say *a* sample space, rather than *the* sample space, since a given experiment may be specified by more than one sample space. If, for example, the experiment consists in tossing a coin twice, a sample space is specified by

$$S_1 = [HH, HT, TH, TT]$$

in which is recorded in order, for the first and second toss, whether the coin fell heads (H) or tails (T). An alternative sample space is

$$S_2 = [0, 1, 2]$$

which applies when only the number of heads that appeared is recorded. This example makes it clear that one sample-space listing may be more fundamental than another in the sense that it contains more detailed information. In the example, S_1 can provide an answer to any question that can be answered by means of S_2, but the converse is not true. Given S_2, upon learning that one head appeared in the two tosses, it is not possible to state whether the head appeared on the first or on the second toss.

I.2.2   Events

Frequently it is convenient to regard several outcomes as corresponding to a single *event*. In the experiment just described, we may be interested in the event "the two tosses have a like result." In this case, HH and TT correspond to outcomes for which this event does occur, and to say that the event "like result" occurs is equivalent to saying that the experiment results in an outcome which corresponds to a point in the subspace:

$$A = [HH, TT]$$

By definition:

An event A is a subspace of the sample space S of an experiment.

I.2.3   Equally likely outcomes

Often an experiment can result in any one of n different, equally likely outcomes. Then, if exactly m of these outcomes corresponds to event A, the probability of event A is

$$P(A) = \frac{m}{n} \tag{I.1}$$

This is the classical definition of probability; the probability of an event is the ratio of the number of sample points in the subspace defining the event to the number of sample points in the entire sample space of the experiment. It is because $P(A)$ can be computed in this situation with only a knowledge of how many sample points are in A that the sophisticated counting techniques (the permutation and combination formulas and the binomial theorem) play such a large role in most presentations of probability theory. It is fortunate for the aim of making this book largely self-contained that we will not have to deal with large numbers of equally likely outcomes and, therefore, a detour through the counting techniques can be avoided.

Treated here are the definitions and theorems that apply even when the outcomes of an experiment are not equally likely. The next task is therefore to determine how probabilities may be assigned to events composed of outcomes, or sample points, which are not equally likely, which do not have probability $1/n$. To accomplish this task, the ideas and the notation of a few formal operations that may be applied to events (or sets) are needed.

I.2.4 Set operations

Consider any two events A and B. A new event may be defined by the condition "either A or B or both occur." The event "A or B," in which "or" is used in the inclusive sense, in the legal sense of "and/or," will be denoted $A + B$. The event $A + B$ consists of all sample points which are in either of the subspaces A and B (the *union* of A and B).

Another new event can be defined by the condition "both A and B occur." The event "A and B" will be denoted $A \cdot B$. The event $A \cdot B$ consists of all sample points which are in both of the subspaces A and B (the *intersection* of A and B). If the events A and B exclude each other, then the event $A \cdot B$ is impossible. We say that $A \cdot B = \varphi$, where by φ is meant the subspace which contains no points (the *null*, or *empty*, set). In this case A and B are said to be *mutually exclusive*.

A third new event can be defined as "the event not-A" This event is denoted A', and contains all of the sample points of the entire sample space S that do not belong to A (the *complement* of A). These events are represented pictorially, by means of a Venn diagram, in Fig. I-1.

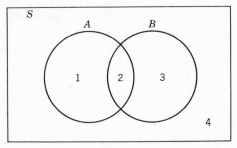

FIG. I-1 The sample space of the experiment *S*, and event *A*, and event *B*, are given. *S* corresponds to the regions 1, 2, 3, and 4; *A* corresponds to the regions 1 and 2; and *B* corresponds to the regions 2 and 3. The event *A* + *B* is represented by regions 1, 2, and 3; the event *A* · *B* is represented by region 2. The event *A'* (see text) would correspond to regions 3 and 4; the event *B'* would correspond to regions 1 and 4. Event *A* and event *B* are mutually exclusive if region 2 is empty.

I.2.5 Assignment of probabilities

We can now proceed with the assignment of probabilities to events that are not composed of equally likely outcomes. This is not a difficult matter. Outcomes or sample points (which are also called *elementary events*) may be assigned numbers (probabilities) in an arbitrary fashion, subject only to the restrictions that the numbers are non-negative and that the sum of the numbers assigned to all of the elementary events of the sample space is 1.

Now, to obtain the probability of an event that is composed of two or more different elementary events, the probabilities of these elementary events are simply added. This procedure is justified by the following three axioms, which are the basic axioms of probability theory:

(1) $P(A) \geq 0$.

(2) $P(S) = 1$.

(3) If *A* and *B* are mutually exclusive events, then $P(A + B) = P(A) + P(B)$.

(An alternative way of stating this is that if *P* is a set function which associates with each subset *A* of *S* a real number denoted by $P(A)$, then the set function *P* is a *probability measure* if it satisfies the requirements just referred to as axioms.)

These axioms serve to specify the scale for a probability, $0 \leq P(A) \leq 1$. They also provide for the unique determination of the probabilities of all other events when the probabilities of the elementary events are known. From the axioms it follows that if A is empty, then $P(A) = P(\varphi) = 0$; that if A is not empty, then $P(A)$ is the sum of the probabilities of the elementary events whose union is A; and that if A and A' are complementary events, then $P(A') = 1 - P(A)$.

I.2.6 Odds

It should be observed in passing that it would have been possible to set up a different scale for measuring uncertainty and that, in fact, a different scale is often employed. This is the scale represented by the use of *odds*. By definition, the odds for A are a to b if and only if

$$P(A) = \frac{a}{a + b} \qquad (I.2)$$

This formula shows how $P(A)$ may be calculated from the odds for A (a to b), or from the odds against A (b to a). Probabilities may be translated into odds by writing them in the fractional form $a/(a + b)$. For example, if $P(A) = 0.75$, then $P(A) = 3/4 = 3/(3 + 1)$, and the odds for A are 3 to 1.

I.2.7 Probability of A + B

According to the third of the axioms just listed, the probability of the occurrence of at least one of two events is the sum of their individual probabilities, if the two events are mutually exclusive. Clearly, it is desirable to be able to specify a relationship that holds between the probabilities of any two events, whether or not they are mutually exclusive, and the probability of their union. The theorem stating this general relationship is

$$P(A + B) = P(A) + P(B) - P(A \cdot B) \qquad (I.3)$$

Reference to Fig. I-1 will make it clear that in the sum $P(A) + P(B)$ the sample points in $A \cdot B$ (region 2) are included twice. Thus, to obtain the sum of the probabilities of all elementary events in $A + B$, each counted once, the quantity $P(A \cdot B)$ must be subtracted from the sum $P(A) + P(B)$. It is clear that Eq. I.3 holds whether or not the events A and B are mutually exclusive; if they are, Eq. I.3 reduces to the equation given in axiom 3, for then $P(A \cdot B) = P(\varphi) = 0$. Moreover, Eq. I.3 can be generalized to an arbitrary number of events.

I.2.8   Conditional probability

We have seen above how the probability of an event, $P(A)$, depends upon the probabilities assigned to the elementary events. Of course, the probabilities assigned to elementary events are not given by probability theory; they depend upon a judgment made about the empirical situation to which the theory is to be applied. Often, different assignments are acceptable for a given problem. We have also noted that the choice of a sample space depends upon a judgment. Again, it is not unusual for different people facing the same problem to define different sample spaces. In general, in probability theory as in the rest of mathematics, or all of science for that matter, the statements made are of the conditional form, that is, "if x is assumed, then y follows." When the context makes it clear which assumptions have been made, the assumptions are usually not made explicit.

Sometimes, however, we want to deal with the probability of an event A when $P(A)$ depends not only upon the choice of a sample space S, and upon the assignment of probabilities to elementary events in S, but also upon the information that another event B has occurred. Thus, in determining the probability that a person selected at random from a population is over six feet tall (event A), the calculation of this probability will be affected by the additional information that the person selected is male (event B). In this case, the space of all possible outcomes of the experiment, at first represented by S (a population of males and females), is now represented by a subspace of S, namely B (a population of males). Since B has occurred, outcomes corresponding to sample points in B' are no longer possible.

The revised or *conditional probability* of A, given B, is denoted by $P(A \mid B)$, and is defined by the equation

$$P(A \mid B) = \frac{P(A \cdot B)}{P(B)} \tag{I.4}$$

Except in certain instances irrelevant to our concern, it is useful to speak of $P(A \mid B)$ only when $P(B) > 0$. $P(B)$ can be less than one, and usually is, since the probabilities in Eq. I.4 are probabilities of the events in the original sample space S. If $P(B) < 1$, we can think of achieving $P(B) = 1$, so that B qualifies as a sample space, by multiplying the probabilities of all elementary events of B by the constant fraction $1/P(B)$. Then the conditional probability of A given B is seen to be the sum of the new probabilities of the points of A that are also in the new, reduced sample space B, that is, in the intersection $A \cdot B$. Since $P(A \mid B)$ is simply a probability associated with a subspace of the new sample space B, the general theorems on (absolute) probabilities apply also to conditional probabilities.

I.2.9 Compound probabilities and the product rule

Equation I.4 is often written in the form:

$$P(A \cdot B) = P(B)P(A \mid B) \tag{I.5}$$

Since order is not important in $A \cdot B$, we may also write:

$$P(A \cdot B) = P(A)P(B \mid A) \tag{I.6}$$

Equations I.5 and I.6 are called the *theorem on compound probabilities* and, sometimes, the *product rule*. These equations are used to assign probabilities in a sample space that corresponds to a compound experiment, that is, an experiment best described as a compounding of two or more trials. A compound experiment is exemplified, given two urns with different compositions of colored balls, by first selecting an urn at random and then drawing one ball at random from that urn. It should be noted that the theorem can be generalized to three or more events.

I.2.10 Independent events

Ordinarily, as suggested in the preceding paragraphs, $P(A)$ and $P(A \mid B)$ are unequal. If

$$P(A \mid B) = P(A) \tag{I.7}$$

then the occurrence of B does not change the probability of A. In this case A is said to be *independent* of B. Substituting Eq. I.7 in Eq. I.5 gives

$$P(A \cdot B) = P(B)P(A) \tag{I.8}$$

Equation I.8 is symmetrical, so that if A is independent of B, then B is independent of A. By definition:

> *Two events A and B are (statistically) independent events if and only if Eq. I.8 holds true.*

Independence is defined in terms of Eq. I.8, rather than in terms of Eq. I.7, since Eq. I.8 does not exclude events with zero probabilities from the definition.

It can be shown that if A and B are independent events, then A and B' are independent, as are A' and B and A' and B'. Three events, A, B, and C, are independent if they are independent by pairs (that is, if Eq. I.8 holds true for each of the pairs of events A and B, A and C, B and C) and if the following equation holds true:

$$P(A \cdot B \cdot C) = P(A)P(B)P(C) \tag{I.9}$$

The definition of independence for any finite number of events requires that the product rule for independent events (exemplified by Eqs. I.8 and I.9) hold for *all* combinations of two or more of the events.

I.2.11 Bayes' rule and a posteriori probabilities

This discussion of the basic theorems of probability theory is concluded by considering an important application of conditional probability: Bayes' rule for the probability of causes. This rule permits the determination of *inverse probabilities*, that is, probabilities that go back along a chain of events. It can provide, for example, conditional upon the color of the ball drawn at random from an urn on trial two, an estimate of the probability that a particular one of two urns was selected on trial one. In general, the rule permits the calculation of the probability that a given hypothesis is true after some evidence has been obtained, that is, after an observation has been made, or after a sample has been taken. The rule thus provides *a posteriori probabilities* which are revised estimates of the *a priori probabilities*, of the probabilities prior to experience.

A posteriori probabilities are basic to statistical inference—the subject of Chapter 1. Although the theory of statistical inference depends directly upon probability theory, there is a fundamental contrast between the two. Probability theory enables one to make deductions about the probable content of a sample from the known content of a population, or to make deductions about probable observations from a mathematical model. The theory of statistical inference, conversely, is a theory of hypothesis testing; it permits inferences to be made about "causes," that is, about the properties of a population or a model, on the basis of observed sample content or data.

Bayes' rule is simply a way of rewriting the equation that defines conditional probability, namely,

$$P(A \mid B) = \frac{P(A \cdot B)}{P(B)} \tag{I.4}$$

Combining the product-rule forms of this equation (Eqs. I.5 and I.6) gives

$$P(B)P(A \mid B) = P(A)P(B \mid A) \tag{I.10}$$

Solving for $P(B \mid A)$ gives

$$P(B \mid A) = \frac{P(B)P(A \mid B)}{P(A)} \tag{I.11}$$

which is Bayes' rule. This rule is also considered, in a more general form, in Chapter 1.

I.2.12   Discrete and continuous sample spaces

To be considered next are random variables and sampling theory. Before proceeding to this discussion, note again that thus far attention has been confined to discrete sample spaces. In these sample spaces probabilities are assigned to isolated points. In continuous sample spaces, probabilities are assigned to intervals of real numbers, or to regions of the space. In the first case, unit probability is divided into portions which are assigned to each point in the sample space; in the second case, the unit of probability is spread over intervals or regions. Thus in discrete sample spaces probabilities of various events are obtained by simple addition, whereas in continuous sample spaces the probabilities must be obtained by integration. Discrete sample spaces will continue to be an adequate basis for subsequent discussion until the normal probability distribution is introduced.

I.3   RANDOM VARIABLES, PROBABILITY FUNCTIONS, AND SOME SAMPLING THEORY

I.3.1   Random variables

A random variable is neither a variable nor random. In fact,

A random variable is a function defined on a sample space.

In general terms, a function is a rule which assigns exactly one number (*value*) to each of a collection of elements. The collection of elements is called the *domain* of the function; all of the values of the function constitute the *range* of the function. Thus, specifically,

A random variable X is a function whose domain is a sample space and whose range is some set of real numbers.

For a discrete sample space a random variable X can be tabulated by listing each point in the sample space (each possible outcome of an experiment) along with its associated value of X. The values assumed by X are represented as x_i, where $i = 1, 2, \ldots, n$, and n is the number of elementary outcomes in the sample space.

I.3.2   Probability functions

Given a random variable X defined on S, we are interested in the probability that the value of X is some number x_i. This probability is designated $f(x_i)$. Thus

$$f(x_i) = P(X = x_i) \qquad i = 1, 2, \ldots, n \qquad (I.12)$$

The set of ordered pairs $[x_i, f(x_i)]$ is called the probability function f of X.

In other words, the probability function of X assigns to each real number x_i in its domain the probability that X has the value x_i. It is clear that $f(x_i) \geq 0$, and $\Sigma f(x_i) = 1$. In practice, probability functions are not

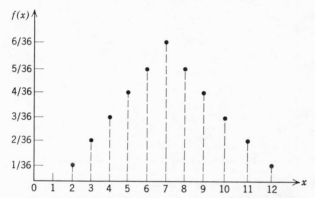

FIG. I-2   An illustrative graph of a probability function. The experiment consists in throwing two dice. Its outcomes correspond to points in a sample space $S = [(1, 1), (1, 2), \ldots, (6, 6)]$ containing 36 elements. This sample space is the domain of the random variable X. The range of X is the set of the sums of the two dice. The range thus consists of 11 values of x of X, namely, 2, 3, \ldots, 12. This same set of 11 numbers is the domain of the probability function f. The range of the probability function, $f(x) = P(X = x)$, is composed of the values given on the ordinate of the graph. The length of the vertical line from the abscissa to the point with coordinates $[x, f(x)]$ represents the probability of the event $X = x$.

usually listed as sets of ordered pairs; they are more conveniently represented by a table, or by a formula for $f(x)$. We shall also have occasion to represent probability functions graphically. An illustrative graph in shown in Fig. I-2.

I.3.3   Distribution functions

It may avoid some confusion if we observe that the terms *probability function* and *probability distribution* are distinguishable, though they are commonly used interchangeably. Technically, the probability *function* lists the probability for each of the elementary events, or sample points, and the probability *distribution* assigns probabilities to each of the possible events, that is, to sets of sample points. Equation I.12 defines the probability distribution of the random variable X if the aggregate of all sample points on which X assumes the fixed value x_i is considered to form the event that $X = x_i$. It is more important to distinguish both of these terms

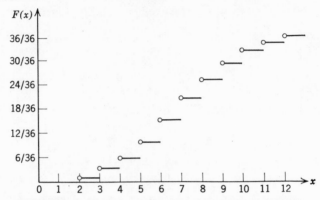

FIG. I-3 An illustrative graph of a distribution function. This distribution function represents the dice experiment discussed in connection with Fig. I-2. The abscissas of the two figures are identical. The ordinate of this figure gives the cumulative probabilities $F(x) = P(X < x)$.

from the term *distribution function*. The distribution function states the probability that a random variable takes on a value *less than or equal to* a prescribed number x. Thus, the (cumulative) distribution function F is defined by

$$F(x) = P(X < x) = \sum_{x_i > x} f(x_i) \tag{I.13}$$

We observe that the distribution function is a nondecreasing function which tends to 0 as $x \to -\infty$ and to 1 as $x \to \infty$, and that the distribution function of a variable can be calculated from its probability distribution and vice versa. Figure I-3 shows an illustrative graph of a distribution function.

Graphs similar to those shown in Figs. I-2 and I-3 can be constructed for cases in which the variable x is continuous. If x is continuous, then, in each type of graph, a line is drawn connecting the points. The probability function of a continuous variable is termed the *probability density function* or, simply, the *density function*.

I.3.4 Joint probability functions

We now consider two random variables defined on the same sample space in order to indicate that the general definitions and theorems discussed earlier apply to probability functions of random variables. The two random variables are denoted X and Y, and the values which they assume are denoted, respectively, by $x_1, x_2, \ldots$, and $y_1, y_2, \ldots$; the corresponding probability functions are $[f(x_i)]$ and $[g(y_j)]$.

The event $X = x_i$ and $Y = y_j$ has a probability denoted by $P(X = x_i, Y = y_j)$.

The function

$$P(X = x_i, Y = y_j) = p(x_i, y_j)$$

is called the joint probability function of the random variables X and Y.

It can be displayed in the form of a double-entry table which lists the values of x_i on the left side, and the values of y_j along the top. The cell entries $p(x_i, y_j)$ have the properties:

$$p(x_i, y_j) \geq 0 \quad \text{and} \quad \sum_{i,j} p(x_i, y_j) = 1$$

The (marginal) probability distributions of X and Y are obtained, respectively, by adding the probabilities in individual rows and columns, for

$$\sum_j p(x_i, y_j) = f(x_i)$$

and

$$\sum_i p(x_i, y_j) = g(y_j)$$

From the definition of conditional probability given in Eq. I.4,

$$P(X = x_i \mid Y = y_j) = f(x_i \mid y_j) = \frac{p(x_i, y_j)}{g(y_j)} \tag{I.14}$$

Again, it is possible to define *independence* in terms of the definition of conditional probability. That is, X is independent of Y if

$$f(x_i \mid y_j) = f(x_i)$$

However, it is again preferable to say that X and Y are independent random variables if and only if

$$p(x_i, y_j) = f(x_i)g(y_j) \tag{I.15}$$

If Eq. I.15 holds, the joint probability table has the form of a multiplication table; the cell entry is the product of the probability in the row margin and the probability in the column margin.

In many cases of interest, X and Y are *dependent;* the joint probability table does not have the form of a multiplication table, and the conditional probability $f(x_i \mid y_j)$ differs from the probability $f(x_i)$. Then an inference about the values of X can be drawn from the values of Y and vice versa. The dependence is strongest when Y is a function of X, or when the value of Y is uniquely determined by the value of X; in each row of the table all of the entries but one are zero. Note that whereas it is always possible to derive the probability functions of X and Y from their joint probability function, it is possible to construct the joint probability table from the marginal probabilities of X and Y only if X and Y are independent. All of these notions are naturally extended to the case where more than two random variables are defined on the same sample space.

I.3.5 Identical distributions

As indicated, random variables and their probability functions depend upon the existence of an underlying sample space and the assignment of probabilities to the elementary events of the sample space. It is permissible, however, and common practice, to make no mention of a sample space or a probability assignment in discussing probability functions. One reason for this is that infinitely many different random variables, defined on different sample spaces, can have the same probability function. Definitions or theorems that depend only on the probability function of a random variable apply therefore to any one of the infinite number of identically distributed random variables. Moreover, it can be shown that if a function f has the properties $f(x_i) \geq 0$ and $\Sigma f(x_i) = 1$, then there exists a finite sample space, an acceptable assignment of probabilities to the elementary events of this sample space, and a random variable having this sample space as its domain, such that f is the probability function of the random variable. Thus, if we are given a function with these properties, we can proceed confidently with no need to be specific about its underpinnings. It is also the case that the original sample space of a random variable X, which assumes the values $x_1, x_2, \ldots$, is in effect supplanted by a new sample space that consists of the sample points $x_1, x_2, \ldots$. Thus, specifying a probability function is equivalent to specifying a sample space whose points are real numbers. In fact, although it would be a conceptual hindrance, it is possible to develop the theory of probability with reference only to sample spaces defined by probability functions.

I.3.6 Expected values: the mean

It is often convenient to summarize some of the properties of a random variable by means of a few numbers that can be computed from its probability function. The two most important summary numbers are the *mean*, denoted $E(X)$, and the *variance*, denoted var (X).

By definition:

> Given a random variable X which assumes the values $x_1, x_2, \ldots$ with probabilities $f(x_1), f(x_2), \ldots$, the mean of X is defined by

$$E(X) = \sum x_i f(x_i) \tag{I.16}$$

In words, the mean of a random variable is the sum of the products of each possible value of the variable and its corresponding probability. It is, then, a *weighted average;* the values of the random variable are weighted by their probabilities of occurrence just as, when obtaining the weighted average of a column of figures, the different figures are weighted by their frequency of occurrence.

The use of E to denote the mean comes from studies of games of chance, in which a player's mean gain was termed his (mathematical) *expectation*. The mean is also sometimes referred to as the *expected value*, a term that is misleading since the mean may well differ from all of the possible values that the random variable can assume. It is desirable to define, in the context of this discussion, an important random variable that is used in Chapter 1. This is the *expected value of a decision*, denoted $E(V)$. The value of a decision having an uncertain outcome, whose possible outcomes differ in desirability, is defined by analogy to the foregoing as the sum of the products of probability of outcome and desirability of outcome. Denoting the desirability, or the value, of the various possible outcomes by V_i, and the probabilities of the various outcomes by P_i, we have

$$E(V) = \sum V_i P_i \tag{I.17}$$

A common objective in decision problems is to make decisions in such a way that the quantity $E(V)$ is maximized.

We are often interested in random variables that are transformations of the random variable X under consideration. It is possible to compute the mean of the probability function of such a related variable directly from the probability function of X, without first determining the probability function of the related random variable. It can be verified that if $Y = g(X)$, then the mean of the new random variable is given by

$$E(Y) = E[g(X)] = \sum g(x_i) f(x_i) \tag{I.18}$$

It follows that if a and b are any numerical constants,

$$E(aX + b) = aE(X) + b \tag{I.19}$$

Thus

$$E(X + b) = E(X) + b$$

and

$$E(aX) = aE(X)$$

That is, adding a constant to every value of a random variable has the same effect as adding this number to the mean of the random variable, and multiplying every value of a random variable by a constant has the same effect as multiplying the mean by that constant.

I.3.7 Expected values: the variance

The mean of a random variable gives us information about the location of the middle, or the center of mass, of the probability function. It summarizes the average result of many repetitions of an experiment. The summary measure of a random variable called the *variance* tells us something about how the outcomes vary from one performance of the experiment to another, about their spread or dispersion. In particular,

If X is a random variable with mean $E(X) = \mu$, then the variance of X is the expected value of $(X - \mu)^2$, that is

$$\text{var}(X) = E[(X - \mu)^2] = \sum (x_i - \mu)^2 f(x_i) \qquad (\text{I.20})$$

In words, the variance of X is the mean squared deviation of X from its mean. Its positive square root is called the *standard deviation* of X. The standard deviation is denoted σ. It provides a measure of variability in the same units as the values of X; for this reason its use is often to be preferred to the use of $\text{var}(X) = \sigma^2$, whose units are squares of the units of X.

An alternative formula for the variance which facilitates its computation is

$$\text{var}(X) = E(X^2) - [E(X)]^2 = E(X^2) - \mu^2 \qquad (\text{I.21})$$

According to this formula the variance of X may be obtained by subtracting the square of the mean of X from the mean of the square of X.

In the discussion of the mean we considered the effect of adding or subtracting a constant, and the effect of multiplying or dividing by a constant (Eq. I.19). Adding or subtracting changes the location of the origin, whereas multiplying or dividing changes the unit of measurement, or the scale. With respect to the variance, adding a constant to every value of a random variable has no effect, but multiplying each value by a constant multiplies the variance by the square of that constant. That is,

$$\text{var}(aX + b) = a^2 \text{var}(X) \qquad (\text{I.22})$$

so that
$$\text{var}\,(X + b) = \text{var}\,(X)$$
and
$$\text{var}\,(aX) = a^2\,\text{var}\,(X)$$

It is clear, from the definition of the standard deviation, that multiplying each value of a random variable by a constant multiplies the standard deviation by the absolute value of that constant.

I.3.8 Standardized random variables

Since the choice of origin and unit of measurement is often arbitrary, it is sometimes convenient to take the mean as the origin and the standard deviation as the unit. This is achieved by defining the random variable X^* as follows:

$$X^* = \frac{X - \mu}{\sigma} \tag{I.23}$$

This random variable X^* has mean 0 and variance (and standard deviation) 1. It is called the *standardized* (or sometimes the *normalized*) random variable corresponding to X. Considerable use is made of such dimensionless quantities throughout this book.

I.3.9 Sums and products of random variables

Consider again two random variables X and Y defined on the same sample space. Given such random variables X and Y, then any function $h(X, Y)$ is also a random variable. Of particular importance are the random variables corresponding to the sum of $X + Y$ and to the product XY. The probability functions of these random variables can be obtained from the joint probability function of X and Y. In general, the probability function of $h(X, Y)$ is determined simply by collecting all possible pairs of X and Y values that lead to the same value of $h(X, Y)$. However, by analogy with Eq. I.18, it is possible to compute the expected value $E[h(X, Y)]$ directly from the joint probability table of X and Y without first obtaining the probability function of $h(X, Y)$. That is, if X and Y have a joint probability function p, then

$$E[h(X, Y)] = \sum h(x_i, y_j)p(x_i, y_j) \tag{I.24}$$

It can be verified on the basis of results given above that:

The mean of the sum of two random variables is equal to the sum of their means;

$$E(X + Y) = E(X) + E(Y) \tag{I.25}$$

This result holds for weighted sums, and for any finite number of random variables.

It can also be verified that:

The mean of the product of two independent random variables is equal to the product of their means;

$$E(XY) = E(X)E(Y) \qquad (I.26)$$

Note that Eq. I.25 holds for any random variables, whereas Eq. I.26 is restricted to *independent* random variables. Note also that the converse of the theorem on products is false; the multiplication rule may hold for *dependent* random variables. The multiplication rule does hold for any number of mutually independent random variables.

If X and Y are independent random variables, then

In words:
$$\text{var}\,(X + Y) = \text{var}\,(X) + \text{var}\,(Y) \qquad (I.27)$$

The variance of the sum of two independent random variables is equal to the sum of their variances.

This result holds for weighted sums, and for any finite number of *independent* random variables.

The detection experiments of principal concern in this book contain a large number of repetitions of the same trial. It is often convenient to regard these repetitions as independent. There is thus occasion to consider the distribution of the sum of many identically distributed variables. It follows from the immediately preceding discussion that, if $X_1, X_2, \ldots, X_n$ are independently and identically distributed random variables with means μ_X and variances $\sigma_X{}^2$, and if $T = X_1 + X_2 + \cdots + X_n$, then

$$\mu_T = n\mu_X \qquad (I.28)$$

and

$$\sigma_T{}^2 = n\sigma_X{}^2 \qquad (I.29)$$

In words:

The distribution of the sum of n independent and identically distributed random variables has a mean equal to n times the mean and a variance equal to n times the variance.

I.3.10   Relation to statistical theory

We are now in a position to consider some applications of probability theory to statistical theory. It was mentioned earlier that the two theories are complementary. Probability theory provides mathematical models which can be used to predict the likely outcomes of an experiment. Given the actual outcomes of an experiment, statistical theory can be used to choose among alternative mathematical models. Specifically, if we know the probability function of a random variable under study in a population, then probability theory will enable us to specify the various possible values that can arise in a sample drawn from the population, and their probabilities. When it is not feasible to determine the probability function for a population, statistical theory will enable us to make inferences about this probability function on the basis of the content of samples drawn from the population.

I.3.11   Statistics: sample mean and variance

Given a sample of values of a random variable, a *statistic* is any function of the sample values. The content of a sample can be summarized by statistics in much the same way as characteristics of a population are described. The statistics of principal importance are those analogous to the two expected values that have been discussed. They are the *sample mean* $\bar{x}$ and the *sample variance* s^2.

The sample mean is a weighted average like the population mean. The weights in the case of a sample, however, are proportions or relative frequencies of occurrence rather than probabilities of occurrence. Thus, in a sample of n values of x_i,

$$\bar{x} = \frac{1}{n} \sum x_i n_i \tag{I.30}$$

Similarly, the sample variance is the average of the squared deviations weighted by their frequencies of occurrence:

$$s^2 = \frac{1}{n} \sum (x_i - \bar{x})^2 n_i \tag{I.31}$$

The *sample standard deviation* s is the positive square root of the sample variance.

An experiment containing many independent repetitions of the same trial may be regarded as an instance of repeated sampling from n independent and identically distributed random variables X_i. A sample value x_i is an observed value of a random variable X_i, and the sample mean (for ungrouped observations),

$$\bar{x} = \frac{x_1 + x_2 + \cdots + x_n}{n} = \frac{1}{n} \sum x_i \tag{I.32}$$

is an observed value of the random variable,

$$\bar{X} = \frac{X_1 + X_2 + \cdots + X_n}{n} = \frac{1}{n} \sum X_i \tag{I.33}$$

Given n independent and identically distributed random variables X_i, each with mean μ_X and variance $\sigma_X{}^2$, and with a mean as defined by Eq. I.33, it can be shown that

$$\mu_{\bar{X}} = \mu_X \tag{I.34}$$

and

$$\sigma_{\bar{X}}{}^2 = \frac{\sigma_X{}^2}{n} \tag{I.35}$$

That is, the expected value of the sample mean is equal to the population mean, and the variance of the sample mean is inversely proportional to the sample size. Although the values of X and $\bar{X}$ have the same mean, the values of $\bar{X}$ have a smaller variance, and their variance decreases as the sample size increases. Chapter 9 presents several experimental applications of the fact that the standard deviation of the sample mean is inversely proportional to the square root of the number of observations,

$$\sigma_{\bar{X}} = \frac{\sigma_X}{\sqrt{n}} \tag{I.36}$$

The application of these results to statistical problems usually requires that more be known of the probability function of $\bar{X}$ than just its mean and standard deviation; this requirement leads to the formulation of problems in terms of continuous random variables. Specifically, in many situations of interest, the additional information about the probability function of $\bar{X}$ is available because this function approximates some probability function which is known in detail. There are a few other concepts to consider before we conclude with a discussion of some specific probability functions.

I.2.12 Law of large numbers

Some additional theoretical results concerning sample size justify a procedure employed in the application of probability theory to empirical experiments—the procedure of taking proportions of events in repeated independent trials as estimates of probabilities. A theorem due to Chebyshev guarantees that, for any random variable, no more than the fraction $1/h^2$ of the probability will be assigned to points more than h standard deviations away from the mean. Chebyshev's theorem, together with the relationships between sample and population means and variances given in Eqs. I.34 and I.35, provides a proof for one form of the so-called *law of large numbers*. According to this law, by taking a sufficient number of sample values, the probability that the sample mean differs from the population mean by less than some arbitrarily small constant can be made as close to unity as desired. According to one application of this law, the sample size can be taken sufficiently large so that the proportion of times the event A occurs in a sample of identical trials will be as close as desired to the probability $P(A)$ of the event A.

It is well known that the interpretation of probabilities as proportions dates back to the beginning of the primitive theory of probability, as far back as the work of Bernoulli in the early 1700's. However, here is an example of the fact that several results of the primitive theory can be incorporated in a strictly mathematical theory by means of some form of the law of large numbers. Because taking observed proportions as estimates of probabilities is essential to the development of probability models for real behavior, the rigorous support of what was at first only a phenomenological interpretation is very welcome.

I.3.13 Covariance and correlation

Consider briefly the interrelated concepts of *covariance* and *correlation*. It was asserted in Eq. I.27 that, for independent random variables X and Y,

$$\text{var}(X + Y) = \text{var}(X) + \text{var}(Y) \tag{I.27}$$

The more general result, one which holds as well for dependent variables, has an additional term which vanishes when X and Y are independent. That is,

$$\text{var}(X + Y) = \text{var}(X) + \text{var}(Y) + 2E[(X - \mu_x)(Y - \mu_y)] \tag{I.37}$$

The last term is twice the number defined as the *covariance* of X and Y:

$$\text{cov}(X, Y) = E[(X - \mu_x)(Y - \mu_y)] \tag{I.38}$$

Thus

$$\text{var}(X + Y) = \text{var}(X) + \text{var}(Y) + 2\,\text{cov}(X, Y) \tag{I.39}$$

Generalizing to more than two variables:

$$\text{var}(X_1 + \cdots + X_n) = \sum_{i=1}^{n} \text{var}(X_i) + 2 \sum_{\substack{\text{all } i,j \\ i<j}} \text{cov}(X_i, X_j) \tag{I.40}$$

It is seen that the covariance is aptly named; it measures the extent to which random variables vary together. It is positive when the variables vary directly with one another, negative when they vary inversely, and zero when they are independent. However, since the covariance can vary over a large range, it is convenient to define it for standardized random variables as given by Eq. I.23. In this form it is called the *correlation coefficient* and denoted $\rho(X, Y)$. Thus

$$\rho(X, Y) = \text{cov}(X^*, Y^*) = \frac{\text{cov}(X, Y)}{\sigma_x \sigma_y} \tag{I.41}$$

The correlation coefficient is bounded by -1 and $+1$.

It must be noted that whereas $\rho(X, Y) = 0$ whenever X and Y are independent, the converse is not true; it is possible for the correlation coefficient to be 0 even when there is a direct functional dependence of Y and X. It follows that the correlation coefficient is not a general measure of dependence between X and Y. In fact, it is meaningful only to the extent that the relationship between X and Y is linear.

I.3.14   The normal distribution

The discussion of random variables to this point applies to all random variables, without regard for the specific form of their probability distributions. Applications of probability theory make considerable use of the fact that a few key distributions occur in a wide variety of measurement problems. These are the *binomial distribution*, the *Poisson distribution*, and the *normal* or *Gaussian distribution*. The normal distribution is the most important distribution in probability and statistics, and it is the most important for the application of probability and statistical theory to detection problems. The next few paragraphs sketch its major properties.

Of the three distributions mentioned, the normal distribution is the only continuous one. As indicated earlier, when dealing with continuous distributions, probabilities are not assigned to single points, but to all of the possible values in an interval of the real line. These probabilities are represented as areas over intervals. For the normal distribution, the probabilities are assigned by means of the normal density function, or the *normal curve*.

The normal or Gaussian probability density function is given by the equation:

$$f(x) = \frac{1}{\sigma\sqrt{2\pi}} e^{-\frac{1}{2}\left(\frac{x-m}{\sigma}\right)^2} \tag{I.42}$$

where m is mean or first moment of the distribution, and σ is the standard deviation or second moment about the mean. A graph of a normal or Gaussian density function is shown in Figure I-4. In this figure the standard deviation is unity and the ordinate is scaled as deviations from the mean. The total area of the curve is, of course, one. As can be seen either in Fig. I-4 or in Eq. I.42, the curve is symmetric about the mean.

If the mean of x is zero and the variance unity, we have, by definition, a *standard normal variable*. This we denote $\phi(x)$:

$$\phi(x) = \frac{1}{\sqrt{2\pi}} e^{-x^2/2} \tag{I.43}$$

We also define

$$\Phi(k) = \int_{k}^{+\infty} \phi(x)\, dx \tag{I.44}$$

which is the complement of the form usually tabulated. (See, for example, Abramowitz and Stegun, *Handbook of Mathematical Functions*, Dover Publications: New York, 1965, page 966.) The area between $\pm\frac{2}{3}$ on the standard normal variable is 0.50, the area between ± 1 is 0.68, and the area between ± 2 is 0.96.

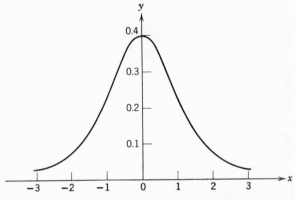

FIG. I-4   The standard normal curve.

The standard normal distribution would be of great importance if it only facilitated the calculation of probabilities for the many measured distributions which are approximately normal. But its importance extends far beyond this. It is often possible to transform variables which are not normally distributed into variables which are. In fact, with the proper adjustment, both the binomial and the Poisson distributions approach normality as the sample size increases, and the standard normal curve provides a good working approximation to these two distributions even for moderate, realistic sample sizes.

I.3.15   Central limit theorem

That the binomial and Poisson distributions can be approximated by the normal distribution is a consequence of a more general *central limit theorem*. According to one version of the central limit theorem, sums of independent and identically distributed random variables, normal or not, are approximately normal. If the mean and variance of the common distribution are known, probabilities for the distribution of the sum can be accurately computed from the normal table without knowing the exact

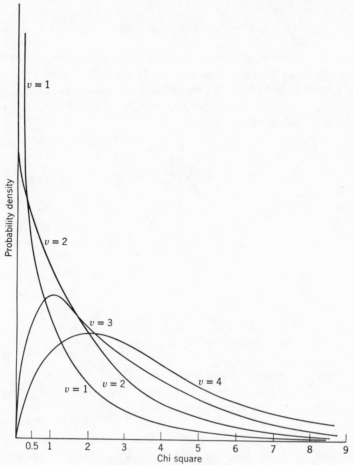

FIG. I-5 Chi-square distribution for various degrees of freedom, v.

distribution of the sum. This result makes practical the application of probability theory to experiments which consist of independent repetitions of the same trial; it is basic to repeated measurement in the sciences.

I.3.16 The chi-square distribution

The chi-square (χ^2) distribution is also used in applications of detection theory. Let $x_1, x_2, \ldots, x_v$ be independent standard normal variables. Then

$$X^2 = \sum_{i=1}^{v} x_i^2 \tag{I.45}$$

will follow a chi-square distribution with v degrees of freedom. The probability that X^2 will be less than χ^2 is

$$P(\chi^2 \mid v) = \left[2^{v/2} \Gamma\left(\frac{v}{2}\right) \right]^{-1} \int_0^{\chi^2} t^{(v/2)-1} e^{-t/2} \, dt \qquad (\text{I.46})$$

$$(0 < \chi^2 < \infty)$$

where Γ is the Gamma function.*

Figure I-5 shows the chi-square distribution for several values of v. Despite the rather unwieldy appearance of the density function, the mean and variance of the distribution are simply defined:

$$E(\chi^2 \mid v) = v$$

$$\text{var}\,(\chi^2 \mid v) = 2v$$

According to the previous section, the sum of independent random variables, whether normal or not, approaches a normal distribution. Equation I.45 represents a sum of nonnormal variables; in fact, each is χ^2 with 1 degree of freedom. But the central limit theorem suggests that, for large v, $P(\chi^2 \mid v)$ will become normal. For $v = 30$, Fig. I-6 shows a χ^2 variable and a normal variable, where the mean of the normal variable is v

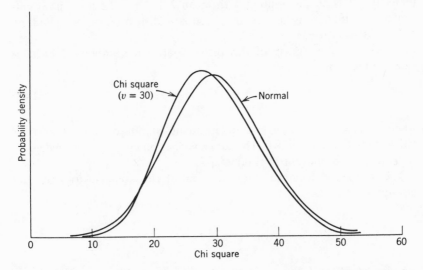

FIG. I-6 A normal variable, and a chi-square variable with 30 degrees of freedom.

* $\Gamma(\tfrac{1}{2}) = \sqrt{\pi}$, $\Gamma(1) = 1$, $\Gamma(\tfrac{3}{2}) = \tfrac{1}{2}\Gamma(\tfrac{1}{2}) = \tfrac{1}{2}\sqrt{\pi}$, $\Gamma(2) = 1$ $\Gamma(\tfrac{5}{2}) = \tfrac{3}{2} \cdot \tfrac{1}{2}\sqrt{\pi}$, and, in general, $\Gamma(n + 1) = n\Gamma(n)$ if n is integer and $n > 0$.

and the variance is $2v$. As can be seen, the normal distribution provides a very satisfactory approximation for the χ^2 distribution, if the number of degrees of freedom is large.

I.3.17   The noncentral chi-square distribution

An important near relative to the χ^2 distribution is the noncentral χ^2 distribution. The distribution function is defined as

$$P(\chi'^2 \mid v, \lambda) = \sum_{j=0}^{\infty} e^{-\lambda/2} \frac{(\lambda/2)^j}{j!} P(\chi^2 \mid v + 2j) \tag{I.47}$$

where χ'^2 is the noncentral variable, v is the number of degrees of freedom, and λ is the noncentral parameter ($\lambda > 0$). This distribution is basically a sum of χ^2 distributions weighted by the term

$$\left[e^{-\lambda/2} \frac{(\lambda/2)^j}{j!} \right]$$

This weight is the probability density function for exactly j events occurring under the Poisson distribution with mean $\lambda/2$. Thus the noncentral chi-square distribution is a sum of chi-square distributions, weighted by Poisson density terms.

A more intuitive grasp of this distribution can be obtained by considering the sum

$$y = \sum_{i=1}^{n-1} x_i^2 + (x_n + \sqrt{\bar{\lambda}})^2 \tag{I.48}$$

where x_i, $i = 1, 2, \ldots, n$, are independent, standard, normal deviates and λ is the constant, $\lambda > 0$. The sum y is distributed as χ'^2 with n degrees of freedom and noncentral parameter λ.

The mean and variance of the noncentral chi-square distribution are also quite simple:

$$E(\chi'^2) = v + \lambda$$

$$\text{var}(\chi'^2) = 2v + 4\lambda$$

I.3.18   The bivariate normal distribution

Often we have two normal or Gaussian variables and we are interested in their joint density function. Consider two normal deviates, x and y, having means m_x and m_y and variance $\sigma_x{}^2$ and $\sigma_y{}^2$. Let ρ be the correlation between the two variables. The joint density function of x and y is then

$$f(x, y) = \frac{1}{2\pi\sigma_x\sigma_y(1 - \rho^2)^{\frac{1}{2}}}$$

$$\times \exp\left\{-\frac{1}{2}\left[\left(\frac{x - m_x}{\sigma_x}\right)^2 - 2\rho\left(\frac{x - m_x}{\sigma_x}\right)\left(\frac{y - m_y}{\sigma_y}\right) + \left(\frac{y - m_y}{\sigma_y}\right)^2\right]\right\}$$

(I.49)

This density is largest at m_x, m_y. If ρ is zero, then the density is an ellipse centered at m_x, m_y and with major and minor axes determined by σ_x

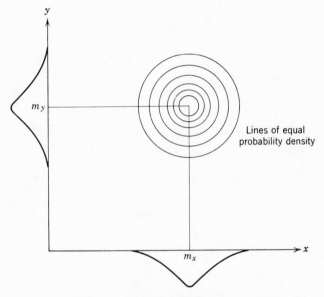

FIG. I-7   A bivariate normal distribution. This is the joint density function of two normal variables, x and y, with means m_x and m_y. Equal variance and zero correlation are assumed in this representation.

and σ_y respectively. A convenient way to represent a two-dimensional distribution is to depict both variables and to indicate the density by lines, tracing changes in density as elevation on a topographical map. Figure I-7 shows such a representation of a bivariate normal distribution, with equal variance and zero correlation.

This concludes the review of the basic concepts of probability theory. The probability concepts applied in this book are, for the most part, precisely the ones treated here; occasionally, a straightforward extension of these basic ideas is developed. We can turn now to the application of probability to the theory of statistical decision in Chapter 1. In Chapter 2 statistical decision theory is used to analyze some common detection problems.

APPENDIX II

Some Basic Concepts
of Waveform Analysis

II.1   INTRODUCTION

The following sections provide a brief introduction to the analysis of signal and noise waveforms and introduce some related terms. This appendix will acquaint the reader with the major definitions and some of the most important results. More extensive and detailed expositions are cited at the end of the relevant sections.

The topic is one of considerable depth and complexity, and many of the issues involved are rather subtle. It is impossible to recommend a single source. Mathematicians are dissatisfied with an engineering treatment and practical persons usually lose patience with mathematical niceties. The references mentioned in the discussion of the individual topics should be consulted for more detail and precision. We present the following as a brief overview for those either unacquainted with the concepts or desiring a small refresher.

II.2   SINUSOIDS

Imagine a pen mounted firmly on the edge of a wheel turning at a uniform rate. See Fig. II-1. Suppose that the wheel turns above a strip of paper that moves to the left at a uniform velocity. The picture traced by such a device is a sinusoid. On the left of Fig. II-1 the tracing has been superimposed on a grid; the coordinates of this grid are t, for time, and y, for displacement. Consider the middle of the wheel as zero displacement and the time at which the picture starts as zero time. Then the picture

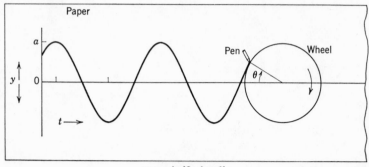

$$y = a \sin [2\pi ft + \theta]$$

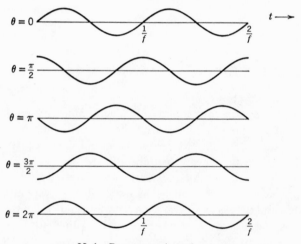

FIG. II-1 Representation of a sinusoid.

traced by the wheel can always be described by three parameters and is of the following form:

$$y(a, f, \theta) = a \sin [2\pi ft + \theta] \tag{II.1}$$

where a is called the amplitude of the waveform and is related to the size of the wheel, and where f is the frequency or number of times the wheel rotates per unit of time. The phase parameter, θ, specifies the initial position of the pen at time zero. For the tracing shown in Fig. II-1, the pen was initially ($t = 0$) in about the same position it occupies at present.

The natural measure for amplitude is a distance: the radius a of the wheel holding the pen. The natural measure for frequency is cycles per second: the rate at which the wheel rotates. The natural measure for phase is an angle: the displacement between the radius and a fixed reference point. The phase angle, θ, is measured as the number of radians between a radius drawn to the pen at $t = 0$ and a horizontal line through the center of the wheel. With angular measure in the range 0 to 2π, we can represent all possible phases; some examples are illustrated in the lower half of Fig. II-1. We are implicitly assuming, in this discussion, a clockwise rotation of the wheel. A negative phase angle would simply refer to the angle measured using counterclockwise rotation. Since radians are ratios of two distances (and are length divided by the radius), the angle is a pure number.

Another way of viewing a sinusoid uses a familiar trigonometric identity to expand Eq. II.1 into a sine component and a cosine component:

$$\sin (\alpha + \beta) = \sin \alpha \cos \beta + \cos \alpha \sin \beta$$

Then

$$y(t) = A \sin 2\pi ft + B \cos 2\pi ft \qquad \text{(II.2)}$$

where $A = a \cos \theta$, $B = a \sin \theta$, $\theta = \tan^{-1} B/A$. Thus a sinusoidal wave can also be considered as the addition of a sine and cosine wave, in which the value of θ determines the relative weight of the two components.

II.3 ADDITION OF TWO SINUSOIDS OF THE SAME FREQUENCY

The second representation of a sinusoidal wave, Eq. II.2, is especially useful in determining the form of the curve that results from adding two sinusoids of the same frequency. Let the two sinusoids be

$$y_1(t) = a_1 \cos \theta \sin 2\pi ft + a_1 \sin \theta \cos 2\pi ft$$

and

$$y_2(t) = a_2 \cos \varphi \sin 2\pi ft + a_2 \sin \varphi \cos 2\pi ft \qquad \text{(II.3)}$$

The sum is

$$y_1(t) + y_2(t) = (a_1 \cos \theta + a_2 \cos \varphi) \sin 2\pi ft$$
$$+ (a_1 \sin \theta + a_2 \sin \varphi) \cos 2\pi ft \quad \text{(II.4)}$$

The terms within the brackets bear an obvious relation to the addition of two vectors. Consider the vector diagram shown in Fig. II-2. Here we have associated the amplitude of the cosine component with the x axis and the amplitude of the sine component with the y axis. The two sinusoids are thus represented by the vectors A_1 and A_2. The projections of the vector A_1 on the x and y axes specify a phase angle, and the same thing is true of A_2. The resultant $A_1 + A_2$ is drawn, giving us the amplitude of the combined waveform, and the projections on the x and y axes give the resultant phase. The combined motion is identical to that of a single sinewave whose amplitude and phase can be determined from the simple sum expressed in Eq. II.4. The utility of this representation is obvious when we consider that the vector representation can be extended to generate the resultant of the sum of an arbitrary number of sinusoids of the same frequency. The same rules are applied as each new component is added to the resultant of the previous additions. The resultant is simply another sinusoid that can be thought of as a rotating wheel in the clockwise direction with a

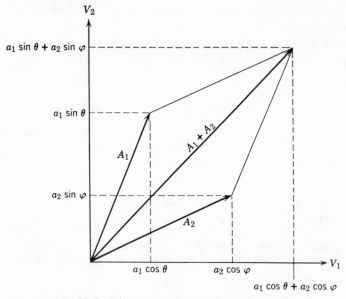

FIG. II-2   Diagram showing addition of two vectors.

uniform velocity. The y projection of each component is the component displacement as a function of time. These component displacements are summed to yield the displacement of the resultant. Thinking of this representation, we find that at $t = 0$ the sine part of the combined waveform is zero, and the cosine part is unity times $a_1 \sin \theta + a_2 \sin \varphi$, as it should be. A quarter of a period later the sine part is unity times $a_1 \cos \theta + a_2 \cos \varphi$ and the cosine part is zero, as it should be. This is, in fact, the basis for the wheel construction used in Fig. II-1.* Almost

* The result of adding two sinusoids of the same frequency could be related to Fig. II-1 if we assume that a second wheel is mounted with a center located at the position of the pen in the figure. Suppose that the second wheel has a pen attached to its rim and both wheels revolve simultaneously. If the frequencies of the two wheels were different, then epicycles would be generated; however, if the frequencies were the same, then another sinusoidal wave would be drawn, and its motion would be the same as the rotation of $A_1 + A_2$ as given in Fig. II-2.

any book on acoustics or communication theory gives a more complete treatment of sinusoidal motion. Chapter 2 of Volume I of Lord Rayleigh's (J. W. Strutt's) *The Theory of Sound* (1894) is particularly clear.

II.4 APPROXIMATION OF A FUNCTION

Before continuing our discussion of sinusoids, let us consider another problem, that of representing some function $f(t)$, $0 < t < T$, by a set of other functions $g_1(t)$, $g_2(t)$, . . . , $g_n(t)$. What we should like to do is to approximate a finite segment of a function $f(t)$ by a linear combination of the g functions. That is,

$$f(t) \approx \sum_{i=1}^{n} a_i g_i(t) \tag{II.5}$$

where the a_i are appropriately chosen constants. Now what do we mean by "appropriately chosen"? We usually mean that the integral from 0 to T of the squared difference between $f(t)$ and our approximation, $\sum_{i=1}^{n} a_i g_i(t)$, will be as small as possible. That is, consider:

$$S = \int_0^T \left[f(t) - \sum_{i=1}^{n} a_i g_i(t) \right]^2 dt \tag{II.6}$$

We want to choose $a_1, a_2, \ldots, a_n$ such that S is a minimum. This is a *least-squares* formulation and is similar to finding the best fitting *regression* line between $g_i(t)$ and $f(t)$. To determine the values of the constant a_i, we should first determine the partial derivatives of S with respect to a_i; the minimum occurs when all these derivations are simultaneously zero. The restriction implies the following identities after differentiation:

$$\int_0^T f(t) g_1(t)\, dt = a_1 \int_0^T [g_1(t)]^2\, dt$$
$$+ a_2 \int_0^T g_1(t) g_2(t)\, dt, \ldots, a_n \int_0^T g_1(t) g_n(t)\, dt$$
$$\cdot$$
$$\cdot \tag{II.7}$$
$$\cdot$$
$$\int_0^T f(t) g_n(t)\, dt = a_1 \int_0^T g_1(t) g_n(t)\, dt$$
$$+ a_2 \int_0^T g_1(t) g_n(t)\, dt, \ldots, a_n \int_0^T [g_n(t)]^2\, dt$$

Remember that $f(t)$ and $g_i(t)$ are given; thus these equations must be solved for the constants $a_1, a_2, \ldots, a_n$. The solution is possible because there are n linear equations in n unknowns, although it might be laborious to carry it out. Suppose, however, that two additional conditions were met by the set of functions $g_1(t), g_2(t), \ldots, g_n(t)$:

$$\int_0^T g_i(t)g_j(t)\,dt = 0 \qquad \text{Condition 1}$$

$$\text{for all } i \neq j$$

$$\int_0^T [g_i(t)]^2\,dt = 1 \qquad \text{Condition 2}$$

$$\text{for all } i$$

The first condition is known as an *orthogonality* restriction. The functions $g_i(t)$ and $g_j(t)$ are said to be orthogonal in the interval 0 to T when Condition 1 applies. It is analogous to independence, or more precisely lack of correlation, of two variables. The second condition is expressed by saying that the functions are *normalized;* hence the set of functions $g_i(t)$ are called *orthonormal functions.*

Given these conditions, the least-squares solutions for the weights in Eq. II.5 are

$$a_i = \int_0^T f(t)g_i(t)\,dt \qquad (II.8)$$

This expression also has a name. The integral is the *cross correlation* between the two functions $f(t)$ and $g_i(t)$. One form of detecting a signal is to compare a received waveform, for instance $f(t)$, with a stored or expected signal waveform, say $g_i(t)$. If the integral of the cross product is large, we may decide that $f(t)$ is indeed a signal and not noise; if the integral of the cross product is very small, we may suspect that $f(t)$ is unrelated to the function $g_i(t)$. Such a detection scheme is called a *cross-correlation detector.*

Let us return to our problem of approximating $f(t)$ with a linear sum of orthogonal functions $g_1(t), g_2(t), \ldots, g_n(t)$. As yet we have simply determined the best constants $a_1, a_2, \ldots, a_n$ to achieve the least-squares objective. We have not yet considered whether the approximation is very good in any absolute sense, or whether additional functions, $g_{n+1}(t)$, $g_{n+2}(t), \ldots, g_{n+m}(t)$, could drive the error to zero. These problems are not discussed here. They depend on the nature of the function $f(t)$ and the set of approximation functions, $g_i(t)$. It should come as no surprise that one set of orthogonal functions used in such approximations is a set of sine and cosine terms. The resulting series is called a *Fourier series.*

Specifically, let

$$g_i^1(t) = \sqrt{2/T} \cos 2\pi \left(\frac{i}{T}\right) t \tag{II.9}$$

$$g_i^2(t) = \sqrt{2/T} \sin 2\pi \left(\frac{i}{T}\right) t \qquad i = 1, 2, \ldots, n$$

Then we can easily show that

$$\int_0^T [g_i^k(t)]^2 \, dt = 1 \qquad \text{for all } i \quad k = 1, 2$$

$$\int_0^T g_i^k(t) g_j^k(t) \, dt = 0 \qquad i \neq j \qquad k = 1, 2.$$

The constants analogous to $a_1, a_2, \ldots, a_n$ of Eq. II.7 are then determined as follows:

$$a_i = \int_0^T f(t) g_i^1(t) \, dt$$

$$b_i = \int_0^T f(t) g_i^2(t) \, dt \qquad i = 1, 2, \ldots, n \tag{II.10}$$

The advantage of this representation, besides the convenient orthonormal property of the set of functions $g_i(t)$, is that for a wide class of functions $f(t)$ we can show that as the number of terms in the series increases, that is, as $n \to \infty$, the error in approximation goes to zero.

A very extensive treatment of this problem is found in *Introduction to the Theory of Fourier's Series and Integrals* by H. S. Carslaw, 3rd ed. (1930).

The foregoing derivation of the Fourier series should make clear that other functions, besides the sine and cosine terms, might be used to approximate a function of time. Bessel functions, Legendre polynomials, exponential series, and $\sin x/x$ are possible. Also, one should note that the approximation is valid only for a segment of the function $f(t)$, namely, that part of the function in the interval 0 to T. (We omit discussion of the end points themselves.)

Suppose $f(t)$ is a nonperiodic function but is otherwise well behaved; then it is not difficult to extend the representation just outlined to the entire time interval $-\infty$ to $+\infty$. The weights $a_1, a_2, \ldots, a_n, b_1, b_2, \ldots, b_n$ are then no longer discrete constants but functions of frequency, that is, $a(f), b(f)$. These functions are called the *Fourier sine and cosine transforms*. We use the finite representation in our discussion of detection systems, so that the transforms need not be discussed here in detail. However, many problems involving the analysis of band-limited noise of finite duration are somewhat easier to understand in the *Fourier integral representation*. Carslaw (1930) should be consulted in such instances.

II.5   NOISE

The final topic of this brief review is *noise*. Probably the most frequent encounter with audio noise is the hiss of a radio when turned off station. We consider a particular audio circuit, as depicted in Fig. II-3, and discuss some of the properties of typical audio noise. The noise generator is assumed to be a voltage source (no internal impedance), and the noise voltage is thus generated across a 1-ohm resistance.

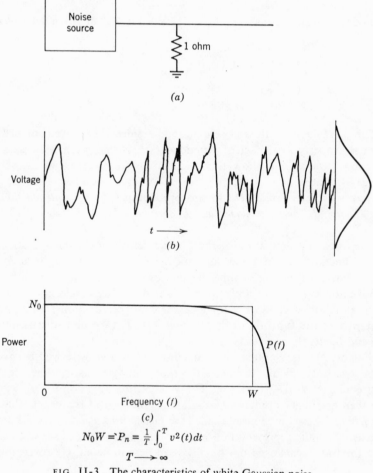

$$N_0 W = P_n = \frac{1}{T} \int_0^T v^2(t)\,dt$$

$$T \longrightarrow \infty$$

FIG. II-3   The characteristics of white Gaussian noise.

We now briefly review some very basic points. By Ohm's law, the current I generated in the resistance R is the voltage V divided by the resistance; $I = V/R$. The power is the voltage times the current (IV), and since $I = V/R$, the power is also V^2/R. The energy E is the integral of the power. The identifying feature of a noise source is its unpredictable output voltage $v(t)$. This voltage is symmetric in probability about zero, going positive and negative with about equal frequency. Figure II-3b shows a typical sample of the voltage measured across a 1-ohm resistor.

Since the noise voltage is irregular, its energy during a time interval 0 to T,

$$E_n = \int_0^T \frac{v^2(t)}{R} \, dt \qquad (II.11)$$

is also irregular. However, if the period of integration increases sufficiently ($T \to T_0$), we expect E_n to be measurable with greater and greater precision, in the sense that the percentage variation will diminish. For the noise sources we are discussing, this will be the case.

The average power of the noise is

$$P_n = \frac{1}{T} \int_0^T V^2(t) \, dt \qquad (II.12)$$

and is one of the fundamental quantities used to describe any noise source. This *power* is proportional to *voltage squared*, rather than to voltage, although if a voltmeter is connected across the 1-ohm resistor the voltmeter will read a roughly steady value on a scale labeled volts. To understand this anomaly, we must realize that a voltmeter does not register average voltage. If it did so, then for a noise voltage the reading should be zero, as consideration of Fig. II-3b will indicate. Rather, the voltmeter reads the average of the voltage squared, or the average of the absolute value of voltage, depending on the specific make of meter. The meter is scaled so that it registers the voltage of a single sinusoid. A true "root mean square" voltmeter (true RMS) registers the square root of the mean voltage squared, that is, a quantity proportional to $P_n^{1/2}$; see Eq. II.12.

There are two other important characteristics of noise besides the average power of the noise. Often we refer to a noise source as a *Gaussian* noise source. This simply indicates that, to a good approximation, the instantaneous voltage of the source has a Gaussian distribution. This is depicted at the right of Fig. II-3b, where the distribution of instantaneous voltage has been accumulated. Any real noise source will only be approximately Gaussian because such a distribution should have finite probability of exceeding any extreme value, either positive or negative. Most noise sources simply limit at extreme voltages, and this limits the tails of the Gaussian distribution. These limit points are called the *peak factor* of the noise source, and this quantity is often quoted in specifying commercially available noise generators. The probability that these limit points will be exceeded is very small, perhaps of order 10^{-6}, and thus, because of the central limit theorem and the natural irregularities in the flow of electrons, many noise sources are very nearly Gaussian.

The last characteristic of the noise is its frequency characteristic. One often hears reference to *white Gaussian noise*. The adjective "white" is borrowed from the visual sense and refers to the fact that a light source radiating nearly the same energy at all the visible wave lengths appears roughly white. When applied to an audio noise source, it means that there is approximately equal energy at all audio frequencies. If the source shown in Fig. II-3 were a white audio noise source it would mean that the power of the noise at the various frequencies would appear as shown in Fig. II-3c. This representation of the noise is called a *power spectrum* and is a very general characterization of the random process generating the noise. A real noise source will not have a perfectly flat spectrum, but will drop off gradually at the higher frequencies such as the curve labeled $P(f)$. The curve $P(f)$ gives the average power as a function of frequency.

We can find the total power of the noise by integrating the average power at each frequency, that is,

$$\overline{P_n} = \int_0^\infty P(f)\, df \tag{II.13}$$

Naturally, the total power will be the same whether we use Eq. II.12 or II.13.

Since the noise is essentially flat over a wide portion, we might approximate the spectrum by two numbers. These two numbers would define a rectangle having an area equal to P_n. The height of the rectangle is chosen to be the maximum power in the noise spectrum (in this case, the power at most of the frequencies), namely, N_0. The width of the rectangle W is chosen such that $WN_0 = P_n$. As Fig. II-3c makes clear, this is a good approximation to the noise spectrum except at high frequencies.

Since N_0 is the total power divided by W, the width of the rectangular band, N_0 must be measured in power per cycle per second, or *noise power density*. The noise power density has as its dimensions power times duration (one second) and hence is an energy, not a power, as its name would imply. The quantity N_0 is especially important in auditory psychophysics because the ability of an observer to hear a sinusoidal signal partially masked by noise depends directly on N_0 and only indirectly on P_n. That is, given equal noise densities, the amount of masking is quite independent of whether the bandwidth W is 10,000, 20,000, or 100,000 cycles per second. In Appendix III precise measurement of N_0 and W is discussed. Chapter 10 contains material on the detection of a sinusoid in noise of various bandwidths.

Although the preceding material describes the important statistics of noise waveforms, we now want to adopt some more specific definition of noise based on the Fourier expression used with sinusoidal waveforms. Since the noise is, by definition, aperiodic, the manner in which this is done is not obvious. The topic that we wish to discuss is the nature of the stochastic process we use to characterize our noise. Thus, before we take up the Fourier representation of noise, let us briefly review the essentials of a stochastic process and give at least one simple example.

II.6   STOCHASTIC PROCESS

A random process that is a function of time is called a *stochastic process*. We might consider a box that generates waveforms $x(t)$ for a short interval of time, $0 < t < T$. To be stochastic, the waveforms must be a function of both time t and a random variable α. Suppose that α is discrete and can be either $\alpha_1, \alpha_2, \ldots, \alpha_n$. Then the waveform generated will be either $x(t, \alpha_1), x(t, \alpha_2), \ldots$, or $x(t, \alpha_n)$, depending on the value of α. The usual probability definitions apply to the sample waveforms. To each

$$x(t, \alpha) = a(\alpha) \cos 2\pi f_1 t + b(\alpha) \sin 2\pi f_1 t$$
$$a(1) = 0, b(1) = 1$$
$$a(2) = 1, b(2) = 0$$

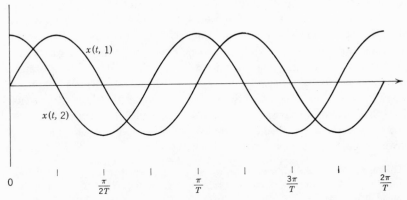

FIG. II-4. An example of a stochastic waveform. The waveform, a function of time, depends upon the parameter value α. If α is equal to 1, a sine wave results; if α is equal to 2, a cosine wave results. If the parameter value α has some probability density associated with it, then a particular value of x at any fixed time also has a probability density associated with it, and thus x becomes a random variable that depends both on time, t, and the value of α.

waveform we associate a probability P, $0 \leq P \leq 1$, such that $P[x(t, \alpha_i)]$ is the probability of the occurrence of the waveform $x(t, \alpha_i)$ and

$$\sum_{i=1}^{n} P[x(t, \alpha_i)] = 1.00$$

The following simple example illustrates a stochastic process. Suppose that we have

$$x(t, \alpha) = a(\alpha) \cos 2\pi f_1 t + b(\alpha) \sin 2\pi f_1 t \qquad 0 < t \leq T$$

where if $\alpha = 1$, then $a(\alpha) = 0$ and $b(\alpha) = 1$; and if $\alpha = 2$, then $a(\alpha) = 1$ and $b(\alpha) = 0$. Assume that $P(\alpha = 1) = P(\alpha = 2) = \frac{1}{2}$. The waveform $x(t, \alpha)$, defined in the interval $[0, T]$, will be either a sine or a cosine wave of unit amplitude and frequency f_1.

Figure II-4 shows the process graphically. Basically, at any fixed time, for instance t_0, the waveform $x(t, \alpha)$ is simply a random variable such as those discussed in Appendix I. The value of the random variable $x(t_0, \alpha)$ depends on α, and the sample space is different for each different time t_0. As time changes, the value of the random variable $x(t, \alpha)$ also changes, so that probabilities such as $P[x(t, \alpha) > k]$ now depend on both t and α.*

II.7   REPRESENTATION OF NOISE

There are several ways in which noise has been represented as a stochastic process. The approach that we use is rather old—its major advantages are its simplicity and the fact that the entire waveform can be represented by a finite set of numbers. For most of our applications we consider only a finite segment of time, $0 < t < T$; thus we are mostly interested in representing the waveform over this brief interval. Given this motivation, we might argue that a good representation of any noise waveform could be achieved by a Fourier series. (See Rice's chapter in Wax, 1954, p. 156.) To make the set of sinusoidal functions orthogonal, the first sinusoid in the series must have a frequency $1/T$. Further, to have a power spectrum that would resemble that shown in Fig. II-3c, the average power at each frequency must be about the same.

---

* On page 23 of Parzen's *Stochastic Processes* (1962), an example of another stochastic process is given. This example and the problem given on page 24 show the equivalence of a wave

$$x(t) = A \cos wt + B \sin wt$$

where A and B are Gaussian, zero mean, variance σ, and the wave

$$y(t) = R \cos (wt + \theta)$$

where θ is uniformly distributed and R has a Rayleigh distribution.

Specifically, we assume that the noise waveform can be approximated by a Fourier series of the form:

$$n(t) = \sum_{k=1}^{WT} a_k \cos\frac{2\pi}{T}kt + b_k \sin\frac{2\pi}{T}kt \qquad 0 \le t \le T \qquad \text{(II.14)}$$

where a_k and b_k are independent Gaussian variables with mean zero and variance N_0/T. This last assumption insures two results. First, the instantaneous amplitude will be approximately Gaussian. (At any specific time the waveform is of the form $\Sigma\, a_k c_k + b_k d_k$, where $c_k = \cos 2\pi/T\,kt_0$ and $d_k = \sin 2\pi/T\,kt_0$ are constant ranging between $+1$ and -1, and a_i and b_i are Gaussian. Thus in the limit $k \to \infty$ the sum will be approximately Gaussian.) Secondly, because the total power at the kth component is N_0/T, and there are WT components, the average total power is N_0W, as it should be.

The reader should not be overly impressed with the accuracy of such a finite representation. According to this approximation there is no component of the noise between k/T and $(k + 1)/T$, where k is an integer. In short, there is only energy at the harmonics of $1/T$. Nevertheless, if $T = 1$ sec and $W = 20,000$ cps, there are 10,000 sine components and 10,000 cosine components from which our approximation is constructed.

We might briefly consider the waveform at a single component of our Gaussian process. This would be roughly the waveform generated by passing the voltage from a Gaussian noise source through an ideal filter of unit bandwidth. The output of such a narrow filter will be nearly a sinusoid whose frequency is the center frequency of the filter. Because the filter bandwidth is very narrow, we know that even if the input of the filter were suddenly removed, the output voltage would continue to oscillate, and these oscillations would diminish in size toward zero at a rate proportional to the reciprocal of the bandwidth. Thus for a filter with a 1-cps bandwidth the decay oscillation would continue appreciably for one second. Despite fluctuations in the power of the noise at the filter's center frequency, the output of the filter is essentially a sinusoid with a slowly changing amplitude.

Figure II-5 shows the typical appearance of the output of a narrow filter excited by noise. Since the narrow-band oscillation occurs at a frequency much higher than the slow fluctuations in amplitude, it is clear that a curve connecting the peaks of the oscillation can be determined. This curve is called the *envelope*. It means that the radius vector a in Fig. II-1 undergoes slow random fluctuations instead of remaining fixed. Hence the curve of the envelope will be poorly defined if the oscillation frequency is very slow—or if the fluctuations in the envelope are fast relative to the frequency of the sinusoidal oscillations.

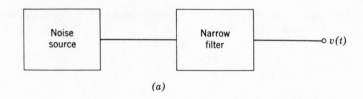

(a)

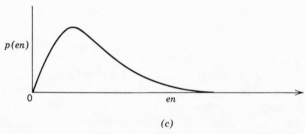

(b)

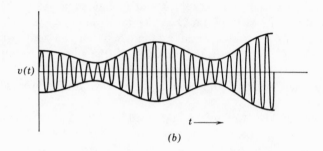

(c)

FIG. II-5   The output of a narrow filter excited by noise.

Referring again to Fig. II-1, we see that the waveform $v(t)$ can be represented as

$$v(t) = en(t) \sin (2\pi f_c t + \theta) \qquad \text{(II.15)}$$

where f_c is the center frequency of the filter, θ is the phase of this oscillation, and $en(t)$ is the envelope. Expanding this equation into a sine and cosine component (see Eqs. II.1 and II.2), we have

$$[en(t) \cos \theta] \sin 2\pi f_c t + [en(t) \sin \theta] \cos 2\pi f_c t \qquad \text{(II.16)}$$

If the filter is narrow enough, then $en(t) \cos \theta$ and $en(t) \sin \theta$ are essentially constant for some brief period of time.

If a brief period of time is about duration T, then, considering the noise as represented by a Fourier series, the output of the filter is

$$v(t) = a_c \sin 2\pi f_c t + b_c \cos 2\pi f_c t \qquad 0 < t < T \qquad \text{(II.17)}$$

The envelope $en(t) = en$ is

$$en = (a_c^2 + b_c^2)^{\frac{1}{2}} \tag{II.18}$$

Since a_c and b_c are both Gaussian variables, the distribution of en can be determined. This derivation is carried out in Chapter 6 (Sec. 6.5.2.1.1.), and there we show that en has a *Rayleigh distribution*, as depicted in Fig. II-5c.

II.8   SUMMARY

This concludes our rather brief review of the concepts of waveform analysis. Again we remind the reader that this is a large area where, unfortunately, there is still argument about the fundamentals. The representation of noise as a stochastic process is particularly subtle. Consultation of the references cited in this appendix is highly recommended.

APPENDIX III

Experimental Techniques

III.1 INTRODUCTION

In order to preserve continuity of the major ideas, the chapters in this book describe theory and experiment with little consideration for details of experimental procedure. This appendix is devoted to procedural matters. We discuss, in turn, collection of data, analysis of data, and measurement of the stimulus.

The general aspects of procedure that are prescribed by detection theory are clear. Enough trials must be presented to provide the desired accuracy in the estimate of response probabilities. The observer's response criterion must be measured. The duration of the signal must be controlled. Noise should be measured in terms of its power in a one-cycle band. And so on. In any experiment, however, it is necessary to add flesh to this skeletal prescription.

Detection theory is, after all, a normative theory. Thus there are probably quite a few variables outside the compass of the theory that actually do have a significant influence on the behavior of human observers. Several of these variables are explicitly recognized and incorporated in the experimental testing session. For example, frequent rest periods are given the observers to minimize the effects of fatigue and boredom. There are probably many other variables whose effects are unknown that influence the observer's behavior significantly; there are no sure recipes for all aspects of experimental procedure. There are some guidelines apart from the theory that may be applied in determining these specific aspects of procedure but, everything considered, there is a good deal of latitude for interpretation—they are, indeed, matters of technique. The specifics of procedure depend upon many factors and must be determined in the context of the particular problem under investigation. It is not useful, therefore, to set down a list of recommendations for procedure. We describe here certain techniques that are used in several laboratories. With minor modifications, these techniques have been used in most of the experiments described in this book.

The ultimate defense of any of these procedures must be a pragmatic one—they work. It may well be that some slight modification of these procedures will produce quite different results. We doubt it, but it is always possible. We have attempted to be as explicit as possible about matters which are seldom as exciting as substantive problems, but which often generate considerable heat when discussed by experimenters. This, then, is frankly an attempt to relate a kind of information that is not ordinarily committed to print—the "kitchen table" knowledge that often seems forbidding in its extent to an investigator as he approaches a specialized field of research that is new to him. It is a small attempt to specify the boundary conditions of the theory, but its omissions and errors may be considerable. Wherever possible, we have cited evidence for our position; in many cases, however, we must appeal to what the reader will see as our intuitions or prejudice, but what we call common sense.

III.2   DATA COLLECTION

III.2.1   Session design

SESSION DURATION AND TRIAL BLOCKS. Typically, an experimental session is scheduled for a period of about two hours. A session of this length can contain eight to ten blocks of trials, with 100 trials in a block, in most auditory and visual experiments. Rest periods of a few minutes between blocks of trials, with a five-to-ten-minute rest midway in the session, are apparently adequate to minimize intrasession trends in the index of sensitivity.

NUMBER OF TRIALS. A given experimental condition, with all parameters fixed, typically includes on the order of 500 trials. Unless the a priori probability of signal occurrence is an experimental variable, it is set at 0.50. That is, in the yes-no and rating tasks about half of the trials are signal trials and about half are noise-alone trials, and in a forced-choice task the signal is equally likely to occur in each interval. When the purpose of the experiment is to define a yes-no ROC curve for a given signal-to-noise ratio, approximately five conditions (each containing about 500 trials) are usually used. Determinants of the response criterion are changed from one condition to another to elicit false-alarm probabilities over a sufficient range. One condition, as we have indicated, suffices for a rating ROC curve. In an experiment undertaken to determine changes in the sensitivity index as a function of some independent variable, a psychometric function based on five or six conditions (with different signal levels) is often obtained for each value of the independent variable. Signal levels are chosen to elicit values of $P(C)$ over a range from near chance to near 1.0. In this case, the two-alternative forced-choice procedure is favored. An index sometimes used is the signal level that corresponds to $d' = 1.0$, which, in the two-alternative procedure, is equivalent to $P(C) = 0.76$.

It is clear that the number of trials mounts rapidly. As few as 500, but as many as 2500, are used in defining an ROC curve at one signal level. A psychometric function might be based on 2500 trials, that is, on two or three experimental sessions. Very clearly, some sensory problems cannot be studied with such large numbers of trials. Severe compromises would be necessary to trace the course of dark adaptation, for example, and in experiments in which stimulus administration is relatively awkward, as in experiments on taste or smell. Again, clinical tests based on these methods are usually impractical. Some efforts are currently being made to devise very efficient schemes of stimulus presentation—schemes in which the choice of signal level on each trial is contingent on previous responses—that will achieve satisfactory reliability with reduced time (for example, Smith, 1961) but, in general, the methods associated with detection theory are fully applicable only when time is not highly critical.

SIGNAL PREVIEWS. It is common practice to allow the observer to observe the signal, with the background noise attenuated enough so that the signal is very clear, a few times at the beginning of each block of trials. This "preview" technique shortens noticeably the period of improvement when a new signal is introduced, and decreases inter- and intra-observer variability. Gundy (1961), in an auditory experiment with a sinusoidal signal and naive observers, found that a preview aided detection by 7 db at a low signal level and by 3 db at a high signal level, in the first block of 50 trials.

Other evidence suggests that the observer can make immediate use of information about signal characteristics, presumably to adjust certain parameters of his sensory system. In one experiment in which relatively strong and weak signals were presented in random sequence, the observer was more likely to be correct on those trials following a correct response to the strong signal than on those trials following a correct response to a weak signal. This result has been interpreted to mean that strong signals provide better cues to the nature of the signal than do weaker signals, and that the observer's perceptual adjustment is better after a strong signal (Shipley, 1959). In another experiment, in which the signal on a given trial could be either of two frequencies, presentation of a cueing signal before each trial increased detectability by the equivalent of approximately one db (Greenberg, 1962). Chapter 7 presents data showing that performance can be changed by continually providing additional cues in the form of a signal "pedestal." Some evidence suggests, on the other hand, that the observer cannot readjust on a moment's notice. Chapter 10 presents the finding that listeners perform less well when a tonal signal is randomly set at either of two frequencies within a block of trials—even when given a preview before each trial of the signal to be presented on that trial—than they do when the signal is fixed in frequency throughout the block of trials. In general, available evidence supports the common practice: when trial-by-trial information is not a variable of interest, signal parameters are fixed over a block of trials, and the block is preceded by a preview.

III.2.2 Trial design

TRIAL EVENTS. A trial consists of some event to alert the observer, one or more observation intervals, and a period during which the observer makes his response. The response is made by pressing a button or throwing a switch. It may, or may not, be followed by an event that gives "knowledge of results," or "feedback." The events that alert the observer, delineate the observation and response intervals, and give feedback are usually innocuous stimuli to a sensory modality other than the one under investigation; lights are suitable in auditory experiments, and tones or clicks in visual experiments.

FEEDBACK. Trial-by-trial feedback is frequently supplied when new observers or new signals are used. It helps to bring about a rapid approach to asymptotic performance (Blackwell, 1953; Lukaszewski and Elliott, 1962), but its effect is relatively small when the signal is previewed prior to each block of trials (Gundy, 1961). Trial-by-trial feedback is often supplied routinely throughout an experiment; in general, observers prefer it. Feedback is sometimes given for larger units of performance; after each block of, say, 100 trials, observers may be told their false-alarm and hit rates in a yes-no test, or their percentage of correct responses in a forced-choice test.

OBSERVATION INTERVALS. The observation intervals, which coincide with the signal's duration, are marked as accurately as possible. Chapter 7 presents data illustrating the benefits of pedestal marking. Chapter 9 shows that an uncertainty of a few seconds concerning the time of the observation interval can produce a decrement in performance of about 2 db.

The length of time separating the two intervals in a two-alternative forced-choice task has a similar effect on performance. In an auditory experiment, performance suffered when the two intervals were separated by less than one half-second or by more than two seconds. Presumably, the observations are not independent if they are too close together, and memory is inadequate if they are too far apart (Tanner, 1961b).

TRIAL DURATION.   In a typical auditory or visual experiment, with one or two observation intervals per trial, and with a signal of a half-second or less in duration, the entire trial cycle lasts for about four to five seconds. Observers who have experienced five-second trials complain of boredom if the trial is lengthened much beyond that. Most experimenters find it difficult to believe that the observer is working conscientiously when the trial cycle is less than 4 or 5 seconds, but the effect of still shorter trials is surprisingly small. Performance has been observed to suffer by less than 2 db when the trial, including warning and feedback, is compressed into a period of only 2 seconds (Green, unpublished data).

III.2.3   Observers

SELECTION.   Almost all the observers represented in this book were college students. The principal criterion for their selection was a class schedule which did not conflict with the experimental schedule. It was established that they were not in academic difficulty, and that they had normal hearing, or vision.

An impression of individual differences among observers selected in this way can be gained from data reported in Chapter 4. Infrequently do two observers in a group of four differ by more than 50% in d' when attempting to detect a signal in noise; this difference is equivalent to approximately 1.5 db in signal power. Thus it is not difficult to find a group of observers such that the same signal levels are appropriate to all—a given range of signal-to-noise ratios will define the psychometric function adequately for each observer. (Somewhat larger individual differences can be expected in the detection of an increment to a sinusoid or in the presence of a sinusoidal masker.) Similarly, in a yes-no task the observers react quite uniformly to variation in the variables that influence the level of the response criterion. Occasionally, as noted in Chapter 4, one observer may be more cautious about saying "yes" than his fellows, but the same range of variables will almost always define an ROC curve adequately for each observer.

LENGTH OF SERVICE.   Typically, the observers work two hours a day, and from three to five days a week. Many observers work, vacations excepted, for an entire academic year. Because most experimental comparisons are made within the data obtained from a given observer, the experimenter obtains a commitment of at least a semester's participation from the observers when they are hired.

INSTRUCTIONS.   The observer is given some general instructions at the beginning of his term of duty. If he begins in a forced-choice task, he is asked to wait until all of the observation intervals in a trial have been presented before making his decision. He is encouraged to maintain, as nearly as possible, a constant "set." He may be asked specifically to refrain from conducting his own experiments—he should not, for example, without telling the experimenter, look at a signal out of the corner of his eye on alternate blocks of trials. The observer is also told something about random sequences. He may be advised of the "gambler's fallacy"—the inexperienced gambler's tendency to move his money from red to black when red has come up on the last several turns of the wheel. He is assured that the experimenter has taken every precaution to prevent him from deriving any information from the sequence of signal and noise-alone events.

In general, the observer is treated as a member of the laboratory staff. His full cooperation is requested, and he is encouraged to report to the experimenter anything that he thinks is relevant. In almost every case, the observer can be told that the variables apparently under study are the ones actually under study. In fact, a strong attempt is made to inform the observer of all significant aspects of the experiment except the hypothesis under investigation; he is given as little latitude as possible for self-instruction.

These thoughts about instructions are certainly not new. Indeed, after the preceding two paragraphs were written, we noticed the very similar comments by Jastrow (1888). Perhaps Jastrow said it better: "It should be stated what knowledge the subject has of the conditions and purposes of the experiment, and the subject should know all the conditions except such as will lead to the use of indications towards forming a judgment other than those furnished by the sensation itself. If he is in doubt as to the several changes that can possibly occur, he will infer them for himself, and will yield to that uncontrollable psychological guessing of what is coming. This mischievous tendency plays havoc with the expectation and throws the attention off the track. When the confidence is low the tendency to prefer one kind of answer is apt to occur, and would be avoided if the subject knew that this tendency had no basis in fact. It is especially necessary for the subject to know that in each case the one stimulus is greater or less than the other (and never equal to it), and that either is as liable to come first as last."

III.2.4 Practice, motivation, and stability

PRACTICE. Few studies of the effect of practice in psychophysical tasks have been published. In a visual task, Blackwell (1953) found a practice effect which lasted for five or six two-hour sessions, with both the

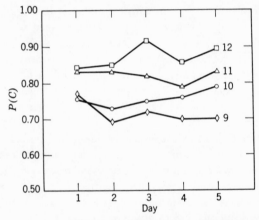

FIG. III-1   Effect of practice in a forced-choice task with a sinusoid signal. The figure shows the average results of three observers at each of four signal intensities, that is, at each of four values of $10 \log E/N_0$. (From Swets and Sewall, 1963.)

forced-choice and yes-no procedures. Auditory studies, in contrast, have shown practice effects of considerably shorter duration. The results shown in Fig. III-1 were obtained with a sinusoid signal in noise and a forced-choice procedure. The figure presents the results of three observers at four signal intensities: $10 \log E/N_0 = 9$, 10, 11, and 12. For both the first and the fifth sessions, the average percentage correct of the four intensities is 0.80 ($d' = 1.20$). The average result ranges from $P(C) = 0.78$ to $P(C) = 0.80$, from $d' = 1.10$ to $d' = 1.20$. This range is the equivalent of less than $\frac{1}{2}$ db in signal power. (The average result in Fig. III-1 does not mask individual differences. Comparing the first and fifth sessions, the changes in $P(C)$ for the individual observers were +0.01, −0.01, and 0.0. The slight decrement in the second and fourth sessions, relative to the other three sessions, was shown by each observer.)

The suggestion of these data that any practice effect is limited to the first session is confirmed by other auditory experiments. Gundy (1961) found a practice effect of 4 to 5 db over the first six blocks of 50 trials, when the observers had not had the benefit of a signal preview. If the observers had been given a preview, the practice effect was again limited to six blocks of 50 trials, and was considerably smaller: approximately 1 db.

TABLE III-1.   EFFECT OF MOTIVATION. THE ENTRIES IN THE TABLE ARE VALUES OF d', AND, IN PARENTHESES, VALUES OF $P(C)$.

Procedure	Observer	Prior to Bonus	With Bonus
Rating	1	0.81	1.00
	2	0.71	0.99
	3	0.93	1.08
	Average	0.82	1.02
2AFC	1	0.90 (0.74)	1.04 (0.77)
	2	1.07 (0.77)	1.11 (0.78)
	3	0.79 (0.71)	0.85 (0.73)
	Average	0.92 (0.74)	1.00 (0.76)

Zwislocki, Maire, Feldman, and Rubin (1958) found a practice effect of 5 db over eight blocks of 100 trials. Lukaszewski and Elliott (1962) report ᴀ practice effect of approximately 2 db lasting over seven sessions; however, there was subsequently some deterioration in performance, so that in the eighth session, for example, the performance was less than 1 db better than in the first session. On the whole, the effect of practice is not a large concern—at least for the simple signals that are typically used. For very complex signals, a word of caution is in order; Tanner and Rivette (1963), using signals that require a very fine temporal discrimination, have found substantial improvements in performance after as many as 50 sessions which showed very little improvement.

MOTIVATION.   The effects of motivation have been studied by offering bonuses for improved performance after asymptotic performance has been reached. Illustrative results are shown in Table III-1. In this experiment both the forced-choice and the rating procedures were used. The bonus offered under the two-alternative forced-choice procedure was one dollar for each increase in $P(C)$ of 0.01 relative to each observer's best

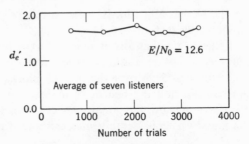

FIG. III-2 Curve showing the long-term stability of the sensitivity index d_e'. The "number of trials" shown on the abscissa refer only to the tests used to determine the stability of performance; experience with other listening conditions also took place during the period of time represented in the figure. The data span a period of nine weeks of nearly daily experimental sessions. (From Egan, Greenberg, and Schulman, 1961a.)

performance up until that time. Under the rating procedure, a bonus of one dollar was offered for each increase in d' of 0.05, which is approximately equivalent to an increase of 0.01 in $P(C)$ under the two-alternative forced-choice procedure. One day was devoted to forced choice, and three days to rating. Thus an increase of 0.10 in $P(C)$, or of 0.5 in d', would bring a return of 10 dollars a day, and 40 dollars for the short week. The table shows that the average improvement in d' under the rating procedure was from 0.82 to 1.02, the equivalent of less than 1 db. The average improvement in d' under the forced-choice procedure was from 0.92 to 1.00, an improvement of from 0.74 to 0.76 in $P(C)$, a difference equivalent to less than $\frac{1}{2}$ db. The standard error of $P(C)$ in this experiment, assuming binomial variance (an underestimation of the actual variance), is about 0.015; thus the difference does not approach statistical significance.

A similar attempt to manipulate motivation by Lukaszewski and Elliott (1962) also led to an improvement of less than 1 db. Blackwell (1953), in a visual study, found a small effect of a bonus if the asymptote of performance previously reached were reached without feedback; when the asymptote had been reached with feedback, the introduction of a bonus did not bring about further improvement.

STABILITY. Informal observations have indicated that the various indices of sensitivity used with detection theory remain constant over relatively long periods of time. Illustrative results are shown in Fig. III-2.

The figure shows the average performance for seven observers over a period of nine weeks. The range is 0.20 in d_e'—the equivalent, in this case, of about $\frac{1}{2}$ db in signal power.

III.3   DATA ANALYSIS

We consider in this section the variance of proportions obtained by experiment; curve-fitting procedures; various measures of sensitivity and means of obtaining them; the effects of response biases in forced choice; and the influence on the response of the stimuli and responses on preceding trials.

III.3.1   Variance of proportions

We have indicated that relatively large numbers of trials are necessary in order to reduce the variance of data to manageable size. Let us consider explicitly the quantities involved.

Assume, for the moment, that the binomial formula yields a valid estimate of the variance of proportions obtained in psychophysical experiments. In this event, the standard deviation is $\sigma = \sqrt{(pq)/N}$, where p is the proportion, $q = 1 - p$, and N is the number of observations. Tracing the one-sigma band about a point in the ROC unit square, therefore, yields an elliptical band.

Figure III-3(a,b,c) shows one-sigma bands for various pairs of proportions in the ROC space. Section (a) of the figure is based on 200 observations for each point: 100 of noise alone, n, and 100 of signal plus noise, s. Section (b) is based on 600 observations per point: 300 of n and 300 of s. It is clear that, even with 600 observations, the degree of precision is not high. Moreover, the calculation of binomial variance is an underestimation of the actual variance; experience shows that the actual variance can be twice the size of binomial variance. Although 600 observations yield a precision that is satisfactory in many applications, it can be seen that distinguishing between two similar, theoretical ROC curves (see Chapters 3 and 5) is very difficult.

Section (c) of Fig. III-3 shows the one-sigma bands for 600 observations on a double-probability graph. As mentioned in Chapter 3, the variance along the edges of such a graph is very large, and thus estimates of the slope of the linear ROC curve are not highly reliable.

A procedure that may mitigate to some extent the somewhat pessimistic conclusions just expressed is the one developed recently by Watson, Rilling, and Bourbon (1964), in which the observer positions a slider along a scale to produce a very detailed rating ROC curve. This procedure resembles the traditional method of adjustment, and it might be that a

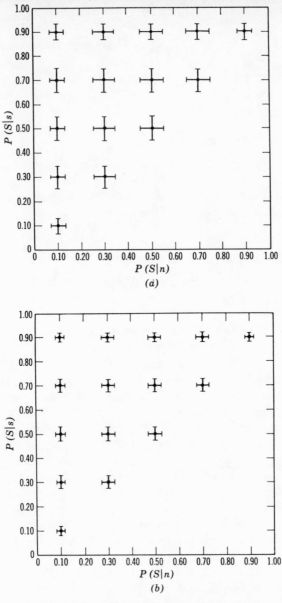

FIG. III-3 Points representing various pairs of proportions in the ROC space, with bands showing plus and minus one standard deviation, assuming binomial variance. (*a*) One-sigma bands based on 200 observations, 100 of signal and 100 of noise alone. (*b*) One-sigma bands based on 600 observations, 300 of signal and 300 of noise alone. (*c*) On double-probability paper, one-sigma bands based on 600 observations, 300 of signal and 300 of noise alone.

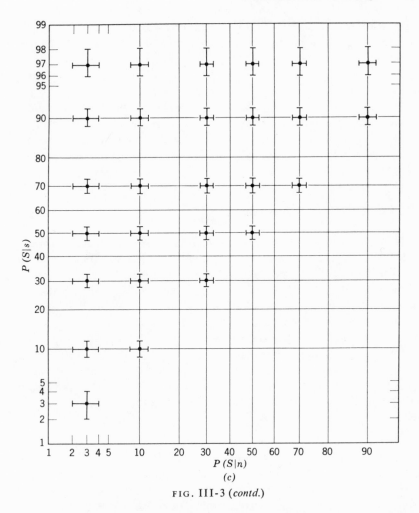

FIG. III-3 (*contd.*)

long-recognized shortcoming of that method, namely, "uncertainty of the hand," introduces variance in the data beyond that obtained with button-pressing or verbal report. Acting to reduce the variance, however, relative to yes-no data, is the cumulation of responses that is made in constructing an ROC curve from rating data (see Chapters 2 and 4). The extent of reduction in variance brought about by the cumulation of responses is not easy to calculate, but the fact is that the procedure proposed by Watson et al. achieves quite a good definition of the ROC curve, as indicated in Fig. 4-8. It is clear, for example, that the data of each of their observers are better fitted by an ROC curve based on Rayleigh distributions (see Fig. 7-2) than by an ROC curve based on normal distributions of unequal variance (Jeffress, 1964). This is a fine distinction, since Fig. 4-8 shows quite a good fit assuming normal distributions of unequal variance.

Psychometric functions are ordinarily defined with somewhat greater accuracy than ROC curves, of course, since variation introduced by the observer occurs only in the y value of the plot, rather than in both x and y values. In Fig. III-3(a,b) the abscissa can be regarded as a normalized scale of signal intensity, and then the vertical bars indicate binomial variance—for 100 observations in Section (a) of the figure, and for 300 observations in Section (b).

III.3.2 Curve-fitting procedures

It is common practice to fit curves to ROC data by selecting from a family of theoretical curves the one that appears upon visual inspection to give the best fit. This procedure is not very satisfactory but, apparently, a more objective one is not available. To our knowledge, optimal statistical procedures for fitting curves to data having variation on both the x and the y coordinates have not yet been devised.

The familiar least-squared-error technique is useful in fitting psycho-metric functions, and a chi-square test will indicate whether the observed function is a chance departure from some specified theoretical distribution. Again, however, the various theoretical functions that have been advanced are so similar that a very large number of observations, often impractical experimentally, is required to distinguish among them.

III.3.3 Measures of sensitivity

In several chapters we use, or allude to, several different measures of sensitivity that have arisen within the framework of detection theory. It might be thought desirable to have a single measure of sensitivity that is appropriate in all experimental situations and for all purposes, but evidently that is not to be. Which measure is most appropriate depends upon the experimental situation, that is, on several stimulus and procedural variables, and upon the investigator's purposes. In this section we bring together the various measures and briefly review their assumptions and calculation.

DISTRIBUTION-FREE MEASURES, $P(C)$ AND $P(A)$. The measures that come closest to being sufficient are defined without regard to hypothetical distributions of sensory events. One of these, applicable to forced-choice results, is the proportion of correct responses, $P(C)$. The other, which applies to yes-no and rating results, is the proportion of area under the ROC curve, $P(A)$. These two measures are equivalent. That is, different models of the detection process, which make different assumptions about the distribution of sensory events, agree on the relationship that holds between $P(A)$ and $P(C)$ for any given number of alternatives in a forced-choice test. In particular, they agree in asserting that $P(A) = P(C)$ in a two-alternative forced-choice test. Thus, taken together, the two measures provide a distribution-free means of relating results from yes-no, rating, and forced-choice tasks (see Chapter 2). The calculation of $P(A)$ circumvents the problem of curve-fitting as discussed in the preceding section: we simply connect the observed ROC points by straight lines and proceed to count squares.

EQUAL-VARIANCE, NORMAL DISTRIBUTIONS AND d'. The appeal of the distribution-free measures is considerable, and we suspect that they will be widely used. However, there are potentially very substantial advantages in making assumptions about the distribution of noise and signal events, particularly when it can be assumed that they are normal and of equal variance. These two assumptions are reasonable when the empirical ROC curves are linear with a slope of one on a double-probability graph, and in this event the measure d' is appropriate. The measure d' is (linearly) related in detection theory to the physical units in which parameters of the signal and noise are measured. A number of models within detection theory provide an analysis of how changes in various signal parameters affect d', and they provide upper bounds on d' for various kinds of signals (see Chapters 6–9). Consequently, insights are gained from observing the nature of the difference between human and ideal detectors. Thus, in a wide range of substantive problems, it is desirable to calculate d' in addition to the distribution-free measures.

A convenient way of calculating d' in yes-no and rating tasks is to plot ROC curves on double-probability graph paper (Codex No. 41,453). The z value associated with the false-alarm proportion is subtracted from the z value associated with the hit proportion, at any point along the curve. A table relating hit and false-alarm proportions to d', appropriate to yes-no and rating tasks, and a table relating $P(C)$ to d' for various numbers of alternatives in a forced-choice task have been presented elsewhere (Elliott, Appendix I, in Swets, 1964). In the ideal detection model for the "signal specified exactly," d' so calculated is equal to $\sqrt{2E/N_0}$ (see Chapter 6).

EXPONENTIAL DISTRIBUTIONS AND k; RAYLEIGH DISTRIBUTIONS AND A; UNEQUAL-VARIANCE, NORMAL DISTRIBUTIONS AND h. Frequently, empirical

ROC curves are approximately linear on a double-probability graph, but with a slope definitely less than one. The evidence in these cases often suggests that the slope decreases with increases in signal strength. At least three detection models predict a decreasing slope with increasing signal strength. One is the model which assumes the noise and signal events to be distributed exponentially. Exponential distributions yield a power-function ROC curve that can be described by a single parameter, denoted k (see Chapter 3). Another is the ideal detection model for a "signal specified exactly except for phase," a model based on amplitude, or envelope, detection. This model assumes Rayleigh distributions for sensory events, and the resulting ROC curve is described by a single parameter which has been denoted A (see Chapters 6 and 7). A third model is the ideal detection model for a "signal a sample of white Gaussian noise"; this model assumes normal distributions of unequal variance. The sensitivity parameter has been denoted h (see Chapter 8). Chapters 6, 7, and 8 show how the sensitivity measures A and h are related to physical measurements of signal and noise.

A graphical calculation of the measure k appears to be suitable. A family of curves can be plotted as in Fig. 3-6 and the best-fitting curve selected by visual inspection. Similarly, a graphical calculation is most convenient for the measure A. Such a graph, for the yes-no and rating tasks, is presented in Fig. 6-3. An alternative is to plot the empirical operating-characteristic curve on double-probability paper; A is closely approximated by $2z + 0.71$ for the z value associated with the intercept of the curve and the negative diagonal (Jeffress, 1964). The value of $P(C)$ in a two-alternative forced-choice test is converted to A by an equation derived by Marill (1956): $A = 2\sqrt{-\ln\{2[1 - P_2(C)]\}}$. The calculation of h depends on the bandwidth of the signal (see Chapter 8). For large bandwidths ($2WT > 10$), the distributions are approximately normal. In this case $P_2(C) = \Phi(h)$. Thus the proportion of correct responses in a two-alternative forced-choice test can be converted to h by means of a table of areas under the normal curve. With h as the argument, the area to the left of h is the equivalent $P_2(C)$. As noted in Chapter 8, h is a parameter of the difference distribution and thus, for distributions of equal variance, $\sqrt{2}h = d'$.

Little use of these three models has been made to date in psychophysics. Notable exceptions in the case of the model for a "signal specified exactly except for phase" are the studies by Marill (1956) and Jeffress (1964); the model for a "signal a sample of white Gaussian noise" was applied by Green (1960a). We may expect to see greater use of both models in the near future. It is certainly reasonable to suppose that the human observer in an auditory experiment is insensitive to phase. The model for a signal containing neither phase nor frequency information is, on the face of it, appropriate to visual signals.

THE EMPIRICAL MEASURES, $D(\Delta m, s)$ AND d_e'. All three of the models discussed in the preceding section predict decreasing slope of the ROC curve with increasing signal strength, but they do not predict precisely the same relationship between slope and signal strength. In many instances, depending on the signal parameters, the model for a "signal a sample of white Gaussian noise" predicts slopes of almost one (see Chapter 6). In general, the model for a "signal specified exactly except for phase" leads to somewhat more shallow slopes, and the model which assumes exponential distributions leads to still more shallow slopes. It is not clear, however, that experimentally determined slopes will serve to distinguish among the three models. As discussed in Section III.3.1, the reliability that can be achieved in estimating experimentally determined slopes leaves something to be desired. It may well be that some other tests will serve adequately to distinguish among the three models, but these tests have not yet been conducted (see Chapters 7 and 8). It is desirable, in any event, to have a measure of sensitivity, for linear ROC curves with slopes less than one, that is not directly tied to a particular model. Such an empirical measure is the measure we denote $D(\Delta m, s)$. This measure gives two parameters of the ROC curve, the intercept, at $P(S \mid s) = 0.50$, and the slope. A measure similar to Δm is d_e'—this measure is read from the point at which the ROC curve intersects the negative diagonal. At this point we take twice the absolute value of either z value. The slope s, in both cases, is measured with respect to the z scale. The conversion formulas for the two measures are given in Chapter 4, Section 4.2.5.

Surplus meaning is sometimes given to this empirical measure by regarding the ROC curve as based upon distributions of noise and signal events of unequal variance. Two of the models just discussed—for a "signal specified exactly except for phase" and for a "signal a sample of white Gaussian noise"—yield slopes of less than one because signal plus noise is conceived of as having greater variance than noise alone. Chapter 4 shows theoretical ROC curves calculated on the assumption of normal distributions where the signal distribution has a variance which increases with its mean. As indicated there, several sets of data are reasonably consistent with the assumption that the ratio of the increment in the mean to the increment in the standard deviation, $\Delta m/\Delta\sigma$, is equal to 4, (that is, $\sigma_s = 1 + \frac{1}{4}\Delta m$). In the instances where normal distributions of unequal variance are assumed, we can take the reciprocal of the slope as the ratio of the standard deviations, $1/s = \sigma_s/\sigma_n$.

SUMMARY. We have discussed the assumptions and calculation of several measures: $P(C)$, $P(A)$, d', k, A, h, $D(\Delta m, s)$ and d_e'. It is likely that reporting more than one of them for any set of data will be helpful. In particular, $P(C)$, $P(A)$, $D(\Delta m, s)$, or d_e' should probably be reported whether or not one of the other, inferred, measures is. It seems likely that ROC curves will come in a variety of forms as more stimulus and procedural variables are explored. An important implication is that forced-choice results cannot be used to predict yes-no behavior until the adequacy of this prediction, for the particular situation, is demonstrated.

III.3.4   Response bias in the forced-choice task

As indicated in several chapters, the forced-choice procedure is typically used in studies of sensory functions, in preference to the yes-no and rating procedures. The reason is that when this procedure is used with equiprobable stimulus alternatives, observers show a relatively small tendency to favor one or another response alternative. Presumably, unlike the yes-no procedure, in which the observer tends to regard the decision outcomes as quite different in value, the decision outcomes in forced choice do not differ intrinsically in value.

If the observer's preference among alternatives is indeed negligible, then an index of sensitivity can be simply and economically obtained. It is not necessary then to determine an ROC curve in order to isolate sensory from extrasensory factors. A satisfactory index of sensitivity is the percentage of correct responses, $P(C)$, or the value of d' that corresponds to this $P(C)$, where these measures are obtained from a single experimental condition with all parameters fixed.

A tendency on the part of the observer to use the response alternatives with different frequencies has been interpreted in two ways. The interpretation that stems from detection theory is that the decision criteria are off center, that is, that the decision criteria are set at values β of likelihood ratio other than one or, equivalently, that the measures of sensory excitation in the various intervals are subjected to different multipliers before the largest is chosen. Decision criteria may be off center because the observer regards the stimulus probabilities, or decision-outcome values, as unequal, and is deliberately attempting to maximize some function of the probabilities and values—or because of asymmetries that inhere in the experimental situation, such as those that may lead to a "time error" or "space error." The interpretation made by the various threshold theories, on the other hand, is that the stimulus configuration (in time or space) may influence the probabilities of detect and nondetect states—or that the observer may deliberately distort the linkage between these sensory events and his responses, perhaps in the interests of a game he is playing with the experimenter.*

Of course, some amount of response bias, however small, is almost always evident in forced-choice data. It may be consistent in direction and, indeed, a preference for later intervals in a temporal forced-choice procedure is frequently observed; phenomenological interpretations of this result are not difficult to come by. Also frequently, the response bias is observed to vary in direction, apparently in accordance with sampling variability. In any event, it is desirable to assess the effect of response bias on the estimate of $P(C)$ that is obtained. The effect might be large enough to warrant a correction. As with yes-no data, we should like an index of sensitivity uncontaminated by response bias.

In the next few pages we consider an analysis of the effect of bias and a means of correcting data for bias that do not require experimental generation of the ROC curve.† Our discussion is limited to the two-alternative forced-choice procedure; the analysis for larger numbers of alternatives is complex and, at this date, has not been accomplished. The discussion is facilitated by thinking of a temporal forced choice; we speak of intervals I_1 and I_2 and responses R_1 and R_2.

It can be assumed that an interval bias will always depress $P(C)$. That is, with the two intervals equally likely to contain the signal, the $P(C)$ obtained with an interval bias will be lower than the $P(C)$ that the same observer, with given sensitivity, would yield if he had no interval bias. It is intuitively clear, and demonstrated in Chapter 1, that the optimal placement of the decision criterion, for maximizing $P(C)$ with equal signal-presentation probabilities, is at the value β of likelihood ratio equal to one. The question is: How much is $P(C)$ depressed; or what is the value of $P(C)$ corrected for bias that corresponds to the biased value of $P(C)$? Our analysis assumes normal density functions of equal variance and thus yields the values of d' that are associated with the biased and corrected values of $P(C)$. We refer to the corrected values as $P(C)_{max}$ and d'_{max}.

Consider the stimulus-response matrix as shown at the top of the following page. These data indicate a rather strong preference (2 to 1) for I_2, or R_2. Ignoring the bias, $P(C) = 134/200 = 0.67$. The corresponding value of d', as determined from the two-alternative forced-choice table (Elliott, Appendix I, in Swets, 1964), is 0.62.

* On occasion, the term "response bias" is used in a narrow sense to apply to the mechanism assumed in the various threshold theories. This usage is unfortunate because neither "response" nor "bias" serves to distinguish the mechanisms assumed in threshold theories from those assumed in detection theory. We use the term here in its general sense.

† This analysis and correction were brought to our attention by Professors James P. Egan and Lloyd A. Jeffress.

	R_1	R_2	
I_1	50	50	100
I_2	16	84	100
	66	134	200

The yes-no table of d' (Elliott, in Swets, 1964), together with a table of areas under the normal curve, provides a means of estimating $P(C)_{max}$ and d'_{max}. We can take $P(R_1 \mid I_1)$ and $P(R_1 \mid I_2)$ as the two probabilities defining the ROC curve, and enter the yes-no table with them. These values, 0.50 and 0.16, give a value for d' of 1.0. (Alternatively, the other two probabilities, $P(R_2 \mid I_2)$ and $P(R_2 \mid I_1)$, or 0.84 and 0.50, can be used; they lead to the same value of d'.) This d' is divided by 2 to obtain the z score corresponding to the symmetrical ($\beta = 1$) criterion. We thus have a z score of 0.50. A table of areas shows 69% of the area under the I_1 distribution to be to the left of $z = 0.50$. Similarly, 69% of the area under the I_2 distribution is to the right of $z = 0.50$. Therefore, under the symmetrical criterion, 69% of the R_1 responses and 69% of the R_2 responses will be correct. The symmetrical matrix for $d' = 1.0$ has 69 and 31 in the top row, and 31 and 69 in the bottom row. $P(C)_{max}$ is then 0.69. The value of d' corresponding to $P(C) = 0.69$, that is, d'_{max}, as obtained from the two-alternative forced-choice table, is 0.71. Note that a severe bias has an effect of 0.02 on the estimate of $P(C)$, and an effect of 0.09 on d'. This effect is the equivalent of approximately $\frac{1}{2}$ decibel in signal power.

An equivalent way of making the correction uses only the d' tables. The $d' = 1.0$ obtained from the yes-no table is divided by $\sqrt{2}$ to obtain the forced-choice $d'_{max} = 0.71$. (See Chapter 3 for a discussion of the $\sqrt{2}$ difference in d' between yes-no and forced-choice tests.) The forced-choice table is then entered with $d'_{max} = 0.71$ to yield $P(C)_{max} = 0.69$.

As another example, consider the matrix with 50 and 50 in the top row, and 5 and 95 in the bottom row. This represents a severe bias of almost 3 to 1 in favor of R_2. $P(C) = 0.73$; $P(C)_{max} = 0.79$. Very few, if any, estimates of $P(C)$ obtained under ordinary conditions will be off by as much as 0.06.

In general, the observed response bias increases as the signal level decreases. This fact suggests that it is important to make the correction whenever the slope of the psychometric function is measured. On the other hand, the effect of response bias is relatively small at low values of $P(C)$. For example, the correction of the matrix with 40 and 60 in the top row and 30 and 70 in the bottom row—which gives $P(C) = 0.55$ and a bias of about 2 to 1—is a change only in the third decimal place.

III.3.5 *Sequential effects in series of responses*

Several studies have shown that the response on a given trial is influenced to some extent by the stimuli and responses on immediately preceding trials (for example, Senders and Soward, 1952; Speeth and Mathews, 1961; Kinchla, 1964). However, the nature of the influence varies from one experiment to another and from one observer to another. Some studies have demonstrated a tendency to alternate responses, and others have demonstrated a tendency to repeat responses. Kinchla (unpublished work, 1964), using the two-interval forced-choice procedure, examined the effects on 20 observers of runs, of lengths up to six, of signals in Interval 1 and, similarly, of runs of signals in Interval 2. Each observer showed a definite effect of preceding stimulus events, but the effect was in one direction for 10 observers, and in the opposite direction for the other 10 observers.

We can assume, as with interval bias, that sequential effects depress $P(C)$. In the simplest case, if the observer shifts back and forth between two decision criteria, or response biases, his ROC point will lie on a straight line connecting the two points that would correspond to the two criteria if each were used consistently, in turn. The straight line, of course, lies below the curvilinear ROC curve (on linear probability scales) which contains the two criteria points. We can also assume, as this example suggests, that sequential effects will serve to increase the variance of the probabilities that are obtained. Again, it is likely that the size of sequential effects increases as the signal level decreases.

Procedures for determining the size of the effect on $P(C)$ of sequential tendencies—procedures which would permit a correction for them—have not been devised. Sequential effects are commonly ignored in sensory studies, for lack of an alternative, and with the belief that they are small. An article by Green (1964) may be consulted for further discussion of the matter.

III.4   STIMULUS MEASUREMENT

Precise measurements of the signal and the background noise are essential, particularly when various parameters of the experimental data are to be compared with quantitative models of the detection process. Since it is impossible to anticipate all the various experimental situations that one might encounter, we limit our discussion of the problems involved in measuring signal and noise to the framework of a single, typical, psychoacoustic experiment.

A generally accepted means of expressing the absolute levels of acoustic waveforms is the sound pressure level (SPL). Sound pressure level is, by convention, 20 times the logarithm of the measured sound pressure divided by the pressure of the reference level, 0.0002 dyne/cm². That is,

$$\text{SPL} = 20 \log_{10}\left(\frac{P}{P_{\text{ref}}}\right)$$

where P is the measured pressure, and P_{ref} is the reference level pressure, 0.0002 dyne/cm².

In point of fact, we generally do not measure sound pressure levels directly; rather, we measure the voltage impressed across the earphones. The rationale for this is as follows. The response of the earphone, a passive device, remains relatively constant over long periods of time. Thus, meaningful calibration curves may be obtained relating the sound pressure generated by the earphone into a standard acoustic impedance to the voltage across the earphone. Such calibration curves usually show that if 1 volt is applied across the earphone, the sound pressure level is about the same (±2 db) over a moderate range of frequencies—for instance, 200 to 4000 cps (see Beranek, 1949). Therefore, if we can insure that the voltage delivered to the earphone is constant over frequency, we may assume that the earphone generates a constant sound-pressure-level output, at least in the frequency range 200 to 4000 cps.

A word of caution is in order regarding the use of calibration curves to determine sound pressure levels. As pointed out above, these calibration curves are generally run on just the earphone, using a standard coupler (of standardized volume and geometry, and consequently of standard acoustic impedance). Then often the phone is incorporated into headsets utilizing ear defenders or some kind of pad. These devices, useful in providing sound attenuation, may yield vastly different acoustic impedances. So drastic is the change with some types of pad that, rather than retaining the flat response (±2 db) over the frequency range 200 to 4000 cps, they exhibit a change of ±6 db, even over the more limited range of 500 to 4000 cps.

Because the acoustic impedance of the earphones changes as a function of frequency, and these changes are in turn reflected by changes in the electrical impedance of the phones, it is wise to drive the earphones from a low-impedance source—for instance, 1 ohm for phones whose nominal impedance is 150 ohms. This technique of driving from a low impedance into a high one is useful, not only in producing a constant voltage source, but also in helping reduce ambient noise. As a rule of thumb, most commercial earphones will generate a pressure of about 110 db in a certain standard volume when a sinusoidal voltage of about 1 volt RMS is impressed across the phone at a frequency of 1000 cps. The exact level, of course, must be determined by measurement for each earphone.

In the discussion that follows we speak only of the electrical measurements. It is assumed that a low impedance source can deliver the voltage in question to the earphone. Equivalently, we treat the earphone as a constant

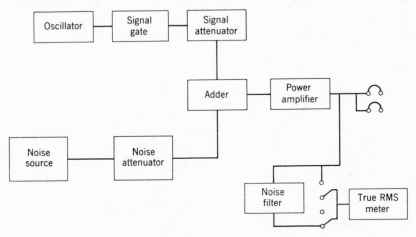

FIG. III-4 Diagram of experimental equipment.

impedance device. Let us call this constant impedance R and, moreover, treat it as purely resistive—that is, as independent of frequency. Inasmuch as most of the measurements are ratios, the exact impedance at the point where the measurement is made is of little consequence. Whatever the impedance, it is approximately the same for both signal and noise, and hence cancels when the ratio is taken.

To fix our ideas, consider a block diagram of the experimental equipment. At the upper left of Fig. III-4 is the oscillator which generates the signal. The sinusoid passes through a signal gate that pulses the signal on for a definite period of time. Next the signal attenuator controls the level of the signal, and then the signal passes into the adder, where the signal is added linearly to the noise.* The noise channel, on the lower left in Fig. III-4, consists of a noise source and of a noise attenuator to control the noise level.

The output of the adder is amplified in power and presented through earphones. The power amplifier is used primarily as a means of achieving

---

* The placement of the signal attenuator after, rather than before, the gate insures that the signal will be large relative to spurious clicks, D.C. pedestals, or other artifacts introduced by the gate itself.

a very low source impedance to drive the earphones. The signal and the noise are measured at the same point in the electrical circuit—at the earphones; this insures that any changes made in the signal or noise circuits will not differentially affect the measurement. By the same token, an even more appropriate measurement might be achieved by using a probe-tube microphone inserted in the ear canal of the subject, but this measurement generally proves impractical. Furthermore, unless abused, the earphones tend to remain stable for long periods of time, although yearly calibration to check their stability is a wise precaution.

III.4.1   Signal measurement

The signal can be measured by turning on the gate and measuring the root-mean-square (RMS) voltage of the sinusoidal signal across the earphones. Since the impedance is R, the signal voltage squared divided by R is the signal power in watts. If the signal gate produces a rectangular pulse for duration T seconds, then the energy of the signal is simply the power of the signal in watts times the duration T in seconds. The signal energy is thus measured in watt seconds. If the signal gate does not produce a rectangular waveform, it is necessary to calculate, either from oscillographic picture or from some other means, the exact envelope of the signal. This envelope, measured in volts squared, divided by R, and integrated over the duration of the signal, is the signal energy. Often the signal turns on and off linearly, and thus the effective signal energy can be calculated quite simply from geometric considerations.

For durations of approximately $\frac{1}{10}$ to $\frac{1}{100}$ of a second the ear integrates power, and thus the integral of signal power is a fairly useful and convenient measurement of the effective signal strength. If the durations are either unusually long or unusually short, some other measurement of the signal might also be required. For very long signal durations, the continuous average power is of interest. For very short signal durations, there is a spread of energy into a range of frequencies because of transients, and a rather exact knowledge of the signal gate is required to express unambiguously the signal measurement. Not to be neglected in these considerations is the fact that the earphone bandwidth and resonance peaks become important for short transient signals, and these may appreciably affect the distribution of signal energy in frequency.

III.4.2   Noise measurement

Measurement of even a flat Gaussian noise is sometimes expressed ambiguously, and we shall therefore develop at some length a practical and convenient method of determining the noise-power density, N_0. For a brief review of noise and the quantity N_0, see Appendix II.

It is well to begin by noting that the overall power in a flat noise is of little practical significance. The overall power produced by such a noise source is the sum of the power produced at all the different frequencies averaged over time. Unless the bandwidth of the noise is known, the overall measurement is nearly useless. Furthermore, when detecting a signal of, for instance, 1000 cps, we know from empirical observations that only the noise components in a narrow region about the 1000-cps signal are effective in masking the signal (see Chapter 10).

For these reasons it is desirable to measure the noise-power density, that is, the power in a one-cycle-per-second band. Also, because the spectrum of the noise source may change with age, we must verify that the noise actually is flat. Therefore, the noise density is measured at several different frequency regions. Hopefully, all these measurements give the same value of noise density, and thus we may be confident of our measured value and confident that the noise density is indeed constant over frequency.

Suppose that our meter is a true RMS meter; that is, the meter shows a value equal to the square root of the average power present at the input. Further, suppose that the noise is flat and has a noise density of N_0/R watt/cps. This is an average power density and corresponds to an average "amplitude" of about $N_0^{1/2}$ per cycle of the noise.

This noise is measured through a filter whose frequency response is given by a function $G(f)$. Assume, for the moment, that the filter has no insertion loss, and thus at center frequency the ratio of output to input is unity. Since the various components of the noise are independent, their powers add (the squares of their amplitudes add); thus, through the filter with no insertion loss we measure a power equivalent to

$$P_G = \frac{1}{R} \int_0^\infty [G(f)N_0^{1/2}]^2 df$$

This is most easily calculated by noting that the above equation can be written:

$$P_G = \frac{N_0}{R} \int_0^\infty [G(f)]^2 df$$

The integral is the effective square bandwidth of the filter, since a rectangular filter of unity response and width Δf would yield the same power as the filter $G(f)$ if

$$\Delta f = \int_0^\infty [G(f)]^2 df$$

We may therefore write

$$P_G = \frac{N_0}{R} \Delta f$$

Actually, our filter may have an insertion loss such that at peak a 1-volt input produces a k-volt output. Then, for our real filter,

$$P_G = \frac{N_0}{R} \Delta f k^2$$

The meter will actually read $P_G^{1/2}$ because it is a true RMS meter.

For a single-tuned (RCL) filter, the equivalent square bandwidth, Δf, is $\pi/2$ times the 3-db bandwidth, W_{3db}.* Hence our basic equation for an RCL filter is

$$P_G = \frac{N_0}{R} \frac{\pi}{2} W_{3db} k^2$$

Solving for N_0 we find:

$$P_G \frac{2}{\pi} \frac{1}{k^2} \frac{1}{W_{3db}} = \frac{N_0}{R}$$

Hence, using logarithms,

$$10 \log \frac{N_0}{R} = 10 \log P_G - 10 \log \frac{\pi}{2} k^2 W_{3db}$$

Often k, the insertion loss, is chosen so that

$$k^2 \frac{\pi}{2} W_{3db} = 10 \quad \text{or} \quad 100$$

Thus, for example,

$$10 \log \frac{N_0}{R} = 10 \log P_G - 20 \; db$$

This means that quantities such as E/N_0 are easily obtained, since the impedance R is the same for both signal and noise. A particularly convenient choice of R is 1 ohm. Then a decibel scale on the voltmeter is easily used to calculate directly the signal energy and the noise-power density. The center frequencies are chosen to represent the range of frequencies used in psychoacoustic experiments. Center frequencies of 500, 1000, 2000, and 4000 cycles are convenient. Noise-power densities are then read at each of the center frequencies to determine whether the noise is indeed flat, that is, if it produces about the same power in equal intervals of frequency throughout the audible spectrum.

---

* For other factors relating the equivalent square bandwidth to the 3-db bandwidth, see Lawson and Uhlenbeck (1950).

References

References preceded by an asterisk are reproduced in the volume of collected papers edited by Swets (1964).

- Abramowitz, M., and Stegun, I. A., *Handbook of Mathematical Functions*. (Eds.) New York: Dover, 1965.
- Anderson, T. W., *An Introduction to Multivariate Statistical Analysis*. New York: Wiley, 1958.
- Atkinson, R. C., "A Variable Sensitivity Theory of Signal Detection," *Psychol. Rev.*, **70**, 91–106 (1963).
- Audley, R. J., "A Stochastic Model for Individual Choice Behavior," *Psychol. Rev.*, **67**, 1–15 (1960).
- Barlow, H. B., "Retinal Noise and the Absolute Threshold," *J. Opt. Soc. Am.*, **46**, 634–639 (1956).
- Becker, G. M., "Sequential Decision Making, Wald's Models and Estimates of Parameters," *J. Exp. Psychol.*, **55**, 628–636 (1958).
- Békésy, G. von, "Ueber das Fechnersche Gesetz und seine Bedeutung für die Theorie der akustischen Beobachtungsfehler und die Theorie des Hörens," *Ann. d. Phys.*, **7**, 329–359 (1930; translated in Békésy, 1960).
- Békésy, G. von, *Experiments in Hearing*. New York: McGraw-Hill, 1960.
- Bellman, R., *Dynamic Programming*. Princeton, New Jersey: Princeton University Press, 1957.
- Beranek, L. L., *Acoustic Measurement*. New York: Wiley, 1949.
- Bertky, W., "Multiple Sampling with Constant Probability," *Ann. Math. Statist.*, **14**, 363–377 (1943).
- Birdsall, T. G., and Roberts, R. A., "Theory of Signal Detectability: Deferred-Decision Theory," *J. Acoust. Soc. Am.*, **37**, 1064–1074 (1965).
- Blackwell, D., and Girshick, M. A., *Theory of Games and Statistical Decisions*. New York: Wiley; London: Chapman and Hall, 1954.
- Blackwell, H. R., "Psychophysical Thresholds: Experimental Studies of Methods of Measurement," *Bull. Eng. Res. Inst. U. Mich.*, No. 36 (1953).
- Blackwell, H. R., "Neural Theories of Simple Visual Discriminations," *J. Opt. Soc. Am.*, **53**, 129–160 (1963).
- Bouman, M. A., and van der Velden, H. A., "Two-Quanta Explanation of the Dependence of the Threshold Values and Visual Acuity on the Visual Angle and the Time of Observation," *J. Opt. Soc. Am.*, **37**, 908–919 (1947).
- Bricker, P. D., and Chapanis, A., "Do Incorrectly-Perceived Tachistoscopic Stimuli Convey Some Information?" *Psychol. Rev.*, **60**, 181–188 (1953).
- Broadbent, D. E., "A Mechanical Model for Human Attention and Immediate Memory," *Psychol. Rev.*, **64**, 205–215 (1957).
- Broadbent, D. E., *Perception and Communication*. London: Pergamon Press, 1958.

- Broadbent, D. E., and Gregory, M., "Vigilance Considered as a Statistical Decision," *Brit. J. Psychol.*, **54**, 309–323 (1963a).
- Broadbent, D. E., and Gregory, M., "Division of Attention and the Decision Theory of Signal Detection," *Proc. Roy. Soc.* (London), **158**, 222–231 (1963b).
- Broadbent, D. E., and Gregory, M., "Effects of Noise and Signal Rate upon Vigilance Analyzed by Means of Decision Theory," *Human Factors*, **7**, 155–162 (1965).
- Bush, R. R., Luce, R. D., and Rose, R. M., "Learning Models in Psychophysics," in Atkinson, R. C. (Ed.), *Studies in Mathematical Psychology.* Stanford University Press, 1964, 201–217.
- Bush, R. R., and Mosteller, F., *Stochastic Models for Learning.* New York: Wiley, 1955.
- Carslaw, H. S., *Introduction to the Theory of Fourier's Series and Integrals*, 3rd rev. ed. London: Macmillan, 1930; New York: Dover, 1952.
- Carterette, E. C., "Message Repetition and Receiver Confirmation of Messages in Noise," *J. Acoust. Soc. Am.*, **30**, 846–855 (1958).
- Carterette, E. C., and Cole, M., "Comparison of the Receiver-Operating Characteristics Received by Ear and by Eye," *J. Acoust. Soc. Am.*, **34**, 172–178 (1962).
- Chocholle, R., "Variation des Temps de Réaction Auditifs en Fonction de l'Intensité à Diverses Fréquences," *Année Psychol.*, **41–42**, 65–124 (1945).
- Christie, L. W., and Luce, R. D., "Decision Structure and Time Relations in Simple Choice Behavior," *Bull. Math. Biophys.*, **18**, 89–112 (1956).
- *Clarke, F. R., "Confidence Ratings, Second-Choice Responses, and Confusion Matrices in Intelligibility Tests," *J. Acoust. Soc. Am.*, **32,**, 35–46 (1960).
- Clarke, F. R., Birdsall, T. G., and Tanner, W. P., Jr., "Two Types of ROC Curves and Definitions of Parameters," *J. Acoust. Soc. Am.*, **31**, 629–630 (L) (1959).
- Collier, G., "Probability of Response and Intertrial Association as Functions of Monocular and Binocular Stimulation," *J. Exp. Psychol.*, **47**, 75–83 (1954).
- Colquhoun, W. P., and Baddeley, A. D., "Role of Pretest Expectancy in Vigilance Decrement," *J. Exp. Psychol.*, **68**, 156–160 (1964).
- Corso, J. F., "The Neural Quantum Theory of Sensory Discrimination," *Psychol. Bull.*, **53**, 371–393 (1956).
- Corso, J. F., "A Theoretico-Historical Review of the Threshold Concept," *Psychol. Bull.*, **60**, 356–370 (1963).
- Cramér, H., *Mathematical Methods of Statistics.* Princeton, New Jersey: Princeton University Press, 1946.
- Creelman, C. D., "Detection of Signals of Uncertain Frequency," *J. Acoust. Soc. Am.*, **32**, 805–810 (1960).
- *Creelman, C. D., "Human Discrimination of Auditory Duration," *J. Acoust. Soc. Am.*, **34**, 582–593 (1962).
- Davenport, W. B., and Root, W. L., *An Introduction to the Theory of Random Signals and Noise.* New York: McGraw-Hill, 1958.
- deBoer, E., "Note on the Critical Bandwidth," *J. Acoust. Soc. Am.*, **34**, 985–986 (L) (1962).
- Decker, L. R., and Pollack, I., "Confidence Ratings and Message Reception for Filtered Speech," *J. Acoust. Soc. Am.*, **30**, 432–434 (1958).
- Decker, L. R., and Pollack, I., "Multiple Observers, Message Reception, and Rating Scales," *J. Acoust. Soc. Am.*, **31**, 1327–1328 (1959).
- Dodge, H. F., and Romig, H. G., "A Method of Sampling Inspection," *B. Sys. Tech. J.*, **8**, 613–631 (1929).
- Egan, J. P., "Monitoring Task in Speech Communication," *J. Acoust. Soc. Am.*, **29**, 482–489 (1957).

- Egan, J. P., "Recognition Memory and the Operating Characteristic," Indiana University: Hearing and Communication Laboratory, Technical Note AFCRC-TN-58-51, 1958.
- *Egan, J. P., and Clarke, F. R., "Source and Receiver Behavior in the Use of a Criterion," *J. Acoust. Soc. Am.*, **28**, 1267–1269 (1956).
- Egan, J. P., and Clarke, F. R., "Psychophysics and Signal Detection," in Sidowsky, J. B. (Ed.), *Experimental Methods and Instrumentation in Psychology*. New York: McGraw-Hill, 1966.
- Egan, J. P., Clarke, F. R., and Carterette, E. C., "On the Transmission and Confirmation of Messages in Noise," *J. Acoust. Soc. Am.*, **28**, 536–550 (1956).
- *Egan, J. P., Greenberg, G. Z., and Schulman, A. I., "Interval of the Time Uncertainty in Auditory Detection," *J. Acoust. Soc. Am.*, **33**, 771–778 (1961a).
- *Egan, J. P., Greenberg, G. Z., and Schulman, A. I., "Operating Characteristics, Signal Detectability, and the Method of Free Response," *J. Acoust. Soc. Am.*, **33**, 993–1007 (1961b).
- *Egan, J. P., Schulman, A. I., and Greenberg, G. Z., "Operating Characteristics Determined by Binary Decisions and by Ratings," *J. Acoust. Soc. Am.*, **31**, 768–773 (1959).
- *Egan, J. P., Schulman, A. I., and Greenberg, G. Z., "Memory for Waveform and Time Uncertainty in Auditory Detection," *J. Acoust. Soc. Am.*, **33**, 779–781 (1961).
- *Eijkman, E., and Vendrick, A. J. H., "Detection Theory Applied to the Absolute Sensitivity of Sensory Systems," *Biophys. J.*, **3**, 65–77 (1963).
- Eriksen, C. W., "Discrimination and Learning Without Awareness: a Methodological Survey and Evaluation," *Psychol. Rev.*, **67**, 279–300 (1960).
- Estes, W. K., "Toward a Statistical Theory of Learning," *Psychol. Rev.*, **57**, 94–107 (1950).
- Estes, W. K., "Learning Theory," *Ann. Rev. Psychol.* Palo Alto: Annual Reviews, Inc., 1962, pp. 107–144.
- Fechner, G. T., *Elemente der Psychophysik*. Leipzig: Breitkopf und Härtel, 1860. English translation of Vol. 1 by Adler, H. E. (Howes, D. H., and Boring, E. G., Eds.). New York: Holt, Rinehart and Winston, 1966.
- Feller, W., *An Introduction to Probability Theory and Its Applications*, Vol. 1, 2nd ed. New York: Wiley, 1957.
- Fernberger, S. W., "Instructions and the Psychophysical Limen," *Am. J. Psychol.*, **43**, 361–376 (1931).
- Fisher, R. A., "The Use of Multiple Measurements in Taxonomic Problems," *Ann. Eug.*, **7**, 179–188 (1936).
- Fitts, P. M., Peterson, J. R., and Wolpe, G., "Cognitive Aspects of Information Processing: II. Adjustments to Stimulus Redundancy," *J. Exp. Psychol.*, **65**, 507–514 (1963).
- *FitzHugh, R., "The Statistical Detection of Threshold Signals in the Retina," *J. Gen. Physiol.*, **40**, 925–948 (1957).
- FitzHugh, R., "A Statistical Analyzer for Optic Nerve Messages," *J. Gen. Physiol.* **41**, 675–692 (1958).
- Fletcher, H., "Auditory Patterns," *Rev. Mod. Phys.*, **12**, 47–65 (1940).
- Fletcher, H., *Speech and Hearing in Communication*, 2nd ed. New York: D. Van Nostrand, 1953 (1st ed. 1929).
- Forgie, J. W., and Forgie, C. D., "Results Obtained from a Vowel Recognition Computer Program," *J. Acoust. Soc. Am.*, **31**, 1480–1489 (1959).
- Gabor, D., "Theory of Communication," *J. Inst. Elec. Engrs.* (London), **93**, 429 (1946).

- Garner, W. R., *Uncertainty and Structure as Psychological Concepts*. New York: Wiley, 1962.
- Gassler, G., "Ueber die Hörschwelle für Schallereignisse mit Verschieden Breitem Frequenzspektrum," *Acustica*, **4**, 408–414 (1954).
- Gnedenko, B. V., and Kolmogorov, A. N., *Limit Distribution for Sums of Independent Random Variables*. Reading, Massachusetts: Addison-Wesley, 1954.
- Goldberg, S., *Probability: An Introduction*. Englewood Cliffs, New Jersey: Prentice-Hall, 1960.
- Goldiamond, I., "Indicators of Perception: I. Subliminal Perception, Subception, Unconscious Perception: An Analysis in Terms of Psychophysical Indicator Methodology," *Psychol. Bull.*, **55**, 373–411 (1958).
- Goldiamond, I., "Perception," in Bachrach, A. (Ed.), *The Experimental Foundations of Clinical Psychology*. New York: Basic Books, 1963.
- Goldiamond, I., and Hawkins, W. F., "Vexierversuch: The Log Relationship Between Word-Frequency and Recognition Obtained in the Absence of Stimulus Words," *J. Exp. Psychol.*, **56**, 457–463 (1958).
- Goldman, S., *Frequency Analysis, Modulation, and Noise*. New York: McGraw-Hill, 1948.
- Goode, H. H., "Deferred Decision Theory," University of Michigan: Cooley Electronics Laboratory, Technical Report No. 123, 1961.
- Granit, R., *Sensory Mechanisms of the Retina*. London: Oxford University Press, 1947.
- Granit, R., *Receptors and Sensory Perception*. New Haven: Yale University Press, 1955.
- Green, B. F., Wolf, A. K., and White, B. W., "The Detection of Statistically Defined Patterns in a Matrix of Dots," *Am. J. Psychol.*, **72**, 503–520 (1959).
- *Green, D. M., "Detection of Multiple Component Signals in Noise," *J. Acoust. Soc. Am.*, **30**, 904–911 (1958).
- *Green, D. M., "Auditory Detection of a Noise Signal," *J. Acoust. Soc. Am.*, **32**, 121–131 (1960a).
- *Green, D. M., "Psychoacoustics and Detection Theory," *J. Acoust. Soc. Am.*, **32**, 1189–1203 (1960b).
- *Green, D. M., "Detection of Auditory Sinusoids of Uncertain Frequency," *J. Acoust. Soc. Am.*, **33**, 897–903 (1961).
- Green, D. M., "Consistency of Auditory Detection Judgments," *Psychol. Rev.*, **71**, 392–407 (1964).
- Green, D. M., "Comments on 'Effects of Waveform Correlation and Signal Duration on Detection of Noise Bursts in Continuous Noise, by Raab, D. H., Osman, E., and Rich, E.,' " *J. Acoust. Soc. Am.*, **39**, 748–749 (1966).
- *Green, D. M., and Birdsall, T. G., "The Effect of Vocabulary Size on Articulation Score," University of Michigan: Electronic Defense Group, Technical Memorandum No. 81 and Technical Note AFCRC-TR-57-58, 1958.
- *Green, D. M., Birdsall, T. G., and Tanner, W. P., Jr., "Signal Detection as a Function of Signal Intensity and Duration," *J. Acoust. Soc. Am.*, **29**, 523–531 (1957).
- *Green, D. M., McKey, M. J., and Licklider, J. C. R., "Detection of a Pulsed Sinusoid in Noise as a Function of Frequency," *J. Acoust. Soc. Am.*, **31**, 1446–1452 (1959).
- Greenberg, G. Z., "Cueing Signals and Frequency Uncertainty in Auditory Detection," Indiana University: Hearing and Communication Laboratory, Technical Report No. ESD-TDR-62-38, 1962.
- Greenwood, D. D., "Auditory Masking and the Critical Band," *J. Acoust. Soc. Am.*, **33**, 484–502 (1961a).

- Greenwood, D. D., "Critical Bandwidth and the Frequency Coordinates of the Basilar Membrane," *J. Acoust. Soc. Am.*, **33**, 1344–1356 (1961b).
- Grenander, U., "Stochastic Processes and Statistical Inference," *Arkiv. Mathematik*, Bd. 1, Nr. 17, p. 195 (1950).
- Guilford, J. P., *Psychometric Methods*, 2nd ed. New York: McGraw-Hill, 1954 (1st ed., 1936).
- *Gundy, R. F., "Auditory Detection of an Unspecified Signal," *J. Acoust. Soc. Am.* **33**, 1008–1012 (1961).
- Haber, R. N., "Repetition as a Determinant of Perceptual Recognition Processes," Symposium on Models for the Perception of Speech and Visual Form, Boston, Massachusetts, November, 1964.
- Hack, M. H., "Signal Detection in the Rat," *Science*, **139**, 758–759 (1963).
- Hake, H. W., "Perception," *Ann. Rev. Psychol.* Palo Alto: Annual Reviews, Inc., 1962, pp. 145–170.
- Hartley, R. V. L., "Transmission of Information," *B. Sys. Tech. J.*, **7**, 535–563 (1928).
- Hawkins, J. E., Jr., and Stevens, S. S., "The Masking of Pure Tones and of Speech by White Noise," *J. Acoust. Soc. Am.*, **22**, 6–13 (1950).
- Hecht, S., "Energy and Vision," in Baitsell, G. A. (Ed.), *Science in Progress*. New Haven: Yale University Press, Series 4, 75, 1945.
- Hecht, S., Shlaer, S., and Pirenne, M. H., "Energy, Quanta, and Vision," *J. Gen. Physiol.*, **25**, 819–840 (1942).
- Helmholtz, H. L. F., *The Sensations of Tone*, 2nd Eng. ed. New York: Longmans, Green, 1885; Dover, 1954.
- Hennon, V. A. C., "The Relation of the Time of a Judgment to its Accuracy," *Psychol. Rev.*, **18**, 186–201 (1911).
- Hodges, J. L., Jr., and Lehman, E. L., *Basic Concepts of Probability and Statistics*. San Francisco: Holden-Day, 1964.
- Hohle, R. H., "Detection of a Visual Signal with Low Background Noise: An Experimental Comparison of Two Theories," *J. Exp. Psychol.*, **70**, 459–463 (1965).
- Howarth, C. I., and Treisman, M., "The Effect of Warning Interval on the Electric Phosphene and Auditory Thresholds," *Quart. J. Exp. Psychol.*, **10**, 130–141 (1958).
- Howes, D. H., "A Statistical Theory of the Phenomenon of Subception," *Psychol. Rev.*, **61**, 98–110 (1954).
- Howes, D. H., "On the Relation Between the Intelligibility and Frequency of Occurrence of English Words," *J. Acoust. Soc. Am.*, **29**, 296–305 (1957).
- Irwin, F. W., and Smith, W. A. S., "Value, Cost, and Information as Determiners of Decision," *J. Exp. Psychol.*, **54**, 229–232 (1957).
- James, W., *The Principles of Psychology*. New York: Holt, 1890; Dover, 1950.
- Jastrow, J., "Critique of Psycho-Physic Methods," *Am. J. Psychol.*, **1**, 271–309 (1888).
- Jeffress, L. A., "Stimulus-Oriented Approach to Detection," *J. Acoust. Soc. Am.*, **36**, 766–774 (1964).
- Jeffress, L. A., Blodgett, H. C., Sandel, T. T., and Wood, C. L., "Masking of Tonal Signals," *J. Acoust. Soc. Am.*, **28**, 416–426 (1956).
- Jerison, H. J., and Pickett, R. M., "Vigilance: A Review and Re-Evaluation," *Human Factors*, **5**, 211–238 (1963).
- Jerison, H. J., and Pickett, R. M., "Vigilance: The Importance of the Elicited Observing Rate," *Science*, **143**, 970–971 (1964).
- Jerison, H. J., Pickett, R. M., and Stenson, H. H., "The Elicited Observing Rate and Decision Processes in Vigilance," *Human Factors*, **7**, 107–128 (1965).
- Jersild, A., "The Determinant of Confidence," *Am. J. Psychol.*, **41**, 640–642 (1929).

- Johnson, D. M., "Confidence and Speed in the Two-Category Judgment," *Arch. Psychol. N.Y.*, **241**, 262–263 (1939).
- Kellogg, W. N., "Experimental Evaluation of Equality Information in Psychophysics," *Arch. Psychol.*, **17**, 112 (1930).
- Kendall, M. G., *Advanced Theory of Statistics*, Vol. 2. New York: Hafner Publishing, 1947, pp. 227–230.
- Kincaid, W. M., and Hamilton, C. E., "An Experimental Study of the Nature of Forced-Choice Responses in Visual Detection," University of Michigan: Vision Research Laboratories, Technical Report No. 2144-295-T, 1959.
- Kinchla, R. A., "A Learning Factor in Visual Discrimination," in Atkinson, R. C. (Ed.), *Studies in Mathematical Psychology*. Palo Alto: Stanford University Press, 1964, pp. 233–249.
- Koopman, B. O., "The Theory of Search: Part II, Target Detection," *Opns. Res.*, **4**, 503–531 (1956).
- Kristofferson, A. B., "Monocular and Binocular Detection Thresholds for Targets Varying in Size and Retinal Position," University of Michigan: Vision Research Laboratories, Technical Report No. 2144-290-T, 1958.
- Kristofferson, A. B., and Dember, W. N., "Detectability of Targets Consisting of Multiple Small Points of Light," University of Michigan: Vision Research Laboratories, Technical Report No. 2144-298-T, 1958.
- Kuffler, S. W., "Neurones in the Retina: Organization, Inhibition, and Excitation Problems," *Cold Spring Harbor Symp. Quant. Biol.*, **17**, 281 (1952).
- Kuffler, S. W., "Discharge Patterns and Functional Organization of Mammalian Retina," *J. Neurophysiol.*, **16**, 37 (1953).
- Kuffler, S. W., FitzHugh, R., and Barlow, H. B., "Maintained Activity in the Cat's Retina in Light and Darkness," *J. Gen. Physiol.*, **40**, 683–702 (1957).
- Larkin, W. D., and Norman, D. A., "An Extension and Experimental Analysis of the Neural Quantum Theory," in Atkinson, R. C. (Ed.), *Studies in Mathematical Psychology*. Palo Alto: Stanford University Press, 1964.
- Lawson, J. L., and Uhlenbeck, G. E., *Threshold Signals*. New York: McGraw-Hill, 1950.
- Lazarus, R. S., and McCleary, R. A., "Autonomic Discrimination Without Awareness: A Study of Subception," *Psychol. Rev.*, **58**, 113–122 (1951).
- Lee, W., "Choosing Among Confusably Distributed Stimuli with Specified Likelihood Ratios," *Percept. Motor Skills*, **16**, 445–467 (1963).
- Lee, Y. W., *Statistical Theory of Communication*. New York: Wiley, 1960.
- Linker, E., Moore, M. E., and Galanter, E., "Taste Thresholds, Detection Models, and Disparate Results," *J. Exp. Psychol.*, **67**, 59–66 (1964).
- Loeb, M., and Binford, J. R., "Vigilance for Auditory Intensity Changes as a Function of Preliminary Feedback and Confidence Level," *Human Factors*, **6**, 445–458 (1964).
- Luce, R. D., *Individual Choice Behavior*. New York: Wiley, 1959, pp. 58–67.
- Luce, R. D., "Detection Thresholds: A Problem Reconsidered," *Science*, **132**, 1495 (1960).
- Luce, R. D., "A Threshold Theory for Simple Detection Experiments," *Psychol. Rev.*, **70**, 61–79 (1963a).
- Luce, R. D., "Detection and Recognition," in Luce, R. D., Bush, R. R., and Galanter, E. (Eds.), *Handbook of Mathematical Psychology*. New York: Wiley, 1963b, pp. 103–189.
- Luce, R. D., "A Model for Detection in Temporally Unstructured Experiments with a Poisson Distribution of Signal Presentations," *J. Math. Psychol.*, **3**, 48–64 (1966).

• Luce, R. D., and Raiffa, H., *Games and Decisions*. New York: Wiley, 1957.
• Lukaszewski, J. S., and Elliott, D. N., "Auditory Threshold as a Function of Forced-Choice Techniques, Feedback, and Motivation," *J. Acoust. Soc. Am.*, **34**, 223–228 (1962).
• Mackworth, J. F., "The Effect of Signal Frequency on the Detection of Two Kinds of Signals," Toronto, Ontario: Defense Research Medical Laboratories, Technical Report No. 234-16, 1962.
• Mackworth, J. F., and Taylor, M. M., "*d'* Measure of Signal Detectability," *Canad. J. Psychol.*, **17**, 302–325 (1963).
• Marill, T. M., "Detection Theory and Psychophysics," Massachusetts Institute of Technology: Research Laboratories of Electronics, Technical Report No. 319, 1956.
• Marill, T. M., and Green, D. M., "Statistical Recognition Functions and the Design of Pattern Recognizers," *IRE Trans. Elec. Computers*, EC-9, No. 4, 1960.
• Martel, H. C., and Mathews, M. V., "Further Results on the Detectability of Known Signals in Gaussian Noise," *B. Sys. Tech. J.*, **40**, 423–451 (1961).
• Martin, W. H., "Rating the Transmission Performance of Telephone Circuits," *B. Sys. Tech. J.*, **10**, 116–131 (1931).
• Mayer, A. M., "Research in Acoustics," *Philosophical Magazine*, **11**, 500–507 (1876).
• McGill, W. J., "Loudness and Reaction Time," *Acta Psychol.*, **19**, 193–199 (1961).
• McGill, W. J., "Stochastic Latency Mechanisms," in Luce, R. D., Bush, R. R., and Galanter, E. (Eds.), *Handbook of Mathematical Psychology*, Vol. 1. New York: Wiley, 1963, pp. 309–360.
• McGill, W. J., *Introduction to Counter Theory in Psychophysics*. 1966 (in press).
• McKnown, F. W., and Emling, J. W., "A System of Effective Transmission Data for Rating Telephone Circuits," *B. Sys. Tech. J.*, **12**, 331–346 (1933).
• Middleton, D., "The Statistical Theory of Detection: I. Optimum Detection of Signals in Noise," Massachusetts Institute of Technology: Lincoln Laboratories, Technical Report No. 35, 1953.
• Middleton, D., "Statistical Theory of Signal Detection," *Trans. IRE Professional Group on Information Theory*, PGIT-3, 26 (1954).
• Middleton, D., "A Note on Singular and Non-Singular Optimum (Bayes) Tests for the Detection of Normal Stochastic Signals in Normal Noise," *Trans. IRE Professional Group on Information Theory*, PGIT-7, 105–113 (1961).
• Miller, G. A., *Language and Communication*. New York: McGraw-Hill, 1951.
• Miller, G. A., and Garner, W. R., "Effect of Random Presentation on the Psychometric Function: Implications for a Quantal Theory of Discrimination," *Am. J. Psychol.*, **57**, 451–467 (1944).
• Miller, G. A., Heise, G. A., and Lichten, W., "The Intelligibility of Speech as a Function of the Context of the Test Materials," *J. Exp. Psychol.*, **41**, 329–335 (1951).
• Miller, J. G., *Unconsciousness*. New York: Wiley, 1942.
• Mosteller, F., Rourke, R. E. K., and Thomas, G. B., Jr., *Probability and Statistics*. Reading, Massachusetts: Addison-Wesley, 1961.
• Munson, W. A., and Karlin, J. E., "The Measurement of Human Channel Transmission Characteristics," *J. Acoust. Soc. Am.*, **26**, 542–553 (1954).
• Murdock, B. B., Jr., "Signal-Detection Theory and Short-Term Memory," *J. Exp. Psychol.*, **70**, 443–447 (1965).
• Nachmias, J., and Steinman, R. M., "Study of Absolute Visual Detection by the Rating-Scale Method," *J. Opt. Soc. Am.*, **53**, 1206–1213 (1963).
• Nachmias, J., and Sternberg, S., "An Analysis of the Recognition Process." Paper presented at Fourth Annual Scientific Meeting, The Psychonomic Society, Bryn Mawr College, Pennsylvania, 1963.

- Nevin, J. A., "A Method for the Determination of Psychophysical Functions in the Rat," *J. Exp. Anal. Behavior*, **7**, p. 169 (abstract) (1964).
- Neyman, J., and Pearson, E. S., "On the Problem of the Most Efficient Tests of Statistical Hypotheses," *Phil. Trans. Roy. Soc. London*, Series A, p. 289 (1933).
- Norman, D. A., "Sensory Thresholds and Response Bias," *J. Acoust. Soc. Am.*, **35**, 1432–1441 (1963).
- Norman, D. A., "A Comparison of Data Obtained with Different False-Alarm Rates," *Psychol. Rev.*, **71**, 243–246 (1964a).
- Norman, D. A., "Sensory Thresholds, Response Biases, and the Neural Quantum Theory," *J. Math. Psychol.*, **1**, 88–120 (1964b).
- Norman, D. A., and Wickelgren, W. A., "Short-Term Recognition Memory for Single Digits and Pairs of Digits," *J. Exp. Psychol.*, **70**, 479–489 (1965).
- North, D. O., "An Analysis of the Factors which Determine Signal-Noise Discrimination in Pulsed Carrier Systems," RCA Laboratory Report PTR-6C, 1943.
- Nyquist, H., "Certain Factors Affecting Telegraph Speed," *B. Sys. Tech. J.*, **3**, 324–346 (1924).
- Parks, T. E., "Signal-Detectability Theory of Recognition-Memory Performance," *Psychol. Rev.*, **73**, 44–58 (1966).
- Parzen, E., *Stochastic Processes*. San Francisco: Holden-Day, 1962.
- Patnaik, P. B., "The Non-Central Chi-Square and F-Distribution and Their Applications," *Biometrika*, **36**, 202–232 (1949).
- Peterson, W. W., and Birdsall, T. G., "The Theory of Signal Detectability," University of Michigan: Electronic Defense Group, Technical Report No. 13, 1953.
- Peterson, W. W., Birdsall, T. G., and Fox, W. C., "The Theory of Signal Detectability," *Trans. IRE Professional Group on Information Theory*, **PGIT-4**, 171–212 (1954).
- Pfafflin, S. M., and Mathews, M. V., "Energy Detection Model for Monaural Auditory Detection," *J. Acoust. Soc. Am.*, **34**, 1842–1852 (1962).
- Pfafflin, S. M., and Mathews, M. V., "Effect of Filter Type on Energy Detection Models for Auditory Signal Detection," *J. Acoust. Soc. Am.*, **38**, 1055–1056 (1965).
- Pierce, J., "Determinants of Threshold for Form," *Psychol. Bull.*, **4**, 391–407 (1963).
- Pirenne, M. H., and Marriott, F. H. C., "The Quantum Theory of Light and the Psycho-Physiology of Vision," in Koch, S. (Ed.), *Psychology: A Study of a Science*, Vol. I. New York: McGraw-Hill, 1959, pp. 288–361.
- Pollack, I., "Message Uncertainty and Message Reception," *J. Acoust. Soc. Am.*, **31**, 1500–1508 (1959a).
- Pollack, I., "Message Repetition and Message Reception," *J. Acoust. Soc. Am.*, **31**, 1509–1515 (1959b).
- Pollack, I., "On Indices of Signal and Response Discriminability," *J. Acoust. Soc. Am.*, **31**, 1031 (L) (1959c).
- *Pollack, I., "Identification of Elementary Auditory Displays and the Method of Recognition Memory," *J. Acoust. Soc. Am.*, **31**, 1126–1128 (1959d).
- Pollack, I., "Message Uncertainty and Message Reception, II," *Language and Speech*, **3**, 174–179 (1960).
- Pollack, I., "Message Probability and Message Reception," *J. Acoust. Soc. Am.*, **36**, 937–945 (1964).
- *Pollack, I., and Decker, L. R., "Confidence Ratings, Message Reception, and the Receiver Operating Characteristic," *J. Acoust. Soc. Am.*, **30**, 286–292 (1958).
- Pollack, I., and Ficks, L., "Information of Elementary Multi-Dimensional Auditory Displays," *J. Acoust. Soc. Am.*, **26**, 155–158 (1954).
- Pollack, I., Galanter, E., and Norman, D., "An Efficient Non-Parametric Analysis of Recognition Memory," *Psychonomic Science*, **1**, 327–328 (1964).

- Pollack, I., and Madans, A. B., "On the Performance of a Combination of Detectors," *Human Factors*, **6**, 523–532 (1964).
- Pollack, I., and Norman, D. A., "A Non-Parametric Analysis of Recognition Experiments," *Psychonomic Science*, **1**, 125–126 (1964).
- Pollack, I., Rubenstein, H., and Decker, L., "Analysis of Incorrect Responses to an Unknown Message Set," *J. Acoust. Soc. Am.*, **32**, 454–457 (1960).
- Pruzansky, S., and Mathews, M. V., "Talker-Recognition Procedure Based on Analysis of Variance," *J. Acoust. Soc. Am.*, **36**, 2041–2047 (1964).
- Raab, D. H., Osman, E., and Rich, E., "Effects of Waveform Correlation and Signal Duration," *J. Acoust. Soc. Am.*, **35**, 1942–1946 (1963).
- Raiffa, H., and Schlaifer, R., *Applied Statistical Decision Theory*. Harvard University: Graduate School of Business Administration, Division of Research, 1961.
- Rayleigh, J. W. S., *The Theory of Sound*, Vol. 1, 2nd ed. London: Macmillan, 1894; New York: Dover, 1945.
- Reich, E., and Swerling, P., "The Detection of a Sine Wave in Gaussian Noise," *J. Appl. Phys.*, **24**, 289–296 (1953).
- Rice, S. O., "Mathematical Analysis of Random Noise," *B. Sys. Tech. J.*, **23**, 282–332 (1944); **24**, 46–156 (1945). (Also avail. in Wax, N. (Ed.), *Selected Papers on Noise and Stochastic Processes*. New York: Dover Publications, 1954.)
- Rilling, M., and McDiarmid, C., "Signal Detection in Fixed-Ratio Schedules," *Science*, **148**, 526–527 (1965).
- Rodwan, A. S., and Hake, H. W., "The Discriminant-Function as a Model for Perception," *Am. J. Psychol.* **77**, 380–392 (1964).
- Sankaran, M., "Approximation to the Non-Central Chi-Squared Distributions," *Biometrika*, **50**, 199–204 (1963).
- Schafer, T. H., "Detection of a Signal by Several Observers," San Diego, California: U.S. Naval Electronics Laboratory, Technical Report No. 101, 1949.
- Schafer, T. H., and Gales, R. S., "Auditory Masking of Multiple Tones by Random Noise," *J. Acoust. Soc. Am.*, **21**, 392–398 (1949).
- Schafer, T. H., Gales, R. S., Shewmaker, C. A., and Thompson, P. O., "The Frequency Selectivity of the Ear as Determined by Masking Experiments," *J. Acoust. Soc. Am.*, **22**, 490–496 (1950).
- Schafer, T. H., and Shewmaker, C. A., "A Comparative Study of the Audio, Visual, and Audio-Visual Recognition Differentials for Pulses Masked by Random Noise," San Diego, California: U.S. Naval Electronics Laboratory, Technical Report No. 372, 1953.
- Scharf, B., "Complex Sounds and Critical Bands," *Psychol. Bull.*, **58**, 205–217 (1961).
- Schoeffler, M. S., "Theory for Psychophysical Learning," *J. Acoust. Soc. Am.*, **37**, 1124–1133 (1965).
- Sebestyen, G. S., *Decision-Making Processes in Pattern Recognition*. New York: Macmillan, 1962.
- Senders, V. L., and Soward, A., "Analysis of Response Frequencies in the Setting of a Psychophysical Experiment," *Am. J. Psychol.*, **65**, 358–374 (1952).
- Shannon, C. E., "The Mathematical Theory of Communication," *B. Sys. Tech. J.*, **27**, 379–423 (1948).
- Shannon, C. E., "Communication in the Presence of Noise," *Proc. IRE*, **37**, 10–21 (1949).
- Shannon, C. E., and Weaver, W., *The Mathematical Theory of Communication*. Urbana, Illinois: University of Illinois Press, 1949.
- Sherwin, C. W., Kodman, F., Jr., Kovaly, J. J., Prothe, W. C., and Melrose, J.,

"Detection of Signals in Noise: A Comparison Between the Human Detector and an Electronic Detector," *J. Acoust. Soc. Am.*, **28,** 617–622 (1956).

- Shipley, E. F., "Cueing as a Determiner of Apparent Variability in Sensitivity," Massachusetts Institute of Technology: Research Laboratory of Electronics, Quart. Prog. Rpt. No. 53; and *J. Acoust. Soc. Am.*, **31,** 834 (abstract) (1959).

- Shipley, E. F., "A Model for Detection and Recognition with Signal Uncertainty," *Psychometrika*, **25,** 273–289 (1960).

- Smith, J. E. K., "Stimulus Programming in Psychophysics," *Psychometrika*, **26,** 27–33 (1961).

- Smith, J. E. K., "Decision-Theoretic Speaker Recognizer," *J. Acoust. Soc. Am.*, **34,** 1988 (abstract) (1962).

- Smith, J. E. K., and Klem, L., "Vowel Recognition Using a Multiple Discriminant Function," *J. Acoust. Soc. Am.*, **33,** 358 (1961).

- Smith, M., and Wilson, E. A., "A Model of the Auditory Threshold and its Application to the Problem of the Multiple Observer," *Psychol. Monogr.*, **67,** No. 9 (Whole No. 359) (1953).

- Solomon, R. L., and Postman, L., "Frequency of Usage as a Determinant of Recognition Thresholds for Words," *J. Exp. Psychol.*, **43,** 195–201 (1952).

- Speeth, S. D., and Mathews, M. V., "Sequential Effects in the Signal-Detection Situation," *J. Acoust. Soc. Am.*, **33,** 1046–1054 (1961).

- Stevens, S. S., "The Direct Estimation of Sensory Magnitudes—Loudness," *Am. J. Psychol.*, **69,** 1–25 (1956).

- Stevens, S. S., "Is There a Quantal Threshold?" in Rosenblith, W. A. (Ed.), *Sensory Communication.* New York: Technology Press and Wiley, 1961.

- Stevens, S. S., Morgan, C. T., and Volkmann, J., "Theory of the Neural Quantum in the Discrimination of Loudness and Pitch," *Am. J. Psychol.*, **54,** 315–335 (1941).

- Stone, M., "Models for Choice-Reaction Time," *Psychometrika*, **25,** 251–260 (1960).

- *Swets, J. A., "Indices of Signal Detectability Obtained with Various Psychophysical Procedures," *J. Acoust. Soc. Am.*, **31,** 511–513 (1959).

- *Swets, J. A., "Is There a Sensory Threshold?" *Science*, **134,** 168–177 (1961).

- *Swets, J. A., "Central Factors in Auditory Frequency Selectivity," *Psychol. Bull.*, **60,** 429–440 (1963a).

- Swets, J. A., "Information Retrieval Systems," *Science*, **141,** 245–250 (1963b).

- Swets, J. A., *Signal Detection and Recognition by Human Observers: Contemporary Readings.* (Ed.) New York: Wiley, 1964.

- *Swets, J. A., and Green, D. M., "Sequential Observations by Human Observers of Signals in Noise," in Cherry, C. (Ed.), *Information Theory.* London: Butterworths, 1961.

- *Swets, J. A., Green, D. M., and Tanner, W. P., Jr., "On the Width of Critical Bands," *J. Acoust. Soc. Am.*, **34,** 108–113 (1962).

- Swets, J. A., Millman, S. H., Fletcher, W. E., and Green, D. M., "Learning to Identify Nonverbal Sounds: An Application of a Computer as a Teaching Machine," *J. Acoust. Soc. Am.*, **34,** 928–935 (1962).

- *Swets, J. A., and Sewall, S. T., "Stimulus vs. Response Uncertainty in Recognition," *J. Acoust. Soc. Am.*, **33,** 1586–1592 (1961).

- Swets, J. A., and Sewall, S. T., "Invariance of Signal Detectability over Stages of Practice and Levels of Motivation," *J. Exp. Psychol.*, **66,** 120–126 (1963).

- *Swets, J. A., Shipley, E. F., McKey, M. J., and Green, D. M., "Multiple Observations of Signals in Noise," *J. Acoust. Soc. Am.*, **31,** 514–521 (1959).

- Swets, J. A., Tanner, W. P., Jr., and Birdsall, T. G., "The Evidence for a Decision-Making Theory of Visual Detection," University of Michigan: Electronic Defense Group, Technical Report No. 40, 1955.
- *Swets, J. A., Tanner, W. P., Jr., and Birdsall, T. G., "Decision Processes in Perception," *Psychol. Rev.*, **68**, 301–340 (1961).
- *Tanner, W. P., Jr., "Theory of Recognition," *J. Acoust. Soc. Am.*, **28**, 882–888 (1956).
- Tanner, W. P., Jr., "Application of the Theory of Signal Detectability to Amplitude Discrimination," *J. Acoust. Soc. Am.*, **33**, 1233–1244 (1961a).
- *Tanner, W. P., Jr., "Physiological Implications of Psychophysical Data," *Ann. N.Y. Acad. Sci.*, **89**, 752–765 (1961b).
- *Tanner, W.P., Jr., and Birdsall, T. G., "Definitions of d' and η as Psychophysical Measures," *J. Acoust. Soc. Am.*, **30**, 922–928 (1958).
- Tanner, W. P., Jr., Clarke, F. R., and Birdsall, T. G., "The Concept of the Ideal Observer in Psychophysics," University of Michigan: Electronic Defense Group, Technical Report No. 98, 1960.
- Tanner, W. P., Jr., and Jones, R. C., "The Ideal Sensor System as Approached Through Statistical Decision Theory and the Theory of Signal Detectability," in Proceedings of the Armed Forces-NRC Vision Committee, held at Washington, D.C., November, 1959.
- Tanner, W. P., Jr., and Rivette, C. L., "Learning in Psychophysical Experiments," *J. Acoust. Soc. Am.*, **35**, 1896 (abstract) (1963).
- Tanner, W. P., Jr., and Swets, J. A., "A New Theory of Visual Detection," University of Michigan: Electronic Defense Group, Technical Report No. 18, 1953.
- Tanner, W. P., and Swets, J. A., "The Human Use of Information: I. Signal Detection for the Case of the Signal Known Exactly," *Trans. IRE Professional Group on Information Theory*, **PGIT-4**, 213–221 (1954a).
- Tanner, W. P., Jr., and Swets, J. A., "A Decision-Making Theory of Visual Detection," *Psychol. Rev.*, **61**, 401–409 (1954b).
- Tanner, W. P., Jr., Swets, J. A., and Green, D. M., "Some General Properties of the Hearing Mechanism," University of Michigan: Electronic Defense Group, Technical Report No. 30, 1956.
- Thurstone, L. L., "A Law of Comparative Judgment," *Psychol. Rev.*, **34**, 273–286 (1927a).
- Thurstone, L. L., "Psychophysical Analysis," *Am. J. Psychol.*, **38**, 368–389 (1927b).
- Titchener, E. B., *Experimental Psychology: Instructor's Manual*, Vol. II, Pt. II. New York: Macmillan, 1905.
- Torgerson, W. S., *Theory and Methods of Scaling*. New York: Wiley, 1958.
- Treisman, M., "Auditory Masking," *J. Acoust. Soc. Am.*, **35**, 1256–1263 (1963).
- Treisman, M., "The Effect of One Stimulus on the Threshold for Another: An Application of Signal Detectability Theory," *Brit. J. Stat. Psychol.*, **XVII**, Pt. 1, 15–35 (1964a).
- Treisman, M., "Noise and Weber's Law: The Discrimination of Brightness and Other Dimensions," *Psychol. Rev.*, **71**, 314–330 (1964b).
- Urick, R. J., and Stocklin, P. L., "A Simple Prediction Method for Signal Detectability of Acoustic Systems," Washington, D.C.: Naval Ordnance Laboratories, Report No. AD274-500, 1962.
- van den Brink, G., "Detection of Tone Pulse of Various Durations in Noise of Various Bandwidths," *J. Acoust. Soc. Am.*, **36**, 1206–1211 (1964).
- Van Meter, D., and Middleton, D., "Modern Statistical Approaches to Reception

in Communication Theory," *Trans. IRE Professional Group on Information Theory*, **PGIT-4,** 119–141 (1954).

· Veniar, F. A., "Signal Detection as a Function of Frequency Ensemble, I," *J. Acoust. Soc. Am.*, **30,** 1020–1024 (1958a).

· Veniar, F. A., "Signal Detection as a Function of Frequency Ensemble, II," *J. Acoust. Soc. Am.*, **30,** 1075–1078 (1958b).

· Voelcker, H. B., "A Decision-Theory Approach to Sound Lateralization," in Cherry, C. (Ed.), *Information Theory.* London: Butterworths, 1961.

· Wald, A., *Sequential Analysis.* New York: Wiley; London: Chapman and Hall, 1947.

· Wald, A., *Statistical Decision Functions.* New York: Wiley, 1950.

· Watson, C. S., Rilling, M. E., and Bourbon, W. T., "Receiver-Operating Characteristics Determined by a Mechanical Analog to the Rating Scale," *J. Acoust. Soc. Am.*, **36,** 283–288 (1964).

· Webster, J. C., Miller, P. H., Thompson, P. O., and Davenport, E. W., "Masking and Pitch Shifts of Pure Tones near Abrupt Changes in a Thermal Noise Spectrum," *J. Acoust. Soc. Am.*, **24,** 147–152 (1952).

· Wegel, R. L., and Lane, C. E., "The Auditory Masking of one Pure Tone by Another and its Probable Relation to the Dynamics of the Inner Ear," *Physical Review*, **23,** Series 2, 266–285 (1924).

· Weintraub, D. J., and Hake, H. W., "Visual Discrimination, an Interpretation in Terms of Detectability Theory," *J. Opt. Soc. Am.*, **52,** 1179–1184 (1962).

· Welch, P. D., and Wimpress, R. S., "Two Multivariate Statistical Computer Programs and Their Application to the Vowel Recognition Problem," *J. Acoust. Soc. Am.*, **33,** 426–434 (1961).

· Woodward, P. M., and Davies, I. L., "Information Theory and Inverse Probability in Telecommunications," *Proc. I.E.E.* (London), Vol. 99, Pt. III, 37–44 (1952).

· Woodworth, R. S., *Experimental Psychology.* New York: Holt, 1938.

· Woodworth, R. S., and Schlosberg, H., *Experimental Psychology.* New York: Holt, 1954.

· Zwicker, E., Flottorp, G., and Stevens, S. S., "Critical Band Width in Loudness Summation," *J. Acoust. Soc. Am.*, **29,** 548–557 (1957).

· Zwislocki, J., Maire, F., Feldman, A. S., and Rubin, H., "On the Effect of Practice and Motivation on the Threshold of Audibility," *J. Acoust. Soc. Am.*, **30,** 254–262 (1958).

Problem Solutions

Answers to Selected Questions

1.1 (a) Table PS1-1 contains the required probabilities and the values of likelihood ratio.

TABLE PS1-1. Probability of Total T Given h_b[a] and h_0[b].

	Multiply Entries by 1/72		
Total Spots, T	Given h_b	Given h_0	$l(T) = \dfrac{P(T \mid H_b)}{P(T \mid H_0)}$
2	0	1	0
3	0	2	0
4	0	3	0
5	2	4	0.50
6	4	5	0.80
7	6	6	1.00
8	8	6	1.33
9	10	6	1.67
10	12	6	2.00
11	10	6	1.67
12	8	6	1.33
13	6	6	1.00
14	4	5	0.80
15	2	4	0.50
16	0	3	0
17	0	2	0
18	0	1	0

[a] h_b: Odd die is black; six sides with "3."

[b] h_0: Odd die is orange; three sides with "0" and three sides with "6."

429

(b) Yes. The likelihood ratio $l(T) \geq 1.5$ if and only if $T = 9$, 10, or 11; similarly, $l(T) < 1.5$ if and only if T is *not* 9, 10, or 11.

1.2 (a) $l(x) = 1.5$ for black hair
$l(x) = 1.0$ for blond hair
$l(x) = 0.66$ for red hair

(b) This problem involves an application of Bayes' rule (Eq. 1.4). Using the relative frequency as an estimate of $P(h_i)$, the answers are:

$$P(\text{black} \mid \text{height} > 5') = 6/13$$
$$P(\text{blond} \mid \text{height} < 5') = 5/12$$
$$P(\text{red} \mid \text{height} > 5') = 2/13$$

1.3 (a) The likelihood ratio is $\lambda e^{-\lambda x}/e^{-x} = \lambda e^{(1-\lambda)x}$.
(b) Using the notation of the text:

$$V_{00} = 0$$
$$V_{01} = 100$$
$$V_{11} = 10^4 \quad \text{and} \quad \frac{P(h_0)}{P(h_1)} = 10^6$$
$$V_{10} = 10^6$$

Thus, using Eq. 1.20 we have $\beta \approx 10^2$. Only if $l(x) > 100$ should a package be inspected.
(c) If $\lambda = \frac{1}{4}$, $l(x) = \frac{1}{4}e^{3/4x}$.

For
$$l(x) = 100$$
$$e^{3/4x} = 400$$

and
$$x = \frac{4}{3}\ln 400 \approx 8$$

1.4 (a) You wish to set the criterion on the number of counts so that the probability of opening the package, given that it is nonradioactive, $P(0 \mid NRA)$, is $10^3/10^7 = 0.0001$.

$$P(0 \mid NRA) = \int_x^{+\infty} e^{-y}\, dy = -e^{-x}\Big]_x^{\infty} = +e^{-x}$$

$$0.0001 = e^{-x} \qquad x \approx 9.30$$

(b) Given that $x = 9.30$, the probability of detecting a radioactive package is:

$$P(0 \mid RA) = \int_{9.30}^{\infty} 1/3 e^{-1/3 y}\, dy = \left[-e^{-1/3 y}\right]_{9.30}^{\infty}$$
$$= +e^{-9.30^{1/3}} = 0.045$$

2.1 The first step is to rank the possible observations according to likelihood ratio. Then, assuming that we respond "black" if $l(T) \geq k$, we consider $P(T \mid b)$ and $P(T \mid o)$ to calculate $P(B \mid b)$ and $P(B \mid o)$. For example, if $k = 1.33$, we say "black" if $T = 8, 9, 10, 11,$ or 12; $P(B \mid b)$ is simply

$$\sum_{T=8}^{12} (T \mid b) = 48/72 = 2/3$$

and $P(B \mid o)$ is simply

$$\sum_{T=8}^{12} (T \mid o) = 30/72 = 5/12$$

As k takes on different values the coordinates (Table PS2-1) for the ROC curve are obtained.

TABLE PS2-1. COORDINATES FOR ROC CURVE.

$l(T)$	$P(B \mid b)$	$P(B \mid o)$
∞	0	0
2.00	0.167	0.083
1.66	0.444	0.250
1.33	0.667	0.417
1.00	0.833	0.583
0.80	0.944	0.722
0.50	1.000	0.833
0.00	1.000	1.000

2.3 The area under the ROC curve is the predicted percentage correct in two-alternative forced-choice: 75%.

2.4 No.

3.1 (a) The likelihood ratio is $f(x \mid s)/f(x \mid n) = l(x) = 2x$ where $0 < x < 1$.

(b) The ROC curve on linear scales starts at (0, 0) with a slope of 2; it has unit slope when $k = \frac{1}{2}$, that is, at coordinates $P(S \mid s) = \frac{3}{4}$, $P(S \mid n) = \frac{1}{2}$; the slope diminishes to zero as the (1.00, 1.00) point is reached. (Notice that the preceding answer was based almost exclusively on the value of likelihood ratio.)

3.2 If $P(R1 \mid \langle sn \rangle) = P(R2 \mid \langle ns \rangle)$, then, since $P(R1 \mid \langle ns \rangle) + P(R2 \mid \langle ns \rangle) = 1$, we know that $P(R1 \mid \langle sn \rangle) = 1 - P(R1 \mid \langle ns \rangle)$. Hence the point lies along the negative diagonal.

3.3 Consider Eq. 3.9. The decision rule of the problem, $x_1 - x_2 > 0$, means that $c = 0$. The first integral, $P(R1 \mid \langle sn \rangle)$, is the area of the difference distribution to the right of zero, given that the mean is at $(m_s - m_n)$. The second integral, $P(R1 \mid \langle ns \rangle)$, is the same area given that the mean is at *minus* $(m_s - m_n)$. By the symmetry of Gaussian distributions, this second probability is one minus the first. Thus

$$P(R1 \mid \langle sn \rangle) = 1 - P(R1 \mid \langle ns \rangle) = P(R2 \mid \langle ns \rangle)$$

which is the condition for symmetry.

3.4 For the symmetric criterion the decision rule is to choose $R1$ if and only if $x_1 - x_2 > 0$. If some error in the criterion is assumed, we have: choose $R1$ if and only if $x_1 - x_2 > \varepsilon$, where ε is a Gaussian variable $E(\varepsilon) = 0$, $E(\varepsilon) = \sigma_\varepsilon^2$.

The probability of the various choices can be determined from the distribution of $x_1 - x_2 - \varepsilon$. For if $x_1 - x_2 - \varepsilon > 0$, we choose $R1$, whereas if $x_1 - x_2 - \varepsilon < 0$, we choose $R2$. The mean of $x_1 - x_2 - \varepsilon$ is

$$E(x_1 - x_2 - \varepsilon) = E(x_1 - x_2)$$

the mean of the difference distribution. The variance of $x_1 - x_2 - \varepsilon$ is

$$\sigma_{x_1-x_2-\varepsilon} = \sigma^2_{x_1-x_2} + \sigma_\varepsilon{}^2$$

assuming that x_1, x_2, and ε are all uncorrelated. The mean of the difference distribution is unchanged; only the variability is increased.

3.5 There are two states: detect (D) and nondetect $(\bar{D})$. The probabilities of each state given a signal, s, or given no signal, n, are $P(D \mid s) = 0.70, P(\bar{D} \mid s) = 0.30, P(D \mid n) = 0.20$, and $P(\bar{D} \mid n) = 0.80$.

In a two-alternative forced-choice task the two intervals can produce the same states, DD or $\overline{DD}$. In either case the chances of being correct are $\frac{1}{2}$. Thus

$$\tfrac{1}{2}(DD) = \tfrac{1}{2}(0.70 \cdot 0.20) = 0.07$$

$$\tfrac{1}{2}(\overline{DD}) = \tfrac{1}{2}(0.30 \cdot 0.80) = 0.12$$

Also, you will be correct if $D\bar{D}$ or $\bar{D}D$ occurs and the s alternative is associated with D. Thus $(0.70 \cdot 0.80) = 0.56$.

In summary, $0.56 + 0.07 + 0.12 = 0.75$.

4.1 We want to test the assumption that $\Delta m/\Delta\sigma = k$, where $k = 2, 4$, and 6. For each obtained value of Δm, and for each of the selected values of k, we obtain a predicted $\Delta\sigma$ from the equation $\Delta\sigma = 1/k(\Delta m)$. We take $\sigma_n = 1$ and $\sigma_s = 1 + \Delta\sigma$; $s = \sigma_n/\sigma_s = 1/\sigma_s$. The results are shown in Table PS4-1.

TABLE PS4-1

Signal Level	Δm	Slope			
		Obtained	Predicted		
			$\Delta m/\Delta\sigma = 2$	$\Delta m/\Delta\sigma = 4$	$\Delta m/\Delta\sigma = 6$
1	0.08	1.03	0.96	0.98	0.99
2	0.49	0.82	0.81	0.89	0.93
3	0.72	0.78	0.74	0.85	0.89
4	1.13	0.84	0.64	0.78	0.84
5	1.64	0.77	0.55	0.71	0.79
6	2.23	0.71	0.47	0.65	0.73

The slopes predicted by $k = 4$ are too steep at the low signal levels (levels 2 and 3) and too shallow at the higher levels (levels 4, 5, and 6). For the lower signal levels, $k = 2$ is closer; for the higher signal levels, $k = 6$ is closer. The data of the other two observers follow a similar pattern.

4.2 Reasonably close. Since the values of Δm obtained from the two-interval-rating procedure are quite similar to the values of Δm obtained from the one-interval-rating procedure, as a quick check the obtained slopes can be compared with the predicted values for $\Delta m/\Delta\sigma = 2$ that are listed in Table PS4-1, given in answer to the preceding question. Compare 0.93 and 0.96, 0.97 and 0.81, 0.74 and 0.74, 0.64 and 0.64, 0.52 and 0.55, and 0.46 and 0.47. The data of another observer are close to $\Delta m/\Delta\sigma = 4$; the results obtained from the third observer are highly variable.

4.3 (a) No. A striking difference between the slopes obtained from the two rating-response procedures and the slopes obtained from the two binary-response procedures is that the latter are quite consistently steeper and do not decrease with increases in Δm. The same pattern was obtained from the two other observers in the experiment.

(b) The data are quite variable, but the slopes vary about 1.0 with no distinct trend, and thus the prediction of symmetrical ROC curves is not rejected by these data. The slopes of the other two observers also vary about 1.0 without a trend.

4.4 (a) Yes. Compare 0.03 and 0.17, 0.52 and 0.40, 0.55 and 0.67, 1.08 and 1.09, 1.10 and 1.11, and 1.49 and 1.50. However, it must be noted that the values of Δm listed here are as read from the ROC plot; that is, they do not take into account, or have not been adjusted for, the factor of $\sqrt{2}$ difference between one-interval and two-interval procedures (see Chapter 3, Section 3.2.4). The similarity of the values of Δm as listed here suggests the possibility that this observer is not observing in both intervals of the two-interval task; the same applies to the data from the two rating-response procedures. The other two observers do not show this particular pattern; one gets very nearly the full value of the two intervals, and the other is intermediate.

(b) Since Δm is approximately proportional to signal power, the difference between the values of Δm obtained at signal level 2 is the equivalent of 1.1 decibels. The ratio $0.52/0.40 = 1.3$; 10 times the log of 1.3 is 1.1. At signal level 3, $0.67/0.55 = 1.2$; $10 \log 1.2$ is 0.9.

4.5 Recall that the two sets of binary-response ROC curves have steeper slopes than the two sets of rating-response ROC curves. Recall also that whereas $P(s) = 0.50$ throughout the rating procedures, $P(s)$ varied from 0.20 to 0.50 to 0.80 for the binary procedures. It is conceivable that the leftmost point on the binary ROC curves was depressed because of a lesser sensitivity in sessions in which the signal occurred relatively infrequently. Similarly, the rightmost point on the binary ROC curves may have been elevated because of greater sensitivity in sessions with relatively frequent signals. The results of such a process would not have much effect on the sensitivity measure $d_e{'}$, which is read from the ROC curve at the negative diagonal, but Δm is read from the curve at $P(S \mid s) = 0.50$. This "cueing" hypothesis is admittedly *ad hoc*; note, however, that it can be tested in an experiment in which ROC curves are fanned out by varying the payoff matrix with constant $P(s)$.

4.6 (a) 15.3

(b) 2.7

5.2 Our inclination is to question the adequacy of the test reported in the second paper. The values of signal strength chosen, and the values of false-alarm proportion obtained, surely did not serve to maximize the difference between the predictions of the two theories; almost all of the data were within ranges of these two variables where the predicted differences are very small. Four of the six ROC plots shown were obtained with a signal level that yielded values of $d' < 0.50$. On these four plots, at the extremes of the range of false-alarm proportions obtained, the difference in hit proportions of the two predictions being compared is approximately 0.04; inside these extremes, the differences are still smaller. On the other two plots, with $d' \approx 1.25$, the range of false-alarm proportions is relatively restricted. On these plots the differences between the two predicted hit proportions, at the extremes of the obtained false-alarm proportions, range from 0.08 to 0.16; the majority of points are well within these extremes, where the differences between the predictions are smaller. Except for the two plots with $d' \approx 0.25$, the variability of the data points about either of the predicted lines is quite large.

5.3 (a) Not obviously.

(b) $k = 4$

5.4 Given the combination of two-state theory and the multithreshold quantal theory, one could assume that the observer shifts his criterion to higher numbers of quanta when the signal intensity is increased. If this assumption is made, the theory includes two mechanisms for adjusting the proportion of false alarms: variation in the quantum criterion and variation in the random response bias. The puzzle remaining is why a priori probabilities and payoffs affect the random response bias, but not the criterion, when the subject can, apparently at will, alter the quantum criterion. McGill's (1966) theory of a counting mechanism in detection also distinguishes a particular type of criterion (the critical number of counts) from other types of response-biasing mechanisms.

6.1 Since the number of samples is $n = 2WT$, there are $2 \cdot 4000 \cdot 1/10 = 800$ sample values in time or frequency. The spacing in frequency is $1/T = 10$ cps apart. The temporal spacing is $1/2W = 1/8000$ sec or 0.125 msec.

6.2 (a) The density of $\vec{X}$ given $\vec{S}$ is

$$g(\vec{X} \mid \vec{S}) = f(\vec{X} - \vec{S} \mid N) = f(\vec{X} - \vec{S})$$

(b) The density is

$$g(\vec{X} \mid \vec{S}_1 \text{ or } \vec{S}_2) = \tfrac{1}{2} f(\vec{X} - \vec{S}_1) + \tfrac{1}{2} f(\vec{X} - \vec{S}_2)$$

6.3 No, as Eq. 6.49 shows, the envelope detector measures X_l, and the energy at the signal frequency is proportional to X_l^2. Thus, since X_l^2 increases monotonically with X_l, $X_l > 0$, we know that the two decision systems will generate equivalent decisions.

6.4 Using Eq. 6.65, we see that

$$\frac{M}{\sigma} = \sqrt{2WT} \quad \text{or} \quad \sqrt{800} = \sqrt{2} \cdot 2 \cdot 10 \approx 28$$

$1/28 \approx 3\%$, so a 10% increase is three sigma from the mean of the average energy value, and hence could be reliably detected with a small false-alarm proportion.

7.1 Consider a background signal $c(t)$, $c(t) \geq 0$. To this background we add a signal; call it $s(t)$. Assuming an impedance of unity, we then have

$$E_s = \int_0^T s^2(t)\, dt$$

as the energy of the signal in the interval T sec. If $s(t)$ is added to $c(t)$, the total energy E_{c+s} is

$$E_{c+s} = \int_0^T [c(t) + s(t)]^2\, dt$$

Thus the increment, $E_{c+s} - E_c = \Delta E$, is

$$\Delta E = 2 \int_0^T c(t)s(t)\, dt + E_s$$

Thus $\Delta E = E_s$ if and only if

$$\int_0^T c(t)s(t)\, dt = 0$$

This condition is known as orthogonality; see Appendix II.

7.2 It depends on the initial level of uncertainty. According to Fig. 7-6, if M changes from $M = 1$ to $M = 4$, a 4.5 db increase in signal level will maintain the percentage of correct detections at 75%. However, an eightfold increase from 4 to 32 requires only a 3 db increase. Thus, as the initial uncertainty increases, less increase in the signal level will be necessary to restore the same percentage of correct detections.

7.3 The optimal detector for a noise signal is the energy detector. Its performance is governed by Eq. 6.67, which states that the performance will be constant if the ratio of signal power to noise power is held constant. However, this same form of detection device, the energy detector, does not predict results consistent with Weber's law for the detection of an increment in a sinusoidal signal. This problem is treated in the next chapter.

8.1 (a) According to Eq. 8.13, $h_1 = 0.69$, whereas according to Eq. 8.15, $h_i = 0.71$.

(b) According to Eq. 8.13, $h = 2.0$; according to Eq. 8.15, $h = 2.3$.

8.2 At parameter values such that $2WT \approx 10$, the approximations made in deriving Eq. 8.13 become less valid; that is, the normal distribution is not a good approximation to the chi-square distribution. Also, unless $2WT > 2E_s/N_0$, Eq. 8.15 is invalid.

Topical Bibliography (1967 — 1973)

ALTERNATIVE THEORIES

Auerbach, C. and Leventhal, G. Evidence for all-or-none preperceptual processing in perceptual set. *Perc. and Psychophys.*, 14, 24-30, 1973.

Baron. J. Perceptual dependence: Evidence for an internal threshold. *Perc. and Psychophys.*, 13, 527-533, 1973.

Broadbent, D. E. The two-state threshold model, and rating scale experiments. *J. Acoust. Soc. Am.*, 40, 244, 1966.

Doherty, M. E. and Keeley, S. M. A Bayesian prediction of four-look recognition performance from one-look data. *Perc. and Psychophys.*, 5, 362-364, 1969.

Dorfman, D. D. Probability matching in signal detection. *Psychon. Sci.*, 17, 103, 1969.

Emerson, P. L. Measurement of low-signal suppression and other parameters of the forced-choice psychometric function. *Perc. and Psychophys.*, 5, 2-6, 1969.

Green, D. M. and Luce, R. D. Detection of auditory signals presented at random times. *Perc. and Psychophys.*, 2, 441-450, 1967.

Green, D. M. and Luce, R. D. Detection of auditory signals presented at random times: III. *Perc. and Psychophys.*, 9, 257-268, 1971.

Keeley, S. M., Doherty, M. E. and Bachman, S. P. A Bayesian prediction of four-look recognition performance from one-look data: II. *Perc. and Psychophys.*, 7, 218-220, 1970.

Krantz, D. H. Threshold theories of signal detection. *Psychol. Rev.*, 76, 308-324, 1969.

Kubovy, M., Rapoport, A. and Tversky, A. Deterministic vs probabilistic strategies in detection. *Perc. and Psychophys.*, 9, 427-429, 1971.

Lee, W. Detection theory, micromatching, and the constant-ratio rule. *Perc. and Psychophys.*, 4, 217-219, 1968.

Lee, W. and Janke, M. Categorizing externally distributed stimulus samples for three continua. *J. Exp. Psychol.*, 68, 376-382, 1964.

Lee, W. and Zentall, T. R. Factorial effects in the categorization of externally distributed stimulus samples. *Perc. and Psychophys.*, 1, 120-124, 1966.

Luce, R. D. and Green, D. M. Detection of auditory signals presented at random times, II. *Perc. and Psychophys.*, 7, 1-14, 1970.

Massaro, D. W. The role of the decision system in sensory and memory experiments using confidence judgments. *Perc. and Psychophys.*, 5, 270-272, 1969.

Meudell, P. R. Two-state threshold theory and the multiple-look k-alternative forced-choice experiment. *J. Acoust. Soc. Am.*, 44, 1139-1140, 1968.

Munsinger, H. and Gummerman, K. Simultaneous visual detection and recognition. *Perc. and Psychophys.*, 3, 383-386, 1968.

Norman, D. A. Neural quantum controversy in sensory psychology. *Science*, 181, 467-469, 1973.

Parducci, A. and Sandusky, A. J. Limits on the applicability of signal detection theories. *Perc. and Psychophys.*, 7, 63-64, 1970.

Tanner, T. A., Jr., Haller, R. W., and Atkinson, R. C. Signal recognition as influenced by presentation schedules. *Perc. and Psychophys.*, 2, 349-358, 1967.

Thomas, E. A. C. and Legge, D. Probability matching as a basis for detection and recognition decision. *Psychol. Rev.*, 77, 65-72, 1970.

Wickelgren, W. A. A test of Luce's two-state decision rule. *Psychon. Sci.*, 9, 91-92, 1967.

Wickelgren, W. A. Testing two-state theories with operating characteristics and a posteriori probabilities. *Psychol. Bull.*, 69, 126-131, 1968.

Yellott, J. I., Jr. Correction for fast guessing and the speed-accuracy tradeoff in choice reaction time. *J. Math. Psychol.*, 8, 159-199, 1971.

ANIMAL OBSERVERS

Blough, D. S. Stimulus generalization as signal detection in pigeons. *Science*, 1958, 940-941, 1967.

Boneau, C. A. and Cole, J. L. Decision theory, the pigeon, and the psychophysical function. *Psychol. Rev.*, 74, 123-135, 1967.

Clopton, B. M. Detection of increments in noise intensity by monkeys. *J. Exp. Anal. of Beh.*, 17, 473-481, 1972.

Coltheart, M. and Irvine, D. The slope of ROCs in the rat. *J. Aud. Res.*, 8, 167-170, 1968.

Eijkman, E. G. Learning and fluctuating behavior experiments with goldfish. *J. Theor. Biol.*, 26, 251-264, 1970.

Elsmore, T. F. Duration discrimination: effects of probability of stimulus presentation. *J. Exp. Anal. of Beh.*, 18, 465-469, 1972.

Hodos, W. and Bonbright, J. S., Jr. The detection of visual intensity differences by pigeons. *J. Exp. Anal. of Beh.*, 18, 471-479, 1972.

Irwin, R. J. and Terman, M. Detection of brief tones in noise by rats. *J. Exp. Anal. of Beh.*, 13, 135-143, 1970.

Kinchla, J. Discrimination of two auditory durations by pigeons. *Perc. and Psychophys.*, 8, 299-307, 1970.

Morrison, G. and Norrison, W. Taste detection in the rat. *Canad. J. Psychol.*, 20, 208-217, 1966.

Nevin, J. A. On differential stimulation and differential reinforcement. In *Animal Psychophysics*, W. C. Stebbins (Ed.), Appleton-Century-Crofts, New York, 401-427, 1970.

Terman, M. Discrimination of auditory intensities by rats. *J. Exp. Anal. of Beh.*, 13, 145-160, 1970.

Terman, M. and Terman, J. S. Concurrent variation of response and sensitivity in an operant-psychophysical test. *Perc. and Psychophys.*, 11, 428-432, 1972.

Wright, A. Psychometric and psychophysical hue discrimination functions for the pigeon. *Vision Res.*, 12, 1447-1464, 1972.

Yager, D. and Duncan, I. Signal-detection analysis of luminance generalization in goldfish using latency as a graded response measure. *Perc. and Psychophys.*, 9, 353-355, 1971.

ATTENTION

Baron, J. Division of attention in successiveness discrimination. In *Attention and Performance IV*, S. Kornblum (Ed.), Academic Press, New York, 703-711, 1973.

Franzén, O., Markowitz, J., and Swets, J. A. Spatially-limited attention to vibrotactile stimulation. *Perc. and Psychophys.*, 7, 193-196, 1970.

Greenberg, G. Z. Frequency-selective detection at three signal amplitudes. *Perc. and Psychophys.*, 6, 297-301, 1969.

Greenberg, G. Z. Frequency selectivity during amplitude discrimination of signals in noise. *J. Acoust. Soc. Am.*, 45, 1438-1442, 1969.

Greenberg, G. Z. and Larkin, W. D. Frequency response characteristic of auditory observers detecting signals of a signal frequency in noise: The probe-signal method. *J. Acoust. Soc. Am.*, 44, 1513-1523, 1968.

Kinchla, R. A. Temporal and channel uncertainty in detection: A multiple-observation analysis. *Perc. and Psychophys.*, 5, 129-136, 1969.

Kinchla, R. A. An attention operating characteristic in vision. Technical Report No. 29, Department of Psychology, McMaster University, Hamilton, Ontario, 1969.

Kristofferson, A. B. and Allan, L. G. Successiveness and duration discrimination. Technical Report No. 45, Department of Psychology, McMaster University, Hamilton, Ontario, 1971.

Lindsay, P. H., Taylor, M. M. and Forbes, S. M. Attention and multidimensional discrimination. *Perc. and Psychophys.*, 4, 113-117, 1968.

Moray, B. Time sharing in auditory perception: Effect of stimulus duration. *J. Acoust. Soc. Am.*, 47, 660-661, 1970.

Moray, N. and Fitter, M. A theory and the measurement of attention: tutorial review. In *Attention and Performance IV*, S. Kornblum (Ed.), Academic Press, New York, 3-19, 1973.

Moray, N. and O'Brien, T. Signal-detection theory applied to selective listening. *J. Acoust. Soc. Am.*, 42, 765-772, 1967.

Pastore, R. E. and Sorkin, R. D. Simultaneous two-channel signal detection. I. Simple binaural stimuli. *J. Acoust. Soc. Am.*, 51, 544-551, 1972.

Shiffrin, R. M., Craig, J. C., and Cohen, E. On the degree of attention and capacity limitation in tactile processing. *Perc. and Psychophys.*, 13, 328-336.

Sorkin, R. D. and Pastore, R. E. Simultaneous binaural signal detection: Comments on "Time sharing in auditory perception: Effect of stimulus duration" [J. Acoust. Soc. Am., 47, 660-661, 1970], *J. Acoust. Soc. Am.*, 49, 1319, 1971.

Sorkin, R. S., Pastore, R. E., and Gilliom, J. D. Signal probability and the listening band. *Perc. and Psychophys.*, 4, 10-12, 1968.

Sorkin, R. D., Pastore, R. E., and Pohlmann, L. D. Simultaneous two-channel signal detection. II. Correlated and uncorrelated signals. *J. Acoust. Soc. Am.*, 51, 1960-1965, 1972.

Sorkin, R. D. and Pohlmann, L. D. Some models of observer behavior in two-channel auditory signal detection. *Perc. and Psychophys.*, 14, 101-109, 1973.

Sorkin, R. D., Pohlmann, L. D., and Gilliom, J. D. Simultaneous two-channel signal detection. III. 630- and 1400-Hz signals. *J. Acoust. Soc. Am.*, 53, 1045-1050, 1973.

Swets, J. A. and Kristofferson, A. B. Attention. *Ann. Rev. Psychol.*, 21, 339-366, 1970.

Taylor, M. M., Lindsay, P. H., and Forbes, S. M. Quantification of shared-capacity processing in auditory and visual discrimination. *Acta. Psychol.*, 27, 223-232, 1967.

Treisman, M. Detection of binaural tone stimuli: time sharing or criterion change? *J. Acoust. Soc. Am.*, 51, 625-629, 1972.

Treisman, A. and Geffen, G. Selective attention: Perception or response? *Quart. J. Exp. Psychol.*, 19, 1-17, 1967.

AUDITION

Abel, S. M. Duration discrimination of noise and tone bursts. *J. Acoust. Soc. Am.*, 51, 1219-1223, 1972.

Ahumada, A., Jr. and Lovell, J. Stimulus features in signal detection. *J. Acoust. Soc. Am.*, 49, 1751-1756, 1971.

Bell, D. W. and Nixon, J. C. Reliability of ratings in an auditory signal-detection experiment. *J. Acoust. Soc. Am.*, 49, 435-439, 1971.

Bourbon, W. T., Evans, T. R., and Deatherage, B. H. Effects of intensity on "critical bands" for tonal stimuli as determined by band limiting. *J. Acoust. Soc. Am.*, 43, 56-59, 1968.

Cuddy, L. L. Training the absolute identification of pitch. *Perc. and Psychophys.*, 8, 265-269, 1970.

Doehring, D. G. and Ling, D. Matching to sample of three-tone simultaneous and successive sounds by musical and nonmusical subjects. *Psychon. Sci.*, 25, 103-105, 1971.

Egan, J. P. Auditory masking and signal detection theory. *Audiology*, 10, 41-47, 1971.

Egan, J. P., Lindner, W. A. and McFadden, D. Masking-level differences and the form of psychometric function. *Perc. and Psychophys.*, 4, 209-215, 1969.

Emmerich, D. S. Receiver operating characteristics determined under several interaural conditions of listening. *J. Acoust. Soc. Am.*, 43, 298-307, 1968.

Emmerich, D. S. Cueing signals in auditory detection and frequency discrimination experiments. *Perc. and Psychophys.*, 9, 129-134, 1971.

Green, D. M. Additivity of masking. *J. Acoust. Soc. Am.*, 41, 1517-1525, 1967.

Green, D. M. Sine and cosine masking. *J. Acoust. Soc. Am.*, 44, 168-175, 1968.

Green, D. M. Masking with continuous and pulsed sinusoids. *J. Acoust. Soc. Am.*, 46, 939-946, 1969.

Hafter, E. R., Bourbon, W. T., Blocker, A. S., and Tucker, A. Direct comparison between lateralization and detection under conditions of antiphasic masking. *J. Acoust. Soc. Am.*, 46, 1452, 1969.

Hafter, E. R. and Carrier, S. C. Masking-level differences obtained with a pulsed tonal masker. *J. Acoust. Soc. Am.*, 47, 1041-1047, 1970.

Henning, B. G. Frequency discrimination in noise. *J. Acoust. Soc. Am.*, 41, 774-777, 1967.

Henning, B. G. A model for auditory discrimination and detection. *J. Acoust. Soc. Am.*, 42. 1325-1334, 1967.

Henning, B. G. Amplitude discrimination in noise, pedestal experiments, and additivity of masking. *J. Acoust. Soc. Am.*, 45, 426-435, 1969.

Henning, B. G. and Bleiwas, S. L. Amplitude discrimination in noise. *J. Acoust. Soc. Am.*, 41, 1365, 1967.

Henning, G. B. and Psotka, J. An extension of some observations of Leshowitz and Raab. *J. Acoust. Soc. Am.*, 45, 785-786, 1969.

Jeffress, L. A. Masking. In *Foundations of Modern Auditory Theory*, J. V. Tobias (Ed.), Academic Press, Inc., New York, 85-114, 1972.

Kinchla, J. Duration discrimination of acoustically defined intervals in the 1- to 8-sec range. *Perc. and Psychophys.*, 12, 318-320, 1972.

Leshowitz, B. and Cudahy, E. Masking with continuous and gated sinusoids. *J. Acoust. Soc. Am.*, 51, 1921-1929, 1972.

Leshowitz, B. and Raab, D. H. Effects of stimulus duration on the detection of sinusoids added to continuous pedestals. *J. Acoust. Soc. Am.*, 41, 489-496, 1967.

Leshowitz, B. and Wightman, F. L. On-frequency masking with continuous sinusoids. *J. Acoust. Soc. Am.*, 49, 1180-1190, 1971.

Long, Glenis R. The role of the standard in an auditory amplitude discrimination experiment. *Perc. and Psychophys.*, 13, 49-59, 1973.

McGill, W. J. and Goldberg, J. P. Pure-tone intensity discrimination and energy detection. *J. Acoust. Soc. Am.*, 44, 576-581, 1968.

Mulligan, B. E. and Adams, J. C. Effect of sound on subsequent detection. *J. Acoust. Soc. Am.*, 44, 1401-1408, 1968.

Mulligan, B. E., Adams, J. C., Mulligan, M. J., and Burwinkle, R. E. Prediction of monaural detection. *J. Acoust. Soc. Am.*, 43, 481-486, 1968.

Nabelek, I. and Hirsh, I. J. On the discrimination of frequency transitions. *J. Acoust. Soc. Am.*, 45, 1510-1519, 1969.

Offutt, G. C. Integration of the energy in repeated tone pulses by man and the goldfish. *J. Acoust. Soc. Am.*, 41, 7-12, 1967.

Patterson, J. H. Masking of tones by transient signals having identical energy spectra. *J. Acoust. Soc. Am.*, 50, 1126-1132, 1971.

Pfafflin, S. M. Detection of auditory signal in restricted sets of reproducible noise. *J. Acoust. Soc. Am.*, 43, 487-490, 1968.

Raab, D. H. and Taub, H. B. Click-intensity discrimination with and without a background masking noise. *J. Acoust. Soc. Am.*, 46, 965-968, 1969.

Rochester, S. Detection and duration discrimination of noise increments. *J. Acoust. Soc. Am.*, 49, 1783-1789, 1971.

Ronken, D. A. Intensity discrimination of Rayleigh noise. *J. Acoust. Soc. Am.*, 45, 54-57, 1969.

Ronken, D. A. Monaural detection of a phase difference between clicks. *J. Acoust. Soc. Am.*, 47, 1091-1099, 1970.

Sandusky, A. and Ahumada, A. Contrast in detection with gated noise. *J. Acoust. Soc. Am.*, 49, 1790-1794, 1971.

Soderquist, D. R. Frequency analysis and the critical band. *Psychon. Sci.*, 21, 117-119, 1970.

Srinivasan, R. Auditory critical bandwidth for short-duration signals. *J. Acoust. Soc. Am.*, 50, 616-622, 1971.

Taylor, M. M. and Clarke, D. P. J. Monaural detection with contra-lateral cue (MDCC). II. Interaural delay of cue and signal. *J. Acoust. Soc. Am.*, 49, 1243-1253, 1971.

Taylor, M. M., Clarke, D. P. J., and Smith, S. M. Monaural detection with contralateral cue (MDCC). III. Sinusoidal signals at a constant performance level. *J. Acoust. Soc. Am.*, 49, 1795-1804, 1971.

Taylor, M. M. and Forbes, S. M. Monaural detection with contra-lateral cue (MDCC). I. Better than energy detector performance by human observers. *J. Acoust. Soc. Am.*, 46, 1519-1526, 1969.

Taylor, M. M., Smith, S. M., and Clarke, D. P. J. Monaural detection with contralateral cue (MDCC). IV. Psychometric functions with sinusoidal signals. *J. Acoust. Soc. Am.*, 50, 1151-1161, 1971.

Tucker, A., Williams, P. I., and Jeffress, L. A. Effect of signal duration on detection for gated and for continuous noise. *J. Acoust. Soc. Am.*, 44, 813-816, 1968.

Viemeister, N. F. Intensity discrimination of pulsed sinusoids: The effects of filtered noise. *J. Acoust. Soc. Am.*, 51, 1265-1269, 1972.

Watson, C. S., Franks, J. R., and Hood, D. C. Detection of tones in the absence of external masking noise. I. Effects of signal intensity and signal frequency. *J. Acoust. Soc. Am.*, 52, 633-643, 1972.

Wilbanks, W. A. and Whitmore, J. K. Detection of monaural signals as a function of interaural noise correlation and signal frequency. *J. Acoust. Soc. Am.*, 43, 785-797, 1968.

CONCEPTUAL JUDGMENT

Hammerton, M. An investigation into changes in decision criteria and other details of a decision-making task. *Psychon. Sci.*, 21, 203-204, 1970.

Lieblich, A. and Lieblich, I. Arithmetical estimation under conditions of different payoff matrices. *Psychon. Sci.*, 14, 87-88, 1969.

Miehle, W. and Siegel, A. I. Defect signal detection model based on variable confidence. *Hum. Fact.*, 12, 409-420, 1970.

Segal, S. J. and Fusella, V. Effects of imaging on signal-to-noise ratio, with varying signal conditions. *Brit. J. Psychol.*, 60, 459-464, 1969.

Segal, S. J. and Fusella, V. Influence of imaged pictures and sounds on detection of visual and auditory signals. *J. Exp. Psychol.*, 83, 458-464, 1970.

Segal, S. J. and Fusella, V. Effect of images in six sense modalities on detection of visual signal from noise. *Psychon. Sci.*, 24, 55-56, 1971.

Segal, S. J. and Gordon, P. E. The Perky effect revisited: paradoxical threshold or signal detection error. *Perc. and Mot. Skills*, 28, 791-797, 1969.

Ulehla, Z. J., Canges, L., and Wackwitz, F. Signal detectability theory applied to conceptual discrimination. *Psychon. Sci.*, 8, 221-222, 1967.

Ulehla, Z. J., Canges, L., and Wackwitz, F. Integration of conceptual information. *Psychon. Sci.*, 8, 223-224, 1967.

Ulehla, Z. J., Little, K. B. and Weyl, T. C. Operating characteristics and realisms of certainty estimates. *Psychon. Sci.*, 9, 77-78, 1967.

EXTENDED THEORY

Berliner, J. E. and Durlach, N. I. Intensity perception. IV. Resolution in roving-level discrimination. *J. Acoust. Soc. Am.*, 53, 1270-1287, 1973.

Braida, L. D. and Durlach, N. I. Intensity perception. II. Resolution in one-interval paradigms. *J. Acoust. Soc. Am.*, 51, 1972.

Cohen, H. S. and Ferrell, W. R. Human operator decision-making in manual control. *IEEE Trans. on Man-Machine Systems*, 10, 41-47, 1969.

Durlach, N. I. and Braida, L. D. Intensity perception. I. Preliminary theory of intensity resolution. *J. Acoust. Soc. Am.*, 46, 372-383, 1969.

Jeffress, L. A. The logistic distribution as an approximation to the normal curve. *J. Acoust. Soc. Am.*, 53, 1296, 1973.

Kinchla, R. A. and Allan, L. G. A theory of visual movement perception. *Psychol. Rev.*, 76, 537-558, 1969.

Larkin, W. Response mechanisms in detection experiments. *J. Exp. Psychol.* 91, 140-153, 1971.

Pynn, C. T., Braida, L. D., and Durlach, N. I. Intensity perception. III. Resolution in small-range identification. *J. Acoust. Soc. Am.*, 51, 559-566, 1972.

Rapoport, A. and Burkheimer, G. J. Models for deferred decision making. *J. Math. Psychol.*, 8, 508-538, 1971.

Swets, J. A. Deferred decision in signal detection. In *Detection and Recognition of Signals*, B. F. Lomov (Ed.), Moscow University Press, Lenin Hills, Moscow, 21-26, 1966.

Swets, J. A. and Birdsall, T. G. Deferred decision in human signal detection: A preliminary experiment. *Perc. and Psychophys.*, 2, 15-28, 1967.

Thijssen, J. M. and Vendrik, A. J. H. Internal noise and transducer function in sensory detection experiments: Evaluation of psychometric curves and of ROC curves. *Perc. and Psychophys.*, 3, 387-400, 1968.

Treisman, M. Relation between signal detectability theory and the traditional procedures for measuring thresholds: An addendum. *Psychol. Bull.*, 79, 45-47, 1973.

Treisman, M. and Leshowitz, B. The effects of duration, area, and background intensity on the visual intensity difference threshold given by the forced-choice procedure: Derivations from a statistical decision model for sensory discrimination. *Perc. and Psychophys.*, 6, 281-296, 1969.

Treisman, M. and Watts, T. R. Relation between signal detectability theory and the traditional procedures for measuring sensory thresholds: Estimating d' from results given by the method of constant stimuli. *Psychol. Bull.*, 66, 438-454, 1966.

Wickelgren, W. A. Unidimensional strength theory and component analysis of noise in absolute and comparative judgments. *J. Math. Psychol.*, 5, 102-122, 1968.

GENERAL SURVEY

Beretta, A. *La Teoria della Detezione del Segnale.* University Degli Studi di Universita Milano, Instituto di psicologia Della Facolta Medica, 1968.

Green, D. M. Application of detection theory in psychophysics, *Proc. of the IEEE*, 58, 713-723, 1970.

Greeno, J. G. An appraisal of mathematical psychology. MMPP 71-13, Michigan Mathematical Psychology Program, The University of Michigan, Department of Psycholgy, Ann Arbor, Michigan, 1971.

Hake, H. W. and Rodwan, A. S. Perception and recognition. In *Experimental Methods and Instrumentation in Psychology*, J. B. Sidowski (Ed.), McGraw-Hill Book Co., New York, 331-381, 1966.

Luce, R. D. What sort of measurement is psychophysical measurement? *Amer. Psychol.*, 96-106, February 1972.

Swets, J. A. Theories of sensory thresholds. In *Sensory Evaluation of Food:*

Principles and Methods, B. Drake (Ed.), A. Rydberg and Co., Gothenburg, Sweden, 17-18, 1969.

Swets, J. A. Theory of signal detection in psychology. In *Encyclopedia of Science and Technology*, McGraw-Hill, New York, 354-355, 1971.

Swets, J. A. The relative operating characteristic in psychology. *Science* (in press).

Tanner, W. P., Jr. and Sorkin, R. D. The theory of signal detectability. In *Foundations of Modern Auditory Theory*, J. V. Tobias (Ed.), Academic Press, Inc., New York, 63-98, 1972.

Watson, C. S. Psychophysics. In *Handbook of General Psychology*, B. B. Wolman (Ed.), Prentice-Hall, New York, 275-306, 1973.

IDEAL OBSERVER

Birdsall, T. G. The theory of signal detectability: ROC curves and their character. Ph.D. thesis, University of Michigan, Ann Arbor, Michigan, i-xxiii, 1-416, 1966.

Green, D. M., and McGill, W. J. On the equivalence of detection probabilities and well-known statistical quantities. *Psychol. Rev.*, 41, 294-301, 1970.

Henning, G. B. A model for auditory discrimination and detection. *J. Acoust. Soc. Am.*, 42, 1325-1334, 1967.

Jeffress, L. A. Stimulus-oriented approach to detection re-examined. *J. Acoust. Soc. Am.*, 41, 480-488, 1967.

Jeffress, L. A. Mathematical and electrical models of auditory detection. *J. Acoust. Soc. Am.*, 44, 187-203, 1968.

Levison, W. H. and Tanner, R. B. A control-theory model for human decision-making. Report No. 2119, Bolt Beranek and Newman Inc., Cambridge, Mass., 1971.

Luce, R. D. and Green, D. M. A neural timing theory for response times and the psychophysics of intensity. *Psychol. Rev.*, 79, 14-57, 1972.

McGill, W. J. A neural counting model with familiar outcomes in auditory detection. *J. Math. Psychol.*, 4, 351-376, 1967.

McGill, W. J. Neural counting mechanisms and energy detection. *J. Math. Psychol.*, 4, 351-376, 1968.

McGill, W. J. Variations on Marill's detection formula. *J. Acoust. Soc. Am.*, 43, 70-73, 1968.

McGill, W. J. and Goldberg, J. P. A study of the near-miss involving Weber's law and pure-tone intensity discrimination. *Perc. and Psychophys.*, 4, 105-109, 1968.

Nolte, L. W. Theory of signal detectability: Adaptive optimum receiver design. *J. Acoust. Soc. Am.*, 42, 773-777, 1967.

Nolte, L. W. Adaptive optimum detection: Synchronous-recurrent transients. *J. Acoust. Soc. Am.*, 44, 224-239, 1968.

Nolte, L. W. and Jaarsma, D. More on the detection of one of M orthogonal signals. *J. Acoust. Soc. Am.*, 41, 497-505, 1967.

Siebert, W. M. Stimulus transformation in the peripheral auditory system. In *Recognizing Patterns*, P. A. Kolers and M. Eden (Eds.), MIT Press, Cambridge, Mass., 104-133, 1968.

Siebert, W. M. Signals and noise in sensory systems. *Technology Rev.*, 23-29, May, 1973.

Wilcox, G. W. Inter-observer agreement and models of monaural auditory processing in detection tasks. Report No. MMPP 68-4, Department of Psychology, The University of Michigan, 1968.

LEARNING

Aiken, E. G. Auditory discrimination learning: Prototype storage and distinctive features detection mechanisms. *Perc. and Psychophys.*, 6, 95-96, 1969.

Bernbach, H. A. and Bower, G. H. Confidence ratings in continuous paired-associate learning. *Psychon. Sci.*, 21, 252-253, 1970.

Cumming, G. D. Theoretical distribution of second choice scores in a paired-associate task if learning is all-or-none. *J. Math. Psychol.*, 5, 463-469, 1968.

Dorfman, D. D. and Biderman, M. A learning model for a continuum of sensory states. *J. Math. Psychol.*, 8, 264-268, 1971.

Eijkman, E. G. The measurement of fluctuation in perceptual and learning tasks. *IEEE Trans. on Man-Machine Systems*, 1, 11-19, 1970.

Fishbein, H. D. and Engel, S. Human eyelid conditioning at detection threshold. *Psychon. Sci.*, 4, 291-292, 1966.

Fishbein, H. D. and Rees, J. F. The interaction effects of CS intensity and CS-UCS interval in human eyelid conditioning. *Brit. J. Psychol.*, 60, 357-361, 1969.

Friedman, M. P., Carterette, E. C., Nakatani, L., and Ahumada, A. Comparisons of some learning models for response bias in signal detection. *Perc. and Psychophys.*, 3, 5-11, 1968.

Grice, G. R. Stimulus intensity and response evocation. *Psychol. Rev.*, 75, 359-373, 1968.

Grice, G. R. A threshold model for drive. (To be published in Kendler, H. H., and Spence, J. T. (Eds.), *Essays in Neobehaviorism: A Memorial Volume to Kenneth W. Spence*, Appleton-Century-Crofts.).

Grice, G. R. Conditioning and a decision theory of response evocation. (To be published in *Psychology of Learning and Motivation; Advances in Research and Theory*, G. H. Bower (Ed.), Academic Press.).

Hickson, R. H. Signal detection in a paired-associate learning task. *Psychon. Sci.*, 12, 253-254, 1968.

Rees, J. F. and Fishbein, H. D. Test of the TSD model in human eyelid conditioning: A priori probability and payoff manipulations. *J. Exp. Psychol.*, 83, 291-298, 1970.

MEDICAL DIAGNOSIS

Kundel, H. L., Revesz, G. and Stauffer, H. M. The electro-optical processing of radiographic images. *Radiolog. Clinics of N. Am.*, 3, 447-460, 1969.

Ling, D., Ling, A. H., and Doehring, D. G. Stimulus, response, and observer variables in the auditory screening of newborn infants. *J. Speech and Hearing Res.*, 13, 9-18, 1970.

Lusted, L. B. *Introduction to Medical Decision Making.* Springfield, Illinois: Charles C. Thomas, 1968.

Lusted, L. B. Perception of the roentgen image: applications of signal detectability theory. *Radiolog. Clinics of N. Am.*, 3, 435-445, 1969.

Lusted, L. B. Signal detectability and medical decision-making. *Science*, 171, 1217-1219, 1971.

Lusted, L. B. Decision-making studies in patient management. *N. E. J. of Med.*, 284, 416-424, 1971.

Lusted, L. B. Observer error, signal detectability, and medical decision making. In *Computer Diagnosis and Diagnostic Methods*, J. A. Jacquez (Ed.), C. C. Thomas, Sprinfield, Ill., 29-44, 1972.

Swets, J. A. Signal detection in medical diagnosis. In *Computer Diagnosis and Diagnostic Methods*, J. A. Jacquez (Ed.), C. C. Thomas, Sprinfield, Ill., 8-28, 1972.

MEMORY

Ackroff, J. M. and Rouse, R. O., Jr. TSD and coding in STM. *Psychon. Sci.*, 21, 231-232, 1970.

Allen, L. R. and Garton, R. F. Detection and criterion change associated with different test contexts in recognition memory. *Perc. and Psychophys.*, 6, 1-4, 1969.

Allen, L. R. and Garton, R. F. The influence of word-knowledge on the word-frequency effect in recognition memory. *Psychon. Sci.*, 10, 401-402, 1968.

Allen, L. R. and Garton, R. F. Manipulation of study trials in recognition memory. *Perc. and Psychophys.*, 7, 215-217, 1970.

Anderson, J. R. and Bower, G. H. Recognition and retrieval processes in free recall. *Psychol. Rev.*, 79, 97-123, 1972.

Atkinson, R. C. and Wickens, T. D. Human memory and the concept of reinforcement. In *The Nature of Reinforcement*, Robert Glaser (Ed.), Academic Press, Inc., New York, 66-119, 1971.

Banks, W. P. Criterion change and response competition in unlearning. *J. Exp. Psychol.*, 82, 216-223, 1969.

Banks, W. P. Signal detection theory and human memory. *Psychol. Bull.*, 74, 81-99, 1970.

Banks, W. P. Confidence-rated recall, d_r, and tests of Bernbach's finite-state theory in recall. *Psychol. Bull.*, 76, 151-152, 1971.

Barr-Brown, M. and White, M. J. Sex differences in recognition memory. *Psychon. Sci.*, 25, 75-76, 1971.

Bernbach, H. A. Decision processes in memory. *Psychol. Rev.*, 74, 462-480, 1967.

Bernbach, H. A. Invariance of d* in memory: response to Banks. *Psychol. Bull.*, 76, 149-150, 1971.

Blick, K. I. Decision and decay processes in the short-term memory for length. *J. Exp. Psychol.*, 82, 224-230, 1969.

Clark, W. C. and Greenberg, D. B. Effect of stress, knowledge of results, and proactive inhibition on verbal recognition memory (d') and response criterion (L_x). *J. Pers. Soc. Psychol.*, 17, 42-47, 1971.

DaPolito, F., Barker, D., and Wiant, J. Context in semantic information retrieval. *Psychon. Sci.*, 24, 180-182, 1971.

Donaldson, W. and Murdock, B. B. Jr. Criterion change in continuous recognition memory. *J. Exp. Psychol.*, 76, 325-330, 1968.

Fischler, I. and Juola, J. F. Effects of repeated tests on recognition time for information in long-term memory. *J. Exp. Psychol.*, 91, 54-58, 1971.

Freund, R. D., Brelsford, J. W., Jr., and Atkinson, R. C. Recognition vs. recall: storage or retrieval differences? *Q. J. Exp. Psychol.*, 21, 214-224, 1969.

Freund, R. D. Loftus, G. R., and Atkinson, R. C. Applications of multiprocess models for memory to continuous recognition tasks. *J. Math. Psychol.*, 6, 576-594, 1969.

Friedman, M. P., Reed, S. K. and Carterette, E. C. Feature saliency and recognition memory for schematic faces. *Perc. and Psychophys.*, 10, 47-50, 1971.

Gibson, K. L. Criterion shifts and the determination of the memory operating characteristic. *Psychon. Sci.*, 9, 207-208, 1967.

Hopkins, R. H. and Schulz, R. W. Meaningfulness in paired-associate recognition learning. *J. Exp. Psychol.*, 79, 533-539, 1969.

Kinchla, R. A. Selective processes in sensory memory: A probe-comparison procedure. In *Attention and Performance IV*, S. Kornblum (Ed.), Academic Press, New York, 87-99, 1973.

Kintsch, W. Memory and decision aspects of recognition learning. *Psychol. Rev.*, 74, 496-504, 1967.

Kintsch, W. An experimental analysis of single stimulus tests and multiple-choice tests of recognition memory. *J. Exp. Psychol.*, 76, 1-6, 1968.

Klatzky, R. L. and Loftus, G. R. Recognition memory as influenced by number of reinforcements and type of test. *Psychon. Sci.*, 16, 302-303, 1969.

Loftus, G. R. Comparison of recognition and recall in a continuous memory task. *J. Exp. Psychol.*, 91, 220-226, 1971.

Lockhart, R. S. and Murdock, B. B., Jr. Memory and the theory of signal detection. *Psychol. Bull.*, 74, 100-109, 1970.

Marley, A. A. J. An observable property of a generalization of Kinchla's diffusion model of perceptual memory. *J. Math. Psychol.*, 8, 481-488, 1971.

Massaro, D. W. The role of the decision system in sensory and memory judgments. *Perc. and Psychophys.*, 5, 270-272, 1969.

McNicol, D. and Ryder, L. A. Sensitivity and response bias effects in the learning of familiar and unfamiliar associations by rote or with mnemonic. *J. Exp. Psychol.*, 90, 81-89, 1971.

Miller, J. D. and Tanis, D. C. Recognition memory for common sounds. *Psychon. Sci.*, 23, 307-308, 1971.

Murdock, B. B., Jr. Serial order effects in short-term memory. *J. Exp. Psychol.*, Monograph supplement, 76, 1-15, 1968.

Nicol, E. H., Roby, T. B., Farrell, F. M. Confidence in recall in paired-associate learning experiments. Technical Report No. ESD-TR-67-457, Decision Sciences Lab., Electronic Systems Div., U.S. Air Force, Hanscom Field, Bedford, Mass., 1967.

Norman, D. A. Acquisition and retention in short-term memory. *J. Exp. Psychol.*, 72, 369-381, 1966.

Norman, D. A. and Wickelgren, W. A. Strength theory of decision rules and latency in retrieval from short-term memory. *J. Math. Psychol.*, 6, 192-208, 1969.

Pappas, B. A., Hepburn, L. K., and Suboski, M. D. A comparison of recall and binary recognition. *Amer. J. Psychol.*, 80, 398-404, 1967.

Raser, G. A. Meaningfulness and signal-detection theory in immediate paired-associate recognition. *J. Exp. Psychol.*, 84, 173-175, 1970.

Rundle, S. A. An experimental and theoretical study of recognition memory. Tech. Report No. 33, Department of Psychology, University of California, Los Angeles, July, 1970.

Schulman, A. I. Word length and rarity in recognition memory. *Psychon. Sci.*, 9, 211-212, 1967.

Schulman, A. I. Recognition memory for targets from a scanned word list. *Brit. J. Psychol.*, 62, 335-346, 1971.

Schulman, A. I. and Lovelace, E. A. Recognition memory for words presented at a slow or rapid rate. *Psychon. Sci.*, 21, 99-100, 1970.

Smith, P. T. The non-monotonicity of the psychometric function in recognition memory. *Perc. and Psychophys.*, 5, 329-337, 1969.

Suboski, M. D. Signal detection analysis of recall paired-associates learning. *Psychon. Sci.*, 7, 357-358, 1967.

Swets, J. A. Signal detection as a model of information retrieval. In *The Simulation of Human Behavior*, F. Bresson and M. deMontmollin, (Eds.), Dunod, Paris, 253-264, 1969.

Treisman, M. and Rostron, A. B. Brief auditory storage: A modification of Sperling's paradigm applied to audition. *Acta Psychologica*, 36, 161-170, 1972.

Tulving, E. and Madigan, S. A. Memory and verbal learning. *Ann. Rev. Psychol.*, 21, 437-484, 1970.

Wickelgren, W. A. Consolidation and retroactive interference in short-term recognition memory for pitch. *J. Exp. Psychol.*, 72, 250-259, 1966.

Wickelgren, W. A. Numerical relations, similarity, and short-term recognition memory for pairs of digits. *Brit. J. Psychol.*, 57, 263-274, 1966.

Wickelgren, W. A. Exponential decay and independence from irrelevant associations in short-term recognition memory for serial order. *J. Exp. Psychol.*, 73, 165-171, 1967.

Wickelgren, W. A. Sparing of short-term memory in an amnexic patient: implications for strength theory of memory. *Neuropsychologica*, 6, 235-244, 1968.

Wickelgren, W. A. Associative strength theory of recognition memory for pitch. *J. Math. Psychol.*, 6, 13-61, 1969.

Wickelgren, W. A. Time, interference, and rate of presentation in short-term recognition memory for items. *J. Math. Psychol.*, 7, 219-235, 1970.

Wickelgren, W. A. Trace resistance and the decay of long-term memory. *J. Math. Psychol.*, 9, 418-455, 1972.

Wickelgren, W. A. and Berian, K. M. Dual trace theory and the consolidation of long-term memory. *J. Math. Psychol.*, 8, 404-417, 1971.

Wickelgren, W. A. and Norman, D. A. Invariance of forgetting rate with number of repetitions in verbal short-term recognition memory. *Psychon. Sci.*, 22, 363-364, 1971.

Wickelgren, W. A. and Whitman, P. T. Visual very-short-term memory is non-associative. *J. Exp. Psychol.*, 84, 277-281, 1970.

Wood, L. E. An objective test of goodness of fit of the continuous strength model in STM. *Perc. and Psychophys.*, 9, 424-426-1971.

Young, R. K., Saegert, J. and Linsley, D. Retention as a function of meaningfulness. *J. Exp. Psychol.*, 78, 89-94, 1968.

METHODS AND MEASURES

Abramson, I. G. and Levitt, H. Statistical analysis of data from experiments in human signal detection. *J. Math. Psychol.*, 6, 391-417, 1969.

Anderson, C. M. B. and Stephens, S. D. G. Automated psychophysical signal detection equipment. Report No. Ac36, National Physical Laboratory, Teddington, Middlesex, U. K., March, 1969.

Bell, D. W. and Nixon, J. C. Reliability of ratings in an auditory signal-detection experiment. *J. Acoust. Soc. Am.*, 49, 435-439, 1971.

Brookes, B. C. The measures of information retrieval effectiveness proposed by Swets. *J. Docum.*, 24, 41-54, 1968.

Calfee, R. C. Effects of payoff on detection in a symmetric auditory detection task. *Perc. and Mot. Skills*, 31, 895-901, 1970.

Clark, W. C. The effect of information feedback and reference tones on d' and L_X: A further analysis of Nash and Adamson's data. *Psychon. Sci.*, 16, 93-94, 1969.

Clark, W. C. and Mehl, L. Signal detection theory procedures are not equivalent when thermal stimuli are judged. *J. Exp. Psychol.*, 97, 148-153, 1973.

Dorfman, D. D. and Alf, E., Jr. Maximum likelihood estimation of parameters of signal detection theory—a direct solution. *Psychometrika*, 33, 117-124, 1968.

Dorfman, D. D. and Alf, E., Jr. Maximum likelihood estimation of parameters of signal-detection theory and determination of confidence intervals—rating method data. *J. Math. Psychol.*, 6, 487-496, 1969.

Dorosh, M. E., Tong, J. E. and Boissonneault, D. R. White noise, instructions, and two-flash fusion with two signal-detection procedures. *Psychon. Sci.*, 20, 98-99, 1970.

Emmerich, D. S. Receiver-operating characteristics determined under several interaural conditions of listening. *J. Acoust. Soc. Am.*, 43, 298-307, 1968.

Emmerich, D. S. ROCs obtained with two signal intensities presented in random order, and a comparison between yes-no and rating ROCs. *Perc. and Psychophys.*, 3, 35-40, 1968.

Friedman, M. P., Carterette, E. C., Nakatani, L. and Ahumada, A., Jr. Feedback and frequency variables in signal detection. Technical Report No. 30, Department of Psychology, Human Communication Laboratory, University of California, Los Angeles, 1968.

Galanter, E. and Holman, G. L. Some invariances of the isosensitivity function and their implications for the utility function of money. *J. Exp. Psychol.*, 73, 333-339, 1967.

Gescheider, G. A., Herman, D. D. and Phillips, J. N. Criterion shifts in the measurement of tactile masking. *Perc. and Psychophys.*, 8, 433-436, 1970.

Goranson, R. E. and Theodor, L. H. Optimal percent correct measures in recognition memory. *Perc. and Mot. Skills*, 31, 848, 1970.

Gourevitch, V. and Galanter, E. A significance test for one-parameter isosensitivity functions. *Psychometrika*, 32, 25-34, 1967.

Grey, D. R. and Morgan, B. J. T. Some aspects of ROC curve-fitting: Normal and logistic models. *J. Math. Psychol.*, 9, 128-139, 1972.

Grier, J. B. Nonparametric indexes for sensitivity and bias: Computing formulas. *Psychol. Bull.*, 75, 424-429, 1971.

Gummerman, K. A response-contingent measure of proportion correct. *J. Acoust. Soc. Am.*, 52, 1645-1647, 1972.

Hammerton, M. and Altham, P. M. E. A non-parametric alternative to d'. *Nature*, 234, 487-488, 1971.

Healy, A. F. and Jones, C. Criterion shifts in recall. *Psychol. Bull.* 79, 3350340, 1973.

Heine, M. H. The inverse relationship of precision and recall in terms of the Swets model. *J. Docum.*, 29, 81-84, 1973.

Heine, M. H. Distance between sets as an objective measure of retrieval effectiveness. *Inform. Stor. Retr.*, 9, 181-198, 1973.

Hershman, R. L. and Small, D. Tables of d' for detection and localization. *Perc. and Psychophys.*, 3, 321-323, 1968.

Herzog, T. R. Effects of amount and kind of prior target-uncertainty reduction in the repeated presentations paradigm. *Perc. and Psychophys.*, 10, 273-277, 1971.

Hochhaus, L. Correct response discrimination as a function of multiple recognition choices: effect of correct guessing on type II d'. *J. Exp. Psychol.*, 84, 458-461, 1970.

Hochhaus, L. A table for the calculation of d' and β. *Psychol. Bull.*, 77, 375-376, 1973.

Hodos, W. Nonparametric index of response bias for use in detection and recognition experiments. *Psychol. Bull.*, 74, 351-354, 1970.

Holloway, C. M. The effects of response bias in two-alternative-forced-choice discrimination matrices. *Behav. Res. Meth. and Instru.*, 1, 175-178, 1969.

Katz, L. A. A comparison of type II operating characteristics derived from confidence ratings and from latencies. *Perc. and Psychophys.*, 8, 65-68, 1970.

LaBerge, D. Effect of type of catch trial upon generalization gradients of reaction time. *J. Exp. Psychol.*, 87, 225-228, 1971.

Leshowitz, B. Receiver operating characteristics and psychometric functions determined under simple- and pedestal-detection conditions. *J. Acoust. Soc. Am.*, 45, 1474-1484, 1969.

Leshowitz, B. Comparison of ROC curves from one- and two-interval rating-scale procedures. *J. Acoust. Soc. Am.*, 46, 399-402, 1969.

Marascuilo, L. A. Extensions of the significance test for one-parameter signal detection hypotheses. *Psychometrika*, 35, 237-243, 1970.

McFadden, D. Three computational versions of proportion correct for use in forced-choice experiments. *Perc. and Psychophys.*, 8, 336-342, 1970.

Miller, H. The FROC curve: A representation of the observer's performance for the method of free response. *J. Acoust. Soc. Am.*, 46, 1473-1476, 1969.

Nachmias, J. Effects of presentation probability and number of response alternatives on simple visual detection. *Perc. and Psychophys.*, 3, 151-155, 1968.

Nash, A. and Adamson, R. Effects of information feedback and reference tones on signal detection. *Psychon. Sci.*, 13, 301-302, 1968.

Ogilvie, J. C. and Creelman, C. D. Maximum likelihood estimation of receiver operating characteristic curve parameters. *J. Math. Psychol.*, 5, 377-391, 1968.

Pastore, R. E. and Sorkin, R. D. Adaptive auditory signal processing. *Psychon. Sci.*, 23, 259-260, 1971.

Penner, M. J. The effect of payoffs and cue tones on detection of sinusoids of uncertain frequency. *Perc. and Psychophys.* 11, 198-202, 1972.

Pollack, I. and Hsieh, R. Sampling variability of the area under the ROC-curve and of d'_e. *Psychol. Bull.*, 71, 161-173, 1969.

Reed, C. M. and Bilger, R. C. A comparative study of S/N_0 and E/N_0. *J. Acoust. Soc. Am.*, 53, 1039-1044, 1973.

Robertson, S. E. The parametric description of retrieval tests. I. The basic parameters. *J. Docum.*, 25, 1-27, 1969.

Robertson, S. E. The parametric description of retrieval tests. II. Overall measures. *J. Docum.*, 25, 93-107, 1969.

Robinson, D. E. and Watson, C. S. Psychophysical methods in modern psychoacoustics. In *Foundations of Modern Auditory Theory*, J. V. Tobias (Ed.), Academic Press, New York, 101-131, 1972.

Rose, R. M., Teller, D. Y. and Rendleman, P. Statistical properties of staircase estimates. *Perc. and Psychophys.*, 8, 199-204, 1970.

Schulman, A. I. and Greenberg, G. Z. Operating characteristics and a priori probability of the signal. *Perc. and Psychophys.*, 8, 317-320, 1970.

Schulman, A. I. and Mitchell, R. R. Operating characteristics from yes-no and forced-choice procedures. *J. Acoust. Soc. Am.*, 40, 473-477, 1965.

Semb, G. and Saslow, M. G. Conformity to experimenter-determined payoff-enforced criterion levels in the method of random staircases. *Perc. and Psychophys.*, 2, 396-398, 1967.

Shipley, E. F. A signal detection theory analysis of a category judgment experiment. *Perc. and Psychophys.*, 7, 38-42, 1970.

Smith, K. A note on the standard error of the estimates of TSD parameters from "Yes-No" experiments. Michigan Mathematical Psychology Program: MMPP 69-8, University of Michigan, Ann Arbor, Michigan, 1969.

Swets, J. A. and Markowitz, J. Factors affecting the slope of empirical ROC curves: Comparison of binary and rating response. *Perc. and Psychophys.*, 2, 15-28, 1967.

Thomas, E. A. C. Sufficient conditions for monotone hazard rate: An application to latency-probability curves. *J. Math. Psychol.*, 8, 303-332, 1971.

Viemeister, N. F. Intensity discrimination: Performance in three paradigms. *Perc. and Psychophys.*, 8, 417-419, 1970.

Watson, C. S. and Clopton, B. M. Motivated changes of auditory sensitivity in a simple detection task. *Perc. and Psychophys.*, 5, 281-287, 1969.

MINOR SENSES

Berglund, B., Berglund, U., Engen, T. and Lindvall, T. The effect of adaption on odor detection. *Perc. and Psychophys.*, 9, 435-438, 1971.

Boyer, W. N., Cross, H. A., Guyot, G. W. and Washington, D. M. A TSD determination of a DL using two-point tactual stimuli applied to the back. *Psychon. Sci.*, 21, 195-196, 1970.

Clark, W. C. Sensory-decision theory analysis of the placebo effect on the criterion for pain and thermal sensitivity (d'). *J. Abnorm. Psychol.*, 74, 363-371, 1969.

Clark, W. C. and Dillon, D. J. SDT analysis of binary decisions and sensory intensity ratings to noxious thermal stimuli. *Perc. and Psychophys.*, 13, 491-493, 1973.

Clark, W. C. and Mehl, L. A sensory decision theory analysis of the effect of age and sex on d', various response criteria, and 50% pain threshold. *J. Abnorm. Psychol.*, 78, 202-212, 1971.

Corbit, T. E. and Engen, T. Facilitation of olfactory detection. *Perc. and Psychophys.*, 10, 433-436, 1971.

Cross, H. A., Boyer, W. N. and Guyot, G. W. Determination of a DL using two-point tactual stimuli: A signal-detection approach. *Psychon. Sci.*, 21, 198-199, 1970.

Gescheider, G. A., Barton, G., Bruce, M. R., Goldberg, J. H., and Greenspan, M. J. Effects of simultaneous auditory stimulation on the detection of tactile stimuli. *J. Exp. Psychol.*, 81, 120-125, 1969.

Gescheider, G. A., Wright, J. H., Weber, B. J., and Barton, W. G. Absolute thresholds in vibrotactile signal detection. *Perc. and Psychophys.*, 10, 413-417, 1971.

McFadden, D., Barr, E. A., and Young, R. E. Audio analgesia: Lack of a cross-masking effect on taste. *Perc. and Psychophys.*, 10, 175-179, 1971.

Pursell, E. D., Sanders, R. E., and Haude, R. H. Sensitivity to sucrose in smokers and nonsmokers: A comparison of TSD and percent correct measures. *Perc. and Psychophys.*, 14, 34-36, 1973.

Rollman, G. B. Detection models: Experimental tests with electrocutaneous stimuli. *Perc. and Psychophys.*, 5, 377-380, 1969.

Semb, G. The detectability of the odor of butanol. *Perc. and Psychophys.*, 4, 335-340, 1969.

Steinmetz, G., Pryor, G. T., and Stone, H. Effect of blank samples on absolute odor threshold determinations. *Perc. and Psychophys.*, 6, 142-144, 1969.

Swets, J. A., Markowitz, J., and Franzén, O. Vibrotactile signal detection. *Perc. and Psychophys.*, 6, 83-88, 1969.

PERSONALITY

Bernstein, I. H. and Eriksen, C. W. Effects of "subliminal" prompting on paired-associate learning. *J. Exp. Res. in Person.*, 1, 33-38, 1965.

Clark, W. C. The psyche in psychophysics: A sensory-decision theory analysis of the effect of instructions on flicker sensitivity and response bias. *Psychol. Bull.*, 65, 358-366, 1966.

Clark, W. C., Brown, J. C., and Rutschmann, J. Flicker sensitivity and response bias in psychiatric patients and normal subjects. *J. Abnorm. Psychol.*, 72, 35-42, 1967.

Dandeliker, J. and Dorfman, D. D. Receiver-operating characteristics curves for taboo and neutral words. *Psychon. Sci.*, 201-202, 1969.

Dorfman, D. D. Recognition of taboo words as a function of a priori probability. *J. Pers. Soc. Psychol.*, 7, 1-10, 1967.

Dorfman, D. D., Grossberg, J. M., and Kroeker, L. Recognition of taboo stimuli as a function of exposure time. *J. Pers. Soc. Psychol.*, 2, 552-562, 1965.

Goldner, J., Reuder, M. E., Riba, B. and Jarmon, D. Neutral vs ego-orientating instructions: Effects on judgments of magnitude estimation. *Perc. and Psychophys.*, 9, 84-88, 1971.

Poortinga, Y. H. Signal-detection experiments as tests for risk-taking: A pilot study. *Psychon. Sci.*, 14, 185-188, 1969.

Price, R. H. Signal-detection methods in personality and perception. *Psychol. Bull.*, 66, 55-62, 1966.

Price, R. H. and Eriksen, C. W. Size constancy in schizophrenia: A reanalysis. *J. Abnorm. Psychol.*, 71, 155-160, 1966.

Rappaport, M. and Hopkins, H. K. Signal detection and chlorpromazine. *Hum. Fact.*, 13, 387-390, 1971.

Rappaport, M., Silverman, J., Hopkins, H. K., Hall, K. Penothiazine effects on auditory signal detection in paranoid and nonparanoid schizophrenics. *Science*, 174, 723-725, 1971.

Stephens, S. D. G. Auditory threshold variance, signal detection theory and personality. *Intern. Audiol.*, VII, 131-137, 1969.

Strickland, B. R. and Rodwan, A. S. Relation of certain personality variables to decision-making in perception. *Perc. and Mot. Skills*, 18, 353-359, 1964.

PHYSIOLOGY

Donchin, E. and Sutton, S. The "psychological significance" of evoked responses: A comment on Clark, Butler, and Rosner. *Commun. in Behav. Biol.*, 5, 111-114, 1970.

Dore, D. and Sutton, S. Evoked potential correlates of response criterion in auditory signal detection. *Science*, 177, 362-364, 1972.

Hillyard, S. A., Hink, R. F., Schwent, V. L., and Picton, T. W. Electrical signs of selective attention in the human brain. *Science*, 182, 177-180, 1973.

Squires, K. C., Hillyard, S. A., and Lindsay, P. H. Cortical potentials evoked by confirming and disconfirming feedback following an auditory discrimination. *Perc. and Psychophys.*, 13, 25-31, 1973.

REACTION TIME

Audley, R. J. Some observations on theories of choice reaction time: Tutorial review. In *Attention and Performance IV*, S. Kornblum (Ed.), Academic Press, New York, 509-545, 1973.

Bindra, D., Williams, J. A., and Wise, J. S. Judgments of sameness and difference: Experiments on decision time. *Science*, 150, 1625-1627, 1965.

Carterette, E. D., Friedman, M. P. and Cosmides, R. Reaction-time distributions in the detection of weak signals in noise. *J. Acoust. Soc. Am.*, 38, 531-542, 1965.

Debecker, J. and Desmedt, J. E. Maximum capacity for sequential one-bit auditory decisions. *J. Exp. Psychol.*, 83, 366-372, 1970.

Emmerich, D. S., Gray, J. L., Watson, C. S., and Tanis, D. C.Response latency, confidence, and ROCs in auditory signal detection. *Perc. and Psychophys.*, 11, 65-72, 1972.

Gescheider, G. A., Wright, J. H., and Evans, M. B. Reaction time in the detection of vibrotactile signals. *J. Exp. Psychol.*, 77, 501-504, 1968.

Gescheider, G. A., Wright, J. H., Weber, B. J., Kirchner, B. M., and Milligan, E. A. Reaction time as a function of the intensity and probability of occurrence of vibrotactile signals. *Perc. and Psychophys.*, 5, 18-20, 1969.

Green, D. M. and Luce, R. D. Speed-accuracy trade off in auditory detection. In *Attention and Performance IV*, S. Kornblum (Ed.), Academic Press, New York, 547-569, 1973.

Grice, G. R. Application of a variable criterion model to auditory reaction time as a function of the type of catch trial. *Perc. and Psychophys.*, 12, 103-107, 1972.

Lappin, J. S. and Harm, O. J. On the rate of acquisition of visual information about space, time, and intensity. *Perc. and Psychophys.*, 13, 439-445, 1973.

Link, S. W. Applying RT deadlines to discrimination reaction time. *Psychon. Sci.*, 25, 355-358, 1971.

Link, S. W. and Tindall, A. D. Speed and accuracy in comparative judgments of line length. *Perc. and Psychophys.*, 9, 284-288, 1971.

Markowitz, J. Optimal flash rate and duty cycle for flashing visual indicators. *Hum. Fact.*, 13, 427-433, 1971.

Murray, H. G. Stimulus intensity and reaction time: evaluation of a decision-theory model. *J. Exp. Psychol.*, 84, 383-391, 1970.

Pachella, R. G. and Pew, R. W. Speed-accuracy tradeoff in reaction time: Effect of discrete criterion times. *J. Exp. Psychol.*, 76, 19-24, 1968.

Pike, R. Response latency models for signal detection. *Psychol. Rev.*, 80, 53-68, 1973.

Pike, R. and Ryder, R. Response latencies in the yes/no detection task: An assessment of two basic models. *Perc. and Psychophys.*, 13, No. 2, 224-232, 1973.

Reed, A. V. Speed-accuracy trade-off in recognition memory. *Science*, 181, 574-576, 1973.

Sanford, A. J. Effects of changes in the intensity of white noise on simultaneity judgments and simple reaction time. *Quart. J. Exp. Psychol.*, 23, 296-303, 1971.

Sekuler, R. W. Signal detection, choice response times, and visual backward masking. *Canad. J. Psychol.*, 19, 118-132, 1965.

Sekuler, R. W. Choice times and detection with visual backward masking. *Canad. J. Psychol.*, 20, 34-42, 1966.

Sternberg, S. and Knoll, R. L. The perception of temporal order: Fundamental issues and a general model. In *Attention and Performance IV*, S. Kornblum (Ed.), Academic Press, New York, 629-685, 1973.

Swensson, R. G. The elusive tradeoff: Speed vs accuracy in visual discrimination tasks. *Perc. and Psychophys.*, 12, 16-32, 1972.

Thomas, E. A. C. On expectancy and the speed and accuracy of responses. In *Attention and Performance IV*, S. Kornblum (Ed.), Academic Press, New York, 613-626, 1973.

Thomas, E. A. C. and Myers, J. L. Implications of latency data for threshold and non-threshold models of signal detection. MMPP 71-10, Michigan Mathematical Psychology Program, Department of Psychology, The University of Michigan, Ann Arbor, Michigan, 1971.

RECOGNITION

Alexander, L. T. and Cooperband, A. S. Visual detection of compound motion. *J. Exp. Psychol.*, 71, 816-821, 1966.

Broadbent, D. E. Word-frequency effect and response bias. *Psychol. Rev.*, 74, 1-15, 1967.

Catlin, J. On the word-frequency effect. *Psychol. Rev.*, 76, 504-506, 1969.

Catlin, J. In defense of sophisticated-guessing theory. *Psychol. Rev.*, 80, 412-416, 1973.

Frederiksen, J. R. Statistical decision model for auditory word recognition. *Psychol. Rev.*, 78, 409-419, 1971.

Hershman, R. L. and Lichtenstein, M. Detection and localization: An Extension of the theory of signal detectability. *J. Acoust. Soc. Am.*, 42, 446-452, 1967.

Hershman, R. L. and Lichtenstein, M. Signal detection and localization by real observers. *Perc. and Psychophys.*, 6, 53-57, 1969.

Hochhaus, L. and Antes, J. R. Speech identification and "knowing that you know." *Perc. and Psychophys.*, 1, 131-132, 1973.

Lindner, W. A. Recognition performance as a function of detection criterion in a simultaneous detection-recognition task. *J. Acoust. Soc. Am.*, 44, 204-211, 1968.

Lowe, G. Auditory detection and recognition in a two-alternative, directional uncertainty situation. *Perc. and Psychophys.*, 4, 180-182, 1968.

Lowe, G. and Earle, D. C. Auditory detection and recognition under conditions of lateral, temporal, and composite uncertainty. *J. Acoust. Soc. Am.*, 45, 1485-1488, 1969.

MacMillan, N. A. Detection and recognition of increments and decrements in auditory intensity. *Perc. and Psychophys.*, 10, 233-238, 1971.

MacMillan, N. A. Detection and recognition of intensity changes in tone and noise: The detection-recognition disparity. *Perc. and Psychophys.*, 13, 65-75, 1973.

Massaro, D. W. Stimulus information vs processing time in auditory pattern recognition. *Perc. and Psychophys.*, 12, 50-56, 1972.

Morton, J. A retest of the response-bias explanation of the word-frequency effect. *Brit. J. Math. Stat. Psychol.*, 21, 21-22, 1968.

Nakatani, L. H. Comments on Broadbent's response bias model for stimulus recognition. *Psychol. Rev.*, 77, 574-576, 1970.

Nakatani, L. H. Confusion-choice model for multidimensional psychophysics. *J. Math. Psychol.*, 9, 104-127, 1972.

Nakatani, L. H. On the evaluation of models for the word-frequency effect. *Psychol. Rev.*, 80, 195-202, 1973.

Reed, S. K. Decision processes in pattern classification. Tech. Report No. 32, University of California, Los Angeles, July, 1970.

Rollman, G. B. and Nachmias, J. Simultaneous detection and recognition of chromatic flashes. *Perc. and Psychophys.*, 12, 309-314, 1972.

Sandusky, A. Signal recognition models compared for random and Markov presentation sequences. *Perc. and Psychophys.*, 10, 339-347, 1971.

Spencer, T. J. Encoding time from iconic storage: a single-letter visual display. *J. Exp. Psychol.*, 91, 18-24, 1971.

Tanner, T. A., Jr., Rauk, J. A., and Atkinson, R. C. Signal recognition as influenced by information feedback. *J. Math. Psychol.*, 2, 259-274, 1970.

Taylor, M. M. Detection and localization experiment: Comments on a paper by Hershman and Lichtenstein [J. Acoust. Soc. Am., 42, 446-452 (1967)] and a note on a table of d' for k=2. *J. Acoust. Soc. Am.*, 43, 884-885, 1968.

Taylor, M. M. and Fraser, W. C. G. A table of d' for a model of the unforced choice experiment. Report No. 534, Defense Research Medical Laboratories, Toronto, Canada, 1965.

Treisman, M. On the word frequency effect: Comments on the papers by J. Catlin and L. H. Nakatani. *Psychol. Rev.*, 78, 420-425, 1971.

Zinnes, J. L. and Kurtz, R. Matching, discrimination, and payoffs. *J. Math. Psychol.*, 5, 392-421, 1968.

VIGILANCE

Baddeley, A. D. and Colquhoun, W. P. Signal probability and vigilance: A reappraisal of the 'signal-rate' effect. *Brit. J. Psychol.*, 60, 169-178, 1969.

Colquhoun, W. P. Training for vigilance: A comparison of different techniques. *Hum. Fact.*, 8, 7-12, 1966.

Colquhoun, W. P. Sonar target detection as a decision process. *J. Appl. Psychol.*, 51, 187-190, 1967.

Colquhoun, W. P. Effects of raised ambient temperature and event rate on vigilance performance. *Aeros. Med.* 40, 413-417, 1969.

Colquhoun, W. P. and Edwards, R. S. Practice effects on a visual vigilance task with and without search. *Hum. Fact.*, 12, 537-545, 1970.

Davenport, W. G. Auditory vigilance: The effects of costs and values on signals. *Austral. J. Psychol.*, 20, 213-218, 1968.

Davenport, W. G. Vibrotactile vigilance: The effects of costs and values on signals. *Perc. and Psychophys.*, 5, 25-28, 1969.

Deaton, M., Tobias, J. S., and Wilkinson, R. T. The effect of sleep deprivation on signal detection parameters. *Quart. J. Exp. Psychol.*, 23, 449-452, 1971.

Guralnick, M. J. Observing responses and decision processes in vigilance. *J. Exp. Psychol.*, 93, 239-244, 1972.

Hatfield, J. L. and Loeb, M. Sense mode and coupling in a vigilance task. *Perc. and Psychophys.*, 4, 29-36, 1968.

Hatfield, J. and Soderquist, D. R. Practice effects and signal detection indices in an auditory vigilance task. *J. Acoust. Soc. Am.*, 46, 1458-1463, 1969.

Hatfield, J. L. and Soderquist, D. R. Coupling effects and performance in vigilance tasks. *Hum. Fact.*, 12, 351-359, 1970.

Jerison, H. J. Signal detection theory in the analysis of human vigilance. *Hum. Fact.*, 9, 285-288, 1967.

Levine, J. M. The effects of values and costs on the detection and identification of signals in auditory vigilance. *Hum. Fact.*, 8, 525-537, 1966.

Loeb, M. and Alluisi, E. A. Influence of display task, and organismic variables on indices of monitoring behavior. *Acta Psychol.*, 33, 343-366, 1970.

Loeb, M. and Binford, J. R. Variation in performance on auditory and visual monitoring tasks as a function of signal and stimulus frequencies. *Perc. and Psychophys.*, 4, 361-367, 1968.

Loeb, M. and Binford, J. R. Examination of some factors influencing performance on an auditory monitoring task with one signal per session. *J. Exp. Psychol.*, 83, 40-44, 1970.

Loeb, M., Hawkes, G. R., Evans, W. O., and Alluisi, E. A. The influence of d-amphetamine, benactyzene, and chlorapromazine on performance in an auditory vigilance task. *Psychon. Sci.*, 3, 29-30, 1965.

Lucas, P. Human performance in low-signal-probability tasks. *J. Acoust. Soc. Am.*, 42, 158-178, 1967.

Mackworth, J. F. Performance decrement in vigilance, threshold, and high-speed perceptual motor tasks. *Canad. J. Psychol.*, 18, 209-223, 1964.

Mackworth, J. F. The effect of true and false knowledge of results on the detectability of signals in a vigilance task. *Canad. J. Psychol.*, 18, 106-117, 1964.

Mackworth, J. F. Deterioration of signal detectability during a vigilance task as a function of background event rate. *Psychon. Sci.*, 3, 421-422, 1965.

Mackworth, J. F. Effect of amphetamine on the detectability of signals in a vigilance task. *Canad. J. Psychol.*, 19, 104-110, 1965.

Mackworth, J. F. Decision interval and signal detectability in a vigilance task. *Canad. J. Psychol.*, 19, 111-117, 1965.

Mackworth, J. F. The effect of signal rate on performance in two kinds of vigilance task. *Hum. Fact.*, 10, 11-18, 1968.

McCann, P. H. Variability of signal detection measures with noise type. *Psychon. Sci.*, 15, 310-311, 1969.

Milosevic, S. Detection du signal en fonction due critere de response. *Le Travail Humain*, 32, 81-86, 1969.

Swets, J. A. Comment: Adaptation-level theory and signal-detection theory and their relation to vigilance experiments. In *Adaptation-Level Theory*, M. H. Appley (Ed.), Academic Press, Inc., New York, 49-53, 1971.

Taylor, M. M. The effect of the square root of time in continuing perceptual tasks. *Perc. and Psychophys.*, 1, 113-119, 1966.

Taylor, M. M. Detectability theory and the interpretation of vigilance data. *Acta Psychol.*, 27, 390-399, 1967.

Thurmond, J. B., Binford, J. R., and Loeb, M. Effects of signal to noise variability over repeated sessions in an auditory vigilance task. *Perc. and Psychophys.*, 7, 100-102, 1970.

Williges, R. C. Within-session criterion changes compared to an ideal observer criterion in a visual monitoring task. *J. Exp. Psychol.*, 81, 61-66, 1969.

Williges, R. C. The role of payoffs and signal ratios in criterion changes during a monitoring task. *Hum. Fact.*, 13, 261-267, 1971.

VISION

Allan, L. G. Visual position discrimination: A model relating temporal and and spatial factors. *Perc. and Psychophys.*, 4, 267-278, 1968.

Allan, L. G., Kristofferson, A. B., and Wiens, E. W. Duration discrimination of brief light flashes. *Perc. and Psychophys.*, 9, 327-334, 1971.

Baron, J. Temporal ROC curves and the psychological moment. *Psychon. Sci.*, 15, 299-300, 1969.

Blake, R. and Fox, R. The psychophysical inquiry into binocular summation. *Perc. and Psychophys.*, 14, 161-185, 1973.

Bruder, G. E. and Kietzman, M. L. Visual temporal integration for threshold, signal detectability, and reaction time measures. *Perc. and Psychophys.*, 13, 293-300, 1973.

Campbell, F. W., Nachmias, J. and Jukes, J. Spatial-frequency discrimination in human vision. *J. Opt. Soc. Am.*, 60, 555-559, 1970.

Clement, D. E. and Hosking, K. E. Scanning strategies and differential sensitivity in a visual signal detection task: Intrasubject reliability. *Psychon. Sci.*, 22, 323-324, 1971.

Cox, S. T. and Dember, W. N. Effects of target-field luminance, interstimulus interval and target-mask separation on extent of visual backward masking. *Psychon. Sci.*, 22, 79-80, 1971.

Creelman, C. D. and Donaldson, W. ROC curves for discrimination of linear extent. *J. Exp. Psychol.*, 77, 514-516, 1968.

Glorioso, R. M. and Levy, R. M. Operator behavior in a dynamic visual signal detection task. *Perc. and Psychophys.*, 4, 5-9, 1968.

Halpern, J. and Ulehla, J. Z. The effect of multiple responses and certainty estimates on the integration of visual information. *Perc. and Psychophys.*, 7, 129-132, 1970.

Handel, S. and Christ, R. E. Detection and identification of geometric forms using peripheral and central viewing. *Perc. and Psychophys.*, 6, 47-49, 1969.

Keller, W. and Kinchla, R. A. Visual movement discrimination. *Perc. and Psychophys.*, 3, 233-236, 1968.

Kinchla, R. A. Visual movement perception: A comparison of absolute and relative movement discrimination. *Perc. and Psychophys.*, 9, 165-171, 1971.

Kinchla, R. A. and Allan, L. G. Visual movement perception: A comparison of sensitivity to vertical and horizontal movement. *Perc. and Psychophys.*, 8, 399-405, 1970.

Leshowitz, B., Taub, H. B., and Raab, D. H. Visual detection of signals in the presence of continuous and pulsed backgrounds. *Perc. and Psychophys.*, 4, 207-213, 1968.

Lowe, G. Interval of time uncertainty in visual detection. *Perc. and Psychophys.*, 2, 278-280, 1967.

Nachmias, J. and Kocher, E. C. Visual detection and discrimination of luminance increments. *J. Opt. Soc. Am.*, 60, 382-389, 1970.

Theodor, L. H. The detectability of a brief gap in a pulse of light as a function of its temporal location within the pulse. *Perc. and Psychophys.*, 12, 168-170, 1972.

Thijssen, J. M. and Vendrik, J. H. Differential luminance sensitivity of the human visual system. *Perc. and Psychophys.*, 10, 58-63, 1971.

Tyson, P. D. Perceptual modification of sensitivity (d'): Modifying temporal resolution by the consistency of the spatial configuration. *Perc. and Psychophys.*, 12, 45-49, 1972.

Westendorf, D. H., Blake, R. R., and Fox, R. Binocular summation of equal-energy flashes of unequal duration. *Perc. and Psychophys.*, 12, 445-448, 1972.

White, M. J. Signal-detection analysis of laterality differences: Some preliminary data, free of recall and report-sequence characteristics. *J. Exp. Psychol.*, 83, 174-176, 1970.

Wickelgren, W. A. Strength theories of disjunctive visual detection. *Perc. and Psychophys.*, 2, 331-337, 1967.

Winnick, W. A. and Bruder, G. E. Signal detection approach to the study of retinal locus in tachistoscopic recognition. *J. Exp. Psychol.*, 78, 528-531, 1968.

Yellott, J. I., Jr. and Curnow, P. F. Second choices in a visual span of apprehension task. *Perc. and Psychophys.*, 2, 307-311, 1967.

VISION AND AUDITION

Baker, E. M. and Schuck, J. R. A signal detection analysis of the effects of hearing on the visual recognition of two-digit numbers. *Perc. and Psychophys.*, 12, 239-240, 1972.

Brown, A. E. and Hopkins, H. K. Interaction of the auditory and visual sensory modalities. *J. Acoust. Soc. Am.*, 41, 1-6, 1967.

Carterette, E. C. and Jones, M. H. Visual and auditory information processing in children and adults. *Science*, 156, 986-988, 1967.

Dougherty, W. G., Jones, G. B., and Engel, G. R. Sensory integration of auditory and visual information. *Canad. J. Psychol.*, 25, 476-485, 1971.

Earle, D. C. and Lowe, G. Channel, temporal, and composite uncertainty in the detection and recognition of auditory and visual signals. *Perc. and Psychophys.*, 9, 177-181, 1971.

Fidell, S. Sensory function in multimodal signal detection. *J. Acoust. Soc. Am.*, 47, 1009-1015, 1970.

Forbes, S. M., Taylor, M. M. and Lindsay, P. H. Cue timing in a multi-dimensional detection task. *Perc. and Mot. Skills*, 25, 113-120, 1967.

Gunn, W. J. and Loeb, M. Correlation of performance in detecting visual signals. *Am. J. Psychol.*, 80, 236-242, 1966.

Kinchla, R. A., Townsend, J., Yellott, J. I., Jr., and Atkinson, R. C. Influence of correlated visual cues on auditory signal detection. *Perc. and Psychophys.*, 1, 67-73, 1966.

Loveless, N. E., Brebner, J. and Hamilton, P. Bisensory presentation of information. *Psychol. Bull.*, 73, 161-199, 1970.

Morton, J. Comments on "Interaction of the auditory and visual sensory modalities" (*J. Acoust. Soc. Am.*, 41, 1-6, 1967). *J. Acoust. Soc. Am.*, 42, 1342-1343, 1967.

Watkins, W. H. and Feehrer, C. E. Acoustic facilitation of visual detection. *J. Exp. Psychol.*, 70, 332-333, 1965.

Name Index

Abramowitz, M., 168, 215, 371, 417
Adler, H. E., 419
Anderson, T. W., 299, 311, 417
Atkinson, R. C., 127, 145, 146, 417, 418, 422
Audley, R. J., 325, 417

Bachrach, A., 420
Baddeley, A. D., 333, 418
Baitsell, G. A., 421
Barlow, H. B., 138, 319, 417, 422
Bayes, T., 14, 357, 430
Becker, G. M., 261, 417
Békésy, G. von, 127, 136, 276, 293, 417
Bellman, R., 260, 417
Beranek, L. L., 412, 417
Bernoulli, J., 369
Bertky, W., 259, 417
Bigelow, J., 195
Binford, J. R., 333, 422
Birdsall, T. G., 1, 41, 69, 94, 102, 103, 104, 105, 107, 109, 127, 132, 139, 152, 172, 241, 260, 261, 298, 301, 302, 307, 335, 344, 417, 418, 420, 424, 427
Blackwell, D., 260, 417
Blackwell, H. R., 127, 336, 395, 398, 400, 417
Blodgett, H. C., 210, 421
Boring, E. G., 419
Bouman, M. A., 138, 417
Bourbon, W. T., 100, 143, 186, 401, 403, 428
Bricker, P. D., 336, 417

Broadbent, D. E., 143, 333, 334, 335, 417, 418
Bush, R. R., 145, 418, 422, 423

Carslaw, H. S., 177, 383, 384, 418
Carterette, E. C., 41, 297, 299, 304, 305, 418, 419
Cattell, J. McK., 124
Chapanis, A., 366, 417
Chebyshev, P. L., 368
Cherry, C., 426, 428
Chocholle, R., 327, 418
Christie, L. W., 325, 418
Clarke, F. R., 11, 41, 134, 152, 297, 298, 299, 300, 301, 302, 303, 304, 306, 418, 419, 427
Cole, M., 297, 304, 305, 418
Collier, G., 248, 418
Colquhoun, W. P., 333, 418
Corso, J. F., 119, 136, 138, 418
Cramér, H., 58, 349, 418
Creelman, C. D., 286, 287, 288, 315, 323, 330, 331, 332, 418

Davenport, E. W., 283, 428
Davenport, W. B., 169, 171, 418
Davies, I. L., 1, 428
deBoer, E., 211, 229, 230, 418
Decker, L. R., 41, 297, 302, 303, 305, 308, 418, 424, 425
Dember, W. N., 243, 244, 245, 246, 422
deMoive, A., 58
Dodge, H. F., 259, 418
Donders, F. C., 325

461

Egan, J. P., 11, 41, 81, 87, 98, 111, 134, 195, 265, 266, 267, 268, 269, 297, 299, 300, 302, 334, 337, 339, 340, 341, 400, 409, 418, 419
Eijkman, E., 110, 116, 140, 419
Elliott, D. N., 395, 399, 400, 423
Elliott, Patricia B., 69, 405, 409, 410
Emling, J. W., 298, 423
Eriksen, C. W., 335, 419
Estes, W. K., 120, 145, 419

Fechner, G. T., 117, 123, 125, 419
Feldman, A. S., 399, 428
Feller, W., 330, 349, 419
Fernberger, S. W., 125, 419
Ficks, L., 344, 424
Fisher, R. A., 419
Fitts, P. M., 325, 419
FitzHugh, R., 137, 319, 320, 321, 322, 323, 419, 422
Fletcher, H., 211, 222, 229, 230, 231, 278, 279, 280, 281, 282, 294, 297, 419
Fletcher, W. E., 232, 344, 426
Flottorp, G., 222, 280, 281, 282, 428
Forgie, Carma D., 312, 419
Forgie, J. W., 312, 419
Fox, W. C., 1, 424

Gabor, D., 154, 419
Galanter, E., 99, 344, 422, 423, 424
Gales, R. S., 210, 248, 289, 290, 292, 425
Garner, W. R., 136, 308, 420, 423
Gassler, G., 282, 290, 291, 292, 293, 420
Girschick, M. A., 260, 417
Gnedenko, B. V., 58, 420
Goldberg, S., 349, 420
Goldiamond, I., 308, 335, 337, 420
Goldman, S., 177, 420
Goode, H. H., 260, 261, 420
Granit, R., 319, 420
Green, B. F., 152, 420
Green, D. M., 69, 88, 92, 95, 97, 110, 175, 188, 193, 195, 196, 210, 220, 221, 248, 254, 255, 256, 257, 261, 263, 264, 281, 282, 286, 288, 291, 292, 294, 298, 299, 307, 344, 396, 406, 411, 420, 423, 426, 427
Greenberg, G. Z., 41, 81, 87, 111, 195, 265, 266, 267, 268, 269, 334, 395, 400, 419, 420
Greenwood, D. D., 281, 420, 421
Gregory, Margaret, 143, 333, 334, 335, 418
Grenander, U., 1, 421
Guilford, J. P., 118, 124, 421
Gundy, R. F., 394, 395, 399, 421

Haber, R. N., 257, 258, 421
Hack, M. H., 316, 317, 421
Hake, H. W., 113, 299, 335, 421, 425, 428
Hamilton, C. E., 110, 422
Hartley, R. V. L., 154, 421
Hawkins, J. E., Jr., 281, 421
Hawkins, W. F., 280, 308, 420
Hecht, S., 125, 138, 319, 421
Heise, G. A., 298, 307, 423
Helmholtz, H. L. F., 191, 210, 277, 278, 421
Hennon, V. A. C., 41, 421
Herbart, J. F., 117
Hodges, J. L., 349, 421
Hohle, R. H., 147, 421
Howarth, C. I., 334, 421
Howes, D. H., 308, 336, 419, 421

Irwin, F. W., 261, 421

James, W., 56, 421
Jastrow, J., 119, 120, 124, 397, 421
Jeffress, L. A., 169, 170, 172, 186, 187, 206, 210, 282, 404, 406, 409, 421
Jerison, H. J., 333, 421
Jersild, A., 41, 421
Johnson, D. M., 327, 422
Jones, R. C., 152, 427

Karlin, J. E., 2, 423
Kellogg, W. N., 125, 422
Kendall, M. G., 215, 422
Kincaid, W. M., 110, 422
Kinchla, R. A., 411, 422
Klem, Laura, 299, 311, 426
Koch, S., 424
Kodman, F., Jr., 210, 425
Kolmogorov, A. N., 58, 420
Koopman, B. O., 240, 422

Kovaly, J. J., 210, 425
Kristofferson, A. B., 243, 245, 246, 247, 422
Kuffler, S. W., 319, 422

Lane, C. E., 278, 428
Larkin, W. D., 136, 137, 422
Lawson, J. L., 1, 416, 422
Lazarus, R. S., 335, 422
Lee, W., 422
Lee, Y. W., 164, 422
Lehman, E. L., 349, 421
Leibnitz, G. W., 117
Lichten, W., 298, 307, 423
Licklider, J. C. R., 220, 248, 281, 291, 294, 420
Linker, E., 99, 422
Loeb, M., 333, 422
Lopes-Cardozo, B., 327, 328
Lorge, I., 258
Luce, R. D., 7, 45, 70, 71, 72, 76, 77, 78, 81, 83, 127, 140, 143, 144, 145, 146, 147, 270, 285, 325, 327, 343, 344, 418, 422, 423
Lukaszewski, J. S., 395, 399, 400, 423

Mackworth, Jane F., 333, 423
Madans, A. B., 241, 245
Maire, F., 399, 428
Marill, T. M., 2, 152, 172, 291, 292, 299, 406, 423
Markowitz, J., 115
Marriott, F. H. C., 319, 424
Martel, H. C., 176, 423
Martin, W. H., 298, 423
Mathews, M. V., 176, 195, 204, 205, 207, 210, 211, 223, 411, 423, 424, 425, 426
Mayer, A. M., 278, 423
McCleary, R. A., 335, 422
McDiarmid, C., 318, 425
McGill, W. J., 315, 323, 324, 326, 327, 423
McKey, Mary J., 220, 248, 254, 256, 257, 281, 288, 291, 294, 420, 426
McKnown, F. W., 298, 423
Melrose, J., 210, 425
Middleton, D., 1, 176, 423, 427
Miller, G. A., 136, 298, 307, 335, 423

Miller, J. G., 306, 423
Miller, P. H., 283, 428
Millman, Susan H., 344, 426
Moore, Mary E., 99, 422
Morgan, C. T., 136, 426
Mosteller, F., 145, 349, 418, 423
Munson, W. A., 2, 423
Murdock, B. B., Jr., 344, 423

Nachmias, J., 106, 137, 143, 147, 148, 343, 344, 423
Nevin, J. A., 317, 318, 424
Neyman, J., 1, 87, 88, 93, 424
Norman, D. A., 68, 136, 137, 143, 342, 343, 344, 345, 422, 424, 425
North, D. O., 1, 424
Nyquist, H., 154, 424

Ohm, G. S., 277, 278, 385
Osman, E., 210, 420, 425

Parks, T. E., 344, 424
Parzen, E., 388, 424
Patnaik, P. B., 215, 424
Pearson, E. S., 1, 87, 88, 93, 424
Peterson, J. R., 325, 419
Peterson, W. W., 1, 172, 424
Pfafflin, Sheila M., 195, 204, 205, 207, 210, 211, 223, 424
Pickett, R. M., 333, 421
Pierce, J., 335, 337, 424
Pirenne, M. H., 125, 138, 319, 421, 424
Pollack, I., 41, 241, 261, 297, 298, 299, 301, 302, 303, 305, 308, 309, 310, 344, 345, 418, 424, 425
Postman, L., 308, 426
Prothe, W. C., 210, 425
Pruzansky, Sandra, 311, 425

Raab, D. H., 210, 420, 425
Raiffa, H., 7, 423, 425
Rayleigh, J. W. S., 169, 381, 425
Reich, E., 1, 425
Rice, S. O., 1, 171, 388, 425
Rich, E., 210, 420, 425
Rilling, M. E., 100, 143, 186, 318, 401, 403, 425, 428
Rivette, C. L., 399, 427
Roberts, R. A., 260, 261, 417

Rodwan, A. S., 299, 425
Romig, H. G., 259, 418
Root, W. L., 169, 171, 418
Rose, R. M., 418
Rosenblith, W. A., 426
Rourke, R. E. K., 349, 423
Rubenstein, H., 308, 425
Rubin, H., 399, 428

Sandel, T. T., 210, 421
Sankaran, M., 215, 425
Schafer, T. H., 210, 248, 249, 254, 289, 290, 292, 425
Scharf, B., 281, 282, 425
Schlaifer, R., 7, 425
Schlosberg, H., 326, 327, 337, 338, 428
Schoeffler, M. S., 78, 425
Schouten, J. F., 327, 328
Schulman, A. I., 41, 81, 87, 111, 195, 265, 266, 267, 268, 269, 334, 400, 419
Sebestyen, G. S., 311, 425
Senders, Virginia L., 411, 425
Sewall, Susan T., 287, 398, 426
Shannon, C. E., 1, 154, 306, 308, 323, 425
Sherwin, C. W., 210, 425
Shewmaker, C. A., 210, 254, 425
Shipley, Elizabeth F., 68, 254, 256, 257, 285, 288, 294, 327, 395, 426
Shlaer, S., 125, 138, 319, 421
Sidowsky, J. B., 419
Siegert, A. J. F., 1
Smith, J. E. K., 299, 311, 394, 426
Smith, M., 2, 131, 249, 250, 251, 426
Smith, W. A. S., 261, 421
Solomon, R. L., 308, 426
Soward, A., 411, 425
Speeth, S. D., 411, 426
Stegun, I. A., 168, 215, 371, 417
Stein, Gertrude, 26
Steinman, R. M., 106, 137, 143, 147, 343, 423
Stenson, H. H., 333, 421
Sternberg, S., 215, 344, 423
Stevens, S. S., 56, 127, 136, 137, 138, 222, 280, 281, 282, 421, 426, 428
Stocklin, P. L., 210, 427
Stone, M., 325, 326, 426
Swerling, P., 1, 425

Swets, J. A., 2, 41, 69, 88, 94, 95, 97, 102, 103, 104, 105, 107, 108, 109, 110, 112, 113, 115, 127, 132, 139, 143, 250, 252, 254, 256, 257, 261, 263, 264, 282, 286, 287, 288, 294, 327, 328, 331, 335, 344, 398, 409, 410, 426, 427

Tanner, W. P., Jr., 2, 41, 88, 94, 95, 97, 102, 103, 104, 105, 107, 109, 127, 132, 139, 152, 195, 207, 282, 286, 298, 301, 302, 331, 335, 344, 396, 399, 418, 420, 426, 427
Taylor, M. M., 333, 423
Thomas, G. B., Jr. 349, 423
Thompson, P. O., 283, 425, 428
Thorndike, E. L., 124, 258
Thrall, R., 139
Thurstone, L. L., 1, 55, 57, 124, 125, 128, 427
Titchener, E. B., 118, 427
Torgerson, W. S., 56, 65, 124, 427
Treisman, M., 227, 334, 421, 427

Uhlenbeck, G. E., 1, 416, 422
Urban, F. M., 119, 120
Urick, R. J., 210, 427

van den Brink, G., 282, 427
van der Velden, H. A., 138, 417
Van Meter, D., 1, 427
Vendrick, A. J. H., 110, 116, 140, 419
Veniar, Florence A., 286, 289, 428
Voelcker, H. B., 152, 428
Volkmann, J., 136, 426

Wald, A., 1, 7, 236, 259, 260, 261, 262, 428
Watson, C. S., 100, 143, 186, 401, 403, 428
Wax, N., 388, 425
Weaver, W., 154, 425
Weber, E. H., 197, 206, 207, 208, 225, 226, 227, 228, 232, 427
Webster, J. C., 283, 428
Wegel, R. L., 278, 428
Weintraub, D. J., 113, 428
Welch, P. D., 311, 428
White, B. W., 152, 420

Wickelgren, W. A., 143, 342, 343, 344, 424

Wilson, Edna A., 2, 131, 249, 250, 251, 426

Wimpress, R. S., 311, 428

Wolf, Alice K., 152, 420

Wolpe, G., 325, 419

Wood, C. L., 210, 421

Woodward, P. M., 1, 428

Woodworth, R. S., 118, 124, 125, 326, 327, 337, 338, 428

Wundt, W., 325

Zwicker, E., 222, 280, 281, 282, 428

Zwislocki, J., 399, 428

Subject Index

A, parameter of ROC curves based on Rayleigh distributions, 170, 406

Absolute threshold, *see* Sensory threshold

Acceptance region, 21

Acoustic impedance of earphones, 412

Addition of sine waves of same frequency, 379-381

Adjustment, method of, *see* Psychophysical method

Animal psychophysics, 315-318, 345

A posteriori probability, 14-15, 357
estimated from independent pieces of information, 27-28
as monotonic with likelihood ratio, 19, 100, 106
and rating categories, 100, 343

A priori probability, affecting stimulus error, 56
and data collection, 393
defined, 14-15
effect of in speech recognition, 308-309
varied to manipulate criterion, 88-99

Articulation test, 297, 302

Attention, model for, 333
and stimulus interaction, 334-335
see also Vigilance

Average error, method of, *see* Psychophysical method

Awareness, perception without, *see* Subliminal perception

Bandwidth, critical, *see* Critical band

effective square, 386, 415-416
of a filter and decay of oscillation, 389
and mean-to-sigma ratio, 231
and signal duration, product of, 206

Basilar membrane, 276

Bayes' rule, 14-15, 357

Beats, 278

β, the criterion value of likelihood ratio, 20-21
correlation between optimal and obtained values of, 91-93
dependence on values, costs, and a priori probabilities, 21-23
in maximizing percentage correct, 23
in satisfying the Neyman-Pearson objective, 23-25
in a weighted combination, 20-21

Bias, response, and correction for chance, 123
in forced-choice, 408-411
in threshold theory, 74-75
see also Stimulus error; Criterion

Binomial distribution, 370

Bivariate Gaussian distribution, 374-375

Blank trials, 122-123
see also False alarms

Categorical judgment method, 55

Category, of certainty, a posteriori probability, 101, 343
see also Rating procedure

Central limit theorem, 57, 371-372

Chance success, *see* Correction for chance success

Chebyshev's theorem, 368

Chi-square, distribution, 214, 372-374
noncentral, 214, 219, 374
variable, 169, 174

Choice theory, and the forced-choice task, 83-84
likelihood ratio and, 81
and reaction time, 327
ROC curves for, 81-82
and uncertain frequency, 285, 287

Classical psychophysics, and method, 121-122
and threshold concept, 117-120
versus objective, 123-124

Combining independent pieces of information, 27-28

Comparative-judgment method, 54-55

Complement of an event, 352

Compound probabilities, 356

Conditional probability, defined, 355-356

Contingent choice of signal levels, 394

Correct confirmation in speech recognition, analogous to a "hit," 297, 299

Correction for chance success, 122-123, 128-129, 131
and recognition memory, 337-338

Correct rejection, 34

Correlation, defined, 369-370

Costs and values of a decision outcome, 10, 21-23, 88-89, 262
see also Expected value

Counting mechanisms, 315, 323, 326, 330-332

Covariance, defined, 369-370

Criterion, 10, 19, 58-59, 118
in the choice model, 81
in forced-choice tasks, 65
manipulated in yes-no experiment, 87-99
optimal versus obtained, 91-94
problem of in reaction time, 324-325
sensory criterion and the threshold, 70
several held simultaneously, see Rating procedure
and slope of ROC curve, 36-40
see also β

Critical band, 278-283

critical-ratio method for determining, 222, 281
and energy summation, 291-292
interpretation and extension of the concept of, 283-289
and multiple-component signal, 290-292
various estimates of, 280

Critical-band experiment, defined, 229
and energy-detection model prediction, 230
reinterpretation of, 229-231

Critical-ratio method, 222, 280-281

Cross-correlation detector, 163-164, 191, 194, 198-200
and the energy detection model, 223
and equal-variance Gaussian assumption, 199
and likelihood ratio, 201
as unrealistic, 206

Cross-correlation of two functions, defined, 382

Cues, 287, 394-395

Curve-fitting procedures, 404

d, index of sensitivity used in physiological experiment, 322-323

d', index of sensitivity based on equal-variance Gaussian distributions, compared to separation of means in two-alternative forced-choice, 68
constancy over different experimental procedures, 110-114
convenient way of calculating, 405
and d_e', $(d_e)^{1/2}$, d_s, $D(\Delta m, s)$, 96-98
defined, 60
and ideal detectors, 165, 173
linear with E/N_o, 191
misuse of term, 301
and signal one-of-M-orthogonal signals, 173
and signal specified exactly, 165
when appropriate, 405

d_e', index of sensitivity determined from negative diagonal of ROC graph, 98, 189-190, 266, 302, 317-318, 407

$(d_e)^{1/2}$, alternative notation for d_e', 98, 302

d'_{max}, index of sensitivity corrected for response bias in 2AFC, 409-410

$d'_{1,2}$, index of recognition sensitivity, 331

d_r, index of performance based on response-response contingencies, 302

d_s, alternative notation for d_e', 98

$D(\Delta m, s)$, index of sensitivity with two parameters, 96-99, 407
    constancy over different experimental procedures, 110-114

ΔE, increment in energy, 184-185, 208 (Problem 7.1), 213

Δm, the difference between the means of Gaussian distributions of unequal variance, 96

$\Delta m/\Delta\sigma$, the "mean-to-sigma" ratio, 95-96, 98-99, 101, 103-106, 110, 115-116 (Problems 4.1 to 4.3), 148 (Problem 5.3)
    see also Mean-to-sigma ratio

Decision, terminal, 259

Decision axis, and likelihood ratio, 62, 79
    possible physical interpretation of, 322

Decision goals, 9
    maximize expected value, 21-23, 88-93
    maximize percentage correct, 9-10, 18, 23, 88
    maximize weighted combination, 20-21
    Neyman-Pearson objective, 23-25, 93-94

Decision outcomes, 10
    expected value of, 21-23
    representation of, 15-19

Decision processes separated from sensory processes, 86-115

Decision rules, equivalence of, 18-19
    optimal, 10, 20-25, 46, 91-94

Decision-threshold model, 235-271
    compared to integration model, 240-243
    predictions of, 239-240

Deferred decision, see Sequential observations

Density function, see Probability distribution

Detectability, index of, see Sensitivity, measures of

Detect state, 70-75, 140-146

Difference threshold, see Sensory threshold

Dimensionality of an observation, 15

Discriminal dispersion, 55

Distribution-free measure, see $P(A)$, $P(C)$

Distribution of the effects of stimulation, 55, 127-128

Double-probability paper, 61, 64, 96, 405

E_s, see Signal energy

E_s/N_o, signal-to-noise ratio, 188

Effective square bandwidth, 415-416

Energy-detection model, 209-232
    and the critical band, 221-222
    and the critical-band experiment, 229-231
        and the cross-correlation detector, 223
        failure to predict Weber's law, 225-226
    flow diagram of, 211
    given noise alone, 213-214
    given pedestal plus noise, 215-217
    given signal plus noise, 214-215
    given signal plus pedestal plus noise, 217
    and the increment-detection experiment, 213, 222-223
    and internal variability, 227
    modified to predict Weber's law, 226-229
    and percent correct in two-alternative forced-choice procedure, 217
    and the psychometric funciton, 220-221
    and the shape of the ROC curve, 224-225
    and signal specified exactly, 223

and the simple detection experiment, 212, 219-222

Energy detector, 194-195, 204
    and envelope detector, 206
    see also Energy-detection model

Energy summation within the critical band, 290-293

Envelope, 389-391

Envelope detector, 167-172, 191, 194
    and data, 186-187
    and energy detector, 206
    and likelihood ratio, 203
    ROC curves of, 170-171, 186, 406
    and the signal-specified-except-for-phase model, 167-172, 191, 202-206

$\epsilon-\eta_0$ as abscissa of psychometric function, 188, 194-196

Equal-variance Gaussian assumption, 59-61, 88-89, 185-186, 342-343, 403
    see also Variance

Equivalent square bandwidth, 415-416

Error, 16-18, 33-35, 44, 123

Event, 351
    complement of, 352
    independent, 356-357
    mutually exclusive, 352
    as a subspace of a sample space, 351

Expected value, 10, 21-23, 362-365
    of decisions, 363
    function, 92
    the mean, 362-364, 367-368
    the variance, 364-365, 367-368
    see also Mean; Variance

Experimental equipment, block diagram of, 413

Experimental techniques, 392-416

Exponential distributions, 301, 406

Exponential model, 78-81

False alarm, 34
    analogy in two-alternative forced-choice task, 44

False alarms, proportion or probability of, 34-35, 38-40, 47, 90, 128, 153
    assumed independence of proportion of hits, 129-130

correlated with reinforcement probability, 318
    dependency on proportion of hits, 133-136
    with temporal uncertainty, 268

False-positives, proportion of, 122-123
    see also False alarms, proportion or probability of

Feedback, 32-33, 44, 395

Filter, bandwidth of and decay of oscillation, 389
    effective square bandwidth of, 415-416
    excited by noise, 389-390
    insertion loss of, 416
    predetection and postdetection, 209

Fixed-observation procedure, 260

Forced-choice procedure, and the choice model, 83-84
    defined, 43-45
    and the Gaussian assumption, 64
    and high-threshold theory, 136
    and invariance of d', 112-113
    reasons for, 43-44, 107-108, 394
    relation to yes-no or rating ROC curves, 45-51
    and response bias, 408-411
    second choices in, 108-110, 116 (Problem 4.6)
    and two-state threshold theory, 74-78
    see also Two-alternative forced-choice procedure

Fourier analysis done by the ear, 277

Fourier integral representation, 384

Fourier series, 156, 382-383

Fourier sine and cosine transforms, 383

Free response, see Vigilance

Frequency analysis, 276-295
    history of, 277-279
    summary of experiments in, 293-295

Frequency of seeing curve, see Phychometric function

Frequency representation of a waveform, 155-157, 160

Frequenzegruppe, see Critical band

Function, approximation of, and cross correlation, 382
    and Fourier series, 382-384
    and least-squares formulation, 381

and orthogonality restriction, 382

Γ, the gamma function, 373
Gaussian assumption, and the central limit theorem, 57
 and forced-choice tasks, 64-69
 history, 54-56
 justification, 57-58
 and the single observation task, 58-64
 see also Equal-variance Gaussian assumption; Unequal-variance Gaussian assumption
Gaussian distribution, 370-371
 as limiting distribution, 58
Gaussian noise, *see* Noise
Gaussian noise source, 385
Goals, *see* Decision goals
Guessing correction, *see* Correction for chance success; High-threshold theory
Guessing mechanism and threshold theory, 71, 129

h, index of sensitivity of the energy-detection model, 219-231, 232 (Problem 8.1), 406
h, measure of precision, 125
High-threshold theory, 69-71, 77, 127-136
 and the correction for chance success, 128-129
 failure of, 130-136
 and the independence of hits and false alarms, 129-130
 interpretation of the threshold, 127-128
 predictions of second choices, 109-110
 rating and forced-choice predictions and data, 136
 rational equation of, 128-129
 ROC curves of, 130-131
 yes-no predictions and data, 130-133
 see also Threshold theory
Hit, 34
 analogy in two-alternative forced-choice task, 44
Hits, proportion or probability of, 34-35, 38-40, 90, 128, 153
 assumed independence of propor-

tion of false alarms, 129-130
 dependency on proportion of false alarms, 133-136
 with temporal uncertainty, 268
Homogeneity-of-noise assumption, 65-66
Hypotheses, 13

Ideal detectors, or ideal observers, 149-179
 basic paradigm of analysis, 152-153
 compared to human observer, 180-207
 criticism and discussion of, 175-178
 as a cross-correlator, 163-164
 and d', 173
 and likelihood ratio, 153
 as a matched filter, 165
 and signal a gated sinusoid, 176
 and signal a sample of noise, 174-175
 and signal one-of-M-orthogonal signals, 172-173
 and signal one-of-M-orthogonal signals of unknown phase, 173-174
 and signal specified exactly, 162-166
 and signal specified except for phase, 167-172
Ideal observers, *see* Ideal detectors
Impedance, acoustic, of earphones, 412
 desirable at source, 413-414
Incorrect confirmation in speech recognition analogous to a "false alarm," 297, 299
Increment-detection experiment, 181-185
 and the cross-correlation detector, 223
 difference distributions for, 218
 and the energy-detection model, 222-223
 and the envelope detector, 186-187
 measurement of quantities in, 184-185
 psychometric functions for, 195-206
 ROC curve for, 224-225
 and temporal uncertainty, 267
 and the unequal-variance Gaussian model, 187

and Weber's law, 225-226
Increment in energy, *see* ΔE
Indices of sensitivity, *see* Sensitivity, measures of
Information theory, 154, 306, 308, 323
Insertion loss, 416
Instructions, 397-398
Integration model, 233-275
    compared to decision-threshold model, 240-243
    derivations for, 271-275
    predictions of, 238-239
Integrator, final and the energy-detection model, 209
    see also Ω
Internal noise, *see* Noise, internal
Internal variability, *see* Noise, internal

Joint probability functions, 361-362
    of Gaussian variables, 374-375
Joint probability of a given hypothesis-response pair, 17-18

k, index of sensitivity based on exponential distributions, 79-81, 301, 406

Law of large numbers, 368-369
Learning theory, 78, 120, 143-145, 147, 324
Likelihood ratio, for the choice model, 81
    and the correlation detector, 201
    criteria, 38-40
    criterion in optimal decision rules, 21-25
    and the decision axis, 62, 79
    defined, 10
    distribution of, 26-27
    and the energy detector, 204
    and the envelope detector, 202-208
    example of, 9
    for the exponential model, 79
    and ideal detectors, *see* Ideal detectors
    and the integration model, 239
    of the likelihood ratio, 26
    logarithm of, 67
    logarithm of assumed normal, 172

as monotonic with a posteriori probability, 19, 100, 106
monotonically related to the cross-correlation of signal with observation, 201
for multiple hypotheses, 16
as optimal linear combination of observations, 274
and percentage correct in two-alternative forced-choice tasks, 46
reported by human observers, 107
and the ROC curve, 36-40, 58-64
and signal a sample of noise, 174
and signal specified except for phase, 168
used in combining information, 27-28
use in optimal decision making, 18-25
and x_t, 168-169
Limits, method of, *see* Psychophysical method
Low-threshold theories, 138-146
$l(x)$, *see* Likelihood ratio

M, the amount of uncertainty, 172-174, 191-196, 306-308
Magnitude estimation, 56
m-alternative forced-choice, *see* Forced-choice procedure
Masking, 278
    and N_o, 386
    see also Critical band
Matched filtering, 165
Mean, 363-364
    of chi-square, 373
    and linear transformations, 363
    of noncentral chi-square, 374
    of a product, 366
    of a sample, 367
    of a sum, 365-366
    as a weighted average, 363
Mean-to-sigma ratio, and bandwidth, 175, 179 (Problem 6.4), 231
    and internal variability, 226-229
    of Ω, 214
    see also $\Delta m/\Delta \sigma$
Measurement, of noise, 414-416
    of signal, 414
    of stimulus, 411-416
Method, *see* Psychophysical method

Method of limits, *see* Psychophysical method
Miss, 34
Monitoring task, 302
Motivation, effect of, 399-400
Multiple-band, or multiband, model, 284-288
  and reaction time, 327-329
Multiple-component signals, auditory, 248, 289-293
  and critical band, 290-291
  and energy summation, 291
  visual, 243-248
Multiple observations, 235-275
  combined linearly, 273-275
  in speech recognition, 309-311
  see also Decision-threshold model; Integration model; Multiple-component signals; Multiple observers; Multiple presentations
Multiple observers, history of research on, 248-250
  ROC data for, 251-253
Multiple presentations: fixed number, and constant noise, 254-257
  and independent noise, 253-254
  and speech recognition, 309-311
Multiple presentations: sequential observation or deferred decision, 259-265, 309-311
Multi-threshold theory, *see* Two-state threshold theory
Multivariate statistical analyses of speech recognition, 299, 311-312

N_o, noise power in a 1-cps band, *see* Noise-power density
Negative sensation, 117
Neural quantum, theory of, 70, 120, 136-138, 141
Noise, average power of, 157, 385
  bandwidth of and masking, 386
  criticism of finite representation of, 175-178
  filtered, 154
  frequency representation of, 155-157, 160
  Gaussian, model of, 155-157
  homogeneity assumption, 65-66

and information theory, 154
internal and Weber's law, 207
measurement of, 414-416
power-spectrum representation of, 386
in psychoacoustic experiments, 89, 156
representation of, 388-391
source, 384-385
as a stochastic process, 154
temporal representation of, 157-161
and true RMS, 385
Noise, constant, and multiple presentations, 254-257, 309-311
Noise, external, adding to internal noise, 255-257
Noise, independent, and multiple presentations, 253-254, 309-311
Noise, internal, adding to external noise, 255
  postulated in energy-detection model, 227-229
  proportional to external noise, 257
Noise generator, assumptions of, 384-385
Noise-power density, 156-175, 197, 213-214, 386, 415-416
Noncentral chi-square, 374
  see also Chi-square
Nondetect state, 70-75, 140-146
Nonparametric measure of recognition memory, 344-345
Normal, curve, 370
  density function, 370
  distribution, 370-371
  ROC curves, *see* ROC curves
  variable, standardized, 370
  see also Gaussian assumption, Gaussian distribution
Normalized random variables, 365

Objective in decision making, *see* Decision goals
Objective psychophysics, early methods of, 124-126
  versus classical, 123-124
Observation interval, 33, 44, 395-396
  extended, *see* Temporal uncertainty
  undefined, *see* Vigilance, Temporal uncertainty

Observation stage, 264
Observers, instructions to, 397-398
  length of service of, 397
  selection of, 396-397
  stability of, 400
Observing response, 333
Odds of hypothesis, 15
  see also Likelihood ratio
Ohm's acoustic law, 277
Ω, integrator output in energy-detection model, 211-217
One-of-M-orthogonal signals, see Signal one-of-M-orthoganol signals
Operating-characteristic curves, see ROC curve, SOC curve
Optimal detector, see Ideal detector
Orthogonality restriction, 382

$P(A)$, proportion of area under ROC curve, 45-50, 217, 404-405
$P(C)$, proportion of correct responses, 45-50, 68-69, 404-405
$P(C)_{max}$, $P(C)$ corrected for response bias, 409-410
$P_m(C)$, proportion of correct responses in m-alternative forced-choice, 69
Payoff matrix, see Costs and values
Pedestal, continuous and gated, 184
  as a cue, 395
Pedestal experiment, see Increment-detection experiment
Percentage correct, see $P(C)$
Perceptual defense and sensitization, 336-337
Phase angle, 378-379
Phase deafness, 191
Φ, integral of standard normal deviate, 59
Physical-quantum theory, 138, 147 (Problem 5.3)
Physiology, sensory, 319-324
Place theory of hearing, 277
Poisson distribution, 370
Postdetection filter, see Integrator, Ω
Power-function ROC curve, 81, 268-269, 301, 406
Power spectrum, 386
Practice, effect of, 398-399
Predetection filter, 209

  see also Critical band
Predetermined-observation procedure, 260
Preview technique, 394-395
Probability density function, see Probability distribution
Probability distribution, 359-360
  binomial, 370
  bivariate normal, 199-203, 374-375
  chi-square, 214, 219, 372-374
  Gaussian, 54-69, 370-371
  joint, 361-362
  non-central chi-square, 215, 219, 374
  Poisson, 147 (Problem 5.3), 370
  Rayleigh, 94, 169-172, 388, 391, 403-406
Probability paper, 61, 64, 96, 405
Probability theory, 349-376
Product rule, 356
Psychometric function, abscissa of, 187-188
  chance correction to, 131
  as a cumulative Gaussian function, 220-221
  for energy detector, 204, 220
  and existence of sensory threshold, 126-127
  fitted by least-squared-error technique, 404
  for ideal visual observer, 125
  for increment-detection experiments, 195-206
  maximum slope of, 125
  models of in simple detection, 191-195
  as an ogive, 118
  ordinate of, 187
  range of, 197
  for simple detection experiments, 187-191, 220-221
  slope of for multiple-components signals, 248
Psychophysical measures, see Sensitivity, measures of
Psychophysical method, of adjustment, 117, 122
  of average error, 117
  of constant stimuli, 117, 121, 124
  correction for chance success, 122
  early objective, 124-126

of limits, 117
of limits and word recognition, 257
of minimal changes, 117
of paired comparisons, 124
relation of classical to detection-theory methods, 122-123
of reproduction, 117
of serial exploration, 117, 119, 122
see also Forced-phase procedure; Two-alternative forced-choice procedure; Rating procedure; Yes-no procedure
Psychophysics, objective versus classical, 56-57, 123-124
see also Psychophysical method

Quantal theory, 70, 120, 136-138, 141

Random strategy, 38
Random variable, 55, 58, 358, 365-366
Rating procedure, compared to yes-no procedure, 40-41
defined, 41-43
and detection data, 99-107
economy of, 43, 106
and high-threshold theory, 136
as irrelevant to two-state theory, 143, 344
and recognition memory, 339, 342
and reduced variance of proportions, 403
relation to two-alternative forced-choice task, 45-49
and the ROC curve, 42-43, 103-106
in speech recognition, 297-305
theoretical justification for, 41
Rayleigh distribution, 94, 169-172, 388, 391, 405-406
Reaction time, and the counting model, 326
the criterion problem in, 324-325
and detection of one of two frequencies, 327-330
as an index of detectability, 326-327
range of compared to $P(C)$, 327
reason for measuring, 327
and the sequential-decision model, 325-326

Receiver, in speech communication compared to sender, 301
Receiver operating characteristic, *see* ROC curve
Recognition memory, 337-346
application to verbal material, 337-344
and correction for chance success, 337-338
and $D(\Delta m, s)$, 340
and Gaussian assumption of equal variance, 342-343
models for, 337-339, 344
nonparametric measures of, 344-345
and nonverbal sounds, 344
and rating scales, 339, 342
and ROC curves, 339-342
Reinforcement, 317-318
Representation, of noise, *see Noise*
of signal, *see* Signal
Reproduction, method of, *see* Psychophysical method
Response, 11
Response bias, *see* Bias, response; Criterion; Stimulus error
ROC curve, from animal psychophysics, 316-317
area under, $P(A)$, 45-50, 217, 404-405
asymmetrical, 94-100, 104-106
and the character of the detector, 185-187
for the choice model, 81-82
and classical psychophysics, 123-124
comparison with SOC, 299-301
data for multiple observers, 251-253
defined, 34-35
empirical, 88-91, 95-100, 103-106
for energy-detection model, 224-225
and the envelope detector, 186
equal-variance Gaussian, 59-63, 88-89, 185-186
for the exponential model, 79-81
for forced-choice tasks, 68
for high-threshold theory, 130-131
for the increment-detection experiment, 224
and likelihood ratio, 36-40, 58-64
for multiple observations, 241

as a power function, 79-81, 268-269, 301, 406
for the rating procedure, 42-43, 101-103
and recognition memory, 339-344
for signal a sample of noise, 175
for signal low-threshold multistate theory, 139
and signal strength, 50-51
slope, *see* Slope of ROC curve on linear coordinates; Slope of ROC curve on probability coordinates
symmetry in two-alternative forced-choice, 49, 68
for three-state theory, 145
and the Thurstone model, 57
for two-alternative forced-choice, 44
for two-state threshold theory, 72-78, 141-142
Type II, 302
unequal-variance Gaussian, 63, 94-100, 104-106, 115-116 (Problems 4.1 to 4.3, 4.5), 186
variance of data points, 401-403
vigilance procedure, 268-270
for the yes-no procedure, 34-36, 87-89, 95-99

Sampling theorem, 154
Scanning model, 327
see also Single-band model
Second choice in intelligibility tests, 298, 303-306, 313
Second choices, 108-110, 116 (Problem 4.6)
Sender in speech communication, 301
Sensitivity, measures of, A, 170, 406
compared empirically, 110-114
d', 60, 405
d_e', 98
$D(\Delta m, s)$, 96-99, 407
distribution free, 45-49, 404-405
empirical, 407
h, 125, 219, 406
k, 79-81, 406
$P(A)$, 45-50, 217, 404-405
$P(C)$, 45-50, 68-69, 404-405
reaction time, 326-327
see also d'; d_e'; d'_{max}

Sensory physiology, 319-324
Sensory threshold, absolute, 121, 147 (Problem 5.2)
difference, 121
existence of, and the psychometric function, 126-127
influenced by "nonsensory" factors, 118
instability of, 118
in physiology, 319
and probable error, 121-122
and psychophysical method, 117-147
as a statistical construct, 127
see also Threshold theory
Sequential effects in series of responses, 411
Sequential observations or deferred decisions, data, 261-265, 309-311
procedure, 259-261
in reaction time, 325-326
Serial exploration, method of, *see* Psychophysical method
σ, the standard deviation, 364-365
σ_s/σ_n, reciprocal of slope of ROC curve, 64, 96
see also Slope of ROC curve on probability coordinates; $\Delta m/\Delta\sigma$
Signal, criticism of finite representation of, 175-178
measurement of, 414
representation of, 162, 377-384
Signal a sample of noise, 174-175, 406
Signal energy, 161-165, 171-175, 183-185, 188, 212-213, 414
Signal one-of-M-orthogonal signals, known phase, 172-173
and psychometric function, 191-195, 208 (Problem 7.2)
in speech recognition, 299, 306-308
and temporal uncertainty, 267
unknown phase, 173-174
Signal specified exactly, 162-166, 200-201, 223
Signal specified except for phase, 167-172, 406
see also Envelope detector
Signal specified statistically, 166-175
Signal strength and ROC curve, 50-51

Signal-to-noise ratio and abscissa of psychometric function, 187-188

Simple detection experiment, 181-185
and the critical band, 221-222
defined, 219
difference distributions for, 218
psychometric functions for, 187-195, 220-221

Single-band model, 284-289, 294-295, 327-329

Single-low-threshold multistate theory, 139-140

Sinusoid(s), addition of two of same frequency, 379-381
representation of, 377-379

Slope of ROC curve on linear coordinates, 36-40, 58-64

Slope of ROC curve on probability coordinates, equal-variance Gaussian distributions, 61, 96-97, 405
exponential distributions, 80, 405-406
Rayleigh distributions, 405-406
unequal-variance Gaussian distributions, 64, 96-97, 405-407
unreliability of estimates of, 401
see also σ_s/σ_n; $\Delta m/\Delta \sigma$

SOC curves, 299-301

Sound pressure level, 412

Space error, 408

Speech communication, see Speech recognition

Speech-intelligibility test, 297

Speech recognition, 296-314
and a priori probability, 308-309
articulation test, 297
and detection model for one-of-M-or-thogonal signals, 299, 306-308
monitoring task, 302
multiple observations, 309-311
operating characteristic curves, 297, 300-301
rating procedure, 297-306
and repetitions, 298-299
speech-intelligibility test, 297
standard procedure for studying, 296-297
stimulus versus response uncertainty, 309

and theory of multivariate statistical analyses, 299, 311-312
use of second choice, 298, 303-306

SPL, sound pressure level, 412

Square-law device, 209

Standard deviation, 364-368

Standardized random variables, 365

Statistical decision theory, an example, 8-11
and the forced-choice procedure, 43-45
and likelihood ratio, see Likelihood ratio
and the rating procedures, 40-43
and the ROC curve, see ROC curve
and yes-no procedure, 32-34

Stimulus, 11

Stimulus alternatives, 33

Stimulus error, 56, 124

Stimulus interaction and attention, 334-335

Stimulus measurement, 411-416

Stimulus-response matrix, 33-34

Stochastic process, 154, 387-388

Sublimal perception, 117, 120, 335-337, 346

Temporal representation of a waveform, 157-161

Temporal uncertainty, 265-270, 332-333

Terminal decision, 269
see also Sequential observations

Theory of ideal observers, see Ideal detectors

Three-state threshold theory, 145-146

Threshold, sensory, see Sensory threshold

Threshold theory, 69-78, 117-120, 127-146, 337-339, 344
and the psychometric function, 126-127

Thurstone's model, 54-57

Time discrimination, 330-332

Time error, 408

Time intervals, judgment of, 345

Trading relationship between time and error, 259

Training of observers, 31

Trial, 11, 32-33, 44

duration of, 396
events in, 395
feedback during, 395
number, 393
observation intervals in, 395-396
True RMS, 385
2AFC, see Two-alternative forced-choice procedure
Two-alternative forced-choice procedure, analogies to hit and false alarm, 44
defined, 44
energy detector and percent correct, 217-219
as an example of comparative judgment, 54-55
in increment-detection, 183-184
with pedestal, 183-184
percentage of correct decisions, 46-48, 50
relation to yes-no or rating ROC curves, 45-50
and the ROC curve, 44
in simple detection, 181-183
Two-category method of constant stimuli, 124
Two-state threshold theory, 69-78, 140-145
and the criterion, 70, 74-75, 148, (Problem 5.4)
and the forced-choice procedure, 74-78
and the guessing mechanism, 71
and learning mechanism, 78
and the likelihood ratio, 70, 73-77
probability densities, 73
and rating data, 143, 343-344
response bias, in, 74-76
and the yes-no ROC curve, 71-74, 141-142
see also Threshold theory
Two-threshold theory, see Three-state threshold theory
Type II ROC curve, 302

Uncertain signal frequency, and the choice model, 285, 287
and Creelman's model, 286
experiments with, 283-289
and the multiple-band model, 284, 287
one-of-two frequencies experiment, 283
and the single-band model, 284, 287
Uncertainty, of the hand, 122, 403
odds as a measure of, 354
one-of-M-orthogonal signals, 166-175
in speech recognition, 306-308
of stimulus versus that of response, 309
temporal, 265-270, 332-333
Unequal-variance Gaussian assumption, 62-64, 79, 94-96, 103-106, 186-187, 403-404

Values and costs of a decision outcome, 10, 21-23, 88-89, 262
see also Expected value
Variable-sensitivity theory, see Three-state threshold theory
Variance, of chi-square, 373
of Gaussian distributions, see Equal-variance Gaussian assumption; Unequal-variance Gaussian assumption
homogeneity assumption in forced-choice tasks, 66
of noncentral chi-square, 374
of proportions, 401-404, 411
see also Expected value
Variance of the signal-plus-noise distribution, see $\Delta m / \Delta \sigma$
Vector addition, 380
Vigilance, 268-270, 332-333, 345
Vocabulary size, 306-308
see also One-of-M-orthogonal signals

W, see Bandwidth
Waveform, finite representation of, 155
frequency representation of, 155-157, 160
temporal representation of, 157-162
Weak-signal suppression, 125
Weber's fraction, 228
Weber's law, 206-207
and increment detection, 225-226
and a modified energy-detection

model, 226-229
 a neurological model for, 227
 at odds with energy-detection model, 208, (Problem 7.3), 225
Weighted combination maximized, *see* Goals in decision making
White Gaussian noise, *see* Noise
Word recognition, visual, 257-259, 303, 305
 see also Speech recognition

x_i, envelope density, 168-171

Yes-no procedure, changing the decision criteria, 87-88
 compared to rating procedure, 40-41

defined, 32-33
and detection data, 88-89, 115-116 (Problems 4.1, 4.2, 4.5)
and early objective methods, 126
as an example of categorical judgments, 55
and high-threshold theory, 130-136
and physical-quantum theory, 138
and quantal theory, 137
relation to two-alternative forced-choice, 45-51
ROC curve, 34-36
simple example of, 37
in speech communication, 299-302
stimulus-response matrix, 33-34
and two-state theory, 141-143